Introducing
Maya® 2011

Introducing Maya® 2011

Autodesk®
Official Training Guide

DARIUSH DERAKHSHANI

Wiley Publishing, Inc.

Acquisitions Editor: Mariann Barsolo
Development Editor: Lisa Bishop
Technical Editor: Keith Reicher
Production Editor: Christine O'Connor
Copy Editor: Tiffany Taylor
Editorial Manager: Pete Gaughan
Production Manager: Tim Tate
Vice President and Executive Group Publisher: Richard Swadley
Vice President and Publisher: Neil Edde
Media Associate Project Manager: Jenny Swisher
Media Associate Producer: Shawn Patrick
Media Quality Assurance: Marilyn Hummel
Book Designer: Caryl Gorska
Compositor: Chris Gillespie, Happenstance Type-O-Rama
Proofreader: Publication Services, Inc.
Indexer: Robert Swanson
Project Coordinator, Cover: Lynsey Stanford
Cover Designer: Ryan Sneed
Cover Image: Dariush Derakhshani, Tayler Hudson

Dear Reader,

Thank you for choosing *Introducing Maya 2011*. This book is part of a family of premium-quality Sybex books, all of which are written by outstanding authors who combine practical experience with a gift for teaching.

Sybex was founded in 1976. More than 30 years later, we're still committed to producing consistently exceptional books. With each of our titles, we're working hard to set a new standard for the industry. From the paper we print on, to the authors we work with, our goal is to bring you the best books available.

I hope you see all that reflected in these pages. I'd be very interested to hear your comments and get your feedback on how we're doing. Feel free to let me know what you think about this or any other Sybex book by sending me an email at nedde@wiley.com. If you think you've found a technical error in this book, please visit http://sybex.custhelp.com. Customer feedback is critical to our efforts at Sybex.

Best regards,

Neil Edde
Vice President and Publisher
Sybex, an Imprint of Wiley

To Max Henry

Acknowledgments

As this book goes into its seventh edition, I am thrilled that the Introducing Maya series is a favorite resource for students and teachers of Maya. Education is the foundation for a happy life, and with that in mind, I'd like to thank the outstanding teachers from whom I have had the privilege to learn. You can remember what you've been taught; or, more important, you can remember those who have taught you. ■ I also want to thank my students, who have taught me as much as they have learned themselves. Juan Gutierrez, Victor J. Garza, Robert Jauregui, and Peter Gend deserve special thanks for helping me complete the models and images for this book. Thanks to the student artists who contributed to the color insert and, of course, thanks to my bosses, colleagues, and friends at work for showing me everything I've learned and making it interesting to be in the effects business. ■ Special thanks to HP for their support and keeping me in the cutting edge of workstations. ■ Thanks to my editors at Sybex and the folks at Autodesk for their support and help and for making this process fun. Thanks to the book team for bringing it all together: Mariann Barsolo, Lisa Bishop, and Christine O'Connor. My appreciation also goes to technical editor, Keith Reicher. ■ Finally, special mad props go to my friends Bill, Mark, Frank, Terry, and Brett. ■ Thank you to my mom and brothers for your strength, wisdom, and love throughout. And a special thank you to my lovely wife, Randi, and our son, Max Henry, for putting up with the long nights at the keyboard; the grumpy, sleep-deprived mornings; and the blinking and buzzing of all my machines in our apartment. Family!

About the Author

Dariush Derakhshani is a Visual Effects Supervisor and Head of CG for Radium|ReelFX - Santa Monica, a creative and design studio with offices in Dallas, Texas, and Santa Monica, California. Dariush has been working in CG for more than 13 years and teaching classes in CG and effects production for close to 11. He is the best-selling author of a handful of books, including the popular Introducing Maya series.

Dariush started using AutoCAD software in his architecture days and then migrated to using 3D programs when his firm's principal architects needed to show their clients' design work on the computer. Starting with Alias PowerAnimator version 6, which he encountered when he enrolled in the University of Southern California Film School's Animation program, and working for a short while in 3ds Max before moving on to Maya jobs, Dariush has been using Autodesk animation software for the past 16 years.

He received an M.F.A. in Film, Video, and Computer Animation in 1997 from USC. Dariush also holds a B.A. in Architecture and Theatre from Lehigh University in Pennsylvania and worked at a New Jersey architecture firm before moving to L.A. for film school. He has worked on feature films, music videos, and countless commercials as a 3D animator and VFX Supervisor, garnering honors from the London International Advertising Awards, the ADDY Awards, the Telly Awards and a nomination from the Visual Effects Society Awards. He is bald and has flat feet.

CONTENTS AT A GLANCE

Contents

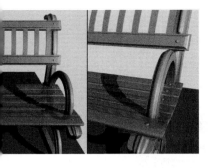

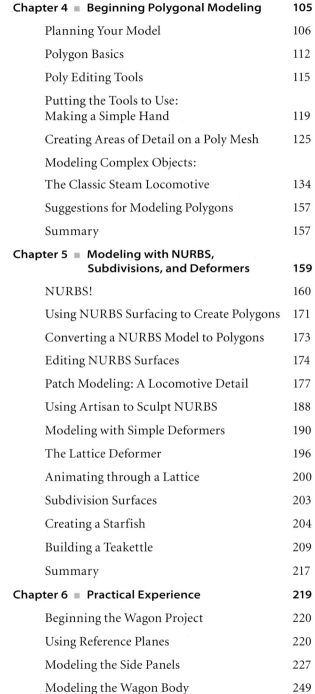

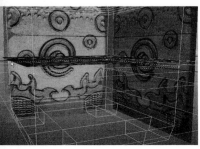

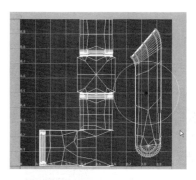

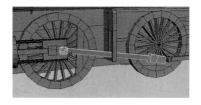

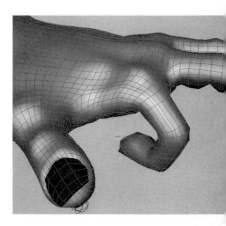

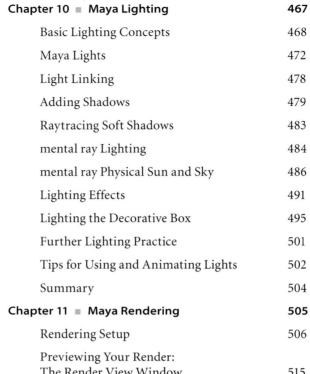

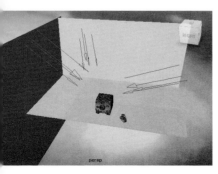

Introduction

Welcome to Introducing Maya 2011 and the world of computer-generated imagery (CGI). Whether you're new to 3D graphics or venturing into Autodesk's powerhouse animation software from another 3D application, you'll find this book a perfect primer. It introduces you to Maya and shows how you can work with Maya to create your art, whether it's animated or static in design.

The first edition of this book was written out of the author's need for a solid, comprehensive, and yet open-ended teaching material about Maya for his classes. This book exposes you to all the facets of Maya by introducing and explaining its tools and functions to help you understand how Maya operates. In addition, you'll find hands-on examples and tutorials that give you firsthand experience with the toolsets. Working through these will help you develop skills as well as knowledge. These tutorials expose you to various ways of accomplishing tasks with this intricate and comprehensive artistic tool.

Finally, this book explains workflow. You'll learn not only how specific tasks are accomplished, but why—that is, how they fit into the larger process of producing 3D animation. By doing that, these chapters should give you the confidence to venture deeper into Maya's feature set on your own or using any of Maya's other learning tools and books as a guide.

It can be frustrating to learn a powerful tool such as Maya, so it's important to remember to pace yourself. The number-one complaint of readers of books like this is a sense that either the pace is too fast or the steps are too complicated or overwhelming. That's a tough nut to crack, to be sure, and no two readers are the same. But this book offers you the chance to run things at your own pace. The exercises and steps may seem challenging at times, but keep in mind that the more you try, even the more you fail at some attempts, the more you'll learn about how to operate Maya. Experience is the key to learning workflows in any software program, and with experience come failure and aggravation. Nevertheless, try and try again, and you'll see that further attempts will be easier and more fruitful.

Above all, this book aims to inspire you to use Maya as a creative tool to achieve and explore your own artistic vision.

What You'll Learn from This Book

Introducing Maya 2011 will show you how Maya works and introduce you to every part of the toolset to give you a glimpse of the possibilities available with Maya.

You'll learn the basic concepts underlying animation and 3D and how to work with the Maya interface. You'll then learn the basic methods of modeling—creating objects and characters that appear to exist in three-dimensional space and that can be animated. You'll also explore shading and texturing—the techniques of applying surfaces to the objects you create—and you'll learn how to create lights and shadows in a scene. Animation is an enormously rich topic, but the practice and theory provided here will give you a solid footing. Then, you'll learn how to control the process of rendering, turning your images into files that can be viewed. Perhaps Maya's most dazzling capability is its dynamics engine, software that allows you to make objects behave as if controlled by the real-world laws of physics.

After you've finished this book and its exercises, you'll have experience in almost everything Maya offers, giving you a solid foundation on which to base the rest of your Maya and CGI experience.

The goal of this book is to get you familiar enough with all the parts of Maya that you can work on your own and start a long, healthy education in a powerful and flexible tool.

You will, however, learn the most from yourself.

Who Should Read This Book

Anyone who is curious about learning Maya or who is migrating from another 3D software package can learn something from this book. Even if you're highly experienced in another 3D package such as Lightwave or XSI, you'll find this book helpful in showing you how Maya operates, so you can migrate your existing skill set quickly and efficiently. By being exposed to everything Maya has to offer, you'll better understand how you can use its toolset to create or improve on your art and work.

If you already have cursory or even intermediate experience with Maya, culled from time spent learning at home, you can fill many holes with the information in this book as well as expand your experience. Self-education is a powerful tool, and the more you expose yourself to different sources, opinions, and methods, the better educated you'll be.

In addition, this book is invaluable for teachers in the CG field. This book was written to cater to those who want to pick up the fundamentals of Maya as well as those who want to teach classes based around a solid body of course material. You won't find a better basis for a class when you combine this book with your own curriculum.

How to Use This Book

Introducing Maya 2011 approaches the subject in a linear fashion that tracks how most animation productions are undertaken. But the book has numerous cross-references, to make sure the chapters make sense in any order you may want to tackle them. You can open this book to any chapter and work through the tutorials and examples laid out for the Maya task being covered. Feel free to browse the chapters and jump into anything that strikes your fancy. However, if you're completely new to CG, you may want to take the chapters in order.

Although you can learn a lot just by reading the explanations and studying the illustrations, it's best to read this book while you're using Maya 2011 so that you can try the exercises for yourself as you read them. If you don't already have Maya, you can download a 30-day trial version of the software at www.autodesk.com/maya. This book also includes a CD that contains all the example and support files you'll need for the tutorials in the text, which is valuable as an educational aid. You can use the example files to check the progress of your work, or you can use them as a starting point if you want to skip ahead within an exercise. The latter can save the more experienced reader tons of time. You'll also find it valuable to examine these files in depth to see how scenes are set up and how some of the concepts introduced in the book are implemented. Because Maya is a complex, professional software application, the tutorials are both realistically ambitious and simple enough for new users to complete. Take them one step at a time, and find your own pace, accepting aggravations and failures as part of the process. Take your time; you're not working on deadline—yet.

How This Book Is Organized

Chapter 1, "Introduction to Computer Graphics and 3D," introduces you to common computer graphics terms and concepts to give you a basic overview of how CG happens and how Maya relates to the overall process. This chapter explores the basics of CG creation and its core concepts. In addition, it describes the process of CG production and discusses how to establish a commonly used workflow.

Chapter 2, "Jumping in Headfirst, with Both Feet," creates a simple animation to introduce you to Maya's interface and workflow and give you a taste of how things work right off the bat. By animating the planets in our solar system, you'll learn basic concepts of creating and animating in Maya and how to use its powerful object structure.

Chapter 3, "The Maya 2011 Interface," presents the entire Maya interface and shows you how it's used in production. Beginning with a roadmap of the screen, this chapter also explains how Maya defines and organizes objects in a scene.

Chapter 4, "Beginning Polygonal Modeling," is an introduction to modeling concepts and workflows in general. It shows you how to start modeling using polygonal geometry to create various objects, from a human hand to a complex locomotive engine.

Chapter 5, "Modeling with NURBS, Subdivisions, and Deformers," takes your lesson in modeling a step further. It will show you how to model with deformers and surfacing techniques, using NURBS to create a patch model detail for the locomotive you modeled in Chapter 4. You'll also use subdivision surfaces, a hybrid between polygons and NURBS, to create a starfish.

Chapter 6, "Practical Experience," rounds out your modeling lessons with two comprehensive exercises showing you how to first model a child's toy wagon using polygons as well as NURBS surfacing, and then build a decorative box to use for detailed photo-real texturing and rendering.

Chapter 7, "Maya Shading and Texturing," shows you how to assign textures and shaders to your models. Using the toy wagon you created in Chapter 6, you'll learn how to texture it to look like a real toy wagon as well as lay out its UVs for proper texture placement. Then, you'll create detailed photo-real textures based on photos for the decorative box model. You'll also learn how to take advantage of Maya 2011's ability to work with layered Photoshop files.

Chapter 8, "Introduction to Animation," covers the basics of how to animate a bouncing ball using keyframes and moves on to creating more complex animation—throwing an axe and firing a catapult. You'll also learn how to import objects into an existing animation and transfer animation from one object to another, a common exercise in professional productions. In addition, you'll learn how to use the Graph Editor to edit and finesse your animation as well as animate objects along paths.

Chapter 9, "More Animation!" expands on Chapter 8 to show you how to use Maya's skeleton and kinematics system to create a simple walk cycle. This chapter also covers how to animate objects by using relationships between them. A thrilling exercise shows you how to rig your locomotive model from Chapter 4 for automated animation, one of Maya's most productive uses.

Chapter 10, "Maya Lighting," begins by showing you how to light a 3D scene as you learn how to light the wagon you modeled and textured earlier in the book. It also shows you how to use the tools to create and edit Maya lights for illumination, shadows, and special lighting effects. mental ray for Maya's Physical Sun and Sky feature is explored in this chapter as an introduction to some sophisticated techniques for mental ray lighting.

Chapter 11, "Maya Rendering," explains how to create image files from your Maya scene and how to achieve the best look for your animation using proper cameras and rendering settings. You'll work with displacement maps to create details in a model. You'll also learn about the Maya renderer, the Vector renderer, and Final Gather using HDRI and Image-Based Lighting through mental ray for Maya, as well as raytracing, motion blur, and depth of field. You'll have a chance to render the decorative box to round out your skills.

Chapter 12, "Maya Dynamics and Effects," introduces you to Maya's powerful dynamics animation system as well as nParticle technology. You'll animate pool balls colliding with each other using rigid body dynamics and, using nParticle animation, you'll create steam to add to your locomotive scene from Chapter 4. This chapter also shows you how to use Paint Effects to create animated flowers and grass within minutes, and it introduces you to using Toon shading for a cartoon look to your renders.

Hardware and Software Considerations

Because computer hardware is a quickly moving target, and Maya now runs on three distinct operating systems (Windows 2000/XP/Vista/Windows 7, Linux, and Mac OS X), specifying which hardware components will work with Maya is something of a challenge. Fortunately, Autodesk has a "qualified hardware" page on its website that describes the latest hardware to be qualified to work with Maya for each operating system. Go to the following site for the most up-to-date information on system requirements:

    www.autodesk.com/maya

Although you can find specific hardware recommendations on these web pages, some general statements can be made about what constitutes a good platform on which to run Maya. First, be sure to get a fast processor; Maya eats through CPU cycles like crazy, so a fast processor is important. Second, you need lots of RAM (memory) to run Maya: at least 2GB, but 8GB is a good to have, especially if you're working with large scene files or are on a 64-bit system. Third, if you expect to interact well with your Maya scenes, a powerful video card is a must—although Maya will mosey along with a poor graphics card, screen redraws will be slow with complex scenes, which can quickly become frustrating. You may want to consider a workstation graphics card for the best compatibility (rather than a consumer-grade gaming video card). Several companies make entry-level through top-performing workstation cards to fit any budget. A large hard disk is also important—most computers these days come with huge drives anyway.

Fortunately, computer hardware is so fast these days that even laptop computers can now run Maya well. Additionally, even hardware that is not officially supported by Autodesk can often run Maya—just remember that you won't be able to get technical support if your system doesn't meet the company's qualifications.

The Next Step

By the time you finish *Introducing Maya 2011,* you'll have some solid skills for using Maya. When you're ready to move on to another level, be sure to check out other Maya titles from Sybex at www.sybex.com.

You can contact the author at www.koosh3d.com. You may also go to the book's website at www.sybex.com/go/intromaya2011.

CHAPTER 1

Introduction to Computer Graphics and 3D

This book is intended to introduce you to the workings of 3D animation (called computer graphics, or CG) with one of the most popular programs on the market, Autodesk Maya. It will introduce you to many of Maya's features and capabilities with the intent of energizing you to further study.

Having said that, let's face a basic fact: The best way to succeed at almost anything is to practice. Prepare to go through the exercises in this book, but also try to think of exercises and projects that can take you further in your learning process. A book, class, or video can take you only so far; the rest is up to you. Imagination and exploration will serve you well.

This is not to say you can't be a casual visitor to working in CG—far from it. Playing around and seeing what you can create in this medium is just flat-out fun. Don't lose sight of that. If you feel the enjoyment slipping away, step away from the screen for a while. Understanding your own learning pace is important.

Throughout this book, you'll learn how to work with Maya tools and techniques at a pace you set for yourself. This chapter will prepare you for the hands-on study that follows by introducing the most important CG concepts and the roles they will play in your Maya work. When you're learning how to work with Maya, the most important concept is discovering how you work as an artist. If you have a basic understanding of the methodology and terms of computer art and CG, you can skim or even skip this chapter and jump right into working with Maya.

Topics in this chapter include:

- **Art?**
- **Computer graphics**
- **The stages of production**
- **The CG production workflow**
- **Core concepts**
- **Basic film concepts**

Art?

Art, in many instances, requires transcendence of its medium; it speaks of its own accord. Art goes beyond the mechanics of how you create it (whether by brush or mouse) and takes on its own life. Learning to look beyond what you're working *with* and seeing what you're working *for* is the key to creating art with CG. Try not to view this experience as learning a software package, but as learning a way of working to an end. As you begin learning 3D with Maya, you acquire a new language—a new form of communication. Keep in mind that the techniques you acquire are only a means to the end.

> Relax and enjoy yourself.

It's hard to relax when you're trying to cram so much information into your brain. But keep in mind that you should try not to make this experience about how a software program works; instead, make it about how you work with the software. Maya is only your tool.

When hiring professional 3D artists, CG studios keenly look for a strong artistic sense, whether in a traditional portfolio or a CG reel. Therefore, it's paramount to fortify the artist within yourself and practice traditional art such as life drawing, photography, painting, or sculpture as you learn CG, beginning with the core principles introduced in this first chapter. Keep in mind that the computer you'll be using for 3D work is nothing more than a tool. You run it; it doesn't run you.

3D is a part of the daily visual lexicon. With the availability of inexpensive and fast computers, everyone can create their own CG projects. Artists everywhere are adding the language of CG to their skill set. So before you start learning a particular CG tool—Maya, in this case—make sure you have a grasp of the fundamental issues underlying CG. It's important.

Computer Graphics

CG and CGI are the abbreviations for *computer graphics* and *computer graphics imagery*, respectively, and are often used interchangeably. CG literally refers to any picture or series of pictures that is generated by an artist on a computer. However, the industry convention is to use the terms *CG* and *CGI* to refer to 3D graphics and not to images created using 2D image or paint programs such as Photoshop.

Most 2D graphics software is bitmap based, whereas all 3D software is vector based. Bitmap-based software creates an image as a mosaic of pixels, filled in one at a time. Vector-based software creates an image as a series of mathematical instructions from one calculated, or graphed, point to another. This much more powerful method for creating graphics is behind all the impressive CG images you've seen in movies, videogames, and so on. It's also the method for the images you'll soon create with Maya. You'll learn more about vectors and bitmaps in the section "Computer Graphics Concepts" later in this chapter.

If you're familiar with 2D graphics software, such as Adobe Illustrator or Adobe Flash, you already know something about vectors. Maya and other 3D graphics tools add the calculation of depth. Instead of drawing objects on a flat plane, they're defined in three-dimensional space. This makes the artist's job fairly cerebral and very different than it is for 2D art; in 3D art, there is more of a dialogue between the left and right sides of the brain. When working with 3D graphics tools, you get a better sense of manipulating and working with objects, as opposed to dealing with the lines, shapes, and colors used to create 2D images.

A Preview of the 3D Process

The process of creating in 3D requires that you either model or arrange prebuilt objects in a scene, give them color and light, and render them through a virtual camera to make an image. In essence, you create a scene that tells the computer what objects are in the scene, where the objects are located, what the colors and textures of the objects are, what lighting is available, and which camera to use in the scene. It's a lot like directing a live-action production, but without any actor tantrums.

> A large community on the Web provides free and for-pay models that you can use in your scenes. Sites such as www.turbosquid.com and www.archive3d.net can cut out a lot of the time you might spend creating all the models for a CG scene. This gives you the chance to skip at least some of the modeling process, if that isn't your thing.

With CG, you work in 3D space—an open area in which you define your objects, set their colors and textures, and position lights as if you were setting up for a live photo shoot. CG is remarkably analogous to the art and practice of photography and filmmaking.

Photographers lay out a scene by placing the subjects into the frame of the photo. They light the area for a specific mood, account for the film qualities in use, adjust the lens aperture, and fine-tune for the colors of the scene. They choose the camera, film, and lens based on their desired result. Then, they snap the pictures and digitally transfer them or develop them to paper. Through this process, a photo is born.

After you build your scene in 3D using models, lights, and a camera, the computer *renders* the scene, converting it to a 2D image. Through setup and rendering, CGI is born—and, with a little luck, a CG artist is also born.

Rendering is the process of calculating lights and shadows, the placement of textures and colors on models, the movement of animated objects, and so on to produce a sequence of 2D pictures that effectively "shoot" your virtual scene. Instead of an envelope of 4×6 glossy prints, you get a sequence of 2D computer images (or a QuickTime or AVI [Audio Video Interleave] movie file) that sit on your hard drive waiting to be seen, and invariably commented on, by your know-it-all friends.

In a nutshell, that is the CG process. You'll need to practice planning and patience, because CG follows conventions that are different from those for painting programs and image editors. The CG workflow is based on building, arrangements, and relationships. But it's an easy workflow to pick up and master in time. It can be learned by anyone with the desire and the patience to give it a try.

Animation

Animation is *change over time.* In other words, animation is the simulation of an object changing over a period of time, whether it's that object's position or size, or even color or shape. In addition to working in the three dimensions of space, Maya animators work with a fourth dimension: time.

All animation, from paper flipbooks to film to Maya, is based on the principle that when we see a series of rapidly changing images, we perceive the changing of the image to be in continuous motion. If you have a chance to pause and step through an animated film, frame by frame, on your DVD player or DVR, you'll see how animation comes together, literally step by step.

To create CG animation yourself, you have to create scene files with objects that exhibit some sort of change, whether through movement, color shift, growth, or other behavior. But just as with flipbooks and film animation, the change you're animating occurs between static images, called *frames,* a term carried over from film. You define the object's animation using a *timeline* measured in these single frames.

You'll learn more in the section "Basic Animation Concepts" later in this chapter. For now, let's move on to the stages of CG production.

The Stages of Production

The CG animation industry inherited a workflow from the film industry that consists of three broad stages: preproduction, production, and post production. In film, *preproduction* is the process in which the script and storyboards are written, costumes and sets are designed and built, actors are cast and rehearsed, the crew is hired, and the equipment is rented and set up. In the *production* phase, scenes are taped or filmed in the most efficient order. *Post production* (often simply called *post*) describes everything that happens afterward: The scenes are edited into a story; a musical score, sound effects, and additional dialogue are added; and visual effects may also be added. (In a film that has special effects or animation, the actual CG creation is usually completed in post production. However, it may start in the preproduction phases of the film or project.)

Although the work performed at each stage is radically different, this is a useful framework for understanding the process of creating CG as well.

Preproduction

Preproduction for a CG animation means gathering reference materials, motion tests, layout drawings, model sketches, and such together to make the actual CG production as straightforward as possible.

Because CG artists are responsible for defining their 3D scenes from the ground up, it's essential to have a succinct plan of attack for a well-organized production. The more time spent planning and organizing for CG, the better. Whether you're working on a small job or a complex film, entering into production without a good plan of attack will not only cause trouble, but also stunt the growth of your project.

In the real world, preproduction is part of every CG animation project. For the tutorial projects in this book, the sketches and other files supplied on the accompanying CD are your preproduction. Even for these tutorials, however, you should try to gather as much information as you can about the objects you'll create, going beyond what is presented. Having different perspectives on a subject is the key to understanding it. Disappointing movies often are the product of terribly flawed preproduction stages; likewise, a poorly thought-out CG production will invariably end in headaches and wasted time.

The Script

To tell a story, CG or not, you should put it in words. A story doesn't need to contain dialogue for it to benefit from a script. Even abstract animations benefit from a detailed explanation of timings and colors laid out in a treatment (because there is likely no dialogue). The script or treatment serves as the initial blueprint for the animation, a place where you lay out the all-important *intent*.

The Storyboard

A storyboard is a further definition of the script. Even a rudimentary storyboard with stick figures on notebook paper is useful to a production. You break the script into scenes, and then you break those scenes into shots. Next, you sketch out each shot in a panel of a storyboard. The panels are laid out in order according to the script to give a visual and linear explanation of the story. Storyboards are useful for planning camera angles (framing a shot), position of characters, lighting, mood, and so on.

The Conceptual Art

Conceptuals are the design elements that you may need for the CG production. Typically, characters are drawn into character sheets in three different neutral poses: from the front, from the side, and from an angle called a *3⁄4 view*. You can also create color art for the various sets, props, and characters to better visualize the colors, textures, and lighting that will be needed. Props and sets are identified from the script and boards and then sketched out into model sheets. The better you visualize the conceptual art, the easier it will be to model, texture, and light everything in CG.

Production

Production begins when you start creating models from the boards, model sheets, and concept art. You model the characters, sets, and props, and then you assign textures (colors, patterns). The animators take the models and animate everything according to the boards and script. The sequences are rendered in low quality for dailies and checked for accuracy and content.

The CG production phase can involve a variety of steps. The specific steps are defined by the needs of the production. Most of the CG techniques you'll learn in this book are part of the production phase. To make a long story short, 3D scenes are created, lit, and animated in the production phase.

Post Production

After all the scenes have been set up with props and characters and everything is animated, post production can begin. Post production for a CG project is similar to post production for a film. This is where all of a CG film's elements are brought together and assembled into final form.

Rendering

Rendering is the process by which the computer calculates how everything in the scene should look and then displays it. As you'll learn throughout this book, the decisions you make in creating the objects in a scene can make a big difference in how the rest of the process goes.

Rendering makes significant processing demands on your computer, usually requiring the full attention of your PC. This can take a considerable amount of time. You can render one scene while another scene is in production, but asking a computer that is rendering to multitask isn't advisable unless you're using a dual-processor machine with plenty of memory.

When everything is rendered properly, the final images are sorted, and the assembly of the CG project begins. Rendering is discussed more fully in Chapter 11, "Maya Rendering."

We'll take a quick look at three more post-production activities: compositing, editing, and adding sound. These are advanced topics, and complete coverage is beyond the scope of *Introducing Maya 2011*. However, a multitude of books are available on these topics for further study.

Compositing

Quite often, CG is rendered in different layers and segments, which need to be put back together. In a particular scene, for example, multiple characters interact. Each character is rendered separately from the others and from the backgrounds. They're then put together in *compositing*, or the process of bringing together scene elements that were created separately to form the final scene. Maya makes this process easier with Render Layers, which you'll experience in Chapter 11.

Compositing programs such as Maya Composite, Nuke, Digital Fusion, and After Effects allow you to compose CG elements together and give you some additional control over color, timing, and a host of other additions and alterations you can make to the images. Compositing can greatly affect the look of a CG project and can be an integral part of CG creation.

> Many new animators try to generate their final images in a single rendering of their scene, but you don't need to do that. Realizing the component nature of CG is important; you can use components to your advantage by rendering items separately and compositing them together in the finishing stage. This gives you a lot of control in finishing the images to your satisfaction without always having to go back, change the scene, and re-render it.

Editing

The rendered and composited CG footage is collected and edited together to conform to the script and boards. Some scenes are cut or are moved around to heighten the story. This is essentially the same process as film editing, with one big difference: the amount of footage used.

To make sure they have adequate coverage for all their scenes and to leave extra room for creativity in editing, live-action filmmakers shoot quite a bit more footage than is needed for a film. The editor and the director sift through all the scenes and arrange them to assemble the film in a way that works best with what they have shot and with the performances they prefer. A typical film uses a fraction of all the film or video that is shot.

Because creating CG is typically more time-consuming and expensive than shooting live action, scenes and shots are often tightly arranged in preproduction boards so not much effort is wasted. The entire production is edited with great care beforehand, and the scenes are built and animated to match the story, almost down to the frame. Consequently, the physical editing process consists mostly of assembling the scenes into the sequence of the story. This is also why a good preproduction process is important. When you plan out what you want to get, you're much more likely to get it.

Sound

Sound design is critical to CG because viewers associate visuals with audio. A basic soundtrack can give a significant punch to a simple animation by helping to provide realism, mood, narrative, and so on, adding a greater impact to the CG.

Sound effects, such as footsteps, are inserted to match the action on the screen. This type of sound is also known in film as *Foley sound*. Music is scored and added to match the film. Quite often, the dialogue or musical score inspires a character's actions or body language. Again, this is much the same procedure as in film, with one exception. In the event that a CG project requires dialogue, the dialogue must be recorded and edited *before* CG production can begin. Dialogue is a part of the preproduction phase as well as a component of post production. This is because animators need to hear the dialogue being spoken so they can coordinate the lip movements of the characters speaking, a process known as *lip-synch*.

How It All Works Together

The process behind making a *South Park* episode is a perfect workflow example. Although the show appears to be animated using paper cutouts, as was the original Christmas short, the actual production work is now done using Maya. In preproduction on a typical episode, the writers hammer out the script, and the voice talent records all the voices before the art department creates the visuals for the show. The script is storyboarded, and copies are distributed to all the animators and layout artists.

At the beginning of the production phase, each scene is set up with the proper backgrounds and characters in Maya and then handed off for lip-synch, which is the first step in the animation of the scene. The voices are digitized into computer files for lip-synch animators who animate the mouths of the characters. The lip-synched animation is then passed to character animators who use the storyboards and the soundtrack to animate the characters in the Maya scene.

The animation is then rendered to start the post, edited together following the boards, and then sent back to the sound department for any sound effects needed to round out the scene. The episode is assembled and then sent off on tape for broadcast.

The CG Production Workflow

Because of the nature of CG and how scenes must be built, a specific workflow works best. Modeling almost always begins the process, which then can lead into texturing, and then to animation (or animation and then texturing). Lighting should follow, with rendering pulling up the rear as it must. (Of course, the process isn't completely linear; you'll often go back and forth adjusting models, lights, and textures throughout the process.) Chapters 4 through 11 follow this overall sequence, presenting the major Maya operations in the same order you'll use in real-world CG projects.

Modeling

Modeling, the topic of Chapters 4 through 6, is usually the first step in creating CG. It's the topic that garners a lot of coverage in publications and captures the interest of most budding CG artists. You most often start a CG scene by creating the objects you need to occupy your space. It can end up taking the majority of the time in your process. This is why downloading or purchasing models from the Internet can often cut down the amount of time you spend on your project. This, of course, assumes you're not a fan of modeling and prefer to spend your time animating or working on texturing and lighting.

There are many modeling techniques, and each could be the subject of its own series of books. The choice of which technique to use usually depends on the modeler's taste and preferred workflow. The choices are among polygonal modeling (Chapter 4, "Beginning Polygonal Modeling"), NURBS modeling, and subdivision surface (SubD) modeling (Chapter 5, "Modeling with NURBS, Subdivisions, and Deformers"). Knowing how an object is used in a scene gives you its criteria for modeling. You never want to spend more time on a model than is needed. Creating a highly detailed model for a faraway shot will waste your time and expand rendering times needlessly. If you need to see a park bench in a wide shot from far away, the model doesn't need abundant detail or complicated surfacing. You can usually create any required details for it by just adding textures. However, if that park bench is featured prominently in a close-up, it needs as much detail as possible because viewers will see more of the bench. You'll learn more about this aspect of modeling in Chapter 4.

The more you use models in scenes, the better you'll develop your eye for exactly how much detail to provide. When you're starting out, however, it's a good idea to lavish as much attention on detail as you can; this can teach you perhaps 70 percent of what you can learn about modeling, which in turn will benefit your overall speed and technique. As you gain more experience, you'll be able to discern exactly how much detail to add to a scene and not go overboard.

Character Modeling

Character modeling usually involves organic forms, such as animals, humans, aliens, and such. Practically anything that is animated and portrays a character in a scene can be referred to as a *character model*. You need to create these with animation techniques in mind, as well as accuracy of form.

Some *organic* characters (for example, critters and people, as opposed to robots with mechanical parts and hard edges) are built with patches of surfaces stitched together or as single objects that are stretched and pulled into shape. Character models need to look seamless because most character animation requires the model to deform in some way—to bend and warp at certain areas such as the joints.

A character modeler needs to keep the future of the character in mind to allow for particular character animation methods that will be used. Quite frequently, you'll create several models for a character to account for different uses of that character and to keep the scene efficient and workable. You may create one character with fine facial detail for close-up speaking scenes and another with hardly any details for walk cycles in distant shots. Listen to your mother: don't get in over your head; do as much as you know you can finish properly.

Architectural and Environment Modeling

Architectural and environmental modeling includes architectural previsualization for the design of buildings as well as the generation of backgrounds for sets and environments. Typically, it involves modeling buildings or interiors as well as mountains or anything that is required for the scenery, such as benches, chairs, lampposts, and so on.

You shouldn't create incredibly detailed environments, especially ones that use a lot of *geometry* (that is, the objects in your scene), if they aren't closely featured in a shot. The greater the amount of geometry, the slower your computer will run and the longer rendering will take. If you reach a critical mass of too much geometry in your scene, it may not even render. You can create much of an environment by using clever textures and *matte paintings* on simple geometry. Matte paintings, which are detailed maps on bare surfaces, are used frequently for game environments. The rule of thumb for all kinds of CG is "use whatever works."

> Because your computer stores everything in the scene as vector math, the term *geometry* refers to all the surfaces and models in a scene.

Props Modeling

Props modeling covers almost everything else needed in the scene. In theater and film terms, a *prop* is an object used by a character in the action; anything relegated to the scenery or background is a *scenic*. For example, a prop can be a purse a character is carrying, a leash on an animated dog, or a car a character is driving. If the car or purse were just sitting in the background, it would be considered a scenic.

Texturing

When the models are complete, it's a good idea to begin *texturing* and *shading*, the process of applying colors and textures to an object to make it renderable. When you create an object in Maya, for example, a simple gray default shader is automatically assigned to it that will let you see the object when you light and render the scene.

Because the textures may look different after animating and lighting the scene, it's wise to leave the final adjustments for later. Just as a painter will pencil in a sketch before adding details, you don't need to make all the shading adjustments right away; you can return to any part of your scene in Maya and adjust it to fine-tune the picture.

You'll learn more about texturing and shading in Chapter 7, "Maya Shading and Texturing."

Animation

You can make or break your scene with animation. We all have an innate sense of how things are supposed to move on a visceral level, if not an academic one. We understand how physics applies to objects and how people and animals move around. Because of this, viewers tend to be critical of CG's motion if it's not lifelike. Put bluntly, you know when something doesn't look right, and so will the people watching your animation.

To animate something properly, you may need to do quite a lot of setup beyond just modeling. Depending on the kind of animating you'll be doing, you may need to set up the models for however you've decided to animate them. For example, for character animation, you'll need to create and attach an armature, or skeleton, to manipulate the character and to make it move like a puppet in order to do your bidding.

Taking the models you've spent hours detailing and reworking and giving them life is thrilling and can make any detailed modeling and setup routine well worth the effort.

Chapter 8, "Introduction to Animation," and Chapter 9, "More Animation!" cover animation techniques in Maya.

Lighting

CG is fundamentally all about light. Manipulating how light is created and reflected is what you're doing with CG. Without light, we wouldn't see anything, so it makes sense that simulating light is the most influential step in CG. Lighting can drastically alter the look of your scene; it greatly affects the believability of your models and textures and creates and heightens mood.

During the lighting step, you set up virtual lights in your scene to illuminate your objects and action. Although you can set up some initial lights during the texturing of the scene, the serious lighting should be the last thing you do, aside from changes and tweaks.

The type and number of lights you use in a scene greatly affect not just the look of your scene, but also the amount of time the scene takes to render. Lighting becomes a careful dance between pragmatics and results. It's perhaps the subtlest part of CG to master.

When you gain more experience with lighting, you'll notice that it affects every part of your CG creation. Before long, you'll start modeling differently—that is, modeling with the final lighting of the scene in mind. Texturing will change when you keep lighting techniques in mind. Even your animation and staging will change a bit to take better advantage of efficient, powerful lighting.

As you'll learn in Chapter 10, "Maya Lighting," virtual lights in Maya are similar to lights used in the real world, from a single point of light, such as a bulb, to directed beams, such as spotlights.

Rendering

At this stage, your computer takes your scene and makes all the computations it needs to create raster (bitmapped) images for your movie. Rendering time depends on how much geometry is used in the scene as well as on the number of lights, the size of your textures, and the quality and size of your output: the more efficient your scene, the shorter the rendering times.

A lot of people ask how long they should expect their renders to take or how long is too long for a frame to render. It's a subjective question with no real answer. Your frames will take as long as they have to for them to look the way you want. Of course, if you have tight time or budgetary constraints, you need simple scenes to keep the render resources and times to a minimum. In production, you're always short on time, so having the most efficient pipeline possible will be your savior. If you don't work efficiently, your producer or supervisor eventually will tire of hearing, "But I'm still rendering."

That being said, it's important to understand *how* a scene is put together before you learn to put a scene together *efficiently*. While you're learning, use as many lights and as much geometry as you think you need for your scenes. The more experience you gain, the more efficient your eye will become.

Core Concepts

CG animation draws from many disciplines. While learning Maya, you'll work with concepts derived not only from computer graphics, but also from design, film and cinematography, and traditional animation. Here's a summary of the most important of those concepts as they apply to Maya.

Computer Graphics Concepts

Knowing a bit about the general terminology and methodology of computer graphics will help you understand how Maya works. Let's begin with the crucial distinction between raster (bitmapped) and vector graphics and how this distinction affects you as a Maya user.

Raster Images

Raster images (synonymous with bitmapped images) make up the world of computer images today. These images are displayed through the arrangements of colored pixels onscreen or dots on a print to display an image. Everything you create in Maya will eventually be seen as a raster image, even though you first create it using vectors.

Raster image programs, such as Photoshop, let you adjust existing settings such as color, size, and position for all or part of an image. They let you paint onto a scanned picture or a virtual canvas to adjust or create the pixels yourself. These programs affect pixels directly, giving you the tools to change pixels to form images. For instance, you can use a scanned photo of your house in Photoshop to paint the side of the house red to see what it might look like before you run down to the local paint store.

A raster or bitmap image is a mosaic of pixels, so the *resolution* of an image is defined by the number of pixels in the horizontal and vertical directions. Because they're based on a grid of a fixed size, raster images don't scale up well. The closer you get to a raster image, the bigger the pixels become, making the image look blocky, or *pixelated*. To make large raster images, you need to begin with a higher resolution. The higher the resolution, the larger the file size will be. Figure 1.1 shows what happens when you blow up a raster image.

Figure 1.1

A raster image at its original size (left) and blown up several times (right)

Most common raster displays are television or computer screens. In fact, the term *raster* originally referred to the display area of a television or computer monitor. To form an image, the electronics in these devices essentially paint it as a grid of red, green, and blue pixels on a glowing screen. Every image generated by a computer, therefore, must either begin as a raster image or be rasterized as part of rendering for display.

Vector Images

Vector images are created in a completely different way. They're formed using mathematical algorithms and geometric functions. Instead of defining the color of each and every pixel in a grid of a raster image, a vector image uses coordinates and geometric formulas to plot points that define *areas*, *volumes*, and *shapes.*

Popular vector-based image applications include Adobe Illustrator and Flash, as well as practically all computer-aided design (CAD) programs, such as AutoCAD and SolidWorks. These programs let you define shapes and volumes and add color and texture to them through their toolsets. They store the results in scene files containing coordinates and equations of points in space and the color values that have been assigned to them. This vector information is then converted into raster images (called *rasterization*) through rendering so you can view the final image or animation.

When scaled, vector graphics don't suffer from the same limitations as raster images. As you can see in Figure 1.2, vectors can be scaled with no loss of quality; they will never pixelate.

Motion in vector programs is stored not by a long sequence of image files, but through changes in positions of the geometry and in the math that defines the shapes and volumes. When a Flash cartoon is played on a website, for example, the information downloaded and fed to your computer is in vector form. Your computer then renders this information on the fly in real time into a raster display of the content that you can (you hope) enjoy on your screen.

When you work in Maya, vectors are displayed as wireframes. When you finish your scene, Maya renders the image, converting the vector information into a sequence of raster images you can play back.

Image Output

When you're done with your animation, you'll probably want as many people as possible to see it (and like it!). To make that happen, you have to render it into a file sequence or a movie file. The file can be saved in any number of ways, depending on how you intend it to be viewed.

COLOR DEPTH

An image file stores the color of each pixel as three values representing red, green, and blue. Image type depends on how much storage is allotted to each pixel (the *color depth*). These are the color depths common to image files in CG production:

Grayscale The image is black and white with varying degrees of gray in between, typically 256 shades of gray. Grayscale images are good for rendering out black-and-white subjects as well as being used for some types of texture maps like displacement maps.

8-Bit Image File (a.k.a. 24-Bit Color Display) Referred to as 24-bit color display or True Color in desktop settings for Windows, each color channel is given 8 bits for a range of 256 shades of each red, green, and blue channel, for a total of 16 million colors in the image. This color depth gives good color quality for an image and is widely used in most animation applications. Most of your renders from Maya will probably be as 8-bit image files, because most monitors are only capable of 8-bit color reproduction in playback.

16-Bit Image File Used in television and film work using such file types as TIFF16, a 16-bit image file holds 16 bits of information for each color channel, resulting in an impressive number of color levels and ranges. Each file can exceed several megabytes even at low resolutions. These files are primarily used in professional productions, although they're being supplanted by the use of 32-bit images.

32-Bit Image File This is where the big kids play. Used primarily for film work but increasingly in general use, 32-bit image files, such as the OpenEXR format, give you an incredible amount of range in each color channel. This lets you adjust a wide range of tones and hues in your rendered output for the fullest detail. They're pretty much standard for film work because outputting CG to film can require high levels of color and brightness range in the image.

High Dynamic Range Imagery (HDRI) HDRI images are 32-bit float images that are created by combining several digital photos into one image file. For example, photos are taken of a subject with different levels of light using various exposures during photography. With a "32 bit float" file format, a lot of information can be stored about the colors in the image; i.e. a very high bit depth is achieved. This way, you have a series of images that range from dark (with very fast exposure) to normal (with proper exposure time) to blown out brightness (with overexposure). These different exposures are then compiled into a single HDR file format (`.hdr`) that represents a wider range of light and dark than a typical photo. These files are traditionally used as lighting setups, especially for scenes in which CG is integrated with a live-action background using image-based lighting (IBL), a concept we'll touch on in Chapter 11.

COLOR CHANNELS

As mentioned, each image file holds the color information in *channels*. All color images have red, green, and blue color channels that, when viewed together, give a color image. Each channel is a measurement of how much red, green, or blue is in areas of the image. A fourth channel, called the *alpha* channel, is used as a transparency channel. This channel, also known as the *matte* channel, defines which portions of the image are transparent or opaque. Not all image files have alpha channels. You can read more about alpha channels in Chapter 7.

FILE FORMATS

In addition to image types, several image file formats are available today. The most common is probably JPEG (Joint Photographic Experts Group), which is widely used on the Internet.

The main difference between file formats is how the image is stored. Some formats compress the file to reduce its size. However, as the degree of compression increases, the color quality of the image decreases.

The popular formats to render into from Maya are TIFF (Tagged Image File Format), Maya IFF (Maya Image File Format), and Targa. These file formats maintain a good 8-bit image file, are either uncompressed or barely compressed (lossless compression), and are frequently used for broadcast or film work. These formats also have an alpha channel, giving you better control when you later composite images together. To see an animation rendered in a file sequence of TIFFs, for example, you must play them back using a frame player such as FCheck (which is included with Maya) or IRIDAS FrameCycler, or compile them into a movie file using a program such as Adobe After Effects.

Ultimately, your final image format depends on the next step in your project. For example, if you plan to composite your CG, you'll need to output a format that can be imported by your compositing or editing program. TIFF files are perhaps the best format to use, because they're widely compatible, store uncompressed color, and have an alpha channel. You might also consider outputting to 16-bit or even 32-bit float images to give you the greatest range of color when you fine tune the image sequences. For the vast majority of your work as a beginner, you'll be working in 8 bit.

MOVIE FILES

Animations can also be output to movie files such as AVI or QuickTime. These usually large files are self-contained and hold all the images necessary for the animation that they play back as frames. Movie files can also be compressed, but they suffer from quality loss the more they're compressed.

Maya can render directly to an uncompressed AVI movie format, saving you the seeming hassle of having to render out a large sequence of files. Although rendering directly to an AVI movie may seem like a good idea, it usually isn't. It's best to render a sequence of files that can easily be compiled into a movie file later using a program such as Adobe After Effects, Premiere, or QuickTime Pro. The primary reason is simple: your render may crash, or your machine may freeze. In such an event, you need to start your AVI render from the beginning, whereas with images (like TIFFs) you can pick up right after the last rendered frame. Rendering frames is just the better way to go.

Color

Color is how we perceive the differences in the wavelengths of light. The wide range of colors that we see (the visible spectrum) results when any of three *primary colors* of light—red, green, and blue—are "mixed" together. You can mix color in two ways: subtractive and additive. These color definitions are most often displayed in *color wheels*, which equally space the primary colors around a ring and place the resultant colors when primaries are mixed in between the appropriate primaries.

Knowing more about color will help you understand how your CG's color scheme will work and help you design your shots with greater authority. (See the reading list at the end of this chapter for some books that expound on color theory and composition.)

SUBTRACTIVE AND ADDITIVE COLOR

Subtractive color mixing is used when the image will be seen with an external light source. It's based on the way reflected light creates color. Light rays bounce off colored surfaces and are tinted by the different pigments on the surface. These pigments absorb and reflect only certain frequencies of the light hitting them, in essence *subtracting* certain colors from the light before it gets to your eyes. Pile up enough different colors of paint, and you get black; all the colors are absorbed by the pigment, and only black is reflected.

When subtractive color mixing is used in painting, the traditional color wheel's primary colors are red, yellow, and blue. These three pigments can be mixed together to form any other color pigment, and they form the basis for the color wheel most people are exposed to in art education in primary school. In the world of print production, however, a CMYK (Cyan, Magenta, Yellow, and blacK) color wheel is used. Cyan, yellow, and magenta ink colors are the primary colors used to mix all the other ink colors for print work.

Projected light is mixed as *additive color*. Each light's frequency adds on to another's to form color. The additive primary colors are red, green, and blue. These three colors, when mixed in certain ratios, form the entire range of color. When all are equally mixed together, they form a white light.

A computer monitor uses only additive color, mixing each color with amounts of red, green, and blue (RGB).

Warm colors are those in the magenta to red to yellow range, and *cool colors* are those in the green to cyan to blue range of the additive color wheel. Warm colors seem to advance from the frame, and cool colors seem to recede into the frame.

HOW A COMPUTER DEFINES COLOR

Computers represent all information, including color, as sets of numeric values made up of binary numbers—0s and 1s (bits). In an 8-bit color file, each pixel is represented by three 8-bit values corresponding to the red, green, and blue channels of the image. An 8-bit binary number ranges from 0 to 255, so for each primary color you have 256 possible levels. With three channels, you have $256 \times 256 \times 256$ (16.7 million) possible combinations of each primary color mixed to form the final color.

Color value can also be set on the hue, saturation, and value (HSV) channels. Again, each channel holds a value from 0 to 255 (in an 8-bit image file); these values combine to define the final color. The hue value defines the actual tint (from red to green to violet) of the color. The saturation defines *how much* of that tint is present in the color. The higher the saturation value, the deeper the color will be. Finally, value defines the brightness of the color, from black to white. The higher the value, the brighter the color will be.

HSV and RGB give you different methods to control color, allowing you to use the method you prefer. All the colors available in Maya, from textures to lights, are defined as either RGB or HSV values for the best flexibility. You can switch from HSV to RGB definition in Maya at any time.

CMYK COLOR

A CMYK color wheel is used for print work, and this is referred to as the *four-color process*. Color inkjet printers produce color printouts by mixing the appropriate levels of these inks onto the paper.

All output from a computer, which is RGB based, to a printer goes through a CMYK conversion as it's printed. For professional print work, specially calibrated monitors are used to enhance previewing the CMYK color of an RGB image before it's printed. Fortunately, only print professionals need to worry about this conversion process, because most of it is handled by graphics software to a fairly accurate degree.

VIEWING COLOR

The broadcast standard for North America is NTSC (National Television System Committee). One joke in the industry is that the acronym means Never The Same Color, referring to the fact that the color you see on one TV screen will be different from what you see on another screen. The same holds true for computer monitors, especially flat-panel displays. All displays are calibrated differently, and what you see on one screen may not be exactly what you see on another screen.

If it's important to have consistent color on different screens, say on your home and school computers, you can use traditional color bars downloaded from the Internet or your own custom-made color chart to adjust the settings of the monitors you work with so they match more closely. If color is absolutely critical when you're working in a group, it's important for everyone to view color output on a single screen.

Resolution, Aspect Ratio, and Frame Rate

Resolution denotes the size of an image by the number of horizontal and vertical pixels, usually expressed as # × # (for example, 640 × 480). The higher the resolution, the finer the image detail will be.

You'll adjust your final render size to suit the final medium for which you're creating the animation. Table 1.1 lists some standard resolutions.

Table 1.1

Typical Video Resolutions

NAME	SIZE	NOTES
VGA (Video Graphics Array)	640 × 480	Formerly the standard computing resolution and still a popular television resolution for tape output.
NTSC D1 (National Television System Committee)	720 × 486	The standard resolution for broadcast television in North America.
NTSC DV	720 × 480	Close to the NTSC D1 resolution, this is the typical resolution of digital video cameras.
PAL (Phase Alternation Line)	720 × 586	The standard broadcast resolution for most European countries.
HDTV (High Definition TV)	1920 × 1080	The emerging television standard, sometimes also referred to as 1080i (interlaced frames) or 1080p (progressive frames).
1K Academy (1K refers to 1000 pixels across the frame)	1024 × 768	Typically the lowest allowable resolution for film production at Academy ratio (see Table 1.2). Because film is an optical format (whereas TV is a raster format), there is no set defined resolution for film. Suffice it to say, the higher the better.
2K Academy (2K refers to 2000 pixels across)	2048 × 1556	Most studios output CG for film at this resolution, which gives the best size-to-performance ratio.
4K Academy (4K is 4000 pixels across)	4094 × 3072	A high resolution for film, used for highly detailed shots.

Any discussion of resolution must include the matter of *aspect ratio*. Aspect ratio is the ratio of the screen's *width* to its *height*. Aspect ratio standards are shown in Table 1.2.

Table 1.2

Aspect Ratio Standards

NAME	SIZE	NOTES
Academy Standard	1.33:1 or 4:3	The most common aspect ratio. The width is 1.33 times the length of the height. This is the NTSC television aspect ratio as well as the aspect ratio of 16mm films and some 35mm films, including classics such as *Gone with the Wind*.
Widescreen TV	1.78:1 or 16:9	With HD and widescreen TVs gaining popularity, the 16:9 standard is commonplace now. This aspect is used in HD programming and is also the aspect ratio of many widescreen computer monitors and laptops. This aspect is very close to the way most films are displayed (1.85:1, as shown next).
Widescreen Film (a.k.a. Academy Flat)	1.85:1	The most-often-used 35mm film aspect today. When it's displayed on a television, horizontal black bars appear above and below the picture so the edges aren't cropped off (an effect called *letterboxing*).
Anamorphic Ratio	2.35:1	Using an *anamorphic* lens, the image captured to 35mm film is squeezed. When played back with a projector with an anamorphic lens, the image is projected with a width at 2.35 times its height. On a standard TV, the letterboxing is more severe to avoid cropping the sides.

The number of frames played back per second determines the *frame rate* of the animation. This is denoted as *fps*, or frames per second. The following are the three standard frame rates for media:

- NTSC: 30fps
- PAL: 25fps
- Film: 24fps

Knowing your output medium is important when beginning an animation project. Although it isn't crucial, it can affect how you design your framing, create your movements, render your project, and so on. You can change the frame rate and render resolution at any time in Maya, but it's always better to know as best you can what the final resolution and fps will be before you begin.

Playing back a 24fps animation at 30fps will yield a slower-moving animation and will necessitate either repeating some frames to fill in the gaps or ending the animation early. Conversely, playing a 30fps animation at 24fps will create a faster-moving animation that will either skip some frames or end later than it should.

3D Coordinate Space and Axes

Three-dimensional space is the virtual area in which you create your models and execute your animation. It's based on the Cartesian coordinate system, a geometric map of sorts developed by the brainy René Descartes. Knowing where you are at all times is essential with a 3D program. You can do so if you understand the toolset you're working with and the 3D space in which you're working.

Space is defined in three axes—*X*, *Y*, and *Z*—representing width, height, and depth. The three axes form a numeric grid in which a particular point is defined by *coordinates* set forth as (#,#,#), corresponding to (*X,Y,Z*), respectively.

At the zero point of these axes is the *origin*. This is at (0,0,0) and is the intersection of all three axes. The 3D space defined by these three axes is called the *World axis,* in which the *XYZ* axes are *fixed references*. The axis in *World Space* is always fixed and is represented in Maya by the XYZ Axis icon in the lower-left corner of the Perspective windows.

Because objects can be oriented in all sorts of directions within the World axis, it's necessary for each object to have its own width, height, and depth axis independent of the World axis. This is called the *Local axis*. The Local axis is the *XYZ*-coordinate space that is attached to every object in Maya. When that object rotates or moves, its Local axis rotates and moves with it. This is necessary to make animating an object easier as it moves and orients about in the World axis.

You'll get a hands-on introduction to Maya's Cartesian coordinate space in the tutorial in Chapter 2, "Jumping in Headfirst, with Both Feet," where you'll re-create the solar system with the Sun placed at the origin, the planets orbiting the World axis and rotating on their own Local axes, and moons orbiting the planets and also rotating (see Figure 1.3).

Figure 1.3

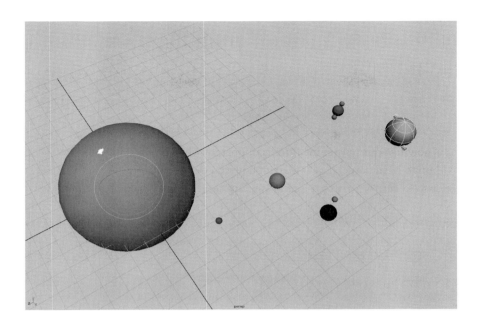

The Sun at the origin, Earth and other planets orbiting the World axis while rotating on their own axes, and the Moon orbiting Earth

Basic Design Concepts

Composition is all about how you lay out your scene and design your colors. Creating a dynamic frame that not only catches the eye but also informs and intrigues is itself an art form.

Some background in basic design is definitely helpful, and you'll want to look at design books as you further your education in 3D. Understanding the fundamentals of layout and design makes for better-looking scenes and easier setup. The concepts presented here will get you started. Design theory may not seem specifically pertinent to CG right now, but recognizing that there is a logical system behind every pretty picture will help you progress, both as an artist and as an animator.

Form, Space, and Composition

Space is your canvas. Because your canvas ultimately will be a rendered image, your composition needs to fit within your rendered image frame. Whether that frame falls into a tiny web window or a huge IMAX screen, the basics of design always apply: how you arrange your forms and divide your space says a lot.

In the design lexicon, *form* means anything you can see; it has some sort of shape, color, or texture that distinguishes it from its frame. How your scene's objects lie in the frame defines your composition. The space behind and between what is rendered out is the ground, or background plane. Objects become *positive space*, and the background becomes *negative space*.

To viewers, positive space tends to proceed forward from the frame, whereas negative space recedes. Playing with the position of positive and negative space greatly affects the dynamics of your frame.

Design a static frame in which the objects are all centered and evenly spaced, and your viewers will wonder why they're looking at your composition. Arrange the composition so that your subjects occupy more interesting areas of the frame in which they play with negative space, and the eye is drawn all over the frame, creating a dynamic composition. This principle applies to still images as well as to animation.

In the tutorial in Chapter 10, you'll use light and shadow to turn a still life of fruit into a dynamic and interestingly composed frame.

Balance and Symmetry

Balance in a frame suggests an even amount of positive space from one side of the frame to the other. A frame that is heavier on one side can create a more dynamic composition.

Symmetrical objects in a frame are mirrored from one side to another and create a certain static balance in the frame. An asymmetrical composition, therefore, denotes movement in the composition.

A popular technique used by painters, photographers, and cinematographers is called *framing in thirds*. With this technique, the frame is divided into a grid of thirds vertically and horizontally. Interesting parts of the frame, or focal points of the subjects, are placed at strategic locations in the grid. Placing your subject in the lower third makes it seem small or insignificant, static, or even boring. Placing it in the upper third makes the image more dynamic, magnifying its perceived scale or importance, and even tells a better story. Figure 1.4 illustrates the difference between a static, symmetric frame and a frame based on thirds.

Figure 1.4

A purely symmetrical frame looks static; the boy seems still with nowhere to go. Framing in thirds helps create or heighten a sense of motion, giving space for the boy to run.

Contrast

Contrast in design describes how much your foreground subject "pops" from the background. As you can see in Figure 1.5, when you create an area in your frame that contains little variation in color and light, the image seems flat and uneventful. Using dark shadows and light highlights increases the perceived depth in the image and helps pop out the subject from the background. Animating contrast can help increase or decrease the depth of your frame.

As you'll see in Chapter 10, light plays an important role in creating dynamic contrasts within your frame.

Figure 1.5

With low contrast, the subject seems to disappear into the background. If you add shadows and highlights, the subject pops out.

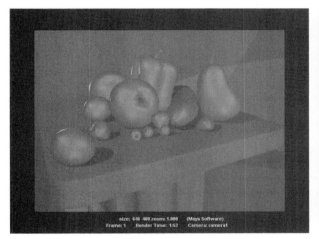 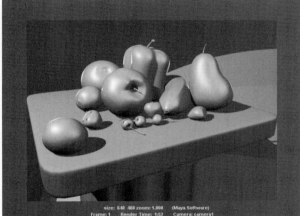

Color

Your use of color also plays a big part in creating impact in your frame. As stated earlier, warm colors tend to advance toward you, and cooler colors seem to recede into the frame. Placing a warm color on a subject on a cool background creates a nice color contrast to help the dynamics of your frame.

Colors opposite each other on the color wheel are *complementary* colors and usually clash when put together. Using complementary colors can create a wide variation of contrast in your scene.

Narrative

A *narrative film* is a film that tells a story of a hero, called a *protagonist,* and that hero's struggle against an *antagonist.* Even in the most abstract concept, there can be a perceived journey: a change that somehow occurs, even if it's a change in the viewer as they view the imagery.

Convincing art creates a sense of change or arc for the audience. This adds an important dimension to your work. When the viewer feels you have something to say, your work becomes that much more touching.

Basic Film Concepts

In addition to the design concepts used in framing a shot, you'll want to understand some fundamental filmmaking concepts.

> There's nothing more important than having a solid, manageable, and achievable plan for your conceptual goal. Almost everybody in production lays out this plan in advance of the principle photography. You can't run into the street with someone else's expensive camera and not know what you're going to shoot. CG takes time. Put together a good plan, and you'll be set for a good production.

Planning a Production

Understanding the paradigm that conventional filmmakers use for their productions will give you a good structure for planning, creating, and managing your own projects. Most narrative films are broken into acts, which comprise sequences made up of scenes, which in turn are made up of shots. By using a similar layout in the scripting and storyboarding of your own short, you'll find that the entire production process becomes easier and the effect of your film is stronger.

Narrative films are typically divided into three *acts*. The first act establishes the main characters and the conflict or struggle that will define the story. The second act covers most of the action of the story as the hero attempts to overcome this conflict. The third act concludes the film by resolving the action in the story and tying up all the loose ends.

Acts can be deconstructed further into *sequences*, which are groups of sequential scenes that unite around a particular dramatic or narrative point.

A *scene* is a part of a film that takes place in a specific place or time with specific characters to present that part of the story. Films are broken into scenes for organizational purposes by their locations (that is, by where or when they take place).

> Don't confuse the filmmaking concept of a scene with the word *scene* in CG terminology. The latter refers to the elements in the 3D file that make up the CG.

Scenes are then broken into *shots*, which correspond to a particular camera angle or *framing*. Shots break up the monotony of a scene by giving different views of the scene and its characters. Shots are separated by *cuts* between each shot.

Shots are defined by angle of view, which is the point of view (POV) of the camera. Shots change as soon as the camera's view is changed.

Lighting

Although CG lighting techniques may seem completely different from lighting in real life, the desired results are quite often the same. The more you understand how real lights affect your subjects in photography, the better you'll be at CG lighting.

Without lights, you can't capture anything on film. How you light your scene affects the contrast of the frame as well as the color balance and overall design impact. If the lights in your scene are too flat or too even, they will weaken your composition and abate your scene's impact.

As a good way to understand the essentials of lighting, you should take a look at the *three-point system*. This method places a *key* light in front of the scene, which is the primary illumination and casts shadows into the scene. The key light is typically placed behind the camera and off to the side to create a highlight on one side of the object for contrast's sake. The rest of the scene is given a *fill* light. The fill acts to illuminate the rest of the scene but typically isn't as bright as the key light. The fill also softens harsh shadows from the key light. To pop the subject out from the background, a *back* light is used to illuminate the subject's silhouette. This is also known as a *rim* light, because it creates a slight halo or rim around the subject in the scene. It's much fainter than the key or fill lights.

You'll learn more about Maya lighting techniques in Chapter 10.

Basic Animation Concepts

As mentioned at the beginning of this chapter, animation is the representation of change over time. This concept is the basis for an amazing art form that has been practiced in one way or another for quite some time. Although this section can't cover all of them, here are a few key terms you'll come across numerous times on your journey into CG animation.

Frames, Keyframes, and In-Betweens

Each drawing of an animation—or, in the case of CG, a single rendered image—is called a *frame*. The term *frame* also refers to a unit of time in animation whose exact chronological length depends on how fast the animation will eventually play back (frame rate). For example, at film rate (24fps), a single frame lasts 1/24 of a second. At NTSC video rate (30fps), that same frame lasts 1/30 of a second.

Keyframes are frames in which the animator creates a pose for a character (or whatever is being animated). In CG terms, a keyframe is a frame in which a pose, a position, or some other such value has been saved in time. Animation is created when an object travels or changes from one keyframe to another. You'll see firsthand how creating poses for animation works in Chapter 9 when you create the poses for a simple walking human figure.

In CG, a keyframe can be set on almost any aspect of an object—its color, position, size, and so on. Maya then interpolates the *in-between* frames between the keyframes set by the animator. In reality, you can set several keyframes on any one frame in CG animation. Figure 1.6 illustrates a keyframe sequence in Maya.

Figure 1.6

Keyframing. In the first frame of this sequence, a keyframe is set on the position, rotation, and scale of the cone. On frame 30, the same properties are again keyframed. Maya calculates all the movement in between.

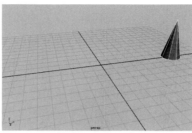

Keyframe at frame 1

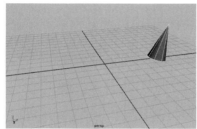

Frame 5

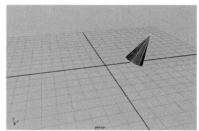

Frame 10

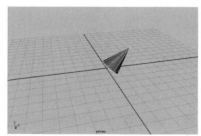

Frame 15

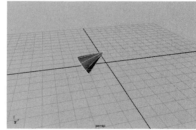

Frame 20

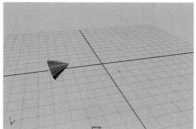

Frame 25

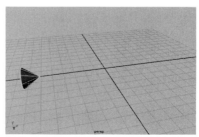

Keyframe at frame 30

Weight

Weight is an implied, if not critical, concept in design and animation. The weight of your subject in the frame is a function of the way it's colored; its contrast, shape, and location in the frame; and the negative space around it, to name but a few ways of looking at it. In animation, weight takes on a more important role. How you show an object's weight in motion greatly affects its believability. As you'll see in the axe tutorial in Chapter 8, creating proper motion to reflect the object's weight goes a long way toward producing believable animation.

Weight in animation is a perception of mass. An object's movement, how it reacts in motion, and how it reacts to other objects together convey the feeling of weight. Otherwise, the animation will look bogus—or, as they say, "cartoonish."

Weight can be created with a variety of techniques developed by traditional animators over the years. Each technique distorts the shape of the object or character in some way to make it look as if it's moving. Although it may seem strange to distort an object's dimensions, doing so makes its motion more realistic. Chapter 8 will touch more on creating weight in animation. Here's a quick preview.

SQUASH AND STRETCH

This technique makes a character, for example, respond to gravity, movement, and inertia by literally squashing it down and stretching it up when it moves. For example, a cartoon character will squeeze down when it's about to jump up, stretch out a bit while it's flying in the air, and squash back down when it lands to make the character look as if it's reacting to gravity.

EASE-IN AND EASE-OUT

Objects never really stop suddenly. Everything comes to rest in its own time, slowing before coming to a complete stop in most cases. This is referred to as *ease-out*.

Just as objects don't stop suddenly, they don't immediately start moving. Most things need to accelerate a bit before reaching full speed. This is referred to as *ease-in*. The bouncing-ball tutorial in Chapter 8 illustrates ease-in and ease-out.

FOLLOW-THROUGH AND ANTICIPATION

Sometimes you have to exaggerate the weight of an object in animation, especially in cartoons. You can exaggerate a character's weight, for instance, by using well-designed follow-through and anticipation.

You should create a bit of movement in your character or object *before* it moves. *Anticipation* is a technique in which a character or object winds up before it moves, like a spring that coils inward before it bounces.

Likewise, objects ending an action typically have a *follow-through*. Think about the movement of gymnasts. When they land, they need to bend a bit at the knees and waist to stabilize their landing. In the same way, a cape on a jumping character will continue to move even after the character lands.

The axe tutorial in Chapter 8 will give you a chance to implement these two concepts.

Physics

In Chapter 12, "Maya Dynamics and Effects," you'll see that one of Maya's most powerful features is its ability to simulate the dynamics of moving objects. To use that capability effectively, you need a general awareness of the properties of physics—how objects behave in the physical world.

Newton's Laws of Motion

You need to know three basic laws of motion. Sir Isaac Newton set forth these three laws, summarized here. Everyone in animation needs to understand the first two laws, because they play a large part in how animations should look. Coming to terms with the third is an art:

- An object in motion will remain in motion, and an object at rest will remain at rest unless an external force acts upon the object. This is called *inertia*, and understanding it is critical to good animation. You'll find more on this in Chapters 8 and 9.

- The more massive an object is, the more force is needed to accelerate or decelerate its motion. This law deals with an object's *momentum*.

- Every action has an equal and opposite reaction. When you press on a brick wall, for example, the wall exerts an equal amount of force on your hand. That way, your hand doesn't smash through the wall.

Momentum

It's important to understand what momentum is all about. When an object is in motion, it has momentum. The amount of momentum is calculated by multiplying the mass of the object by its velocity. The heavier something is, or the faster it's moving, the more momentum it has, and the bigger the bruise it will leave if it hits you. Duck!

That's why a tiny pebble on the highway can cause such a significant impact on your windshield, for example. Its sheer speed greatly increases its momentum. Likewise, a slow-moving garbage truck can bash your car, relying on its sheer mass for its tremendous momentum.

When one moving object meets another object—moving or not—momentum is transferred between them. So, when something hits an object, that object is moved if sufficient momentum is transferred to it. For more on this notion, see the axe-throwing exercise in Chapter 8.

SUGGESTED READING

The more you know about all the arts that make up CG, the more confident you'll feel among your peers. To get started, check out the following excellent resources.

ART AND DESIGN

These books provide valuable insights into the mechanics and art of design. The more you understand design theory, the stronger your art will be.

Bowers, John. *Introduction to Two-Dimensional Design: Understanding Form and Function*. New York: John Wiley & Sons, 2008.

Itten, Johannes. *Design and Form: The Basic Course at the Bauhaus and Later*. New York: John Wiley & Sons, 1975.

Ocvirk, Otto G., et al. *Art Fundamentals: Theory and Practice*. New York: McGraw-Hill, 2008.

Wong, Wucius. *Principles of Form and Design*. New York: John Wiley & Sons, 1993.

CG

CG has an interesting history, and it's evolving at breakneck speed. Acquiring a solid knowledge of this history and evolution is as important as keeping up with current trends.

Keller, Eric and Eric Allen. *Mastering Maya 2009*. New York: John Wiley & Sons, 2009.

Kerlow, Isaac. *The Art of 3D Computer Animation and Effects*. New York: John Wiley & Sons, 2009.

Kuperberg, Marcia. *Guide to Computer Animation*. Burlington, MA: Focal Press, 2002.

Masson, Terrence. *CG 101: A Computer Graphics Industry Reference*. Williamstown, MA: Digital Fauxtography, 2007.

PERIODICALS

Computer Graphics World (free subscription for those who qualify)
www.cgw.com

Cinefex
www.cinefex.com

HDRI 3D
www.hdri3D.com

3D World
www.3Dworldmag.com

WEBSITES

www.animationartist.com
www.awn.com
www.creativecrash.com
www.learning-maya.com

FILM

Block, Bruce. *The Visual Story: Seeing the Structure of Film, TV, and New Media*. Burlington, MA: Focal Press, 2001.

MUST-READ

Myers, Dale K. *Computer Animation: Expert Advice on Breaking into the Business*. Milford, MI: Oak Cliff Press, 1999.

Summary

In this chapter, you learned the basic process of working in CG, called a *workflow* or *pipeline,* and how it relates to the process of working on a typical live film production. In addition, you were introduced to the core concepts of CG creation and the fundamentals of digital images. Some important ideas in design as well as traditional animation concepts were also covered.

Now that you have a foundation in CG and 3D terminology and core concepts, you're ready to tackle the software. Maya is a capable, intricate program. The more you understand how *you* work artistically, the better use you'll make of this exceptional tool.

There is a lot to think about before putting objects into a scene and rendering them. With practice and some design tinkering, though, all this will become intuitive. As you move forward in your animation education, stay diligent, be patient, and never pass up a chance to learn something new. Above all else, have fun.

CHAPTER 2

Jumping in Headfirst, with Both Feet

In this chapter, you're going to start using Maya and get your groove on. This will be a quick primer on the Maya interface so you experience tasks right away. The next chapter will show you more details and provide additional explanations and a reference of how the entire Maya interface works.

This chapter will take you through the creation of a Solar System project and the mechanics of animating orbits. With this exercise, you'll dive into creating simple objects, setting keyframes, and stacking your animation to get planets and moons to orbit each other and the Sun. This will expose you to object creation, simple modeling, object components, pivot-point placement, grouping and hierarchies, basic keyframing, and timing.

Topics in this chapter include:

- **You put the U in UI**

- **Project overview: the Solar System**

- **The preproduction process: planning**

- **Creating a project**

- **The production process: creating and animating the objects**

- **Hierarchy and Maya object structure**

- **The Solar System resumed**

- **Using the Outliner**

- **Outputting your work: playblasting**

You Put the U in UI

Fire up your computer, and let's get this project going. This section will introduce you to getting around the Maya user interface (UI). It may seem difficult at first, but it will make sense as you move along.

You'll find everything you ever wanted to know about the interface and more in Chapter 3, "The Maya 2011 Interface." The overall goal of *this* chapter is to expose you to Maya UI basics as well as important scene creation and editing tools. You can consider the next chapter a debriefing of sorts, to fill in UI details that aren't covered in this chapter. If you prefer, you can skip ahead and get a more detailed rundown of the UI first and then return to this chapter for your first Maya project experience.

KEYBOARD AND SYMBOL CONVENTIONS USED IN THIS BOOK

The following terms are used throughout this book:

Click and *LMB+click* refer to a mouse click with the primary (left) mouse button.

RMB+click refers to a mouse click with the right mouse button.

MMB+click refers to a mouse click with the middle mouse button.

Shift+click indicates that you should hold down the Shift key as you click with the primary (left) mouse button.

Shift+select indicates that you're holding down the Shift key as you select the next object for multiple selections.

Right-click refers to clicking with the right mouse button.

The ❑ symbol next to a menu command indicates that you should click the box (❑) next to the menu command to open the Options for that command.

A Quick Screen Roadmap

Let's get to the basics of how Maya is laid out (see Figure 2.1). Running across the top of the screen, right under the application's title bar, are the UI elements: the *Main Menu bar*, the *Status line*, and the *Shelf*. On a Macintosh system running OS X, note that the Main Menu bar runs at the very top of the screen, above the application's title bar.

Figure 2.1 shows the major parts of the UI. In the middle of the interface is the *workspace*, which is host to your *panels* (or Scene windows) and their menu options (known as *views* or *viewports* in some other 3D packages). This is where most of your focus will be; this is where you create and manipulate your 3D objects.

Click inside the large perspective view panel (named *persp*) with the mouse to activate the panel, highlighting its border slightly. Press the spacebar to display a four-panel layout, which gives you top, front, and side views as well as the perspective view. Press the spacebar in any of the panels to display a large view of that panel.

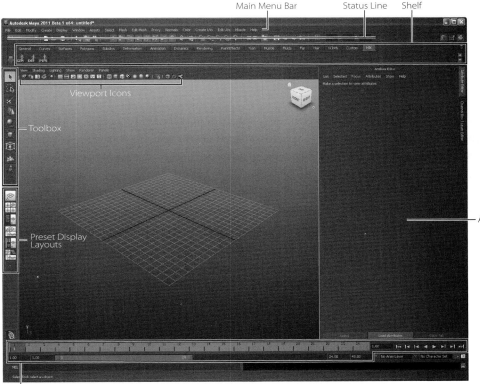

Figure 2.1

The initial Maya screen

To the right of the panels is the Attribute Editor / Channel Box. This is where most of the information (attributes) about a selected object is displayed and edited. Pressing Ctrl-A toggles between the Attribute Editor and the Channel Box. In short, the Attribute Editor gives you access to all of an object's attributes, whereas the Channel Box is a quicker display of the most commonly animated attributes of the selected object. The Attribute Editor is typically wider than the Channel Box, so you'll notice a shift in your view panels when you toggle between them. You can set Maya's preferences to treat the Attribute Editor as its own window, to prevent it from displaying on the right side of the UI. More on this in the next chapter.

Keys and Syntax in Maya

Maya is case sensitive in that it distinguishes between lowercase and uppercase letters. The conventions of this book will be to always print an uppercase letter to denote which key you must press, but to specify "Shift + the letter" when you must press the uppercase of that key. In other words, when we ask you to press the E key, for example, you should simply press the E key on your keyboard, lowercase. When an uppercase letter is called for, the book tells you to press Shift+E, requiring you to enter the uppercase letter E into Maya. Make sure your Caps Lock key is turned off.

Mouse Controls

Maya requires the use of a three-button mouse, even on a Macintosh system. The clickable scroll wheel found on most mice can be used as the third button by pressing down to click with the wheel. Scrolling the wheel lets you zoom into or out of a view panel.

In Maya, you press and hold the Alt key on a PC (or the Option key on a Mac) along with the appropriate mouse button to move in the view panel:

- The left mouse button (LMB) acts as the primary selection button and allows you to orbit around objects when used with the Alt key.
- The right mouse button (RMB) activates numerous shortcut menus and lets you zoom when used with the Alt key.
- The middle mouse button (MMB) used with the Alt key lets you move within the Maya interface panels, and the mouse's wheel can be used to zoom in and out as well.

SHORTCUTS TO NAVIGATING

Here's a rundown of how to navigate Maya. Keep in mind that the Option key is used on a Macintosh in place of the Alt key on a PC:

Alt+MMB+click Tracks around a window. Tracking moves left, right, up, or down in two dimensions; hold down the Alt key, press and hold the MMB, and drag the mouse.

Alt+RMB+click Dollies into or out of a view. A *dolly* moves the scene's camera in and out of the view, essentially zooming the view in and out. To dolly, hold down the Alt key, press and hold the RMB, and drag the mouse.

Scroll Wheel The scroll wheel, in addition to acting as a middle mouse button, can also dolly into or out of a view just like the Alt+RMB+click combination. Scrolling up dollies in, and scrolling down dollies out.

Alt+click Rotates or orbits the camera around in a Perspective window. Orbiting lets you get around your object to observe it from different vantage points. To orbit, hold down the Alt key and the LMB. This move is called a *tumble*. You can't tumble your view in an orthographic panel.

Alt+Ctrl+click and drag Dollies your view into the screen area specified in your mouse drag. Hold down the Alt and Ctrl keys while using the LMB to outline a window in the panel to execute this *bounding box dolly*. This action is commonly referred to as a *window zoom* in other applications.

Making Selections

Selecting objects in a view panel is as easy as clicking them. If the object is displayed in Wireframe mode, its wireframe turns green while it's selected. If the object is displayed in a Shaded mode, the object's wireframe will appear around the object. Shaded mode is a way of seeing your objects in the view panel with a basic surface, as opposed to a wireframe that you can see through. You'll see this as you do the following exercise.

As you select an object, its attributes appear in the Attribute Editor or Channel Box on the right.

To select multiple objects, simply hold the Shift key as you click objects to add to your current selection. The previous selection's wireframe turns white, and the new selection is now green. If you press Ctrl+LMB (that is, press the Ctrl key and click) on an active object, you'll deselect it. To clear all of your current selections, click anywhere in the empty areas of the view panel.

Manipulating Objects

When you select an object and enable one of the transformation tools (tools that allow you to move, rotate, or scale an object), you'll see a Manipulator appear at or around the selected object. Figure 2.2 shows the three distinct and most common Manipulators for all objects in Maya: Move, Rotate, and Scale as well as the Universal Manipulator. You use these Manipulators to adjust attributes of the objects visually and in real time.

Figure 2.2

The Maya Manipulators

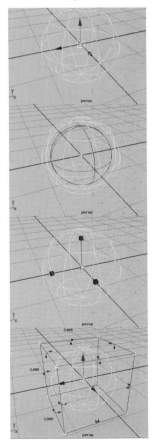

Figure 2.3

The Transform tools in the Tool Box

Transform
Tools

To activate a Transform tool, select an object and then click one of the Transform tool icons in the Tool Box, shown in Figure 2.3.

Try This Let's put some of this into action, shall we?

Choose Create → NURBS Primitives → Sphere. Drag in a view panel anywhere on its grid to create a wireframe sphere, and then size it to your liking. In one of the view panels, press the 5 key on your keyboard, and the display of the sphere will become solid gray, as opposed to open wireframe. This is called Shaded mode. Press the 4 key to return to Wireframe mode.

With the sphere selected, select the Move tool ( ) from the Tool Box. The first Manipulator shown in Figure 2.2 should appear in the middle of the sphere. The three arrows represent the three axes of possible movement for the object.

Red is for the X-axis, green is for the Y-axis, and blue is for the Z-axis. Cyan is for free movement in both axes of the active panel view.

Clicking any one of the three arrows lets you move the object only on that particular axis. The square in the middle of the Manipulator lets you move the object freely about the plane of the view panel, regardless of the axis. When you select a Manipulator handle for movement, it turns yellow. The Free Movement box in the center then turns back to its regular color, cyan.

Next, select the Rotate tool ( ) from the Tool Box, and you'll see the second Manipulator in Figure 2.2. The three colored circles represent the three axes of rotation for the object—red for X, green for Y, and blue for Z. Select a circle to rotate the object on that axis. The yellow circle surrounding the three axis circles lets you freely rotate the object on all three axes. The Free rotation handle also turns cyan when an axis handle is active.

Now, try selecting the Scale tool ( ) to see the third Manipulator in Figure 2.2. By selecting one of the axis handles and dragging the mouse, you can scale the object in a nonuniform manner in that axis. The middle cyan box scales the object uniformly on all three axes.

Try selecting the Universal Manipulator ( ). This tool acts in place of all three Manipulators you just tried. Grabbing the familiar arrows translates the sphere. Selecting any of the curved arrows in the middle of the edges of the Manipulator box lets you rotate the sphere in that axis. Finally, selecting and dragging the cyan boxes in the corners of the Manipulator box lets you scale the sphere. If you hold down the Ctrl key as you drag, you can scale the sphere in just one axis.

Go ahead and click around the interface some more. Create more primitive objects, and tool around a bit. Move around the view panels, and see how it feels. Give the tires a good kick.

Enough chatting—let's jump into the Solar System project.

Project Overview: The Solar System

This project focuses on familiarizing you with the fundamentals of navigating Maya, object creation, hierarchy, and pivots, all of which are important concepts for scene manipulation and animation within Maya. In this exercise, you'll create and animate a simple simulation of our working Solar System. (You may have done this in school using coat hanger wire and Styrofoam balls.) This time-tested tutorial is great practice for getting used to object creation, hierarchies, scene manipulation, UI navigation, and working with objects and selections. It will show you how to set up hierarchies and give you experience in working with the proper nodes within a group to create hierarchically layered animation.

The Preproduction Process: Planning

Every smooth operation begins with a good plan. The more research and focused information you gather, the better off you'll be in your work. For this exercise, you need to find out where each of the planets is in relation to the Sun and to the other planets and also how many moons it has.

Starting with the Sun in the center, the planets in order are Mercury, Venus, Earth, Mars, Jupiter, Saturn, Uranus, Neptune, and Pluto. (We'll label Pluto a planet for old time's sake, even though it was reclassified as a "dwarf planet" by the scientific community in 2006.) All these planets actually orbit the Sun in ellipses, but we'll give them circular orbits for this exercise. Most planets have a number of moons that orbit them, and one, Saturn, has large rings that circle around it.

Earth	1 moon
Mars	2 small moons
Jupiter	16+ moons
Saturn	3 large rings and 18+ moons
Uranus	18 moons
Neptune	8 moons
Pluto	1 moon

Creating and animating all those objects may seem overwhelming, but it's a great way to become comfortable with Maya and animation. Because the goal of the project is achievable without making every moon, you'll cut most of them out of your scene and make a maximum of two moons per planet.

You can redo this exercise in more detail when you feel more comfortable with Maya. For instance, if, after you've worked through the exercises in this book, you feel like creating a much more accurate Solar System with beautifully textured planets and a perfect starry backdrop, go for it! It will still be a good idea to set up and animate the scene carefully, just as you did (or should have done) the first time you worked on this exercise.

The more you run this exercise, the clearer Maya's scene manipulation and hierarchy structure will become to you. Art is a marriage of inspiration, hard work, and practice.

Creating a Project

Projects are Maya's way of managing a scene's assets. A file and folder structure keeps your files organized according to projects. You'll have a project for the Solar System exercise.

Start by creating a new project for this assignment. Choose File → Project → New to open the New Project window. (Figure 2.4 shows the Windows version; the Mac OS X version has the same fields.) Files are organized in a particular way in Maya. The top level of this organization is the *Project folder.* Within the Project folder are numerous file folders that hold your files. The two most important types are the Scenes and Images folders. The Scenes folder stores your scene files, which contain all the information for your scene. The Images folder stores images you've rendered out from your scene. As with clothing and other items around your house, keeping your files and projects organized is a good practice.

Figure 2.4

The New Project window

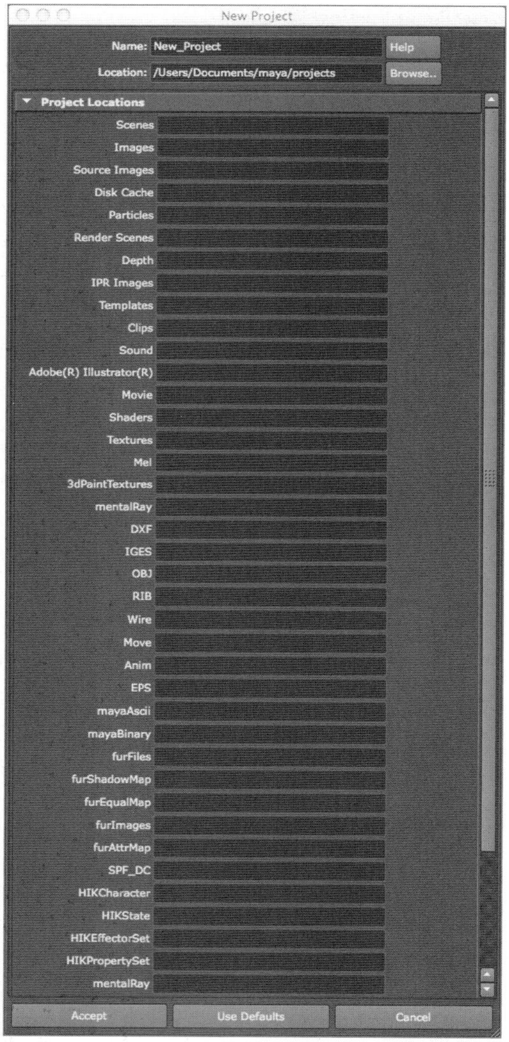

NAMING OBJECTS AND KEEPING THE SCENE ORGANIZED

In Maya and most other CG packages, keeping things organized and as clean as possible is more important than you probably realize. Picking up a scene from a disorganized colleague is annoying because it's very time consuming to figure out exactly what is in their scene and how everything works together. Many professional studios have strict naming procedures and conventions to minimize the confusion their artists may have when working in a pipeline. These procedures and conventions are beneficial because many artists will touch the same digital files and assets in the course of a production. Even if you're the only person who will ever see your scene in Maya, it's still a good idea to name and organize your objects. Get into the habit of naming your objects and keeping a clean scene. You'll waste a lot of time if you don't, and you'll be bombarded by dirty looks from other artists when they have to handle your cluttered scenes.

The scene files discussed in this chapter are included on the CD in a project layout explained in the following text. Copy the scene files on the CD for this project into your own Project folders after you create the project.

To create a new project, follow these steps:

1. In the Name field in the New Project window, enter **Solar_System** as the name for your project. In the Location box, type the location where you want to store your projects.

   The default location for Windows XP, Vista, and Windows 7 is in the current user's `My Documents` folder: `My Documents\maya\projects`; for Macs, the default location is `Home (/Users/<yourname>)` in the `Documents/maya/projects/default` folder. If you prefer, you can put projects in a folder on a secondary or external hard drive to keep them separate from your operating system; this allows for easier backup and is generally a safer environment.

2. If you're using a Windows system, create a folder on your hard drive called **Projects** using Windows Explorer. If you're using a Mac, select a drive in the Finder and create a folder on the drive called **Projects**. In the New Project window, click the Browse button and select `D:\Projects` (Windows) or `<Hard Drive Name>/Projects` (Mac) for the location. Maya will fill in all the other fields for you with defaults; just click the Use Defaults button. Click Accept to create the necessary folders in your specified location. Figure 2.5 shows the completed New Project window in Windows; except for the drive name, the values are the same on a Macintosh.

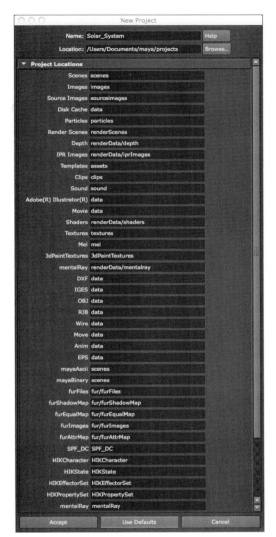

After you create projects, you can switch between them by choosing File → Project → Set and selecting the new project. Maya will then use that project's folders until you switch to or create another project. You may also select a recent project by choosing File → Recent Projects. Maya by default will list four of your recent projects and scene files on the File menu for easy access.

Figure 2.5
The completed New Project window

DON'T FORGET TO SET YOUR PROJECT!

You should make sure to set your project before continuing with your work. The exercises in this book are based on projects, and you'll need to set your project whenever you start a new exercise—otherwise, the scene may not load properly or your files may not save to the proper locations for that project.

The Production Process: Creating and Animating the Objects

As discussed in Chapter 1, "Introduction to Computer Graphics and 3D," production is typically divided into phases to make workflow easier to manage. In this project, you'll first create the Sun, the planets, and their moons; then, you'll animate their respective orbits and rotations.

Creating the Sun and the Planets

The first thing you're going to do is create the Sun and the planets. Follow these steps:

1. Choose File → New Scene (or press Ctrl+N). Maya asks if you want to save your current scene. Save the file if you need to, or click Don't Save to discard the scene.

2. By default, Maya's screen should begin in an expanded perspective view. Press the spacebar to enable the four-panel view. When you're in the four-panel view, press the spacebar with the cursor inside the top view panel to select and maximize it.

3. To create the Sun, you need a primitive sphere. A *primitive* is a basic 3D shape. First, let's turn off a Maya feature called Interactive Creation that is on by default. Turning off Interactive Creation allows you to create the sphere at the center of the grid (the

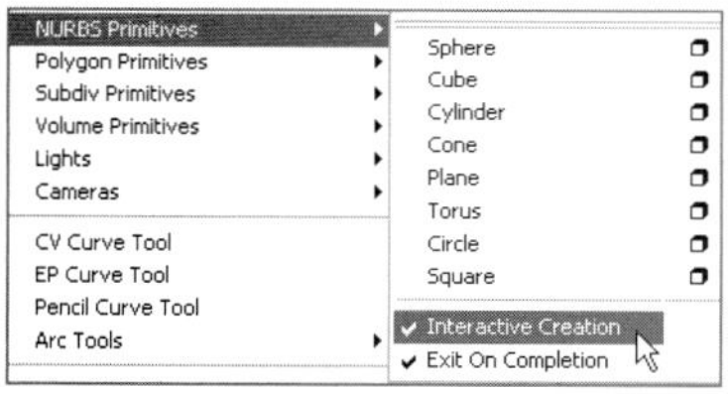

Figure 2.6

Turning off Interactive Creation

origin) without having to click and drag its size and then reposition it manually. Uncheck Create → NURBS Primitives → Interactive Creation to toggle it off, as shown in Figure 2.6. For more on how to create primitives with interactive feedback, see the section on primitives in Chapter 3.

4. With Interactive Creation turned off, choose Create → NURBS Primitives → Sphere. Doing so places a NURBS sphere exactly at the origin—that is, at a position of 0,0,0 for *X,Y,Z*. This is good, because the origin of the workspace will be the center of the Solar System, too.

5. Select the word *nurbsSphere1* in the Channel Box to the right of the Maya UI (shown in Figure 2.7), and enter **Sun** to rename it. If you don't see the Channel Box in your Maya window, please refer to the section on the Channel Box in Chapter 3.

NURBS AND POLYGONS

NURBS and polygons are two types of geometry that you can create and edit in Maya. We'll explore the uses of each modeling type in Chapter 4, "Beginning Polygonal Modeling," Chapter 5, "Modeling with NURBS, Subdivisions, and Deformers, and Chapter 6, "Building the Red Wagon."

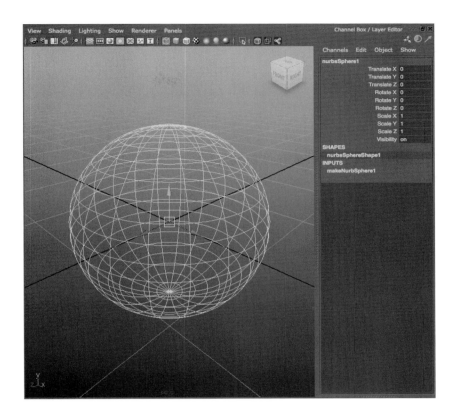

Figure 2.7

Renaming the sphere in the Channel Box

Always keep in mind that Maya is case sensitive. An object named "sun" is different from an object named "Sun."

Naming your objects right after creation is a good habit to develop. Doing so makes for a cleaner scene file and a more organized workspace. This is particularly important if anyone needs to alter your scene file; proper naming will keep them from getting frustrated when they work on your scene.

Maya typically uses an object-naming structure called a *humpback style,* where words are slung together without spaces. The first letter of a new word in the humpback name is capitalized. An example of humpback style is the name indoorPatioScene. Maya uses this structure when naming nodes, such as the node name nurbsSphere1.

6. Choose the Scale tool in the Tool Box to activate the Scale Manipulator, and uniformly scale the Sun sphere up to about four times its creation scale of 1. (Make it a scale of about 4 in all three axes.) For more precision, you can do one of two things: You can select the sphere and enter a value of **4** in all three entry fields (the white window next to the attribute) for the Scale X, Scale Y,

and Scale Z channels in the Channel Box shown in Figure 2.8. Alternatively, you can enter a value of **4** in the Input box on the Status line along the top of the UI, as shown here. Don't worry; we'll take an in-depth look at both of these methods in the next chapter.

7. After you enter the final value through either method, press Enter, and the sphere will grow to be four times its original size (at a scale of 1). When you enter the values in either the Channel Box or the Input box, a scale of 4 appears in all three fields, as shown in Figure 2.8, and your Sun expands in size by a factor of 4. Entering exact values in the Channel Box or Input box is a way to scale the sphere precisely; using the Manipulator isn't as precise.

Figure 2.8

The Sun's Scale values in the Channel Box

Creating the Planets

Next, you'll create the primitive spheres you'll be using for the planets. Leave Interactive Creation off, and follow these steps:

1. Create a NURBS sphere for Mercury just as you did before, by choosing Create → NURBS Primitives → Sphere. A new sphere appears at the origin. Click its name in the Channel Box, and change it to **Mercury**.

2. Choose the Move tool from the Tool Box to activate the Move Manipulator, and move Mercury a few grid units away from the Sun in the positive *X* direction. (Click the red arrow and drag it to the right.) Leave about two grid units between Mercury and the Sun.

3. Because Mercury is the second smallest planet and is tiny compared to the Sun, scale it down to ½₀ the size of the Sun, or type in 0.2 in all three axes of scale if you choose to enter the values manually in the Channel Box.

4. Repeat steps 1 through 3 to create the rest of the planets and line them up, placing each one farther out along the *X*-axis. Be sure to keep about two grid units of space between them. Scale each one proportionally as follows:

Venus	0.5
Earth	0.5
Mars	0.4
Jupiter	1.0
Saturn	0.9
Uranus	0.7
Neptune	0.7
Pluto	0.15

These proportions aren't exactly the same as those found in the real Solar System, but they will do nicely here. Figure 2.9 shows how your Solar System should look now.

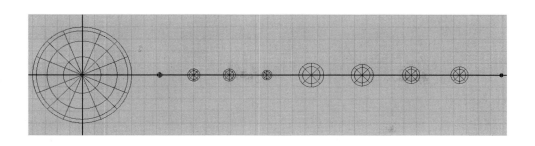

Figure 2.9

All the NURBS spheres are lined up in place (top view).

No, Pluto isn't actually a planet anymore, but for nostalgia's sake, we'll include it here in our Solar System. Poor Pluto!

Using Snaps

Now is the perfect time to start using *snaps*. Some common snap icons are shown in Table 2.1. Snap icons are explained in greater depth in the next chapter. These icons run across the top of the UI just below the Main Menu bar, as shown here.

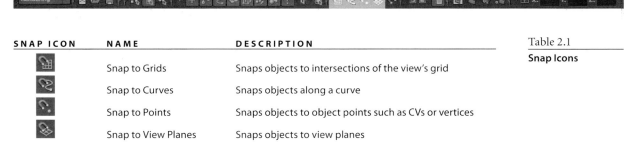

SNAP ICON	NAME	DESCRIPTION
	Snap to Grids	Snaps objects to intersections of the view's grid
	Snap to Curves	Snaps objects along a curve
	Snap to Points	Snaps objects to object points such as CVs or vertices
	Snap to View Planes	Snaps objects to view planes

Table 2.1

Snap Icons

You use snaps to snap objects into place with precision, by placing them by their pivot points directly onto grid points, onto other object pivots, onto curve points, and so on. Here you'll reposition all the planets slightly to center them on the nearest grid line intersection. To do so, follow these steps:

1. Select the first planet, Mercury. Choose the Move tool from the Tool Box, and toggle on *grid snaps* by clicking the Snap to Grids icon ( ).

2. The center of the Move Manipulator turns from a square to a circle, signaling that some form of snapping is active. Grab the Manipulator in the middle by this circle, and move it slightly to the left or right to snap it onto the closest grid intersection on the *X*-axis.

3. Select the remaining planets, and snap them all to the closest grid intersection on the *X*-axis, making sure to keep about two grid spaces between each of them. Because the Sun was created at the origin and you haven't moved it, you don't need to snap it onto an intersection.

SAVING MULTIPLE VERSIONS OF YOUR WORK AND INCREMENTAL SAVING

As you're working on a project, you may want to save multiple versions of your files at various stages of completion. When working in the professional world, you'll find that clients and art directors often reconsider animations you've created, sometimes, it seems, just to make you crazy. So, it's always good to keep as many versions of an animation as you can. Scene files are reasonably small, and hard disk space is inexpensive. Just keep your Scene folder organized well—for example, by keeping older versions of scenes in separate subfolders—and you should have no problems.

Maya's Incremental Save feature makes a backup of your scene file every time you save your scene. To enable it, choose File → Save Scene ❑, and click the Incremental Save box. After you've done this, Maya will create a new folder within your Scenes folder with the name of your current scene file. It will then create a backup of your scene in that folder and append a number to the filename: for example, `planets_001.mb`. Every time you save your file, Maya will create a new backup until you disable the feature by choosing File → Save Scene ❑.

The scene files for the projects in this book are provided on the accompanying CD to give you a reference point for the major stages of each project. These files use a slightly different naming system than the names generated by Incremental Save (for example, the file on the CD is `planets_v1.mb` instead of `planets_001.mb`), so there is no risk of files overwriting each other.

For important real-world projects, you may decide to supplement the Incremental Save backups by using Save Scene As to create named files manually, perhaps following a similar naming system with a version number appended, at the stages where you've made significant changes. Whether you do this or use Incremental Save, it's a good idea to keep written notes about the differences in each version of a scene file so that whenever you make a significant change to a file, you have a record of your work.

If you prefer to name files manually, be sure to use an underscore (_) between the filename and version number instead of a space. Using spaces in your filenames can create problems with the software and operating system, especially when you're rendering out a scene.

Making Saturn's Ring

Now, create the ring for Saturn. To do so, follow these steps:

1. Choose Create → NURBS Primitives → Torus to place a donut shape at the origin. Remember, Interactive Creation is turned off. You can also try creating the torus with the Interactive Creation option. In that case, click and drag the mouse to create the donut shape as you prefer. When you have a ring, use the Move tool to snap it to the same grid intersection as Saturn. This ensures that both the planet and its ring are on the same pivot point and share the same center.

2. Select the torus shape you've created, and name it **Ring** (if you haven't already done so) in the Channel Box.

3. While the torus shape is still selected in the top view, press the spacebar to display the four-panel layout. Place the mouse cursor in the persp view, and press the spacebar to maximize the Perspective window.

4. Press the F key to focus the perspective display on the ring and on Saturn. Pressing F centers and zooms in the panel on just the selected object(s).

5. Press 5 to get into Shaded mode, and, with the torus selected, press 3 to increase the resolution display for the ring. Display resolutions are achieved by pressing the 1, 2, or 3 key and are further explained in the next chapter. Pressing 3 gives you the smoothest view of the torus in the view panels. That's a good thing.

6. From the Tool box, select the Scale tool, and scale the torus down to 0 or close to 0 in the *Y*-axis (the torus's height, in this case) to flatten it.

   You'll notice that the ring is too fat and is cutting into the planet. You need to edit the attributes of the ring to increase the inside radius of the donut shape and create a gap between the planet and the ring.

7. Press Ctrl+A (Ctrl+A will also work on a Mac) to toggle the Attribute Editor if it's not on, and then click the makeNurbTorus1 tab to select its creation node. (See Figure 2.10.)

8. Increase the Radius attribute to about 1.5, and decrease the Height Ratio attribute to about 0.25 to get the desired effect.

Now all your planets are complete, and you can move on to the moons.

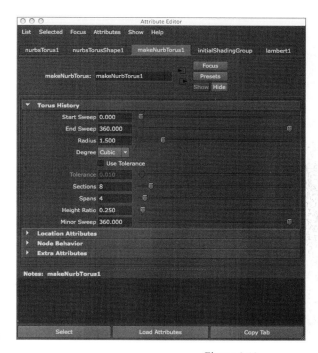

Figure 2.10

Changing the creation attributes of the NURBS torus in the Attribute Editor

> Changing the original attributes or parameters of an object, as you've just done with Saturn's ring, is often referred to as *parametric modeling*.

Saving Your Work

Save your work, unless you like to live on the edge. Saving frequently is a critical habit to develop. Power failures and other unforeseen circumstances (such as your pet jumping onto your keyboard) may not happen often, but they do happen, and usually at the wrong time. (As mentioned in the sidebar "Saving Multiple Versions of Your Work and

Incremental Saving," Maya's Incremental Save feature makes it easy to maintain backups of your work.) Because you created this as a new project, the Save File window will direct you to the Scenes folder of that project. Save your scene as **planets** in the .mb (Maya Binary) format. (If you're working in Maya PLE, you can only save your files as .mp files, which may not be compatible with full versions of Maya 2011. Maya PLE saves scenes as .mp files simply to differentiate them from full Maya-version saved files.)

The file Planets_v1.mb in the Scenes folder of the Solar_System project on the CD shows what the scene should look like at this point.

Creating the Moons

For the planets with moons, create a new NURBS sphere for each moon. For simplicity's sake, create a maximum of only two moons for any planet. However, feel free to make all the moons for all the planets after you get a handle on this exercise.

The first moon will be Earth's. Use the top view to follow these steps:

1. Create a NURBS sphere, and scale it to about half the size of Earth using the Scale tool. Visually estimate the size of the moon.

2. Move the sphere to within half a unit of Earth, using the Move tool by the *X*-axis. There's no need to snap it to a grid point, so toggle off the Snap to Grids icon (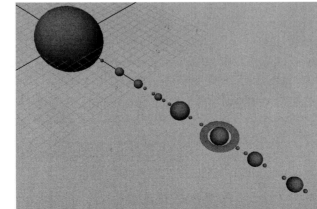).

3. Repeat steps 1 and 2 for the remaining moons, placing them each within half a grid unit from their respective planets. When placing two moons, place them on opposite sides of the planet.

4. After you're done with all the moons, their placements, and their sizes, select all the elements in the scene and press 3 to increase the display resolution on all the spheres. This gives you a smoother view of the NURBS spheres. When you're finished, you should have a scene similar to Figure 2.11 in perspective view. If you don't, it's clear Maya doesn't like you.

Figure 2.11

The planets and moons in position in perspective view

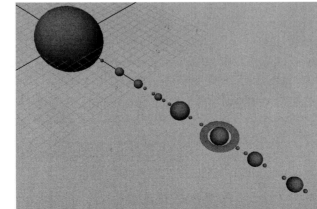

Applying a Simple Shader

To help distinguish one gray planet from another, attach simple shaders to each of the planets to give them color. You can easily take care of this task using the Hypershade window. Follow these steps:

1. Choose Window → Rendering Editors → Hypershade to open the Hypershade window. This window lists and allows you to edit all the shaders and textures in the scene. With this window, you create the look of your objects by assigning colors, surface properties, and so on. You'll notice three default (or initial) shader icons already loaded. (See Figure 2.12.) For more on the Hypershade window, see Chapter 3.

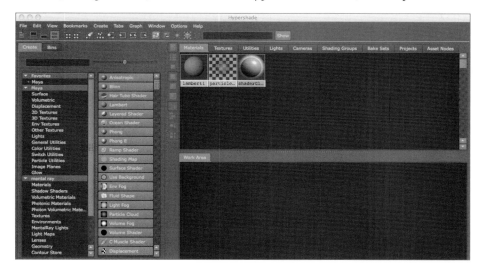

Figure 2.12

The Hypershade window

2. In the Create Maya Nodes panel on the left of the Hypershade window and under the Surface heading, click the Lambert icon (a gray sphere) to create a new Lambert shader node. It appears in the top and bottom of the Hypershade window. Click this icon eight more times to create a total of nine Lambert shading groups in the Hypershade window.

3. Click the first of the new Lambert nodes (lambert2) in the Hypershade window, and you should notice its attributes display in the Attribute Editor on the right of the UI. If you have the Channel Box displayed instead, double-click the shader's icon to open the Attribute Editor. At the top, replace lambert2 with **Mercury_Color** to identify this material as the one you'll use for Mercury.

4. Name each of the remaining planets in your animation (Venus, Earth, Mars, Jupiter, Saturn, Uranus, Neptune, and Pluto).

To rename a node in the Hypershade window, you can also right-click the node's icon and choose Rename from the shortcut menu that appears.

Again, keeping a well-named and organized scene is critical to a smooth animation experience. It's much more of a chore to root through dozens of unnamed nodes to find the one you want. When you've finished naming all the material nodes, save your work.

After you've created the shaders, you can assign the appropriate colors to each of them according to the planet they represent:

1. Double-click Mercury to open its Attribute Editor, if it's not currently open (see Figure 2.13).

2. To change the color of the shader, click the gray box next to the Color attribute. This opens the Color Chooser window, where you can choose a new color from the color wheel or by adjusting values with the HSV sliders. Because Mercury has a brownish red appearance, go with an orange color, such as in Figure 2.14 (take note of the HSV values).

Figure 2.13

Mercury's shading group in the Attribute Editor

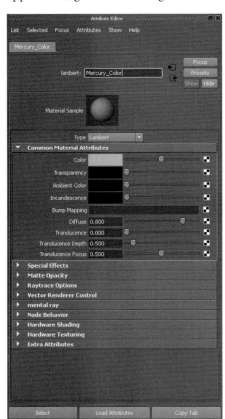

Figure 2.14

The Color Chooser window

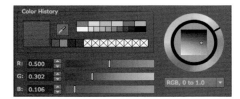

SETTING KEYFRAMES

As with many other functions in Maya, you can set a keyframe in several ways. Switch to the Animation menu set by pressing F2. When you're first starting to learn Maya, the best way is to choose Animate → Set Key ❑ to display the Set Key Options dialog box. Here, you're selecting the Option box for that menu item by clicking the little empty box to the right of the menu item. The Option box for any particular menu item allows you to set the options for that function. In this case, you're changing the options for the Set Key function.

If you choose Animate → Set Key without first changing those options, Maya sets a keyframe for all the keyable attributes for the selected object. Although this may seem convenient, it makes for a sloppy scene, especially if the scene must be heavily animated.

Having keyframes for attributes that may not actually be animated creates unnecessary clutter. In the Set Key Options dialog box shown here, set the Set Keys On option to All Keyable Attributes instead of the default All Manipulator Handles and Keyable Attributes. Set Channels to From Channel Box instead of the default All Keyable. (These attributes will remain grayed out until you change to All Keyable Attributes.) Now, when you choose Animate → Set Key, you'll set a keyframe only for the channels that you specify explicitly through the Channel Box, giving you greater control and efficiency. All you have to do is highlight the channel you want to keyframe in the Channel Box and then choose Animate → Set Key. Save your settings by choosing Edit → Save Settings, and then click Close to close the dialog box.

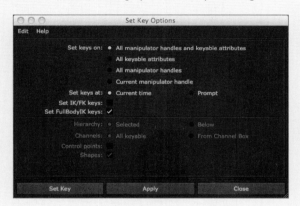

3. Change the remainder of the shaders as follows:

Mercury	Orange-brown
Venus	Beige-yellow
Earth	Blue
Mars	Red-orange
Jupiter	Yellow-green
Saturn	Pale yellow
Uranus	Cyan
Neptune	Aqua blue
Pluto	Bright gray

Figure 2.15 shows the shading groups.

Figure 2.15

The Hypershade window with all the colored planet shading groups

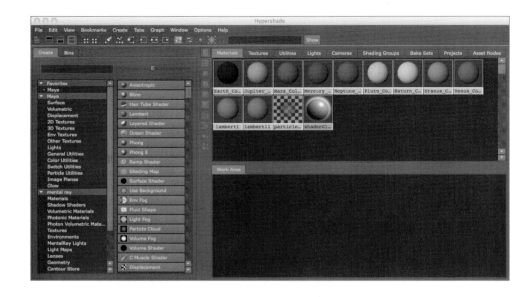

4. Next, apply shaders to the planets. Select a planet in the Perspective window, and right-click its corresponding material in the Hypershade window to open a marking menu. Drag up to highlight Assign Material to Selection, and release the button to select it. You can also use the middle mouse button to drag the material from the Hypershade window to its planet. Leave the moons set to the default gray color. When you're finished, you should have a scene similar to Figure 2.16.

Figure 2.16

The shaded planets in perspective view

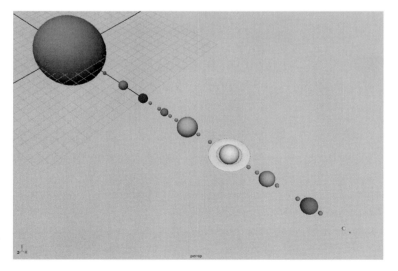

Now that you're finished, you're ready to animate. Save this file; if you enabled Incremental Save as recommended earlier, your file won't be replaced with subsequent saves. This way, if you get lost in your animation and need to start fresh, you won't have to re-create everything from scratch. You can return to a previous version of the file and start your animation over.

Creating the Animation

To begin this phase of the project, load the file Planets_v2.mb in the Scenes folder of the Solar_System project on the CD to your hard drive, or continue with your own scene file.

The animation you'll do for the orbits is straightforward. You'll rotate the planets around their own axes for their self-rotation, and then you'll animate the moons around the planets for their lunar orbits, and finally you'll make the planets and their moons orbit the Sun.

The premise of this exercise deals with hierarchy and pivot points. A *pivot point* is an object's center of balance of sorts. Every object or node that is created in Maya has a pivot point set at the origin. Because most objects, such as the spheres you created for the planets, appear at the origin upon creation, their pivot points are automatically centered.

When you move an object, as you've done to position the planets and moons, the pivot point moves with it. Therefore, all your planets' and moons' pivot points are already correctly positioned at the center of each planet and moon.

Now, you need to set up your scene file's animation settings:

1. Press F2 to open the Animation menu set. *Menu sets* are groupings of menu headings in the Main Menu bar. They're organized according to the type of task at hand. You'll see the first several menu headings change when you switch from one menu set to another.

2. At the bottom of the UI, you'll notice a slider bar (the Range slider) directly below the strip of numbers counting off the frames (the Time slider) in the scene. Using the Range slider, you'll set the length of your animation to go from 1 to 240. Enter **1** in the Scene Start Frame and Range Start Frame boxes (Figure 2.17). Enter a value of **240** in the Scene End Frame and Range End Frame boxes, also as called out in Figure 2.17.

Figure 2.17

The Time and Range sliders

3. To the right of the Range slider, click the Animation Preferences icon () (shown here in the context of the lower-right corner of the Maya screen), click Settings, and set Time to NTSC (30fps), which is 30 frames per second, or NTSC video speed. Also see Figure 2.18.

Figure 2.18

**Set Time to 30fps
in the Settings tab
of the Preferences
window.**

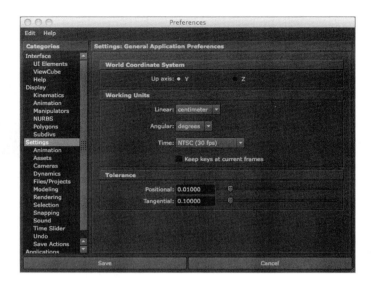

Figure 2.18

Set Time to 30fps in the Settings tab of the Preferences window.

4. Also verify that Up Axis is set to *Y* and not *Z*, as shown in Figure 2.18. This ensures that you've designated the *Y*-axis to be pointing "up" in the perspective window or pointing out at you from the monitor in the top view. *Y up*, as it's called, is Maya's default, but it never hurts to make sure, especially if you're on a shared computer.

Choose Window → Settings/Preferences → Preferences to open the Preferences window. Under Settings: Undo, make sure Undo is on (if it isn't already), and set Queue to Infinite. Setting Queue to Infinite takes a little more system memory, but it's worth it. With this configuration, you can undo (press Ctrl+Z, Command+Z, or just Z if you're using a Mac) as many times as it takes to undo any blunders. To close the Preferences window, click Save.

Mercury's Rotation

Now you're ready to animate Mercury's rotation. Follow these steps:

1. Select Mercury, and press E to activate the Rotate tool. The E key is the hotkey to invoke the Rotate tool in Maya; pressing it is the same as clicking the Rotate Tool icon in the Tool Box, as you've been doing so far. Press F to focus on Mercury in the perspective view, or zoom in on it manually.

2. Make sure you're on frame 1 of your animation range by clicking and dragging the Scrub bar (refer back to Figure 2.17) to place it at the desired frame. You can also manually type the frame value of **1** in the Current Frame box.

3. For Mercury, you'll set your initial keyframe for the *Y*-axis rotation. Click the Rotate Y's attribute name in the Channel Box to select it (it's then highlighted in gray, as

shown in Figure 2.19), and, in the Main Menu bar, choose Animate → Set Key. This places a keyframe for a rotation of 0 in the Y-axis at frame 1 for the Mercury sphere. If you followed the advice in the sidebar "Setting Keyframes," earlier in this chapter, only the Rotate Y attribute's Value box turns from white to orange to indicate that a keyframe exists for that attribute. If you left the Set Key command at its defaults, choosing Animate → Set Key sets keys on all the attributes for the sphere, turning all their values orange in the Channel Box.

Figure 2.19

Setting the initial keyframe for Mercury's Y-axis rotation

4. Using the Scrub bar in the Time slider, go to frame 240. Grab the Rotation Manipulator handle by the Y-axis (the green circle), and turn it clockwise a few times to rotate the sphere clockwise. You'll notice that you can rotate the object only so far in one direction before it seems to reset back to its original starting rotation. Rotate it as far as it will go, and release the mouse button. Then, click the Manipulator again, and drag to rotate the sphere as many times as necessary until you're satisfied.

5. Choose Animate → Set Key with the Rotate Y attribute still selected in the Channel Box. This sets a keyframe for the new Y-axis rotation at frame 240 for the Mercury sphere.

6. To play back your animation, you can scrub your Time slider. *Scrubbing* is using the mouse to move the Scrub bar back and forth so you can watch the animation play back in a window. Click in the Time slider on the Scrub bar, hold down the left mouse button, and move your cursor from side to side to scrub in real time. You see Mercury rotating in your active view panel, if you set your two keyframes as described.

Clicking so many things just to set two keyframes may seem like a lot of work, but you're doing this the long way right now; you're not yet using any shortcuts or hotkeys. You'll start using those for the next planet.

You have the self-rotation for Mercury worked out. Mercury has no moon, so let's get Mercury orbiting the Sun.

Grouping Mercury for a New Pivot Point

You've learned that every object in Maya is created with a pivot point around which it rotates, from which or to which it scales, and which acts as the placement point for its X-, Y-, and Z-coordinates. To orbit Mercury around the Sun, the sphere must revolve around a pivot point that is placed in the middle of the Sun. If the pivot point for Mercury is already at the center of itself, how can you revolve it around the Sun?

One idea is to move its current pivot point from the center of itself to the center of the Sun. That would, however, negate Mercury's own rotation, and it would no longer spin around its own center, so you can't do that. You need to create a new pivot point for this object. This way, you have the original pivot point at Mercury's center so it can self-rotate, and you have a second pivot point at the Sun so that Mercury can revolve around that point around the Sun. You'll accomplish this by creating a new *parent node* above Mercury in the hierarchy. What does that mean?

In order not to get too confusing, we'll take time in the following section to introduce the concept of Maya object structure: nodes and hierarchies. Save your progress so far, and open a new blank scene. After this explanation, we'll resume the Solar System exercise.

Hierarchy and Maya Object Structure

Let's take a timeout from the Solar System exercise and look at how objects and hierarchies work in Maya. On top of everything that you see in Maya—its interface—is a layer you don't see: the code. The layer of code keeps the objects in Maya organized through a network of nodes. How you relate these nodes defines how you've built your scene. In short, using Maya is essentially programming your computer directly to create 3D objects and animation.

So, having a solid understanding of how Maya defines objects and how they interact is essential to an efficient and successful animation process. This involves getting an intrinsic understanding of how nodes relate, whether it's a straightforward parent-child hierarchy in which one affects the other directly or a more complicated script-driven expression connecting 15 attributes of several objects to simplify a task.

Understanding Nodes

At its core, Maya relies on packets of information called *nodes*, and each node carries with it a group of attributes that in combination define an object. These attributes can be spatial coordinates, geometric descriptors, color values, and so on. Taken together, an object's attributes define it and how it animates. You can define, animate, and interconnect any or all of these attributes individually or in concert, which gives you amazing control over a scene.

When you're beginning to work with a robust program, the learning curve occasionally spikes. With Maya, these spikes typically involve nodes and their interconnections. Although the interface automates much of the node creation and relationship process, the sooner you're exposed to the implications of the node level of objects, the easier it will be for you to overcome the typical learning curve. Even though you may not actively see that you're making root-level connections between nodes and attributes, that is exactly what you're doing every time you click a command.

Nodes that define the shape of a surface or a primitive are called *creation nodes* or *shape nodes*. These nodes carry the information that defines how that object is created. For example, a sphere's creation node has an attribute for its radius. Changing that attribute changes the radius of the sphere at its base level. Shape nodes are low on the hierarchy chain and are always child nodes of *transform nodes*. The sphere listens to its creation node attributes first and then moves down the chain to its other nodes' attributes (such as position, rotation, or scale).

> Not all primitives are created with shape nodes, so changes at the creation level may not be possible on certain objects; some objects are created without a creation node. When you create a new primitive or an object, make sure the History button (⬛) is turned on in the Status line (see Chapter 3 for more about the Status line and its icons). If it displays a small red X in the icon, History is off, and the primitive will be created without a shape node.

The most visible and used nodes are the transform nodes, also known as DAG nodes (Directed Acyclic Graph nodes). These nodes contain all the transformation attributes for an object or a group of objects below it. *Transformations* are the values for translation (position), rotation, and scale. These nodes also hold hierarchy information about any other children or parent nodes to which they're attached. When you move or scale an object, you adjust attributes in this node.

Try This As an example of working with transform nodes, you can create a sphere and see what happens in the Attribute Editor as you adjust its position and size. Follow these steps in a new Maya scene:

1. Press Ctrl+A to toggle the Attribute Editor on the right of the UI or to open it as its own window if you've set it up to do so in Maya's preferences. (Ctrl functions the same on a Mac as on a PC, so Mac users can also use their Ctrl key when called for in the text.)

   The tabs along the top of the window let you switch between the nodes that are attached to this object. The current tab should be on the sphere's shape node, called nurbsSphereShape1. This node contains specific information about the object, but it isn't typically a node that you edit.

2. Press W to select the Translate tool. With the sphere still selected, click the nurbsSphere1 tab in the Attribute Editor to access the sphere's transforms node. Move the sphere a little in the *X* direction. Notice in the Attribute Editor that the Translate attribute for *X* has changed. You should also see the change in the Channel Box.

3. Press R to select the Scale tool. R is the hotkey by default in Maya for the Scale tool and is the same as clicking the Scale tool icon in the Tool Box (⬛). Scale the sphere uniformly, meaning equally, in all directions by clicking and dragging the Center Manipulator handle (the cyan box). Notice that the Scale X, Scale Y, and Scale Z

attributes of the sphere change in the Attribute Editor. In the Attribute Editor, enter **1.0** for the *X, Y,* and *Z* Scale values to reset the sphere back to its original size.

4. In the creation node of makeNurbsSphere1, change the radius from 1.0 to 2.0. The sphere doubles in size because its radius is doubled. Switch back to the transform node (nurbsSphere1), and note that the Scale X, Scale Y, and Scale Z attribute values are unchanged. This is because you affected the size of the sphere through its Radius attribute in the creation node at its root level, not through the Scale attributes in a higher node. Any changes you make to the Scale attributes take effect after changes in the lower node. This is a perfect example of how one node's output (here, the Radius attribute) changes another node.

Parents and Children

A *parent node* is simply a node that passes its transformations down the hierarchy chain to its children. A *child node* inherits the transforms of all the parents above it. So, by using hierarchies for the Solar System exercise, you'll create a nested hierarchy of parents and children to animate the orbital rotation of the nine planets and some of their moons.

By creating parent-child relationships, you can easily animate the orbit of a moon around a planet while the planet orbits the Sun. With the proper hierarchy, the animation of the planet orbiting the Sun automatically translates to the moon. In effect, the planet takes the moon with it as it goes around the Sun.

Child nodes have their own transformations that can be coupled with any inherited transforms from their parent, and these transformations affect them and any of their children down the line.

The revolution of one of the planets around the Sun takes into account its moons, but those moons can have their own animation to spin themselves around their planets. You're about to experience this firsthand as you continue the Solar System exercise. The more you hear about these concepts in different contexts, the easier they will be to master.

Figure 2.20 shows the Outliner and Hypergraph views with a simple hierarchy of objects for your reference. The Outliner and Hypergraph show you the objects in your scene in an outline and flowchart format, respectively. Both of these windows allow you to access the different levels of nodes (the hierarchy) in a scene and are discussed further in Chapter 3.

A top parent node called group1 holds its children *nurbsCone1, nurbsSphere3,* and the nested group node *group2.* The node group2 is the parent node of nurbsSphere2 and nurbsSphere1.

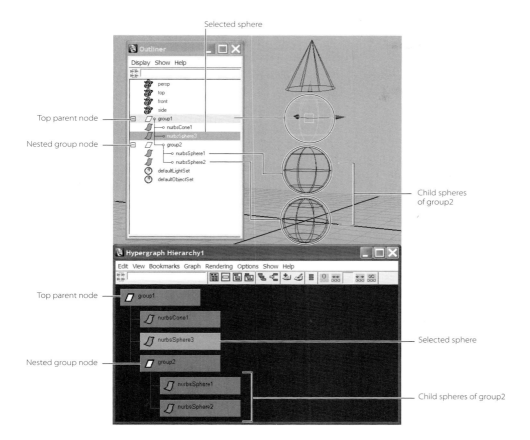

Figure 2.20

A simple hierarchy in both the Outliner and Hypergraph windows

The Solar System Resumed

If you still feel a little unsure about nodes and hierarchies, take the time to reread the previous section and try the short exercise again. You'll practice these concepts as you resume the Solar System exercise. By the time you've finished this exercise, you'll have a strong sense of how hierarchies work in Maya, although you should feel free to repeat the entire exercise if you think that will help you master hierarchies. Understanding nodes and hierarchies is important to animating in Maya.

   If you're new to CG animation, take your time with the following section.

Animating Mercury's Orbit Around the Sun

Load up your scene from where you last saved it. When you left off, you had created the self-rotation animation for Mercury and were about to create a second pivot point for the planet to orbit around the Sun by creating a new parent node for the Mercury sphere.

To create a new pivot point by making a new parent node, follow these steps:

1. With Mercury selected, press E for the Rotate tool, and then choose Edit → Group from the Main Menu bar. The Channel Box displays attributes for a new node called group1. Notice that nothing about the Mercury sphere changed, except that the Rotation Manipulator handle jumped from where it was originally centered on Mercury all the way back to the origin, where the zero points of the *X*-, *Y*-, and *Z*-axes collide. Figure 2.21 shows the new Mercury group and its new pivot location.

Figure 2.21

Grouping Mercury to itself creates a new pivot point at the origin.

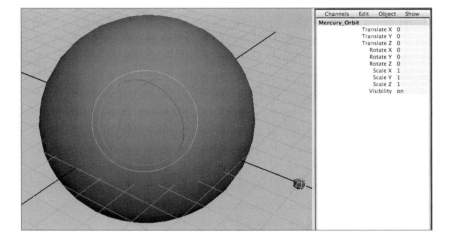

You just created a new Maya object by grouping Mercury to itself. In doing so, you also created a second pivot point for Mercury, in effect, which was placed by Maya at the origin by default. Because an object's Manipulator always centers on its pivot point when it's selected, Mercury's Rotate Manipulator jumped to the origin when the new parent node became selected upon its creation. That is fortunate for you, because that happens to be the center of the Sun—exactly where you need it to be for Mercury to orbit the Sun properly.

2. Without unselecting Mercury, click group1 in the Channel Box, and change the name of this new group to **Mercury_Orbit**. It's important to make the distinction between node names so you never get confused. Now you know that the Mercury node is the planet sphere itself, whereas Mercury_Orbit is the name of the new parent node, with which you'll orbit Mercury around the Sun.

3. Click anywhere in an empty space in your view window to unselect Mercury_Orbit. Try selecting it again. Notice that when you click Mercury, you select only the planet and not the new parent node Mercury_Orbit, the group that has its pivot point at the center of the Sun. This happens because you're in Object Selection mode (a.k.a.

Object mode). To select the group Mercury_Orbit, you need to switch into Hierarchy mode by toggling its icon (![icon]) on the Status line at the top of the UI, as shown in Figure 2.22. Make sure you switch back to Object mode by clicking its icon (![icon]) in the Status line. For more on selection modes, see Chapter 3.

Figure 2.22

Toggling on the Hierarchy mode

4. Go back to frame 1 of your animation. Set a keyframe for Mercury_Orbit's Rotate Y attribute by selecting its name in the Channel Box and then choosing Animate → Set Key from the Main Menu bar.

5. Go to frame 240, grab Mercury_Orbit's Rotate Manipulator handle by the green Y-axis, and spin it around the Sun twice in either direction. (It doesn't matter if you go clockwise or counterclockwise.) You can also enter **720** (or **-720** Object Selection mode to go in the other direction) in the Rotate Y attribute field in the Channel Box.

6. Choose Animate → Set Key to set a keyframe at frame 240 for Mercury_Orbit. Scrub your animation to play it back.

Does that make good sense? You'll have the chance to do this a few more times as you animate the other planets and their moons. However, if you still find yourself a little fuzzy on this concept (which is perfectly normal), repeat the steps to animate Mercury in a new scene file if need be. One down, eight to go.

Creating Venus

For your next planet, Venus, follow the same procedure as for Mercury's self-rotation, and animate it so that it rotates about itself. Then, create a new pivot point (placed by default at the origin) by grouping Venus to itself to create a new parent node for that sphere, and call the new parent node **Venus_Orbit**. Last, animate Venus_Orbit to revolve around the Sun just as you did with Mercury_Orbit in the previous steps.

Earth and the Moon

Now you need to animate the third planet, the Earth, in much the same way, except that this time there will be the added complication of a moon. In addition, instead of choosing Animate → Set Key to set your keyframes, you'll use the keyboard hotkey S. (The Earth? Hey, I can see my house from here!)

> Whenever you press S when an attribute is highlighted in the Channel Box, you're essentially choosing Animate → Set Key. In the Set Key Options dialog box, be sure you've changed Set Keys On to All Keyable Attributes instead of the default All Manipulator Handles and Keyable Attributes. Also make sure you've set Channels to From Channel Box instead of the default All Keyable, as mentioned in the earlier sidebar.

To animate Earth and the Moon, follow these steps:

1. Select Earth, and give it its self-rotation animation as you did for Mercury. But this time, select the rotation channel names in the Channel Box and press S, instead of choosing Animate → Set Key to set rotation keyframes. Again, if you left the Animate → Set Key ❐ at its defaults, pressing S sets keys for all attributes; but if you followed the advice given previously in the sidebar, only the selected channels are keyframed.

2. Select the Moon, and give it its self-rotation animation by spinning it around itself and keyframing it as you've just done with Earth.

3. To spin the Moon around Earth, do what you did earlier in this chapter to spin a planet around the Sun: group the Moon to itself by choosing Edit → Group, and name the new parent node **Moon_Orbit**.

This time, however, you need the pivot point to be at the center of Earth and not at the center of the Sun object, where it is currently. Follow these steps:

1. Turn on the grid snap, and then press the Insert key to activate the pivot point. If you're using a Macintosh, press the Home key. The Moon's Manipulator changes from a rotation handle to the *Pivot Point Manipulator*. This Manipulator acts just like the Move Manipulator, but instead of moving the object, it moves the object's pivot point.

2. Grab the yellow circle in the middle of the Manipulator, and move the pivot point to snap it to the grid point located at the center of Earth (see Figure 2.23).

3. Press the Insert key again (or the Home key on a Macintosh) to return to the Rotation Manipulator for Moon_Orbit. At frame 1, set a keyframe for the Moon's *Y*-axis rotation. Then, at frame 240, rotate the Moon about the *Y*-axis and set a keyframe. Return to frame 1.

Figure 2.23

Moving the Moon's pivot point to the center of Earth

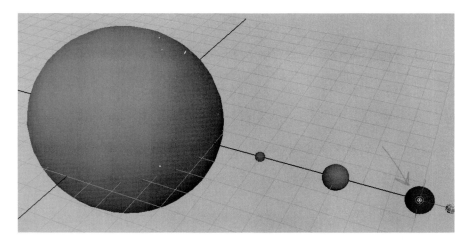

Grouping the Moon with Earth

To animate Earth's orbit of the Sun, you need to make sure the Moon will also follow Earth around the Sun. Instead of just selecting Earth and grouping it to itself as you've done for the other two planets, you need to include the Moon_Orbit node in that group. Follow these steps:

1. Select Earth. Shift+click the Moon_Orbit group while in Hierarchy mode () to make sure you get the topmost node of the Moon, and then choose Edit → Group. Name this new parent node **Earth_Orbit**. Remember, when you select just Earth or the Moon in Object mode (), the Earth_Orbit node isn't selected. If you select Earth and then Shift+click the Moon, you select both objects, but you still don't select the parent node Earth_Orbit, which is the group that contains both these objects and has its pivot point at the center of the Sun. Make sure you select the right group. Keep an eye on where the Manipulator is when you make your selection. If you have the Earth_Orbit node selected, its Manipulator should be in the middle of the Sun. We'll deliberately illustrate this mistake and its consequences when you animate Pluto a little later.

> Make sure you use Hierarchy mode () when you click the moon object to select Moon_Orbit and not just the moon sphere. Otherwise, you'll lose the animation of the Moon orbiting Earth.

2. Set a keyframe for Earth_Orbit's Rotate Y attribute at frame 1 by highlighting Rotate Y in the Channel Box and pressing S for the Set Key command. This assumes you've changed the defaults in Animate → Set Key ❒ as discussed in the earlier sidebar.

3. Go to frame 240, spin Earth and the Moon around the Sun a few times in whichever direction and for however many revolutions you want, and set a keyframe at frame 240 as well.

Now the first three planets are going around themselves and around the Sun, with a moon for the Earth. If you haven't been saving your work, save it now. Just don't save over the un-animated version from earlier.

Creating the Other Planets' Moons

Repeat this animation procedure for the remaining planets and moons, but leave out Pluto for now. (Poor Pluto: first it loses out on being a planet, and now it has to wait for last.)

> If you find that one of your moons is left behind by its planet or that it no longer revolves around the planet, you most likely made an error when grouping the moon and planet. Undo until you're at the point right before you grouped them, and try again. If that still doesn't work, start over from the earlier version of the file you saved just before you began animating it. You'll learn how to fix it in the section "Using the Outliner," later in this chapter.

Auto Keyframe

You can also use the Auto Keyframe feature when animating the planets and moons. Auto Keyframe automatically sets a keyframe for any attribute that changes from a previously set keyframe. For example, an initial keyframe for an attribute such as Y-Axis Rotation needs to be set at some point in the animation. The next time the Y-Axis Rotation is changed, Maya will set a keyframe at the current frame automatically.

To turn on Auto Keyframe, click the Auto Keyframe icon ( ), which is to the right of the Range slider. When the icon is red, Auto Keyframe is active.

To use Auto Keyframe to animate the moon orbiting Mars, follow these steps:

1. Turn on Auto Keyframe.

2. Start at frame 1. Select Mars's moon, and set a keyframe for its *Y*-axis orbit by highlighting Rotate Y in the Channel Box and pressing S.

3. Go to frame 240. Revolve the moon around Mars several times in a direction of your choosing. Maya automatically sets a frame for *Y* rotation at frame 240. Save your file.

USE CUBES INSTEAD OF SPHERES

Feel free to create the planets and moons as cubes instead of spheres. That way, you can see each of their individual rotations much more easily, so you can tell whether the animation is working properly for you.

Using the Outliner

The Outliner is an outline format listing of all the objects and nodes in your scene. For an in-depth look at the Outliner, see Chapter 3. For now, let's look at how to use the Outliner to illustrate the hierarchies for the planets and moons. When all is good and proper, the Outliner should look like Figure 2.24. Choose Window → Outliner to open the Outliner window and take a peek at what you have. If you haven't yet properly named everything, including the moons, take this opportunity to do so by double-clicking a name in the Outliner and entering a new name.

Let's look at the planet Mars and its layout in the Outliner to better understand the hierarchy for all the planets. All the other planets should be laid out exactly like Mars (except the planets that have just one or no moons).

At the bottom of the hierarchy are Mars's two moons, mars_moon and mars_moon2. Each of those moons is spinning on its own pivot point. You grouped each moon to itself,

Figure 2.24

The Outliner view of the planet hierarchies

created the mars_moon_orbit and mars_moon2_orbit nodes, and placed their pivot points at the center of Mars to animate their orbits around Mars.

Mars is spinning on its own pivot point, but it needed another pivot point to be able to orbit the Sun. Because you had to make the moons go with it around the Sun, you selected Mars, mars_moon_orbit, and mars_moon2_orbit (the top nodes of the moons that circle the planet Mars) and grouped them all together, placing that pivot point at the center of the Sun. You called this node Mars_Orbit. This is the *parent node* because it's the topmost node for this group. Wherever this parent node goes, the child nodes that are under it will follow.

Hierarchies such as this are a cornerstone of Maya animation. It's imperative that you're comfortable with how they work and how to work with them. If you find yourself scratching your head even a little, try the exercise again. A proper foundation is critical. Remember, this learning 3D thing isn't easy, but patience and repetition help a lot.

Correcting Hierarchy Problems Using the Outliner

One of the most common problems you'll run into with this project is a planet revolving around the Sun without its moon. To illustrate how to fix it using the Outliner, as opposed to undoing and redoing it as suggested earlier, the following steps will force you to make this error with Pluto. Usually, people learn more from mistakes than from doing things correctly.

Go to Pluto, start the same animation procedure as outlined earlier, and then follow these steps to force an error:

1. Create Pluto's own self-rotation by spinning it around itself and keyframing as before.

2. Do the same for Pluto's moon's rotation.

3. Group the moon to itself, and grid-snap the pivot point at the center of Pluto to create the moon's orbit of Pluto.

   When Pluto's moon (pluto_moon) is orbiting Pluto, you're ready to group the moon's orbit and Pluto together to create an orbit of the Sun for both.

4. Here is where you make your mistake. In Object mode, select the sphere for Pluto's moon, and select the sphere for Pluto. Your error is that you're remaining in Object mode instead of switching to Hierarchy mode.

5. Choose Edit → Group to group them together, and call that new node **Pluto_Orbit** (following the naming convention you used for the others).

6. Animate Pluto_Orbit revolving around the Sun.

7. Play back the animation.

Notice that the moon is no longer orbiting the planet. This is because you didn't include pluto_moon_orbit in your group Pluto_Orbit. The animation of the moon going around Pluto is stored in that node; and because it's no longer attached to Pluto_Orbit, there's no moon orbit of Pluto.

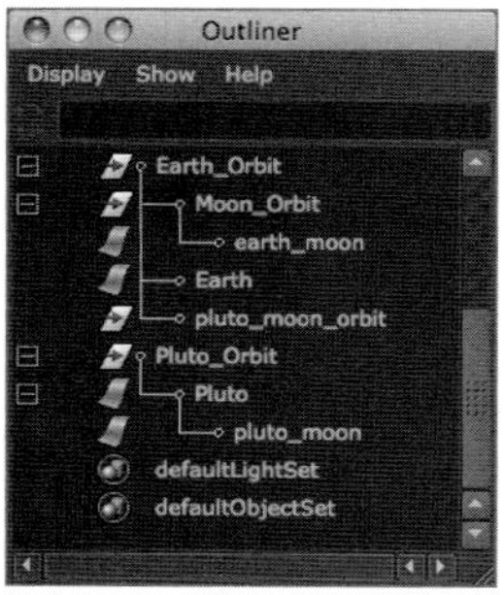

Figure 2.25
Pluto's incorrect hierarchy

Figure 2.25 shows the hierarchy of Pluto and how it's different from that of the other planets: the moon's orbit node has been left out of the group. (Earth has been expanded as a contrasting example.)

Using the Outliner, you can easily fix this problem. Place the pluto_moon_orbit node under the Pluto_Orbit node. Go to frame 1 of the animation, grab the pluto_moon_orbit node in the Outliner, and use the middle mouse button to drag it to the Pluto_Orbit node so that it has a black horizontal line above and below it to show a connection, as in Figure 2.26.

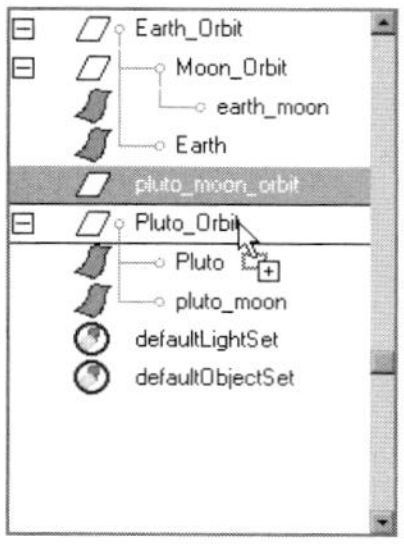

Figure 2.26
Regrouping objects in the Outliner

You've just grouped pluto_moon_orbit under Pluto_Orbit, a practice known as *parenting*. Now you need to parent pluto_moon under pluto_moon_orbit as well. Use the middle mouse button to drag pluto_moon onto pluto_moon_orbit. When you play back the animation, you'll see that the moon is revolving around the planet, while at the same time Pluto and the moon are orbiting the Sun.

Now that you've corrected Pluto's layout in the Outliner, it's similar to the layouts for the other properly working planets.

The file Planets_v3.mb in the Scenes folder of the Solar_System project on the CD will give you an idea of how this project should look. The first five planet systems are grouped and animated as a reference, leaving the final four for you to finish.

You can add objects to a group by MMB+dragging their listing onto the desired parent node in the Outliner. You can also remove objects from a group by MMB+dragging them out of the parent node to a different place in the Outliner.

GROUPING TERMINOLOGY

Grouping terminology can be confusing. Grouping Node A under Node B makes Node A a child of Node B. Node B is now the parent of Node A. Furthermore, any transformation or movement applied to the parent Node B will be inherited by the child Node A.

When you group Node A and Node B, both nodes become siblings under a newly created parent node, Node C. This new node is created just to be the parent of Nodes A and B and is otherwise known as a *null node*. To group objects, select them and choose Edit → Group. Parenting nodes together places the first selected node under the second selected node. For

GROUPING TERMINOLOGY *(continued)*

example, if you select Node A, Shift+select Node B, and then choose Edit → Parent, Node A will group under Node B and become its child. This is the same procedure as MMB+dragging Node B to Node A in the Outliner, as you did with Pluto's moon and Pluto itself.

Outputting Your Work: Playblasting

What's the use of animating all this work and not being able to show it? There are several ways of outputting your work in Maya, most of which involve rendering to images. One faster way of outputting your animation in a simple shaded view is called *playblasting*. Playblasting creates a sequence of images that play back on your computer at the proper frame rate. Only if your PC is slow, or if you're playblasting a large sequence of frames, will your playback degrade. In this case, playblasting 240 frames shouldn't be a problem.

A *playblast*, as it's called in Maya, outputs the view panel's view into an image sequence or AVI movie. You can also save the image sequence or AVI to disk if you like. Playblasting is done mainly to test the look and animation of a scene, especially when its playback is slow within Maya.

When you have your Solar System animated, output a playblast by following these steps:

1. With your animation completed, click in the Perspective panel to make it active in the four-panel layout (don't maximize the Perspective window). Press 5 to enter Shaded mode.

2. RMB+click in the Time slider, and select Playblast ❒ from the menu, as shown in Figure 2.27. The Options dialog box is shown for the Playblast options in Figure 2.28.

3. In the Playblast options, set the Viewer to Movieplayer (displayed as QuickTime when using a Macintosh) and the Display Size to From Window. Check the Save to File option, and give your Playblast a name. Set the Scale to 1.0.

Figure 2.27

Select the Option box for Playblast.

Figure 2.28

Options for creating a Playblast preview

4. Because you checked the Movieplayer (or QuickTime on a Mac) option, Maya runs through the animation and creates an AVI movie file on a PC or a QuickTime movie file on a Mac that is based on the Shaded-mode appearance of the currently active view panel (which should be the Perspective panel). Because you also checked the Save to File option, the movie file is saved to disk. By default, it's saved to the Images folder for the Solar_System project you created on your hard drive. You can also click the Browse button to store the playblast video file anywhere you like. For now, click Browse, and place the file on your desktop. Click the Playblast button.

5. When Maya runs through the animation, Windows Media Player on Windows and QuickTime on a Mac (or whatever your default movie player is set to in your OS) automatically opens and plays the move file of the animation at the proper speed of 30fps, as shown in Figure 2.29. Now you can share your animation with others without having to open Maya and play it back in the scene.

When you're creating a playblast, make sure you don't cover the view panel with any other windows, such as an Internet browser, as you wait for the animation to complete. Doing so will create a display error in the playblast output. It's best to allow Maya to complete the playblast before you use the system again.

Figure 2.29

Creating a playblast movie file is easy.

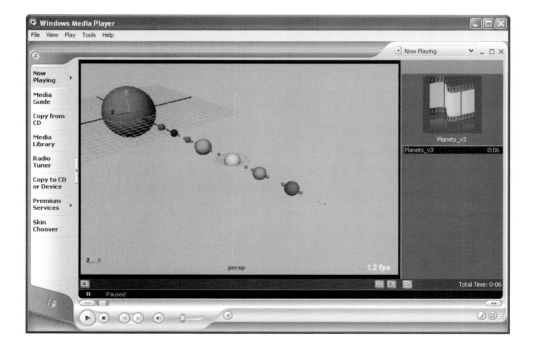

Summary

In this chapter, you learned how to start working in Maya by getting around the interface a bit and learning how to navigate the UI. Then, you began working by creating a new project, creating basic objects such as primitives, and placing objects in the scene. You learned how to place pivot points for objects and how to use snaps to place points precisely. You had some experience with the Channel Box and Attribute Editor to set an object's attributes. You then went on to create simple shaders for your objects and set keyframes to animate a Solar System. You went over object hierarchy and grouping conventions to organize and set up your scene better, and finally you learned how to output a basic playblast video file of your completed animation.

The planet animation you created is based on a system of layering simple actions on top of each other to achieve a more elaborate result. If you work slowly and in segments, animation is more straightforward to produce and generally of higher quality. Much of your time in actual animation, as opposed to setup or modeling, will be spent adjusting the small things. These small things give the scene life and character. You'll find that finishing 85 percent of a scene will take about 15 percent of the time. The remaining 85 percent of the time goes into perfecting the final 15 percent of the scene.

CHAPTER 3

The Maya 2011 Interface

This chapter takes you on a guided tour of all the elements visible on the Maya 2011 screen. It draws from the experience you had in Chapter 2, "Jumping in Headfirst, with Both Feet," with the Solar System exercise. You'll visit the menus, icons, and shelves, to become familiar with the interface basics; you'll learn how to work with these tools later in this book. For now, while you're first getting into this, knowing the name of everything and its purpose is a good idea. Don't get nervous; you won't need to retain a lot of information. Think of this more as a nickel tour.

This chapter also serves as a good reference when you're wondering about the purpose of a particular icon. If you're already familiar with the Maya interface, you may want to skip this chapter.

Topics in this chapter include:

- **Navigating in Maya**
- **Maya's layout**
- **Panels and frequently used windows**
- **Customizing Maya**

Navigating in Maya

The key to being a good digital artist or animator isn't necessarily knowing exactly where to find all the tools and buttons, but knowing *how* to find the features you need. Don't let the interface intimidate you; it's much friendlier than you may initially think, and there is more than one way to get something done through the user interface (UI).

Maya is intricate, with layers of function sets and interface options separated into categories. The purpose of this chapter is to help you get to know Maya and how it operates, building on your experience so far. This chapter will also answer the questions you may have about the UI from the previous chapter.

The best way to start is to explore the interface. Using your mouse, check out the menus and the tools. Just be careful not to change any settings; the rest of this book and its projects assume your Maya settings are all at their defaults. If you do change some settings inadvertently, reverting to the defaults is easy. Choose Window → Settings/Preferences → Preferences. In the Preferences window, choose Edit → Restore Default Settings. Now all the settings and interface elements are restored to their default states.

Maya's Layout

Let's take another look at the initial Maya screen in Figure 3.1—this time with the Full Perspective window, and not the four-panel layout you saw in the previous chapter.

Figure 3.1

The initial Maya screen

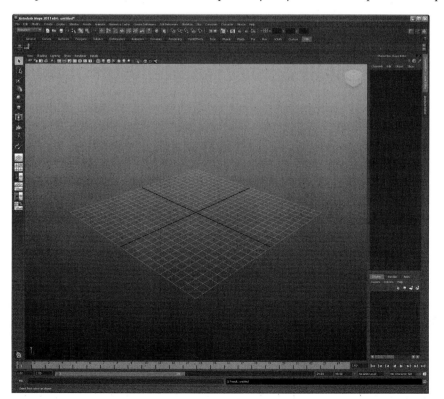

The *Main Menu bar*, *Status line*, and *Shelf* all run across the top of the screen. The Tool Box runs vertically on the left side of the screen. It contains icons for your transform tools (such as Move and Rotate) as well as quick-view selections to allow you to customize your panel layouts quickly. The Attribute Editor and Channel Box/Layer Editor (the Channel Box is displayed in Figure 3.1, and not the Attribute Editor) run down the right side of the screen. Finally, listed from the top down, the Time slider, the Range slider, the Character Set menu, the Auto Keyframe button, and the Animation Preferences button, some of which you've already used, run across the bottom of the screen.

REMINDER: MAYA'S MOUSE CONTROLS

In Maya, holding the Alt key on a PC or the Option key on a Mac along with the appropriate button allows you to move in the view panel. The left mouse button (LMB) acts as the primary selection button (as it does in many other programs) and lets you orbit around objects when used with the Alt key. The right mouse button (RMB) activates numerous shortcut menus and lets you zoom with the Alt key. The middle mouse button (MMB) with the Alt key lets you move within the Maya interface, and the mouse's wheel can be used to zoom in and out as well.

The Main Menu Bar

In the Main Menu bar, shown in Figure 3.2, you'll find a few of the familiar menu choices you've come to expect in many applications, such as File, Edit, and Help.

One difference in Maya, however, is that menu choices are context sensitive; they depend on what you're doing. By switching menu sets, you change your menu choices and hence your available toolset. The menu sets in Maya are Animation, Polygons, Surfaces, Dynamics, Rendering, and nDynamics. No matter which menu set you're working in, the first six items are constant: File, Edit, Modify, Create, Display, and Window. The last menu, Help, is also constantly displayed no matter which menu set you choose.

Some plugins can also add menu items to the Menu Bar. For example, Maya Muscle is a plugin that comes with Maya and is on by default; it adds the Muscle menu to the Menu Bar. If the plugin is turned off, that menu item is removed. So, don't panic if you don't see the same exact Menu Bar pictured throughout this book.

Figure 3.2

The Main Menu bar is where the magic happens!

In Maya, you can create your own menu sets by choosing Customize from the Menu Set pull-down menu. Here you can select which menu headings to display. Customizing Maya is a powerful way to optimize your workflow; however, you should keep your settings at their defaults until you feel comfortable with the UI.

When searching for a particular tool, keep in mind that each menu set controls particular functions. You'll notice two different demarcations to the right of some menu items: arrows and boxes (called *option boxes*). Clicking an arrow opens a submenu that contains more specific commands. Clicking an option box (❐) opens a dialog box in which you can set the options for that particular tool.

As noted, the following menus are always visible:

File Deals with file operations, from saving and opening to optimizing scene size and export/import.

Edit Contains the commands you use to edit characteristics of the scene (for example, deleting and duplicating objects or undoing and redoing actions).

Modify Lets you edit the characteristics of objects in the scene, such as moving or scaling them or changing their pivot points.

Create Lets you make new objects, such as primitive geometries, curves, cameras, and so on.

Display Contains commands for adjusting elements of the graphical user interface (GUI) in Maya as well as objects in the scene, allowing you to toggle, or switch on or off, the display of certain elements as well as components of objects, such as vertices, hulls, pivots, and so on.

Window Gives you access to the many windows you'll come to rely on, such as the Attribute Editor, Outliner, Graph Editor, and Hypergraph. This menu is broken into submenus according to function, such as Rendering Editors and Animation Editors.

Assets Gives you access to Maya Assets, which gives you the tools to better organize and manage productions in Maya, especially with multiple artists working on the same project. Assets are beyond the scope of this book.

Muscle Contains the tools you would need to create muscle systems for your characters. Muscles are an advanced topic and beyond the scope of this text.

Help Gives you access to the help files.

ADVANCED TIP: FLOATING MENUS

In Maya, you can *tear off* menus to create separate floating boxes that you can place anywhere in the workspace, as shown here. This makes accessing menu commands easier, especially when you need to use the same command repeatedly. Let's say, for example, that you need to repeatedly access polygonal editing tools. You can tear off the Edit Mesh menu and place it at the edge of your screen. You can then click the commands you need as many times as necessary without opening the menu every time. To tear off a menu, click the dashed line at the top of the menu, and drag the menu where you want it.

Click and drag

The Status Line

The Status line (see Figure 3.3) contains a number of important and often-used icons.

The Status line begins with a drop-down menu that gives you access to the menu sets in Maya. Selecting a menu set changes the menu headings in the Main Menu bar according to the type of work you're doing (modeling with polygons, rendering, animating, and so on). You'll notice immediately after the Menu Set drop-down menu, and intermittently throughout the Status line, white vertical line breaks with either a box or an arrow in the middle. Clicking a break opens or closes sections of the Status line.

Figure 3.3

The Status line

Scene File Icons

The tools in the first section of the Status line deal with file operations:

ICON	NAME	DESCRIPTION
	New Scene	Creates a new, blank scene file
	Open Scene	Displays a window in which you can find and open any scene file you've saved
	Save Scene	Displays a window in which you can specify a filename and location to save a new scene; or, if the current scene has already been saved and named, saves it to that location

Selection Modes

The second section between the black horizontal lines is the Selection Mode field. This drop-down menu lets you use presets for *selection masks*. Selection masks give you the chance to pick one kind of object but not another—you can, for example, select all the particles in the scene and none of the polygon models.

> Using a selection mask, you can select some object types in a scene and not others. For example, in a heavily layered scene, you might want to select only the faces of a polygon and not any other object or object component. You can use a selection mask to isolate polygonal faces as the only selectable object on the screen and click away.

This Selection Mode field gives you some presets that optimize the Selection modes for your convenience. However, you may prefer to use the individual selection mask icons farther down the Status line, which give you more control. You can turn on and off select-ability for individual object types, such as particles, NURBS, polygons, and so on.

The next group of icons lets you click into three distinct selection modes. Selection modes allow you to select different levels of an object's hierarchy. For example, using a selection mode, you can select an entire group of objects, only one of the objects in that group, or even points on the surface of that object, depending on the selection mode you're in:

ICON	NAME	DESCRIPTION
	Hierarchy mode	Lets you select groups of objects or parts of a group
	Object mode	Lets you select objects such as geometry, cameras, lights, and so on
	Component mode	Lets you select an object's components, such as vertices, faces, or the control vertices (CVs) of NURBS surfaces

> To switch between Object and Component mode, press the F8 key, which is Maya 2011's default hotkey.

Click the Hierarchy Mode icon, for example, to select the topmost node of a hierarchy or group of objects. If you've grouped several objects together, being in this mode and clicking any of the member objects selects the entire group. For more on hierarchies, see the section "Hierarchy and Maya Object Structure" in Chapter 2.

Individual Selection Masks

The next set of icons between the section breaks deals with individual selection masks, which give you control over which objects or components you want to select. Exactly which icons are displayed here depends on your current selection mode. If you have many objects in your scene and you're having difficulty selecting a certain type of object with your mouse pointer, you can use these filters to single out the object(s):

ICON	NAME	DESCRIPTION
	Set Object Selection Mask	Turns on or off all selection icons
	Select by Handles	Allows selection of object handles
	Select by Joints	Allows selection of joints
	Select by Curve	Allows selection of curves
	Select by Surfaces	Allows selection of surfaces
	Select by Deformations	Allows selection of lattices and other deformers
	Select by Dynamics	Allows selection of particles and dynamic objects
	Select by Rendering	Allows selection of rendering nodes and objects such as lights and cameras
	Select by Miscellaneous	Allows selection of miscellaneous objects such as locators and dimensions
	Lock Selection	Keeps selected objects locked in as selected
	Highlight Selection Mode	Turns off the automatic display of components when selecting in a selection mode

You'll work with these filters throughout the book. For a quick preview, hover your cursor over each of the icons to see a tool tip that gives the icon's name and describes its function. As you gain experience, you'll find these masks helpful in your workflow.

Snapping Functions or Snaps

The icons with the magnets are called *snaps*. They allow you to snap your cursor or object to specific points in the scene. You can snap to other objects, to CVs or vertices, and to grid intersections and other locations by toggling these icons. Therefore, you can place your objects or points precisely. You made good use of the snapping functions in the previous chapter in making the Solar System:

ICON	NAME	DESCRIPTION
	Snap to Grids	Lets you snap objects to intersections of the view's grid.
	Snap to Curves	Lets you snap objects along a curve.
	Snap to Points	Lets you snap objects to object points such as CVs or vertices.
	Snap to View Planes	Lets you snap objects to view planes.
	Make the Selected Object Live	This icon has nothing to do with snapping but is grouped with the Snap To icons. It lets you create objects such as curves directly on a surface.

Input and Output Connections

The first two icons following the filters list the input and output connections of an object. Objects in Maya can connect with each other to create relationships between them for animation, modeling, rendering, or what have you. When an object is influenced by an attribute of another object or node in Maya, it has an *input connection*. When the node's own attribute(s) influence another object, it has an *output connection*. Clicking either of these icons shows you the connections for a selected object.

The third icon following the filters toggles Construction History on and off. Construction History is a feature that keeps track of the nodes and attributes that help make up an object, making it easier to edit those objects that have history. These subjects are covered in more detail later in this book:

ICON	NAME	DESCRIPTION
	Input Connections	Lets you select and edit all the input connections for the selected object
	Output Connections	Lets you select and edit the output connections for the selected object
	Construction History	Toggles the object's Construction History on/off

Render Controls

The next four icons give you access to render controls:

ICON	NAME	DESCRIPTION
	Open Render View	Opens the Render View window
	Render Current View	Renders the active viewport at the current frame to the Render View window
	IPR Render Current View	Renders the active view at the current frame into Interactive Photorealistic Rendering (IPR), a feature that lets you change certain shading and texturing settings and view real-time updates
	Render Settings	Opens a window that gives you access to all the rendering switches, such as resolution, file type, and frame range

The Input Line Operations Menu and Fields

In this section, you can input values directly into Maya to affect the selected object(s). You have a few functions here at your disposal. Clicking the icon for the menu of line input operations ( ) gives you access to the following features:

Absolute Transform Allows you to type in the *XYZ* values for how you want to move, rotate, or scale the selected object in the scene absolutely. This lets you give the object coordinates that are absolute to the coordinates of the 3D space. For instance, selecting a sphere and typing in *XYZ* values of **2**, **8**, and **10** for the Move tool places the sphere exactly at these coordinates (2,8,10) in the 3D space.

Relative Transform Entering the same values for Relative Transform adds 2, 8, and 10 to the current position of the sphere.

Rename Allows you to rename the selected object easily.

Select by Name Allows you to type the name of an object that you want Maya to select for you in a scene. This is handy when you have a large scene and don't want to spend time hunting around in the view panels for an object. You can enter exact names as well as wildcards such as **sphere***, which is handy if you only remember part of the object's name.

The Channel Box/Layer Editor

The last part of the Status line deals with the area defined earlier in the chapter as the Attribute Editor and Channel Box/Layer Editor. These buttons toggle through three views in that area on the right side of the screen. Clicking the first button displays the Attribute Editor, with which you can edit Maya's object attributes. Clicking the second button turns on a window called Tool Settings in that column, giving you access to options for the currently active tool. Clicking the last icon restores the Channel Box/Layer Editor, showing you the commonly keyed attributes of an active object as well as the display layers in your scene.

Pressing Ctrl+A toggles between the Attribute Editor and the Channel Box/Layer Editor by default. Additionally, at the top of these windows is a dotted bar. Clicking and dragging that bar undocks the window from the main user interface, so you can have a floating Attribute Editor, for example. You can redock the Attribute Editor by dragging the title bar back to where the dotted line is. These windows are discussed in detail later in this chapter. Feel free to skip ahead and then come back for the next area of the interface, the Shelf.

ICON	NAME	DESCRIPTION
	Show/Hide Attribute Editor	Displays the Attribute Editor in this area
	Show/Hide Tool Settings	Displays the current tool's settings
	Show/Hide Channel Box/Layer Editor	Displays the Channel Box and Layer Editor

The Shelf

The *Shelf*, shown in Figure 3.4, is an area where you keep icons for tools. It's divided into tabs that define functions for the tool icons in the Shelf. Whenever you start Maya, the tab you used in your previous session of Maya will be selected and displayed.

Figure 3.4

The Shelf

Each tab is broken out into different function sets, showing you icons that are useful for a particular set of functions such as creating surfaces or creating lights and textures. You can change the Shelf display to show the functions you'll be using by clicking the tabs. Click the Surfaces tab, and you'll see icons to create often-used NURBS primitives (such as spheres and cubes) and often-used tools (such as Loft and Extrude). For more on these NURBS surface tools, see Chapter 5, "Modeling with NURBS, Subdivisions, and Deformers."

The Custom tab is empty so that you can create your own custom Shelf, populating it with the tools you find most useful.

Pointing to an icon in the Shelf displays a tool tip that gives you the name and a description of that tool.

Don't worry too much about the Shelf right now; it may be better to use the commands from the menus first before turning to icons and shelves. Doing so will build your proficiency at finding the tools you need, and it will also give you the chance to explore further every time you open a menu. After you've used Maya for a while, you'll probably use the Shelf feature to create a group of your favorite tools; you'll find it to be a key feature of your workflow.

ADVANCED TIP: CUSTOMIZING THE SHELF

When you've established a set of favorite Maya tools for routine tasks, you may want to customize the Shelf to make those tools immediately accessible. Clicking the Menu icon (▼) opens a menu that you can use to edit the Shelf to your liking. To add a menu item to the Shelf, press Ctrl+Alt+Shift, and select the command from the menu (for Mac users, press Ctrl+Option+Shift). The command appears on the current Shelf. To get rid of an item, MMB+click to drag it to the Trash icon. You can create multiple shelves, stack them on top of each other, and access them by clicking the Shelf Tab icon (▢) above the Menu icon to the left of the Shelf. For more, see the section "Customizing Maya" at the end of this chapter.

The Tool Box

The Tool Box, shown in Figure 3.5, displays the most commonly used tools: Select, Lasso Select, Translate (or Move), Rotate, Scale, Universal Manipulator, Soft Modification, and Show Manipulator. In addition to the common commands, it displays several choices for screen layouts that let you change the interface with a single click. This is convenient because different animations call for different view modes. Experiment with the layouts by clicking any of the six presets in the Tool Box.

Figure 3.5

The Tool Box

ICON	NAME	DESCRIPTION
	Select	Lets you select objects
	Lasso Select	Allows for a free-form selection using a lasso marquee
	Paint Selection Tool	Enables the Paint Selection tool
	Translate (Move)	Moves the selection
	Rotate	Rotates the selection
	Scale	Scales the selection
	Universal Manipulator	Allows for translation, rotation, and scale within one tool
	Soft Modification	Allows you to modify an area with a gradual drop-off of its effect
	Show Manipulator	Displays an object's specific manipulators
	Current Tool display	Shows the currently selected tool (shown as blank)

The Channel Box/Layer Editor

The area running vertically to the right of the screen is usually used for the *Channel Box*. This key element of the interface lists an object's *channels*: that is, the attributes of an object that are most commonly animated and used for keyframing, as well as an object's input and output connections. When an object is selected in one of the main views, its name appears at the top of the Channel Box and its channels are listed vertically below with their names to the left and their values to the right in text boxes. In the Channel Box, you can edit all the channel values and rename the object itself. Below these values are the names of the nodes or objects to which the selection has input and output connections.

Immediately under the Channel Box is the Layer Editor. This arrangement is convenient for scenes that require multiple objects and require layered objects, renders, and animations. Each type of layer is designated by the radial check box (Display, Render, and Anim).

You can place some objects on Display layers that can be turned on or off to help organize a scene. Become familiar with this feature early, because it will be a valuable asset when you animate complicated scenes.

Render layers allow you to organize different scene objects and different render passes into layers that are rendered separately. You'll be introduced to rendering in layers later in this book. Finally, in this space you can access the use of Animation layers. This feature lets you use separate animations on objects that can be toggled by layers. Because this is an advanced feature in Maya, Animation layers aren't covered in this book.

To create a new layer, click the Create New Layer icon (). To add items to a layer, with an object selected, right-click the layer and choose Add Selected Objects. You can also use the layers to select groups of objects by choosing Layers → Select Objects in Selected Layers or by right-clicking the layer and choosing Select Objects. To change the name and color of a layer, double-click the layer to open the Edit Layer dialog box, as shown in Figure 3.6.

Figure 3.6

The Edit Layer window

Figure 3.7

The Channel Box/ Layer Editor

You can easily resize this area by clicking and dragging the left side wall of the panel. (See Figure 3.7)

This area of the screen is usually used for the Channel Box and the Layer Editor. You can replace this panel with one of two other windows—the Attribute Editor or the Tool Settings—by clicking one of the three icons in the upper-right corner, as shown in the Channel Box/Layer Editor section. This gives you quick access to the three windows you find most useful to have onscreen all the time. You may want to display the Channel Box all the time.

Time Slider/Range Slider

Running horizontally across the bottom of the screen are the Time slider and the Range slider, as shown in Figure 3.8. The Time slider displays the range of frames available in your animation and gives you a gray bar, known as the *Current Time indicator*. You can click it and then drag it back and forth in a scrubbing motion to move through time in your sequence. (When instructed in this book to *scrub* to a certain point in your animation, use this indicator to do so.)

The text box to the right of the Time slider gives you your current frame, but you can also use the text box to enter the frame you want to access. Immediately next to the current time readout is a set of DVD/DVR-type playback controls that you can use to play back your animation.

Below the Time slider is the Range slider, which you use to adjust the range of animation playback for your Time slider. The text boxes on either side of this slider give you readouts for the start and end frames of the scene and of the range selected.

Figure 3.8

The Time slider and the Range slider

You can adjust any of these settings by typing in these text boxes or by lengthening or shortening the slider with the handles on either end of the bar. When you change the range, you change only the viewable frame range of the scene; you don't adjust any of the animation.

This lets you zoom into sections of the timeline, which makes adjusting keyframes and timing much easier, especially in long animations. When you zoom into a particular section of your time frame, the Time slider displays only the frames and keyframes for that portion, making it easier to read.

To the right of the Range slider are the Character Set Selection menu (which deals with the automation of character-animated objects), the Auto Keyframe button (which sets a keyframe automatically when an animated value is changed), and the Animation Preferences button. You'll find information about these features later in this book.

Command Line/Help Line

Maya Embedded Language (MEL) is the user-accessible programming language of Maya. Every action you take invokes a MEL command or script that runs that particular function. You can write your own commands or scripts using either the Command line or the Script Editor. Use the Command line (see Figure 3.9) to enter single MEL commands directly from the keyboard in the white text box portion of the bar. The Command line also displays command feedback and messages from the program in the gray portion of the bar. Try entering the following into this box: **sphere**. A new sphere should pop up in your Maya panels. You've created a basic sphere using the MEL command. To delete it, click it to select it, and then press Delete.

Toggle between MEL and Python scripting   Script Editor button

Help line   Command line   Command feedback

Figure 3.9
The Command line and the Help line

OPENING THE ATTRIBUTE EDITOR IN ITS OWN WINDOW

By default, the Attribute Editor opens in the right side of the UI area of the screen when you start Maya. The preferred configuration in this book is to open the Attribute Editor as a separate window instead. To follow along in this book, you'll want this configuration.

To configure the Attribute Editor to open in its own window, choose Window → Settings/Preferences → Preferences to open the Preferences dialog box.

Under the Interface → UI Elements heading, uncheck the Attribute Editor and Tool Settings check boxes in the Editor in Main Window section, as shown here.

If any of your screen elements are missing, you can toggle them on and off through this dialog box.

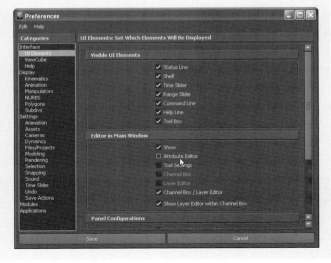

Clicking the icon at the end of the Command line opens the Script Editor, in which you can enter more complicated MEL or Python commands and scripts.

Below the Command line is the Help line. This bar provides a quick reference for almost everything on the screen. For the most part, it's a readout of functions when you point to icons. It also prompts you for the next step in a particular function or the next required input for a task's completion.

The Help line is very useful when you're not really sure about the next step in a command, such as which object to select next or which key to press to execute the command. You'll be surprised by how much you'll learn about tool functions by reading the prompts displayed here.

Panels and Frequently Used Windows

The main focus of Maya is, of course, its work windows (called *panels*)—the perspective and orthographic views. You use these windows to create, manipulate, and view 3D objects, particles, and animations. By using the mouse, you can navigate in these views easily. Navigation in almost all panel views involves a combination of mouse control and keyboard input.

Perspective/Orthographic Windows

The default Maya layout begins with a full-screen perspective view, as shown in Figure 3.10. This is essentially a camera view and expresses real-world depth through the simulation of perspective. In this window, you can see your creation in three dimensions and move around it in real time to get a sense of proportion and depth.

Figure 3.10

The full perspective view

SHORTCUTS TO VIEWING

Here's a summary of the most important keyboard shortcuts. Keep in mind that the Option key is used on a Macintosh in place of the Alt key on a PC. See Chapter 2 for more details.

Alt+MMB+click Tracks around a window.

Alt+RMB+click Dollies into or out of a view.

Scroll Wheel Dollies into or out of a view.

Alt +LMB+click Rotates or orbits the camera around in a Perspective window.

Alt+Ctrl+click and Drag Dollies your view into the screen area specified in your mouse drag.

ViewCube Allows you to change views in a panel easily.

Macintosh Keys The Option key on a Mac is used as the Alt key on a PC.

By pressing the spacebar, you can switch your view from the full-screen perspective to the four-panel layout shown in Figure 3.11. Pressing the spacebar again returns your active view panel to Full-Screen mode.

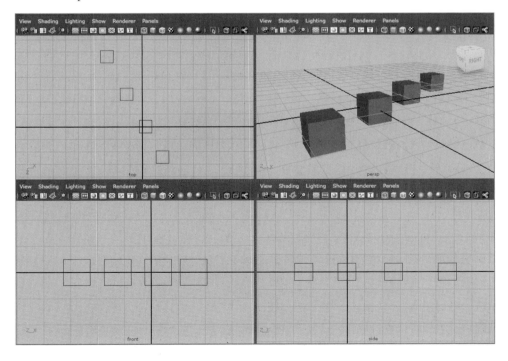

Figure 3.11

The four-panel layout

Orthographic views (top, front, and side) are most commonly used for modeling, because they're best at conveying exact dimensions and size relationships. Even though the cubes in the Perspective window are all the same size, the perspective view, by definition, displays the cubes farther away as being smaller than those closer to you. Orthographic views, however, display exact proportions so that you can see the four cubes as being identical in size and shape.

The four-panel layout gives you accurate feedback on the sizing and proportionality of your models. In general, you'll probably prefer to start your modeling in orthographic view and use the perspective view(s) for fine-tuning and finishing work and for setting up camera angles for rendering. You can also easily change from perspective to any of the orthographic views in the current panel by using the ViewCube (⬛) in the upper-right corner of any active panel. For more information about this topic, see Chapter 2.

You can easily adjust the panel layouts of your screen by using any of the six presets in the Tool Box on the left side of the screen or by choosing Window → Saved Layouts. Furthermore, you can replace each view panel by choosing another panel name from the list in the Panels menu in the bar at the top of each view. From this menu, you can choose any modeling view, orthographic or perspective, or another window to best suit your workflow. You can also change the size of these windows by clicking and dragging the separating borders between the panels.

By default, each panel displays a grid that you can adjust by choosing Display → Grid ❑. The grid is made of actual units of measure that you can adjust. Choose Window → Settings/ Preferences → Preferences to open the Preferences dialog box; and, in the Settings section, make your adjustments.

Levels of Detail

Try This In the four-panel layout (click the second Layout icon in the Tool Box), create a NURBS sphere by choosing Create → NURBS Primitives → Sphere. Your cursor turns into a small black cross, and "Drag on the grid" appears in the middle of your panels.

> Creating a primitive by clicking and dragging to specify its size and position only works when Interactive Creation is turned on. You'll find this option when you choose Create → NURBS Primitives or Create → Polygon Primitives. When this option, at the top of each of those menus, is selected, you can click and drag the primitive you're creating. When it's unselected, the primitive appears at the origin in 3D space.

Click and drag the cursor to create a sphere of any size, as shown in Figure 3.12. You'll notice its primary attributes in the Channel Box.

Press 2, and you'll see the wireframe mesh get denser. Press 3, and the mesh will get even more dense. You can view all NURBS objects, such as this sphere, in three levels of display. Pressing 1, 2, or 3 toggles between detail levels for any selected NURBS object.

NURBS is a type of surface in Maya that lets you adjust its detail level at any time to become more or less defined as needed. The display detail keys (1, 2, 3) adjust the level of NURBS detail shown in the panels only.

When you have a polygonal object selected, you may also press 1, 2, or 3 for levels of detail on the smoothness of the polygonal mesh. In this case, the level of detail is a preview of what the polygon object will look like after you apply a smoothing function on it. It isn't a display of the level of detail of the current object, but again just a preview of what it would look like when you smooth it. Polygonal modeling and smoothing objects are covered in Chapter 4.

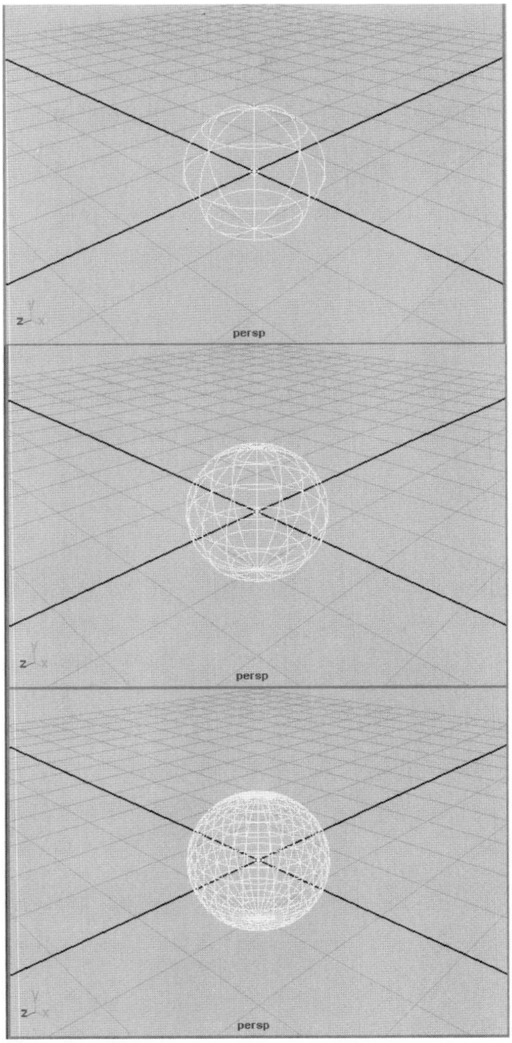

Figure 3.12

NURBS display smoothness

Wireframe and Shaded Modes

When you're working in the windows, you can view your 3D objects as either wireframe models (as in Figure 3.12) or as solid, hardware-rendered models called *Shaded mode* (see Figure 3.13). Wireframe mode is the fastest because it makes fewer processing demands on your computer. However, Shaded mode can be pretty quick too, depending on your graphics card and your system processor.

Within Shaded mode, you can select varying degrees of shading detail. You can cycle through the levels of detail by pressing 4, 5, 6, and 7. Wireframe mode is 4, Shaded mode is 5, Texture Shaded mode is 6, and Lighted mode is 7.

Pressing 4 or 5 toggles between Wireframe and Shaded mode in any of the Modeling windows. Texture Shaded mode (6) displays the image textures that have been applied to the object as long as Hardware Texturing is already enabled. (In the view panel, choose Shading → Hardware Texturing, and make sure it's checked on.) Lighted mode (7) is a hardware preview of the object or objects as they're lit in the scene. The detail level hot-keys for NURBS objects (1, 2, 3) apply in Shaded mode as well. Here's a summary:

KEY	FUNCTION
4	Toggles into Wireframe mode
5	Toggles into Shaded mode
6	Toggles into Textured mode
7	Toggles into Lighted mode

It's always good to toggle between the Wireframe and Shaded modes to get a feel for the weight and proportion of your model as you're building it. The Texture mode is good for the rudimentary lining up of textures, but typically it's better to rely on fully rendered frames for that. The IPR renderer in Maya is also great for previewing work because it updates areas of the frame in good-quality renders at interactive speeds. Chapter 11, "Maya Rendering," covers IPR.

The Lighted mode is useful for spotting proper lighting direction and object highlights when you first begin lighting a scene. It helps to see the direction of lights in your scene without having to render frames all the time. How many lights you see in the Modeling window depends on your computer's graphics and overall capabilities. Chapter 10, "Maya Lighting," covers lighting and makes frequent use of this mode.

Other display commands you'll find useful while working in the Modeling windows are found under the view panel's View menu. Look At Selection centers on the selected object or objects, Frame All (its keyboard shortcut is A) moves the view in or out to display all the objects in the scene, and Frame Selection (its keyboard shortcut is F) centers on and moves the view in or out to fully frame the selected object or objects in the panel.

Figure 3.13

Shaded NURBS display detail

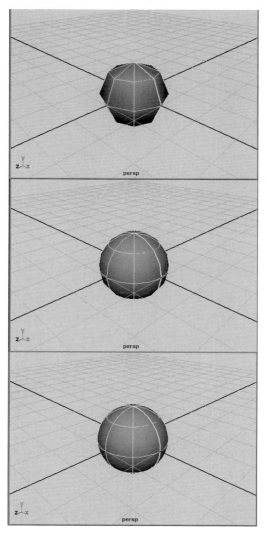

When you're using the keyboard shortcuts discussed in this subsection, don't press the Shift key to generate the letter A or F. Keyboard shortcuts in Maya are described as *case sensitive* because in many cases, pressing a single letter key has a different effect than pressing Shift + that letter (which makes the letter uppercase). This book shows all single letters as capitals in the text (the same way they appear on your keyboard). The Shift key is included in the text only when it's part of an uppercase shortcut. So if you find yourself wondering why pressing a hotkey isn't working, make sure you aren't pressing Shift or that the Caps Lock isn't enabled, capitalizing your entries when they should be lowercase.

The Manipulators

The next thing you should know about the interface deals directly with objects. *Manipulators* are onscreen handles that you use to manipulate the selected object. Figure 3.14 shows three distinct and common Manipulators for all objects in Maya: Move, Rotate, and Scale. You use these Manipulators to adjust attributes of the objects visually and in real time. In addition, the fourth icon shown in Figure 3.14 is the Universal Manipulator, which allows you to move, rotate, or scale an object all with one Manipulator. Additionally, you can use special Manipulators, or special *manips*, to adjust specific functions while using certain tools or with some objects, such as a spotlight.

You can access the Manipulators using either the icons from the Tool Box or the following hotkeys:

KEY	FUNCTION
W	Activates the Move tool
E	Activates the Rotate tool
R	Activates the Scale tool
Q	Deselects any Translation tool to hide its Manipulator, and reverts to the Select tool

It may seem strange for the default hotkeys to be W, E, and R for Move, Rotate, and Scale; but because the keys are next to each other on the keyboard, selecting them is easy. These are without a doubt the hotkeys you'll use most often, because they activate the tools you'll use the majority of the time.

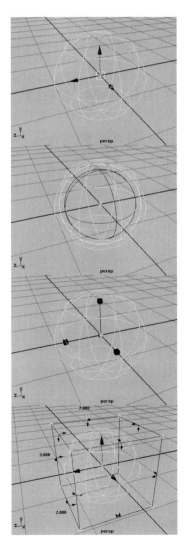

Figure 3.14

Using Manipulators

In the last chapter, you made ample use of the Manipulators. In the following short exercise, you'll look at the remaining Manipulators in the Tool Box.

Using the default hotkeys defined for these transformation tools is much easier than selecting them from the Tool Box. If the keys don't work, make sure Caps Lock is off. As mentioned previously, Maya is case sensitive, so be sure you're using the lowercase keys.

Try This Choose Create → NURBS Primitives → Sphere, drag in a view panel on its grid to create a sphere, and then size it however you like. If you have Interactive Creation already turned off for NURBS primitives, a sphere appears at the origin. Press the 5 key on your keyboard in one of the view panels for Shaded mode. In the last chapter, you tried out the Manipulators on a sphere to get a feel for how they work. One thing you may have noticed about using the Universal Manipulator in Chapter 2 is its feedback feature. Select the Universal Manipulator from the Tool Box (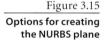), manipulate the sphere in the view panel, and take a look.

The Universal Manipulator interactively shows you the movement, rotation, or scale as you manipulate the sphere. Notice the coordinates that come up and change as you move the sphere. When you rotate using this Manipulator, you see the degree of change. Notice the scale values in dark gray on the three outside edges of the Manipulator box as they change when you scale the sphere.

Next, let's try using the Soft Modification tool ( ) from the Tool Box. This tool allows you to select an area on a surface or model and make any adjustments in an interesting way. The adjustments you make gradually taper off away from the initial place of

Figure 3.15
Options for creating the NURBS plane

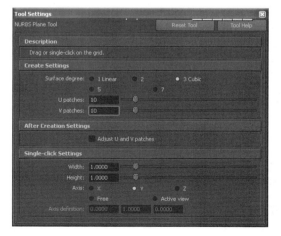

selection, giving you an easy way to soft-modify an area of a model, like lifting up a tablecloth from the middle, for example. First, turn off Interactive Creation. To try the Soft Modification tool, create a NURBS plane by choosing Create → NURBS Primitives → Plane ❏. Doing so opens the options for creating a plane, as shown in Figure 3.15. Set both the U Patches and V Patches sliders to 10, and click Create.

Click and drag a plane on the grid. (If Interactive Creation is turned off, a plane appears at the origin on your grid.) Select the Scale tool, and scale the plane up to about the size of the grid. Then, select the Soft Modification tool ( ) from the Tool Box, and click the plane somewhere just off the middle. Doing so creates an S and a special

Manipulator to allow you to move, rotate, or scale this soft selection (see Figure 3.16). You also see a yellow-to-red-to-black gradient around the S manipulator. This shows you the area and degree of influence, where yellow moves the most and black the least.

Grab the cone handle, and drag it up to move the soft selection up. Notice that the plane lifts up in that area only, gradually falling off. This effect resembles what happens when you pick up a section of a tablecloth with one hand.

Grabbing the cube handle scales the soft selection, and dragging on the circle rotates it. After you're done making your soft adjustments, you can go back to that soft selection by selecting the S on the surface for later editing. You can place as many soft selections as you need on a surface. Figure 3.17 shows the soft modification adjusting the plane.

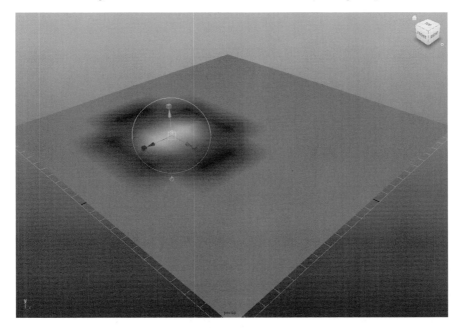

Figure 3.16

Creating and manipulating a soft modification

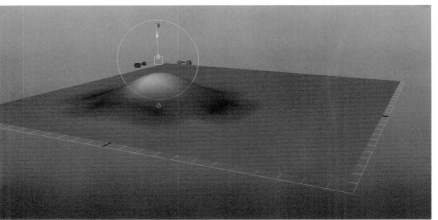

Figure 3.17

Lifting an area of the NURBS plane

> You can scale the Manipulator handles to make them more noticeable or less obtrusive. Press the plus key (+) to increase a Manipulator's size, and press the minus key (–) to decrease it.

The Attribute Editor Window

To use the Attribute Editor, select Window → Attribute Editor (Ctrl+A). The Attribute Editor window is arguably the most important window in Maya. Every object is defined by a series of attributes, and you edit these attributes using the Attribute Editor. This window displays every attribute of an object, and you can use it to change them, set keyframes, connect to other attributes, attach expressions, or simply view the attributes.

> **ATTRIBUTE EDITOR IN A FLOATING WINDOW**
>
> We'll assume for the course of the book that you've set the Attribute Editor to open in its own window, as advised earlier in this chapter. Most figures reflect that assumption.

The Attribute Editor has tabs that correspond to the object's node structure. You'll learn more about Maya's object structure later in this chapter, so don't worry about what the tabs mean just yet. As you can see, each tab displays different attributes of the object.

Try This Press Ctrl+A to open the Attribute Editor for the sphere (shown in Figure 3.18), and click the makeNurbSphere1 tab.

Figure 3.18
The Attribute Editor

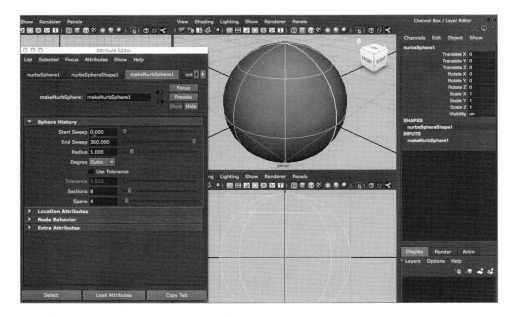

You'll notice that the Channel Box now has the primary attributes (Translate X, Translate Y, Translate Z, Rotate X, and so on) of the sphere listed. Below them, you'll find the shapes node named *nurbsSphereShape1* and the inputs node *makeNurbSphere1* listed. If you click the makeNurbSphere1 entry in the Channel Box, it will expand to show you Select attributes from the tab of the same name in the Attribute Editor. These attributes, despite being shown in two places, are the same. If you edit one in the Channel Box, it will be reflected in the Attribute Editor, and vice versa. The Channel Box is essentially a quick reference, giving you access to the most likely animated attributes of an object. The Attribute Editor goes into detail, giving you access to everything that makes up that object and the other nodes that influence it.

Try changing some of the settings in this window and see how doing so affects the sphere in the view panels. For example, changing the Radius attribute under the nurbsSphereShape1 tab changes the size of the sphere. Click the nurbsSphere1 tab next, and you'll see the primary attributes listed. Try entering some different values for the Translate or Scale attributes to see what happens to the sphere in the view panels.

On the flip side, press W to activate the Move tool, and move the sphere around one of the view planes. Notice that the respective Translate attributes update in almost real time in both the Attribute Editor and the Channel Box. You'll see an area for writing notes at the bottom of the Attribute Editor. This is handy because you can put reminders here of important events, such as how you set up an object or even a birthday or an anniversary. If you drag the horizontal bar, you can adjust the size of the notes space, as shown in Figure 3.19.

Because you'll use the Attribute Editor constantly, you may want to keep the window open all the time and just move it around. You can also press the Ctrl+A hotkey to open the window more easily.

Figure 3.19

You can keep notes with an object's attributes in the Attribute Editor.

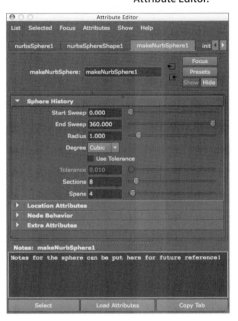

Outliner/Hypergraph

These two very different windows serve similar functions. They're both used for organizing and grouping scene objects. These windows let you see every object node in your scene in either outline or flowchart/graph form.

When you're well into an animation or a model, you'll invariably have several elements in your scene. Without a roadmap, finding the correct object to select or manipulate can be difficult. Both windows provide this service.

How do you choose between the Outliner and the Hypergraph? It depends on exactly what you need to do. The Outliner is perfect for organizing, grouping objects, renaming nodes, and so forth. The Hypergraph displays all the connections between nodes, and it's perfect for editing the relationships between nodes and locating hard-to-find nested nodes in a big scene.

The Outliner

To use the Outliner, select Window → Outliner (see Figure 3.20). It displays all the objects in your scene as an outline. You can select any object in a scene by clicking its name.

The objects are listed by order of creation within the scene, but you can easily reorganize them by MMB+clicking and dragging an object to a new location in the window; doing so lets you group certain objects in the list. This is a fantastic way to keep your scene organized.

Additionally, you can easily rename an object by double-clicking its Outliner entry and typing a new name. It's crucial to an efficient animation process to keep things well named and properly organized. By doing so, you can quickly identify parts of your scene for later editing and troubleshooting.

A separator bar in the Outliner lets you split the display into two separate outline views. By clicking and dragging this bar up or down, you can see either end of a long list, with both ends having independent scrolling control.

The Hypergraph

By contrast, the Hypergraph: Hierarchy (referred to as just the Hypergraph from here on) displays all the objects in your scene in a graphical layout similar to a flowchart (see Figure 3.21). Select Window → Hypergraph: Hierarchy to see the relationships between the objects in your scene more directly. This window will perhaps be somewhat more difficult for a novice to decipher, but it affords you great control over object interconnectivity, hierarchy, and input and output connections. The Hypergraph Input and Output Connections window is technically called the Hypergraph window, but it shows you the interconnections of attributes among nodes as opposed to the layout of nodes and node hierarchy within the scene. For the most part, throughout this book we'll be dealing with the Hypergraph Scene Hierarchy and referring to it as the Hypergraph.

Figure 3.20

The Outliner

Figure 3.21

The Hypergraph

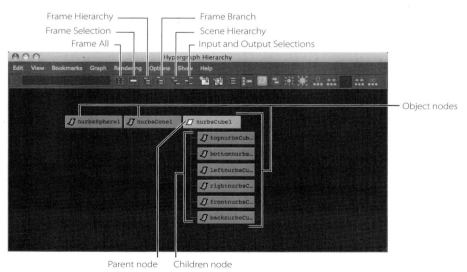

Navigating the Hypergraph is the same as navigating any Modeling window using the familiar Alt key and mouse combinations for tracking and zooming. Subsequent chapters will focus much more on these two windows. Let's have a quick look at the windows and their icons. Later, you can refer back to this section as needed.

Hypershade

Just as the Outliner and Hypergraph windows list the objects in the scene, the Hypershade window lists the textures and shaders of your scene. Shaders are assigned to objects to give them their visual appearance—their look and feel, in other words. Through the Hypershade, you can create and edit custom shaders and assign them to any object in the scene.

> Maya uses render nodes to create shaders and shader networks for assignment to objects. Render nodes define the characteristics of shaders, which in turn are applied to objects to define how they will look when they're rendered. Shader networks are complex shaders that rely on a network of render nodes to achieve special rendering or texturing effects.

The Hypershade (Window → Rendering Editors → Hypershade) displays the shaders and textures in your scene in a graphical flowchart layout similar to the Hypergraph window. (See Figure 3.22.) You can easily connect and disconnect render nodes to create anything from simple to complex shading networks. The Hypershade window has three main areas: the *Create/Bins panel*, the *render node display*, and the *work area*. The three icons at upper right let you easily switch views:

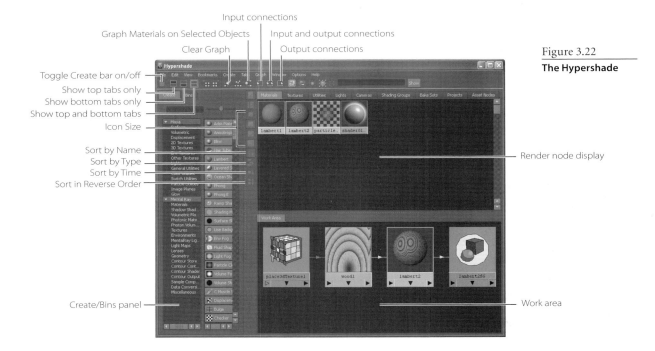

Figure 3.22

The Hypershade

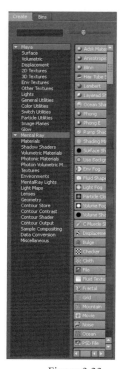

Figure 3.23

The Create/Bins bar

The Create/Bins Bar   The Create/Bins bar or panel is divided into two tabs: Create and Bins, as shown in Figure 3.23. Selecting the Create tab gives you access to a variety of render nodes. The Bins tab adds a level of organization by letting you store sets of shaders in different bins to sort them. By default, Maya selects the Create tab. Here you can create any render node and its supporting textures by clicking the icon for the desired shader or texture. The bar at the top switches between Create Maya Nodes and Create Mental Ray Nodes. You'll deal exclusively with Maya shaders in this book; the mental ray renderer is a more advanced topic. In the Create Maya Nodes panel, render nodes are divided into sections for their types, such as Surface (or material nodes), 2D Textures, Lights, and so on.

The Render Node Display Area   After you create a render node, it appears in the display area as a thumbnail icon as well as in the work area and is available for editing. Clicking a render node's icon selects that node for use. Double-clicking the icon opens the Attribute Editor. You can also use the middle mouse button to drag the icon to the work area, where you can create or edit the render node's connections to other nodes to form shading networks. Navigating in this area of the Hypershade, as well as in the work area, is similar to navigating the Hypergraph and work windows in that you use the Alt/Option key and mouse controls.

The Work Area   The work area is a free-form workspace where you can connect render nodes to form-shading networks that you can assign to your object(s) for rendering. This is by far the easiest place to create and edit complex shaders, because it gives you a clear flowchart of the network. You can add nodes to the workspace by MMB+clicking and dragging them from either the display area of the Hypershade or the Multilister window.

The Graph Editor

To use Maya's Graph Editor, select Window → Animation Editors → Graph Editor. It's an unbelievably powerful tool for the animator (see Figure 3.24), that you use to edit keyframes in animation.

Because 3D data is stored digitally as vector information in mathematical form, every movement that is set in Maya generates a graph of value versus time. The Graph Editor gives you direct access to the curves generated by your animation, which means you have unparalleled access to editing and fine-tuning your animation.

The Graph Editor is divided into two sections. The left portion, which is much like the Outliner, displays the selected objects and their hierarchy with a listing of their animated channels or attributes. By default, all of an object's keyframed channels are displayed as colored curves in the display to the right of the list. However, by selecting an object or an object's channel in the list, you can isolate only those curves that you want to see.

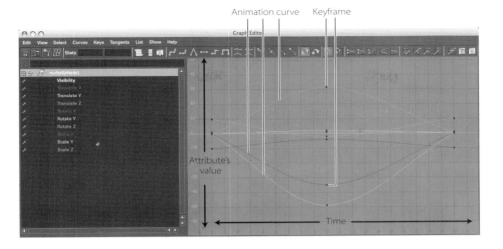

Figure 3.24

The Graph Editor

The Graph Editor displays these animation curves, also known as *function curves*, as value versus time, with value running vertically and time horizontally. Keyframes are represented on the curves as points that can be freely moved to adjust timing or value. You'll want to tune and refine animation through the Graph Editor, because doing so gives you the utmost in control over value, timing, and finesse.

The concept of the Graph Editor, and the process of editing animation using graph curves, may seem daunting at first, especially if you aren't mathematically inclined. However, this window is truly an animator's best friend. Intimate knowledge of this process will come to you as you use the Graph Editor, and you'll find it much easier to deal with animation. Most if not all animation programs make extensive use of a graph or a function-curve editor. You'll be making significant use of the Graph Editor a little later on in the book.

The Script Editor

To use the Script Editor, select Window → General Editors → Script Editor. You can also access it (see Figure 3.25) by clicking the icon in the bottom-right corner of the screen at the end of the Command line or by choosing it from the menu. Because almost everything in Maya is built on MEL, every command you initiate generates some sort of MEL script or MEL argument. A history of these comments is available in the Script Editor.

This window is handy when you need to reference a command that was issued or an argument or a comment that was displayed. It's also useful in *scripting*, or creating macros of MEL or Python commands to execute compound actions. When you want to create a custom procedure, you can copy and paste MEL from this window to form macros. You can also click the Python tab to switch to scripting in the popular Python language.

Figure 3.25

The Script Editor

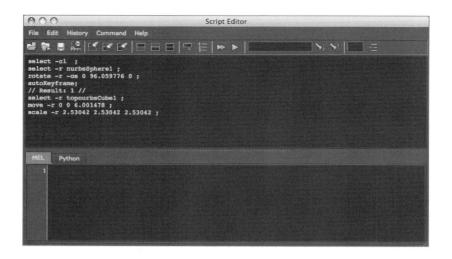

The Script Editor is essential in learning how to script. However, scripting is a fairly advanced function that you may never need for your work. In any case, tackle scripting only after you establish a comfortable working repertoire in Maya.

The window has two halves. The top half is the Script Editor's feedback history, and the bottom half is its Command line, where new MEL commands can be issued. By highlighting text in the upper window, you can copy and paste the command back into the Command line. You can easily add newly issued commands or macros of commands to the Shelf by choosing File → Save Script to Shelf or by clicking the Save Script to Shelf icon (⬚) in the Script Editor's top line.

Using the Script Editor is also a good way to check on error messages that are too long to view fully in the Command line's Feedback box. If you see an error message pop up and something goes wrong, open the Script Editor to see what sort of error(s) have occurred.

The Connection Editor

To use the Connection Editor, select Window → General Editors → Connection Editor. You can use the Connection Editor (see Figure 3.26) to connect attributes between almost any two objects easily. Therefore, you can set up almost any sort of relationship between any number of objects. For example, the scale of a cube in the Y-axis could control the Y-axis rotation of a sphere through a simple click of the mouse to connect the two attributes. You can set up more complicated connections to rotate the tires of a car automatically as the car moves forward, for example.

The Connection Editor window is separated into two vertical columns, each representing one of two objects. By selecting an object and clicking the Reload Left button, you can load all the attributes of the selected object into the Connection Editor's left column. By selecting a second object and clicking Reload Right, you can load the attributes of the second object. Clicking attributes in both columns creates a direct relationship between the two objects' attributes.

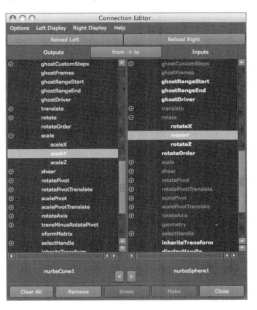

Figure 3.26

The Connection Editor shows a newly created connection between a cone and a sphere.

Connections are the cornerstone of animation and a significant reason for it being so open-ended in Maya. You can create any kind of relationship between almost any attributes of almost any object to create highly complex, interconnected animations as well as automate animations to simplify a job—and who wouldn't want to simplify a job?

The Hotbox

The Hotbox gives you convenient access to Maya's menus and commands. Figure 3.27 shows the Hotbox configured to show all the menus in Maya 2011.

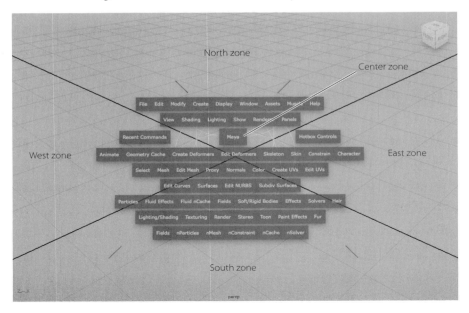

Figure 3.27

The Hotbox and marking menus

To display the Hotbox, press and hold down the spacebar in any panel view. All the menu commands that are available from the Main menu bar are also available through the Hotbox. To access a command, simply click it. You can display some or all of the menu headings to give you quick access to whatever commands and features you use most by clicking Hotbox Controls and selecting the menus.

As you can see in Figure 3.27, the Hotbox is separated into five distinct zones—North, East, West, South, and Center—delineated by black diagonal lines. Activating the Hotbox and clicking a zone displays a set of shortcut menu commands called *marking menus*, discussed in the next section.

If you don't see all the menu options when you invoke the Hotbox, or if you want to restrict the menu display to specific menu sets, simply invoke the Hotbox by pressing the spacebar, click Hotbox Controls, and mark the selection of menus you would like, such as Hide All or Show All, from the marking menu.

Marking Menus

In addition to menu selections, the Hotbox has marking menus in each of the five zones. Using marking menus is yet another way to quickly access the commands you use the most. By default, the marking menus deal with changing your selection masks (which objects you can and can't select), Control Panel visibility, and the type of panel that is being displayed. You can also access predefined (but customizable) key/mouse strokes through the Hotbox.

A WORD TO THE WISE ABOUT THE HOTBOX

You should use the Hotbox/marking menus only when you're comfortable with the interface and you've begun to establish a workflow for yourself. After you begin using them, however, you'll find them pleasantly efficient. Many animators prefer to turn off the menu bar to increase screen space for modeling and animating, and use the Hotbox exclusively. Others use both.

Again, use the Main Menu bar at the top of the screen instead of the Hotbox when you're learning. It's better to find out where the commands are first. It also helps cut down the clutter of commands and potential confusion about where and how to find them.

Menu Sets

Recall that menu sets are organized according to function. These menu sets are Animation, Polygons, Surfaces, Dynamics, Rendering, and nDynamics. Each menu set gives you access to the commands associated with its broader function set. The Animation menu set, for example, displays in the Main Menu bar all the menu headers that correspond to animation functions, such as the Deform and Skeleton menus.

The Menu Set drop-down is the first thing on the Status line, as shown in Figure 3.28. Changing between menus is easier if you use the default hotkeys:

KEY	FUNCTION
F2	Animation menu set
F3	Polygons menu set
F4	Surfaces menu set
F5	Dynamics menu set
F6	Rendering menu set

Figure 3.28

The menu sets help organize the menu headings.

Switching back and forth between menu sets may feel a little strange at first, but it makes for a much more organized workspace than having all the menu headers staring at you across the top of the window as you animate. Besides, you can access all the functions through the Hotbox anywhere on the screen.

When you're wondering where a particular toolset is, all you need to do is ask yourself, "What CG phase would that function fall under?" Because the menu sets are organized in phases of computer animation workflow—modeling (Polygons and Surfaces), animating, dynamics, and lighting/rendering—the task dictates which menu includes its toolset.

Customizing Maya

One of Maya's most endearing features is its almost infinite customizability. Maya includes many tools, features, and functions to fulfill a variety of artistic needs, which appeals to a wide cross-section of people. Everyone has different tastes, and everyone works in their own way. Part of what makes Maya powerful is the fact that anyone can shape how they work with Maya.

You've probably noticed that we've run into the same tools more than once as we've gone through the different aspects of the user interface. Simply put, for everything there is to do in Maya, there are several ways of doing it; there are at least a couple of different ways to access Maya's tools, features, and functions, as well.

Most of Maya's commands and tools can be found in at least two different places. This may be confusing at first, but you'll discover that in the long run it's very advantageous. This enables the greatest flexibility in individual workflow and is partly why Maya is as customizable and flexible as it is.

It's best to use Maya at its defaults as you go through this book. However, when you feel comfortable enough with your progress, you can refer back to this section to change some of the interface elements in Maya to better suit how you like to work.

User Preferences

All the customization features are found under Window → Settings/Preferences, which displays the window shown in Figure 3.29.

Figure 3.29

The Settings/ Preferences menu

Figure 3.30

The Preferences window

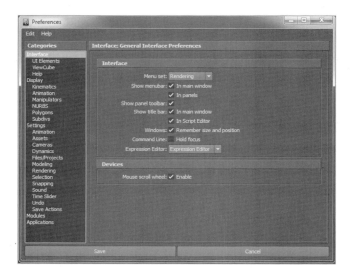

Figure 3.30

The Preferences window

The Preferences window (see Figure 3.30) lets you make changes to the look of the program as well as to toolset defaults by selecting from the categories listed in the left pane of the window. You've already changed some settings here when you set the Attribute Editor to open in a separate window.

The Preferences window is separated into categories that define different aspects of the program. Interface and Display deal with options to change the look of the program. Interface affects the main user interface, whereas Display affects how objects are displayed in the workspace.

The Settings category lets you change the default values of several tools and their general operation. An essential aspect of this category is Working Units: these options set the working parameters of your scene (in particular, the Time setting).

By adjusting the Time setting, you tell Maya your frame rate of animation. If you're working in film, you use a frame rate of 24 frames per second. If you're working in NTSC video (the standard video/television format in the Americas), you use the frame rate of 30 frames per second. This Category window is also accessed through the Animation Preferences icon at the end of the Range slider (⊞).

The Modules category allows you to enable or disable Dynamics and Paint Effects.

The Applications category lets you specify which applications you want Maya to start automatically when a function is called. For example, while looking at the Attribute Editor for a texture image, you can press a single button to open that image in your favorite image editor, which you specify here.

> Under the Settings section, click the Undo header and set the undo Queue to Infinite. This allows you to undo as many actions as have occurred since you loaded the file. This is an unbelievably handy feature, especially when you're first learning Maya.

Shelves

Under the Shelf Editor command (Window → Settings/Preferences → Shelf Editor) lurks a window that manages your shelves (see Figure 3.31). You can create or delete shelves, or manage the items on the Shelf with this function. This is handy when you create your own workflow for a project. You prob-ably won't customize your own Shelf until you're very comfortable with Maya. Simply click the Shelves tab to display the icons on that Shelf in the Shelf Editor win-dow. Click in the Shelf Contents section to edit the icons and where they reside on that selected Shelf. Clicking the Command tab gives you access to the MEL command for that icon when it is single-clicked in the Shelf. Click the Double Click Command tab for the MEL command for the icon when it is double-clicked in the Shelf.

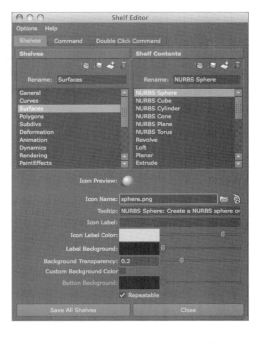

Figure 3.31

The Shelf Editor

You can also edit Shelf icons from within the UI; you don't need to load the Shelf Editor. For example, to add items to your Shelf, you merely have to drag its icon to the Shelf. To add a menu com-mand to the current Shelf, hold down Ctrl+Alt+Shift, and click the function or command directly from its menu. Items from the Tool Box, pull-down menus, or the Script Editor may be added to any Shelf:

- To add an item from the Tool Box, MMB+drag its icon from the Tool Box into the appropriate Shelf.

- To add an item from a menu to the current Shelf, hold down the Ctrl+Alt+Shift keys while selecting the item from the menu.

- To add an item (a MEL command) from the Script Editor, highlight the text of the MEL command in the Script Editor, and MMB+drag it onto the Shelf. A MEL icon will be created that will run the command when you click it.

- To remove an item from a Shelf, MMB+drag its icon to the Garbage Can icon at the end of the Shelf, or use Window → Settings/Preferences → Shelf Editor.

Hotkeys

Hotkeys are keyboard shortcuts that can access almost any Maya tool or command. You've already encountered a few in your exploration of the interface and in the Solar

System exercise in the previous chapter. What fun! You can create even more hotkeys, as well as reassign existing hotkeys, through the Hotkey Editor, shown in Figure 3.32 (Window → Settings/Preferences → Hotkey Editor).

Through this monolith of a window, you can set virtually any key combination to be used as a shortcut to virtually any command in Maya. This is the last customization you want to touch. Because so many tools have hotkeys assigned by default, it's important to get to know them first before you start changing things to suit how you work.

Every menu command is represented by menu categories on the left; the right side allows you to view the current hotkey or assign a new hotkey to the selected command. Ctrl and Alt key combinations may be used with any letter keys on the keyboard. Keep in mind that Maya is *case sensitive*, meaning that it differentiates between uppercase and lowercase letters. For example, one of my personal hotkeys is Ctrl+H to hide the selected object from view; Shift+Ctrl+H unhides it. (I'm sharing.)

When you're ready to start setting your own hotkeys, you should query your intended hotkey with the Query button to find out if it's assigned to a command that better suits that hotkey.

Figure 3.32

The Hotkey Editor

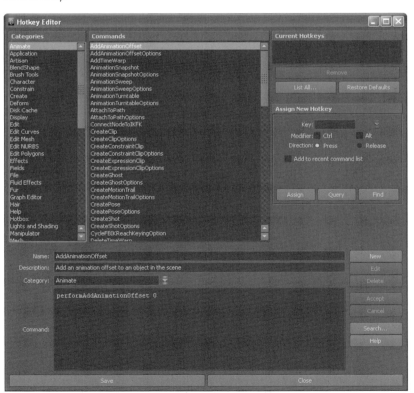

The lower section of this window displays the MEL command that the menu command invokes. It also allows you to type in your own MEL commands, name them as new commands, categorize them with the other commands, and assign hotkeys to them.

> The important thing to focus on right now is *discovering how to use the tools* to accomplish the tasks you need to perform and *establishing a basic workflow.* Toward that end, I strongly suggest learning Maya in its default configuration and *only* using the menu structure and default shelves to access all your commands at first, with the exception of the most basic hotkeys.

Color Settings

You can set the colors for almost any part of the interface to your liking through the Colors window shown in Figure 3.33 (Window → Settings/Preferences → Color Settings).

The window is separated into different aspects of the Maya interface by headings. The 3D Views heading lets you change the color of all the panels' backgrounds. For example, color settings give you a chance to set the interface to complement your office's décor as well as make certain items easier to read.

Customizing Maya is important. However—and this can't be said enough—it's important to get your bearings with default Maya settings before you venture out and change hotkeys and such. When you're ready, this section of this chapter will still be here for your reference.

Summary

In this chapter, you learned about the user interface and the primary windows used in Maya. The user interface combines mouse and keyboard input as well as plenty of menu and tool icons that you can select and use to accomplish your tasks. It also gives you a host of options to customize Maya to suit your needs.

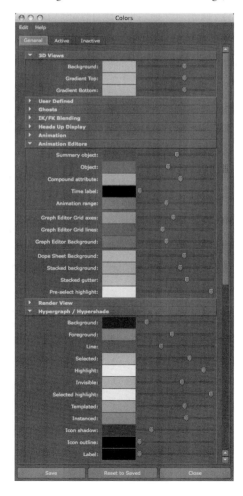

Figure 3.33

Changing the interface colors is simple.

You'll be quizzed in 10 minutes. Do you have it all memorized? Don't worry if you haven't absorbed all the information in this chapter. Now that you've had some exposure to the Maya user interface, you'll be familiar with the various windows when you really get to work.

You can always come back to this chapter to refresh your memory. Remember, you should learn the Maya program using its default settings. When in doubt, remember to access the Maya Help system, as shown in Figure 3.34.

Figure 3.34

The best menu…ever!

To start, concentrate on using the menus to access most commands. After you're comfortable working in Maya, you can begin using hotkeys and shortcuts, and eventually you may even customize them. At this stage, though, focus on getting a clear understanding of the tools and what they do. You'll be introduced to various hotkeys and shortcuts as you work through the exercises in this book.

CHAPTER 4

Beginning Polygonal Modeling

Modeling is the process of creating 3D objects, whether for animation or other purposes. Simple objects call for simple models, and complicated objects call for a complex of simple models. One of the toughest decisions is how to represent an object in 3D. Like a sculptor, you analyze the object and deconstruct its design to learn how to create it.

Maya uses three types of modeling: polygons, NURBS, and subdivision surfaces. All three require a process that begins with deciding how best to achieve your design, although it's common to mix modeling methods in a scene.

To help you decide where to begin, this chapter starts with an overview of modeling, briefly describing the three methods and how they differ. You'll also learn about Maya's primitives, which are available with all three modeling methods. The second part of the chapter takes a detailed look at modeling with polygons. (The next two chapters cover the process of modeling with polygons and subdivision surfaces and how to bring them together in one model.)

Topics in this chapter include:

- **Planning your model**
- **Polygon basics**
- **Poly editing tools**
- **Putting the tools to use: making a simple hand**
- **Creating areas of detail on a poly mesh**
- **Modeling complex objects: the classic steam locomotive**
- **Suggestions for modeling polygons**

Planning Your Model

The first step in making any object is to understand how it's constructed. The best training for a CG modeler is to visualize the elements that make up an object. Dissecting the components of an object into primitive shapes will help you translate and re-create it in 3D terms. You create the elements in Maya and then join them together to form the desired object.

Figure 4.1

The level of detail you need to include in a model depends on how it will be seen in the animation.

Gather as much information as you can about the object you want to model. Take pictures from many angles, get sizes and dimensions, and even write down a description of the object. Try to re-create it in a different medium, such as a charcoal sketch or a simple clay or balsa-wood model. Why go through these steps before you start the model in Maya? The more perspectives from which you see your subject, the better you'll understand and be able to interpret your model.

Maya has a rich toolset for creating models, so it's important to choose the methodology that best matches the modeling task at hand. Be prepared with sketches, pictures, and whatever information you can gather before you sit down to realize your CG model.

How detailed should your model be? This is a crucial question, because a model that's too complex, or a scene that has too much detail, wastes precious computing time and power, which will greatly increase render times.

Begin by deciding the purpose for your model. Then, determine the level of detail at which it will be seen in your CG scene. For example, consider the two scenes in Figure 4.1. If you need to create a park bench that is shown in a far shot (left), it will be a waste of time and effort to model all the details such as the grooves in the armrest. If, however, your park bench is shown in a close-up (right), you'll need those details. It's important to plan your model in accordance with the level of detail it requires.

If you aren't certain how much detail you'll need, it's better to create a higher level of detail rather than skimping. You can easily pare down the detail if it becomes unnecessary in the scene.

Keep in mind that you can add detail to your model in the texturing phase of production. You would be amazed at the richness of detail a model can achieve with simple geometry and well-painted texture maps. (Chapter 7, "Maya Shading and Texturing," covers texturing.) It's also important to keep in mind that in the rendering phase, you can run into memory shortages if you have too many scene models or they're overly detailed. Finding the right balance is tough, but it will come with time and experience.

As the geometry detail increases in a model, the performance demands on your PC can skyrocket. If you're working with a slower machine or with a low-end graphics card, your models must be especially well thought out in terms of their level of detail. Equipped with this decision and a number of photos, web pictures, and sketches, your modeling experience will be more productive.

An Overview of Polygons, NURBS, and Subdivision Surfaces

A fundamental decision you'll make in planning is choosing a modeling method. Maya can define a model in three ways: polygons, NURBS, and subdivision surfaces. (Polygons are the subject of this chapter. NURBS and subdivision surfaces are the subjects of Chapter 5, "Modeling with NURBS, Subdivisions, and Deformers.") Although NURBS modeling is what Maya modeling is renowned for, polygons are the simplest to describe.

Polygon Modeling

Polygons are made up of *faces*. A single polygon *face* is a flat surface made when three or more points called *vertices* are connected. The position of each *vertex* defines the shape and size of the face, usually a triangle. The line that connects one vertex to another is called an *edge*. Some polygonal faces have four vertices instead of three, creating a square face instead of a triangular one.

Polygonal faces are attached along their polygonal edges to make up a more complex surface that constitutes your model (as shown with the polygonal sphere in Figure 4.2).

A camping tent is a perfect example. The intersections of the poles are the faces' vertices. The poles are the edges of the faces, and the cloth draped over the tent's frame is the resultant surface.

Polygon models are the simplest for a computer to render. They're used for gaming applications, which need to render the models as the game is running. Gaming artists create models with a small number of polygons, called *low-count poly models*, which a PC or game console can render in real time. Higher-resolution

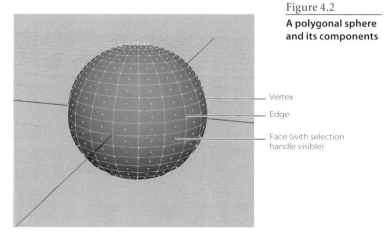

Figure 4.2

A polygonal sphere and its components

Vertex

Edge

Face (with selection handle visible)

polygon models are frequently used in television and film work. In fact, a number of science fiction TV shows use polygonal models almost exclusively for their special effects. Because even complex polygon models can be made of a single surface, they're useful for character animation work as well. Models in character animation bend and warp a good deal, so having a single surface that won't separate at the seams can be advantageous. You'll get hands-on practice with polygon modeling later in this chapter.

NURBS Modeling

NURBS is an acronym for *Non-Uniform Rational B-Spline. NURBS modeling* is based on mathematics that is more complicated than the mathematics for polygons. Because NURBS modeling requires more processing, this method is typically used for applications in which the rendering is done in advance, such as animation for film or television. NURBS modeling excels at creating curved shapes and lines, so it's most often used for organic forms such as animals and people, as well as highly detailed cars and the like. These organic shapes are typically created with a quilt of NURBS surfaces, called *patches*. Patch modeling can be powerful for creating complex shapes such as characters.

NURBS geometry is based on Bézier curves, a math concept originally developed by the French engineer Pierre Bézier. Bézier curves are drawn between *control vertices (CVs)* based on equations using cubic polynomials.

In essence, Bézier curves are created with a starting and an ending CV and at least two CVs in between that provide the curvature. As each CV is laid down, the curve or spline tries to go from the previous CV to the next one in the smoothest possible manner.

As shown in Figure 4.3, CVs control the curvature. The *hulls* connect the CVs and are useful for selecting multiple rows of CVs at a time. The starting CV appears in Maya as a closed box. The second CV, which defines the curve's direction, is an open box, so you can easily see the direction in which a curve has been created. The curve ends, of course, on the end-point CV. The start and end CVs are the only CVs that are always actually on the curve.

Figure 4.3

A Bézier curve and its components

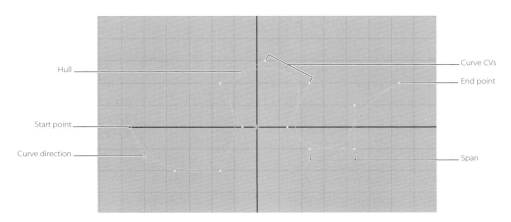

Whereas CVs control the curvature of a Bézier spline, NURBS surfaces are defined by curves called *isoparms*, which are created with CVs. The surface is created between these isoparms to form *spans* that follow the surface curvature defined by the isoparms, as in Figure 4.4. The more spans, the greater the detail and control over the surface; but this added detail makes greater demands on the computer, especially during rendering.

Control vertices, or CVs

Isoparms

Figure 4.4

NURBS surfaces are created between isoparms. You can sculpt them by moving their CVs.

Unlike a polygonal model, a NURBS surface deformation is based on the interpolation of curves, which must interpret a deformation of polygons as a collection of faces created from straight edges. For that reason, it's easier to get a smooth deformation on a NURBS surface with few CVs. To get the same smooth look on a polygon would take much more surface detail.

As you can see in Figure 4.5, NURBS modeling yields a smoother deformation, whereas polygons can become jagged at the edges.

If your model requires smooth curves and organic shapes, use NURBS. When in doubt, however, it's better to begin modeling with NURBS. You can convert NURBS to polygons at any time, but converting back to NURBS can be tricky.

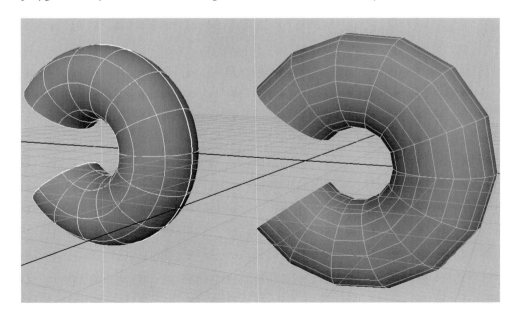

Figure 4.5

A NURBS cylinder (left) and a polygonal cylinder (right) bent into a C shape. The NURBS cylinder remains smooth, and the polygon cylinder shows its edges. A NURBS object retains its smoothness more easily, although it's possible to create a smooth polygon bend with increased surface faces.

NURBS modeling is losing its popularity overall to newer and better polygonal modeling and subdivision techniques. It is, however, an excellent way to create smooth surfaces and difficult organic shapes, even though the resulting geometry is frequently converted to polygons for rigging, texturing, and rendering.

You'll get important hands-on practice with NURBS surface modeling with NURBS patching in the next chapter.

Try This Open a new scene (choose File → New Scene). In the new scene, you'll create a few curves on the ground plane grid in the Perspective (*persp*) panel. Maximize the perspective view by moving your cursor to it and pressing the spacebar. Choose Create → CV Curve Tool. Your cursor turns into a cross. Lay down a series of points to define a curved line on the grid. Notice how the actual Bézier curve is created between the points (CVs) as they're laid down.

Subdivision Surfaces

Subdivision surfaces incorporate the best of polygons and NURBS modeling to give you the ease of polygon creation plus the smoothness and organic forms of NURBS geometry.

Subdivision surfaces usually start as polygonal surfaces. You then use NURBS math to smooth the rough polygon surfaces by subdividing them according to how the model needs to look. For example, you can easily turn a poly cube into a sphere by using subdivisions to subdivide the faces into smaller and smaller faces that are rearranged to form the sphere along smooth curves used to define this new surface.

With this technique, you can create simple poly models quickly and then overlay them with levels of detail to define the new smooth surface. You can go back to the original poly model at any time to make large-scale changes quickly and efficiently.

Furthermore, with subdivision surfaces, you have the added advantage that your surface won't tend to crease or tear at the seams as NURBS models made of patches of surfaces are prone to do. This leads to better models with which to animate organics.

The disadvantage of subdivision surfaces is that they require even more computation than NURBS, and keeping models in subdivisions will cost you a lot of memory. It's almost always the best practice to convert subdivisions (SubDs) back to polygons. You'll also get hands-on practice with subdivision surface modeling in the next chapter.

Choosing a Method

Maya provides highly effective tools for all three types of modeling, so you can make a model with any technique in as much detail as necessary. The choice depends on how you prefer to model.

Polygons are a welder's tool. Polygon modeling involves tearing and extruding from larger pieces and welding several surfaces together to form a desired whole. Orthogonal models (models with straight lines and sharp corners) are created more easily with polys.

A clay sculptor might prefer NURBS. Pushing and pulling CVs to create subtle curves on the surface is like working soft clay with your fingertips; you're nurturing something into shape with the fine art of pressure.

Subdivision surfaces combine the best of both worlds. An artist can begin with a rough shape, chisel it out coarsely, and then switch to finely detailed sculpting by adding levels of detail to the sculpture only when and where needed. Subdivision surface modeling excels at creating organic shapes out of single surfaces.

In the end, converting everything back to polygons is almost always preferable. Why? The available rendering applications all turn everything to polygons (a process called *tessellation*) when they render the scene. You can save yourself some memory and time and be the master of your own models by trying to go back to polygons as often as is reasonable.

Using Primitives

Primitives are the simplest objects that you can generate in Maya (or in any 3D application). Primitives are simple geometric shapes—polygons, subdivisions, or NURBS. Typically, they're used to sculpt models, as you saw with the Solar System project in Chapter 2, "Jumping in Headfirst, with Both Feet."

Because you can define the level of detail of the primitive's surface, primitives offer great sculpting versatility through vertex or CV manipulation. You can create polygonal primitives using practically any level of subdivisions to define the number of vertices and faces. NURBS primitives can be created with almost any number of *sections* and *spans* to define the number of isoparms and CVs.

> *Spans* are isoparms that run horizontally in a NURBS surface; *sections* are isoparms that run vertically in the object.

Starting with primitives, a modeler can create highly complex and detailed models. You may find it helpful to analyze your modeling subjects into forms and shapes that fit in with Maya primitives to get a better sense of how to begin a modeling assignment. Figure 4.6 shows all of Maya's primitives, NURBS, polygons, subdivisions, and volume primitives. Quite different from geometry primitives, volume primitives are used for lighting and atmosphere effects such as fog or haze and don't play a part in modeling.

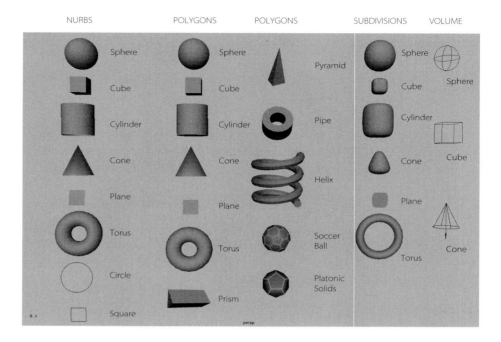

Polygon Basics

In addition to using less bandwidth to render, polygon modeling is popular because its resulting models are usually one piece of geometry with many facets. You can, therefore, deform polygon models without fear of patches coming apart, as can happen with NURBS. Polygons, however, have a finite detail limitation and can look jagged up close or when scaled up. One solution to this problem in the Maya software is the Smooth tool. Many 3D applications support only this form of modeling, so it's a popular exchange method among platforms.

Polygons are inherently better for orthogonal models, mechanical objects, and the like. But character modeling with polygons is quite powerful when you understand the tools to edit polygons. A popular method of polygonal modeling, sometimes called *box modeling,* involves creating a base object, such as a simple cube, and then pulling and pushing faces to draw out angles to create more faces. Whereas NURBS typically need the creation of curves to start, complex polygons are usually created from basic-shaped polygons such as primitives.

Another method for creating poly surfaces uses the same curves that NURBS surfaces use or even converts a completed NURBS surface model to polygons. A third method is to create poly surfaces directly with the Polygon tool, which allows you to outline the shape of each face. We'll look at these procedures in the next chapter.

Creating Polygonal Primitives

The most notable difference between the options for a NURBS primitive and a poly primitive are the options for surface detail. With a NURBS surface, sections and spans define detail. With a poly surface, detail is defined by *subdivisions*, which are the number of rows and columns of poly faces that run up, down, and across. The more subdivisions, the smoother the surface will be.

Choosing Create → Polygon Primitives gives you access to the poly version of most of the NURBS primitives. Opening the option box for any of them gives you access to their creation options. To see an example, choose Create → Polygon Primitives → Sphere, and open the option box.

To get started, first make sure History is turned on, or there will be no creation node; then, click Create to make the poly sphere. Open the Attribute Editor, and switch to its creation node, called polySphere1. In the creation node polySphere1, just as in the option box, you'll find the Subdivisions Axis and Subdivisions Height sliders, which you can use to change the surface detail retroactively.

The Polygon Tool

You use the Polygon tool (switch to the Polygons menu set, and then choose Mesh → Create Polygon Tool) to create a single polygon face by laying down its vertices. When you select this tool, you can draw a polygon face in any shape by clicking to place each point or vertex. Aside from creating a polygon primitive by choosing Create → Polygon Primitives, this is the simplest way to create a polygon shape. Figure 4.7 shows some simple and complex single faces you can create with the Polygon tool.

After you've laid down all your vertices, press Enter to create the poly face and exit the tool. For complex shapes, you may want to create more than just the single face so that you can manipulate the shape. For example, you may want to fold it.

Figure 4.7

Polygon faces created with the Polygon tool

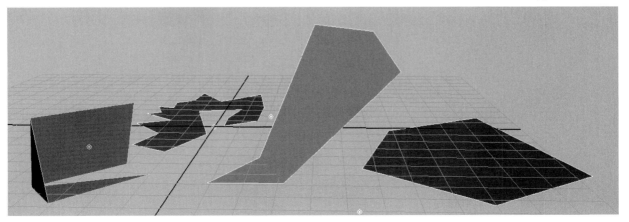

Try This The poly shown in Figure 4.8 was created with the Polygon tool and has only one face. Therefore, adjusting or deforming the surface is impossible. To fold this object, you need more faces and the edges between them. Make your own intricate poly shape with the Polygon tool by clicking vertices down in the different views to get vertices in all three axes.

With the surface selected, choose Mesh → Triangulate. The surface has more faces and edges and is easier to edit, but it's still simple to create because you start with a single face. If you need a uniquely shaped poly, start with this tool, and then triangulate your surface into several faces as shown in Figure 4.9.

Figure 4.8

A single-faced polygon with a complex shape

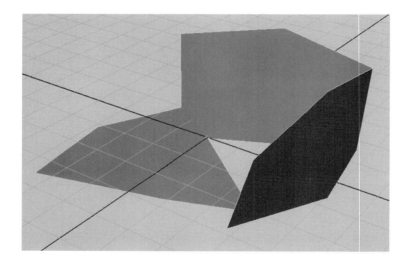

Figure 4.9

Complex shapes are better with more faces.

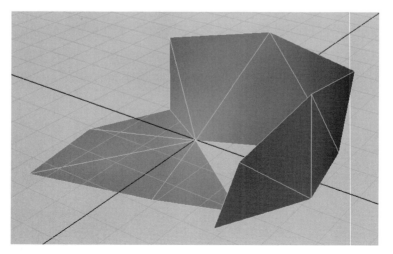

Poly Editing Tools

As you've learned, you can easily create complex models by adjusting existing, simpler poly objects with some of the poly editing tools that Maya provides. Here's a brief preview of what to expect in the world of poly editing. You should experiment with each tool on a primitive sphere as it's introduced, so saddle up to your Maya window and try each tool as you read along.

Later in this chapter, you'll deploy these new skills on two different poly models. In Chapter 6, "Practical Experience," you'll create a red wagon to exercise your modeling skills. For most of the work in this chapter, you'll use the Polygons menu. Open the Edit Mesh menu, tear it off, and place it somewhere on your screen so you can get a good look at the tools and functions. You can access all of the following tools from that menu.

The Poly Extrusion Tools

The most commonly used poly editing tool has to do with extrusion. You can use Extrude to pull out a face or an edge of a polygon surface to create additions to that surface. You access the tool at Edit Mesh → Extrude. Maya distinguishes between edge or face Extrude based on whether you've selected edges or faces. Follow these steps:

1. Select a face or multiple faces of a polygon, and choose Edit Mesh → Extrude. The regular manipulator changes to a special manipulator, as shown in the left image in Figure 4.10.

2. Grab the Z-axis move handle (the blue arrow), and drag it away from the sphere, as shown in the center of Figure 4.10.

3. Using the scale handles (the boxes) scales the faces of the extrusion. The cyan circle rotates the face. The image at right in Figure 4.10 shows the faces extruded, rotated, and scaled.

4. Choosing the Extrude command again without deselecting the faces lets you extrude even more, keeping the original extrusion shape and building on top of that.

5. Selecting the edges of the poly surface instead of the faces and choosing Edit Mesh → Extrude extrudes flat surfaces from the edges selected. The special manipulator works the same way as Extrude does for poly faces.

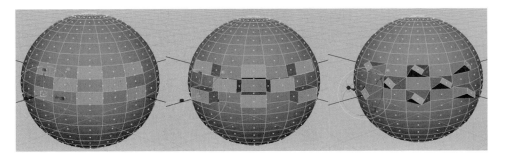

Figure 4.10

Extruding several faces at once on a sphere. The left image shows the selected faces, the middle image shows those faces extruded, and the right image shows those faces extruded with a rotation and smaller scale.

The face(s) you select pull out from the sphere, and new faces are created on the sides of the extrusion(s). The Extrude tool is an exceptionally powerful tool in that it allows you to easily create additions to any poly surface in any direction. It's particularly useful for modeling characters and creatures. Later in this chapter, you'll use it to make a simple human hand.

You can also use the direction and shape of a curve to extrude faces. Create a curve in the shape you want your extrusion to take, select the curve along with the face(s), and choose Extrude ❑. Taper decreases or increases the size of the face as it extrudes. Twist rotates the face as it extrudes, and Divisions increases the smoothness of the resulting extrusion. When you have your settings for those attributes, click Use Selected Curve For Extrusion (see Figure 4.11).

Figure 4.11

Extruding a face along a path curve

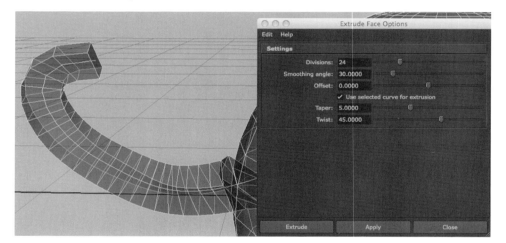

This seems to be strange behavior, but the Twist and Taper values are taken into account in the extrusion. You can edit these values when you uncheck Use Selected Curve For Extrusion, or you reselect this option after you enter values for Twist and Taper. If your faces aren't extruding to the shape of the curve, increase the number of divisions.

The Wedge Face Tool

Similar to extruding faces, Wedge Face pulls out a poly face, but it does so in an arc instead of a straight line. For this tool, you need to select a face and an edge of the selected face for the pivot point of the corner. Here's how to do this.

Select a face, Shift+select one of its edges, and choose Edit Mesh → Wedge Face ❑. (To select a face and Shift+select an edge, right-click the sphere to display the marking menu. Choose Face, and select a face. Right-click again, and choose Edge on the marking menu. Then, Shift+select one of the face's edges.)

In the option box, you'll notice some help for the tool under the Description heading. Under the Settings heading, you can select the degree of turn in the arc angle (90 degrees is the default) as well as the number of faces used to create the wedge (by moving the Divisions slider), as shown in Figure 4.12.

To access selection filters more easily, you can right-click an object to display a marking menu. Drag the cursor in the direction of the selection type you want, and release the mouse button. Then, click or Shift+click your selection.

The Wedge Face tool is useful for items such as elbows, knees, archways, and tunnel curves.

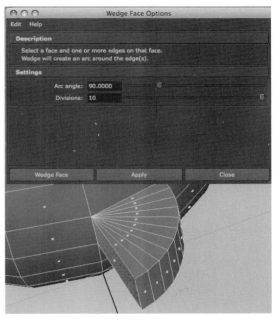

Figure 4.12

Executing a Wedge Face on a face of a sphere

The Poke Face Tool

Poke Face is great for creating detailed sections of a mesh (poly surface) and bumps or indentations. To use the Poke Face tool to add detail to a face, select a face, and then choose Edit Mesh → Poke Face.

A vertex is added to the middle of the face, and the Move manipulator appears on the screen, as shown in Figure 4.13. This lets you move the point to where you need it on the face. You can add bumps and depressions to your surface as well as create regions of extra detail. By selectively adding detail, you can subdivide specific areas of a polygon for extra detailed work, leaving lower poly counts in less-detailed areas for an efficient model.

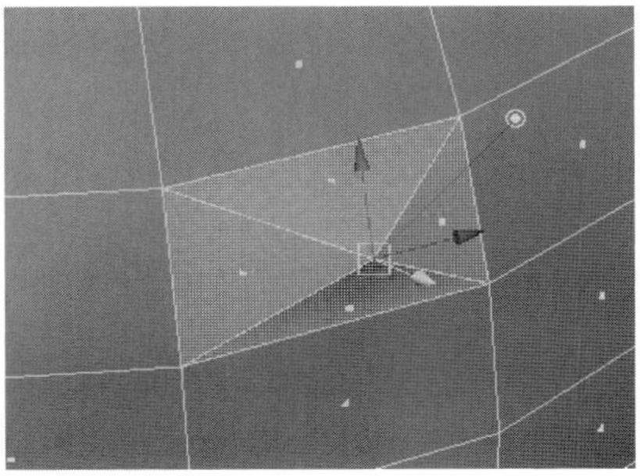

Figure 4.13

Poke Faces helps create areas of detail in your model.

The Bevel Tool

Use the Bevel tool to round sharp corners and edges. The Bevel tool requires that you select an edge or multiple edges and then use them to create multiple new faces to round that edge or corner.

Select an edge or edges, and choose Edit Mesh → Bevel ❑ to adjust your bevel. The Width slider sets the distance from the edge to the center of where the new face will be. This basically determines the size of the beveled corner. The Segments number defines how many segments are created for the bevel: the more segments, the smoother the beveled edge. Leaving Segments at 1 creates a sharp corner. See Figure 4.14.

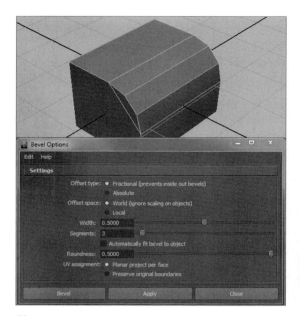

Figure 4.14

Increase Segments to create a rounder corner.

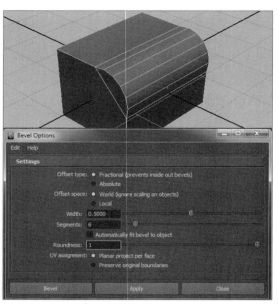

Figure 4.15

A poly bevel's roundness set too high

The setting of the Roundness slider specifies the roundness of the corner. Setting the number too high will make the beveled edge stick out, as shown in Figure 4.15, although that can be a valid design choice. You can allow Maya to set the roundness automatically based on the size of the geometry being beveled. Select the Automatically Fit Bevel to Object check box to disable the Roundness slider. Move the Segments slider to set the number of new faces that are created on the bevel: the more segments, the smoother the bevel.

Use the Bevel tool to round polygonal edges. You can also use it to add extra surface detail, because Bevel creates more faces on the surface.

Having even a *slightly* rounded edge on a model—a box, for example—greatly enhances the look of that box when it's lighted and rendered, because the edges catch much more light, helping define the shape of the box. A perfectly flat corner with no bevel doesn't catch any light, making the model look weaker.

Putting the Tools to Use: Making a Simple Hand

Starting with a simple polygonal cube, you'll create a basic human hand.

Either create a new project called Poly_Hand or copy the entire project from the CD and use that. Follow these steps:

1. Create a polygonal cube. Open the Attribute Editor and, in the polyCube1 tab, set Subdivisions Width to **4**, Subdivisions Height to **1**, and Subdivisions Depth to **3**. If you don't have that tab in the Attribute Editor, click Undo, turn on History, and re-create the cube.

2. Scale the cube to $X = 1$, $Y = 0.25$, and $Z = 1.3$, so that it looks as shown in Figure 4.16.

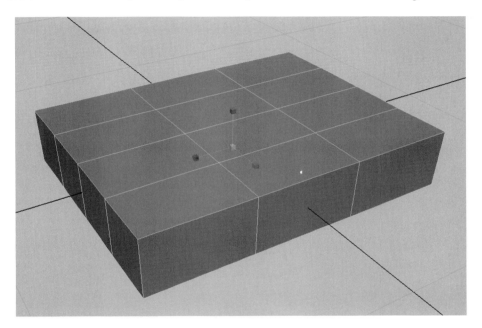

Figure 4.16

The poly cube in position to make the hand

3. Enter Component mode (F8), and turn on the Faces filter ( ) in the Status line. (For more on selection filters, see Chapter 3, "The Maya 2011 Interface.") You can also right-click the object and choose Face from the marking menu, although it may be easier to use the icons for a little while until you're more accustomed to the interface.

4. Select the front face that is in the corner closest to you by clicking its little blue handle box. You'll extrude the face to make the first part of the index finger. Before you extrude, though, rotate the face a bit in the Y-axis, away from the rest of the hand, to angle the extrusion toward where the thumb would be.

5. Choose Edit Mesh → Extrude, and use the Z-axis translate handle to pull out the face to a distance of 0.4 in the Local Translate Z attribute in the Channel Box. This is

the first segment of the index finger. Select the Extrude command for a new extrusion. Extrude the second segment of the finger out to 0.4 in Local Translate *Z*. Use Extrude again for the tip of the index finger, pulling that out to 0.3. Figure 4.17 shows the full index finger with the slight rotation away from the hand.

Save your work, and compare it to the scene file `poly_hand_v1.mb` in the Poly_Hand project on the CD.

6. Repeat steps 4 and 5 for the remaining three fingers. Remember, if you rotate the initial face of each finger slightly away from the previous finger, the extrusions will have small gaps between them, as shown in Figure 4.18. Otherwise, the fingers will extrude right up against each other, like a glove with the fingers glued together.

Use Table 4.1 as a guide for the extrusion lengths for the different parts of each finger.

Table 4.1

**Extrusion
Length Guide**

FINGER	1ST	2ND	TIP
Middle	0.45	0.45	0.3
Ring 0.45	0.4	0.3	
Pinkie	0.35	0.3	0.3

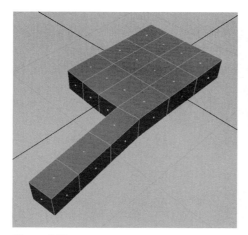

Figure 4.17

The index finger

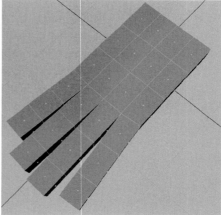

Figure 4.18

Four fingers

When you're done with the four fingers, select the hand; in the Perspective panel, press 2 to give you a smooth preview of the hand. Back in Chapter 3, we discussed levels of detail in the view panels. With a polygonal object, pressing the 1, 2, and 3 keys previews the smoothness your model will likely have when it's smoothed (a polygonal modeling operation about to be discussed). When you press 2, your hand is previewed smoothed. Doing so also shows the original shape of the hand as a wireframe cage (see Figure 4.19).

With the hand still selected, press 3. The original wireframe cage disappears, as shown in Figure 4.20. This doesn't alter your model in any way; if you render, your hand will still be blocky just as you modeled it. Press 1 to exit the smooth preview and return to the original model view. The scene file poly_hand_v2.mb shows the hand with the four fingers created.

7. Let's work on the thumb. First, you need to move a couple of edges to make room for where the thumb attaches to the hand. Select the three edges on the index finger side of the hand, and move them up toward the tip of the hand, as shown in Figure 4.21. This creates an elongated face to start the thumb.

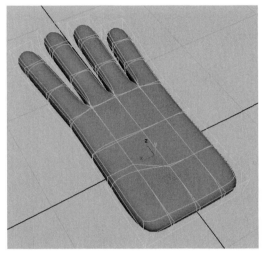

Figure 4.19

A smoothed preview of the hand, with the original shape shown as a cage

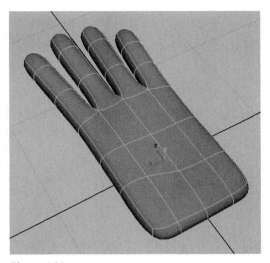

Figure 4.20

A full smooth preview of the hand

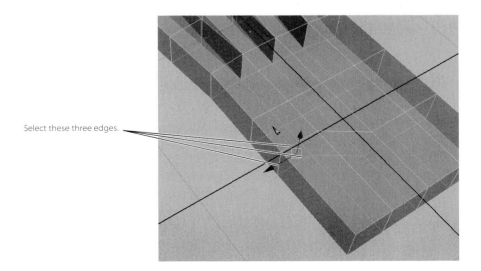

Select these three edges.

Figure 4.21

Creating an elongated face for the thumb

8. You'll use the Wedge Face tool to start the thumb. Select the elongated face. Right-click the object to display the marking menu, and choose Edge. Shift+select the edge on the left side of that face. (See Figure 4.22.)

9. Choose Edit Mesh → Wedge Face ❐. In the option box, set Arc Angle to **65**, and set Divisions to **5**. Click Wedge Face. With that wedged face still selected, scale it down in the *X*-axis to just under half its width to make it less broad, and rotate it toward the hand a bit so it looks like the first image in Figure 4.23.

Figure 4.22

Select the face and edge for the Wedge Face function.

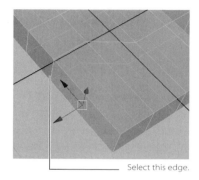

Figure 4.23

Rounding out the side for the thumb

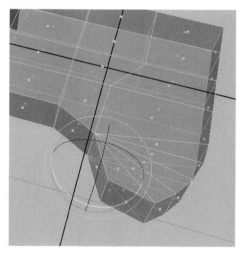 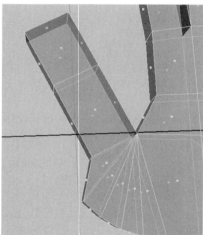

10. To make the thumb itself, extrude that face first to 0.5 and then to 0.4 in Local Translate *Z*. The hand looks awkward right now, especially the thumb area (see the second image in Figure 4.23).

11. Select the faces along the meaty part of the thumb, and move and rotate them to round out the hand. While you're at it, squeeze in the tips of the fingers to point them all, by selecting and scaling the very top face of each finger.

12. Select the pinkie finger edges (not faces), and scale them in to narrow the pinkie.

13. Select the edges that make up the knuckle of each finger (one by one), and scale them out in the *X*-axis to fatten the knuckles a bit. Your results should be similar to Figure 4.24.

14. To add more detail to the hand, you'll raise the knuckles. You need to create new vertices for the knuckles where each finger meets the hand. For this, the Split Polygon tool is perfect. Go back into Object mode (F8), and select the hand. Choose Edit Mesh → Split Polygon Tool. Your cursor changes to a sharp triangle. Use it to select a point on the hand where the index finger starts. Click the opposite edge on that face along the back of the hand. A line is drawn between the two points (the first image in Figure 4.25).

15. If you press Enter, that line becomes a single new edge on that face. While you have the Split Polygon tool active, select three more points along the back of the hand, as shown (the second image in Figure 4.25).

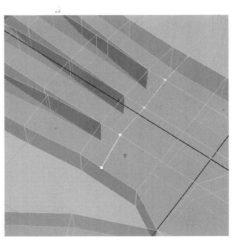

Figure 4.24

Better-proportioned fingers and knuckles

Scale these edge pairs out for bigger knuckles.

Figure 4.25

A new poly edge is drawn between the two points.

16. Press Enter to add four new edges and hence four new faces along the back of the hand for the knuckles. Select each of those new faces, and choose Edit Mesh → Poke Face to subdivide them into four triangles, with a vertex in the center. A special manipulator appears. Use the *Z* translate handle to pull those middle vertices up to make knuckles (see Figure 4.26).

17. Now that you have a simple hand, you can smooth out the mesh to make it less boxy. In Object mode, select the hand, and press 2 to see a preview of what the hand will look like after it's smoothed. Press 1 to exit the smooth preview. Choose Mesh → Smooth □; in the option box, set Division Levels to 2, and leave the other options at their defaults (see Figure 4.27).

18. Click Smooth. Your hand should take on a smoother, rounder look—more like a real hand—and it should roughly resemble the preview. This time, however, you've altered the geometry and actually made the mesh smoother and given it a higher density of polygons. Notice all the nodes listed under INPUTS in the Channel Box in Figure 4.28. This is because History has been on for the entire duration of this exercise. At any time, you can select one of those nodes and edit something—the extrusion of the pinkie, for example. You don't need to do any of this now, so with the hand selected, choose Edit → Delete By Type → History to get rid of all those extra nodes. (Feel free to edit any of those nodes through the Attribute Editor if you like.)

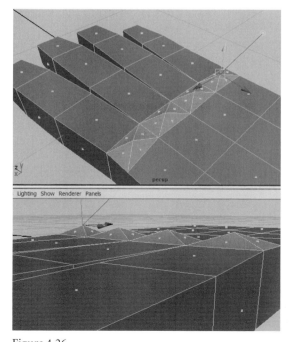

Figure 4.26

Use the Poke Face tool to raise the knuckles.

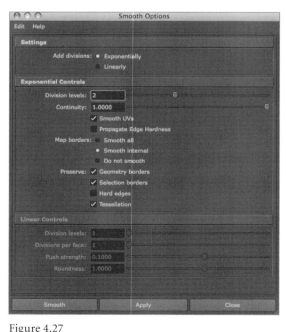

Figure 4.27

Set the options for the Smooth operation.

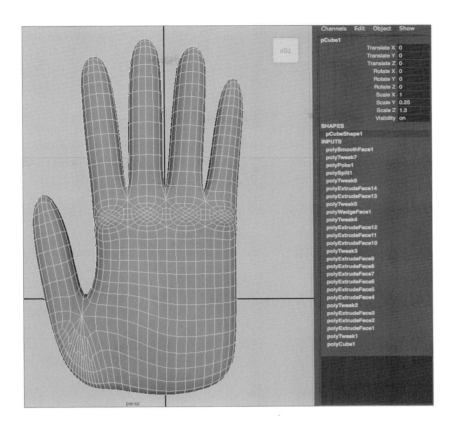

Figure 4.28

The smoothed hand with all its history nodes

Save your file again. To verify that you've been working correctly, you can load the finished hand file (with its history intact): `poly_hand_v3.mb` from the CD.

Creating Areas of Detail on a Poly Mesh

As you saw with the hand, it became necessary to add more faces to parts of the surface to create various details. The hand takes on better form when you devote time to detailing it. We began the hand shown in Figure 4.29 using the previous steps, but we detailed it by creating faces using the tools discussed in this section, moving vertices, and adding fingernails. The most intricate of objects begin from the simplest models. You merely need time and effort to create them. Don't expect to be able to model intricately right from the start unless you already have modeling experience from another package. Recognizing how to detail models takes a good amount of time and experience; start with simple objects, work your way up, and stay with it.

Maya provides several ways to add surface detail or increase a poly's subdivisions.

Figure 4.29

This detailed hand can be modeled from a simple cube, given a lot of time and love.

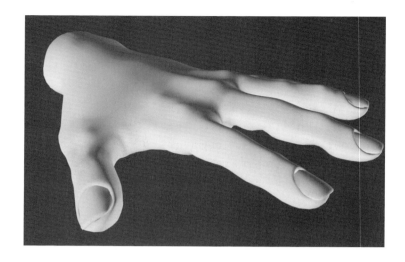

The Add Divisions Tool

You can use the Add Divisions tool to increase the number of faces of a poly surface by evenly dividing either all faces or just those selected. Select the poly surface face or faces, and choose Edit Mesh → Add Divisions. In the option box, you can adjust the number of times the faces are divided by moving the Division Levels slider. The Mode drop-down menu gives you the choice to subdivide your faces into quads (four-sided faces, as on the left of Figure 4.30) or triangles (three-sided faces, as on the right in Figure 4.30).

You can also select a poly edge to divide. Running this tool on edges divides the edges into separate edges along the same face. It doesn't divide the face; rather, you use it to change the shape of the face by moving the divided edges, as shown in Figure 4.31.

Figure 4.30

The Mode drop-down menu of the Add Divisions tool lets you subdivide faces into quads or triangles.

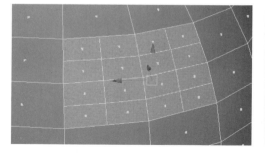
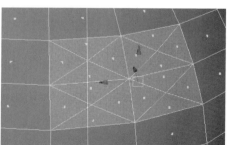

Figure 4.31

Dividing edges

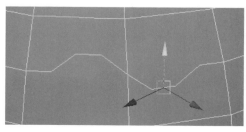

You use the Add Divisions tool to create regions of detail on a poly surface. This is a broader approach than using the Poke Face tool, which adds detail for more pinpoint areas.

The Split Polygon Tool

Another way to create detail is to use the Split Polygon tool, which does exactly what its name suggests. As you've seen, when you choose Edit Mesh → Split Polygon Tool, your cursor changes to a triangle. Use this cursor to select two points along two edges of a face. Doing so creates a straight line from the first to the second point, which serves as a new edge to divide the face into two halves, as shown in Figure 4.32. Notice at lower left in the Help line that a percentage readout gives you the relative position of the tool along the current edge. You can use this readout to help position the new split.

Figure 4.32

Splitting a Polygon allows you to draw the new edge(s) to split the face.

Press Enter to create the new edge and faces, or right-click to continue selecting new points for more edges to split the polygon face. When you're adding multiple new edges, right-clicking makes for a much faster workflow. Simply pick the first two points, and then right-click. The tool remains active for the next split.

Using the Split Polygon tool is a flexible, accurate, and fast way to create surface subdivisions for your model.

The Insert Edge Loop Tool

This handy tool adds edges to a poly selection, much like the Split Polygon tool, but it does so more quickly by working along the entire poly surface, along common vertices. The Insert Edge Loop tool automatically runs a new edge along the poly surface perpendicular to the subdivision line you click, without requiring you to click multiple times as with the Split Polygon tool. You'll use this tool in the locomotive exercise shortly. You'll find it indispensable in creating polygonal models because it creates subdivisions quickly.

For instance, subdividing a polygonal cube is quicker than using the Split Polygon tool. With a poly cube selected, choose Edit Mesh → Insert Edge Loop Tool. Click an edge, and the tool places an edge running perpendicular from that point to the next edge across the surface and across to the next edge, as shown in Figure 4.33. If you click and drag along an edge, you can interactively position the new split edges.

Figure 4.33

Using the Insert Edge Loop tool

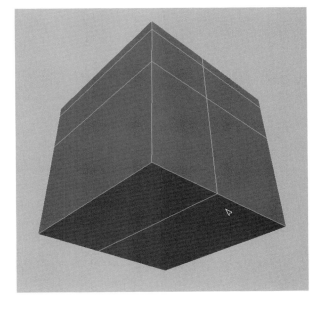

The Offset Edge Loop Tool

Much like the Insert Edge Loop tool, the Offset Edge Loop tool inserts not one, but two edge loop rings of edges across the surface of a poly. Edges are placed on either side of a selected edge, equally spaced on both sides. For example, create a polygon sphere, and select one of the vertical edges, as shown in Figure 4.34. Maya displays two dashed lines on either side of the selected edge. Drag the mouse to place the offset edge loops, and release the mouse button to create the two new edge loops.

The Offset Edge Loop tool is perfect for adding detail symmetrically on a surface quickly.

Figure 4.34

The Offset Edge Loop tool

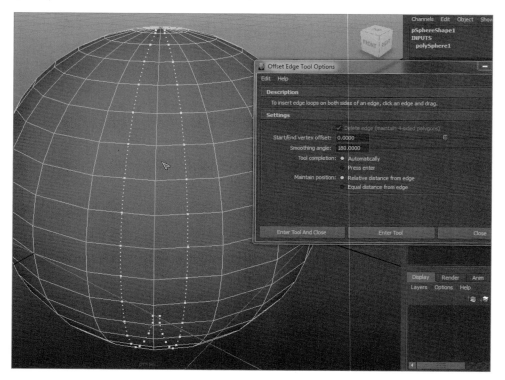

The Combine and Merge Functions

The Combine function is important in cleaning up your model and creating a unified single mesh out of the many parts that form it. When modeling, you'll sometimes use several different polygon meshes and surfaces to generate your final shape. Using Combine, you can create a single polygonal object out of the pieces.

The Merge tool is important when you're creating a polygon model because it fuses multiple vertices at the same point into one vertex on the model. Frequently, when you're modeling a mesh, you'll need to fold over pieces and weld parts together. Doing so often leaves you with several vertices occupying the same space. Merging them simplifies the model and makes the mesh much nicer to work with, from rigging to rendering.

In the following simple example, you'll create two boxes that connect to each other along a common edge and then combine and merge them into one seamless polygonal mesh. To begin, follow these steps:

1. In a new scene, create two poly cubes, and place them apart from each other, more or less as shown in Figure 4.35.

2. Select the bottom edge of the cube on the right that faces the other cube, and choose Edit Mesh → Extrude. Pull the edge out a little to create a new face, as shown in Figure 4.36. This will be a flange connecting the two cubes. It isn't important how far you pull the edge out; you'll connect the two cubes by moving the vertices manually.

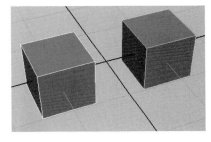

Figure 4.35

Place two polygonal cubes close to each other.

Figure 4.36

Extrude the bottom edge to create a flange.

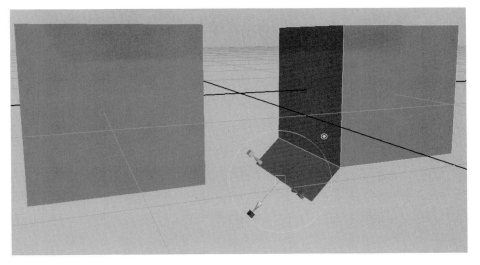

3. Select the first corner vertex on the newly extruded face, and snap it into place on the corner vertex of the other cube, as shown in Figure 4.37. Remember, you can click the Snap to Points icon ( ) to snap the vertex onto the cube's corner.

4. Snap the other vertex to the opposite corner, so that the cubes are connected with a flange along a common edge, as shown in Figure 4.38.

Figure 4.37

Snap the first corner vertex to the newly extruded face.

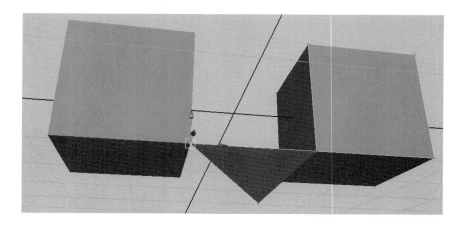

Figure 4.38

Snap the other corner vertex.

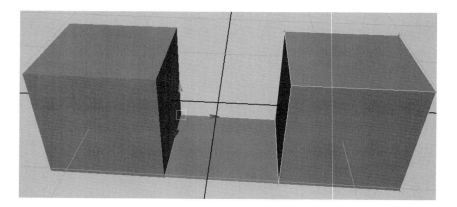

Even though the cubes seem to be connected at a common edge, they're still two separate polygonal meshes. You can easily select just one of the vertices and disconnect the connective face of the two cubes. You need to merge the common vertices of the cubes. However, the Merge function won't work on vertices from two separate meshes. Therefore, you must first combine the cubes into a single poly mesh. The following steps continue this task.

5. Select the two cubes (one has the extra flange on the bottom, of course), and choose Mesh → Combine. Doing so makes a single poly mesh out of the two cubes. You can now use the Merge function.

6. Even though the cubes are now one mesh, you still have two vertices at each of the connecting corners of the cube on the left. As you can see in Figure 4.39, you can disconnect the flange by selecting a single vertex at the corner and moving it. (Click the vertex to select just one. Don't use a marquee selection, because that will select both vertices at once.) If you move one of the corner vertices, press the Z key to undo and return the flange to its connected position.

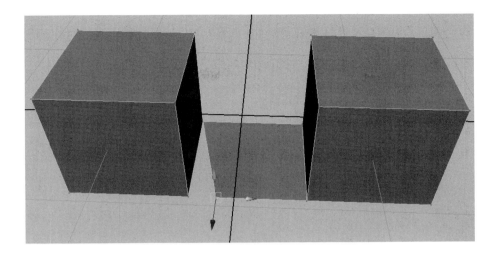

Figure 4.39

There are still two different vertices at the corner, and the boxes aren't really connected.

7. To merge the vertices at the corners, select both the vertices at the near corner (you can use a marquee selection), and then choose Edit Mesh → Merge. The two vertices become one. Repeat the procedure for the far corner. Your connected cubes become a single mesh with no redundant vertices. As you can see in Figure 4.40, if you select a vertex at a corner and move it, the cube and the flange both move: there is no disconnect.

> If you need to separate a poly mesh back into its component meshes after you combine them, you can select the mesh and choose Mesh → Separate. But you can't use Separate if the mesh you've combined has merged vertices.

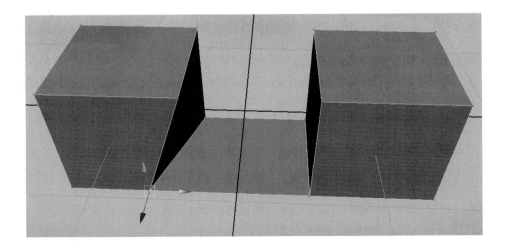

Figure 4.40

The cubes are now connected properly at the corners.

Keeping your meshes simple and organized is important to maintaining a clean and efficient workflow. You'll notice fewer errors and issues with clean models when you animate, light, and render them. Combining meshes makes them easier to deal with, and Merge cuts down on unwanted vertices and makes working with the mesh cleaner and the surface easier. You'll find that the more you model with polys, the more useful Merge becomes for creating great models.

> If the Merge function isn't working on vertices in your model, make sure the model is a single mesh; merging vertices with this tool doesn't work on separate meshes. You must combine them into one poly mesh first.

The Cut Faces Tool

Known as a *poly knife* in other 3D applications, the Cut Faces tool lets you cut across a poly surface to create a series of edges for subdivisions, pull off a section of the poly, or delete a section. (See Figure 4.41.) Select the poly object, and choose Edit Mesh → Cut Faces Tool. Click the option box if you want to extract or delete the section.

You can use the Cut Faces tool to create extra surface detail, to slice portions off the surface, or to create a straight edge on the model by trimming off the excess.

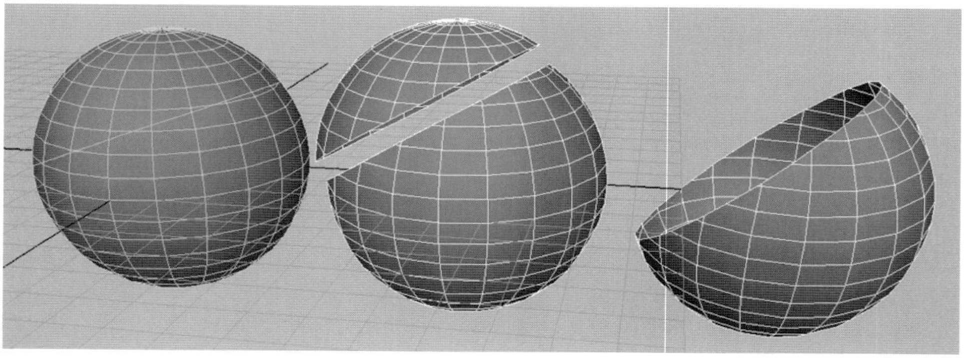

Figure 4.41

You can use the Cut Faces tool to create the edges, to pull apart the poly object, or to cut off a whole section.

The Duplicate Face Tool

Select one or more faces, and choose Edit Mesh → Duplicate Face to create a copy of the selected face(s). You can use the manipulator that appears to move, scale, or rotate your copied face(s).

The Extract Tool

The Extract tool is similar to the Extrude tool, but it doesn't create the extra faces. Select the face(s), and choose Mesh → Extract to pull the faces off the surface (see Figure 4.42).

If the Separate Extracted Faces option is enabled, the extracted face will be a separate poly object; otherwise, it will remain a part of the original.

You can use the Extract tool to create a hole in an object and still keep the original face(s). When you use this tool with the Split Polygon tool to make custom edges, you can create cutouts of almost any shape.

The Smooth Tool

The Smooth tool (choose Mesh → Smooth) evenly subdivides the poly surface or selected faces, creating several more faces to smooth and round out the original poly object.

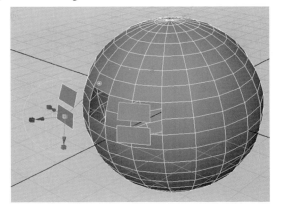

Figure 4.42
Pull off the faces.

The Sculpt Geometry Tool

You can use a Maya feature called *Artisan* to sculpt polygonal surfaces. Artisan is a painting system that allows you to paint attributes or influences directly onto an object. With the Sculpt Geometry tool usage of Artisan, you paint on a polygon surface to move the vertices in and out, essentially to mold the surface.

To access the tool in polygon modeling, select your poly object and choose Mesh → Sculpt Geometry Tool □.

For more on sculpting, see the section "Using Artisan to Sculpt NURBS" in Chapter 5. The workflow is much the same as for sculpting with NURBS; the only difference when sculpting polygons is that the surface behaves in a slightly different manner when sculpted. Unlike the NURBS sphere, where the brush strokes give smooth curves in and out, a polygon surface is more jagged. Of course, if you create the poly with a large number of subdivisions, you'll have a smoother result when using the Sculpt Geometry tool. (See Figure 4.43.)

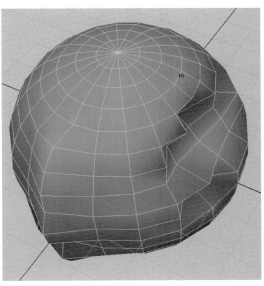

Figure 4.43
The Sculpt Geometry tool deforms the surface.

Modeling Complex Objects: The Classic Steam Locomotive

This exercise will demonstrate the following polygonal modeling techniques:

- Extrusion
- Insert Edge Loop and Wedge Face tools
- Object duplication
- Pivot placement
- CV curves and revolved surfaces
- Complex model hierarchy

You'll start to create a rather complex-looking object, an old-fashioned steam locomotive, using mostly polygons. (You'll create one of the more detailed parts using NURBS patches in the following chapter.) You'll use a schematic printout of the final model as a reference for your model. Because this is a complicated object, it's much better to start with good plans. This involves research, web surfing, image gathering, and/or sketching to get a feel for what you're trying to make.

To begin, create a new project called Locomotive for all the files, or copy the Locomotive project from the CD to your hard drive. If you don't create a new project, set your current project to the copied Locomotive project on your hard drive. Choose File → Project → Set, and select Locomotive.

> If you forget to set your project, your rendered images and scene files will be saved into your last project. When you create a new project, Maya automatically sets it as the current project.

Remember that you can enable Incremental Save to make backups at any point in the exercise.

Now, on to modeling a design that's already sketched and modeled. To begin, study the schematic printout of the final model included in the project's sourceimages folder. This will help orient you to what you're building. Typically, you'll use sketches or downloaded images and such.

Beginning in Chapter 8, "Introduction to Animation," and following into Chapter 9, "More Animation!" you'll set up and animate the locomotive. When you're building any model, it's important to keep animation in mind, especially as it impacts grouping related objects in the scene hierarchy so that they will move as you intend. Creating a good scene hierarchy will be crucial to a smooth animation workflow; so throughout this exercise, you'll use the Outliner to keep the locomotive's components organized as you create them.

The Production Process

The trick with a complex object model is to approach it part by part. Deconstruct the major elements of the original into distinct shapes that you can approach one by one. The locomotive can be broken down into three distinct objects, each with its own subobjects:

- Engine
  - Boiler
  - Undercarriage
  - Cowcatcher
- Cabin
- Wheels

You'll model each part separately based on the detailed schematic in Figure 4.44.

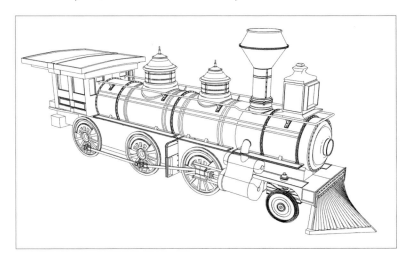

The Boiler Engine

The most prominent part of a steam locomotive is the steam engine, or boiler. Look at its shape. You can start with a simple cylinder, and work from there. To begin building the boiler, follow these steps:

Figure 4.44

A schematic diagram of the finished model

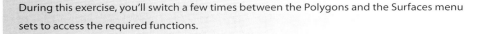
During this exercise, you'll switch a few times between the Polygons and the Surfaces menu sets to access the required functions.

1. Create a polygonal cylinder by choosing Create → Polygon Primitives → Cylinder. Leave all the creation option settings at their defaults (don't enable Interactive Creation).

2. Rotate the cylinder 90 degrees in the *X*-axis to place it on its side. Scale the cylinder to about 1.8 in all axes. Then, lengthen the cylinder until Scale *Y* is at about 8.9. You can either use the Scale manipulator or enter the values in the Channel or Input Box.

3. You can use the Insert Edge Loop tool mentioned earlier in this chapter to insert edges into the cylinder to make one end smaller. Select the cylinder, and choose Edit Mesh → Insert Edge Loop Tool ❑. In the option box, make sure Maintain Position is set to Relative Distance From Edge, and Auto Complete is turned on. Your cursor turns into a triangle pointer. In two separate actions, click one of the horizontal subdivisions to create two new vertical edges about one-third of the way in from the right end of the cylinder, as shown in Figure 4.45.

Figure 4.45

The Insert Edge Loop tool creates subdivisions quickly.

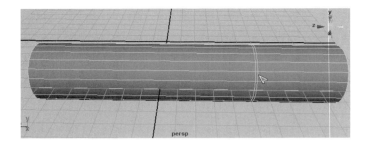

4. Right-click the cylinder, and choose Face from the marking menu. Select the end faces, and scale them down a bit as in Figure 4.46. This gives you the main part of the boiler.

5. Make a new poly cylinder as before. Scale the cylinder to make it a flat plate, and place it on the boiler. The cylinders need to be scaled to fit snugly over the boiler as you see fit. This gives you a simple weld plate to provide the boiler with some detail. Choose Edit → Duplicate Special ❐ to copy the plate four times in one action. In the option box, set Number Of Copies to 4. Move these duplicates one by one back along the boiler cylinder, and place them through the skinny section of the boiler. Arrange a total of five plates along the boiler, as shown in Figure 4.47.

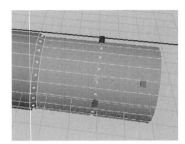

Figure 4.46

Scale the end faces.

Figure 4.47

Arrange five plates along the boiler.

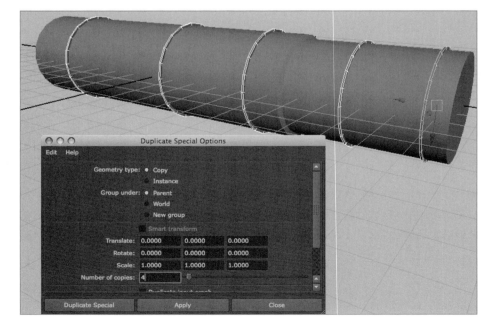

Boiler Front Cap

Now you'll create the boiler's front cap. You'll use a NURBS curve to create a NURBS surface using a technique called *Revolve,* which we'll discuss in more detail in the next chapter.

Switch to the Surfaces menu, and then follow these steps:

1. Choose Create → CV Curve Tool. In the Side view panel, lay down CVs as shown in Figure 4.48 from the top of the curve down. Make sure you begin the curve about 1.5 units from the *Z*-axis so you can end the curve on the *Z*-axis line, as shown in Figure 4.48. When you've placed your last CV, press Enter to complete the curve. Don't worry if it isn't exactly like the curve shown.

Figure 4.48

Draw a curve to create an outline for the boiler front cover.

   When you finish the curve in step 1, you should notice that Maya no longer displays its CVs in the panel. To display the CVs on a NURBS object, such as this curve, select the object and choose Display → NURBS → CVs. You can toggle the CVs off by choosing the same menu items again.

2. This curve is called the *profile curve,* and it will spin around to sweep a surface for the boiler cap. You need to revolve the curve around its bottom end to sweep a proper surface. Because you created the curve to end on the *Z*-axis, and the pivot point for the curve is by default at the origin, select the curve and, while still in the Surfaces menu set, choose Surfaces → Revolve ❏. Set Axis Preset to *Z*. Click Revolve to create the boiler cap. With the new surface selected, press 3 to display its highest level of detail in the view panels.

Figure 4.49

Fit the boiler cap onto the boiler engine.

   Now that you've created the boiler cap, select the curve and move it in the scene. Notice that the surface changes. This is how the history is displayed on the resulting surface. As we touched on earlier in the book, Maya's History functionality keeps a record of how the object was made, as long as the Construction History icon in the Status line is on.

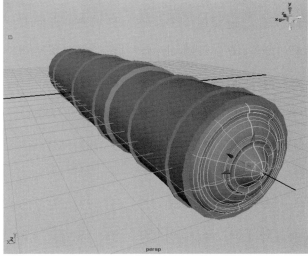

3. You don't want history on the object, so select the boiler cap and choose Edit → Delete by Type → History. Doing so erases the history so the curve no longer affects the surface. Move the boiler cap into place at the front of the boiler. Scale it as needed to fit the cylinder's skinny end. (See Figure 4.49.)

Adding Details

You'll include some detail by adding bolts to the front boiler cap and the weld plates. This will introduce you to the process of copying multiple objects into position automatically, otherwise known as *copying into an array*. To create the bolts, follow these steps:

1. Create a poly sphere by choosing Create → Polygon Primitives → Sphere ❑. In the option box, set both Axis Divisions and Height Divisions to 6. Click Create. This makes a crude sphere at the origin, perfect for a bolt. Scale the sphere down to 0.07 in all axes to make it the right size.

2. You need to duplicate this bolt many times to place bolts around the boiler cap and the weld plates. Instead of moving them into position one by one, you'll create a circular array of bolts that you can group together and snap on the boiler. Move the bolt to the boiler cap, and place it on the left side of the boiler cap, halfway into the surface, as shown in Figure 4.50.

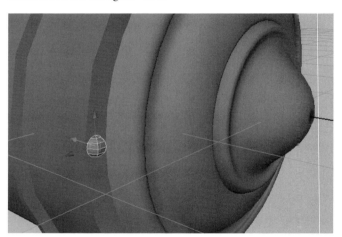

Figure 4.50

Place the bolt on the left side.

3. Enter Pivot Placement mode by pressing Insert (Home on a Mac, or fn + Home on a Mac laptop) to move the pivot of the bolt to the center of the boiler cap, and then exit Pivot Placement mode by pressing Insert (Home) again.

4. You need to copy 19 more bolts to go around the boiler cap at 18-degree intervals, pivoting around the center of the cap. To do so, select the bolt, and choose Edit → Duplicate Special ❑. In the option box, set Number Of Copies to 19, and set a value of 18 for Rotate Z, as shown in Figure 4.51. Click Apply to copy the bolts all the way around the boiler cap. The copies array themselves around their common pivot point (the center of the boiler plate) at 18-degree intervals.

If you make the copies without moving the pivot point of the original bolt to the center of the boiler cap, none of the 19 copies will be arrayed into a nice circle around the boiler. They will end up in different configurations.

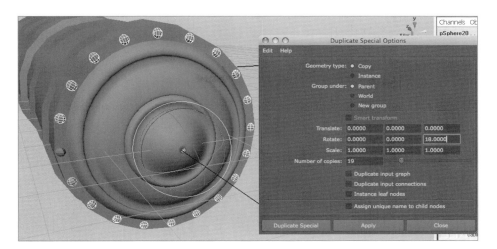

Figure 4.51

Multiple copies of the bolt are placed automatically.

5. Notice that the option box doesn't close when you click Apply. Make sure to reset Duplicate Special Options back to default. Otherwise, the next time you try to duplicate an object, you'll get 19 instances of it! In the option box, choose Edit → Reset Settings.

6. In the Outliner, select the 20 bolts, and choose Edit → Group (or press the hotkey combination Ctrl+G) to group them. Call the new group **boiler_bolts** or something similar to keep it organized. Center the pivot on the new group by choosing Modify → Center Pivot.

7. Select the boiler_bolts group, and duplicate it once to create another set of bolts you can place on the welding plates. You'll have to scale the duplicated boiler_bolts group up a bit to make all the bolts fit around the weld plates. Repeat for the other plates, as shown in Figure 4.52. Make sure you reset the duplicate options when you're finished, to keep from making 19 copies next time.

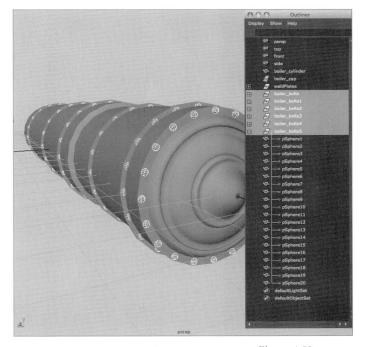

Figure 4.52

Duplicate the boiler bolts for all the plates.

To check your work, or if you've skipped ahead to this point, you can load the scene file locomotive_model_v1.mb from the Locomotive project on the CD.

The Undercarriage

Now, you can tackle the base on which the boiler sits. Look at Figure 4.53, which shows a schematic view of the boiler sitting on the undercarriage of the train. Luckily, you have the luxury of referring to the final model here, to visualize what you're modeling.

Figure 4.53

The schematic view of the boiler and undercarriage

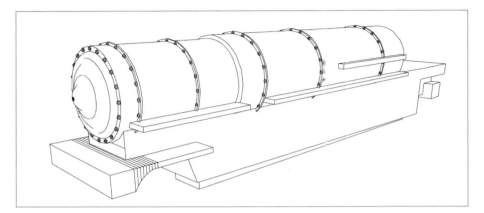

Follow these steps to continue with the engine:

1. Create a poly cube, and scale it to $X = 2.7$, $Y = 2.95$, and $Z = 17.55$. This forms the main length of the undercarriage you saw in the sketch in Figure 4.44, earlier in the chapter. You'll use extrusions to create the ends. To make viewing easier while you create the undercarriage, you can select all the boiler elements and place them on a display layer to hide them as you work on this section. Alternatively, you can move the cube away from the boiler for the time being and move it back when you're finished.

2. Switch back to the Polygons menu, and right-click the cube you just created. Choose Face from the marking menu, and select the left end of the face. Choose Edit Mesh → Extrude. Using the Transform manipulator on the special Extrude manipulator, pull out the face slightly. Use the Scale Y manipulator (the green box) to scale the new face smaller in the Y-axis, and move it up as shown in the left image in Figure 4.54.

3. With the new face still selected, choose the Extrude tool again. Pull a new face out about 2.5 units to create a lip, as shown in the right image in Figure 4.54.

4. At the other end, you need to make a thinner lip. Select the poly object, and choose Edit Mesh → Insert Edge Loop Tool. Place a horizontal edge about one-fifth of the way down from the top edge. Choose the Extrude tool (from the Edit Mesh menu or from the Polygons tab of the Shelf, using the ![icon] icon) and pull out the newly divided face 3.5 units (see Figure 4.55). This completes the main undercarriage piece.

5. Create three polygon cubes, and scale and position them at the right end of the undercarriage, as shown in Figure 4.56. For now, fit them in without worrying about overlapping or interpenetrating geometry.

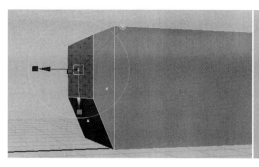

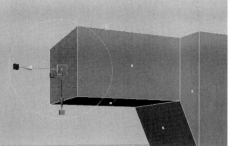

Figure 4.54

Extrude the face and scale it down (left), and then extrude that new face again (right).

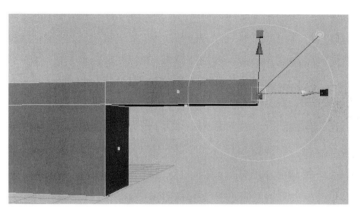

Figure 4.55

Extrude to complete the undercarriage piece.

Figure 4.56

Place three cubes into the undercarriage. The cubes are shown here, highlighted.

If you want to make your models look like the preceding image, with the wireframe lines showing in Shaded mode, enable Shading → Wireframe On Shaded in the panel view. Doing so helps delineate the model.

6. For a finishing touch, you can round out the lip you created in step 4. Select the face on the end of the lip, and then right-click it again. This time, choose Edge from the marking menu, and Shift+select the bottom edge as shown in Figure 4.57. Choose Edit Mesh → Wedge Face ❑. Set Arc Angle to **90** and Divisions to **6**. Click Wedge Face, and you see a result similar to that shown in Figure 4.58. These little impromptu details help make your model nicer.

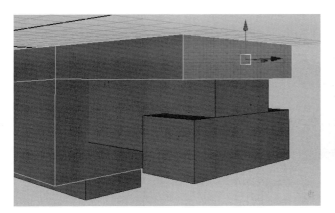

Figure 4.57

Select the end face for a Wedge Face operation.

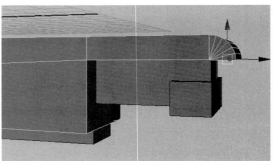

Figure 4.58

The rounded back lip of the undercarriage

7. The next piece of the undercarriage fits on the left or front end and eventually attaches to the locomotive's cowcatcher. Create a polygon cube, and scale it to $X = 4.45$, $Y = 0.16$, and $Z = 4.0$. Using the Insert Edge Loop tool, place nine equidistant subdivisions on the polygon slab, as shown in Figure 4.59. Notice that if you click and hold with the Insert Edge Loop tool, you can drag the location of the new edge line. This way, you can more easily position the lines.

8. Select the bottom faces, and move them down individually to create an arc, as shown in Figure 4.60. There is no need to extrude the faces; moving them one by one is fine. Place the new piece at the front of the undercarriage, as shown in Figure 4.61.

Figure 4.59

Place nine subdivisions on the poly slab.

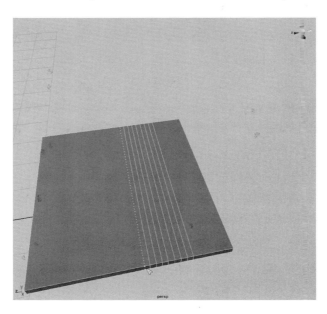

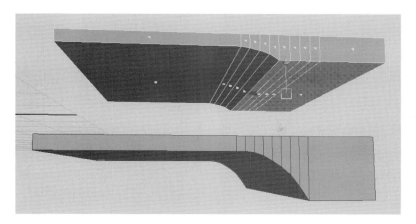

Figure 4.60

Create an arc by moving the bottom faces down individually.

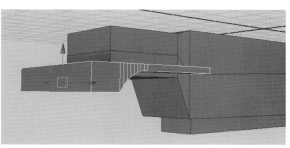

Figure 4.61

Attach the new piece beneath the front of the train.

9. Let's tackle the cowcatcher. Create a polygon cube with eight subdivisions along its width. Scale the cube to 4.4 in X, 2.15 in Y, and 1 in Z. You'll use this subdivided cube to pull vertices to make a cowcatcher shape. Enter Component Selection mode, pick the front top vertices, and move them down to make a wedge, as shown in Figure 4.62.

10. Select all the front vertices and the middle five back vertices along the bottom. Scale them in together in the Z-axis and then in the X-axis. Move them all forward to create the cowcatcher, as shown in Figure 4.63. Place the cowcatcher at the front of the undercarriage, as shown in Figure 4.64.

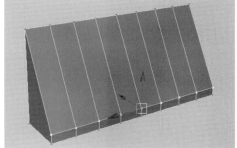

Figure 4.62

Begin the cowcatcher with a simple wedge.

11. Place three poly cube slabs approximately as shown in Figure 4.65 for the boiler platforms. Group all these undercarriage pieces together, and name them in a way that will help you stay organized. Also, make sure you group the parts of the boiler in a logical manner. The Outliner is shown in Figure 4.66 with the organization of the model so far.

You can load the scene file `locomotive_model_v2.mb` from the Locomotive project on the CD to check your work.

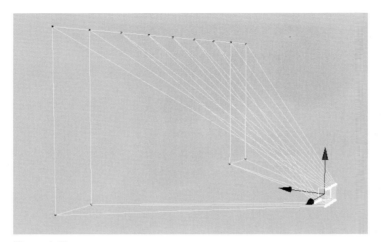

Figure 4.63
Scale down the front vertices.

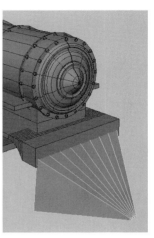

Figure 4.64
The cowcatcher in place

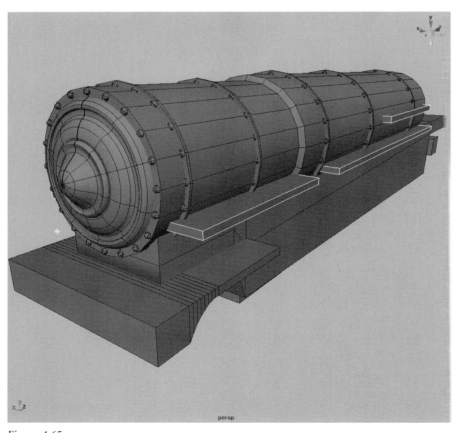

Figure 4.65
The boiler platforms are simple cubes.

Figure 4.66
The Outliner view of the locomotive geometry

Finishing the Boiler

The fun parts of a steam locomotive are all the chimneys on top of the boiler. To create the main steam chimney and give it a revolving surface, follow these steps:

1. You need to draw a profile curve for the smokestack/chimney. Choose Create → CV Curve Tool ❑. In the option box, set Curve Degree to 1 Linear. This lets you create straight curves. In the Top view panel, start from the bottom, and lay down CVs similar to those shown in Figure 4.67. Press Enter when you finish. Make sure you reset the options to the defaults when you're done.

2. This profile curve should be about five units tall in the *Z*-axis in the Top view panel and have its pivot point at the origin. Enter the Surfaces menu set, select the curve, and choose Surfaces → Revolve ❑.

   Change Axis Preset to *Z*. Also, at the bottom of the window, change Output Geometry to Polygons. You won't create a NURBS surface as you did before with the boiler cap but instead will go for a poly revolve. Change Type from Triangles to Quads. This creates polygon faces that are rectangular rather than triangular.

   Under Tessellation Method, select Standard Fit. Click Revolve, and you should have a chimney similar to the one shown in Figure 4.68. You may need to orient the chimney to fit the boiler properly if it's lying flat.

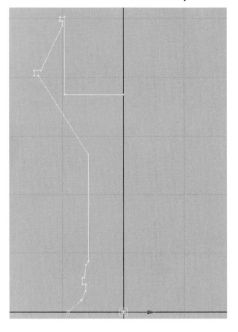

Figure 4.67

The profile curve for the chimney

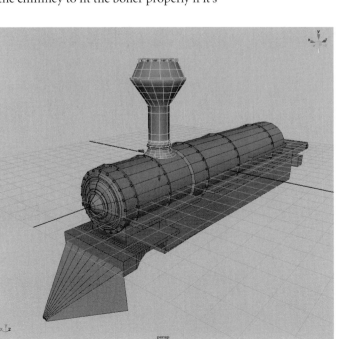

Figure 4.68

The engine's chimney

3. Delete the history by selecting the chimney and choosing Edit → Delete By Type → History. Place the chimney as shown in Figure 4.68. You can move the vertices at the bottom of the chimney to fit it to the round engine boiler, as shown in Figure 4.69.

Figure 4.69

Edit vertices to fit the boiler around the body of the boiler.

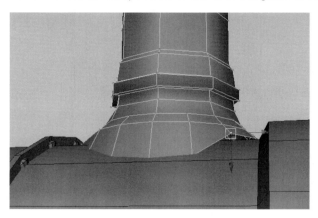

Go Get 'Em, Cowboy (or Cowgirl)!

Here is where I kick you out into the cruel hard world and make you create the remaining pieces for the engine boiler before you move on to the steam pumps, main cabin, wheels, and drive axles. You'll find suggestions on how to create the individual pieces in this section. (You'll set up the wheels in the animation chapters that follow.)

Study the following figures and graphics to get an idea of how to create these pieces using the Revolve tool and the other polygon toolsets used in this exercise and in this chapter. Figure 4.70 shows the extra pieces for you to build.

Figure 4.70

You're on your own!

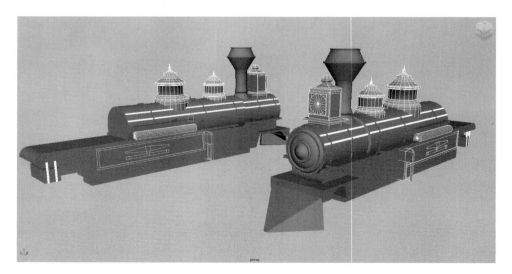

You can build the lantern shown in Figure 4.71 from a polygon cube by adding subdivision edges with the Insert Edge Loop tool and extruding or moving faces in and out. The light itself is a simple cylinder set into this shape.

You can draw the two top boiler caps by drawing a profile curve and then revolving the boiler caps as you did for the chimney (see Figure 4.72).

The piping and small tanks along the length of the engine boiler are cylinders placed in position, as shown in Figure 4.73.

Figure 4.71
Create the lantern from a simple cube.

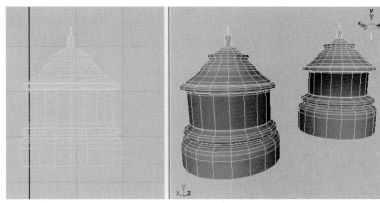

Figure 4.72
Use Surfaces → Revolve to create the boiler caps.

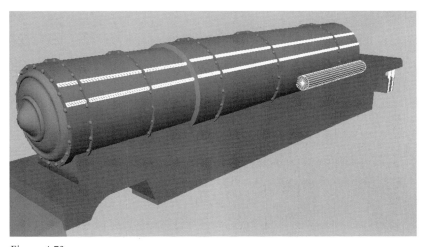

Figure 4.73
Place the piping on the boiler.

Figure 4.74

The side panels

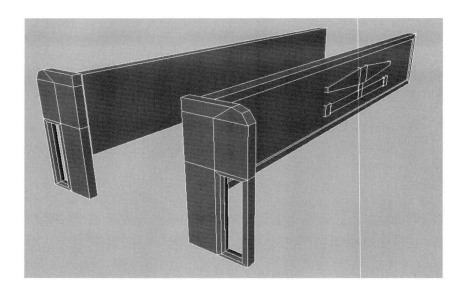

Figure 4.74

The side panels

The side panel details are poly cubes that have some faces extruded, with a few faces cut out (see Figure 4.74).

You can load the scene file `locomotive_model_v3.mb` from the Locomotive project on the CD to go over the models firsthand and get a much closer look. You can use the scene file to help build the pieces shown in this section to complete the engine boiler and its details.

The following sections will cover the cabin and wheels.

The Cabin

All that remains now, as shown in Figure 4.75, are the main cabin, the wheels, and their drive system. You'll finish those parts in the following sections; you'll set up, or *rig*, the wheels for animation in Chapter 9.

Figure 4.75

The remaining parts to make for the locomotive

You'll start with the main cabin. It has two sections: the cabin itself and the roof. You'll begin with the roof and work your way down. Follow these steps:

1. Make a poly cube, and scale it so that $X = 5.6$, $Y = 1$, and $Z = 7.7$. Select the front vertices (at the right side of the cube in Figure 4.76), and move them back a tad in Z to angle the edge. Do the same to the rear bottom vertices, giving the cube a tapered look in the Z-axis.

2. You need to subdivide the cube. This time, you'll use the Add Divisions tool. Select the cube, and choose Edit Mesh → Add Divisions ❏. Make sure Division Levels is set to 1 and Mode is set to Quads. Click Add Divisions. Maya places edges that cut through the middle of the faces.

3. Right-click the cube to enter Component Selection mode, and choose Edge from the marking menu. Select the edges as shown in Figure 4.77, and move them toward the back (to the left of the image in the figure) of the roof.

4. Using vertices, shape the roof to match the one in Figure 4.78.

5. Select the bottom two faces, and extrude them down once. Select the back face again, and extrude that down one more time to match the shape shown in Figure 4.79.

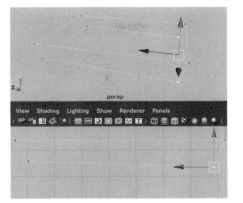

Figure 4.76

Taper the cube by moving the vertices.

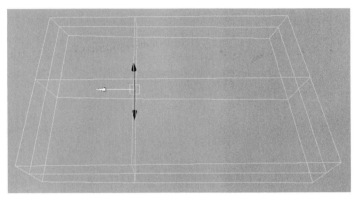

Figure 4.77

Select and move these edges.

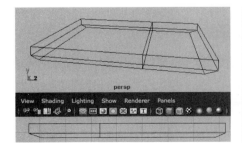

Figure 4.78

Shape the roof to match this shape.

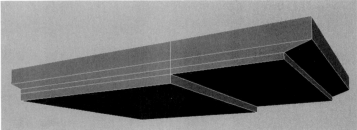

Figure 4.79

Continue to shape the roof.

6. Use the Insert Edge Loop tool to create more subdivisions along the long sides of the roof. Then, move the corner vertices down to angle the side edges of the roof down a little to complete the roof, as shown in Figure 4.80.

7. The cabin is a simple cube that is subdivided with the Insert Edge Loop tool, as shown in Figure 4.81. To make the windows and the open back, select the faces that make up the openings in Component mode, and delete them.

8. Place the roof on top of the cabin, and you're finished. Figure 4.81 shows the completed main cabin from two sides.

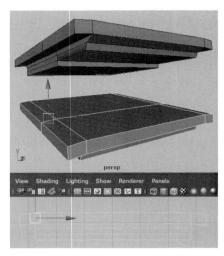

Figure 4.80

The roof is finished.

Figure 4.81

The cabin is a cube with some deleted faces.

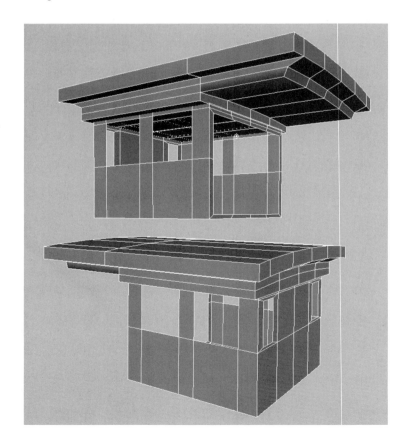

The Wheels

What's a locomotive without wheels? You'll have two types of wheels: large ones that are driven by the steam pumps and a pair of small wheels in front of the boiler (see Figure 4.82).

To make the large wheels, follow these steps.

1. To create the outer rim of the wheels, create a poly cylinder with Cap Divisions set to 5 in the option box and Axis Divisions set to 20. Scale the cylinder to $X = 1.87$, and squash it down to $Y = 0.145$. Turn it up on its side by rotating it 90 degrees in Z.

2. To hollow it out, select the inner faces on the caps, as shown in Figure 4.83, and delete them.

3. You should see a wheel rim similar to that in Figure 4.84. It's hollow on the inside, so you need to close the inside rim. Select the front edges of the inside rim, as shown in Figure 4.84, and choose Edit Mesh → Extrude. Extrude the edges toward the back side of the rim to close the inside rim.

Figure 4.82

The wheels of the locomotive

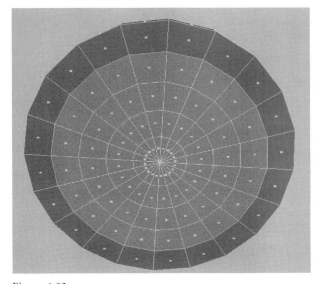

Figure 4.83

Select the inner faces.

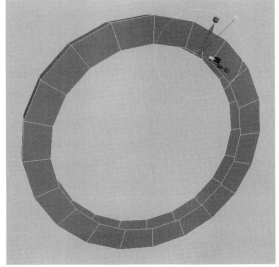

Figure 4.84

Close the inside rim using Extrude.

4. The wheel spokes are next. You'll create the hub of the spokes with a poly cylinder scaled to X and $Z = 0.25$ and $Y = 0.12$, so it's slightly thinner than the rim. Rotate the hub 90 degrees in Z, and place it in the middle of the rim. It helps to snap both the hub and the rim to the same grid point to make sure they're centered and aligned (see Figure 4.85).

5. Choose the Edit Mesh menu, and make sure the Keep Faces Together option at the top of the menu is unchecked. Select the outer ring of faces on the hub, and extrude them out to meet the rim, as shown in Figure 4.86.

6. Create a poly cube, and shape it as shown in Figure 4.87 to place it against the rim of the wheel on one side. This is where the steam drive's arm will connect to the wheel.

7. Group the pieces together, and name the node **large_wheel**. Center the pivot on the hub by choosing Modify → Center Pivot. If your geometry isn't perfectly symmetrical, the pivot may not center properly; you'll have

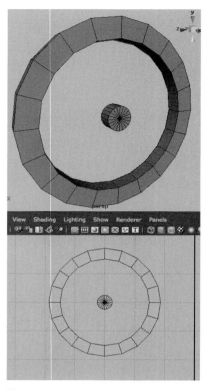

Figure 4.85
Create the hub for the wheel's spokes.

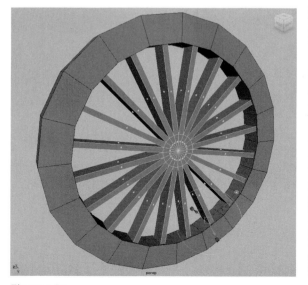

Figure 4.86
Extrude the outer faces of the hub to create the spokes.

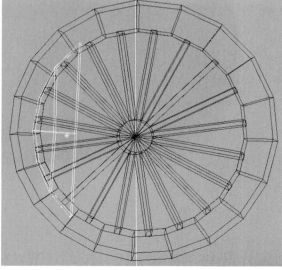

Figure 4.87
Create a plate to which the steam drive's arm will connect.

to enter Pivot mode (press Insert/Home) and move it manually to the center of the hub. If the top wheel node's pivot isn't centered properly, animation will look weird. Duplicate and place the wheels as shown in Figure 4.88. Make sure they all face out properly and align as in the figure.

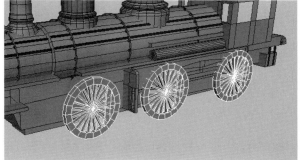

Figure 4.88

Duplicate and place the wheels.

8. The wheel arms are next. These connect the wheels to the steam drive that runs the locomotive. You can use simple poly cubes to make the arms shown in Figure 4.89. Place them as shown, and then rotate the appropriate wheels (using the top large_wheel node) so that they align with the connecting plates. Notice that the arms go through the side panel detail you created earlier with the undercarriage. Group the arms together so you have one group on either side of the train.

Figure 4.89

Add the wheel arms to the wheels to drive the locomotive.

The Small Wheels, the Axle, and the Steam Pumps

They sound like a trio of fifties rockabilly bands, but they're actually the last parts of the locomotive that you'll build in this chapter. The small wheels up front are the same as the larger wheels, except they don't have the connector plate and they have a solid background. You just need to copy one of the large_wheel groups and scale the top node down from 1.0 to 0.575. Delete the connector plate on the side, and place a cylinder behind the wheel to close the back. Remember to group this new closing cylinder into the top node. Call the group **small_wheel**.

Figure 4.90 shows a small wheel in position.

Figure 4.90

A small wheel in position

The axle that holds the front wheels is easy to make using basic shapes. Using Figures 4.91 and 4.92 as guides, build the axle assembly using simple poly shapes made with primitives and a few subdivision tools and extrusions.

The steam pumps provide drive power to the wheel arms, which in turn rotate the wheels to move the locomotive. These pumps are located on the sides of the engine between the small wheels and the first of the large wheels. They connect down from the boiler and through a drive mechanism to the first set of large wheel on both sides.

Figure 4.91

The front axle

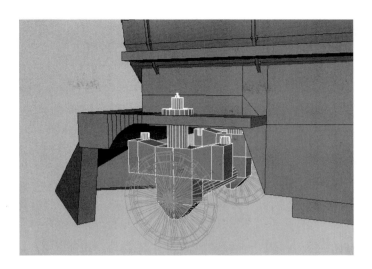

Figure 4.92

The front axle connected to the undercarriage

This drive mechanism rotates the first wheel, which drives the wheel arm to turn the other wheels on the engine. We'll look at how to set up this relationship in the animation chapters later in the book. For now, let's make the steam pumps using poly objects, as shown in Figures 4.93 and 4.94.

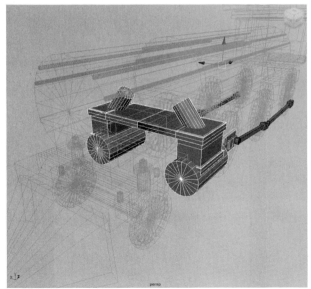

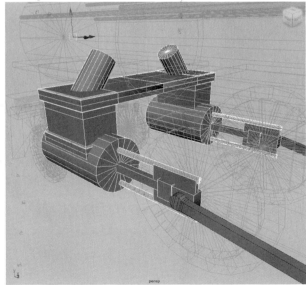

Figure 4.93

The steam pump is made of two cylinders and an extruded cube.

Figure 4.94

The drive mechanism is made of a couple of extruded cubes flanked by poly cylinder rods.

Connect the drive mechanism to the end of the wheel arm. Considering how your model will animate is an important aspect to modeling. This unit will animate in and out of the large pump cylinder, pulling the drive arm back and forth with it.

The completed model is shown in Figure 4.95.

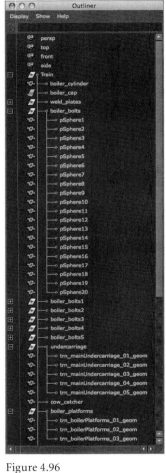

Figure 4.95
You built the whole thing!

Figure 4.96
The Outliner view of the organized scene

Carefully go through your scene and name everything. OK, maybe not everything, but at least name the top nodes and important pieces of the model. Group items neatly so that everything makes sense. In Chapter 8, you'll learn how best to organize the hierarchy of the model to suit your animation needs.

Figure 4.96 shows the Outliner view of the organization of the final scene on the CD.

Open the scene file `locomotive_model_v4.mb` from the Locomotive project on the CD to compare with your work and to guide you as you complete your work. Comparing and contrasting are valuable learning aids. Sometimes, figuring out how something was done by starting at the end and working backward (*reverse engineering* it) will give you a great deal of information.

Suggestions for Modeling Polygons

Poly modeling lends itself nicely to a wide range of objects—practically anything you can think of, and some things you can't. Try modeling the following objects to fine-tune your skills and explore the toolset:

Dining Room Table and Chairs This is an easy place to start. There is good amount of leeway in the design, which will give you as much of a challenge as you feel you can handle.

Computer Monitor With all its angles and overall surface details, a monitor makes for a great extrusion and face-editing exercise.

Desk Lamp or Floor Lamp This can be a quick exercise, so try to keep it highly detailed.

Car This exercise can be a real challenge, so keep it simple at first and increase the amount of detail the next time. Try to keep your model to the overall shape of the car, and don't worry making doors and windows that actually operate. Try to model the faces so that different parts of the car have different faces. Use NURBS surface tools to create poly patches to form the body of the car.

Summary

In this chapter, you learned about the basic modeling workflows and how best to approach a model. This chapter dealt primarily with polygon modeling and covered several polygon creation tools as well as several polygon subdivision tools. You put those tools to good use by building a hand and smoothing it out, as well as making a complex model of an old-fashioned steam locomotive. The latter exercise stressed the importance of putting a model together step by step and understanding how elements join together to form a whole model. You'll have a chance to make another model of that kind in Chapter 6, when you create a little red wagon.

Complex models become much easier to create when you recognize how to deconstruct them into their base components. You can divide even simple objects into more easily managed segments from which you can create a model.

The art of modeling with polygons is like anything else in Maya: your technique and workflow will improve with practice and time. It's less important to know all the tricks of the trade than it is to know how to approach a model and fit it into a wireframe mesh.

Modeling with NURBS, Subdivisions, and Deformers

As you saw in the previous chapter, NURBS are based on organic mathematics that allows you to create smooth curves and surfaces. NURBS models can be made of a single surface molded to fit, or they can be a collection of patches connected like a quilt. In any event, NURBS provide ample power for creating smooth surfaces for your models.

Now that you've learned the basics of creating and editing poly meshes, getting into NURBS models and more advanced modeling techniques will easily become part of your toolbox. This chapter explains how to use deformations to adjust a model, as opposed to editing the geometry directly as you did with the previous modeling methods. It also introduces subdivision surface modeling, which fully incorporates this concept.

Topics in this chapter include:

- NURBS!

- Creating polygons

- Converting a NURBS model to polygons

- Editing NURBS surfaces

- Patch modeling: the locomotive

- Sculpting NURBS

- Modeling with simple deformers

- The lattice deformer

- Animating through a lattice

- Subdivision surfaces

- Creating a starfish

- Building a teakettle

NURBS!

NURBS modeling depends on surfaces that are created using curves. Just as control vertices (CVs) are connected to form curved lines, NURBS surfaces are created by connecting (or *spanning*) curves. Therefore, typical NURBS modeling pipelines first involve the creation of curves that define the edges, outline, paths, and/or boundaries of surfaces.

When a surface is created, its shape is defined and governed by its *isoparms.* These surface curves, or curves that reside solely on a surface, show the outline of a surface's shape much as the chicken wire in a wire mesh sculpture does. CVs on the isoparms define and govern the shape of these isoparms just as they would regular curves. Adjusting a NURBS surface involves manipulating the CVs of the object, somewhat like sculpting.

You can create a NURBS surface in several ways. The easiest way is to create a NURBS primitive. You can sculpt the primitive surface by moving its CVs, but you can also cut it apart to create different surface swatches or patches to use as needed, which you'll see in a steam pump model for the locomotive later in this chapter. A primitive need not retain its original shape, and it frequently can be shaped to fit the artist's needs. Using the surfacing tools available under the Surfaces menu set, you can detach, cut, and attach pieces into and out of a primitive to get the exact shapes you need.

You can also make surfaces in several ways without using a primitive. All these methods involve first creating or using existing NURBS curves, or curves on another surface, to define a part or parts of the surface, and then using one of the methods described in the following sections to create the surfaces.

Lofting

The most common surfacing method is *lofting*, which takes at least two curves and creates a surface span between each selected curve in the order in which they're selected. Figure 5.1 shows the result of lofting two curves together.

Figure 5.1

A simple loft created between two curves

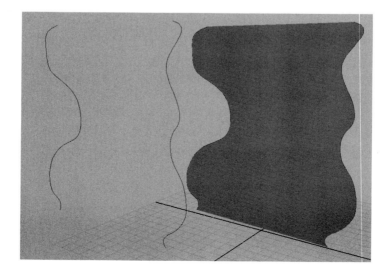

To create a loft, follow these steps:

1. Switch to the Surfaces menu set (press F4).

2. Draw the two curves.

3. Select the curves in the order in which you want the surface to be generated.

4. Choose Surfaces → Loft, or click the Loft icon in the Surfaces shelf ().

When you define more curves for the loft, Maya can create more complex shapes. The more CVs for each curve, the more isoparms you have, and the more detail in the surface. Figure 5.2 shows how four curves can be lofted together to form a more complex surface. You can use almost any number of curves for a lofted surface.

Lofting works best when curves are drawn as cross-sectional slices of the object to be modeled. Lofting is used to make a variety of surfaces, which may be as simple as tabletops or as complex as human faces.

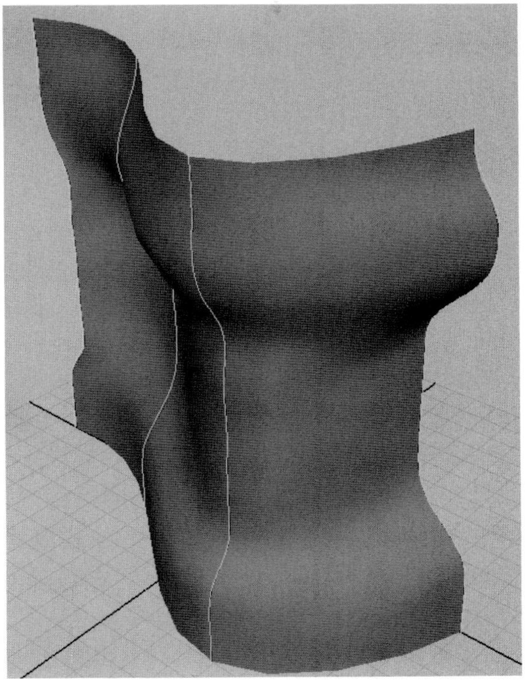

Figure 5.2

A loft created with four curves that are selected in order from left to right

Revolved Surface

A *revolved surface* requires only one curve that is turned about a point in space to create a surface, like a woodworker shaping a table leg on a lathe. First you draw a *profile curve* to create a profile of the desired object, and then you revolve this curve (anywhere from 0 degrees to 360 degrees) around a single point in the scene to create the surface. The profile revolves around the object's pivot point, which is typically placed at the origin but can be moved (as seen in the Solar System exercise in Chapter 2, "Jumping in Headfirst, with Both Feet"), and sweeps a new surface along its way. Figure 5.3 shows the profile curve for a wine glass.

The curve is then revolved around the Y-axis a full 360 degrees to create the wine glass. Figure 5.4 is the complete revolved surface with the profile revolved around the Y-axis.

To create a revolved surface, draw and select your profile curve, and then choose Surfaces → Revolve.

Figure 5.3

A profile curve is drawn in the outline of a wine glass in the Y-axis.

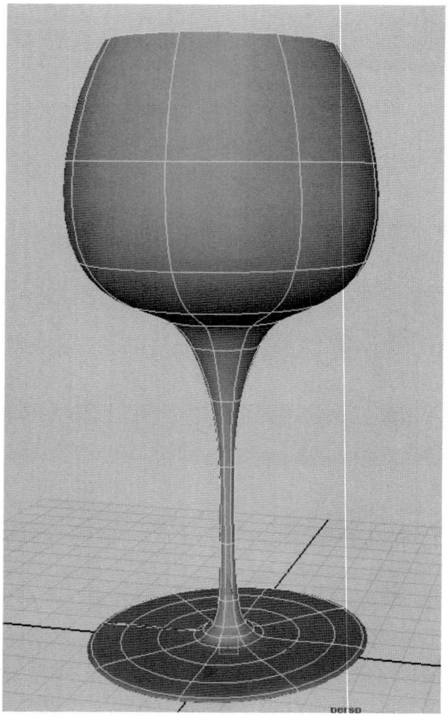

Figure 5.4

The revolved surface

A revolved surface is useful for creating objects such as bottles, furniture legs, and baseball bats—anything that is symmetrical about an axis.

Extruded Surface

An *extruded surface* uses two curves: a profile curve and a path curve. The profile curve is drawn to create the profile shape of the desired surface. It's then swept from one end of the path curve to its other end, creating spans of a surface along its travel. The higher the CV count on each curve, the more detail the surface will have. An extruded surface can also take the profile curve and simply stretch it to a specified distance straight along one direction or axis, doing away with the profile curve. Figure 5.5 shows the profile and path curves, and Figure 5.6 shows the resulting surface after the profile is extruded along the path.

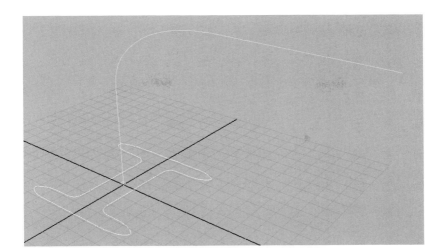

Figure 5.5

The profile curve is drawn in the shape of an *I*, and the path curve comes up and bends toward the camera.

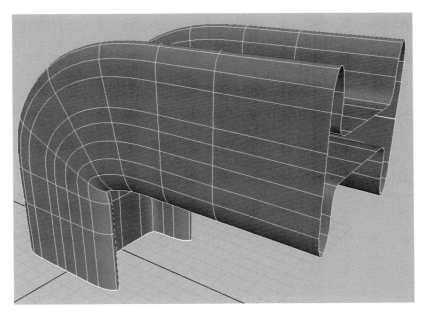

Figure 5.6

After extrusion, the surface becomes a bent I-beam.

To create an extruded surface, follow these steps:

1. Draw both curves.
2. Select the profile curve.
3. Shift+click the path curve.
4. Choose Surfaces → Extrude.

An extruded surface is used to make items such as winding tunnels, coiled garden hoses, springs, and curtains.

Planar Surface

A *planar surface* uses one perfectly flat curve to make a two-dimensional cap in the shape of that curve. It does this by laying down a NURBS plane (a flat, square NURBS primitive) and carving out the shape of the curve like a cookie cutter. The resulting surface is a perfectly flat, cutout shape, also known as a *trimmed surface* because the "excess" outside the shape curve is trimmed away.

To create a planar surface, draw and select the curve and then choose Surfaces → Planar.

You can also use multiple curves within each other to create a planar surface with holes in it. A simple planar surface is shown on the left side of Figure 5.7. When a second curve is added inside the original curve and both are selected, the planar surface is created with a hole. On the right side is the result when the outer curve is selected first and then the inner curve is selected before Surfaces → Planar is chosen.

Figure 5.7

A planar surface based on a single curve (left). A planar surface based on a curve within a curve to create the cutout (right).

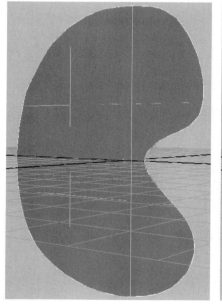

A planar surface is great for flat lettering, for pieces of a marionette doll or paper cutout, or for capping the ends of a hollow extrusion. Planar surfaces are best left as flat pieces, however, because deforming them may not give the best results. In addition, it's sometimes best to create the planar surface as a polygon. You'll see how to convert surfaces to polygons later in this chapter. The following quick exercise will give you an idea of what to look out for when creating polygons from surfacing techniques:

1. In the Surfaces menu set, select Create → NURBS Primitives → Circle twice to create two circles.

2. Scale the second circle to about three times its original size, as shown in Figure 5.8.

3. Select the larger circle first, then the smaller circle, and finally select Surfaces →
    Planar ❑. In the option box, check Polygons for Output Geometry, Quads for Type,
    and General for Tessellation Method, as shown in Figure 5.9.

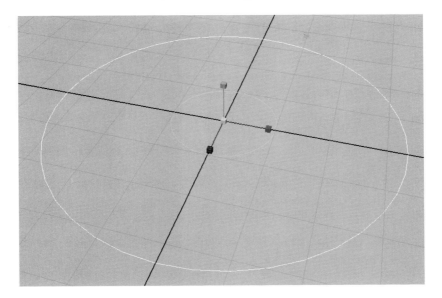

Figure 5.8

Scale the circle up.

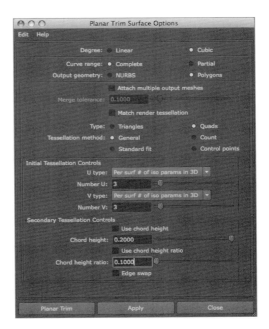

Figure 5.9

Choose these options.

4. Depending on how you create the geometry as polygons, you'll get different results—particularly around curves. Because Maya has to figure out where to put more faces to create a smoother outline, you have to set the Number U and Number V settings to best fit the curves of your resulting surface. At the current settings, your planar surface looks as shown in Figure 5.10. Notice the small gaps between the original outer NURBS circle and the surface outline.

5. Increase the Number U and Number V values, and you'll get tighter results at curves, although you'll have more faces on your model.

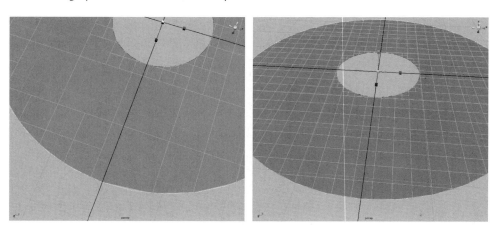

Figure 5.10

Notice the gaps between the outer NURBS circle and the outline.

Keep this exercise in mind as you continue modeling. Whenever you need to create polygons from NURBS surfaces, which should be quite often for some people, try the different creation methods for the best output. No one way works best all the time.

If you try creating a planar surface using a curve and notice that Maya doesn't allow it, verify that the curve(s) is perfectly flat. If any of the CVs aren't on the same plane as the others, the planar surface won't work.

Beveled Surface

The Bevel Surface function takes an open or a closed curve and extrudes its outline to create a side surface. It creates a bevel on one or both corners of the resulting surface to create an edge that can be made smooth or sharp (see Figure 5.11). The many options in the Bevel tool allow you to control the size of the bevel and depth of extrusion, giving you great flexibility. When a bevel is created, you can easily cap the bevel with planar surfaces.

To create a bevel, draw and select your curve, and then choose Surfaces → Bevel.

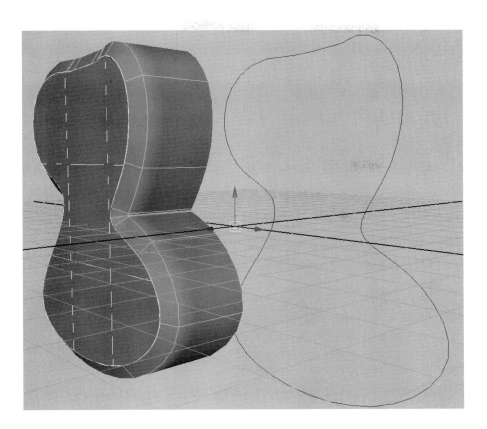

Figure 5.11
A curve before and
after it's beveled.
The beveled surface
has been given a
planar cap.

Maya also offers a Bevel Plus surface, which has more creation options for advanced bevels. A beveled surface is great for creating 3D lettering, for creating items such as bottle caps or buttons, and for rounding out an object's edges.

Boundary Surface

A *boundary surface* is so named because it's created within the boundaries of three or four surrounding curves. For example, two vertical curves are drawn opposite each other to define the two side edges of the surface. Two horizontal curves are then drawn to define the upper and lower edges. These curves can have depth to them; they need not be flat for the boundary surface to work, unlike a planar surface. Although you can select the curves in any order, it's best to select them in opposing pairs. In Figure 5.12, four curves are created and arranged to form the edges of a surface to be created. First, select the vertical pair of curves, because they're opposing pairs; then, select the second two horizontal curves before choosing Surfaces → Boundary.

A boundary surface is useful for creating shapes such as car hoods, fenders, and other formed panels.

Figure 5.12

**Four curves
arranged to cre-
ate the edges for a
surface (left). The
resulting bound-
ary surface formed
from the four curves
(right).**

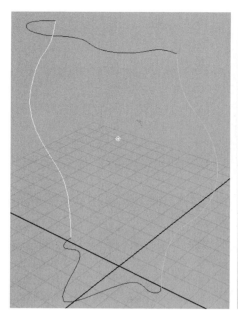
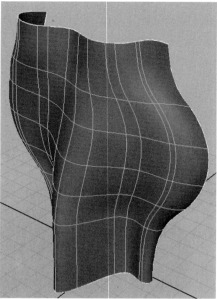

Figure 5.12

Four curves arranged to create the edges for a surface (left). The resulting boundary surface formed from the four curves (right).

Combining Techniques

You can use certain surfacing techniques in combination to create intricate models. For example, whenever a curve is required for a surface, you can use an isoparm instead to create a surface between two existing surfaces.

Try This Take a couple of lofted surfaces, and connect them with a third surface. Figure 5.13 shows two surfaces with two intermediate curves between them. (Notice that the view panel's option Shading → X-ray is turned on so you can see through the shaded surfaces.) You'll select an isoparm from the first surface (on the left) and then the curve on the left, the curve on the right, and finally an isoparm on the second surface:

1. Either create two lofted surfaces and curves as shown in Figure 5.13, or load the Chap_5_Lofting_Exercise_1.ma file from the Lofting_Exercise project on the CD.

2. To select the first isoparm, press F8 for Component Selection mode, and click the Lines Selection Filter button (▨) in the Status line to allow you to select isoparms. You can also right-click the surface and choose Isoparm from the marking menu to enter Component mode for isoparms.

3. Select an isoparm close to the left edge. Press F8 to return to Object Selection mode (or right-click the first curve and choose Object Mode from the marking menu), Shift+click the first curve, and then Shift+click the second curve. Press F8 again or use the marking menu again for Component mode, and Shift+click an isoparm toward the left edge on the second surface, as in Figure 5.14.

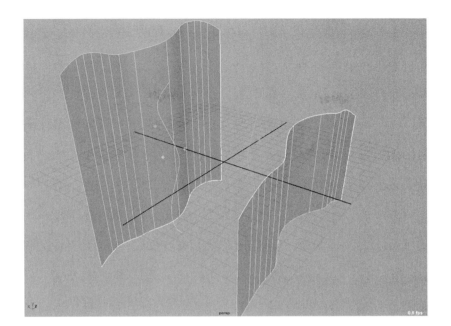

Figure 5.13

Two lofted surfaces with two curves in between

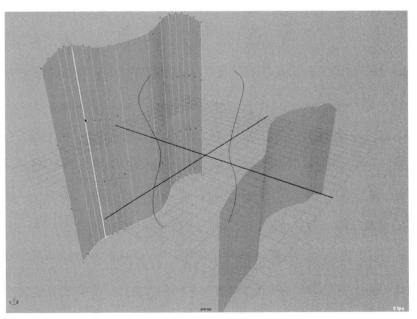

Figure 5.14

Selecting the isoparm

4. Choose Surfaces → Loft to create the intermediate surface between the existing lofts. Figure 5.15 shows how the new surface snakes from the first loft to the second loft by way of the two curves.

Figure 5.15

The spanning loft between the existing surfaces snakes from the first isoparm to the curves to the second isoparm.

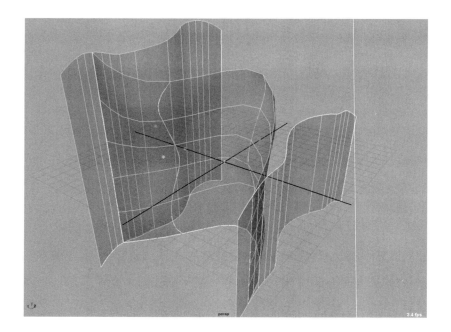

Surface History

In Chapter 3, "The Maya 2011 Interface," you learned that clicking the History icon ( )
toggles History on and off. *History* has to do with how objects react to change. Leaving
History on when creating primitives, as you did in Chapter 2, allows you to access an
object's original parameters.

Leaving History on when creating NURBS surfaces allows the surface to update when
any of its creation pieces change. For example, the loft you just created will update whenever the two original surfaces or curves you used to create the loft move or change shape.
If you were to move the original loft on the left and rotate it back a bit, the new loft would
adjust to keep its one side attached to the same isoparm. If one or more of the input
curves were to change, the loft would bend to fit.

> You must toggle History on before you create the object(s) if you want History to be on for
> the object(s).

By lofting using isoparms and with History toggled on, you can keep the new surface permanently attached to the original loft, no matter how the isoparms move, as in
Figure 5.16. This technique works with all surface techniques, not just with lofting, as
long as History is turned on. History is useful for making adjustments and fine-tuning
a surface, and it can be handy in animation if several surfaces need to deform but stay
attached.

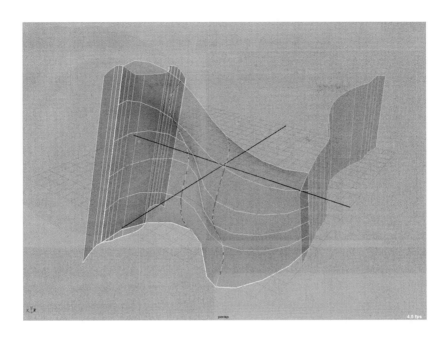

Figure 5.16

History updates the newly created loft to keep it attached to the isoparms and curves used to create it, even when they've been moved or altered.

Why wouldn't you want History turned on for everything? After a long day of modeling, having History on for every single object can slow down your scene file, adding unnecessary bloat to your workflow. But it isn't typically a problem on most surface types unless the scene is huge, so you should leave it on while you're still modeling.

If you no longer want a surface or an object to retain its History, you can selectively delete it from the surface. Select the surface, and choose Edit → Delete by Type → History. You can also rid the entire scene of History by choosing Edit → Delete All by Type → History. Just don't get them mixed up!

Using NURBS Surfacing to Create Polygons

You can create swatches of polygon surfaces by using NURBS surfacing tools, as you saw with the exercise on creating a planar surface.

To create a polygonal surface with any of the surfacing techniques in this chapter, open the option box for that particular NURBS tool. For example, create two simple curves. With both curves selected, choose Surfaces → Loft ❏. In the options for Output Geometry, click the Polygons button to display the options for creating the polygon surface and its detail level.

History for the surface will adjust the new polygonal surface. The detail of the surface will try to adjust as changes to the input curves are made. If you anticipate significant changes to the input curves, make sure you create the poly surface with a high poly count to accommodate major changes. This is probably the best way to create a single poly surface, especially if you prefer a NURBS workflow.

Try This Draw two CV curves as you did at the beginning of this chapter, both with the same number of CVs. Open the Loft options box, and click the Polygons option for the Output Geometry.

The creation options that appear at the bottom of the window affect the tessellation of the resulting surface; that is, you use them to specify the level of detail and the number of faces with which the surface is created. Generally speaking, the more faces there are, the more detail you'll need. (That doesn't mean a detailed surface can't be efficient, with areas of high tessellation placed only where needed.)

The default Tessellation Method, Standard Fit, uses the fewest faces to create the surface without compromising overall integrity. The sliders adjust the resulting number of faces in order to fit the finer curvature of the input curves.

The lower the Fractional Tolerance, the smoother the surface and the greater the number of faces you need.

The Chord Height Ratio determines the amount of curve in a particular region and calculates how many more faces to use to give an adequate representation of that curved area with polygons. This option is best used with surfaces that have multiple or very intense curves.

It isn't uncommon to create a surface, undo it, change the slider settings, re-create it, and repeat, to get just the right tessellation. That's why you should click the Apply button, which keeps the window open, rather than the Loft button, which closes the window after applying the settings.

The General Tessellation Method creates a specific number of lines, evenly dividing the horizontal (U) and vertical (V) into rows of polygon faces.

The Control Points method tessellates the surface according to the number of points on the input curves. As the number of CVs and spans on the curves increases, so does the number of divisions of polygons.

The Count method simply relies on how many faces you tell it to make—the higher the count, the higher the tessellation on the surface. Experiment with the options to get the best poly surface results.

TESSELLATION

In the rendering phase, all 3D objects are broken into polygonal triangles that form the surfaces that shape your objects. This process, called *tessellation*, happens on all rendered surfaces, whether polygonal, subdivided, or NURBS.

The computer calculates the position of each significant point on your surface and connects the points to form a skin representing your surface.

Converting a NURBS Model to Polygons

Some people prefer to model on NURBS curves and either create poly surfaces or convert to polygons after the entire model is done with NURBS surfaces. Ultimately, you'll find your own workflow preference, but it helps greatly if you're comfortable using all surfacing methods. Most modelers choose one way or another but are familiar with both methodologies. In the following section, you'll convert a NURBS model to polygons.

Try This Convert a NURBS modeled axe into a poly model like one that might be needed in a game.

Open axe_model_v1.mb in the Scenes folder of the Axe project on the CD. The toughest part of this simple process is getting the poly model to follow all the curves in the axe with fidelity, so you'll have to convert parts of the axe differently. Follow these steps:

1. Grab the handle, and choose Modify → Convert → NURBS to Polygons ❒. Use the default presets. If need be, reestablish your settings by choosing Edit → Reset Settings; the handle converts well to polygons. Click Apply, and a poly version of the axe handle appears on top of the NURBS version. Move it eight units to the right to get it out of the way. You'll move the other parts 8 units as well to assemble the poly axe properly.

Figure 5.17

A faithful high-poly conversion (on the right) of the NURBS axe (on the left)

2. Select the back part of the axe head. All those surfaces are grouped together to make selection easy. The default settings will work for this part as well, so click Apply and move the resulting model eight units to the left.

3. The front of the axe head holds a lot of different arcs, so you'll have to create it with finer controls. Change Fractional Tolerance from 0.01 to 0.0005. This yields more polygons but finer curved surfaces. Figure 5.17 shows the result.

If you were following this process for a conventional game engine, you'd normally be restricted to a low number of polygons, and your axe design would be different to better handle a low poly count.

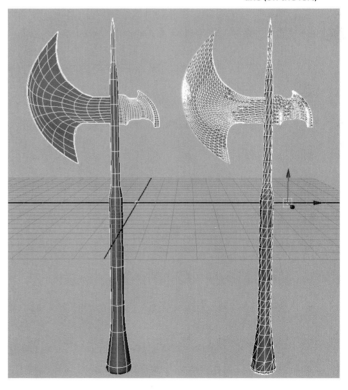

Editing NURBS Surfaces

As you've experienced, Maya provides numerous NURBS tools that you'll find useful when editing your surfaces. In addition to tools for moving CVs, some important functions and tools allow you to add realism to your model. This section gives you a quick overview of these tools—some you've already used, and others you'll need to try out for yourself.

The following functions are all accessed through the Edit NURBS menu. Open and tear off the Edit NURBS menu so it remains open as you follow along. (For more on tear-off menus, see Chapter 3.)

Project Curve on Surface

The ability to project a curve onto a surface allows you to cut holes in the surface using the Trim tool (choose Edit NURBS → Trim Tool). It also lets you create, using History, another surface that is attached, following the outline of your projected curve, as you saw in the section "Combining Techniques" earlier in this chapter.

Similar to drawing a curve on a surface, projected curves project an existing curve onto the selected surface. That curve on the surface is now useful for patch modeling as well as tracing animation paths for objects to follow along a surface. For example, you can project a curve around a hilly landscape surface and assign a car to animate (drive) along that projected curve. The car will stick to the surface of the road with ease.

To use Project Curve on Surface, select the surface and the curve to project, and then choose Edit NURBS → Project Curve on Surface.

Trim and Untrim Surfaces

Trimming a surface (choose Edit NURBS → Trim Tool) creates holes in the surface using curves that are either drawn or projected onto the surface.

If you have a surface that has already been trimmed, and it's too late to reverse the function with Undo, you can use Untrim Surfaces to remove either the last trim performed or all the surface trims. Choose Edit NURBS → Untrim Surfaces.

Attach Surfaces

Attach Surfaces does exactly that—it attaches two contiguous NURBS surfaces along two selected isoparms. Select an isoparm on the edge of the first surface, Shift+click an edge isoparm on a second surface, and choose Edit NURBS → Attach Surfaces to create a new surface from the two. As shown in Figure 5.18, the attach point is along the selected isoparms.

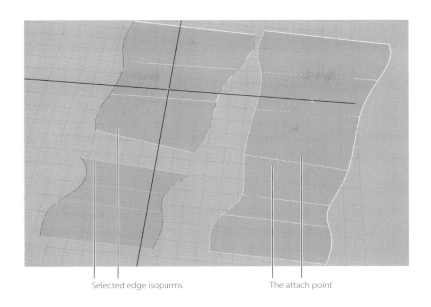

Selected edge isoparms   The attach point

Detach Surfaces

Detach Surfaces is a highly useful tool for generating specific areas of a NURBS surface, or patches. Select an isoparm to define the line of detachment, and choose Edit NURBS → Detach Surfaces. The surface is cut along that isoparm to create two distinct surfaces (see Figure 5.19). You'll see plenty of Detach and Attach tools later in this chapter.

Selected isoparms   Detached patch

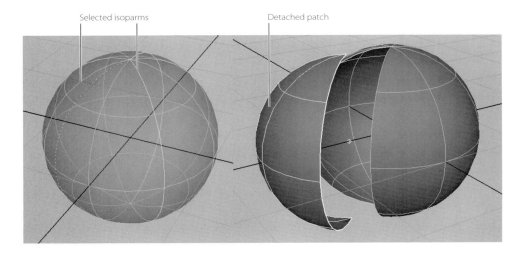

To select an isoparm that isn't displayed on the surface, click a viewable isoparm and drag the mouse to place the isoparm selection elsewhere on the surface. Release the button to make the selection; a dashed isoparm line is now selected. This is a valid surface isoparm, but it isn't one used to define the number of spans in the surface.

Insert Isoparms

You've already come upon a modeling assignment for which you needed extra surface definition (that is, more spans) on a NURBS object. As you've seen, it's a matter of selecting an isoparm and choosing Edit NURBS → Insert Isoparms. Doing so creates an isoparm and redefines the surface to add more spans. This function is used to make extra detailed parts of a NURBS surface, to allow for smoother deformations—for example, adding an isoparm or two to the elbow joint of a model to make the arm bend with a cleaner crease (see Figure 5.20). You can either create a new isoparm between two existing ones or add isoparms to your own defined area.

Figure 5.20

Inserting isoparms for a smoother deformation

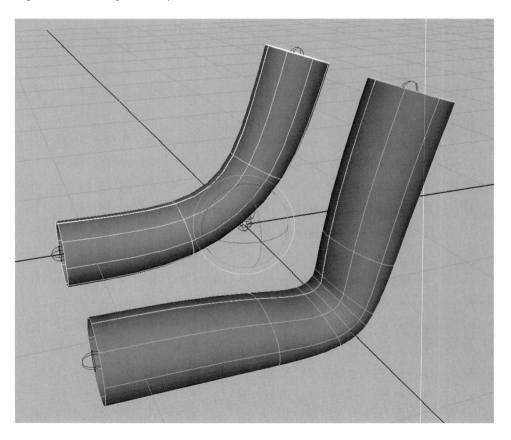

Patch Modeling: A Locomotive Detail

With NURBS modeling, you frequently need to attach surfaces so that a model doesn't split at the seams. This process of aligning and attaching NURBS patches is called *stitching*, and this kind of modeling is called *patch modeling.*

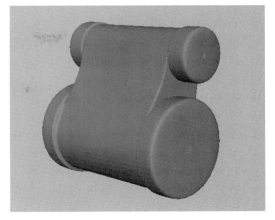

In this exercise, you'll jump back in time to create an element for the locomotive modeling exercise in the previous chapter. You'll create a pump for the polygonal locomotive you made in Chapter 4, "Beginning Polygonal Modeling," using patches that you'll stitch together. This exercise gives you more of an idea of how patches work to pull together an organic shape using NURBS shapes. To show you what you're seeking to build, the finished model is shown in Figure 5.21.

Figure 5.21

The finished pump elements for the previous chapter's locomotive model are created in NURBS patches.

Keep in mind that patch modeling is a fairly involved process. If you don't feel comfortable with modeling quite yet, skip this tutorial and move on to the next section in this chapter, "Using Artisan to Sculpt NURBS." You can always return to this section to bone up on your patch modeling later.

Starting the NURBS Pump

First, create a new project called Locomotive, or copy the Locomotive project from the CD to your hard drive and set it as your current project.

To start creating the locomotive pump, follow these steps:

1. Create a NURBS cylinder with no caps by choosing Create → NURBS Primitives → Cylinder ❒. Under Caps in the Options box, select None to create an open-ended cylinder. Set Axis to *Z* to create the cylinder on its side, and then click Create.

2. Size the cylinder down to 0.72 in *X* and *Y* and to 0.9 in *Z*.

3. Reset the cylinder so that its attributes are set back to normal. With the cylinder selected, choose Modify → Freeze Transformations ❒. In the Options box, choose Edit → Reset Settings to set to reestablish the defaults, and then click Freeze Transform. The cylinder, resized and after the application of Freeze Transformations, is shown in Figure 5.22.

Figure 5.22

The first NURBS cylinder, after Freeze Transformations

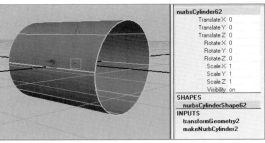

4. You'll create slightly larger end pieces for the cylinder. Duplicate the cylinder once, move the copy, and scale it as shown in Figure 5.23. Repeat to create the other end piece. The end pieces are roughly 1.075 in Scale X and Y and 0.18 in Scale Z and are moved slightly past the ends of the cylinder, leaving a slight gap as shown. You should freeze transforms on the ends to reset their scale and positions back to the default.

5. Create a second copy of this assembly that is smaller in radius but is the same length (see Figure 5.24). Duplicate the three cylinders, and change their respective scales to 0.55 in *X* and *Y*, but leave Scale *Z* set to 1. Remember, you froze their transforms, so their starting scales should have been at 1. Position the three cylinders as shown in Figure 5.24, slightly to the side and above the original larger cylinders. Freeze their transforms.

Figure 5.23

Create the end pieces.

Figure 5.24

Create a smaller copy of the first cylinders, and place them higher for the top of the steam pump assembly.

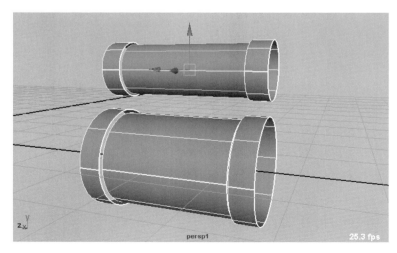

6. Cut a couple of holes in the main cylinders. Cut at the top two isoparms on the sides of the larger cylinder first, as shown in Figure 5.25. To select the first isoparm, right-click the cylinder, choose Isoparm from the marking menu, and click the isoparm to select it. Next, Shift+click the isoparm on the other side so that both are selected.

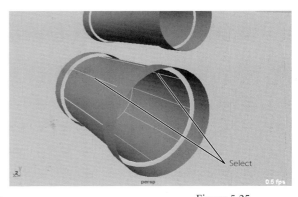

7. In the Surfaces menu set, choose Edit NURBS → Detach Surfaces. The surface between the isoparms you just selected is now its own surface and can be deleted. This gives your first cut, as shown in Figure 5.26.

8. Use the same procedure to cut the smaller cylinder, but at the sides so you can remove the bottom half. Select the isoparms on the sides of the smaller cylinder, and detach the surface by choosing Edit NURBS → Detach Surfaces again. Delete the bottom surface. Now your model should look like Figure 5.27.

Figure 5.25

Select these isoparms to cut the top of the cylinder.

Figure 5.26

Cutting the cylinder's top

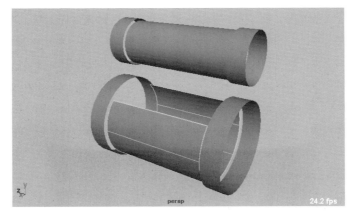

Figure 5.27

The cut cylinders

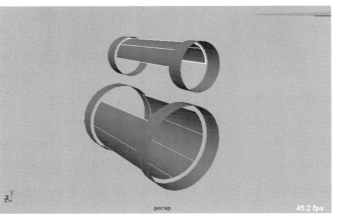

If detaching the surface doesn't work the first time, select the same isoparms again and detach surfaces again. This sometimes happens when you try to cut a NURBS surface at a side isoparm where the surface is beginning and ending.

Adding End Caps

At this point, you'll cap the ends of the cylinders to close them off. You can continue with your own file or load the file NURBS_pump_v01.mb from the Locomotive project on the CD and check your work so far. The trick will be to add four isoparms using the Insert Isoparms function you read about earlier in this chapter to create the caps.

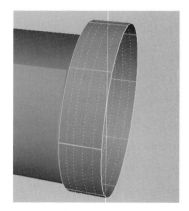

Figure 5.28

Select these four isoparms.

To cap the ends, follow these steps:

1. Select the end cylinder, right-click the geometry, and select Isoparm from the marking menu. Select four isoparms (make sure you hold down Shift while selecting the isoparms so as not to deselect them), as shown in Figure 5.28, and choose Edit NURBS → Insert Isoparms ❑.

    Make sure your settings match those in Figure 5.29. This inserts four isoparms into the end cylinder that you can use to close the end to make the cap.

Figure 5.29

The default Insert Isoparm settings

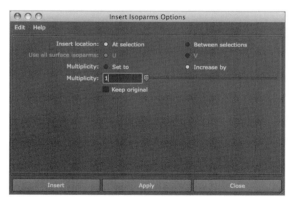

2. Select the end CVs to scale them down to close the cap. The easiest way to do this is to select the hull that controls all the edge CVs. Right-click the end cylinder, and select Hull. Select the very outermost hull, and scale it down as shown in Figure 5.30. Doing so closes the end cap. Don't worry about leaving a small hole in the cap; you'll complete this pump when you finish the locomotive model.

3. Repeat the previous procedures to close off the other three end cylinders to create caps for both ends of both objects, as shown in Figure 5.31.

4. Connect and patch the end caps to their cylinders. To do this, you need to line up a few new isoparms on the cylinders so you can stitch everything together properly. Using the previous workflow, add new isoparms to the bottom cylinder, as shown in Figure 5.32. (You may have to hide the end caps to create the isoparms on the cylinder. Select the end caps and use Display → Hide → Hide Selection. After you create the isoparms, select Display → Show → Show All.)

Figure 5.30
Scale down the outermost hull.

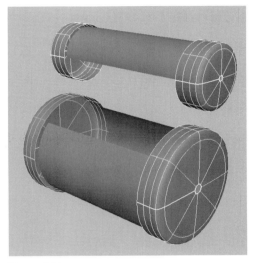

Figure 5.31
End caps for the pump pieces

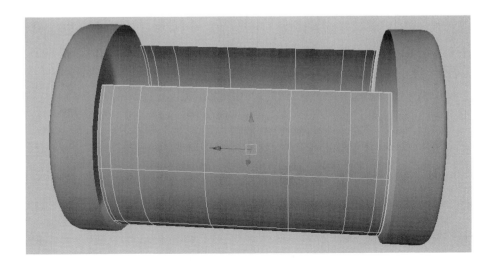

Figure 5.32
Add isoparms as shown.

5. You need to prep the end cap to connect to the cylinder, by cutting a pie piece out of the cap, to line it up with the cut cylinder. On the end cap, select two isoparms to form a V that lines up with the cut edges of the main cylinder, as shown in Figure 5.33. Then, choose Edit NURBS → Detach Surfaces. Doing so cuts the V section out of the end cap. This aligns the end cap and the cylinder geometry at the edges so you can create a smooth connection between them in the next few steps.

Figure 5.33

Select two isoparms and detach the surfaces.

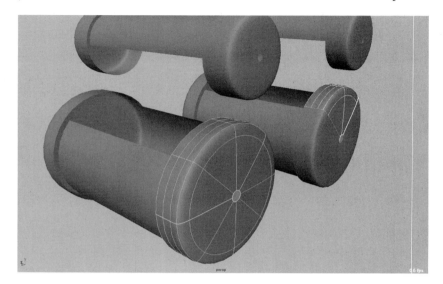

 You can load the file NURBS_pump_v02.mb from the Locomotive project to compare your work with it; or, if you skipped the previous steps, you can proceed from here to attach the end cap.

6. You need to pull the end of the cylinder to line it up with the edge of the end cap. Select the end four vertical hulls, as shown in Figure 5.34, and move them so that the edges of the cylinder and end cap align. Repeat this to line up the other end of the cylinder with the other cap.

7. Create the pieces to connect the caps to the cylinder using lofts. Right-click the cylinder, and choose Isoparm from the marking menu. Select the edge isoparm on the cylinder. Right-click the end cap, and choose Isoparm from the marking menu. Shift+click the edge isoparm of the end cap, as shown in Figure 5.35. Choose Surfaces → Loft ❑. Make sure you're using the default settings for the loft: in the Options box, choose Edit → Reset Settings.

8. The previous step creates a surface to bridge the cylinder and the end cap. You'll notice that it's rather jagged—almost a diamond shape as opposed to a smooth ring. With the loft selected, press 3 on the keyboard to see it with a smooth display in the panel. Figure 5.36 shows the loft.

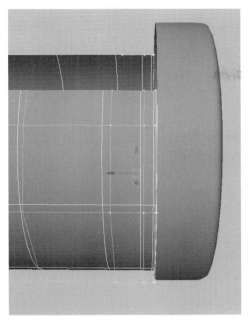

Figure 5.34

Select the four end hulls, and move them to line up.

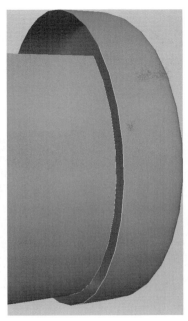

Figure 5.35

Shift+click the edge isoparm.

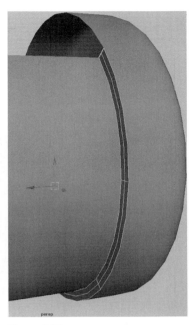

Figure 5.36

Lofting the end cap to the cylinder

Stitching and Tangency

In the next series of steps, you'll get further into the real meat of patch modeling, which is all about creating smooth seams. Smooth seams are essential to organic modeling. The trick in creating a good patch model is to make sure all the patches line up; this is called *tangency*. In animation setup, it's important—for characters that have been made with NURBS patches and for textures, to name but two instances—that tangency be correct; otherwise, you may notice tearing at seams during deformations or texture maps that don't line up quite right. It's a tedious process, but here is a taste of it. To continue with the patch model of the locomotive pump, follow these steps:

1. Create a smooth piece that connects the cylinder and the end caps using the lofts created in steps 7 and 8 in the previous section and shown in Figure 5.36. Select the cylinder and the connector loft, as shown in Figure 5.37, and attach them by choosing Edit NURBS → Attach Surfaces ❏. Make sure the tool is set to default (choose Edit → Reset Settings). Turn off Keep Originals, and click Attach. This blends the two surfaces into one, creates a smooth transition between them, and deletes the original surfaces.

Figure 5.37

Attach the patches.

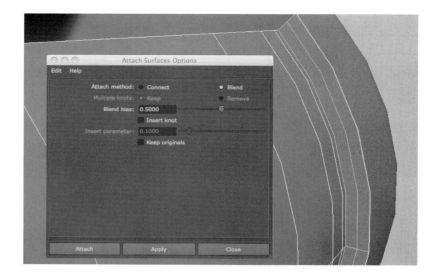

2. Here's the funny part: you need to disconnect the surfaces. Select the isoparm at the location where the patches originally met, and choose Edit NURBS → Detach Surfaces. Again, make sure the tool is reset to default so as not to keep the original patches. This gives you tangency across the two patches as well as a smooth transition in the model.

3. Repeat steps 1 and 2 for the other end of the cylinder and its end cap and also for the upper cylinder and its two end caps. You should now have end caps with smooth attachments to the cylinders, as shown in Figure 5.38.

Figure 5.38

The end caps attach to the cylinders— smooth as low-cholesterol butter!

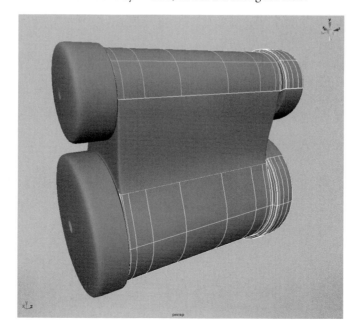

4. Connecting the upper and lower cylinders is next. Select the edge isoparms of both cylinders, and choose Surfaces → Loft ❑. Check to make sure to keep Section Spans to 2 in the Options box and click Apply. Repeat to create a loft on the back side of the cylinders as well. Figure 5.39 shows the resulting surfaces.

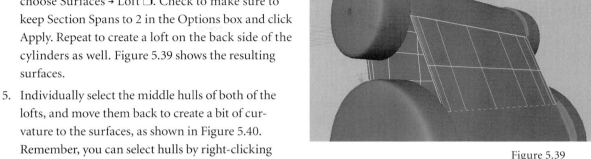

Figure 5.39

Lofting the two cylinders together

5. Individually select the middle hulls of both of the lofts, and move them back to create a bit of curvature to the surfaces, as shown in Figure 5.40. Remember, you can select hulls by right-clicking the surface and using the marking menu.

6. Select the edge isoparms of the lofts you just created, and loft between them with two spans. Make sure you reset the settings by choosing Edit → Reset Settings in the Options box, and then set Section Spans to 2 spans before you create the loft. Repeat for the other side. Figure 5.41 shows the closed ends.

Figure 5.40

Move back the middle and lower-middle hulls.

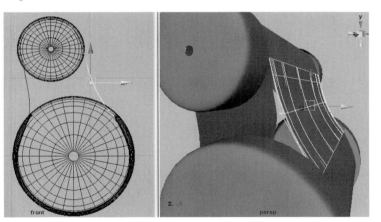

Figure 5.41

Closing the sides

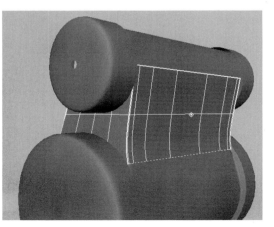

7. Go into CV mode, and move the CVs to line up the edges of the newly formed closed ends with the bottom and top cylinders. Repeat for the other side, as shown in Figure 5.42.

8. As you did in steps 1 and 2, attach and then detach the loft you just edited with CVs (we'll call it the side panel) and the front panel, as shown in Figure 5.43, to set up a smooth transition and a tangency. Repeat for the back panel and the other end of the cylinders to make the other side panel.

Figure 5.42

In CV mode, line up the ends and cylinders.

Figure 5.43

Create a smooth transition between the surfaces.

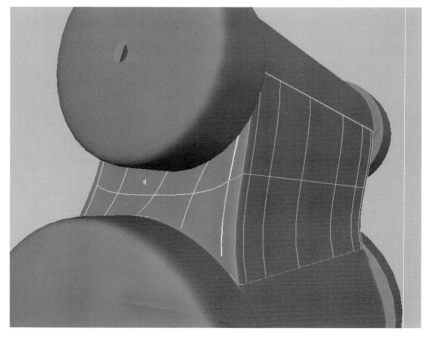

9. Shift your attention to one of the end caps on the lower cylinder. In step 5 in the previous section, and as shown in Figure 5.33, you detached a pizza-slice shape out of the end caps. Select the detached slice, and insert two isoparms between the existing ones. Your model should resemble the one in Figure 5.44 with the added isoparms. This is set up for another attachment in a moment. Repeat for the other end cap on the lower cylinder.

10. Select isoparms on the edges of the end cap and the side panel, and loft between them with two spans. Repeat for the other side. Doing so plugs the hole between the end cap and the side panels. You can, if you like, run another attach and detach to smooth out the groove between the end caps and the side panels. Figure 5.45 shows the end result of the groove.

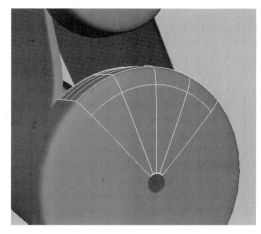

Figure 5.44

Insert isoparms into the end cap slice.

Figure 5.45

The groove connecting the end cap with the side panel

11. You're getting kicked out into the cold now to run the same set of procedures on the upper cylinder and its end caps. These should be simpler, because there are fewer sections to deal with. Go ahead and finish the model from here to form the connections shown in Figure 5.46 and to form the final model shown in Figure 5.47.

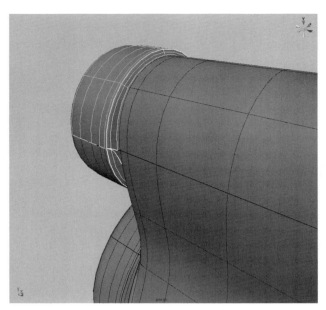

Figure 5.46

Finishing the top part of the NURBS pump

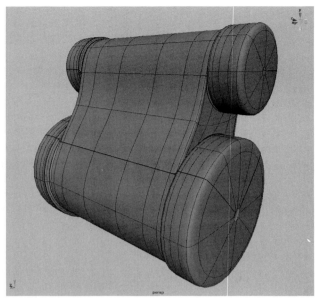

Figure 5.47

The finished pump

As you can see, there is quite a bit of lofting, attaching, and detaching between surface patches in patch modeling. The key to becoming good at it is to be able to line up isoparms easily and cleverly and to be able to attach them again smoothly. This type of modeling isn't for the faint of heart, and it takes a lot of practice to get used to this technique. You'll make a lot of mistakes along the way, but that is how you'll learn the most! It's easy to see how this kind of modeling is useful for making organic shapes such as faces.

Using Artisan to Sculpt NURBS

Imagine that you can create a NURBS surface and sculpt it using your cursor the way hands are used on wet clay to mold the surface. You can do just that with a Maya module called Artisan—and without the mess!

Try This Artisan is basically a 3D painting system that allows you to paint directly onto a surface. By painting on the surface with the Sculpt Geometry tool, you move the CV points in and out, effectively molding the surface.

1. In Shaded mode (press 5), maximize the Perspective window (press the spacebar) for a nice big view. Create a NURBS sphere, and open the Attribute Editor. In the sphere's creation node (makeNurbSphere1), set Sections to 24 and Spans to 12. The greater the surface definition, the more detailed the sculpting.

2. Select the sphere, and choose Edit NURBS → Sculpt Geometry Tool ❑. Clicking the Options box opens the tool settings. You'll need those almost every time you paint with Artisan to change brush sizes and so forth.

Your cursor changes to the Artisan brush, as shown in Figure 5.48. The red circle around the brush cursor and the lettering displays the type of brush you're currently using. When the red lines point outside the circle and the lettering reads *Ps*, you're using the *push* brush that pushes in the surface as you paint it. The black arrow pointing toward the sphere's center is a measurement of the Max Displacement slider in the tool settings. This sets how far each stroke pushes in the surface. The lower the number, the less the brush affects the surface.

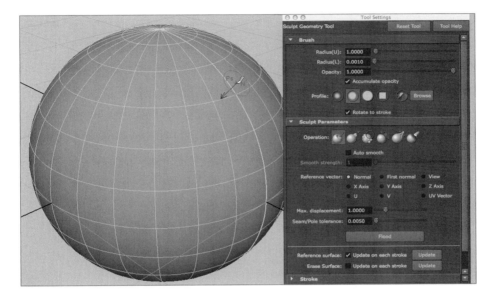

Figure 5.48

The Sculpt Geometry tool lets you mold your surface by painting on it. Here the brush is set to push in the surface of the sphere as you paint.

3. Click and drag the cursor across the surface of the sphere to get a feel for how the surface deforms under your tool. Use the Max Displacement slider to control the force of the brush, and use Radius (U) and Radius (L) to set the size of the brush.

4. Switch your brush type to *pull*. Your cursor changes to read *Pl*, and the red lines appear on the inside of the circle (see Figure 5.49). You can then pull out the surface.

> The Opacity slider also controls the force of the brush, but it's subtler than Max Displacement to give you greater control. Because this is after all a 3D painting tool, Opacity controls how much value you paint onto the surface. The value in this case isn't a color, but how far the surface is deformed. You'll see how Artisan comes into play in other aspects of Maya later in the book.

5. *Smooth* blends the pushed in and pulled out areas of the surface to yield a smoother result. *Erase* simply erases the deformations on the surface, setting it back to the way it was before.

Figure 5.49

With a pull brush, your cursor changes to read *PI*.

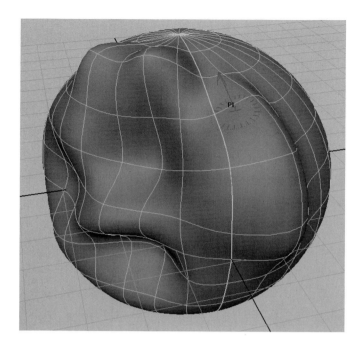

If you plan to sculpt a more detailed surface, be sure to create the surface with plenty of surface spans and sections. If you only want to paint a specific area of a NURBS surface, choose Edit NURBS → Insert Isoparms to add extra detail to that area before you begin painting, although you can add isoparms after you paint. When you begin to sculpt this way, going back into the surface's creation node to increase its sections and spans will ruin your results.

> **AUTODESK MUDBOX AND PIXOLOGIC ZBRUSH FOR SCULPTING**
>
> Although sculpting a surface in Maya with Artisan is convenient, the tool can take you only so far with your sculpture. For intricate sculpting and modeling, artists frequently use Autodesk's Mudbox or Pixologic's ZBrush programs. Both interface with Maya easily and give you very intricate control while sculpting your model. The workflow can start with a basic model shaped out in Maya, transferred to the sculpting package, and then detailed. It's then exported from that package and reimported into Maya to be integrated back into the scene as needed.

Modeling with Simple Deformers

In many ways, deformers are the Swiss Army knives of Maya animation, except you can't open a bottle with them. *Deformers* are handy for creating and editing modeled shapes in Maya. These tools allow you to change the shape of an object easily. Rather than using

CVs or vertices to distort or bend an object manually, you can use a deformer to affect the entire object. Popular deformers, such as Bend and Flare, can be powerful tools for adjusting your models quickly and evenly, as you're about to see.

Nonlinear deformers, such as Bend and Flare, create simple shape adjustments for the attached geometry, such as bending the object. You can also use deformers in animation to create effects or deformations in your objects. We'll explore this later in the book.

Modeling Using the Bend Deformer

Let's apply a deformer. In a new Maya scene, you'll create a polygonal cylinder and bend it to get a quick idea of how deformers work. Follow these steps:

Figure 5.50

Create a cylinder to bend.

1. Choose Create → Polygon Primitives, and turn on Interactive Creation. Then, choose Create → Polygon Primitives → Cylinder. Click and drag to create the base. Make it a few units in diameter; the exact sizing isn't important here. Click and drag to make the height of the cylinder 7 or 8 units, as shown in Figure 5.50. Make sure your create options are set to the defaults so that they're consistent with these directions.

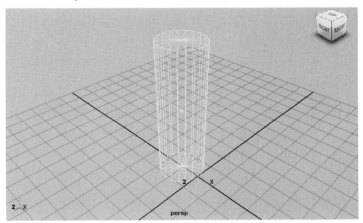

To make sure the settings are at their defaults, open the command's Options box and click the Reset Settings button.

2. Let's jump right in and create the Bend deformer. With the cylinder selected, switch to the Animation menu set by pressing F2 and choosing Create Deformers → Nonlinear → Bend. Your cylinder turns magenta, and a thin line appears at the center of the cylinder, running lengthwise. Figure 5.51 shows the deformer and its Channel Box attributes. Depending on your settings, your deformer may be created in a different axis than the one pictured. You can reset

Figure 5.51

Creating the Bend deformer

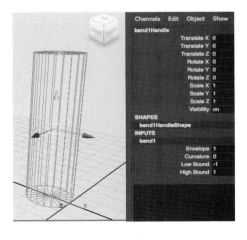

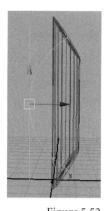

Figure 5.52

Notice the problem with this cylinder?

the deformer's options as needed. Click bend1 in the Channel Box to expand the deformer's attributes shown in the figure.

3. Click Curvature, and enter a value of **1**. Notice that the cylinder takes on an odd shape, as shown in Figure 5.52. The Bend deformer itself is bending nicely, but the geometry isn't. As a matter of fact, the geometry is now offset from its original location. It's offset because there aren't enough divisions in the geometry to allow for a smooth bend.

4. Select the cylinder, and click polyCylinder1 in the Channel Box to expand the shape node's attributes. Enter a value of **12** for the Subdivisions Height attribute (see Figure 5.53), and your cylinder will bend with the deformer properly, as shown in Figure 5.54.

5. Try adjusting the Bend deformer's Low and High Bound attributes. This allows you to bend one part of the cylinder without affecting the other. Figure 5.55 shows the cylinder with the Bend deformer's High Bound set to 0.25 instead of 1. This causes the top half of the cylinder to bend only one quarter of the way up and continue straight from there.

Experiment with moving the Bend deformer, and see how doing so affects the geometry of the cylinder. The deformer's position plays an important role in how it shapes an object's geometry.

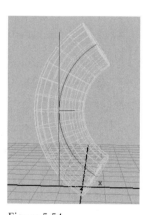

Figure 5.54

The cylinder bends properly now that it has the right number of divisions.

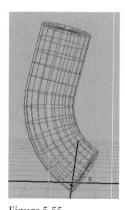

Figure 5.55

Using the High Bound to change the effect of the Bend deformer

Figure 5.53

Increase Subdivisions Height to 12.

Adjusting an Existing Axe Model

In this exercise, you'll take an existing NURBS model of an axe and fine-tune the back end of the axe head. In the existing model, the back end of the axe head is blunt, as you can see in Figure 5.56. You'll need to sharpen the blunt end with a nonlinear deformer. Open the AxeHead_v01.ma file in the Scenes folder of the Axe project on the CD, and follow these steps:

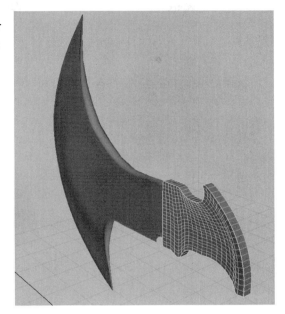

Figure 5.56

The axe head is blunt.

1. Select the top group of the axe head's back end. To do so, open the Outliner, and select axeHead_Back (see Figure 5.57).

2. Click F2 to switch to the Animation menu set.

3. Create a Flare deformer by choosing Create Deformers → Nonlinear → Flare. The Flare deformer appears as a cylindrical object (see Figure 5.58).

Figure 5.57

Select the back of the axe head.

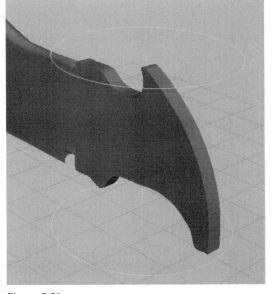

Figure 5.58

The Flare deformer appears as a cylinder.

Figure 5.59

Rotate the deformer 90 degrees in the Z-axis.

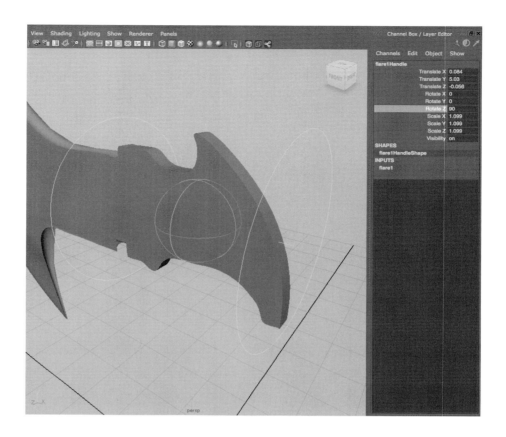

4. Rotate the deformer 90 degrees in the *Z*-axis, as shown in Figure 5.59.

5. Open the Attribute Editor (Ctrl+A), click the flare1 tab to access the Flare controls, and enter the following values:

ATTRIBUTE	VALUE
Start Flare Z	0.020
High Bound	0.50

These values taper in the end of that part of the axe head, as shown in Figure 5.60. This is a much easier way of sharpening the blunt end than adjusting the individual CVs of the NURBS surfaces.

Deformers use History to distort the geometry to which they're attached. You can animate any of the attributes that control the deformer shapes, but in this case you're using the deformer as a means to adjust a model. When you get the desired shape, as shown in Figure 5.61, you can discard the deformer. However, simply selecting and deleting the deformer will reset the geometry to its original blunt shape. You need to pick the

axeHead_Back geometry group (not the deformer) and delete its History by choosing
Edit → Delete by Type → History.

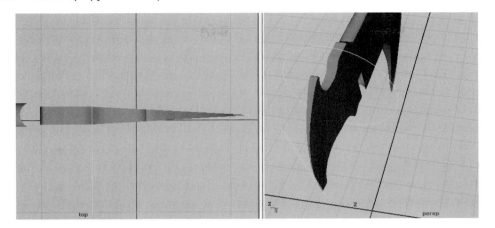

Figure 5.60

**Sharpen the axe's
back edge.**

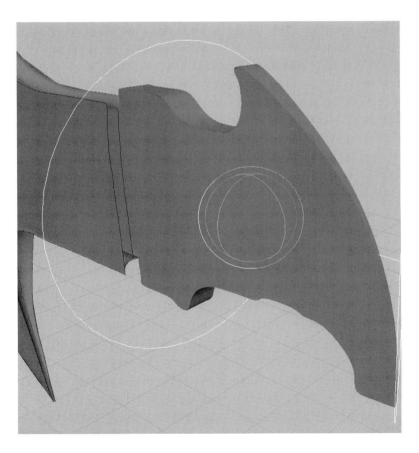

Figure 5.61

**Another view of
the back of the axe
head with the Flare
deformer**

The Lattice Deformer

A simple deformer, such as a Bend or Flare, will get you only so far; when a model requires more intricate editing with a deformer, you'll need to use a lattice.

A *lattice* is a scaffold that fits around your geometry. The lattice object controls the shape of the geometry. When you adjust the Lattice deformer, the geometry deforms to match. When a lattice point is moved, the lattice smoothly deforms the underlying geometry. The more lattice points, the greater control you have. The more divisions the geometry has, the more smoothly the geometry will deform, as you saw with the bending cylinder in the previous example.

Lattices are especially useful when you need to edit a relatively complex poly mesh or NURBS surface that is too dense to edit efficiently directly with CVs or vertices. Instead, you assign a lattice and use it to create changes. This way, you don't have to move the individual surface points.

Lattices can work on any surface type, and a single lattice can affect multiple surfaces simultaneously. You can also move an object through a lattice (or vice versa) to animate a deformation effect, such as a golf ball sliding through a garden hose.

Creating an Alien Hand

Make sure you're in the Animation menu set. To adjust an existing model or surface, select the model(s) or applicable groups to deform, and choose Create Deformers → Lattice. Figure 5.62 shows a polygonal hand model with a default lattice applied. The top node of the hand has been selected and the lattice applied.

Figure 5.62

A lattice is applied to the polygonal hand model.

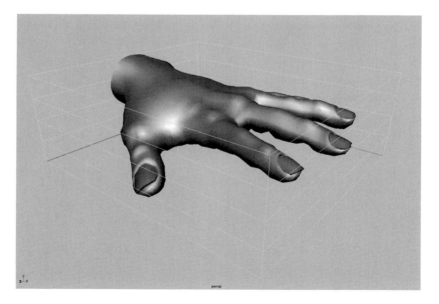

To experience how this works, you'll remodel the poly hand using a few different lattices. Your objective is to create an alien hand by thinning and elongating the hand and each of the fingers—we all know aliens have long gawky fingers. Because it would take a lot of time and effort to achieve this by moving the vertices of the poly mesh, using lattices here is ideal.

To elongate and thin the entire hand, load the scene file `detailed_poly_hand.ma` from the Poly_Hand project on the CD, and follow these steps:

1. Select the top node of the hand (poly_hand) in the Outliner, and choose Create Deformers → Lattice. Doing so creates a default lattice that affects the entire hand, fingernails and all, as shown in Figure 5.62. Although you can change the lattice settings in the Options window upon creation, you'll edit the lattice after it's applied to the hand.

2. The lattice is selected after it's created. Open the Attribute Editor, and click the ffd-1LatticeShape tab. The three attributes of interest here are S Divisions, T Divisions, and U Divisions. These sliders control how many divisions the lattice uses to deform its geometry. Set S Divisions to 3, set T Divisions to 2, and set U Divisions to 3 for the result shown in Figure 5.63.

Figure 5.63

Changing the number of divisions in the lattice

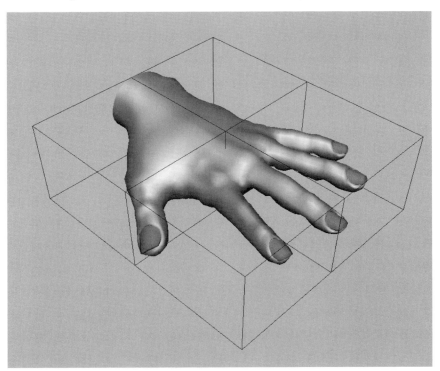

A 3 x 2 x 3 lattice refers to the number of division lines in the lattice as opposed to the number of sections; otherwise, this would be a 2 x 1 x 2 lattice!

3. With the lattice selected, press F8 to switch to Component mode and display the lattice's points. These points act just like the vertices on a polygonal shape. You'll use them to change the overall shape of the hand without moving the vertices of the hand. Select the vertices on the thumb side of the hand, and move them to squeeze in that half of the hand. Notice how only that zone of the model is affected by that part of the lattice.

4. Toggle back to Object mode (press F8 again), and scale the entire lattice to be thinner in the *Z*-axis and longer in the *X*-axis. The entire hand is deformed in accordance with how the lattice is scaled (see Figure 5.64).

5. Now that you've altered the hand, you have no need for this lattice. If you delete the lattice, the hand will snap back to its original shape. You don't want this to happen. Instead, you need to delete the construction history on the hand to get rid of the lattice, as you did with the axe head exercise earlier in this chapter.

Select the top node of the hand, and choose Edit → Delete by Type → History.

Figure 5.64

Lengthen the hand using the deformer.

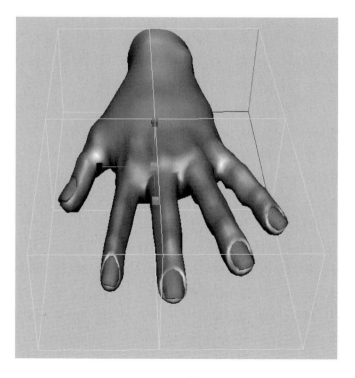

Creating Alien Fingers

The next step is to elongate the individual fingers and widen the knuckles. Let's begin with the index finger. Follow these steps:

1. Select the top node of the hand, and create a new lattice as before. It forms around the entire hand.

   Although you can divide the lattice so that its divisions line up with the fingers, it's much easier and more inter-active to scale and position the entire lattice so it fits around the index finger only.

Figure 5.65
Select the lattice and base nodes.

2. Simply moving and scaling the selected lattice will deform the hand geometry. You don't want to do this. Instead, you need to select the lattice and its base node. This lets you change the lattice without affecting the hand. In the Outliner, select both the ffd1Lattice and ffd1Base nodes (see Figure 5.65).

3. Scale, rotate, and transform the lattice to fit around the index finger, as shown in Figure 5.66.

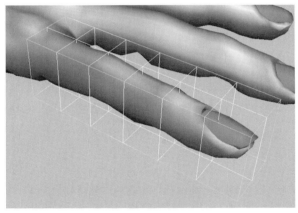

Figure 5.66
Position the lattice and its base to fit around the index finger.

4. Deselect the base, and set the lattice S Divisions to 7, T Divisions to 2, and U Divisions to 3.

5. Adjust the lattice to lengthen the finger by pulling the lat-tice points (see Figure 5.67). Pick the lattice points around each of the knuckles individually, and scale them sideways to widen them.

6. To delete the lattice and keep the changes to the finger, select the top node of the hand and delete its His-tory. Repeat this entire procedure for the rest of the fingers to finish your alien hand. (Try to creep out your younger sister with it.)

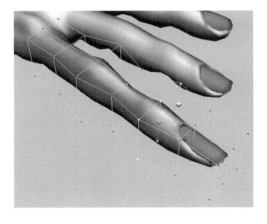

Figure 5.67
Flare out the knuckles.

The alien hand in Figure 5.68 was created by adjusting the polygonal hand from this exercise using only lattices.

As you can see, lattices give you powerful editing capabilities without the complication of dealing with surface points directly. Lattices can help you reshape an entire complex model quickly or adjust minor details on parts of a larger whole.

In Chapter 8, "Introduction to Animation," you'll animate an object using another type of deformer. You'll also learn how to deform an object through a path.

Figure 5.68

The human hand model is transformed into an alien hand by using lattices to deform the geometry.

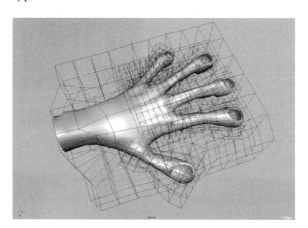

Animating through a Lattice

Lattices don't only work on polygons; they can be used on any geometry in Maya and at any stage in your workflow to create or adjust models. You can also use lattices to create animated effects. In the next exercise, you'll animate an object through a simple lattice.

In the previous example, if you moved the hand geometry through the lattice while it was still applied to one of the fingers, you should have seen an interesting effect before you deleted the last of your lattices. The parts of the geometry of the hand deformed as the hand traveled through the lattice. Think of ways you can use this warping effect in an animation. For example, you can create the effect of a balloon squeezing through a pipe by animating the balloon geometry through a lattice.

In the following exercise, you'll create a NURBS sphere with 8 sections and 16 spans, and an open-ended NURBS cylinder that has no end caps:

1. Choose Create → NURBS Primitives → Sphere ❏, and set the Sections to 8 and Spans to 16 and create the sphere.

2. Choose Create → NURBS Primitives → Cylinder ❏, and check None for the Caps option. Scale and arrange the sphere balloon and cylinder pipe as shown in Figure 5.69.

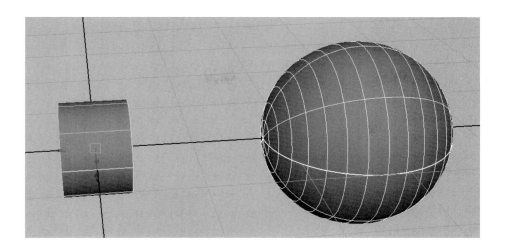

Figure 5.69
Arrange the balloon and pipe.

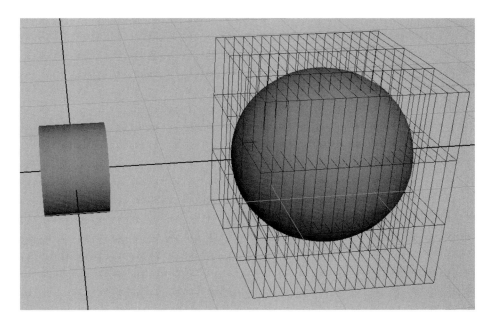

Figure 5.70
Create a lattice for the sphere.

3. Select the balloon, and create a lattice for it (see Figure 5.70). (From the Animation menu set, choose Create Deformers → Lattice.) Set the S, T, and U Divisions to 4, 19, and 4, respectively. You set this number of lattice divisions to create a smoother deformation when the sphere goes through the pipe.

4. Select the lattice and its base in the Outliner (ffd1Lattice and ffd1Base nodes), and move the middle of the lattice so it fits over the length of the pipe (see Figure 5.71).

Figure 5.71

Relocate the lattice to the cylinder.

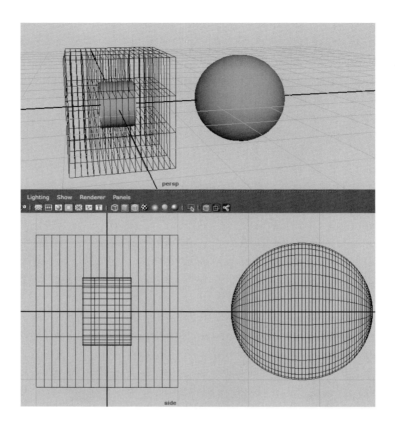

5. Deselect the lattice base, and go to Component mode for the lattice. Select the appropriate points, and shape the lattice so the middle of the lattice fits into the cylinder (see Figure 5.72).

6. Select the sphere, and move it back and forth through the pipe and lattice. Notice how it squeezes to fit through. If you look closely, you'll see that the sphere starts to squeeze a little before it enters the pipe. You'll also see parts of the sphere sticking out of the very ends of the pipe. This effect, in which geometry passes through itself or another surface, is called *interpenetration*. You can avoid this by using a more highly segmented sphere and lattice. If you try this exercise with a lower-segmented sphere and/or lattice, you'll notice the interpenetrations even more. Figure 5.73 shows the balloon squeezing through the pipe.

In a similar fashion, you can create a lattice along a curve path and have an object travel through it. You'll try this in Chapter 8.

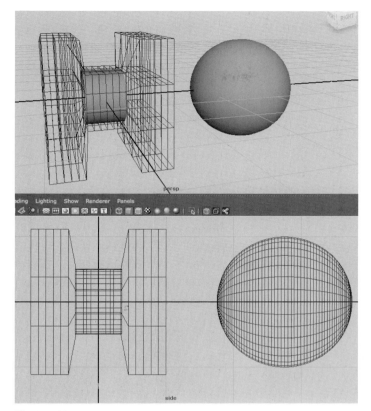

Figure 5.72
Squeeze in the lattice points to fit the cylinder.

Figure 5.73
Squeezing the balloon through the pipe using a Lattice deformer

Subdivision Surfaces

Subdivision surfaces combine the best features of NURBS and polygonal modeling and are useful for intricate surfaces such as faces. Using subdivision surfaces, you can model complex characters and create models from single primitives (as in polygonal modeling) but with perfectly smooth surfaces (as in NURBS modeling).

Like lattices, subdivision surfaces rely on varying levels of editing detail that allow you to adjust a surface from a global level, where large parts of the model are modified, to a micro level, where you have control over the most dense surface points.

Typical subdivision workflow begins when you create a simple polygonal mesh of your model. The polygon is converted to a subdivision surface that you can edit using any number of subdivision detail levels. More often than not, the resulting subdivision surface is then converted back to a polygonal object for use in production. Subdivision surfaces can also be converted to NURBS patches.

The Subdivision Surfaces (or *SubD,* as they're called) toolset is found in the Surfaces menu set (press F4). You'll find yourself switching back and forth within the Polygons menu set (press F3). Just remember these hotkeys, and you'll be switching like a pro in no time.

Creating a Starfish

Now, you'll create a starfish model starting with polygons, like the models you created in Chapter 4. You'll then convert the polygon mesh to a subdivision surface to mold it into a proper starfish. Follow these steps:

1. Create a new scene, and switch into the Polygons menu set. With Interactive Creation turned off, create a polygon cube and scale it to be 8 wide, 8 deep, and 1.2 high.

2. Use the Split Polygon tool (Edit Mesh → Split Polygon Tool) to split one side of the box into halves (see Figure 5.74). You can right-click every time you finish one of the splits without exiting the tool. When you do this, center the new edge by using the readout display in the Feedback bar (at lower-left on the screen) to place the split at 50 percent along each edge.

Figure 5.74

Split the sides.

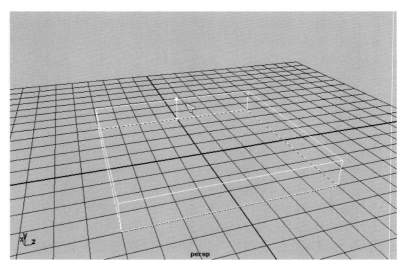

When you invoke the Split Polygon tool, Maya's view panel prompts you to select along the first edge.

3. Reshape the box into an irregular pentagon, as shown in Figure 5.75, by selecting the polygonal edges of the box in Component mode (F8) and moving them one by one. You needn't make all five sides exactly the same size—real starfish are irregular— but be careful not to move any of the edges up or down in the *Y*-axis because you want the pentagon to be flat.

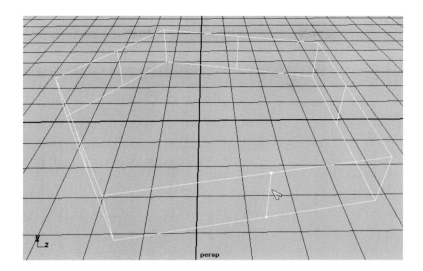

Figure 5.75

After the pentagon is created, split each face into two.

4. Use the ever-popular Split Polygon tool again to cut all five sides in half, as shown in Figure 5.75. You'll use these edges to create a polygonal star, which you'll then convert to the subdivision surface.

5. Use the newly created edges to shape the pentagon into a star by moving the edges in toward the center (see Figure 5.76). This will be the basis for your starfish subdivision surface.

6. Save your work, and compare it to the scene file Starfish_v01.ma in the Starfish project on the CD.

Figure 5.76

Create a star shape.

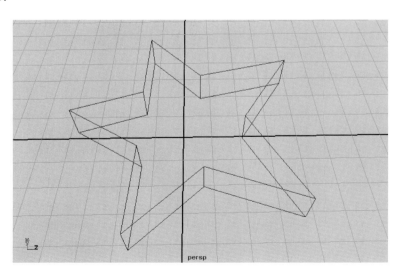

Converting to a Subdivision Surface

Now that you have the basic polygonal shape for the starfish, convert it to a subdivision surface. Follow these steps:

1. Select the star, and then choose Modify → Convert → Polygons to Subdiv. The star turns into a smooth subdivision surface, as shown in Figure 5.77.

2. Although you've all but lost the points of the star by converting it to smooth subdivisions, you have far greater control. Press the 3 key to increase the display resolution of the surface. As they do with NURBS objects, the 1, 2, and 3 keys set the display resolution of a subdivision surface.

3. With the starfish still selected, switch to the Surfaces menu set (F4) and choose Subdiv Surfaces → Polygon Proxy Mode. This switches Maya to a low-level editing mode and restores the shape of the star as a cage around the starfish (see Figure 5.78). Note that the star here isn't the surface of the starfish, but a proxy that shapes the subdivision surface, much as a lattice does. Switch to Component mode (F8), and you see vertices on the polygon proxy (sometimes called a *cage*) that you can move to shape the starfish.

4. Change the display of the vertices of the subdivision surfaces before continuing. To do so, click Window → Setting/Preferences → Preferences and select Display → Subdivs in the Categories list on the left. Set the Component display to Numbers for this exercise.

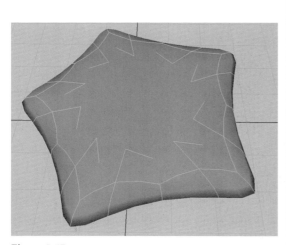

Figure 5.77

Converting the star shape to a subdivision

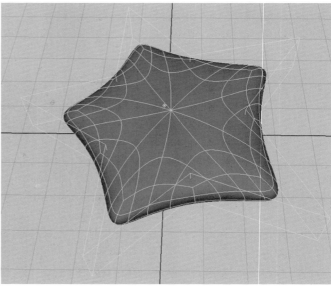

Figure 5.78

The starfish's cage

5. Using the *polygon proxy* to shape the starfish is a good way to create broad strokes when creating your final model. It won't yield good results by itself, however.

    Press F8 to go back to the Object Selection mode, where you can select the starfish and not its vertices, and then switch back to Standard mode (choose Subdiv Surfaces → Standard Mode). With the starfish still selected, enter Component mode to select vertices. The vertices of the starfish appear in the same locations as the points on the polygon proxy and are represented with zeros, as in Figure 5.79.

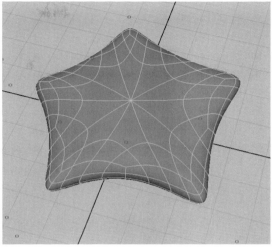

Figure 5.79

The zeros represent the zero level of detail on this subdivision starfish and correspond to the vertices on its polygon proxy.

6. Right-click the starfish to open a marking menu, and choose Display Level → 1. You'll define the arms of the fish at this level of detail. Select the vertices (now represented with 1s, as in Figure 5.80) between each point, and pull them in toward the center of the fish. This level of detail is automatically generated when you convert a poly image to a subdivision surface. Maya also has another level of detail (Display Level → 2), which you'll use later.

    If by chance you don't see Display Level → 2 as an option and Display Level → 1 is the highest detail level you have, you can create a higher level of display by selecting all the level 1 vertices on the starfish in Component mode and choosing Subdiv Surfaces → Refine Selected Components to create level 2 vertices. You'll then be able to choose Display Level → 2 when needed.

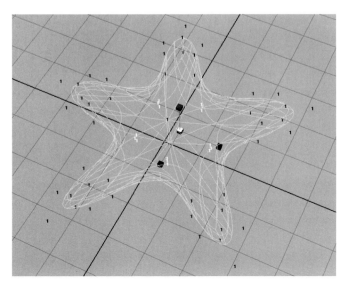

Figure 5.80

Level 1 of the starfish

7. Save your file, and compare your work to the scene file `Starfish_v02.ma` in the Starfish project on the CD.

8. Right-click the starfish, and choose Display Level → 2. The vertices on the next higher detail level appear and are represented by 2s. At this level of detail, you can move these vertices to give your starfish more character. Try making the areas between the points on the star smoother, as shown in Figure 5.81. Also try to flatten the bottom of the starfish using either level 1 or level 2 vertices.

9. To achieve the appearance shown in Figure 5.81, you may need to detail your starfish further in some areas. As it stands now, the starfish can be edited up to level 2. To create another level of detail, select the areas you want to refine by selecting the level 2 vertices along the outside of each star point, as shown in Figure 5.82.

10. With those vertices selected, right-click the selection, and choose Refine Selected from the marking menu. Maya adds another level of detail to that area of the starfish with vertices marked as 2s. This allows you to make more detailed adjustments to the surface to mold it to your liking. Work the vertices at all levels to sculpt your starfish so it looks similar to the one in Figure 5.81.

Right-clicking the starfish and choosing Refine Selected is the same as selecting the vertices and choosing Subdiv Surfaces → Refine Selected Components. Choosing vertices in an area of your model and refining them beyond a display level of 2 creates more vertices for that area only. You can continue to refine your selection as needed. At any time, you can go back to Polygon Proxy mode to access the lowest level of detail and adjust the broad strokes of the model.

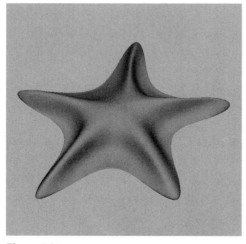

Figure 5.81

A molded starfish

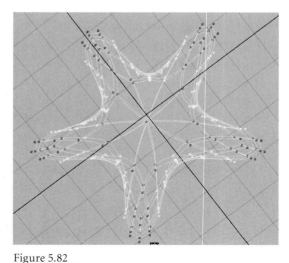

Figure 5.82

Select the area to be refined.

11. Save your work again, and open the scene file `Starfish_v03.ma` in the Starfish project on the CD to compare your work with the model.

> You can use these same techniques to re-create the polygon hand from Chapter 4 with subdivision surfaces.

Building a Teakettle

Now that you've experienced the mechanics of subdivision surface modeling and editing, you're ready to work on another model. The next subdivision exercise asks you to create a teakettle. You'll fashion the kettle from simple polygon shapes and then refine it using subdivisions.

Creating the Base Polygon Model

To create the base poly mesh for the kettle, follow these steps:

1. The main body of the kettle begins as a poly cylinder. Choose Create → Polygon Primitives → Cylinder → ❐ to open the Options box. Set Axis Divisions to 8, and set Height Divisions to 4.

2. To create the lid, create another poly cylinder with 8 subdivisions around the axis and 2 for the height. Scale it to fit as a lid on the first cylinder.

3. Select the upper row of poly edges on the lid, and scale them all in to create a bevel, as shown in Figure 5.83. Select every other edge on the top surface and delete them, as shown in Figure 5.84.

4. Select the poly edges of the main cylinder, and scale them out increasingly larger as you work your way down. Delete every other edge of the top surface as you did with the lid. Your kettle should look like the one in Figure 5.85.

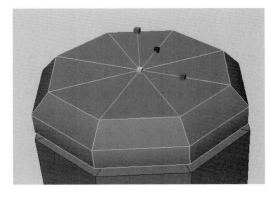

Figure 5.83

Scale the outer edges inward.

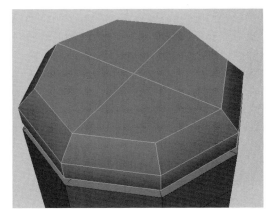

Figure 5.84

Delete every other edge of the top surface.

Figure 5.85

Creating the overall shape

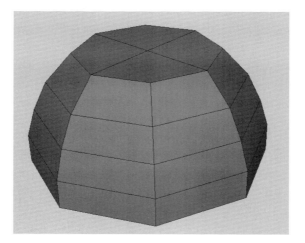

5. Select the lid's top four faces. You can create a handle by extruding these faces and scaling them in. First, make sure the option Edit Mesh → Keep Faces Together is enabled. This option lets you extrude these faces properly by keeping the poly faces together during the extrude operation. Now, select the four faces again, and choose Edit Mesh → Extrude → ☐. Choose Edit → Reset Settings to make sure the settings are correct, and click Extrude. Use the scale handles to scale the extruded faces in, as shown in Figure 5.86.

If instead of following these directions you chose Edit Mesh → Extrude and use the special scale handles shown in Figure 5.87, your faces may all separate.

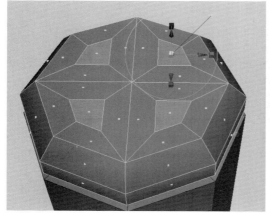

Figure 5.86

By default, faces extrude separately.

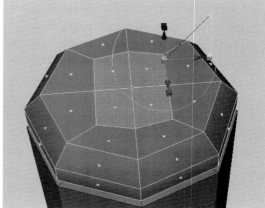

Figure 5.87

The Keep Faces Together command allows you to extrude the faces together.

6. With those four faces still selected, extrude the faces again, but this time pull them up and scale them in a bit, as shown in Figure 5.88.

7. Select the side faces of the lid's new handle, and extrude the faces inward using the scale handle to create detail on the handle.

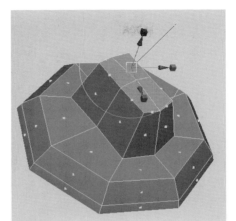

Figure 5.88

Pulling up the lid's handle

8. Select the edges that make up the lid handle, and move them to round out the handle, as shown in Figure 5.89.

9. Select the four faces on the top of the kettle, and extrude them. Scale the faces in, and pull them up to round the top of the kettle, as shown in Figure 5.90.

10. Select the kettle, and apply a lattice to it by choosing Create Deformers → Lattice (in the Animation menu set). In the Channel Box, with the new lattice select, set S Divisions to 2, T Divisions to 3, and U Divisions to 2. Adjust the lattice to bend the kettle back to create the front. Figure 5.91 shows the lattice's final position. When you have the proper shape, select the kettle, and delete its History to delete the lattice.

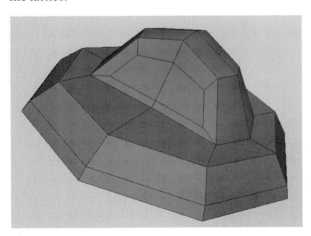

Figure 5.89
Round out the handle by moving the edges.

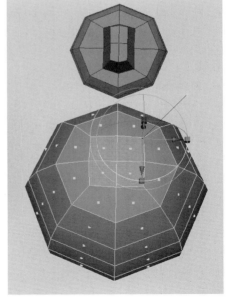

Figure 5.90
Round off the top of the kettle.

Figure 5.91

Use the lattice to bend the kettle.

11. Just before you convert the kettle to a subdivision surface, you need to create more detail at the bottom of the kettle so the subdivision surface won't round out and you'll still have a flat bottom. In the Side or Front view panel, select the kettle. Go to the Polygons menu set (F3), choose Edit Mesh → Insert Edge Loop Tool, and use the Insert Edge Loop tool to create a new division along the bottom of the kettle, as shown in Figure 5.92.

Figure 5.92

Use the Insert Edge Loop tool to create a straight division line across the bottom.

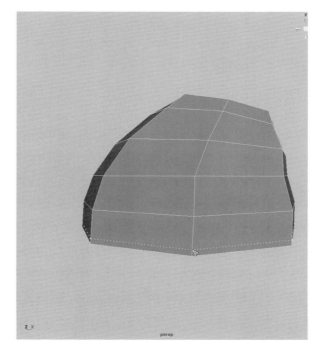

12. Select all the new faces along the bottom, and extrude them to create a lip that runs around the kettle's bottom, as shown in Figure 5.93. Be sure that Edit Mesh → Keep Faces Together is still selected; otherwise, the faces will separate. Luckily, the Keep Faces Together option appears at the top of the Edit Mesh menu whenever you access the tools in that menu, so you can verify that it's enabled without too much bother.

13. Save your scene file, and load the `Kettle_Model_v01.ma` file from the Tea_Kettle project on the CD to compare your work up to this point.

Figure 5.93
Creating the base

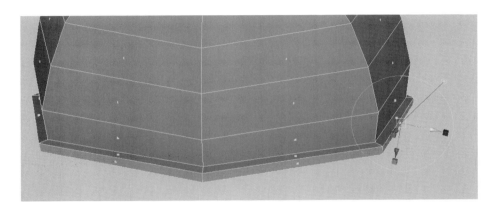

Converting to Subdivisions

When you complete the base polygon model for the kettle, you can convert it to a subdivision surface to round it out and make it smooth. To convert the kettle, follow these steps:

1. Select the kettle, and choose Modify → Convert → Polygons to Subdiv. Select the lid, and convert it as well.

2. Select the converted kettle and the lid, and press 3 to view them in High-Resolution mode. Position the lid on top of the kettle. Your model should be similar to that in Figure 5.94.

3. The only items you still need to model are the spout and a handle. For the handle, create a subdivision torus (choose Create → Subdiv Primitives → Torus). Scale, rotate, and place the torus above and around the lid on top of the kettle.

4. With the handle selected, choose Subdiv Surfaces → Polygon Proxy Mode in the Surfaces menu set. Using the vertices on the polygon proxy, make the handle thinner and elongate it upward, as shown in Figure 5.95.

Figure 5.94

The subdivision kettle and lid

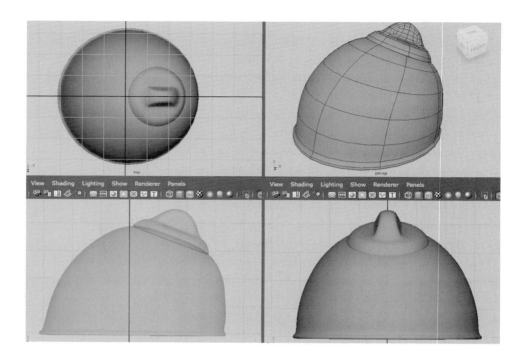

Figure 5.95

The kettle's handle

5. Return to Standard mode with the handle selected (choose Subdiv Surfaces → Standard Mode). To make the handle smoother, you can refine it and add more subdivisions. Switch to Component mode so the vertices of the handle display as 0s. Right-click the handle, and choose Refine Selected from the marking menu. New vertices appear as 1s. The handle should now be much smoother. Make any modeling adjustments to your liking. Using the right mouse button and the marking menu's Display Level command, switch between level 0 and level 1 displays as needed.

6. To create the spout, create a subdivision cylinder. Switch to Component mode to select the faces (not the vertices). Right-click the cylinder, and choose display level 2. Select the inside circle of faces on the top of the cylinder, as shown in Figure 5.96. Move them down into the cylinder to hollow it out, but create a thickness to the spout at the same time, as also shown in Figure 5.96.

7. Position the spout on the kettle. Move the vertices to flare out at the bottom of the spout where it meets the kettle. Figure 5.97 shows the completed kettle. Save your file.

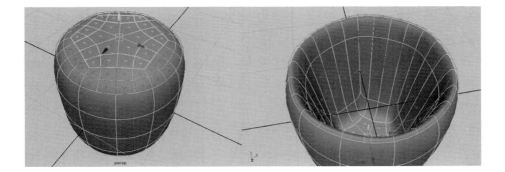

Figure 5.96

Hollow out the spout.

Figure 5.97

The completed subdivision teakettle

Converting Back to Polygons

Most models created with subdivision surfaces should be converted back to polygons after the modeling is finished and rendering setup is ready to begin. Because subdivisions are a more intricate surface type than polygons, you'll probably have better performance while animating if you work with a polygonal model rather than a subdivision. Professionals frequently use subdivision tools and surfaces to create their models but then convert back to polygons after they're finished to avoid excessive memory usage while rendering.

This is a simple procedure, similar to the earlier exercise in which you converted NURBS surfaces to polygons. Here you'll convert the kettle back to polygons:

1. Select the subdivision kettle and its handle, spout, and lid, and choose Modify → Convert → Subdiv to Polygons ❑ to open the Options box shown in Figure 5.98.

Figure 5.98

The Convert Subdiv to Polygons Options box

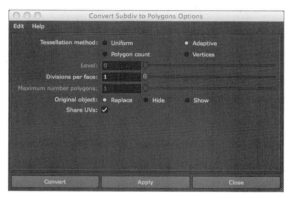

2. Select Adaptive for Tessellation Method. This option usually yields the best results.

3. The Divisions Per Face slider controls how smoothly the object is converted to polygons. For the best results, select each piece of the kettle separately and convert the pieces one by one, adjusting the Divisions Per Face value appropriately. A division value of 2 will work for everything but the handle, which requires a division value of at least 3 to remain fairly smooth.

> At a division factor of 1, your kettle will look jagged. Turn it up to 2, and you'll notice a faithful conversion to polygons.

More often than not, you'll want to take a model as far as possible before you convert it to polygons, but you should always save the original subdivision version in case it needs to be modified. This way, you can revert to your subdivision file, make your changes, and reconvert to polygons to render out the changes.

Taking the Kettle Further

Try creating more detail for the kettle or experimenting with your own designs. An easy addition is a whistle cap for the spout. You can also create a matching set of teacups and saucers with subdivision surfaces. With the skills you've acquired here, you should feel confident to tackle an entire kitchen full of models.

Summary

In this chapter, we tackled NURBS modeling by going through the usual surfacing tools, from lofting and revolving to bevels and boundary surfaces. Then, we explored the implications of surface History and how surfaces adjust to changes when History is enabled. You learned about different editing methods for NURBS surfaces, such as inserting isoparms and attaching surfaces together as well as converting those surfaces to poly meshes. You then put those lessons to work on creating a NURBS patch model for a steam pump for the locomotive model. Also in this chapter, we introduced you to the Artisan tool and how to use it to sculpt a NURBS surface.

This chapter covered various modeling techniques to help you break away from typical ways of thinking. You learned how to use a lattice to adjust a polygon hand model into an alien hand as well as how to animate a balloon pushing through a pipe. Moving on to a starfish model, you explored subdivision modeling techniques that are based on polygon modeling methods. Using polygons and SubDs hand-in-hand, you first made a teakettle out of polygons and then refined the model using subdivision modeling. Finally, you learned how to convert SubD models back to polygons.

Modeling is usually the first step of CG production. It's also almost always the first CG procedure at which students try to excel before moving on to other aspects of CG.

Using other tools such as a lattice to shape your model is not only a fantastic way of making gross or overall changes to a model, but also an excellent technique for adding fine detail in certain areas.

As you've seen in this and in the previous chapter, and as you'll see in the next chapter, you can accomplish a modeling task in several ways. Different workflows give you the flexibility to choose your own modeling style. To make good choices, however, you'll need to practice. Good modelers have a strong eye for detail and a high tolerance for work that is repetitious. They also love assembling a complex object, and they're thrilled by the eventual outcome.

Keep at it; model everything you get your hands and eyes on. Try the same model a few different ways; switch between NURBS, polygons, and subdivisions to become comfortable with Maya's toolset. As you're doing that, stay on top of how you organize your nodes, and keep everything named and organized: the organization of your scenes is extremely important.

For further practice, use this chapter as a reference to create some of the following NURBS or subdivision models:

Bathroom Sink Snap a few digital stills of your bathroom sink, or find some pictures on the Internet. A sink will give you a great chance to explore NURBS surfacing, making pristine curves and smooth surfaces. It may be a bit involved, but it's not overwhelming.

Couch or Love Seat Cushy furniture is great for NURBS as well as SubDs. Use lofting to make plush cushions, or use a primitive. It's up to you, but try it. You'll only get better with practice.

Disposable Lighter Sounds simple, but try to get detailed with it.

Cartoon Head Use Maya Artisan and the Sculpt Geometry tool to turn an ordinary sphere into a cartoonish head. It's fun to use Sculpt Geometry to model. Try to make the head using only Artisan.

Human Hand Use the polygon model exercise in Chapter 4, but this time convert the base poly model you create to subdivisions and then add detail to it.

Computer Mouse A PC or Mac mouse makes a great SubD or NURBS model.

Office Chair This will require a few different components. Start with a good ergonomic chair to reference. Then, try to make the major (if not all) components out of SubDs. Afterward, convert it to polygons for additional practice.

CHAPTER 6

Practical Experience

It's time to put what you've learned so far into action. In this chapter, you'll build a toy called the red wagon and a little wooden decorative box. The wagon project uses poly and NURBS modeling techniques to give you some practical experience with a larger project, and the decorative box exercise paves the way for extensive texturing, lighting, and rendering in Chapter 7, "Maya Shading and Texturing," Chapter 10, "Maya Lighting," and Chapter 11, "Maya Rendering."Topics in this chapter include:

- Using reference planes
- Polygonal modeling in action
- NURBS surfacing techniques
- Booleans
- Hierarchies

Beginning the Wagon Project

Copy the entire RedWagon project folder structure to your computer's hard drive. Set your current project to RedWagon on your local machine; don't set your project to the RedWagon project on the CD itself. That would be bad news.

Figure 6.1

The red wagon

Figure 6.1 shows the red wagon you'll be modeling first in this chapter. There's certainly enough detail in this object to make it a good exercise, but it won't be difficult to complete. You can always come back to this exercise to add more of your own detail or even redesign it for more challenge, which is something I highly recommend.

Study the wagon closely to get a good idea of what you'll be modeling.

Using Reference Planes

References aren't just for fun! You can also import images into Maya to work directly on the reference. For a model like this, it's best to create three different image views of the model (front, side, and top) to give you the most information as you build the model. The first step, of course, is to take pictures of your intended model from these three angles. Figures 6.2, 6.3, and 6.4 show photos taken of the front, side, and top views of the wagon.

Figure 6.2

The wagon's front

Figure 6.3

The wagon's side view

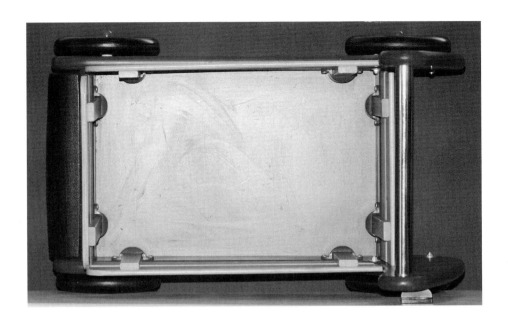

Figure 6.4

The wagon's top view

The trick here is to bring the photos into an image-editing program, such as Adobe Photoshop, and scale the images to line them up as shown in Figure 6.5. The figure has the added benefit of a view of the wagon taken from the back. The images have been copied and pasted into a larger frame, and grid lines are used to line up the major portions of the wagon, such as its wheels.

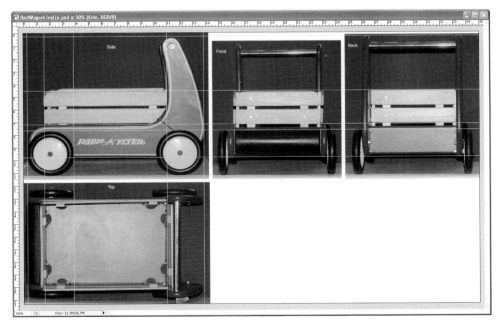

Figure 6.5

The views of the wagon roughly lined up in Photoshop

Keep in mind that when you take a photo, in most cases, there will be *perspective shift* or parallax in the image. Because of that shift, the different views of the same object will never exactly line up. As you can see in Figure 6.5, the height of the wagon doesn't line up between the front view and the back view, even though all the other major elements of the wagon are in alignment. This is due to perspective shift. Because the handle of the wagon is farther back from the lens of the camera in the front view, it appears lower in the frame than the handle in the back view.

Complete accuracy isn't what you're after in this situation. You just want to have a reasonable reference, and this will be more than adequate. Now, you'll import the images and create the model reference planes on which to work.

Creating Reference Planes for the Images

The reference views of the wagon have already been created for you. You can find them in the `Sourceimages` folder of the RedWagon project. They're shown in Table 6.1. Hoorah!

Table 6.1
Reference Views and Sizes

FILENAME	VIEW	IMAGE SIZE	ASPECT RATIO
RedWagonFront.jpg	Front	714 × 783	0.912:1
RedWagonSide.jpg	Side	1024 × 829	1.235:1
RedWagonTop.jpg	Top	1024 × 687	1.490:1

Why is the image resolution important? Well, it's not so much the resolution of the photos, but rather the aspect ratio of each image. To properly map these images onto the planes you'll use in Maya, each plane has to be the same ratio in scale as its image. For example, an image that is 100 × 50 pixels has an aspect ratio of 2:1 and is, therefore, a wide horizontal rectangle. For it to map properly, the plane on which it's mapped in Maya must also have a scale ratio of 2:1, so that it's also a wide horizontal rectangle. Otherwise, the image may distort. The more accurate your model needs to be, the more accurate your photos and their planes need to be.

You'll need to create three planes for each of the three views. First, make sure Interactive Creation is turned off, and then follow these steps:

1. In the Front view panel, create a polygonal plane by choosing Create → Polygon Primitives → Plane ❑. This plane is for the front image, so in the Options box set Axis to Z, Width to 0.912, and Height to 1.0. Make sure the check box for Preserve Aspect

Figure 6.6
Creating a plane for the top view

Ratio is deselected, as shown in Figure 6.6. Setting Axis to Z will place the plane properly in the front view.

2. Switch to the Side view panel. Create a second plane, this time with Width of 1.235 and Height of 1. Set Axis to X, and make sure the Preserve Aspect Ratio check box is unchecked.

3. Switch to the Top view panel. Create a third plane with Width of 1.49, Height of 1, and Axis set to Y. Make sure the Preserve Aspect Ratio box is still unchecked. Your Perspective panel should look like Figure 6.7.

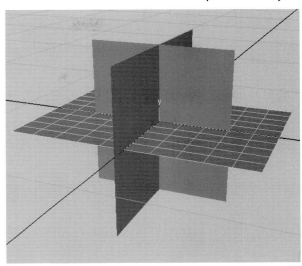

Figure 6.7

The three view planes are ready.

Now that all three image planes have been created with the proper aspect ratios, you're ready to map the photos to them to create the reference for the model.

Mapping the Reference Planes

To map the photos of the wagon to the reference planes, follow these steps:

1. Open the Hypershade (Window → Rendering Editors → Hypershade). Open a file browser, and navigate to the Sourceimages folder of the RedWagon project on your hard drive.

2. Click the first image in your file browser, and drag it into the work area of the Hypershade window to import the file image. Drag the other two images into the Hypershade, as shown in Figure 6.8.

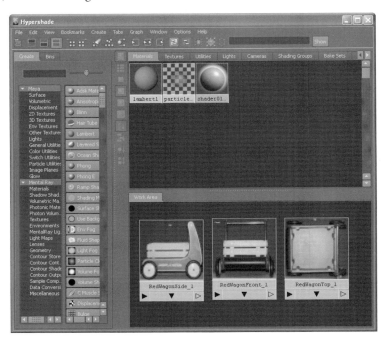

Figure 6.8

Importing the photos into the Hypershade window

3. Before you can assign the images to their respective planes, you must create shaders for each of the planes. In the left panel of the Hypershade window, click the Lambert icon three times to create three new Lambert shaders, as shown in Figure 6.9. For more information about shaders and texturing, see Chapter 7.

4. While still in the Hypershade work area and while holding down the Ctrl key, MMB+drag the side-view photo swatch onto the first Lambert shader icon. Maya automatically maps the image to the color of the Lambert shader, as shown in Figure 6.10. You can also MMB+drag the image to the Lambert Shader icon and then choose Color from the context menu that appears.

Figure 6.9

Create three new Lambert shaders.

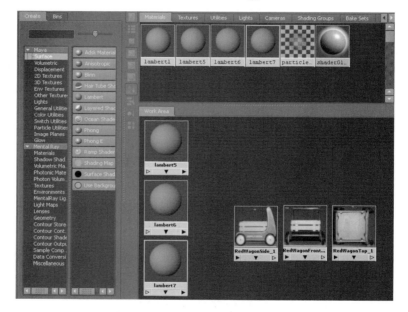

Figure 6.10

Connecting the image to the shader's color

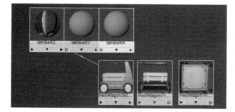

5. Ctrl+MMB+drag the other two images onto their respective Lambert shaders to connect them.

6. Assign the shaders to the reference planes. To do so, MMB+drag the Lambert shader that is connected to the side-view image to the side-view plane in the Perspective panel. Switch the perspective view into Texture mode by pressing 6 while in that panel. You should see the image of the wagon appear, as shown in Figure 6.11.

Figure 6.11

The side-view photo is mapped to the side-view plane.

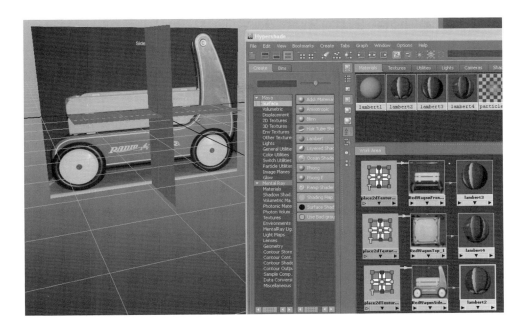

7. Drag the top-view Lambert shader to the top reference plane and the front Lambert shader to the front reference plane to assign the other two views. You should now have the three reference planes laid out as shown in Figure 6.12.

Figure 6.12

All three reference planes are mapped.

8. All isn't rosy yet! The front reference view and the side reference view seem to match up, but the top reference view is off. Select the top reference plane, and rotate it 90 degrees in the Y-axis. Although it's oriented properly now, the top view is larger than the side-view plane, and the images still don't line up.

9. Scale the top reference plane to match the width of the side-view plane, as shown in Figure 6.13.

10. Remember that the scale of these planes is small right now. You don't need to use real-world units for this project. However, you should scale the reference planes so that you have a larger scale with which to work. Select all three reference planes, and scale them to about four times their previous size. Don't enter values in the Channel Box; you should scale them by sight. Remember to scale all three reference planes together.

11. To give yourself more room to work, select the front-view plane and move it back, as shown in Figure 6.14.

12. Create a display layer for the planes to make it easy to manage them later. To do so, in the Layer Editor below the Channel Box, click the Create a New Layer icon ( ). Double-click the new layer, and name it **referencePlanes** in the window that pops up (see Figure 6.15). Click Save. Your Layer Editor should resemble the one shown in Figure 6.16.

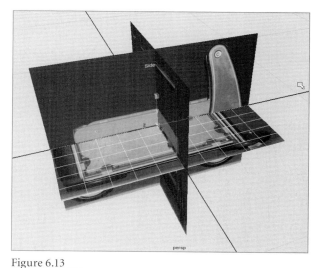

Figure 6.13

Scale the top reference plane to match the side reference plane.

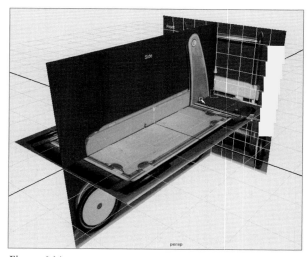

Figure 6.14

Scale up the planes together, and then move the front reference plane back.

Figure 6.15

Name the new layer.

Figure 6.16

**The new layer in
the Layer Editor**

13. Select all three reference planes, RMB+click the referencePlanes layer, and choose
    Add Selected Objects from the context menu. For more on the Layer Editor, see
    "The Channel Box/Layer Editor" section in Chapter 3, "The Maya 2011 Interface."
    To toggle the display of the reference planes to get them out of the way, simply toggle
    the box to the extreme left of the layer name. It's currently checked with a V for
    Visible in Figure 6.16.

Save your work, and "version up" so you don't write over your previous scene files. You
can load the scene file RedWagonModel_v01.ma from the Scenes folder of the RedWagon project on the CD to check your work or skip to this point. Just make sure to set your project
to the RedWagon project on your hard drive after copying the entire project from the CD.

> To remain in step with this chapter, make sure Interactive Creation is turned off when you
> create a new primitive.

Modeling the Side Panels

Now that your reference is all set, let's get to work building the model. Here is where the
sweat comes in. There are many ways to model the same object, but they all basically stem
from the same procedures you've seen in the previous chapters.

Shaping the A Panel

You'll start with the first side piece, marked A in Figure 6.17. Follow these steps:

1. Enter the Polygons menu set. Create a default poly cube, and place it in the side view
   in front of the A piece, as shown in Figure 6.18.

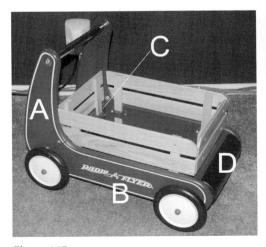

Figure 6.17

You'll build the wagon in this order.

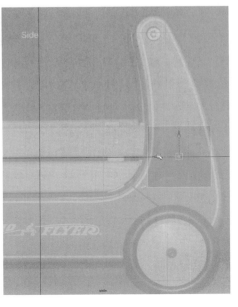

Figure 6.18

**Place a poly box for
the first side.**

MENU SET HOT KEYS

You can use the following hot keys to toggle between menu sets:

F2	Animation
F3	Polygons
F4	Surfaces
F5	Dynamics
F6	Rendering

2. RMB+click the cube, and select Vertex from the marking menu to enter Vertex Selection mode. Carefully move the corners to place them as shown in Figure 6.19. To place the vertices, use only the Z- and Y-axis handles for the Move tool so that you don't accidentally move the vertices in X as well.

3. To be able to see the texture view of the reference planes through the shaded gray cube you just created, you need to enter X-Ray mode. In any of the view panels, click Shading → X-Ray, as shown in Figure 6.20.

Figure 6.19

Place the four corners of the box to fit the A piece.

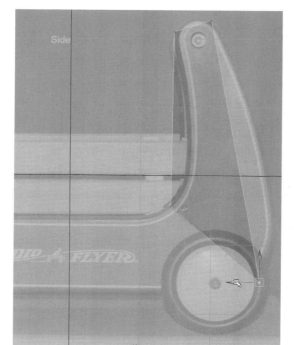

Figure 6.20

In the view panels, turn on X-Ray Shading mode. (The side view is shown here.)

4. This shape obviously won't fit the A panel. You need to add edges to define this mesh better. Choose Edit Mesh → Insert Edge Loop Tool. With the Triangular Tool icon,

click along the vertical edges to place seven new edge loops, as shown in Figure 6.21. RMB+click the cube, select Vertex to enter Vertex Selection, and move the new vertices to fit the shape of the A panel, also shown in Figure 6.21.

5. The area around the bend just above the back wheel needs more edge loops to fit the curvature better. Using the Insert Edge Loop tool, insert seven more edge loops as shown in Figure 6.22. In Vertex mode, move the vertices to fit the curvature as shown in Figure 6.23.

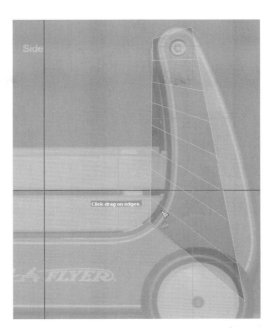

Figure 6.21

Insert edge loops to create more edges and vertices, and then shape the cube to match the A panel as shown here.

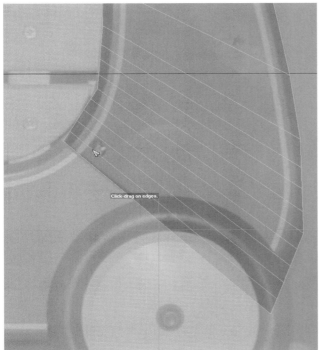

Figure 6.22

Insert more edge loops.

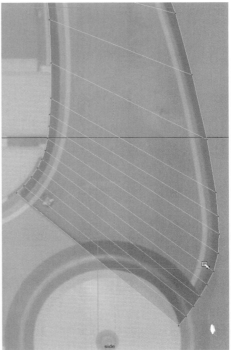

Figure 6.23

Move the new vertices to match the curvature.

6. Turn your attention to the top curvature. Using the Insert Edge Loop tool, add four new edge loop divisions to the top of the A panel (see Figure 6.24). Move the vertices to match the curvature, as shown in Figure 6.25.

7. You need to match the very top curvature by adding vertical edge loops to the mesh. Using the Insert Edge Loop tool, click and drag to add five new vertical edge loop divisions, as shown in Figure 6.26.

8. Move the vertices to match the top curvature, as shown in Figure 6.27. Try to place the vertices evenly.

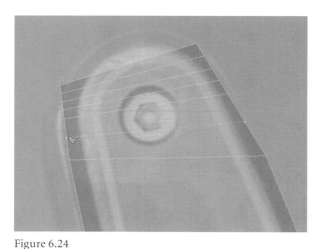

Figure 6.24
Add new edge loop divisions to the top curvature.

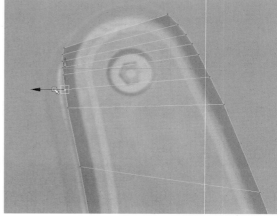

Figure 6.25
Move the new vertices to match the top curvature.

Figure 6.26
Insert five new vertical edge loop divisions.

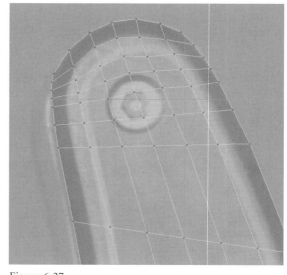

Figure 6.27
Match the curvature of the top.

9. The mesh for the A panel should look like Figure 6.28. It's too wide and not in place. Using the front view, position the mesh to fit where the A panel goes. Scale the width down to match the width of the panel. See Figure 6.29.

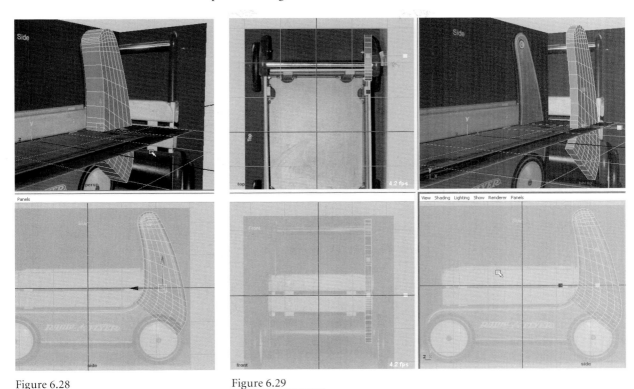

Figure 6.28
The current state of the mesh

Figure 6.29
Scale and position the mesh in the front view to match the actual A panel.

Fixing Problem Areas

You may notice an awkward polygon face at the top corners of the mesh, as shown in Figure 6.30. This polygon will break apart when you try to round the edges as you can see with the real wagon (Figure 6.17).

Let's add a couple of edges to these faces to circumvent any problems that may arise when you bevel the edges to round them to match the real wagon:

1. Choose Edit Mesh → Split Polygon Tool, and click and drag to place the first end of the edge at the corner shown in Figure 6.31. Place the other end of the new edge as shown in Figure 6.32.

2. Use the Split Polygon tool to place a new edge for the awkward polygon on the reverse side of the A panel, as shown in Figure 6.33.

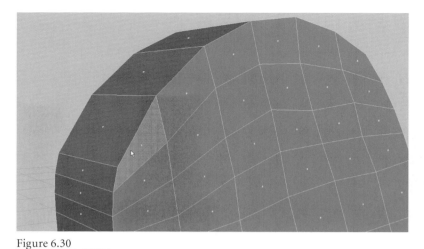

Figure 6.30
An awkward polygon corner may cause problems when you round the edges.

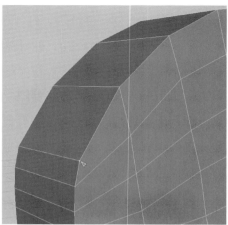

Figure 6.31
Begin the new edge here.

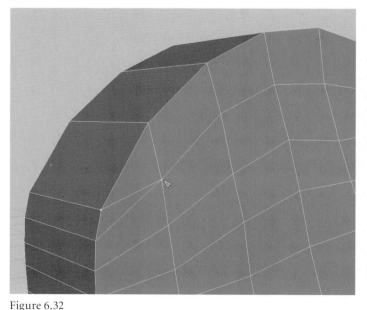

Figure 6.32
The new edge

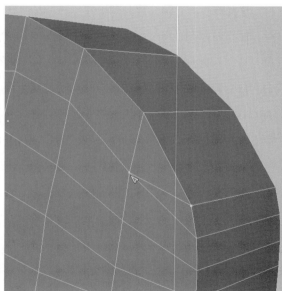

Figure 6.33
Add an edge to the reverse side's awkward polygon face.

3. Use the Split Polygon tool to place new edges for the awkward polygons on the front and back sides for the right side of the A panel, as shown in Figure 6.34.

4. As you can see in Figure 6.17, the panels on the real wagon are rounded at the edges. You can use Bevel to round the three topside edges of the panel, leaving the bottom rim of the panel flat for now. In the Polygons menu set, choose Select → Select Edge Loop Tool. Double-click one of the edges to select the entire edge loop for the front

of the panel. Double-click one of the edges to select the loop of edges on the back side of the panel, as shown in Figure 6.35. Notice that the bottom loop of edges isn't selected; this is fortunate for you in this case. You can always select each of those edges individually; however, the Select Edge Loop tool makes it quite a bit easier.

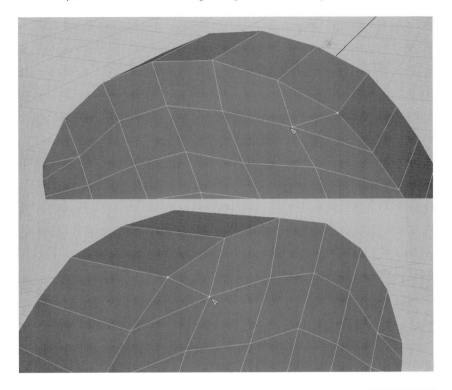

Figure 6.34

Add edges to the awkward polygons on the right side (front and back shown; top and bottom, respectively).

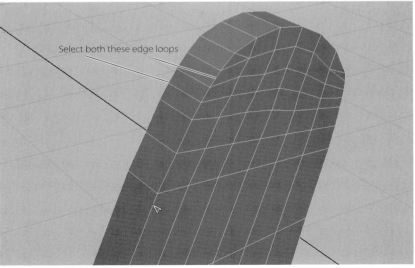

Figure 6.35

Select the edge loops for the front and back.

5. With those edge loops selected, choose Edit Mesh → Bevel ❑ to open the Options box for the Bevel command. Set Width to 1.0 and Segments to 2, as shown in Figure 6.36. Click Bevel to create the beveled edge shown in Figure 6.37. It's not quite as round as it should be, but you'll tackle that with a Smooth operation in the following steps.

Figure 6.36

Settings for the Bevel operation

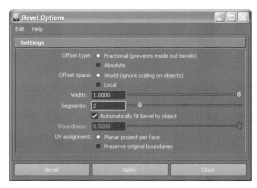

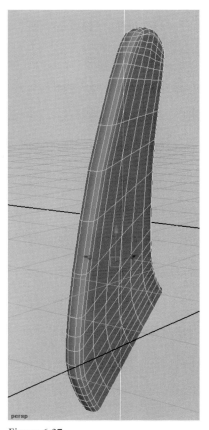

Smoothing the Panel

Next, you'll smooth the panel for a better fit to the real panel and a nicer look overall. Because the panel isn't as rounded as you'd like, you'll want to add a Smooth to the mesh, as you did in Chapter 4, "Beginning Polygonal Modeling" with the hand model. With the panel mesh selected, press 3 to display the panel as it will look after it's smoothed. Notice that the panel looks subtly but appreciably better with the Smooth preview. However, the bottom of the panel becomes too smooth, as you can see in Figure 6.38. To fix this, you'll add divisions to the bottom in the next step:

Figure 6.37

The rounded edges after the Bevel

1. Press 1 to return to the normal view of the mesh.

2. Use the Insert Edge Loop tool to insert three new edge loops at the bottom of the panel, as shown in Figure 6.39. Toggle between previews 1 and 3 to see how much better the smoothing will look at the bottom.

3. Now for the Smooth operation. Select the panel, and make sure you're back in normal mesh view by pressing 1. Choose Mesh → Smooth ❑. In the Options box, make sure Exponentially is selected and Division Levels is set to 1 (the default settings), as shown in Figure 6.40. Click Smooth. The A panel should look much nicer. Check it against the reference planes, and it should fit better.

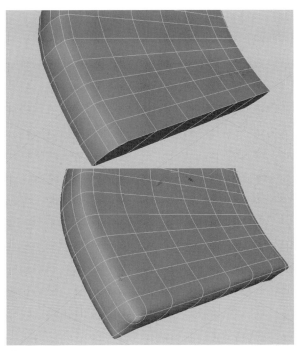

Figure 6.38

In the preview, the bottom of the A panel becomes too smooth when you press 3.

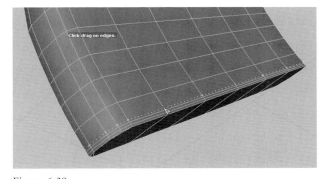

Figure 6.39

Insert three new edge loops at the bottom of the panel.

Figure 6.40

The Smooth options

4. Look in the Channel Box to see the history of all the work you did on the project (see Figure 6.41). Let's work cleanly and get rid of this history. With the mesh still selected, choose Edit → Delete by Type → History.

5. Select the mesh, and name it **Apanel** in the Attribute Editor or Channel Box. Your finished panel shape is shown in Figure 6.42. While you're at it, name the reference planes as well: **sideRef**, **topRef**, and **frontRef**.

Save your work, and version it up so you don't write over your previous scene files. You can load the scene file RedWagonModel_v02.ma from the Scenes folder of the RedWagon project on the CD to check your work or to skip to this point.

To keep track of your progress, you can save the file of your wagon scene manually and rename it with new version numbers, or you can use Incremental Save to let Maya make backups for you. (Make sure the option is turned on through File → Save Scene ❑.)

Figure 6.41

So much history!

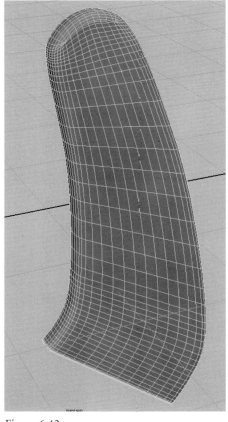

Figure 6.42

The finished panel shape

Using Booleans

Now that you've worked out the shape of the A panel and the model is clean and named, you'll use a Boolean operation to cut a hole in the top of the panel for the handlebar that crosses between the panels (see Figure 6.43).

Booleans are very impressive operations that allow you to, among other things, cut holes in a mesh fairly easily. Basically, a Boolean is a geometric operation that creates a shape from the addition of two shapes together (Union), the subtraction of one shape from another (Difference), or the common intersection of two shapes (Intersection).

Be forewarned, however, that Boolean operations can be problematic.

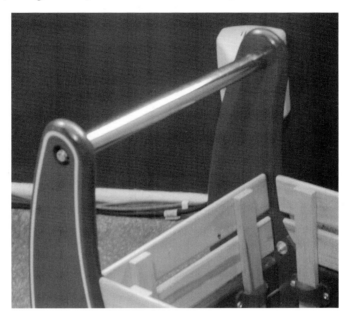

Figure 6.43

The handlebar

Sometimes you get a result that is wrong—or, even worse, the entire mesh disappears and you have to undo. Use Booleans sparingly and only on a mesh that is clean and prepared. You've cleaned and prepped your panel mesh, so there should be no problems. (Actually, there will be a problem; but that is half the fun of learning, so let's get on with it.)

Creating the Boolean Object

For the red wagon, you need to cut a hole into the panel to bolt in the handlebar, as you can see in Figure 6.43. In this case, you'll use a Difference Boolean. You need to cut a cylindrical hole out of the mesh at the location of the handlebar (refer to the side reference plane in the Side view panel). For a Boolean, you need two meshes. The panel is the first mesh to be affected, and the second mesh will be a polygonal cylinder to represent the handlebar.

Make sure Interactive Creation is turned off, and follow these steps:

1. In your scene, create a polygonal cylinder with Axis Divisions of 24 and Height Divisions of 2 (choose Create → Polygon Primitives → Cylinder ❒), as shown in the Polygon Cylinder Options box in Figure 6.44.

Figure 6.44

The Polygon Cylinder creation Options box

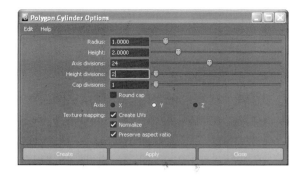

2. Using the side view as reference, scale, orient, and place the cylinder to match up with the handlebar. Scale the cylinder to go all the way through the panel mesh, as shown in Figure 6.45. Try to center the cylinder's middle at the center line of the width of the mesh.

3. First select the panel mesh, and then select the handlebar cylinder. Choose Mesh → Booleans → Difference. The cylinder disappears, and the panel mesh now has a hole cut through it, as shown in Figure 6.46.

Figure 6.45

Place the handlebar cylinder.

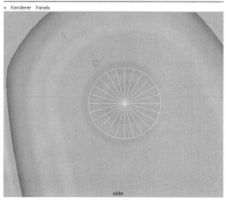

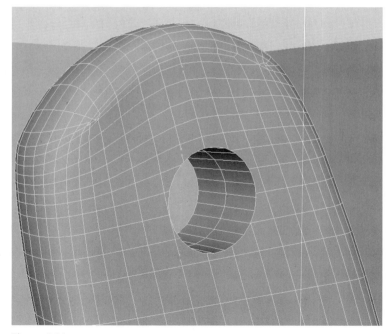

Figure 6.46

The Boolean cuts a hole in the mesh.

4. But now you have a problem! It's not easily seen, but there is a tear in the mesh, close to the rounded edge. Figure 6.47 shows the location of the tear, and Figure 6.48 shows a closer rendered view of the tear. It goes all the way through. If you don't see a tear in your mesh, you can skip the next section, "Fixing Tears," if you wish.

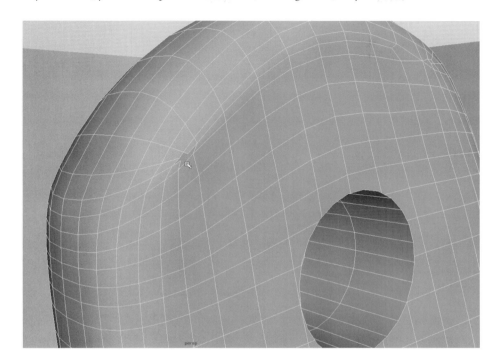

Figure 6.47

There is a tear between the faces.

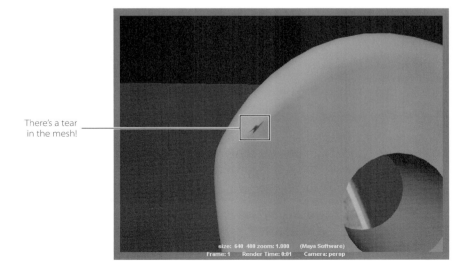

There's a tear in the mesh!

Figure 6.48

A render of the mesh shows the tear on both sides of the mesh panel.

Fixing Tears

Remember when I said Booleans can be problematic? Here is a perfect example. You'll work on fixing the tear by first moving and merging vertices. Let's begin on the front side of the mesh. You'll have to repeat these steps for the tear on the back side of the mesh:

1. Select the entire mesh object, and delete its history (Edit → Delete by Type → History).

2. Select the vertex shown on the left in Figure 6.49, and snap it (with Point Snap) to the vertex just above it, shown on the right.

3. Select both those vertices to merge them. Choose Edit Mesh → Merge. The vertices don't become one, as you saw in an earlier exercise in Chapter 4.

4. Select the vertex shown on the left in Figure 6.50, and snap it onto the vertex just below it, as shown on the right.

Figure 6.49

Select and snap the vertex to begin cleaning the tear.

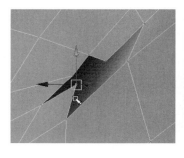 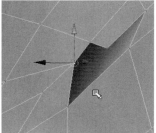

Figure 6.50

Select and snap the second vertex to clean the tear.

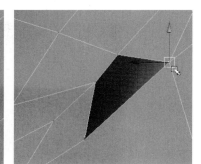

5. Select both vertices, and merge them as in step 3. Now you have a clean hole in the front of your panel's mesh that can be filled with a simple four-sided polygon face.

6. Use the same procedures in steps 2 through 5 to clean the tear in the back of the panel's mesh, as shown in Figure 6.51.

7. You now should have two simple four-sided holes in your mesh, front and back. Select the entire mesh, and choose Mesh → Fill Hole. *Bam!* Maya fills in both tears in the front and back of the panel mesh with a simple four-sided polygonal face. Figure 6.52 shows the newly formed face on the front side of the mesh.

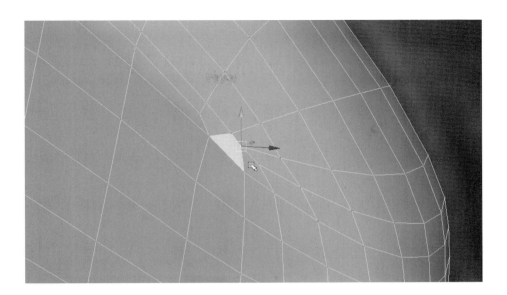

Figure 6.51

To clean up the tear, snap the vertices on the back side of the panel's mesh.

Figure 6.52

The tears are filled in with new faces.

8. There is a little scar from the tear that you can probably see in the Shaded mode of the mesh (see Figure 6.53). This scar won't show up in your renders after you texture and shade the wagon in the next chapter. Otherwise, your fix works great. Select the mesh, and delete its history. Rename the mesh back to **Aplane**, because the Boolean operation changed the mesh's name to polySurface1.

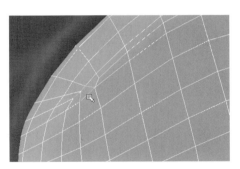

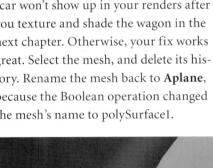

Figure 6.53

The fix works great. It leaves a little scar that won't show in your renders later in the book.

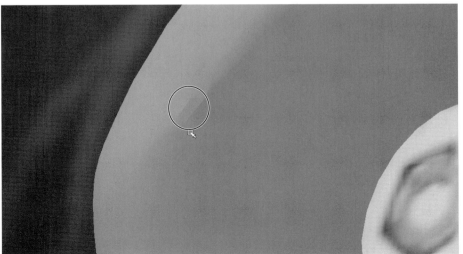

Cleaning the Faces Around the Handlebar Hole

With the tears fixed, turn your attention to the faces that surround the hole you cut for the handlebar. Although there are no longer any glaring issues evident, several faces that border the hole have more than four sides. This isn't always an immediate problem, but rendering and modeling issues may crop up further down the road of you don't clean up these faces:

1. Select the faces that surround the handlebar hole one by one for the front side of the mesh. Then, with the Shift key depressed, select the faces around the hole on the back side of the mesh. Don't select the faces that make up the inside tunnel of the hole. See Figure 6.54.

2. With the faces selected, choose Edit Mesh → Add Divisions ❐, and set the options as shown in Figure 6.55.

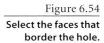

Figure 6.54

Select the faces that border the hole.

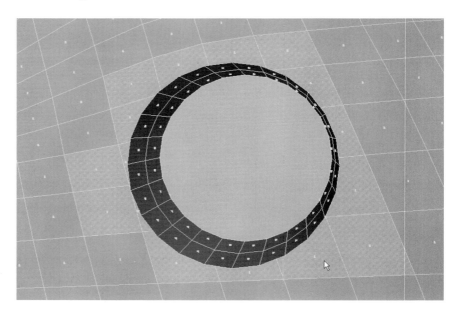

Figure 6.55

The Add Divisions settings

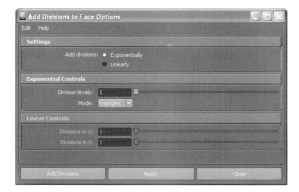

Figure 6.56

Add Divisions cleans up the faces by aligning the segments with new edges and faces.

3. The faces around the hole fill in with new divisions that match the way the hole is segmented and cut. See Figure 6.56.

4. Select the mesh, and delete its history.

Figure 6.57 shows the final A panel in perspective view. Save your work! You can load the scene file RedWagonModel_v03.ma from the Scenes folder of the RedWagon project on the CD to check your work or to skip to this point.

Shaping the B Panel

Now that everything is nice and clean and your A panel mesh is finished, you're ready to move on to the B panel (shown earlier in Figure 6.17):

1. Create a new polygon cube, and place it in the side view to line up with the B panel. Move the corner vertices in the side view to roughly line up, as shown in Figure 6.58.

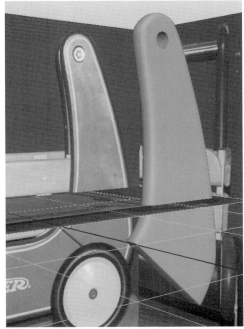

Figure 6.57

Final A panel in perspective view

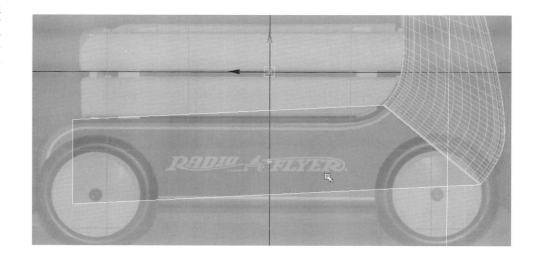

2. You need to add edge loops as you did with the A panel to match the curvatures of the B panel in the real wagon. Add six edge loops as shown in Figure 6.59 for the right side of the panel.

3. Move the vertices to match the curvature of the B panel, as shown in Figure 6.60.

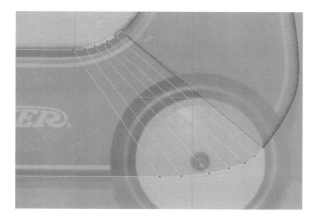

4. Select the B panel mesh, and scale and position it in the front view to line up with the B panel of the real wagon in the front reference plane, as shown in Figure 6.61.

5. To make the curvature of the B panel at the front of the wagon, use the Wedge procedure you used in the hand exercise in Chapter 4. First, look at the end face of the B panel. You need to split that into two faces for a proper Wedge.

6. Select Edit Mesh → Split Polygon Tool. Click and drag a point on one edge of that end face to put it at exactly 50 percent, as shown to the left in Figure 6.62. Release the mouse button to place the point, and then click and drag the opposite edge to place the other point for the new edge also at 50 percent as shown on the right in Figure 6.62. Notice that the readout in the very bottom-left corner of the UI shows the percentage as you drag the point on either edge, also shown in the bottom-left corner of both sides in Figure 6.62.

7. Right-click the mesh, and choose Face from the marking menu to enter Face Selection. Select the top face of the newly split end. Then, RMB+click the mesh, and select Edge to enter Edge Selection mode. With the Shift key depressed, Shift+select that new middle edge, as shown in Figure 6.63.

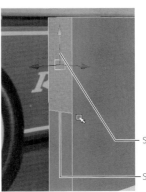

Figure 6.61

Line up the position and size of the panel.

Figure 6.62

Split the end face in half to prep for the Wedge.

Figure 6.63

Select the top face as well as its bottom edge.

Select this face

Shift+select this edge

Figure 6.64

Wedge the face at the end to create the curvature of the panel.

8. Choose Edit Mesh → Wedge Face ☐. Set Arc Angle to 180 and Divisions to 10. Click Wedge Face, and the end of the B panel is rounded at the end. See Figure 6.64.

9. In the side view, select all the vertices at the end and position the arc to match the curvature of the wagon's real B panel. See Figure 6.65.

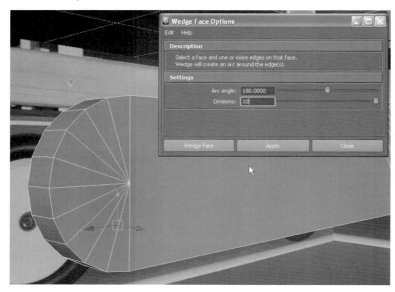

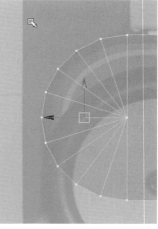

Figure 6.65

Move the vertices as a whole to fit the end curvature to the real curve of the wagon's panel.

Rounding the Edges

Now, you'll round the edges of the B panel in these continuing steps:

1. Using the Select Edge Loop tool (Select → Select Edge Loop Tool), select the edges that run along the B panel mesh. Don't select the edges where the B panel meets the A panel. See Figure 6.66.

Figure 6.66

Select these edge loops that run along both edges of the panel.

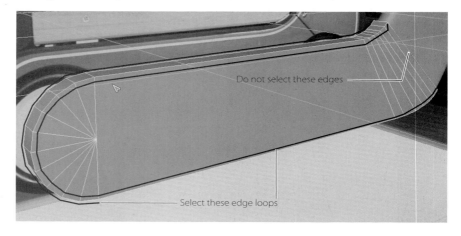

2. Choose Edit Mesh → Bevel ❏, and set Width to 0.5 and Segments to 2 as shown. Click Bevel, and your B panel edges will be rounded as shown in Figure 6.67.

3. With the mesh selected, toggle in and out of smooth mesh preview using the 1 and 3 keys to see how the mesh would look after being smoothed. You'll have issues with the end that meets the A panel, so you'll have to insert edge loop divisions at that end to prevent the model from becoming too smooth. Using the Insert Edge Loop tool, insert three new edge loops at the very end of the B panel where it meets the A panel, as shown in Figure 6.68.

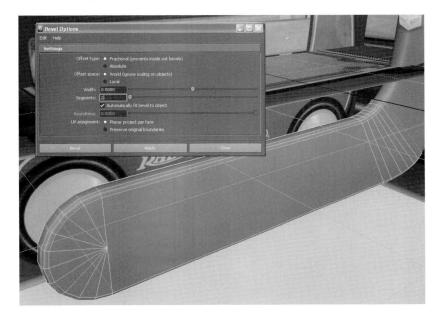

Figure 6.67

Bevel to round the edges of the B panel.

Figure 6.68

Insert edge loops to prevent this end from smoothing too much.

4. Select the B panel mesh, and choose Mesh → Smooth □. Set Add Divisions to Exponentially and Division Levels to 1. Click Smooth, and your B panel is done! See Figure 6.69.

5. Select the mesh, name it **Bpanel**, and delete its history.

Figure 6.69

**Smooth the
B panel mesh.**

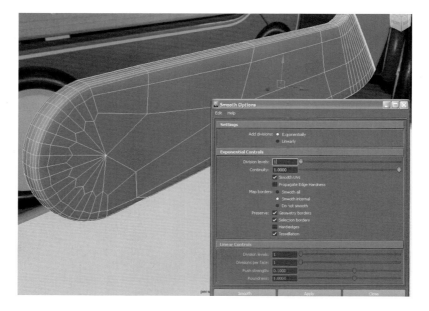

Cleaning Up the Scene

Now, let's put these objects into a good hierarchy and clean everything up. Select both the A and B panels, and freeze their transforms: choose Modify → Freeze Transformations. This resets the *values* for the mesh's position and the rotation to 0 in all axes and sets the scale values back to 1. It doesn't adjust the objects in the slightest; it only resets their values back to an original value to keep things nice and clean. After you froze the transformations, the meshes stayed in place, but their values in the Channel Box reverted back to 0s (Translate and Rotate) and 1 (Scale).

> Freeze Transformations (also referred to as *freezing transforms*) sets the values of the object's settings back to their defaults (that is, it sets Translate and Rotate back to 0 and Scale back to 1). It doesn't reset the size or positions—just the number values in the attributes. This is useful for getting an object back to default conditions without losing all the work done to it. Using Freeze Transformations keeps things clean as you work, and doing so is usually a good idea when you're working with patches.

With both the panels still selected, group them together by choosing Edit → Group or by pressing Ctrl+G. Name the new group **rightSidePanels**.

With the rightSidePanels top node selected, duplicate the panels by pressing Ctrl+D or by choosing Edit → Duplicate. Move them in the front view to line up with the left side of the wagon, as shown in Figure 6.70. Name the duplicated group **leftSidePanels**. Notice that the panels don't line up perfectly to the reference images. This is due to the perspective in the photos and is to be expected. Use the upper part of the panels to line everything up, as shown in Figure 6.70.

Save your work to another version number. You may want to load the scene file RedWagonModel_v04.ma from the Scenes folder of the RedWagon project on the CD to check your work or to skip to this point.

Modeling the Wagon Body

Now that you've finished the hardest part of the process, you can concentrate on getting the body of the wagon built between the two side panels (called out as C in Figure 6.17 earlier in the chapter).

Look in the top view, and you probably won't see all the side panels. This is because the top reference plane is blocking it. Select the top reference plane, and move it down as shown in Figure 6.71 to give you a little more room in which to work.

Creating the Floor

To begin the floor of the wagon, follow these steps:

1. In the top view, create a polygonal cube. Scale and position it to fit the bottom of the wagon body using all the views as reference, as shown in Figure 6.72.

2. Using the Insert Edge Loop tool, insert edge loops at the ends of the wagon's floor at about the same thickness as the side panels, as shown in Figure 6.73.

3. Select both the new faces created on top of the floor. Choose Edit Mesh → Extrude to pull up the ends to just under the lip of the panels to make a box, as shown in Figure 6.74.

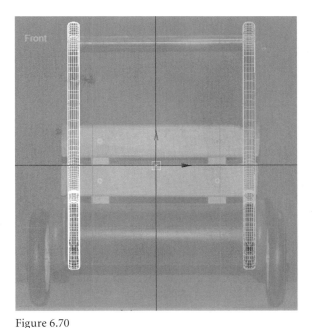

Figure 6.70

Duplicate and position the panels to the other side of the wagon.

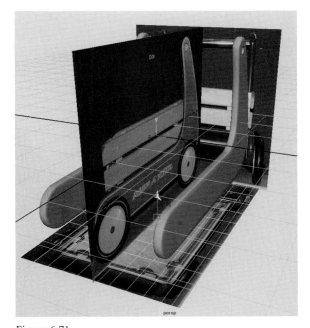

Figure 6.71

Move the top reference plane down a bit.

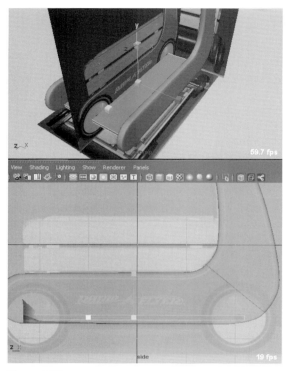

Figure 6.72

Place and scale the box to be the bottom of the wagon body.

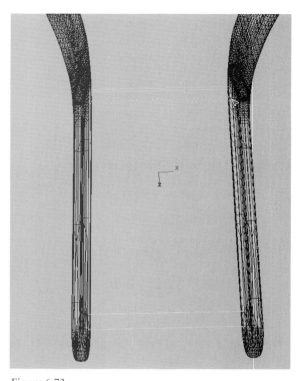

Figure 6.73

Insert Edge Loop divisions at both ends of the floor.

Figure 6.74

Extrude the top faces to make an open-faced box.

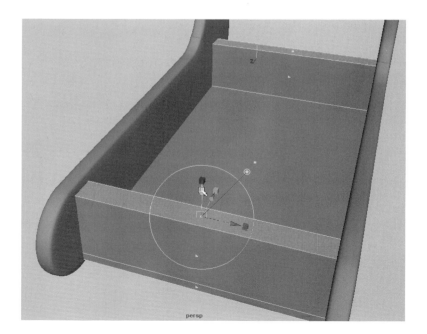

4. You need to round the new edges of the box to match the panels. Select the edges of the front and back box ends, as shown in Figure 6.75.

5. Choose Edit Mesh → Bevel ❏. Set Width to 1.0 and Segments to 12. Click Bevel, and your edges are e rounded beautifully, as shown in Figure 6.76. Name the cube **wagonFloor**.

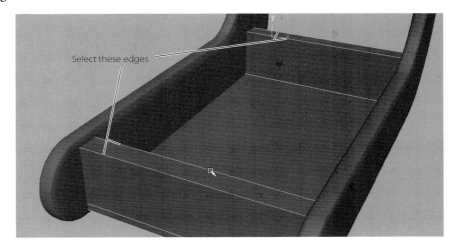

Figure 6.75
Select these edges.

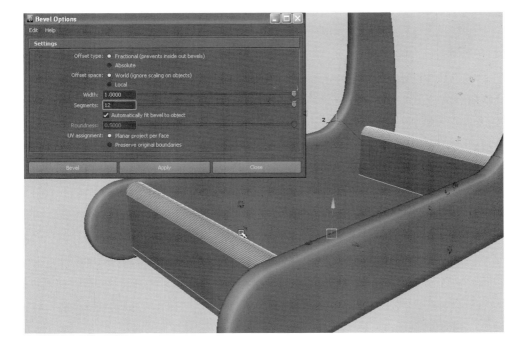

Figure 6.76
Bevel does a great job of rounding these edges.

Creating the Bullnose

Next, let's create the bullnose in front of the wagon body (part D, called out earlier in Figure 6.17), as shown in Figure 6.77.

1. Create a polygonal cylinder with the options shown in Figure 6.78. Set Radius to 1, Height to 2, Axis Divisions to 48, Height Divisions set to 1, Cap Divisions to 2, and Axis to X.

Figure 6.77

The bullnose

Figure 6.78

**Create a poly
cylinder with
these settings.**

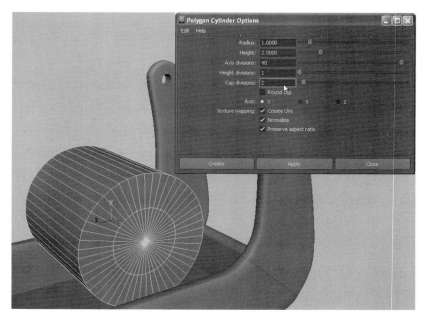

2. You only need the front half of the cylinder. In the top view, select the cylinder, and choose Edit Mesh → Cut Faces Tool ❑. In the Options box, set Cut Direction to XY plane, and select the Delete Cut Faces check box. Click Cut, and half of the cylinder immediately deletes at the center line, as shown in Figure 6.79. You could use the special manipulator to move the cut plane back and forth to cut the cylinder at a different place; but because it's already at the center, you're fine.

3. Press W to enter the Move tool and exit the Cut Faces tool. Move and scale the cylinder to fit into the front of the wagon, as shown in Figure 6.80. Name the cylinder **bullnose**. The bullnose is ready!

4. Select both the wagonFloor and bullnose objects, and delete their histories.

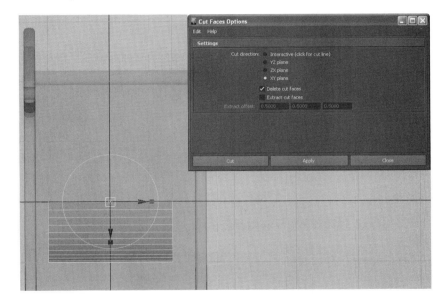

Figure 6.79
Cut the cylinder in half.

Figure 6.80
The bullnose is in place.

Save your work to a higher version number. You may want to load the scene file `RedWagonModel_v05.ma` from the `Scenes` folder of the RedWagon project on the CD to check your work or to skip to this point.

The wagon's body is finished. You can insert the handlebar into the side panels.

Inserting the Handlebar

The handlebar is a pretty easy affair to create. It's a simple cylinder that fits in the holes at the top of the side panels. However, each end has a bolt that holds the bar in place. Although you don't have to be completely accurate and create a washer and bolt, it's nice to add the detail of a bolt at either end of the handlebar.

Making the Handlebar

To begin the handlebar, follow along here:

1. Create a poly cylinder with Axis Divisions of 24, Height Divisions of 2, and Cap Divisions of 1.

2. Scale, rotate, and position the cylinder to fit between the side panels, fitting into the holes. For the best effect, make sure the cylinder is a little smaller than the holes. Figure 6.81 shows the handlebar in place.

3. Make sure the ends of the handlebar are about halfway through the holes to make room for the bolts. Name the cylinder **handlebar**.

Figure 6.81

Place the cylinder.

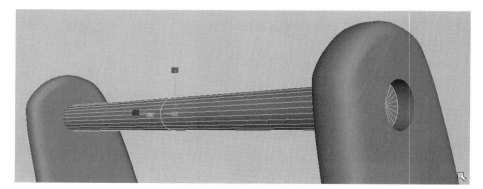

Making the Bolts

Now, you'll make a bolt for the handlebar in these continuing steps:

1. Create a poly cylinder with the following options: Axis Divisions = 6, Height Divisions = 1, Cap Divisions = 2, and Axis = X. (See Figure 6.82.)

2. Select the inner faces of the cap facing forward, as shown in Figure 6.83, and move them back into the cylinder to create a depression.

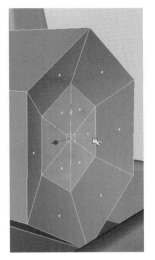

Figure 6.83

Create an indent in the cap of the bolt head.

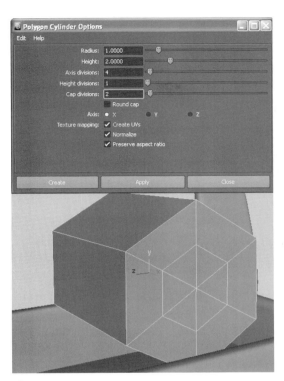

Figure 6.82

Starting the bolt model

Figure 6.84

Shorten the bolt cylinder.

Select and move all the back vertice

3. Select the back vertices of the cylinder, and move them closer to the front to shorten the cylinder, as shown in Figure 6.84. It's still a rather large bolt, but don't worry about that yet.

4. Create another cylinder, this time with Axis Divisions set to 16 and Cap Divisions set to 1. Scale and orient the new cylinder to fit through the bolt head slightly, as shown in Figure 6.85.

5. Let's make the bolt head a lot nicer. Using the Select Edge Loop tool, select the outer loop of edges all the way around the bolt head, as shown in Figure 6.86.

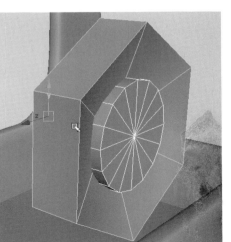

Figure 6.85

Place a cylinder slightly through the bolt head.

Figure 6.86

**Select the outer
loop of edges.**

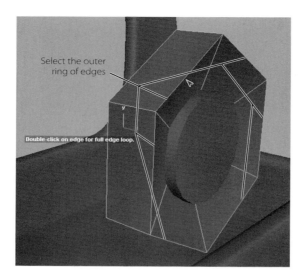

6. Bevel the outer loop of edges with a Width setting of 0.3 and a Segments value of 3, as shown in Figure 6.87.

7. Select the outer loop of edges for the inner cylinder, and bevel them with the same settings. Figure 6.88 shows the result.

Figure 6.87

**Bevel the end of
the bolt head.**

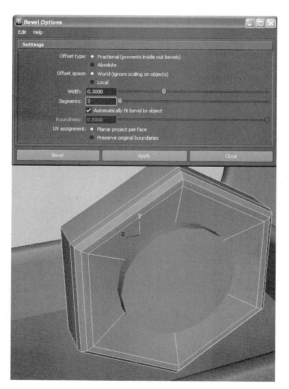

Figure 6.88

Bevel the inner cylinder.

8. Select the bolt head object, and name it **boltHead**. Select the inner cylinder for the bolt, and name it **boltBody**.

9. Select both the boltBody and boltHead objects and group them together (Ctrl+G). Name the new group **bolt**.

10. Scale the bolt group down to a good size, and place it inside the hole in the side panel up against the handlebar's end, as shown in Figure 6.89.

Figure 6.89

Size and position the bolt.

11. With the bolt group in place and still selected, freeze its transforms by choosing Modify → Freeze Transformations.

12. To make another bolt for the other side of the handlebar, simply duplicate the bolt group by pressing Ctrl+D. Then, with the duplicate group (bolt1) selected, enter a scale of **-1.0** in the ScaleX value in the Channel Box. (See Figure 6.90.)

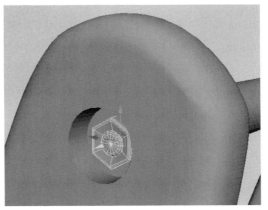

Figure 6.90

Place the duplicated bolt on the other end of the handlebar.

Figure 6.91 shows the progress of the wagon so far. With the body of the wagon pretty much finished, you can move on to the wheels.

Figure 6.91

The wagon so far...

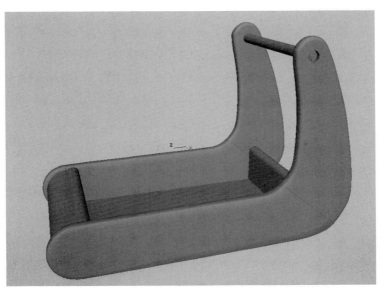

Modeling the Wheels

What's a kid's wagon without wheels? That would be no fun. How else would it smash into all your expensive stuff? You're going to make a wheel for the wagon and then duplicate it. Figure 6.92 shows the object of your design. You'll complete the wheel model by revolving a NURBS surface and converting it to a poly.

Figure 6.92

Ensign, take the
wheel! (The author
is a dork.)

Creating the Profile Curve

You'll begin the first wheel by creating a profile curve to match the cross-section of the wheel on the wagon. This is where coloring between the lines in kindergarten comes into play. You did color inside the lines, right?

1. Select Create → CV Curve Tool. In the top view, lay down the first CV on the grid. As you'll notice, the first CV is displayed as a closed box. Lay down the second CV a little lower in the Z-axis, and you see the second CV displayed as an open-sided box. This display shows you the direction of a curve. Lay down a third CV to the right of the second CV in the X-axis, as you see in the upper-right CVs shown in Figure 6.93.

    It's important to create the curve in the top view.

    No curve is displayed between the three CVs. A NURBS curve based on CVs will begin to appear after you've laid down the fourth and all subsequent CVs.

2. To match the profile shape, continue laying down the rest of the CVs counterclockwise to the curve, as shown in Figure 6.93.

3. After you lay down the last CV at the upper-left corner, press Enter to complete the curve. The CV display turns off, and you have a bare curve.

4. You can adjust the curve by entering Component mode and moving the CVs to taste. Make sure the first and last CVs line up. Use the grid to help you. The final profile shape is essentially a big U with a small notch cut out of the lower-right side where the tire meets the rim. Check the size of the profile curve, and make sure it's about the size of half the wheel in the top reference image in the top view. This profile curve will be revolved around an axis and will fill in a surface for the entire wheel. You can always scale the finished wheel later, so getting this step perfect isn't critical.

5. As you can see in Figure 6.94, the pivot point of the curve is at the origin, no matter where on the top grid you drew the curve. You need to move the pivot to the first CV of the curve. First, to display the CVs of the curve without entering Component mode, select the curve and choose Display → NURBS → CVs.

6. Press W to activate the Move tool, and then press Insert (Home on a Mac system or fn+Home/Left Arrow key on a Macbook Pro) to enter Pivot mode, as you did in the Solar System exercise earlier in the book. Hold down the V key to enable Snap to Points, and snap the pivot to the first CV of the curve (the upper-right corner of the curve), as shown in Figure 6.95.

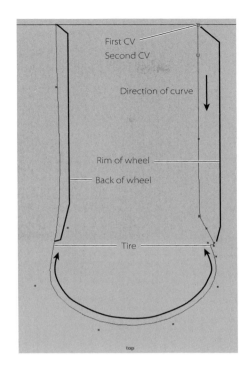

Figure 6.93

Match this profile shape with a CV curve in the top view.

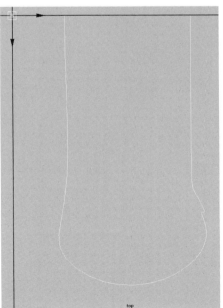

Figure 6.94

The pivot point for the profile curve you just created is at the origin.

Figure 6.95

Place the pivot at the beginning CV of the curve.

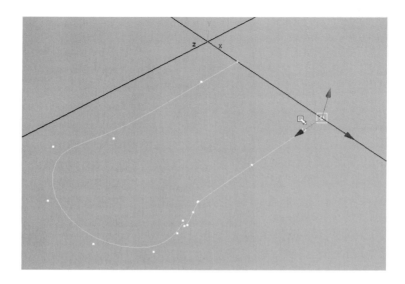

Creating the Revolved Surfaces

Now you can revolve the profile curve to make the base shape of the wheel as you continue by following these steps:

1. Select the curve, and move it to the origin; now its first CV lies on the origin. Turn off CV display by selecting Display → NURBS → CVs.

2. Enter into the Surfaces menu set, select the curve, and choose Surfaces → Revolve ❑. In the Options box, set the options as shown in Figure 6.96. Click Revolve, and your wheel appears, as shown in Figure 6.97. For more on these tessellation settings, see the "Wheel Tessellation" sidebar *before* you move on to the next steps and before you delete the surface history on the wheel mesh.

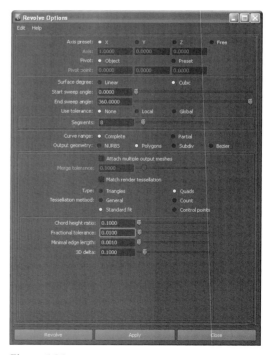

Figure 6.96

Revolve options for the wheel

Figure 6.97

The wheel!

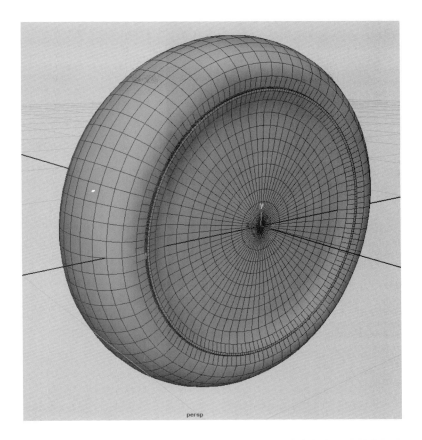

WHEEL TESSELLATION

What are all those numbers you input for the revolve surface? Because you're generating the wheel surface as a polygon mesh using a NURBS surfacing technique, you have to tell Maya the proper parameters for the poly surface. If the tessellation values, which are determined by the Tessellation method and the attribute values below it (as shown in Figure 6.96) aren't just right, the wheel's mesh will be revolved without all the details you need. These settings are deemed to be the best tessellation for the wheel through trial and error by creating the wheel, changing the tessellation values interactively, and seeing the results update through surface history.

As a test (save your scene first!), select the newly revolved wheel mesh before you delete history on it. In the Attribute Editor, you'll see a tab for the recently created mesh called something like nurbsTessellate1. Click that tab to open its attributes, and change some of the values under the Advanced Tessellation Options → Standard Fit Options heading. Because history is still attached to this mesh, it changes the mesh interactively as you change the tessellation options. After you've had your fill, revert back to your saved file, and continue with the exercise at hand.

3. Move the pivot point of the wheel to the center of the rim. Name the surface **wheelMesh**.

4. You need to add the little nub of the wheel at the rim, as you can see in the photos back in Figure 6.92. Just as you did with the wheel's profile curve, create a profile curve for the little inset cap. As best you can, match the shape and position to the one shown in Figure 6.98. This time, start the curve on the lower-left of the curve shown, and work your way counterclockwise up to the upper-right corner, ending the curve at the same height as the wheel at the *X*-axis.

5. Move the pivot point of the new profile curve to its last CV, as shown in Figure 6.99. Put the curve at the origin; its last CV should now rest at the origin.

Figure 6.98

Create a new profile curve for the hubcap detail.

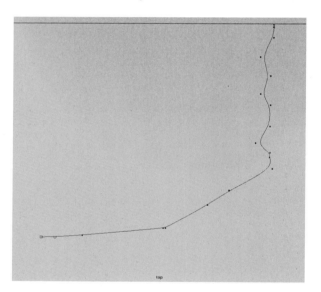

Figure 6.99

Move the pivot point.

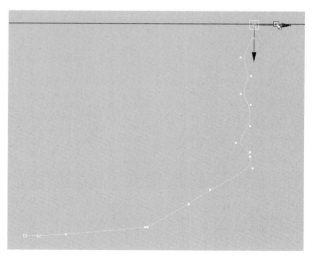

6. Select the new profile curve, and revolve a new surface using the same settings as before in Figure 6.96 (see Figure 6.100).

7. Select and move the new cap mesh into the middle of the wheel's rim, and size the cap to fit using the side-view reference. Name the object **capMesh**. See Figure 6.101.

8. If you want to adjust the shape of the wheel or the hubcap nub, you can adjust the CVs on your profile curves; the surfaces will adjust, provided history is still intact. Delete both the profile curves for the wheel and the cap, if you haven't already. Doing so also deletes the history on the surfaces, which is fine after you're pleased with the shape of both surfaces.

9. Select both the wheel and the cap meshes, and group them together by pressing Ctrl+G. Name the group node **wheel**.

10. With the wheel node selected, center the pivot by choosing Modify → Center Pivot. This places the pivot for the wheel assembly properly in the center of the wheel.

11. Using the side-view reference, position the wheel to the back of the wagon using the top wheel node to place it, as shown in Figure 6.102. If you need to, scale the wheel's top node to fit it to the real wheel using both the side and front reference planes for sizing.

12. Duplicate the wheel, and place it on the other side of the wagon's back end. Select the top node (wheel1), and scale it in the X-axis to -1.0 to mirror it properly.

13. Duplicate both the rear wheels, and place them at the front of the wagon, as shown in Figure 6.103. Don't worry about placing the wheels exactly where they're shown in the front reference plane; use the side view for positioning. Due to the perspective of the photo, they won't line up accurately in both reference planes, so it's best to keep all the wheels lined up in the Maya scene, as you can see from Figure 6.103.

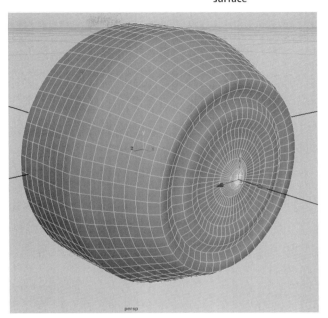

Figure 6.100

The hubcap detail surface

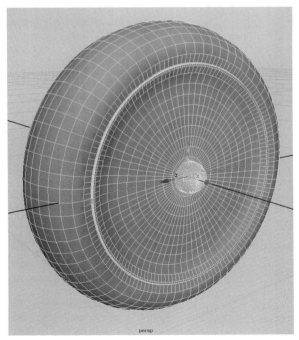

Figure 6.101

The wheel is complete!

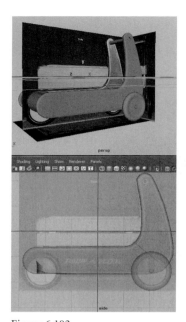

Figure 6.102

Place the first wheel.

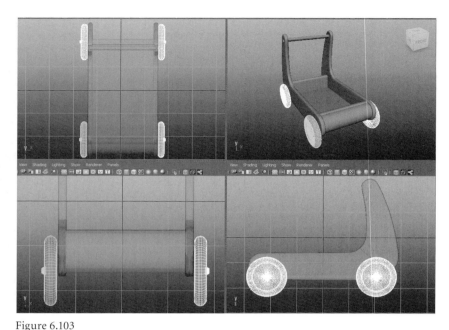

Figure 6.103

Duplicate and place the other three wheels.

14. After you've placed the wheels, freeze their transforms: select the four top wheel nodes, and choose Modify → Freeze Transformations. Doing so sets the transform values for the wheel nodes to 0 in translation and rotation and 1 in scale without altering them in any way.

Because the axles of the wheels aren't very noticeable, there is no need to build them. Simply placing the wheels close to the body in the correct positions will suffice. Now you have a wagon that can roll; and, if you have a kid, you know it'll end up rolling over your toes pretty soon. The red wagon is really starting to take shape. Enjoy a frosty beverage—perhaps a smoothie—save your work, and get ready to finish this wagon in the next sections.

You may want to load the scene file RedWagonModel_v06.ma from the Scenes folder of the RedWagon project on the CD to check your work or to skip to this point. You'll move on to the wooden railings in the next section.

Modeling the Wood Railings

Remember Figure 6.17? Take a peek at that figure again; I'll wait. You'll see that all that remains to do for your model are the wood railings placed around the four sides of the wagon.

These models will be pretty simple; they're all based on poly cubes with some slight alterations to round a corner here or there. To start modeling the rails, begin with these steps:

1. Switch back to the Polygons menu set. In the Side view panel, create a poly cube; use the side and front reference planes to scale and place the cube to fit the top rail on the side, as shown in Figure 6.104. Again, use the side reference view primarily to position the railing, because the front and top view will be a little off due to perspective in the photos.

2. To round the one corner of the railing, select the top edge at the end to be rounded and choose Edit Mesh → Bevel ❏. Reset your Bevel settings by selecting Edit → Reset Settings in the Options box. Set Segments to 12, and bevel that edge. See Figure 6.105.

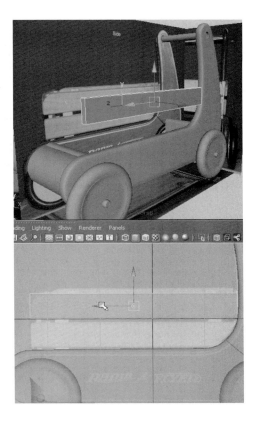

Figure 6.104

Create a cube, and position it to be the top rail on the side of the wagon.

Figure 6.105

Bevel the end of the rail.

3. It's unseemly to leave the rest of the edges of the mesh sharp. Adding a slight bevel to the edges will enhance the look and fidelity of the railings in your model. Especially when you begin lighting, beveled edges and corners are much nicer than perfectly sharp edges and corners, even if it's a small bevel. Select the outer edges that run all the way around the cube, as shown in Figure 6.106.

4. Set the Bevel options to a Width of 0.25 and Segments of 3, and bevel those outer edges, as shown in Figure 6.107.

Figure 6.106

Select the outer edges, but not the inner edges.

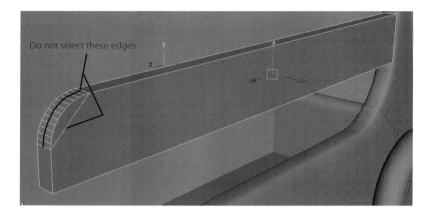

Figure 6.107

Put a slight bevel around the railing.

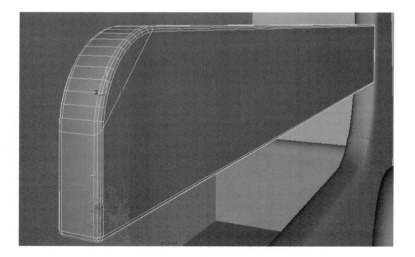

5. Delete the history from the top railing, and freeze its transforms (Modify → Freeze Transformations).

6. Create another cube. Scale and position it as the bottom rail under the one you just created. See Figure 6.108.

7. You need to bevel the end of the bottom railing to match the real railing on the wagon. But the cube is resting inside the wagon mesh right now, because you already lined it up perfectly. The easiest thing to do here is to freeze transforms on the cube so its position values reset to 0,0,0 in *X*, *Y*, *Z* space.

8. Move the cube out of the way of the wagon, anywhere in the scene you'd like. I suggest you move it just above the wagon so you can see the obscured end more easily, as shown in Figure 6.109.

9. Select the bottom edge at the right end of the cube, as shown in Figure 6.110.

10. Set your Bevel options to Width 1.0 and Segments 12, and bevel that end, as shown in Figure 6.111.

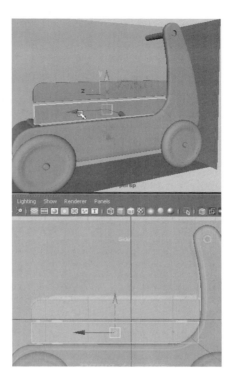

Figure 6.108

Place a second cube for the bottom railing.

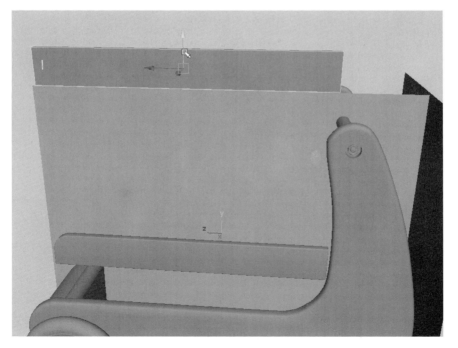

Figure 6.109

After you freeze transformations, move the cube to a better space in which to work.

Figure 6.110

Select the bottom edge on the right end of the cube to round that end.

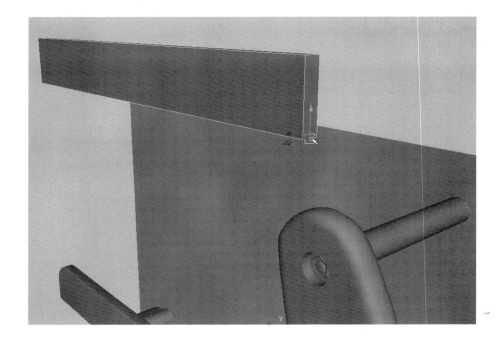

Figure 6.111

Bevel the end to round it out.

11. While the object is still clear of the wagon, bevel the outside edges as you did on the other railing. Select all the outer edges, being careful not to select the inner edges, and bevel them with Width 0.25 and Segments 3, as before. See Figure 6.112.

12. What good is the railing if it's nowhere near the wagon? That's easy to fix. Earlier, you froze its transforms so that, in its proper place, the railing was at location (0,0,0) in 3D space. Therefore, you can enter those values in the Channel Box to place the railing exactly where it was before. Figure 6.113 shows the bottom railing back in place; however, it's still cutting into the wagon. You'll fix it in place with a lattice.

Figure 6.112

Bevel the rest of the edges.

13. With the bottom railing still selected, switch to the Animation menu set (F2), and choose Create Deformers → Lattice ❏. Set Divisions to 2, 2, 2, and click Create.

14. Enter X-Ray mode in the Perspective panel (choose Shading → X-Ray in the persp panel's menu bar). You see the lattice sticking into the wagon body, as shown in Figure 6.114.

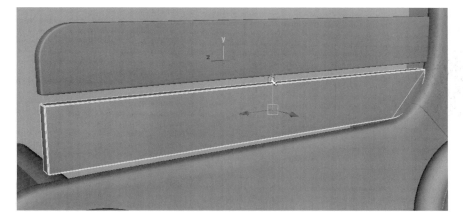

Figure 6.113

Put the railing back.

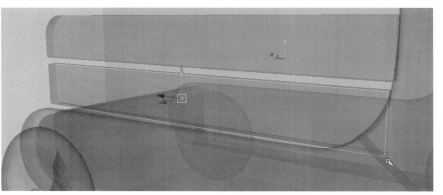

Figure 6.114

Create a lattice.

15. With the lattice still selected, RMB+click one of the lines of the lattice, and select Lattice Point from the marking menu. You may have to RMB+click around to get the correct marking menu that displays Lattice Point as a selection option. Try not to RMB+click the wagon itself, to avoid having the wrong marking menu appear. Select the two bottom lattice points, as shown in Figure 6.115.

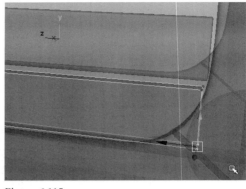

Figure 6.115

In X-Ray mode, select the bottom lattice points on the end buried in the wagon.

16. Exit X-Ray mode with the lattice points still selected by choosing Shading → X-Ray to toggle it off in the persp panel. Move the two lattice points to deform the bottom rail's end properly to create a gap between the railing and the wagon, as shown in Figure 6.116.

Figure 6.116

Use the lattice to put a gap between the curved railing and the wagon.

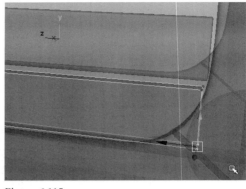

17. Select the railing mesh object, and delete its history to remove the lattice but keep the deformation. Switch back to the Polygons menu set (F3).

18. You need to make the braces behind the railings. Create a poly cube, and then scale and position it to match the front end brace behind the railings, as shown in Figure 6.117. The brace should reach the floor of the wagon and should extend to just below the top railing edge.

19. With the cube selected and in position, choose Edit Mesh → Bevel ❒. Set Width to 0.25 and Segments to 3. This puts a slight bevel around the entire edge of the brace, as shown in Figure 6.118. Having edges beveled helps light catch the edges of an object when you light and render it, even for seemingly inconsequential parts of the model.

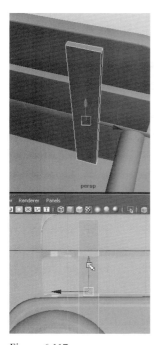

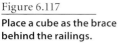

Figure 6.117
Place a cube as the brace behind the railings.

Figure 6.118
Bevel the brace.

20. Duplicate the brace, and place it toward the back of the wagon according to the side reference image. See Figure 6.119.

21. Select the top rail, and name it **topRail**. Name the bottom rail **bottomRail**, and name the braces **brace1** and **brace2**. Select all four objects (two rails and two braces), and group them together. Name the group **sideRailing**. Center the pivot (Modify → Center Pivot).

Figure 6.119
Duplicate and place the second brace.

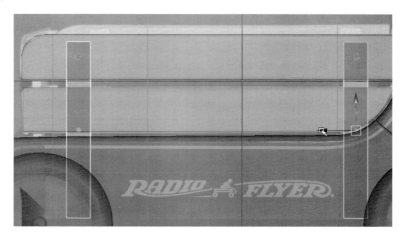

22. With the sideRailing group selected, duplicate the group and move it to the other side of the wagon. Set its X scale to **-1.0** to mirror it. Place it properly against the other side of the wagon, as shown in Figure 6.120. Feel free to adjust the length of the side railings to make them fit your model best; they don't need to line up exactly to the side reference image plane. Do what looks best for your model if you find you're deviating a bit from the reference images, which is easy to do.

23. Use the same procedures as in the previous steps to create the front and back railings. Figure 6.121 show these railings in a more detailed photo. The front railing is shown on the left, and the back railing is shown on the right.

Figure 6.120

Duplicate, mirror, and place the other side's railing.

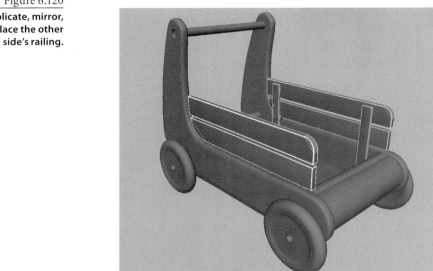

Figure 6.121

The front (left) and rear (right) railings of the wagon

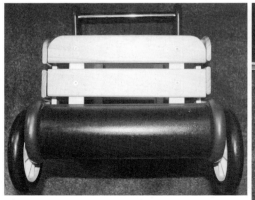

24. After you've created the railings, make sure to name them properly. Group the front railing objects together, and name the group **frontRailing**. Group the objects for the rear railing together, and name that group **rearRailing**. Figure 6.122 shows the railings in place, and Figure 6.123 shows the Outliner view of the scene.

And that's it! Save your work. The red wagon has taken shape and looks pretty good. Figure 6.124 shows the wagon in the persp panel, and Figure 6.125 shows a render of the wagon. Just wait until you render this puppy!

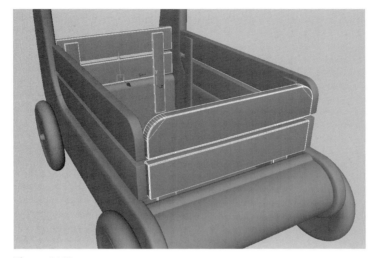

Figure 6.122

The railings are in place.

Figure 6.123

Keep everything properly named and grouped.

Figure 6.124

The completed wagon model

Figure 6.125

A render of the wagon!

You can load the scene file RedWagonModel_v07.ma from the Scenes folder of the RedWagon project on the CD to check your work or to skip to this point.

Adding Extra Details

Did I say you were done? For the best impact, let's add a few details to the railings and wagon body—namely screws and bolts. The little details of a model are always what make it look real. You may not miss the screws and bolts initially, but after you see them in the render, you'll know you did the right thing by spending the extra time.

Railing Screws

First, let's add screws to the railings. You can plainly see them in the reference photos in the scene, as well as in the photos of the real wagon throughout this chapter. The trick for the railing screws is that they're slightly indented into the wood. Instead of placing a screw model on the surface of the railings, let's go all the way and cut a small indentation into the wood where each screw is placed. For this, you'll turn to your sometimes dubious friend, the Boolean:

1. Using the side reference as a marker, create a cylinder (16 segments around are all you need), and size it to match the head of one of the screws in the wood railing. Duplicate this cylinder, and place one at every screw location on the railings. Set the cylinders just a bit into each railing, as shown in Figure 6.126.

Figure 6.126

Place the cylinders where the screws are, so you can Boolean a small notch into the wood.

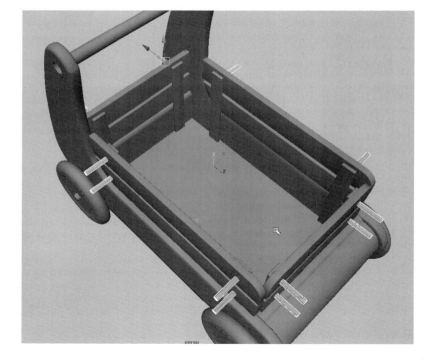

2. One at a time, select the first rail and then *one* of its cylinders, and choose Mesh → Booleans → Difference. A notch is cut into the wood rail, as shown in Figure 6.127. Repeat the procedure for the remaining rails, doing one cylinder at a time. You can't cut both cylinders out of one rail at once.

3. When all the notches are cut into the railings, as shown in Figure 6.128, select all the railing meshes and delete their history.

4. After you delete the history, look in the Outliner. All the railing meshes are removed from their proper hierarchy due to the Boolean operations. You have to place them back into the correct groups in the Outliner by MMB+dragging each railing node into its proper group, as shown in Figure 6.129. You can also rename them back to their original names.

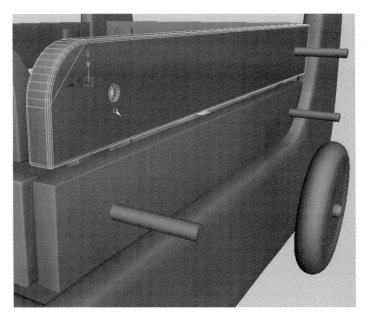

Figure 6.127

A shallow notch is cut into the wood.

Figure 6.128

Notches? We don't need no stinking notches!

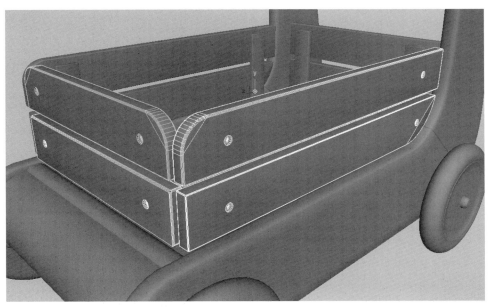

Figure 6.129

Place the railing meshes back in their proper groups.

Figure 6.129

Place the railing meshes back in their proper groups.

5. Now that you have notches, you need screws in them. You don't need to model the entire screw, just a screw head that you replicate many times. Create a poly cylinder with Axis Divisions of 16 and Height and Cap Divisions of 1. Size the cylinder to be a touch smaller than the diameter of the notches. Scale it down to make the cylinder into a fairly flat disk, as shown in Figure 6.130.

6. Create a poly box, and scale it down to fit into the screw head. Push the cube slightly into the disk. Copy the cube, and rotate it 90 degrees to create a cross in the screw head, as shown in Figure 6.130. Don't set the cross through the screw head, but about ¾ deep into it.

7. Select the disk and then the first cube, and choose Mesh → Booleans → Difference to cut a slit into the screw head. Select the screw head mesh and the next cube, and apply another Difference Boolean to cut a cross in the disk, as shown in Figure 6.131.

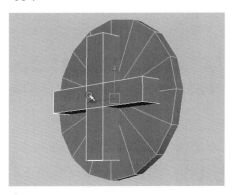

Figure 6.130

Create a disk and a cross for the screw head.

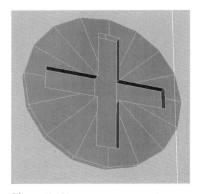

Figure 6.131

The screw head is almost finished.

8. Delete the history on the screw head.

9. You must do one more little thing for the screw head. Select the vertices at the middle of the cross, and scale them away from each other to add a bit of eccentricity to the screw head, as shown in Figure 6.132.

10. Select the top vertices at the end of each notch, and squeeze them together to taper in the tips of the notch in the screw head. See Figure 6.133. Center the pivot point, and name the mesh **screw**.

11. Duplicate the screw head and place one into each notch of the railings. You can use Snap to Points if you'd like to place them exactly into the notches in the wood, but make sure they sink only a little into the notch. You don't want the surface of the

wood railing to show through the screw's cross notch. Make sure you mirror the screws for the other side of the wagon so that the notched side of the screw is visible.

12. Place the screws in their appropriate groups, as shown in Figure 6.134. Figure 6.135 shows some of the screws in place.

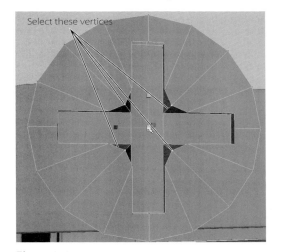

Figure 6.132

Add a touch of detail to the screw head.

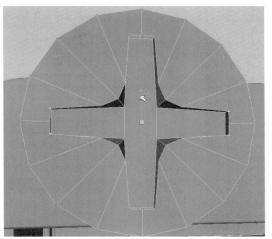

Figure 6.133

Taper the ends of the notches.

Figure 6.134

Group the screws under their respective railings.

Figure 6.135

The screws are in place!

Screws for the Wagon Body

While you're at it, let's add a couple of round-headed screws to the body of the wagon where the A and B panels meet:

1. To make that screw, create a poly sphere. Cut it in half with the Cut Faces tool (Edit Mesh → Cut Faces Tool), as you did earlier in the chapter with a cylinder to create the bullnose piece for the front of the wagon. Scale it down to flatten the hemisphere somewhat.

2. Select the faces of the hemisphere, as shown in Figure 6.136.

3. Extrude those faces into the screw head by choosing Edit Mesh → Extrude. Use the special manipulator to push in the faces and create a notch for the rounded screw head, as shown in Figure 6.137.

4. Delete the history, and freeze the transformations on the screw head.

5. Duplicate the rounded screw, and place copies on the wagon body as needed according to the reference images in your scene. You definitely need a couple of these screws at the junction of the A and B panels, which you created at the beginning of this modeling exercise, as shown in Figure 6.138.

6. Freeze all of the screws' transformations, and then group the rounded screws under the existing leftSidePanel and rightSidePanel groups to place them with their respective panels.

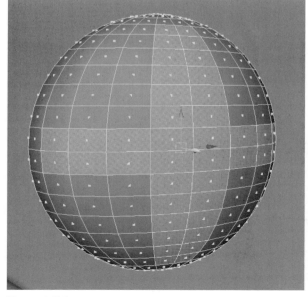

Figure 6.136

Creating a rounded screw head for the body of the wagon

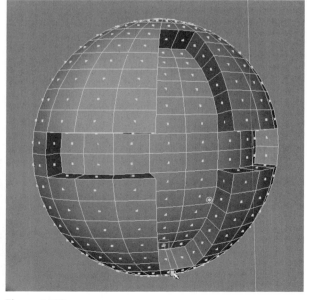

Figure 6.137

Extrude the faces to create the notch for the screw head.

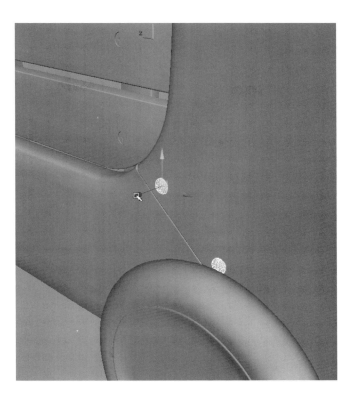

Figure 6.138
More screws

Taking the Wagon Model Further

That will do it—at least for this exercise. If you want, you can continue to add your own details to the wagon model, including the flanges on the inside that hold the braces for the rails as well as all the little bolts and screws on the body of the wagon. The back rims of the wheels are also a challenge to model. Figure 6.139 shows some of the additional details you may want to add.

Figure 6.139
When you're learning to model, adding more detail is never a bad idea.

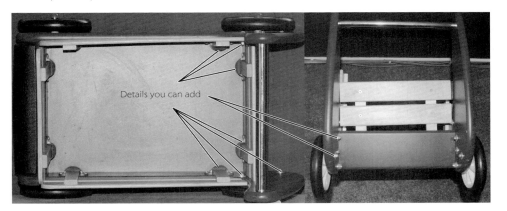

Details you can add

Compare Figure 6.140 to Figure 6.125. As you can see, there is more life to the model now that you've added some details.

Figure 6.140

Adding details, even small details, adds life to a model. Compare this to Figure 6.125, which has no screws.

Building a Decorative Box

In this thrilling exercise, you'll build a decorative box, shown in Figure 6.141. This box will be a fairly simple model to make, but you'll use it extensively in the following chapters about texture, light, and rendering.

Notice that the box has intricately carved grooves and surface features. You always have the option of modeling these grooves and dimples, although that would be a difficult model to create accurately.

Instead, you'll build the box to fit the reference, as you did with the wagon, and then rely on accurately created texture maps in the next chapter to create the details on the surface of the box.

You'll begin by creating the reference planes in the next section.

Figure 6.141

A photo of the decorative box

Creating Reference Planes

The image reference views of the decorative box have been created for you. You can find them in the Sourceimages folder of the Decorative_Box project. Table 6.2 lists their names, along with their statistics. Call over your neighbor; they may want to see this, too.

FILENAME	VIEW	IMAGE SIZE	ASPECT RATIO
boxFrontRef.jpg	Front	1749 × 2023	0.865:1
boxSideRef.jpg	Side	1862 × 2046	0.910:1
boxTopRef.jpg	Top	1782 × 1791	1.005:1

Table 6.2

Reference Views and Image Sizes

Just as you did with the wagon model early in this chapter, create three planes for each of the three views of the box. Use the ratios in Table 6.2 to size your reference planes as shown in Table 6.3, and place them as shown in Figure 6.142.

REFERENCE PLANE	WIDTH	HEIGHT
Front	0.865	1
Side	0.910	1
Top	1.005	1

Table 6.3

Reference Planes and Sizes

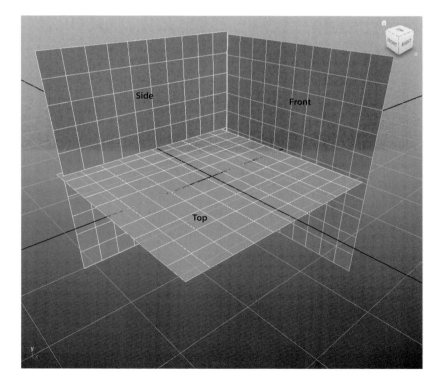

Figure 6.142

Arrange the reference planes for the box model.

Next, import the three reference JPEG images from the Sourceimages folder into the Hypershade window by dragging them into it, and map the photos to them to create the reference for the model.

Create three Lambert shaders just as you did for the wagon exercise, and connect one image to each Lambert shader. Assign the respective Lambert shader to the appropriate reference plane so you have the three model views set up. Press 6 for texture mode in the Perspective window, as shown in Figure 6.143.

Figure 6.143

The reference planes are fully set up for the box.

For a refresher on creating reference planes for the box, refer to the "Mapping the Reference Planes" section for the wagon tutorial toward the beginning of this chapter.

Modeling the Box

To model the box to fit the references, begin here:

1. Create a polygonal cube, and position and size it to roughly match the reference pictures of the decorative box.

2. To make it easier to see the reference planes in relation to the box you just created, in the Perspective panel's menu bar, select Shading → X-Ray, as shown in Figure 6.144.

3. Scale and position the cube to match the size of the main part of the box, as shown in Figure 6.145. Don't bother sizing the box to include the little feet on the bottom of the box. Use X-Ray mode in the side, front, and top modeling panels in Maya to line up the cube as best as you can. This will be the base model for the decorative box.

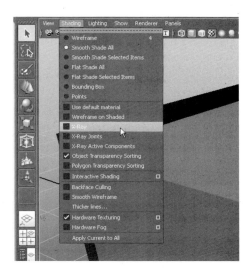

Figure 6.144

Set the display to X-Ray mode so you can see better how the poly cube and the decorative box line up.

Figure 6.145

Size the cube to fit the box references.

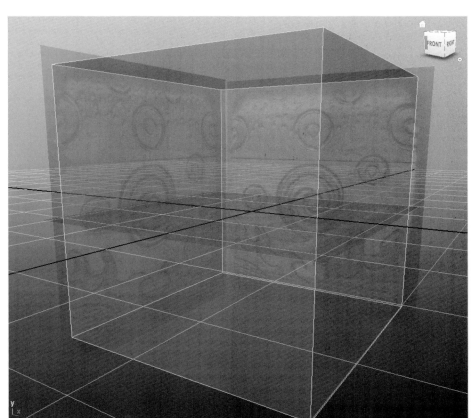

4. Switch off X-Ray mode in your views. Let's work on the rounded bevel on top of the box, where the lid is. Select the poly cube, open the Attribute Editor, and click the pCubeShape1 tab to access the shape node attributes. Under Object Display → Drawing Overrides, check Drawing Overrides to enable it. Uncheck Shading to display the poly cube as a wireframe while the reference planes remain displayed as textured planes. This way, you can more easily match the cube to the decorative box. (See Figure 6.146.)

5. Select the top four edges of the cube, and switch to the front view, as shown in Figure 6.147. Using the front view, you'll shape the top of the cube.

Figure 6.146

Display the cube as a wireframe.

Figure 6.147

Select the top four edges.

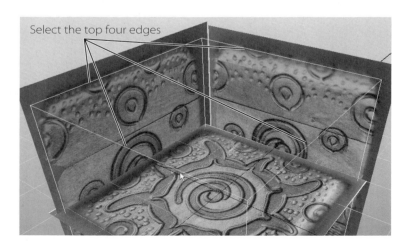

Select the top four edges

6. In the Polygons menu set, select Edit Mesh → Bevel. Don't worry about the settings; you'll adjust them after the fact. You should now have something like Figure 6.148 if your bevel options were at the defaults.

7. Select the cube. In the Attribute Editor, select the new polyBevel1 tab. Using the Front view panel, set Offset so that it lines up with the rounded top of the box, at about 0.26. Set Segments to 12. Make sure Auto Fit, Offset as Fraction, and World Space are all checked. Also make sure UV Assignment is set to Planar Project Per Face. (See Figure 6.149.)

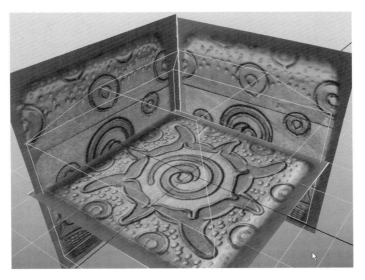

Figure 6.148

Default bevel

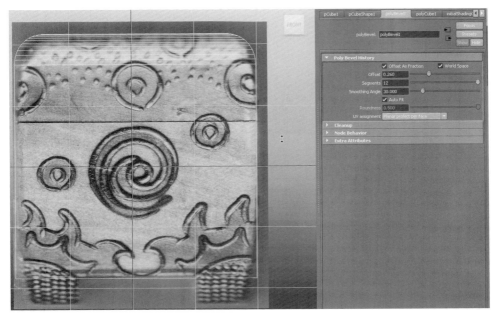

Figure 6.149

Set the bevel to fit the rounded top of the box in the front panel.

8. Move the vertices on the cube in the front and side panels to line up the other corners of the box to the reference images. (Don't worry about the curvature in the middle of the box or the feet just yet.) Doing so tapers the box slightly toward the bottom, as shown in Figure 6.150. Save your work.

9. Select Edit Mesh → Split Polygon Tool, and create four separate splits in the bottom face of the cube that line up with the legs of the box, as shown in Figure 6.151.

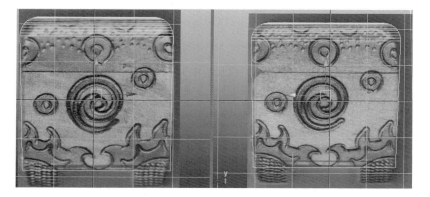

Figure 6.150

Taper the bottom of the cube.

Figure 6.151

Split the bottom face four times to create divisions for the box's feet.

10. Select the four corner faces on the bottom that you just created, and extrude them straight down to create the feet, as shown in Figure 6.152.

11. Using vertices, taper the feet to match the reference images in the front and side views.

12. There is a little curve to the middle of the box. Select the box, and then select Edit Mesh → Insert Edge Loop Tool ❐. You insert the edge loop manually because some geometry in Maya doesn't work properly with the automatic edge loop insertion you've used before. Turn off Auto Complete in the tool settings. Click a vertical edge of the

box toward the middle to select the first point. Click the other three vertical edges of the box to outline the edge loop, as shown in Figure 6.153. Press Enter to insert the edge loop.

Figure 6.152
Extrude the feet.

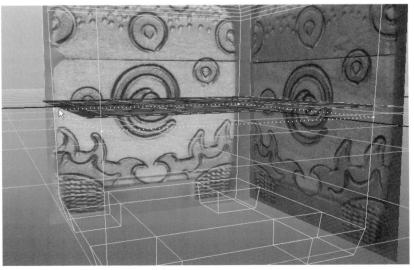

Figure 6.153

Insert an edge loop around the middle of the cube.

13. Use the new vertices to bow out the box in the middle slightly. Adjust the rest of the vertices to match the model to the box images in the side and front views. (See Figure 6.154.)

14. Now bevel the edges of the box throughout, to soften the crisp corners of the cube that the real box doesn't have. Select all the outer edges of the cube shown in Figure 6.155.

Figure 6.154
Adjust the cube to fit the box images.

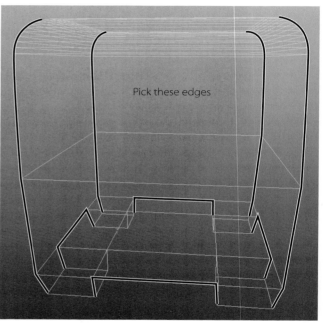

Figure 6.155
Select these edges for beveling.

15. Select the reference images, and hide them by selecting Display → Hide → Hide Selection or by pressing Ctrl+H. You can unhide them by selecting them again in the Outliner and selecting Display → Show → Show Selection or by pressing Shift+H. Notice that when an object is hidden, its Outliner entry is grayed out.

16. With those edges selected, select Edit Mesh → Bevel ❏. Set everything to the defaults, but change Segments from 1 to **3**. Click Bevel, and your box should resemble the one shown in Figure 6.156.

17. Select the cube, and delete its history by selecting Edit → Delete by Type → History. Save your work.

18. You have one final detail to tend to on the lid. You need to add the hinge area you can see in the Side view panel's reference image. Select the reference planes in the Outliner (pPlane1, pPlane2, and pPlane3), and press Shift+H to unhide them. Make sure you're in Textured mode in your views (press 6).

Figure 6.156

The beveled edges of the box

19. Select the box. Turn its display back to wireframe by going into the Attribute Editor and, in the pCubeShape1 tab, turning off Shading under the Object Display → Drawing Overrides heading.

20. Select Edit Mesh → Insert Edge Loop Tool ❑, and turn Auto Complete back on. In the side panel, insert five horizontal edge loops as shown in Figure 6.157, starting with the bottom one and going up. This gives you edges with which to create the wedge cutout where the box is hinged and that gives you a little indentation where the lid meets the box. You won't create a separate lid because you won't animate the box to open or close, and you don't need to see the inside.

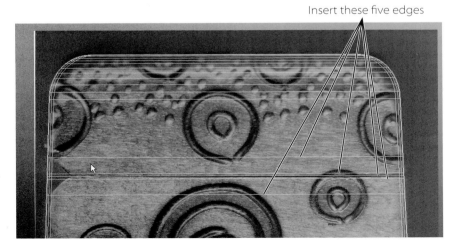

Insert these five edges

Figure 6.157

Insert these five edge loops for the lid of the box.

21. In the Side view panel, select the appropriate vertices (see Figure 6.158), and move them to create the wedge-shaped indentation as shown.

22. Choose Select → Select Edge Loop Tool. Select the middle edge loop you created earlier for the indent where the lid meets the box, as shown in Figure 6.159. Press R to scale the edge loop very slightly inward as shown.

Select this edge loop

23. Hide the reference planes again, and turn Shading back on for the cube in the Attribute Editor. Figure 6.160 shows the completed box. But there's still a little snag. Notice the dark area where the lid meets the box, where you just created the slightly indented line. This is due to Normals. It makes the lid look like it's angled inward.

24. Select the box, and choose Normals → Set Normal Angle. In the Set Normal Angle window that pops open, set the Angle to the default of 30, and click Apply and Close. Doing so fixes the darkening. For more on Normals, see the note in this section. Select the box, and delete its history.

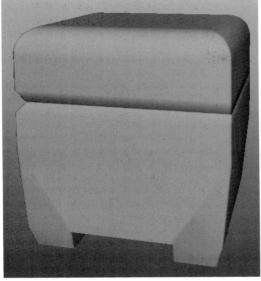

Figure 6.160

The completed box needs one more adjustment.

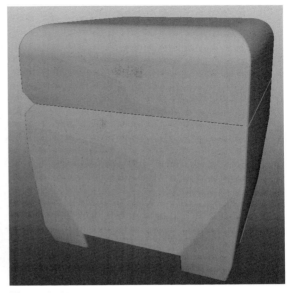

Figure 6.161

The box now looks right.

You're finished with the modeling portion of this decorative box. In the following chapters, you'll texture, light, and render the box with photorealism in mind. You can load boxModel.mb from the Scenes folder in the Decorative_Box project on the CD to compare your work.

NORMALS

Normals are imaginary lines that are perpendicular to a mesh's poly face and that define sides for that face. They also help determine how a renderer, such as mental ray, shades the surface. In some cases when you're modeling, you may notice an action that causes part of your model to display a darkened area as you see in the decorative box in Figure 6.160. By manually setting a Normal angle for the box as you did in step 24 of the exercise, you override the seeming display error. You'll learn more about Normals in Chapter 7.

Summary

In this chapter, you flexed your knowledge from the previous chapters and concentrated on creating a model of a child's toy wagon. You used many of the tools discussed in the previous chapters, from extruding, to adding edge loops, to using a lattice to finesse a shape, and even to sculpting by moving vertices and welding them together. You also used Booleans to create the notches and holes you needed in the wagon's railings and side panels, and then you fixed the problems that Booleans sometimes create.

You moved on to a simple model of a decorative box, leaving the intricate detailing of textures for the following chapter.

Creating a model can be a lot of hard and sometimes tedious work; but when you start seeing it take shape, the excitement begins to build. From the basic shaping of the wagon's parts to the detail of adding screws and bolts, you rolled up your sleeves and worked hard in this chapter to create the red wagon.

In the following chapter, you'll tackle some simple texturing for the wagon to see how to work with UVs. You'll then add detail to the decorative box by creating maps for displacement as well as color. Further on in the book, you'll light and render the wagon to make it look as photo-real as possible.

This doesn't mean your modeling experience is over! There's still plenty of detailing you can add to the wagon model. Or, you can take the procedures you used in this chapter to build your own wagon or decorative box design. The important lesson to take away from this chapter is how in-depth you can get with a model and how a lengthy modeling process takes shape. Along the way, don't forget to name your pieces and group everything in a sensible fashion.

CHAPTER 7

Maya Shading and Texturing

Shading is the Maya term for applying colors and textures, known in Maya as shaders. A shader defines an object's look—its color, tactile texture, transparency, luminescence, glow, and so forth.

Topics discussed in this chapter include:

- **Maya shading**
- **Shader types**
- **Shader attributes**
- **Texturing the axe**
- **Textures and surfaces**
- **Texturing the red wagon**
- **Working with and creating UVs**
- **Photoreal mapping: the decorative box**

Maya Shading

After you model your objects, Maya assigns a default shader to them with a neutral gray color. This is to allow them to render and display properly. If no shader is attached to a surface, an object can't be seen.

Shading is the proper term for applying a renderable color, surface bumps, transparency, reflection, shine, or similar attributes to an object in Maya. It's closely related to, but distinct from, *texturing,* which is what you do when you apply a map or other node to an *attribute of a shader* to create some sort of surface detail. For example, adding a scanned photo of a brick wall to the Color attribute of a shader that you assign to a model in Maya is considered applying texture. Adding another scanned photo of the bumps and contours of the same brick wall to the Bump Mapping attribute is also considered applying a texture. Nevertheless, because textures are often applied to shaders, the entire process of shading is sometimes informally referred to as *texturing.* Applying textures to shaders is also called *texture mapping* or simply *mapping.* You map a texture to the color node of a shader that is assigned or applied to a Maya object.

Shaders are based on nodes. Each node holds the attributes that define the shader. With shaders, akin to the hierarchies and groups of models, you create shader networks of interconnected nodes. These networks can be simple, or they can be intricate and involved, as when several render nodes are used to create complex shading effects.

Each shader, also known as a *shading group*, comprises a set of material nodes. *Material nodes* are the Maya nodes that hold all the pertinent rendering information about the object to which they're assigned, such as their color, opacity, or shininess. The shading groups are the nodes that allow the connection between the surface and the material you've created. When you edit the shader through the Attribute Editor, as you'll do later in this chapter, you edit its material node.

As you learn about shading in this chapter, you'll deal at length with the Hypershade window. See Chapter 2, "Jumping in Headfirst, with Both Feet," and Chapter 3, "The Maya 2011 Interface," for the layout of this window and for a hands-on introduction. You can access the Hypershade window by choosing Window → Rendering Editors. Shading in Maya is almost always done hand-in-hand with lighting. At the very least, textures are tweaked and edited in the lighting stage of production. Because the appearance of an object depends on light, in this chapter's exercise you'll create some lights as you create textures. You'll learn more about lighting in Chapter 10, "Maya Lighting."

Shader Types

Open the Hypershade by choosing Window → Rendering Editors → Hypershade. In the left column of the Hypershade window, you'll see a listing of Maya shading nodes

(Figure 7.1). The first section displays surface nodes, a.k.a. material nodes or shader types. Of these shader types, five are common to other animation packages as well. You'll use two of these later in this chapter.

To understand a bit more about shaders, consider what makes objects appear as they do in the real world. The short answer is light. The way light bounces off an object defines how you see that object. The surface of the object may have pigments that affect the wavelength of light that reflects off it, giving the surface color. Other features of that object's surface also dictate how light is reflected.

For the most part, shader types address the differences in how light bounces off surfaces. Most light, after it hits a surface, *diffuses* across an area of that surface. It may also reflect a hot spot called a *specular* highlight. The shaders in Maya differ in how they deal with specular and diffuse parameters according to the specific math that drives them. As you learn about the shader types, think of the things around you and what shader type would best fit them. Some Maya shaders are specific to creating special effects, such as the Hair Tube shader and the Use Background shader. It's important to learn the fundamentals first, so we'll cover the shading types you'll be using right off the bat.

Figure 7.1

The Maya shading nodes

The Lambert Shader Type

The most common shader type is *Lambert*, an evenly diffused shading type found in dull or matte surfaces. A sheet of paper, for example, is a Lambert surface.

A Lambert surface diffuses and scatters light evenly across its surface in all directions. (See Figure 7.2.)

Figure 7.2

A Lambert shader

The Phong Shader Type

Phong shading, named after its developer, Bui Tuong-Phong, who created it in 1975, brings to a surface's rendering the notions of specular highlight and reflectivity. A Phong surface reflects light with a sharp hot spot, creating a specular highlight that drops off sharply. (See Figure 7.3.) You'll find that glossy objects such as plastics, glass, and most metals take well to Phong shading.

Figure 7.3

A Phong shader

Figure 7.4

A Blinn shader

Figure 7.5

A Phong E shader

The Blinn Shader Type

Also named after its developer, James Blinn, the *Blinn* shading method brings to the surface a highly accurate specular lighting model that offers superior control over the specular's appearance. (See Figure 7.4.) A Blinn surface reflects light with a hot spot, creating a specular that diffuses somewhat more gradually than a Phong. The result is a shader that is good for use on shiny surfaces and metallic surfaces.

The Phong E Shader Type

The Phong E shader type expands the Phong shading model to include more control over the specular highlight. A Phong E surface reflects light much as a regular Phong does, but it has more detailed control over the specular settings to adjust the glossiness of the surface. (See Figure 7.5.) This creates a surface with a specular that drops off more gradually and yet remains sharper than a Blinn. Phong E also has greater color control over the specular than do Phong and Blinn, giving you more options for metallic reflections.

The Anisotropic Shader Type

The Anisotropic shader is good to use on surfaces that are deformed, such as a foil wrapper or warped plastic. (See Figure 7.6.)

Anisotropic refers to something whose properties differ according to direction. An Anisotropic surface reflects light unevenly and creates an irregular-shaped specular highlight that is good for representing surfaces with directional grooves, like CDs. This creates a specular highlight that is uneven across the surface, changing according to the direction you specify on the surface. In contrast with Blinn and Phong types, the specular highlight is evenly distributed to make a circular highlight on the surface.

The Layered Shader Type

A *Layered* shader allows the stacking of shaders to create complex shading effects, which is useful for creating objects composed of multiple materials. (See Figure 7.7.) By using the Layered shader to texture different materials on different parts of the object, you can avoid using excess geometry.

You control Layered shaders by using transparency maps to define which areas show which layers of the shader. You drag material nodes into the top area of the Attribute Editor and stack them from left to right, the left being the topmost layer assigned to the surface.

Figure 7.6
An Anisotropic shader

Figure 7.7
A Layered shader

Layered shaders are valuable resources to control compound and complex shaders. They're perfect for putting labels on objects or adding dirt to aged surfaces. You'll use a Layered shader in the axe-texturing exercise later in this chapter.

The Ramp Shader Type

A *Ramp texture* is a gradient that can be attached to almost any attribute of a shader as a *texture node*. Ramps can create smooth transitions between colors and can even be used to control particles. (See Chapter 12, "Maya Dynamics and Effects," for how a ramp is used to control particles.) When used as a texture, a ramp can be connected to any attribute of a shader to create graduating color scales, transparency effects, increasing glow effects, and so on. You'll use Ramp textures later in this chapter.

The *Ramp shader* is a self-contained shader node that automatically has several Ramp texture nodes attached to its attributes. These ramps are attached within the shader itself, so there is no need to connect external Ramp texture nodes. This makes for a simplified editing environment for the shader because all the colors and handles are accessible through the Ramp shader's own Attribute Editor, as shown in Figure 7.8.

To create a new color in any of the horizontal ramps, click in the swatch to create a new ramp position. Edit its color through its Selected Color swatch. You can move the position by grabbing the circle right above the ramp and dragging left or right. To delete a color, click the box beneath it.

Ramp textures are automatically attached to the Color, Transparency, Incandescence, Specular Color, Reflectivity, and Environment attributes

Figure 7.8
A Ramp shader in its Attribute Editor

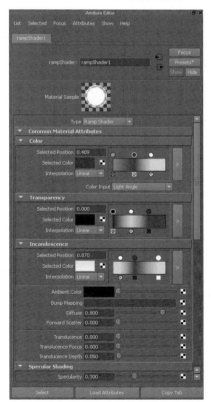

of a Ramp shader. In addition, a special curve ramp is attached to the Specular Roll Off to allow for more precise control over how the specular highlight diminishes over the surface.

Shader Attributes

Shaders are composed of nodes just like other Maya objects. Within these nodes, attributes define what shaders do. Here is a brief rundown of the common shader attributes with which you'll be working:

Color An RGB or HSV value defines what color the shader is when it receives a neutral color light. For more on RGB and HSV, see Chapter 1, "Introduction to Computer Graphics and 3D."

Transparency The higher the Transparency value, the less opaque and more see-through the object becomes.

Although usually expressed in a black-to-white gradient, with black being opaque or solid and white being totally clear, transparency can have color. In a color transparency, the shader's color shifts because only some of its RGB values are transparent, as opposed to the whole.

Ambient Color This color affects the Color attribute of the shader as more ambient light is created in the scene. Ambient color tends to flatten an object because this attribute evenly colors the object. This attribute is primarily used to create flat areas and should be used with care. The default is black, which keeps the darker areas of a surface dark. The lighter the ambient color, the lighter those areas are. A bright Ambient Color setting flattens out an object, as shown in Figure 7.9.

Figure 7.9

Ambient color values

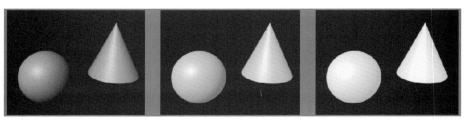

Ambient Color = Black   Ambient Color = Medium Gray   Ambient Color = White

Incandescence This is the ability to self-illuminate. Objects that seem to give off or have their own light, such as an office's fluorescent light fixture, can be given an Incandescence value. Incandescence doesn't, however, light objects around it in regular renders, nor does it create a glow. It also serves to flatten the object into a pure color. As you'll see in Chapter 11, "Maya Rendering," incandescence can also help light a scene in mental ray's

Final Gather rendering. The value of Incandescence (as well as the color) of an object is used to calculate the overall brightness in a Final Gather scene. (See Figure 7.10.)

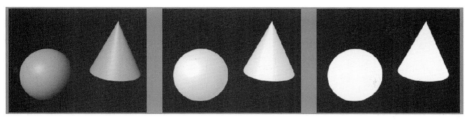

Incandescence = 0   Incandescence = 0.5   Incandescence = 1

Figure 7.10
Incandescence values

Bump Mapping This attribute creates a textured feel for the surface by adding highlights and shadows to the render. It doesn't alter the surface of the geometry, although it makes the surface appear to have ridges, marks, scratches, and so forth. The bump map has to be a texture node such as a ramp, a fractal noise, or an image file. The more intense the variation in tones of that map, the greater the bump. Bump maps are frequently used to make surfaces look more real, because nothing in reality has a perfectly smooth surface. Using bumps very close up may create problems; bumps are generally good for adding inexpensive detail to a model that isn't in extreme close-up. (See Figure 7.11.)

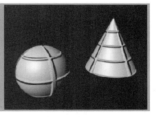

No Bump Map   Fractal Texture Bump Map   Grid Texture Bump Map

Figure 7.11
The effects of a bump map

Close-up geometry, where you have to change the topology of the model physically using texture maps, requires displacement maps. We'll cover displacement maps in Chapter 11.

Diffuse This value governs how much light is reflected from the surface in all directions. When light strikes a surface, light disperses across the surface and helps to illuminate it. The higher this value, the brighter its object is when lit, because more of the striking light is reflected from the surface. The lower the Diffuse value, the more light is "absorbed" into the surface, yielding a darker result, especially in areas that aren't well lit. Metals have very low Diffuse values because they rely on reflections and direct light. (See Figure 7.12.)

Figure 7.12

How a Diffuse value affects a shader's look

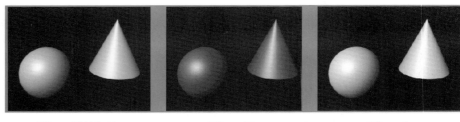

Diffuse = 0.8 (default)   Diffuse = 0.3   Diffuse = 1

Translucence and Translucence Focus The Translucence and Translucence Focus attributes give the material the ability to transmit light through its surface, like a piece of canvas in front of a light. At a value of 1 for Translucence, all light shines through the object; at 0, none does. The Translucence Focus attribute specifies how much of that light is scattered. A light material such as paper should have a high translucence focus, and thicker surfaces should have low focus rates.

Glow Intensity Found in the Special Effects section of the Attribute Editor, the Glow Intensity attribute adds a glow to the object, as if it were emitting light into a foggy area. (See Figure 7.13.) You'll add glow to an object in Chapter 10.

Figure 7.13

Adding a glow

Glow = 0   Glow = 0.5   Glow = 1

Matte Opacity Objects rendered through Maya generate a solid *matte*. Where there is an object, the matte is white; where there is nothing, the matte is black. This helps compositing programs, which bring together elements created independently into a single composite scene, to separate rendered CG from their backgrounds. Turning down the slider decreases the brightness of the object's matte, making it appear more transparent. This is usually used for compositing tricks or to make an object render in RGB but not appear in any composites. For more information about mattes, see both the sidebar "Image Mattes" in this chapter and Chapter 11.

Raytrace Options With raytracing, you can achieve true reflections and refractions in your scene. This subset of attributes allows you to set the shader's raytracing abilities. See Chapter 11 for more on raytracing.

Beginners' Gallery

On the following pages, you'll find some images from the book as well as images created by a few artists fairly new to Maya. We hope these images will inspire your own creativity as you become more familiar with 3D in general and Maya specifically.

Some of these artists have been using Maya for only a short period of time, and already they've been able to use the tools and techniques they've learned to channel their artistic eye and creativity into some beautiful and interesting imagery. (All images are used with permission.)

This still life from Chapter 10 was modeled and textured by Maya students Juan Guitierrez and Robert Jauregui. The fruit still life was modeled by Guitierrez using mostly polygons. The textures were created by Jauregui, who took this opportunity to learn all about UV texture space and mapping polygons because this was his first texturing experience inside Maya. Dariush Derakhshani laid out the scene, lit it, and rendered it to demonstrate some rendering concepts.

ABOVE: This pool table was modeled by Victor Garza to demonstrate modeling techniques in an introductory Maya class and to show the students how to be creative when combining surfaces to form a complex object. After Garza modeled the table, he and Dariush Derakhshani textured and lit the scene.
BELOW: Dariush Derakhshani created this box full of marbles to test indirect lighting options with mental ray for Maya. The scene is made of very simple geometry, with the majority of the work going into lighting and rendering using mental ray for Maya.

ABOVE: This living room scene was modeled by Huyen Dang of The Art Institute of California—Los Angeles for a lighting class, and it was lighted by Dariush Derakhshani using global illumination in mental ray. The color render can be enhanced with the addition of an Ambient Occlusion pass to add detail and contact shadows. BELOW: The Ambient Occlusion render creates contact shadows and some further detail in the dark areas of the image to enhance the look of the color render. This pass is multiplied in a compositing package to add realism.

ABOVE: This is a photo of the real decorative box modeled and textured in Chapters 6 and 7, lit in Chapter 10, and finally rendered with mental ray for Maya in Chapter 11. BELOW: The decorative box model from Chapter 6 was lit and rendered with mental ray for Maya and placed into a photographed background plate.

ABOVE: Brittany Biggs' intent with her student film *A Tall Tail* was to create a 2D fairytale storybook in a 3D setting. She first drew the characters in their different views and scanned them to apply as textures to animatable cut-out models created in Maya. Here, she used lighting cleverly to create a moody atmosphere. Brittany created her characters with animation rigs to simulate stop-motion animation style as part of the aesthetic of her film.
BELOW: Sepehr Dehpour from University of Southern California's John C. Hench Division of Animation and Digital Arts (DADA) depicts a barren landscape for his fantastical character as part of his thesis film. He achieved the tactile feel of the stone through clever texturing.

ABOVE: Tayler Hudson from Art Institute of California—Los Angeles created this impressive library for her Advanced Materials and Lighting Class. Using carefully painted textures, she achieved a nice level of detail. **BELOW:** This is an otter character modeled and textured by Ben Knox at Piedmont Com munity College (North Carolina) for his 3D modeling class. Originally a Blender user, Ben is working in Maya on creating different otter face shapes to create a talking character.

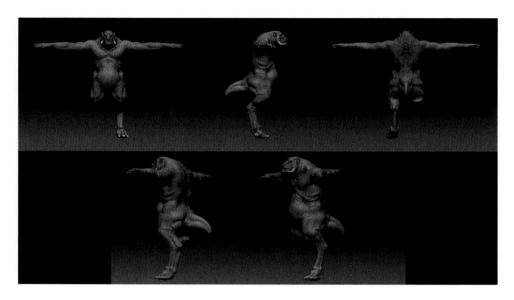

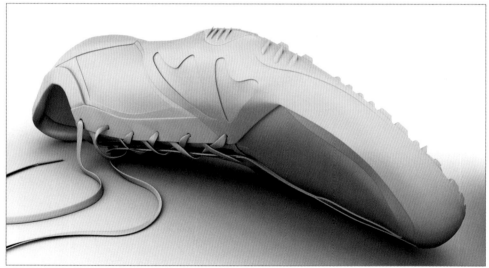

ABOVE: Kami Solomon modeled this character at The Art Institute of California—Los Angeles in Maya and used ZBrush for texturing. **BELOW:** Brian Lee of USC's John C. Hench Division of Animation and Digital Arts created this model of a golf shoe while attending his graduate-level courses. His choice to render the shoes as Ambient Occlusion black-and-white proofs showed off his clean models. A recent graduate, Brian focused on creating solid models because he knew that a good scene always starts with solid assets.

Some attributes are available only with certain shader types. The following are the attributes for the Phong, Phong E, and Blinn shaders:

Specular Color The color of the highlights on a shiny surface. Black produces no specular, and white creates a bright one.

Reflectivity The amount of reflection visible in the surface. The higher the value, the more reflective the object will render. Increasing this value increases the visibility of the Reflected Color attribute or of true reflections in the scene when raytraced.

Reflected Color Gives the surface a reflection. Texture maps are generally assigned to this attribute to give the object a reflection of whatever is in the image file or texture without having to generate time-consuming true reflections with a raytraced render. Using ray-tracing to get true reflections, however, is the only way to generate reflections of other objects in the scene.

Cosine Power Only available with a Phong shader. This attribute changes the size of the shiny highlights (a.k.a. specular) on the surface. The higher the number; the smaller the highlight looks.

IMAGE MATTES

As you learned in Chapter 1 (and will explore further in Chapter 11), image files are stored with a red, a green, and a blue channel that keep the amount of each color in each pixel of the image. Some image formats, including TIFF and TARGA, also have an alpha channel, known as a *matte channel* or *image matte*. This is a grayscale channel that controls the opacity of an image. Completely white parts of the matte make those parts of the image opaque (solid), whereas black parts make those parts of the image fully transparent. Gray in the matte channel makes those parts of the image partly transparent. These mattes are used in *compositing*—bringing together elements created separately into a single composite scene. See Chapter 11 for an example of how an alpha channel works.

Roughness, Highlight Size, Whiteness Control the specular highlight on a Phong E surface only. They control specular focus, amount of specular, and highlight color, respectively.

mental ray Attributes Because Autodesk now integrates features of its mental ray rendering engine into Maya, an object's Attribute Editor usually includes a set of mental ray options. Shaders are no different. If you open the Mental Ray heading in the Attribute Editor for a shader, you'll see attributes such as Reflection Blur and Irradiance, as well as a few ways to override Maya's shading attributes with mental ray's own.

An in-depth discussion of the mental ray attributes is beyond the scope of this introductory text. But it's a good idea to know that this brief section is available to you after you have more experience with rendering and you want to work with mental ray at its more advanced levels in Maya. You'll work with mental ray in Chapters 10 and 11.

Texturing the Axe

In this section, you'll add shaders to a NURBS modeled axe to make it look real; in the next chapter, you'll import this axe into an animation exercise. Starting animation on a project and then replacing it with a finished and textured model is a fairly common practice with Maya.

Load axe_texture_A.mb from the Axe project on the CD.

You'll start by texturing the metal parts of the axe. Even though you can find a good metal to use for your axe head in Maya's shader library or on Autodesk's website, for this exercise you'll make a simple metal from scratch. Because the look of real metals is greatly affected by their surroundings (that is, by the reflections of the environment), metal is one of the toughest materials to create and to light. In many cases, metals are lighted and rendered with HDR Image Based Lighting, a technique too advanced for this book. It will be easier to learn when you're more familiar with lighting and rendering with Maya.

> Autodesk's website lists several premade shaders for your use. Maya also includes a shader library on its installation CD.

The Metal Axe Head

First, set up your render parameters so that you can render out your axe while you're tweaking the Metal shader to get it right:

1. Choose Window → Rendering Editors → Render Settings, or click (⬛) in the menu bar to open the Render Settings window. Make sure Render Using is set to Maya Software.

2. In the Image Size section under the Common tab, set Presets to 640 × 480. In the Anti-Aliasing Quality section under the Maya Software tab, use the Intermediate Quality preset. This will give you a good look for the final render with a short render time.

3. Open the Hypershade window, and click Phong under the Create pane on the left. A new Phong shader shows up in both the top and the bottom parts of the Hypershade window.

4. Double-click the phong1 shader node in the Hypershade window to open the Attribute Editor, and name the shader **Metal**.

5. Click the gray swatch next to the Color attribute to open the Color Chooser. Select a light blue-gray. In the Slider section, the HSV values should be something like H: 207, S: 0.085, and V: 0.80. Click Accept.

6. Back in the shader's Attribute Editor, click the gray swatch for Specular Color. By changing this color, you control the hue and brightness of the highlights on this surface. Use a bright faded blue with HSV values of H: 208, S: 0.20, and V: 0.90.

7. Increase the spread of the specular highlights by changing Cosine Power from the default of 20 to 2.0. Doing so creates a large area for the bright highlights, implying a polished reflective surface.

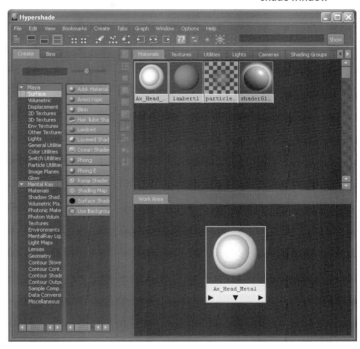

Figure 7.14

The Metal shader's material node, as shown in the Hypershade window

8. To assign the shader to the surfaces, select both sides of the axe head. In the Hypershade, right-click the shader node (in either the upper or lower window), and choose Assign Material to Selection from the shortcut menu. Figure 7.14 shows the shader.

9. Make sure your perspective view is active, and click the Render the Current Frame button ( ) in the menu bar. Check out different angles of the axe, and render them to see how the metal axe head responds to the default lights that Maya inserts into the scene for your render.

   This procedure creates a simple Metal shader that works well overall. To create a more polished look for the axe head, you can add a reflection to it using an Environment texture node. This node creates a 3D texture node in the scene that projects its contents onto the Material attribute to which it has been connected. As an object animates through the scene, different parts of the texture are reflected on its surface.

10. In the Metal shader's Attribute Editor, click the Map button next to the Reflected Color attribute, as shown in Figure 7.15. Doing so attaches a new node to create a reflection and opens the Create Render Node window. Click the Env Textures section, and select Env Chrome. An environment texture will provide an interesting reflection.

Figure 7.15

You can add a texture to a shader's attribute by clicking the checkered Map button.

11. Move the Reflectivity slider from 0.50 to 0.85. The higher this number, the more prominent the Reflected Color in the surface. Figure 7.16 shows the axe before and after a reflection. The Env Chrome reflection texture makes the axe look polished by reflecting a grid representing the ground and a bright blue sky.

Figure 7.16

The axe head before and after a reflection is mapped onto the shader

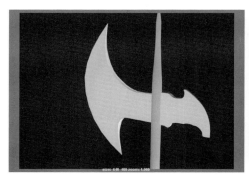
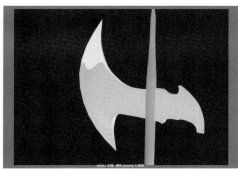

Figure 7.17

Use placement nodes in the scene to scale and position textures.

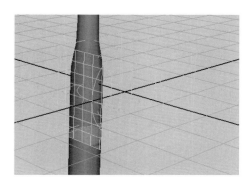

After you create the Env Chrome texture, you'll see a green object in the Modeling windows at the origin, as shown in Figure 7.17. This is the Env Chrome's placement node. You can manipulate this node just as you manipulate other Maya objects—in other words, move, rotate, and scale it.

Altering this will change how the environment chrome projects itself in the scene. For example, if you increase the size of this placement node, the grid showing in the reflection of the axe will get larger. For more on projections and placement nodes, see the "Texture Nodes" section later in this chapter.

The Wooden Handle

A glossy cherry wood would look good for the handle, so a Phong shader will be best:

1. In the Hypershade, choose Create → Materials → Phong. Set Diffuse to 0.70, Specular Color to a light gray, and Cosine Power to 50.

2. Click the Map button for the color. In the Create Render Node window, select Wood in the 3D Textures section. Figure 7.18 shows this texture in the Attribute Editor.

3. In the Wood Attribute Editor, adjust Filler Color to a nice reddish brown with an HSV of 8.5, 0.85, and 0.43. Change Vein Color to a darker version of the filler with HSV color values of 8.5, 0.75, and 0.08, respectively.

4. Change Vein Spread to 0.70, change Layer Size to 0.119, and darken Grain Color a bit by pulling the slider to the left, but not all the way, as shown in Figure 7.19. This gives you a nice dark cherry wood.

The Wood texture is a projected 3D texture; it's projected from a source onto the object using a placement node, just like the Env Chrome on the axe head's reflection. To assign the Wood texture from the Hypershade, select the handle, and right-click the shader to select Assign Material to Selection; or MMB+click and drag the icon onto the handle in the viewport. For more on projected textures, see the "Texture Nodes" section later in this chapter.

You can assign a shader to any object by MMB+clicking and dragging its icon from the Hypershade to the object in the viewport.

5. To see this dark texture on your object, create a new light in the scene. In the main menu, choose Create → Lights → Ambient Light. (For more on lights, see Chapter 10.) Open the Attribute Editor for the light by pressing Ctrl+A or by double-clicking its icon on the Lights tab in the Hypershade. Increase the Intensity attribute to 2.5.

6. Render a frame of the axe handle up close, as shown in Figure 7.20. Notice how the wood repeats on the handle and creates an undesirable texture. You need to adjust the Wood texture's placement.

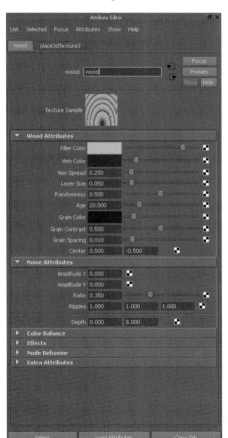

Figure 7.18

The Wood texture in its Attribute Editor

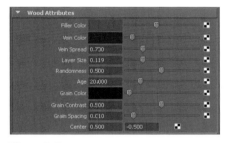

Figure 7.19

Set the Wood texture's attributes.

Figure 7.20

The Wood texture repeats too much by default.

7. To get to the Wood texture's placement node, open the Hypershade. Drag the Wood shader to the Hypershade work area (bottom half). Right-click the wood, and choose Graph Network from the shortcut menu. You can also select it and click the Input Connections button (📥) at the top of the Hypershade. Figure 7.21 shows the shader nodes for the Wood Shader network in the Hypershade work area. The place3dTexture2 node connects to the wood2 node and gives it position information. The wood2 node then connects to the phong3 material node as a Color texture map.

Figure 7.21

The Wood Shader network

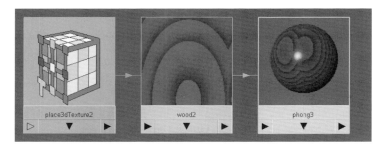

8. Double-click the place3dTexture node to open its Attribute Editor.

9. Click the Fit to Group BBox button to position the placement node for the wood around the handle automatically. In your viewport, you see the green placement node around the handle, as shown in Figure 7.22.

10. Rendering a frame reveals that the wood still doesn't look quite right. Select the placement node in the viewport, and rotate it in *Z* to 90. Click the Fit to Group BBox button again to rescale it to fit the handle. This doesn't rotate it back to the way it was; it only scales it to fit the extent of the object to which it's assigned.

11. Render another frame, and you see the wood veins running the length of the handle. It looks more like wood now, but it still repeats too much.

Instead of moving and scaling the texture placement node and rendering multiple times to get the wood placement just right,

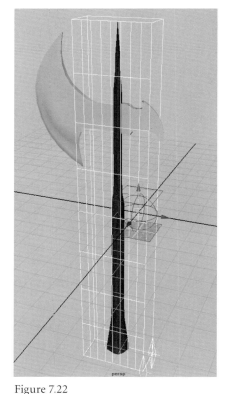

Figure 7.22

The wood's placement node

you can use Maya's Interactive Photorealistic Rendering (IPR) to see your changes in real time. Choose the camera panel to render, and click the IPR Render the Current Frame button () in the Status line; or choose Render → IPR Render Current Frame.

The Render View window shows a lower-quality render of the axe. It prompts you to select a region to begin tuning. Drag a marquee selection in the Render View window around the handle. IPR refreshes that part of the window. Every change you make to the texture placement node prompts IPR to update that section of the render, giving you a fast update on the positioning and scale of the Wood texture.

12. Select the texture placement node, and scale it up in the three axes until you get a good-looking grain. Figure 7.23 shows a well-spaced wood grain.

The scene file `axe_texture_B.mb` in the Axe project on the CD will bring you up to this point.

Layered Shaders: The Metal Spike

Currently, the entire length of the handle is shaded as wood, including the top spike. The spike on the axe head should be metal like the axe head.

You can approach this in two ways: with geometry or with shaders. If you manipulate the NURBS geometry, you select a horizontal isoparm and detach the spike portion of the handle to make it a separate surface. You then assign a Metal shader to the new tip surface.

Using a shader instead of cutting up or creating more geometry can be desirable in many instances. For example, you may not be able to detach surfaces like this all the time.

The Layered shader is a normal surface shader that allows you to stack materials on top of each other to assign to a surface. You control which layer of material is exposed, and by how much, by assigning transparency values or textures to each layer. Use a Ramp texture to specify where on the handle the wood stops and the metal starts.

To create a Layered shader, follow these steps:

1. Select the axe handle, and in the Rendering menu set, choose Lighting/ Shading → Assign New Material → Layered Shader to open the Attribute Editor, as shown in Figure 7.24. By default, the Layered shader contains a green layer in the top of the Attribute Editor window. From left to right, the layers are displayed in the order in which they appear from top to bottom as they're assigned to the surface. (This means the left-most shader in the Layered shader is on top of all the others.)

Figure 7.23

The wooden handle after the texture has been scaled and placed

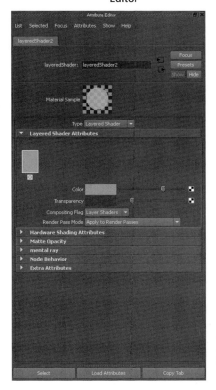

Figure 7.24

The Layered shader in the Attribute Editor

Choosing Lighting/Shading → Assign New Material is an easy way to create and assign a material without having to open the Hypershade.

2. Using the Hypershade, MMB+click and drag the metal material you've made into the top region of the Layered shader's Attribute Editor window, under the Layered Shader Attributes section. To delete the default green material, click the Xed square beneath it. The Material Sample icon in the Attribute Editor turns into the metal.

3. MMB+click and drag the wood material into the Layered shader's Attribute Editor. Make sure it's placed to the left of the metal material. If the materials are already in place, you can rearrange their order by MMB+clicking and dragging them left or right of the other materials in the Attribute Editor. Notice in Figure 7.25 that the Material Sample icon changed to the wood material. The wood is now the top layer, so only it will show until you give it some transparency to reveal metal at the tip.

You can see the names of the materials in the Layered shader by pointing to the icons.

4. Click the Wood Shader icon in the Layered shader's Attribute Editor to highlight it. Notice that the Transparency Map button (as well as Color) is now a square with an arrow ( ) as opposed to the checkerboard you've seen before. Click this button to open the Attribute Editor for the wood material.

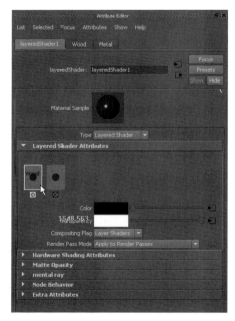

When an attribute is already mapped, its Map button turns from a checkerboard to an Input Connection icon. Clicking it opens the Attribute Editor for whatever node is attached to that attribute. In this case, clicking the Map button opens its Attribute Editor because the wood material was assigned to this layer. Here you need to attach a transparency ramp to control where the metal tip starts and the wooden handle ends.

Figure 7.25

The Layered shader with the wood on top of the metal

5. Click the Map button for the wood's Transparency attribute. Create a Ramp texture node. Make sure the Normal radio button is checked and not the As Projection or As Stencil radio button.

6. In the ramp's Attribute Editor, change Interpolation to None, and change Type to U Ramp.

7. Delete the middle (green) color by clicking the square to the right of green's position. Select the bottom (red) color by clicking its round handle on the left of the ramp. Change the Selected Color attribute to white. Drag it all the way to the bottom of the ramp.

8. Select the top color (blue), and change it to black. Drag the handle down the ramp to a Selected Position of 0.105. Figure 7.26 shows the ramp position and the axe. If you're in Texture Display mode in the perspective view (press the 6 key), you see that the tip of the model is a blue-gray color (metal) and the bottom of the handle is a reddish brown (wood). As you adjust the position of the white color on the ramp, notice how the spike and handle change.

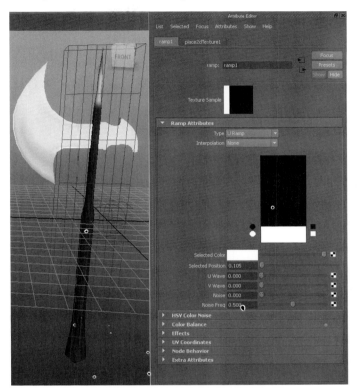

Figure 7.26

The Ramp texture is set on the wood's Transparency attribute controls where the wood and metal meet.

9. In the Hypershade, choose Edit → Delete Unused Nodes to purge all unused shading nodes from your scene. Make sure your Layered shader and Metal shader are assigned, of course.

10. Render out a frame of the axe. Save this frame in the render buffer by clicking Keep Image (📷) in the Render View window. This keeps the image so you can scroll back to it for reference. A scroll bar appears at the bottom of the Render View window.

11. Select the axe's top node, and rotate it about 45 degrees in *Z* to angle it. Render a frame at this point. Notice how the grain of the wood has changed. Use the scroll bar to toggle back and forth and compare these two images, as shown in Figure 7.27.

When a projected texture, such as the wood, doesn't "stick" to an object, and the object seems to move through the texture, the object is said to be *swimming* through the projection. The wood is being projected by the 3D placement node

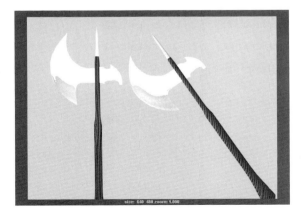

Figure 7.27

The wood grain changes as the axe moves.

that you positioned to get the grain just right, so you need to group the texture node under the axe's top node. When the axe moves, the texture will stick with it, maintaining its orientation with the axe.

12. Rotate the axe back to 0 in *Z*. Select the place3dTexture2 node from either the viewport (it's the green texture you scaled to fit the handle as you see here) or the Outliner. Be careful not to use the Env Cube's 3D placement node you used for the axe head reflection. In the Outliner, MMB+click and drag it under the axe's topmost node, as shown in Figure 7.28.

The file axe_texture_C.mb, in the Scenes folder of the Axe project on the CD has the final textured axe for your reference.

Now you have a fully textured axe. Because you used a Layered shader, you didn't need to build another piece of geometry to represent a metal tip. You can embellish a model a lot at the texturing level. Although you may first consider using geometry, you can accomplish a number of tasks by using simple texturing tricks, such as those you used for the axe handle and its metal spike. The more you explore and experience shaders and modeling, the better you'll be at juggling modeling with texturing to get the most effective solution.

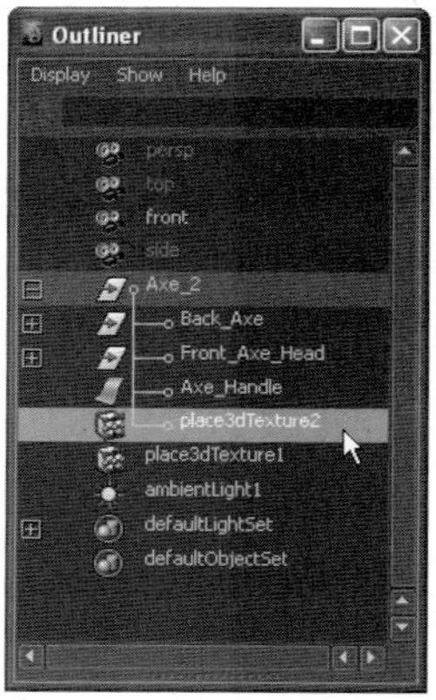

Figure 7.28

Group the placement node for the handle under the axe geometry's group node.

You'll begin texturing the red wagon from Chapter 6, "Practical Experience," later in this chapter and then go into more detailed texturing with the decorative box, which you'll then light and render in mental ray. For even more practice, try loading the locomotive model from Chapter 4, "Beginning Polygonal Modeling," and texturing it from top to bottom. A great deal of independent geometry needs textures, some of which must be carefully placed with 3D placement nodes. Experiment with as many different ways of shading the locomotive as you can figure out.

Textures and Surfaces

Texture nodes generate maps to connect to an attribute of a shader. There are two types of textures: procedural and bitmapped (sometimes called maps). *Procedural* textures use Maya's own nodes' attributes to generate an effect, such as ramp, checkerboard, or fractal noise textures. You can adjust each of these procedural textures by changing their attribute values.

A *map*, on the other hand, is a saved image file that is imported into the scene through a File texture node. These files are pregenerated through whatever imaging programs you have and include digital pictures and scanned photos. You need to place all texture nodes onto their surfaces through the shader. You can map them directly onto the surfaces' UV values or project them.

BAKING A TEXTURE PROJECTION

In the axe handle texturing exercise, you grouped the 3dplacement node for the wood grain to the handle of the axe to make the texture stick to the handle. But you can also *bake* the texture onto the axe handle by converting the texture projection to a file node. By baking the texture node, you convert the 3dplacement node into an image file that is then mapped to the color channel of the material, discarding the projection node, so you needn't group it with the handle as you did earlier.

Follow these steps to bake the wood-grain texture to the axe:

1. Open the Hypershade.

2. Click to select the axe handle's Layered shader node, and MMB+click and drag it to the work area of the Hypershade.

3. Right-click it, and select Graph Network to see all the nodes of the Layered shader (shown here).

4. Select the axe handle geometry, and then Shift+click the texture node wood2node in the Hypershade.

5. Choose Edit → Convert to File Texture (Maya Software) ❒. In the option box, select an X Resolution and a Y Resolution of 512 each, and click Convert and Close. If you get an error when you convert, you can choose Edit → Delete Unused Nodes and try again. The shader rebuilds itself to create a texture file, a material, and a shading group node that is automatically assigned to the selected geometry. Delete all unused nodes again to clean up the Hypershade window. Your new Shader network should appear as pictured here.

Notice that the 3dplacement node, as well as the Hypershade view, is removed from the scene. Your axe handle's texture now sticks to the handle as a mapped-file texture instead.

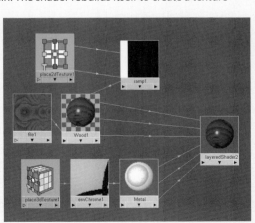

Figure 7.29

Selecting the type of map layout

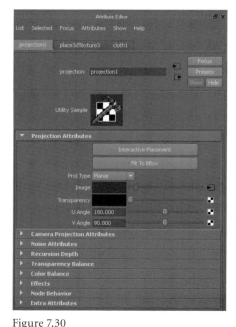

Figure 7.30

The projection node in the Attribute Editor

UV Mapping

UV mapping places the texture directly on the surface and uses the surface coordinates for its positioning (called UVs). In this case, you must do a lot of work to line up the UVs on the surface to make sure the created images line up properly. What follows is a brief summary of how UV mapping works. You'll get hands-on experience with UV layout with the red wagon and decorative box exercises later in this chapter.

Just as 3D space is based on coordinates in *XYZ*, surfaces have coordinates denoted by *U* and *V* values along a 2D coordinate system for width and height. The UV value helps a texture position itself on the surface. The *U* and *V* values range from 0 to 1, with (0,0) UV being the origin point of the surface.

Maya creates UVs for primitive surfaces automatically, but frequently you need to edit UVs for proper texture placement, particularly on polygonal meshes after you've edited them. In some instances, placing textures on a poly mesh requires projecting the textures onto the mesh, because the poly UVs may not line up as expected after the mesh has been edited. See the next section, "Using Projections."

If the placement of your texture or image isn't quite right, simply use the 2D placement node of the texture node to position it properly. See the section "Texture Nodes" later in this chapter for more information.

Using Projections

You need to place textures on the surface. You can often do so using UV placement, but some textures need to be projected onto the surface. It's common to project textures (when texturing polys, for example). A *projection* is what it sounds like. The file image, ramp, or other texture being used can be *beamed* onto the object in several ways.

You can create any texture node as either a normal UV map or a projected texture. In the Create Render Node window, clicking a texture icon creates it as a normal mapped texture. To create the texture as a projection, you must right-click the icon and select Create as Projection. (See Figure 7.29).

When you create a projected texture, a new node is attached to the texture node. This projection node controls the method of projection with an attached 3D placement node, which you saw in the axe exercise. Select the projection node to set the type of projection in the Attribute Editor. (See Figure 7.30.)

Setting the projection type will allow you to project an image or a texture without having it warp and distort, depending on the model you're mapping. For example, a planar projection on a sphere will warp the edges of the image as they stretch into infinity on the sides of the sphere.

Try This In a new scene, create a NURBS sphere and a NURBS cone, and place them side by side. Create a Blinn shader, and assign it to both objects. In the Blinn shader's Attribute Editor, set its Color attribute to a checkerboard pattern, as shown in Figure 7.31.

Figure 7.31

Assign a checkerboard pattern to the sphere and cone with Normal checked.

Try removing the color map from the Blinn shader. In the Blinn shader's Attribute Editor, right-click and hold the attribute's title word *Color*, and then choose Break Connection from the shortcut menu. Doing so severs the connection to the checker and resets the color to gray. Now, re-create a new checker map for the color, but this time create it as a projection by right-clicking the icon in the Create Render Node

window. In the illustration on the left in Figure 7.32, you see the perspective view in Texture mode (press the 6 key) with the two objects and the planar projection placement node.

Try moving the planar placement object around in the scene to see how the texture maps itself to the objects. Figure 7.32 on the right shows the rendered objects.

Try the other projection types to see how they affect the texture being mapped.

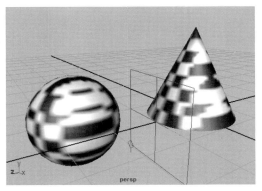

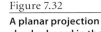

Figure 7.32

A planar projection checkerboard in the view panel (top) and rendered (bottom)

Projection placement nodes control how the projection maps its image or texture onto the surface. Using a NURBS sphere with a spherical projected checker, with *U* and *V* wrap turned off on the checker texture, you can see how manipulating the place3dTexture node affects the texture.

In addition to the Move, Rotate, and Scale tools, you can use the Special Manipulator tool (press T to activate or click the Show Manipulator Tool icon in the toolbar) to adjust the placement. Figure 7.33 shows this tool for a spherical projection.

Figure 7.33

The spherical projection's Manipulator tool

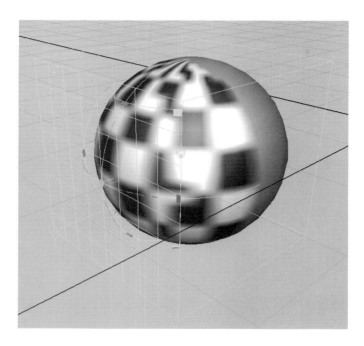

Drag the handles on the special manipulator to change the coverage of the projection, orientation, size, and so forth. All projection types have special manipulators. Figure 7.34 shows the special manipulator wrapping the checker in a thin band all the way around the sphere.

To summarize, projection textures depend on a projector node to position the texture onto the geometry.

Figure 7.34

The manipulator wrapping the Checker texture around the sphere (left, perspective view; right, rendered view)

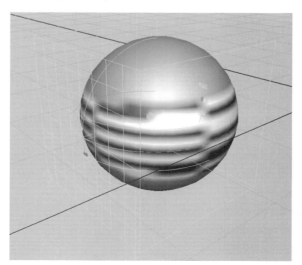 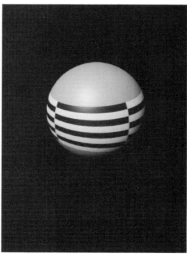

Texture Nodes

You can create a number of texture nodes in Maya. This section covers the most important. All texture nodes, however, have common attributes that affect their final look. Open the Attribute Editor for any texture node. (See Figure 7.35.) The two top sections affect the color balance of the texture. The Color Balance and Effects sections are described here:

Color Balance This set of attributes adjusts the overall brightness and color balance of your texture. Use these attributes to tint or brighten a texture without having to change all the individual attributes of the shader.

Effects You can invert the texture's color space by clicking the Invert check box. This changes black to white and white to black in addition to inverting the RGB values of colors.

You can map textures to almost any shader attribute for detail. Even the tiniest amount of texture on a surface's bump, specular, or color increases its realism.

Place2dTexture Nodes

The 2D texture nodes come with a 2D placement node that controls their repetition, rotation, size, offset, and so on. Adjust the setting in this node of your 2D texture in the Attribute Editor, as shown in Figure 7.36, to position it within the Shader network. You used a similar approach when dealing with the wood's 3D placement node in the axe exercise earlier in this chapter.

The Repeat UV setting controls how many times the texture is repeated on whatever shader attribute it's connected to, such as Color. The higher the wrap values, the smaller the texture appears but the more times it appears on the surface.

The Wrap U and Wrap V check boxes allow the texture to wrap around the edges of their limits to repeat. When these check boxes are turned off, the texture appears only once, and the rest of the surface is the color of the Default Color attribute found in the texture node.

The Mirror U and Mirror V settings allow the texture to mirror itself when it repeats. The Coverage, Translate Frame, and Rotate Frame settings control where the image is mapped. They're useful for positioning a digital image or a scanned picture.

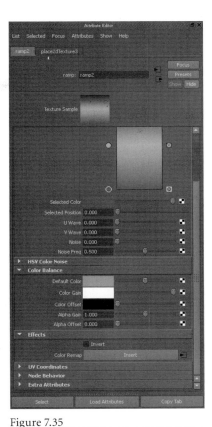

Figure 7.35

Some common attributes for all texture nodes

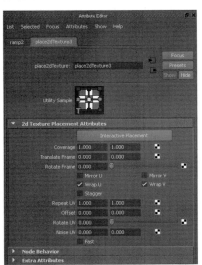

Figure 7.36

A 2D placement node in the Attribute Editor

Ramp Texture

A *ramp* is a gradient in which one color transitions into the next color. You've already seen how useful a ramp can be in positioning materials in a Layered shader. It's also perfect for making color gradients, as shown in Figure 7.37.

Use the round handles to select the color and to move it up and down the ramp. The square handle to the right deletes the color. To create a new color, click inside the ramp.

The Ramp texture is different from the Ramp shader. The Ramp shader automatically has several Ramp textures mapped to some of its attributes.

Figure 7.37

The Ramp texture

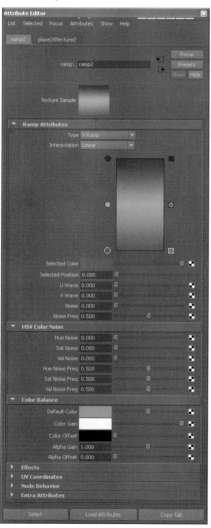

The Type setting allows you to create a gradient running along the U or V direction of the surface, as well as to make circular, radial, diagonal, and other types of gradients. The Interpolation setting controls how the colors grade from one to the next.

The U Wave and V Wave attributes let you add a squiggle to the *U* or *V* coordinate of the ramp, and the Noise and Noise Freq (frequency) attributes specify randomness for the placement of the ramp colors throughout the surface.

Using the HSV Color Noise attributes, you can specify random noise patterns of Hue, Saturation, and Value to add some interest to your texture. The HSV Noise options are great for making your shader just a bit different, to enhance its look.

Fractal, Noise, and Mountain Textures

These textures are used to create a random noise pattern to add to an object's Color, Transparency, or any other shader attribute. For example, when creating a surface, you'll almost always want to add a little dirt or a few surface blemishes to the shader to make the object look less CG. These textures are commonly used for creating bump maps.

Bulge, Cloth, Checker, Grid, and Water Textures

These textures help create surface features when used on a shader's Bump Mapping attribute. Each creates an interesting pattern to add to a surface to create tactile detail, but you can also use them to create color or specular irregularities.

When used as a texture for a bump, Grid is useful for creating the spacing between tiles, Cloth is perfect for clothing, and Checker is good for rubber grips. Placing a Water texture on a slight reflection makes for a nice poolside reflection in patio furniture.

The File Node

You use the file node to import image files into Maya for texturing. For instance, if you want to texture a CG face with a digital picture of your own face, you can use the file node to import a Maya-supported image file.

Importing an Image File as a Texture

To attach an image to the Color attribute of a Lambert shader, for example, follow these steps:

1. Create the Lambert shader. (Phong, Blinn, or any of the shaders will do.)

2. Click the Map button to map a texture on the Color attribute of the new Lambert shader. Select the file node as a normal texture. (You can also use a projected texture with an image file.) The Attribute Editor shows the attribute for the file node. See Figure 7.38.

3. Next to the Image Name attribute, click the Folder icon to open the file browser. Find the image file of choice on your computer. (It's best to put images to use as textures in the project's Sourceimages folder. As a matter of fact, the file browser defaults directly to the Sourceimages folder of your current project.) Double-click the file to load it.

4. After you import the image file, it connects to the Color attribute of that shader and also automatically connects the alpha to transparency if there is an alpha channel in the image. You can position it as you please by using its Place2dTexture node or by manipulating the projection node if you created the File texture node as a projection.

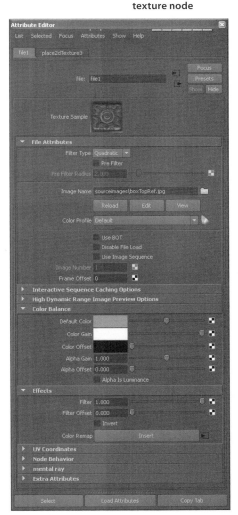

Figure 7.38

The File texture node

You can attach an image file to any attribute of a shader that is *mappable*, meaning it's able to accept a texture node. Frequently, image files are used for the color of a shader as well as for bump and transparency maps. You can replace the image file by double-clicking the File texture node in the Hypershade and choosing another image file with the file browser. Maya disconnects the current image file and connects the new file.

Using Photoshop Files: The PSD File Node

Maya can also use Adobe Photoshop PSD files as image files in creating shading networks. The advantage of using PSD files is that you can specify the layers within the

Photoshop file for different attributes of the shader, as opposed to importing several image files to map onto each shader attribute separately. This, of course, requires a modest knowledge of Photoshop and some experience with Maya shading. As you learn how to shade with Maya, you'll come to appreciate the enhancements inherent in using Photoshop networks.

Try This You'll create a single Photoshop file that will shade this sphere with color as well as transparency and a bump. Again, this is instead of creating three different image files (such as TIFFs) for each of those shading attributes:

1. Create a NURBS sphere in a new scene, and assign a new Lambert shader to it. You can do this through the Hypershade or by choosing Lighting/Shading → Assign New Material → Lambert in the Rendering menu set. This creates a new shader and assigns it to the selection, in this case your sphere.

2. Select the sphere, and choose Texturing → Create PSD Network. In the option box that opens, select color, transparency, and bump from the list of attributes on the left side, and click the right arrow to move them to the Selected Attributes list on the right, as shown in Figure 7.39.

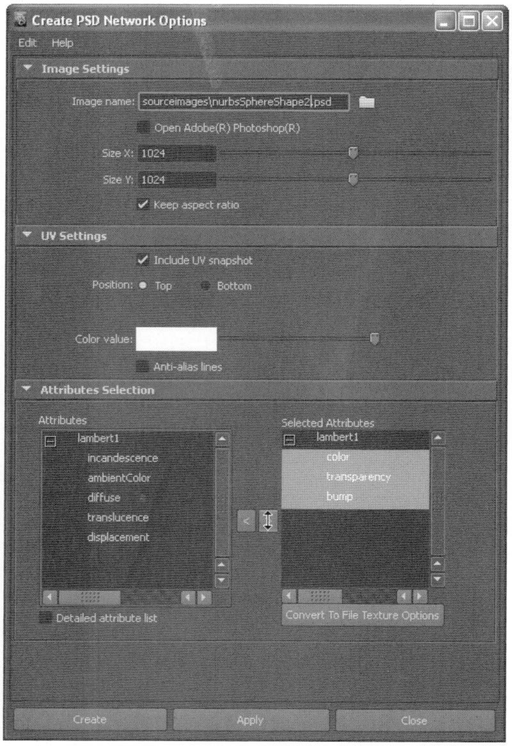

Figure 7.39

The Create PSD Network Options window

3. Select a location and filename for the image. By default, Maya places the PSD file it generates under the Sourceimages folder of your current project, named after the surface to which it applies. Click Create.

4. In Photoshop, open the newly created PSD file. You see three layers grouped under three folders named after the shader attributes you selected when creating the PSD file. There are folders for lambert2.bump, lambert2.transparency, and lambert2.color, as well as a layer called *UVSnapShot*.

   The UVSnapShot layer gives you a wireframe layout of the UVs on the sphere as a guideline to paint your textures. Because the sphere is an easy model, you don't need this layer, so turn it off. You'll use UVSnapShots later in this chapter.

   You can now paint whatever image you want into each of the layers to create maps for each of the shader attributes, all in one convenient file. Save the PSD file. You can save over it or create a new filename for the painted file.

5. In Maya, open the Hypershade, and open the Attribute Editor for the Lambert shader assigned to the sphere (in

this case, *Lambert2*). If you graph the connections to the Lambert shader in the Hypershade window's work panel, you see that the PSD file you generated is already connected to the Color, Bump, and Transparency attributes of the shader, with the proper layering set for you as shown in Figure 7.40.

6. Open the file nodes for the shader, and replace the PSD file with your new painted PSD file. If you saved your PSD file with the same name, all you need to do is click the Reload button to update the psdFilenode.

If you decide that you need another attribute added to the PSD file's layering, or if you need to remove an attribute, you can edit the PSD network. Select the shader in the Hypershade, and choose Edit → Edit PSD Network. In the Options window, you can select new attributes to assign to the PSD file, or you can remove existing attributes and their corresponding Photoshop layer groups. When you click Apply or Edit, Maya saves over the PSD file with the new layout.

Figure 7.40

The PSD network for the Lambert shader in the Hypershade shows the connections to Color, Bump, and Transparency.

3D and Environment Textures

As you saw earlier with the axe, 3D textures are projected within a 3D space. These textures are great for objects that need to reflect an environment, for example.

Instead of simply applying the texture to the plane of the surface as 2D textures do, 3D textures create an area in which the shader is affected. As an object moves through a scene with a 3D placement node, its shader looks as if it swims, unless that placement node is parented or constrained to that object, as you saw with the wooden handle of the axe. (For more on constraints, see Chapter 9, "More Animation!")

Figure 7.41

Right-clicking a shader's attribute allows you to disconnect a texture node from the shader.

Disconnecting a Texture

Sometimes, the texture you've applied to an object isn't what you want, and you need to remove it from the shader. To do so, double-click the shader in the Hypershade to open its Attribute Editor.

You can then disconnect an image file or any other texture node from the shader's attribute by right-clicking the attribute's name in the Attribute Editor and choosing Break Connection from the context menu, as shown in Figure 7.41.

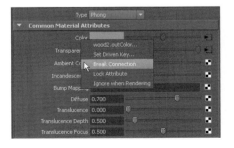

Texturing the Red Wagon

Using the wagon model from Chapter 6, you'll now assign shaders to the red wagon shown in Figure 7.42. Take a good look at the image of the toy wagon in the Color

Figure 7.42

The red wagon

Section of the book to see how the red wagon is colored. The wagon is fairly simple; it will need a few colored shaders (Red, Black, Blue, and White) for the body, along with a few texture maps for the decals—which is where the real fun begins. The wagon will also require some more intricate work on the shaders and textures for the wood railings and silver metal screws, bolts, and handlebar; these will be a good foray into image maps and UVs.

This exercise is a prime example of how lighting and shading go hand in hand.

Assigning Shaders

Load the file RedWagonModel_v08.ma from the Scenes folder of the RedWagon project to begin shading the finished model of the wagon.

Shading is the common term for adding shaders to an object.

Study the color images of the wagon, and see how light reflects off its plastic, metal, and wood surfaces. Blinn shaders will be perfect for nearly all the parts of the wagon. Follow these steps:

1. Open the Hypershade window, and create four Blinn shaders.

2. Assign the following HSV values to the Color attribute of each Blinn shader, and name them as shown in Table 7.1 and in Figure 7.43. You'll create the Chrome Metal and Wood shaders later.

Figure 7.43

Create the four-colored Blinn shaders.

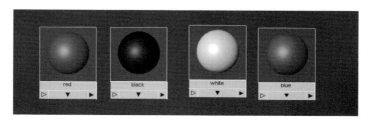

WAGON COLOR	SHADER NAME	H VALUE	S VALUE	V VALUE
Red	Red	355	0.910	0.650
Black	Black	0	0	0
White	White	0	0	1
Blue	Blue	220	0.775	0.560

Table 7.1

HSV Color Values for the Wagon's Colors

Initial Assignments

Look at the photo of the wagon in the Color Section in the middle of this book. The bull-nose and tires are black, the wheel rims are white, the floor is blue, the screws and bolts and handlebar are chrome metal, the railings are wood, and the main body is red. Assign shaders to the wagon according to the color photo and the following steps:

1. In the view panel, select the side panels (the A and B panels, without the screws and bolts) and the wheel rim caps, as shown in Figure 7.44, and assign the Red Blinn shader to them. Press 6 to enter into Texture Display mode.

2. Select the wheelMesh objects for all four wheels, and assign them the White shader. The tires also turn white, but you'll fix that shortly; don't worry about it now. See Figure 7.45.

Figure 7.44

Assign the Red shader.

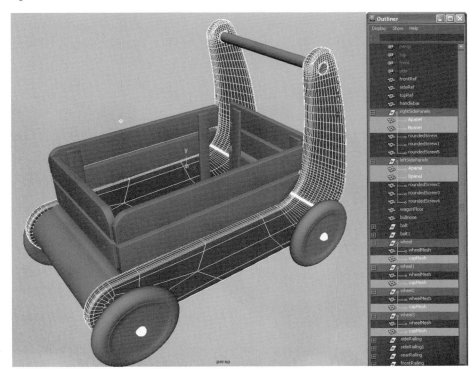

Figure 7.45

Assign the White shader.

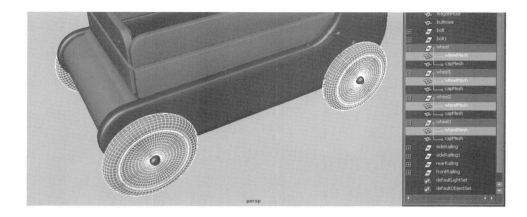

3. Select the bullnose (the rounded cylinder in front of the wagon), and assign it the Black Blinn.

4. Select the wagon floor object, and assign it the Red shader, as shown in Figure 7.46. You'll notice that the front and back body of the wagon turn red as they're supposed to, but so does the floor of the wagon, which should be blue according to the photo in the Color Section. If you try to assign the Blue shader to the wagon floor mesh, the floor will be correct, but the front and back body of the wagon will be blue and not red. You'll fix this later.

Now you have initial assignments for the basic colors of the wagon's body. Let's tweak these shaders' colors next.

Figure 7.46

Assign the Red shader to the wagon floor for now.

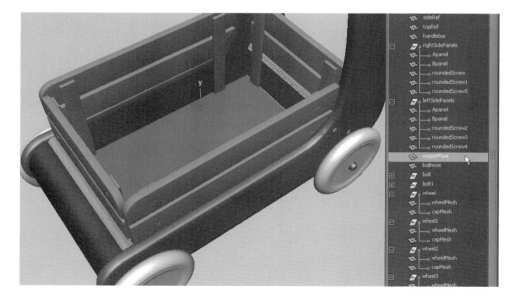

Creating a Shading Network for the Wheels

Refer to Figure 7.47 to observe how the materials are different between the rim and the tire for the wheels. The rim is glossier and has a tighter, sharper specular, whereas the tire has a very diffuse specular and is quite bumpy. As you did for the axe exercise, you'll create a Layered shader for the wheels with white feeding into the rim portion and black into the tire.

Figure 7.47

The tire on the wagon

Coloring the Wheel

First, you need to determine where the white ends and the black starts on the surface of the wheel mesh:

1. Select the White shader in the Hypershade window. Click the Map button (▣) next to the Color attribute. Make sure that Normal is checked. Click Ramp to create a Ramp texture. The wheel's color turns to a red, green, blue gradient, but in the wrong direction; you need the gradient to run from the center to the edge and not clockwise across the wheel. In the Ramp texture's Attribute Editor, set the Type to U Ramp, as shown in Figure 7.48.

> If the ramp doesn't show up in your view panels, make sure you press 6 to enter Texture Display mode. If the colors and ramp texture still don't display, make sure Use Default Material isn't checked in the view panel's Shading menu.

2. Now the color gradient is running from the center (red) to the outside edge (green) to blue on the reverse side of the wheel. Move the blue ramp's handle in the ramp's Attribute Editor until its Selected Position value is about 0.6, as shown in Figure 7.49.

Figure 7.48

Set the ramp to a U Ramp type.

3. Delete the red handle in the ramp by clicking the checked box on the right of the handle. Change the blue color to black and the green color to white. Set the Interpolation attribute (found above the ramp color) to None so you get clean transitions from white to black, instead of a soft linear gradient where the black slowly grades to white. Name this ramp **wheelPositionRamp**.

4. The backs of the wheels are solid black. In the wheelPositionRamp, click toward the top of the ramp to create a new color. Set that color to white, and set its position to about .920 to place white behind the wheels, keeping the black only where the tire is. See Figure 7.50.

Now that you've pinpointed where the white rim ends and the black tire begins, you'll use this ramp as a transparency texture to place the Tire shader on top of the Rim shader in a Layered shader that you'll create later.

Figure 7.49

Move the blue handle.

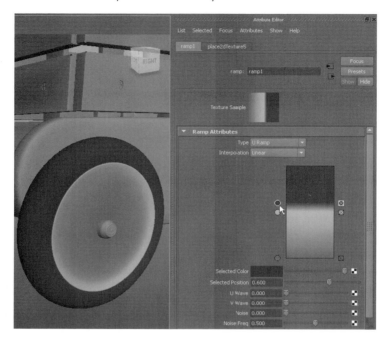

Figure 7.50

Setting the tire location using a ramp

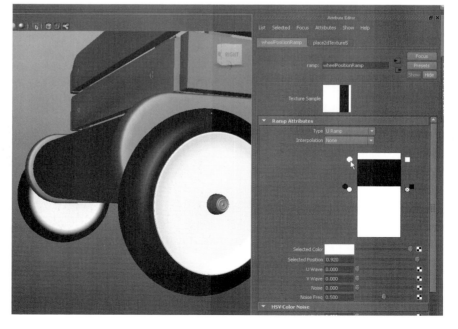

5. You don't need this Ramp shader on the color of the shader anymore—you did this so you could easily see the ramp color positions in the view panels. In the Hypershade, select the White shader, and click the Input and Output Connections icon (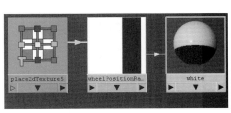) to graph the shader, as shown in Figure 7.51.

6. In the Attribute Editor, RMB+click the Color attribute, and select Break Connection from the context menu to disconnect the ramp from the color. Set the Color back to white. Notice that the link connecting the Ramp texture node to the White shader node disappears in the Hypershade window.

Figure 7.51

The White shader has the ramp attached as color.

7. Create a Layered shader. MMB+drag the White shader from the Hypershade to the top of the Layered Shader Attributes window, as shown in Figure 7.52. Delete the default Green shader in the Attribute Editor by clicking the checked box below its swatch.

Figure 7.52

Drag the White shader to the Layered shader, and delete the default Green shader from it.

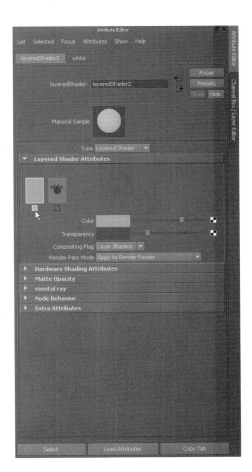

8. Create a new Blinn shader, and set its color to black. Name the shader tireShader. Select the Layered shader, and then MMB+drag the new tireShader from the Hypershade to the Layered shader's Attribute Editor, placing it to the left of the White shader, as shown in Figure 7.53. Name the Layered shader **wheelShader**.

9. Select the wheels, and assign the wheelShader Layered shader to them. The wheels should appear all white. This is where the ramp you created earlier (wheelPositionRamp) comes into play.

10. Select the wheelShader, and click Input and Output Connections to graph the network in the Work Area of the Hypershade window. In the top panel of the Hypershade, click the Texture tab to display the texture nodes in the scene, so you can see wheelPositionRamp's node.

Figure 7.53

Add the black tireShader.

11. In the wheelShader's Attribute Editor, click the tireShader swatch on the left. MMB+drag the wheelPositionRamp node to the Transparency attribute, as shown in Figure 7.54.

12. When you attach the ramp, the wheelShader icon turns white on top and black on the bottom. Render a frame in the persp panel to make sure the black tires line up properly, as shown in Figure 7.55. The wheel coloring is complete!

Figure 7.54

Attach the ramp to the Transparency of the tireShader in the wheelShader.

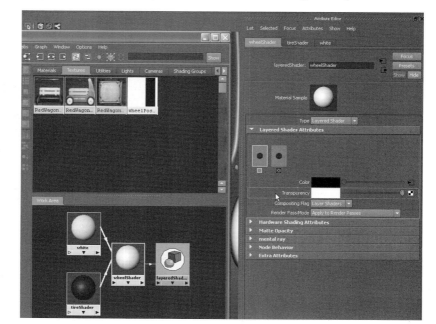

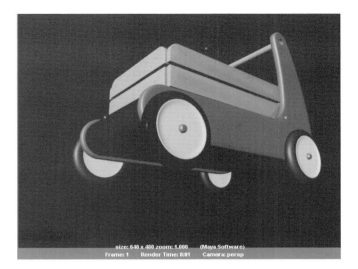

Figure 7.55

The tires are done!

HEY, HOLD ON A MINUTE...

Why did you go through a Layered shader with two different shaders (one white and one black) when you could more easily use one shader and assign the same black to white ramp to its color? Because the white rim and the black tire are different materials, and you need to use two different shaders to properly show that in renders.

Setting the Feel for the Materials and Adding a Bump Map

Because the material look and feel on the real wheels differs quite a bit between the rim and the tire, you'll further tweak the white rim and the black tire shaders. The rim is a smooth, glossy white, and the tire is a bumpy black with a broad specular. Follow these steps:

Figure 7.56

Set your view to this angle, and render a frame.

1. Let's set up a good angle of view for your test renders. Position your persp view to resemble the view in Figure 7.56. Render a frame.

2. Select the White shader, and set Eccentricity to 0.05 and Specular Roll Off to 0.5. Doing so sharpens the specular highlight on the rim.

3. Select the black tireShader, and set Eccentricity to 0.375 and Specular Roll Off to 0.6 to make the highlight more diffuse across the tire. Set Reflectivity to 0.05. Render a frame, and refer to Figure 7.57 to see how the specular highlight is broader and less glossy than in Figure 7.56.

Figure 7.57
Setting specular levels

Figure 7.58
The whole wheel becomes bumpy!

4. Open the Attribute Editor for the tireShader, and click the Map icon (▉) next to the Bump Mapping attribute. In the Create Render Node window, click to create a Fractal texture map. Notice that the entire wheelShader icon becomes bumpy. Render a frame, and you'll see that the entire wheel is bumpy—not just the tire. (See Figure 7.58.) Argh!

5. You have to use the wheelPositionRamp to prevent the bump from showing on the rim. Select the wheelShader, and click the Input and Output Connections icon (▶▶) in the Hypershade to graph its network (Figure 7.59).

Figure 7.59
Graph the wheel-Shader network.

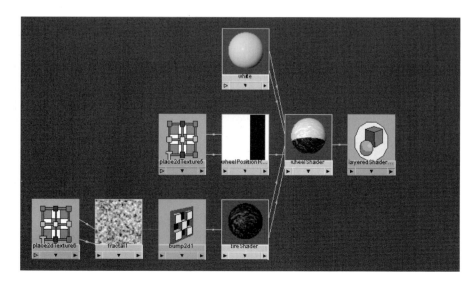

Notice the single, blue connecting line between the fractal1 node and the bump2d1 node in the Hypershade. This means the alpha channel of the fractal feeds the amount of bump that is rendered on the tireShader. You have to alter the alpha coming out of the fractal node with the positioning ramp to block the rim from having any bump. The white areas of the ramp allow an output in alpha from the fractal, which creates a bump for the surface; whereas the black area of the ramp keeps any bump from appearing. Because you already used this ramp to position the Rim shader and the Tire shader on the wheel, it will work perfectly for the bump position as well.

Figure 7.60

MMB+drag the ramp to the Alpha Gain of the fractal.

6. Select the fractal to display it in the Attribute Editor, and MMB+drag the wheelPositionRamp in the Hypershade to the Alpha Gain attribute for the fractal, as shown in Figure 7.60.

7. Render a frame, and you see that now the tire has no bump and the rim is bumpy (Figure 7.61).

8. This is easy enough to fix. All you need to do is reverse the ramp and then feed it into the Alpha Gain of the fractal so that the tire is bumpy and the rim is smooth. In the Hypershade, in the Create pane on the left, click the Maya → General Utilities heading, and then select the Reverse icon to create a reverse node in the Hypershade window. See Figure 7.62.

9. In the Hypershade, MMB+drag the wheelPositionRamp node onto the Reverse node, and select Input from the context menu when you release the mouse button. This connects the output of the ramp into the reverse node, which will then reverse the effect of the ramp on the fractal when you connect it in the next step.

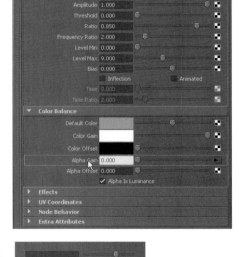

Figure 7.61

The tire is smooth and now the rim is bumpy.

Figure 7.62

Create a reverse node.

Figure 7.63

**Connecting the
reverse node to the
fractal node**

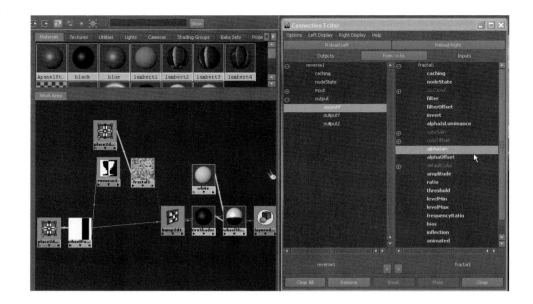

10. MMB+drag the reverse node on top of the fractal1 node, and select Other from the context menu. This opens the Connection Editor, which you first saw in Chapter 3. On the left is loaded the reverse1 node, and on the right is the fractal1 node. In the left pane, click the plus sign next to the Output attribute, and select output.X. In the right pane, select the alphaGain attribute, as shown in Figure 7.63.

11. Open the Render Settings window by choosing Window → Rendering Editors → Render Settings. Click the Maya Software tab, and set Quality to Production Quality in the pull-down menu. (See Figure 7.64.) Render a frame: you finally have a bump on the tire and a smooth rim. See Figure 7.65.

12. It's not a very convincing bump yet, so select the fractal node and set Ratio to 0.85. Click the Placement tab for the fractal (it should be called something like *place2d-Texture6*), and set the Repeat UV values to 18 and 48, as shown in Figure 7.66. Doing so makes the fractal pattern finely speckled on the tire.

13. Render a frame: the fractal's scale on the bumpy tire looks too strong. Double-click the bump2d node in the Hypershade, and, in the Attribute Editor, set Bump Depth to 0.04. Render, and check your frame against Figure 7.67. The bump looks much better, if not a little strong from this angle; you can finesse it to taste from here.

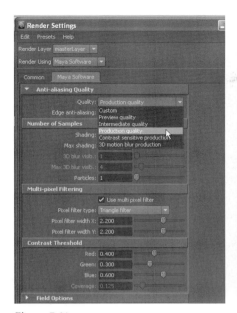

Figure 7.64

Set Quality to Production Quality.

Figure 7.65

Now you've got the bump where you need it.

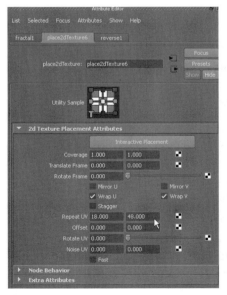

Figure 7.66

Set the Repeat UV values for the fractal map.

Figure 7.67

The wheel looks pretty good.

Tire Summary

Congratulations! You've made your first somewhat complex shading network, as shown in Figure 7.68. By now, you should have a pretty good idea of how to get around the Hypershade and create shading networks. To recap, you're using a ramp to place the two Tire and Rim shaders on the wheel, as well as using it to place the bump map on just the tire by using a reverse node. The more you make these shading networks, the easier they will become to create.

Figure 7.68

Your first complex shading network

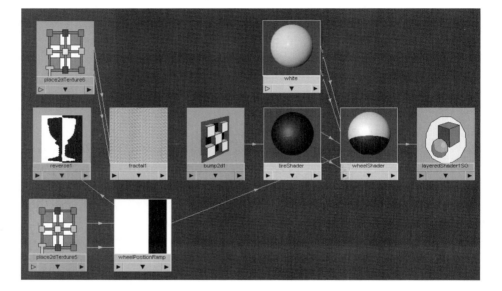

This type of shading is called *procedural shading*, because you used nothing but stock Maya texture nodes to accomplish what you needed for the wheels. In the following sections, you'll make good use of image mapping to create the decals for the wagon body as well as the wood for the railings.

You can load the file RedWagonTexture_v01.ma from the Scenes folder of the RedWagon project to check your work or skip to this point.

Putting Decals on the Body

Figure 7.69 shows you the decals that need to go onto the body of the wagon. They include the wagon's logo, which you'll replace with your own graphic design, and the white stripe that lines the side panels.

Instead of trying to make a procedural texture as you did with the wheel, you'll create an image map that will texture the side panels' white stripe. The stripe is far too difficult to create otherwise. You'll create an image file using Photoshop (or other such image editor) to make sure the white stripe (and later the red wagon logo) lines up correctly.

Figure 7.69
**You need to add
the body decals.**

Working with UVs

Mapping polygons can involve the task of defining UV coordinates for them so that you can more easily paint an image map for the mesh. When you create a NURBS surface, UV coordinates are inherent to the surface. At the *origin* (or the beginning) of the surface, the UV coordinate is (0,0). When the surface extends all the way to the left and all the way up, the UV coordinate is (1,1). When you paint an 800×600–pixel image in Photoshop, for example, it's safe to assume that the first pixel of the image (at $X = 0$ and $Y = 0$ in Photoshop) will map directly to the UV coordinate (0,0) on the NURBS surface, whereas the topmost right-corner pixel in the image will map to the UV (1,1) of the surface. Toward that end, mapping an image to a NURBS surface is fairly straightforward. The bottom of the image will map to the bottom of the surface, the top to the top, and so on. Figure 7.70 shows how an image is mapped onto a NURBS plane and a NURBS sphere.

The locations in the image, marked by text, correspond to the positions on the NURBS plane. The sphere, because it's a surface bent around spherically, shows that the origin of the UV coordinates is at the sphere's pole on the left and that the image wraps itself around it (bowing out in the middle) to meet at the seam along the front edge as shown.

When you're creating polygons, however, this isn't always the case. You must sometimes create your own UV coordinates on a polygonal surface to get a clean layout on which to paint in Photoshop. Although poly UV mapping becomes fairly involved and complicated, it's a concept that is important to grasp early. When poly models are created, they have UV coordinates; however, these coordinates may not be laid out in the best way for texture-image manipulation.

Figure 7.70

An image file is mapped to a NURBS plane and a NURBS sphere. Notice the locations marked in the image and how they map to the locations on the surface, with the pixel coordinates directly corresponding to the surface's UV coordinates.

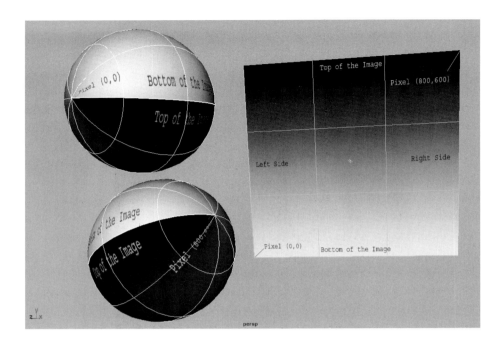

Working with the A Panels

This section assumes that you have some working knowledge of Adobe Photoshop. You can skip the creation of the maps and use the maps already on the CD, which are called out in the text later in the exercise.

First, let's look at how the UVs are laid out for the A panel that you modeled in Chapter 6:

1. Using your scene or the scene file RedWagonTexture_v01.ma from the Scenes folder of the RedWagon project, select the A panel on one side of the wagon, and choose Window → UV Texture Editor, as shown in Figure 7.71.

    The UV Texture window works almost like any other view panel. You may navigate the window and zoom in and out using the familiar Alt + mouse button combinations.

2. RMB+click any part of the wireframe layout in the UV Texture Editor window, and select UV to enter the UV selection. Select the entire wireframe mesh at lower right, as shown in Figure 7.72. Notice that green points are selected—almost as if they were vertices. These are UV points, and they're what define the UV coordinates on that part of the mesh. Look in the Perspective view panel; the entire front face of the A panel is selected as well the green UV points (also in Figure 7.72).

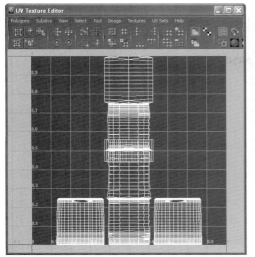

Figure 7.71
The A Panel in the UV Texture Editor

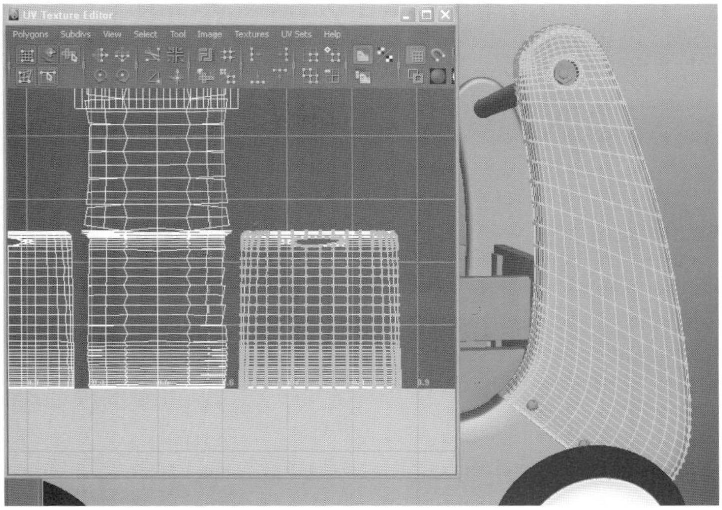

Figure 7.72
Select the UVs on this part of the A panel mesh.

Feel free to select parts of the UV layout in the UV Texture Editor to see what corresponding points appear on the mesh in the persp panel. This will help orient you as to how the UV layout works on this mesh.

3. You need to again lay out just this area of the mesh's UVs. Because you already have the entire front side of the panel selected in UVs, let's convert that selection to poly faces on the model. In the Polygons menu set and in the main Maya menu bar, choose Select → Convert Selection → To Faces. The front faces of the A panel mesh are selected, as shown in Figure 7.73. You can always manually select just the front faces of the mesh, but this conversion method is much faster. The UV Texture Editor shows just those faces now.

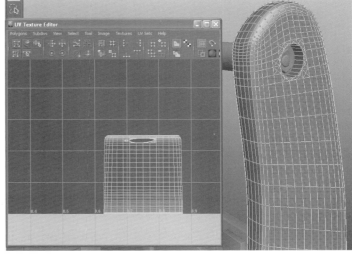

Figure 7.73
Convert the UVs you just selected to a face selection. This method easily isolates the front faces of the A panel for you to lay out their UVs again.

4. With those faces selected, make sure you're in the Polygons menu set. Choose Create UVs → Planar Mapping ❏ from the Main Menu bar. In the option box, set the Project From option to X Axis, check the Keep Image Width/Height Ratio option, and then click Project. (See Figure 7.74.) The UV Texture Editor shows the front A panel face.

Figure 7.74

Create a planar projection for the UV layout.

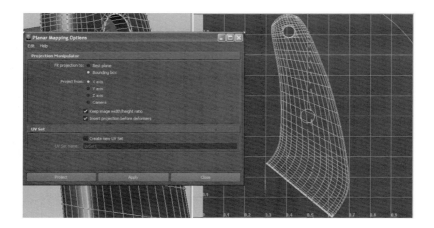

5. Now the front face has a much simpler UV layout from which to paint. However, it's centered in the UV Texture Editor and will overlap the other UVs of the same mesh. You should move and size it to fit into its original corner, more or less, to make sure no UVs double up on each other. In the UV Texture Editor, right-click the wireframe, and select UV to enter UV selection. Select all the UVs on those faces; all the UVs for the A panel mesh appear in the UV Texture Editor, and you can see the overlap. See Figure 7.75.

6. Press W for the Move tool, and move the selected UVs to the side of the UV Texture Editor. Press R for the Scale tool, and scale them down a bit to fit into the corner, as shown in Figure 7.76.

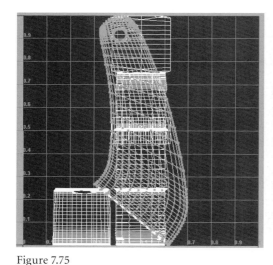

Figure 7.75

The UVs for the A panel, with the front side's UVs still selected

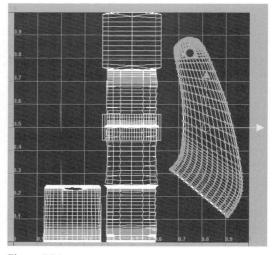

Figure 7.76

Position these UVs to make sure they don't overlap the rest of the A panel mesh's UVs.

7. Earlier in the chapter, you saw how to write out a PSD file with a UV snapshot as one of its layers. You'll use a similar technique to paint the decal for the panel. Click an empty area of the UV Texture Editor to deselect everything. Then, in Object Selection mode (press F8 if you need to exit Component Selection), select the A panel mesh in the persp panel.

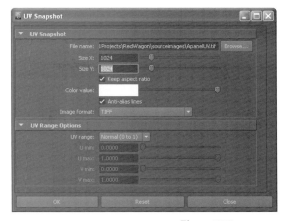

8. In the UV Texture Editor window, select Polygons → UV Snapshot to open the Options window. Set both Size X and Size Y to 1024. Change the image format to TIFF, click the Browse button at the top next to the File Name field, and navigate to the RedWagon project's `Sourceimages` folder on your hard drive. Name the file **`ApanelUV.tif`**, and click Save. Leave UV Range set to Normal (0 to 1), and click OK. See Figure 7.77.

Figure 7.77
Settings for the UV snapshot

WORKING IN PHOTOSHOP

Next, you'll go into Photoshop to paint your map according to the UV layout you just output:

1. In your OS file browser, navigate to the RedWagon project's `Sourceimages` folder, and open the file `ApanelUV.tif` in Photoshop. Figure 7.78 shows the layout of the UVs that you'll use to create the white stripe for the front of the A panel.

Figure 7.78
Working with the UV layout for the A panel will be easy.

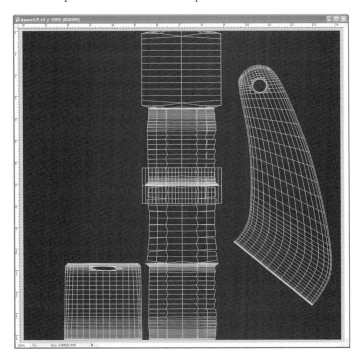

2. In Photoshop, create a new layer on top of the background layer that is the UV layout (white on black, as shown). Using the Bucket tool, fill that new layer with the same red you used on the shader in your scene. To do so, click the foreground color swatch in Photoshop, and set H to 355, S to 91 percent, and B to 65 percent, as shown in Figure 7.79. Click OK.

3. Using the Bucket tool, click to fill the entire image with the red you just created. The trouble is that now you can't see the UV layout. Set the Opacity of the red layer in Photoshop to 50 percent, as shown Figure 7.80.

4. Set Photoshop's foreground color to white. Using the Line and Brush tools set to a width of about 6 pixels, draw a stripe following the UV layout lines, as shown in Figure 7.81. Doing so places that white stripe along the A panel's outer edge, because the UV lines you're following correspond to that area of the mesh. The rest will be left red.

Figure 7.79

In Photoshop's Color Picker, create the same red you used for the wagon.

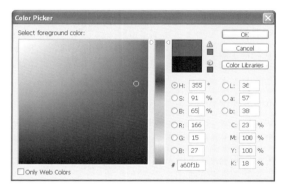

Figure 7.80

Set the opacity for the red layer in Photoshop so you can see the UV layout on the layer below.

Figure 7.81

Follow the UV lines to draw the white stripe.

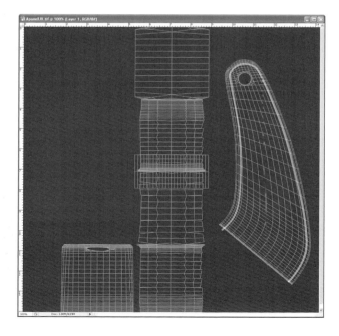

5. You may have drawn directly on the red layer in Photoshop or created a new layer for the stripe. In either case, set the Opacity of the red layer back to 100 percent so you can no longer see the UV layout. Your image file should look like the one in Figure 7.82. Save the image as `ApanelStripe.tif` in the `Sourceimages` folder of your RedWagon project. You may keep the layers in the TIFF file, or you may choose to flatten the image or merge the layers. It may be best to keep the stripe and red on separate layers so that you can go back into Photoshop and edit the stripe as needed.

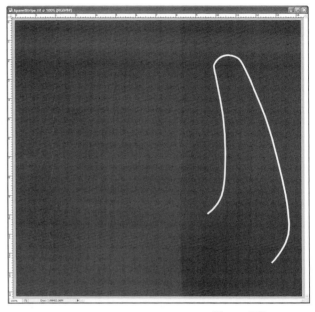

Figure 7.82

The striped image file

CREATING AND ASSIGNING THE SHADER

Now, let's create the shader and get it assigned to the geometry:

1. Back in Maya, open the Hypershade, and select the Red shader. Duplicate it by choosing Edit → Duplicate → Shading Network in the Hypershade window, as shown in Figure 7.83.

Figure 7.83

Duplicate the original Red shader.

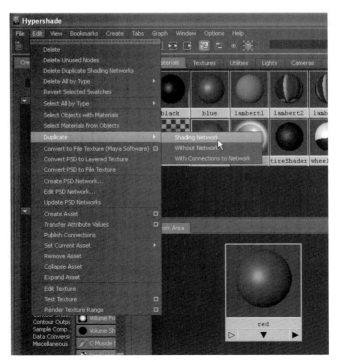

2. Name the new shader (called red1) **ApanelStripe**. Open the Attribute Editor, click the Map button (■) next to Color, and choose File. In the Attribute Editor, click the Folder icon next to the Image Name field. Navigate to your Sourceimages folder, and select ApanelStrip.tif, as shown in Figure 7.84.

3. In the Hypershade, you may see that the Shader icon has turned somewhat transparent. Maya is automatically mapping the Transparency attribute of the shader as well as the color. Double-click the shader to open its Attribute Editor, RMB+click Transparency, and select Break Connection from the context window. Doing so sets the shader to the same red you used earlier, but now it gives you a stripe along the side A panel.

4. Assign the ApanelStripe shader to the A panel mesh, and press 6 for Texture Display mode in the persp panel. See Figure 7.85. The stripe lines up well.

You may skip the image creation using Photoshop and use the ApanelStripe.tif image file found in the Sourceimages folder of the RedWagon project on the CD instead.

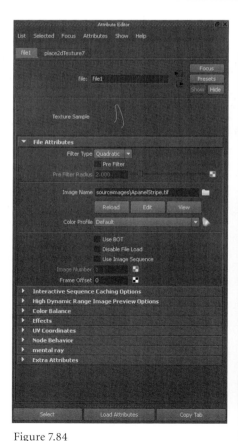

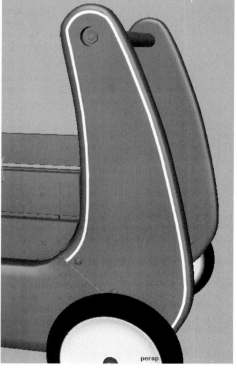

Figure 7.84

Select the ApanelStripe.tif **file.**

Figure 7.85

The stripe

COPYING UVS

You need to put the stripe on the other side's A panel. Select the other A panel, and assign the ApanelStripe shader to it. You'll notice that no stripe appears. (See Figure 7.86.) This is because the UV layout for this A panel hasn't been set up yet. Don't worry; you don't have to redo everything you did for the first A panel. You can essentially copy the UVs from the first A panel mesh to this one:

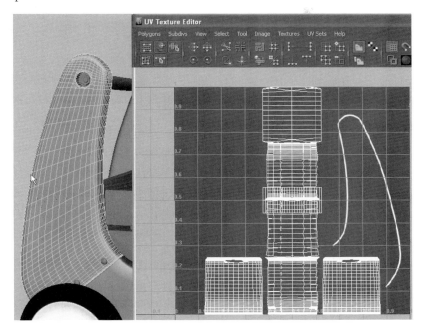

Figure 7.86

Assign the Apanel-Stripe shader to the other side's A panel.

1. Select the first A panel (with the stripe) and the second panel (without the stripe). In the Polygons menu set, choose Mesh → Transfer Attributes □. In the option box, set Sample Space to Local, as shown in Figure 7.87, and click Transfer.

2. The stripe appears on the inside of the back A panel, and not on the outside as you need. Select that A panel, and choose Modify → Center Pivot.

3. In the Channel Box, enter a value of **-1.0** for Scale X. The stripe flips to the correct side, as shown in Figure 7.88.

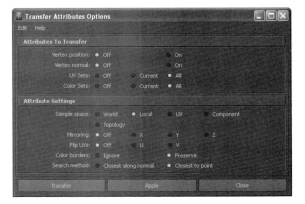

Figure 7.87

The Transfer Attributes settings

4. With that A panel still selected, choose Modify → Freeze Transformations.

You can load the file RedWagonTexture_v02.ma from the Scenes folder of the RedWagon project to check your work or skip to this point.

Figure 7.88

The stripe is on the correct side now.

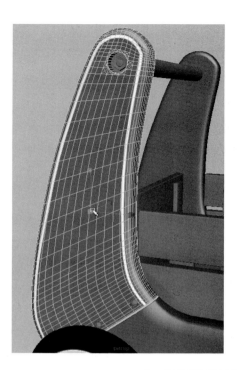

The file texture you'll use for the panels were painted in Photoshop to place the stripes and logo properly on the wagon using their UV layouts. Study the image file, and see how it fits on the mesh of the wagon. Try adjusting the image file with your own artwork to see how your image map affects the placement on the mesh.

Working with the B Panels

With the A panels done, you'll move on to the B panels, using much the same methodology you did with the A panels. To begin, follow these steps:

1. Select one of the B panels, shown in Figure 7.89, and open the UV Texture Editor window.

2. As you did with the front face of the A panel, select the UVs on the lower-right side of the layout in the UV Texture Editor, as shown in Figure 7.90, to isolate the front face of the B panel.

3. Choose Select → Convert Selection → To Faces. You've isolated the front face of the B panel.

4. Choose Create UVs → Planar Mapping ❑. In the Options box, set the Project From option to X Axis, and make sure the Keep Image Width/Height Ratio option is checked, just as before. Your B plane shows up nicely laid out in the UV Texture Editor. See Figure 7.91.

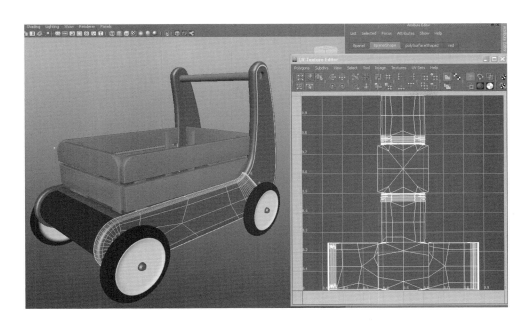

Figure 7.89

**Starting on
the B panels**

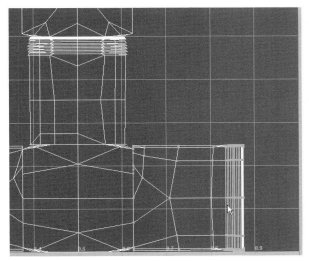

Figure 7.90
Select the front face UVs for the B panel.

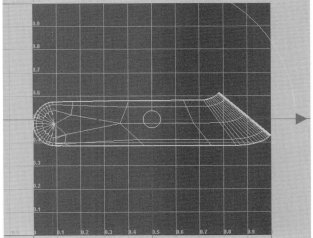

Figure 7.91
**The planar projection creates a nice UV layout for the front faces
of the B panel.**

5. Convert the selection to UVs, and use Move (W), Scale (R), and Rotate (E) to position the UV layout for that front face, as shown in Figure 7.92.

6. Press F8, and select the B panel mesh. In the UV Texture Editor, save a UV snapshot called **BpanelUV.tif** to the Sourceimages folder of the RedWagon project.

Figure 7.92

Put the front face UVs on the side.

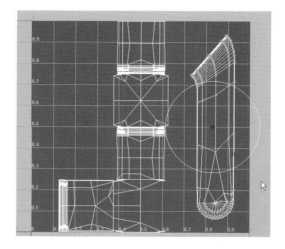

Figure 7.92

Put the front face UVs on the side.

7. Open the `BpanelUV.tif` image in Photoshop, and follow the same steps as you did for the A panel to lay down a red layer and paint a stripe along the layout, as shown in Figure 7.93. It's best to save the stripe on its own layer in Photoshop, because you'll probably need to edit and reposition the stripe to make sure it lines up with the A panel stripe after you assign the shader.

8. Create your own logo to place in the middle of panel B, and place it in the Photoshop image file, as shown in Figure 7.94. Save the image file as **BpanelStripe.tif** into the Sourceimages folder.

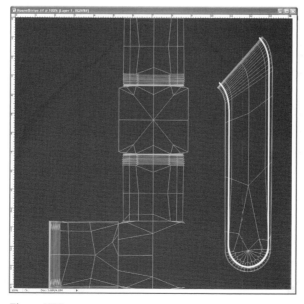

Figure 7.93

Create the B panel's stripe in Photoshop using the UV snapshot.

Figure 7.94

Create the logo in Photoshop.

9. Duplicate another Red shader, and, as you did previously, assign the BpanelStripe.tif as its color map. If necessary, disconnect the transparency from the shader as you did with the A panel's shader. Name the shader **BpanelStripe**.

10. Assign the BpanelStripe shader to the B panel, as shown in Figure 7.95.

Figure 7.95

The B panel has its decals.

You may skip the image creation in Photoshop and use the BpanelStripe.tif image file found in the Sourceimages folder of the RedWagon project on the CD.

CREATING THE OTHER B PANEL TEXTURE

Finally, you need to create the shader for the other side's B panel. Assign the BpanelStripe shader to the other B panel. Nothing happens, because the UVs for the second B panel aren't set up yet.

However, because there is a logo with text, setting up its UVs won't be as simple as copying the UVs from the first B panel and then mirroring the mesh, as you did with the A panel with a Scale X value of −1.0. Doing so will make the logo and text read backward. First, let's copy and flip the UVs to the other B panel:

1. Select the first B panel with the correct texture, and then select the other side's B panel and choose Mesh → Transfer Attributes ❑. Make sure Sample Space is still set to Local, and set Flip UVs to U. Click Transfer to copy the UVs, flipping them over as you can see in Figure 7.96.

Figure 7.96

Copying and flipping the UVs to the other B panel

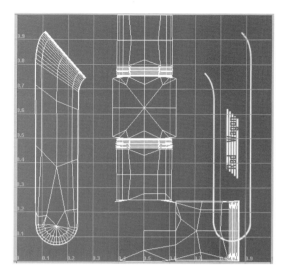

2. You have to go back to Photoshop and create a second `BpanelStripe.tif` image file with a mirrored logo. In Photoshop, create a marquee around the logo, and mirror or flip the canvas horizontally. See Figure 7.97.

3. Select the logo portion of the image, and flip that vertically, as shown in Figure 7.98. Save the image as `BpanelStripe_2.tif`.

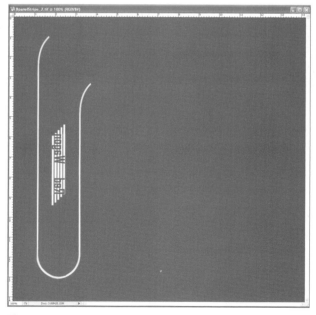

Figure 7.97

Flip the original image horizontally to fit the new UV layout of the second B panel.

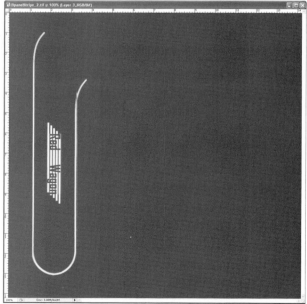

Figure 7.98

Flip the logo vertically, and save the image as its own file.

4. Duplicate the BpanelStripe shader in the Hypershade by selecting the shader and choosing Edit → Duplicate → Shading Network. The copy is called BpanelStripe1.

5. Select the newly copied BpanelStripe1 shader, and graph its input and output connections (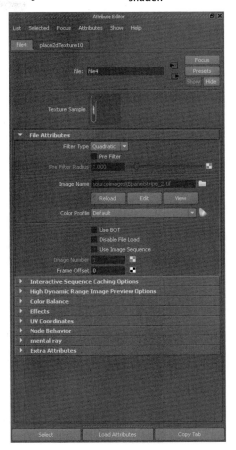) in the Hypershade. Select its file node, and open the Attribute Editor. Click the Folder icon to select a new image file, and then select the BpanelStripe_2.tif you just created in the Sourceimages folder. See Figure 7.99.

Figure 7.99

Assign the new image file to the new BpanelStripe1 shader.

6. The stripe and logo display on the wrong side of the B panel. Select the mesh, and center its pivot.

7. Set the Scale X attribute for the B panel to -1.0 to mirror it. The stripe and logo decals now show up on the correct side of the panel. Select the mesh, and freeze its transforms. Figure 7.100 shows the wagon so far.

Figure 7.100

The wagon has decals on both sides.

Texturing the Floor

Right now, the floor of the wagon is red, like the rest of its body. However, the real wagon has a blue floor, not red. If you select the mesh for the wagon's floor (named wagonFloor) and assign the Blue shader you created, the whole body of the wagon turns blue, and that isn't what you want. You only need the inside and bottom of the floor to be blue, not the front and back sides of the wagon's body.

You'll make a face assignment instead of dealing with UVs and image files. RMB+click the wagon floor mesh, and select Face from the marking menu. Select the two faces for the floor, as shown in Figure 7.101.

Figure 7.101

**Select the
floor faces.**

With the faces selected, assign the Blue shader from the Hypershade window, and you're done! You have a blue floor. All that remains now are the screws, bolts, handle, and wood railings.

You can load the file RedWagonTexture_v03.ma from the Scenes folder of the RedWagon project to check your work or skip to this point.

Shading the Wood Railings

You'll go back to procedural shading and use the Wood texture available in Maya to create the wood railings, as you did with the axe exercise earlier in the chapter. Begin here:

1. In the Hypershade, create a new Phong material.

2. Click the Color Map icon (■), and choose the Wood texture from the 3D Textures heading in the Create pane in the Hypershade.

3. In the Attribute Editor for the Wood texture, set the Filler Color and Vein Color attributes according to Table 7.2.

Table 7.2

**Color and Vein
Attributes**

ATTRIBUTE	H VALUE	S VALUE	V VALUE
Filler Color	43	0.25	1.0
Vein Color	10.7	0.315	0.9

4. Set Vein Spread to 0.5, Layer Size to 0.5, Randomness to 1.0, Age to 10.0, and Grain Contrast to 0.33. In the Noise Attributes heading, set Amplitude X to 0.2 and Amplitude Y to 0.1, as shown in Figure 7.102. Name the shader **wood**.

5. Select all the wood railings and posts, and assign the Wood shader to them. Render a frame, and compare it to Figure 7.103. Notice the green cube place3dTexture node that is now in your scene. (See Figure 7.104.)

6. The side wood railings look fine; however, the wavy pattern on the front and back wood railings looks a bit odd. In the Hypershade, duplicate the shading network for the Wood shader, and call the new shader **woodFront**.

7. Assign that shader to the front and back railings and posts. Graph the network on the woodFront shader in the Hypershade window.

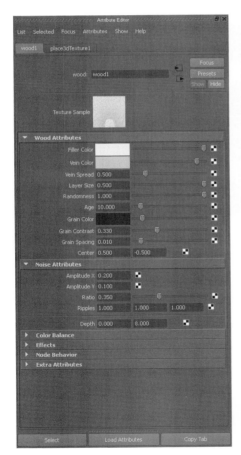

Figure 7.102

Setting the Wood texture

Figure 7.103

Assign the Wood shader.

Figure 7.104

The place3dTexture node for the wood texture

8. In the Hypershade, select the place3dTexture2 node (Figure 7.105) and the green cube in the view panels.

9. Rotate that placement node in the persp panel 90 degrees to the right or left. Render a frame, and compare it to Figure 7.106. The wood should no longer have that awkward wavy pattern.

Figure 7.105

Select the placement node for the second Wood texture.

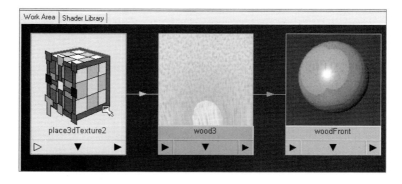

Figure 7.106

The wood on the front and back railings looks better.

The wood railings are finished. Now, for some extra challenge, you can use pictures of real wood to map onto the railings for a more detailed look. The procedural Wood texture can give you only so much realism. If you create your own wood maps, use your experience with the side panels to create UV layouts for the railings so you can paint realistic wood textures using Photoshop. You'll use custom photos and texture image maps next to simulate the rich wood in the decorative box.

Finishing the Wagon

Now that the railings are done and you have test renders, there are only two parts left to texture: the bullnose front of the wagon and the metal handle and screws. From here, take your time and create a bump map based on a fractal, as you did for the tires, and apply it to the bullnose's black shader. Figure 7.107 shows a nice subtle bump map on the bullnose.

Figure 7.107

A nice bump for the bullnose

Figure 7.108

Select all the metal screws, the bolts, and the handlebar, and assign the Metal shader to them.

And last, you'll need a metal shader for the screws, bolts, and handlebar for the wagon, just as you did for the axe exercise earlier in the chapter. Use a Phong shader with a blue-gray color and a low diffuse value, and assign it to all the metal parts of the wagon, as shown in Figure 7.108. You can then add an environment map to the reflection color, as you did for the axe earlier in this chapter to give the metal a reflective look.

Because metal is a tricky material to render, and a lot of metal's look is derived from reflections, you'll finish setting the Metal shader's attributes in Chapter 11 when you render the wagon. You'll enable raytracing to get realistic reflections and gauge how to best set up the Metal shader for a great look.

Figure 7.109 shows the wagon with all its parts assigned to shaders. Figure 7.110 shows a quick render of the wagon as it is now.

You can load the file `RedWagonTexture_v04.ma` from the `Scenes` folder of the RedWagon project to check your work or skip to this point.

Figure 7.109

The wagon in the Perspective panel

Figure 7.110

A current render of the wagon

Photoreal Mapping: The Decorative Box

With all the references you can find to any given object on the Internet, why not use real photos to create the textures for a model? That's exactly what you'll do here, with the decorative box you modeled in Chapter 6, using pictures of the real box.

You'll take this texturing exercise one important step further in Chapter 11 and experience how you can add detail to an object through displacement mapping, after you assign the colors in this chapter. This will allow you to add finer detail to a model without modeling those details.

Setting Up UVs (Blech!)

The UVs on the decorative box aren't too badly laid out by default, as you can see in Figure 7.111. The only parts of the box that are missing in the UV layout are the feet. That is a common issue when extruding polygons: their UVs are rarely laid out automatically as you extrude them. Frequently, they're bunched up together in a flat layout that is difficult, if not impossible, to see in the UV Texture Editor.

First, you have to make room for the feet UVs:

1. Select all the UVs for the entire box in the UV Texture Editor. Press R for the Scale tool, and scale everything down uniformly to gain some space in the normalized UV space, shown in Figure 7.112.

2. Now for the tedious part: you have to create new UVs for the four feet and then move them to where they should be in the full box's UV layout. Go into Component mode, and select the poly faces for the four feet, as shown in Figure 7.113.

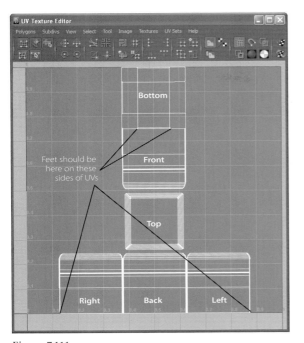

Figure 7.111

The feet UVs are missing from the box model.

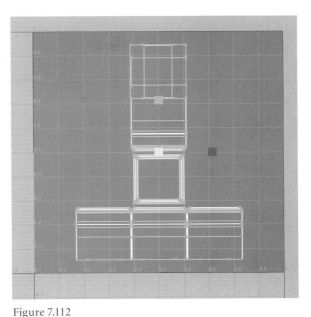

Figure 7.112

Scale all the UVs down a bit.

Figure 7.113

Select the faces for the feet.

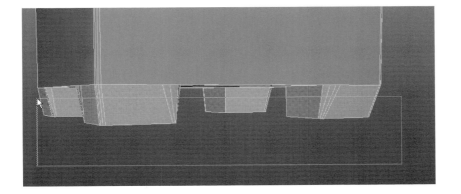

3. With the faces selected, go to the main Maya window. In the Polygons menu set, select Create UVs → Automatic Mapping. The feet now have UVs that you can see in Figure 7.114. However, they're all over the place. You have to individually select and move each face of each foot to its appropriate place on the box's overall UV layout.

4. Select all the feet UVs in the UV Texture Editor, scale them all down uniformly together, and move them off to the side. (See Figure 7.115.) You'll position and scale them to fit properly soon.

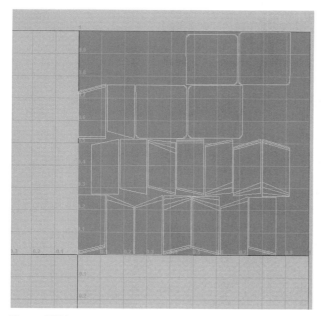

Figure 7.114

The automatic UV creation puts the UVs everywhere.

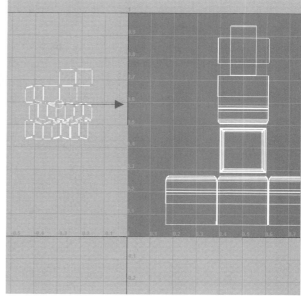

Figure 7.115

Separate the feet UVs to the side, and scale them down.

Laying out UVs can be a time-consuming affair, as you've seen with the wagon. Although it's recommended that you follow along with this exercise to lay out UVs for the box, because doing so will give you more practice and experience with UVs, you can skip straight to color-mapping the box in the next section by loading the file boxTexture01.mb in the Scenes folder of the Decorative_Box project on the CD.

5. Now comes the task of figuring out which UV fits where. Start with the left foot on the front of the box. In the persp window, select one front face of the front foot, left side on the front of the box. (See Figure 7.116.)

6. Right-click in the UV Texture Editor, and choose UV from the marking menu. Select a single UV point on the face that appears in the UV Texture Editor window, as shown in Figure 7.117. As soon as you make the selection, the UV Texture Editor shows you the UVs for the entire box. Because you moved the feet UVs to the side, your UV Texture Editor should look like the one in Figure 7.118, with a green point showing the single selected UV.

7. In the UV Texture Editor, choose Select → Select Shell. The UVs for the entire front part of that foot are selected. The UVs are sideways, so choose Polygons → Rotate ❑. Set the rotation angle to 90, and click Rotate UVs. The front of this foot should now resemble the actual foot, although the scale is still off.

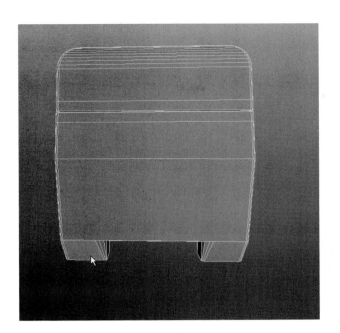

Figure 7.116

Select the one face on this foot on the front of the box.

Figure 7.117

Select one UV point on that face in the UV Texture Editor window.

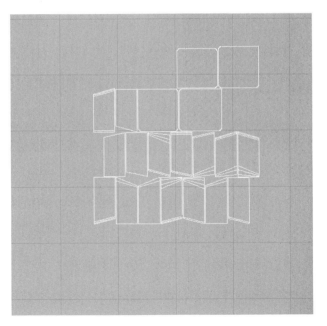

Figure 7.118

The UV Texture Editor shows you that one selected UV as well as the UV layout for the rest of the box.

Position the UV layout of this foot onto the front of the box, as shown in Figure 7.119. Scale down the UVs to match the size of the foot in the model, more or less. Keep in mind that the box-front UV layout is upside down in the UV Texture Editor.

Figure 7.119

Move these UVs to the front of the box where that foot belongs.

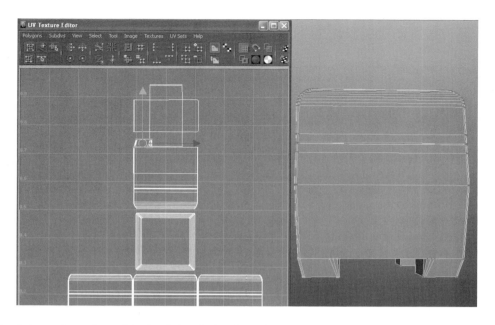

8. Select a front face of the back foot behind the front foot, as shown in Figure 7.120. Sounds confusing, but the figure shows you which face to select. In this figure, you're looking at the front of the box. The UV Texture Editor shows the UV layout for that part of the foot. Choose Select → Select Shell to grab the entire front of that back foot. (See Figure 7.121.)

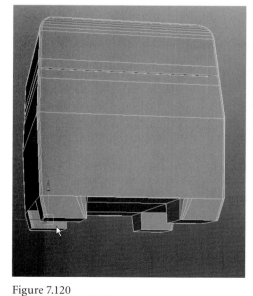

Figure 7.120

Select a front face of the back foot.

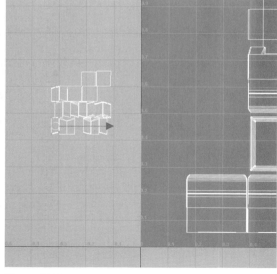

Figure 7.121

The UV Texture Editor shows the UV layout for that part of the back foot.

9. The back foot's UVs lie directly behind the front foot's UVs, which you laid out in step 7. Rotate the UVs (90 degrees again) with the Polygons → Rotate command, as you did before, and then position and scale the UVs as shown in Figure 7.122. They fit exactly behind the front foot.

10. Repeat steps 5 through 9 for the front and back feet on the front right side of the box.

Figure 7.122

Place the front of the back foot's UVs.

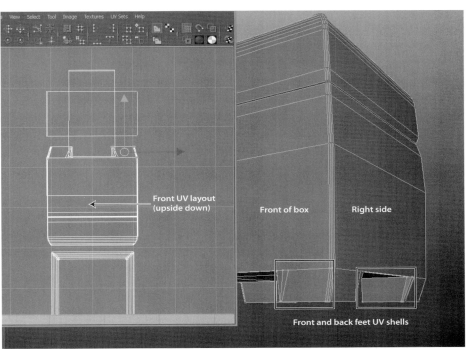

Figure 7.123

Place the UVs for the fronts of the two feet on the right side of the box's front.

11. Let's move to the right side of the box. Select a front face for the foot on the left on the right side of the box. Again, it sounds confusing, but reference Figure 7.124 for clarification. You should be getting the hang of what you're doing. Save your work.

12. In the UV Texture Editor, select one UV from the selected face, and then choose Select → Select Shell. (See Figure 7.125.)

13. Check to see where the UVs for the right side of the box are laid out in the UV Texture Editor in the earlier Figure 7.111. Rotate, scale, and place these foot UVs as shown in Figure 7.126.

Figure 7.124

Selecting a face for the left foot on the right side of the box

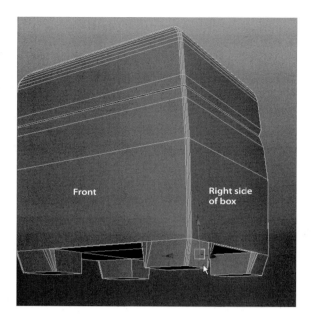

Front   Right side of box

Figure 7.125

The UV shell for the foot you're working on

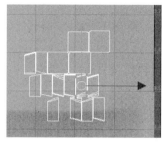

Figure 7.126

Place the right side foot UVs.

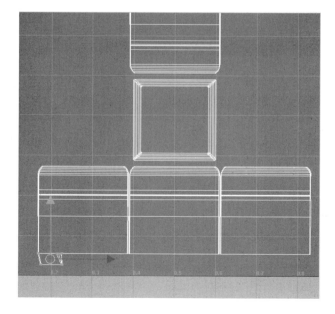

14. Repeat the procedures to move the UVs for the front and back feet for the right side of the box, as shown in Figure 7.127. Make sure you're using Select → Select Shell, to ensure that you have the entire UV shell selected before orienting and moving the feet UVs.

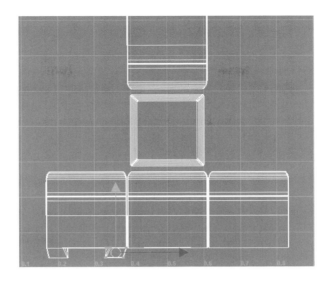

Figure 7.127
**Placing the feet
for the right side
of the box**

15. Repeat the procedures for the feet seen from the back side of the box, so the foot UVs are all laid out similar to Figure 7.128.

16. Repeat the procedures to lay out the UVs for the feet seen from the left side of the box, as shown in Figure 7.129.

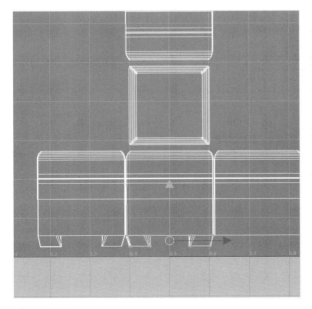

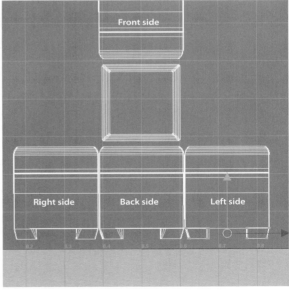

Figure 7.128
The feet are laid out for the back side of the box.

Figure 7.129
The feet are laid out for the left side of the box.

17. All that remain are the bottoms of the feet, as seen in the UV Texture Editor in Figure 7.130. Move the entire shell of the box bottom up to get some space between it and the box front layout.

18. Using the same procedures as before (selecting the shell, and rotating, moving, and scaling each UV shell), place the bottoms of the feet where they belong, as shown in Figure 7.131.

When you're all done, your UV Texture Editor should resemble the one shown in Figure 7.132. Because the box's decorations are seamless from the top of the box down to the four sides, let's layout the UVs to make painting and editing in Photoshop easier.

Figure 7.130

The bottom UVs for the feet are selected and shown in the small square highlights in the image on the right and are also shown selected in the UV Texture Editor on the left.

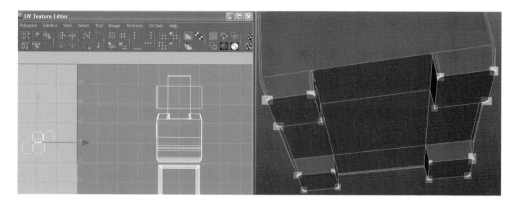

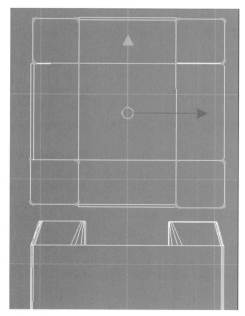

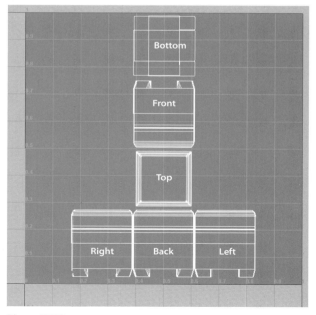

Figure 7.131

Move the bottom UVs to the underside of the box.

Figure 7.132

Finally, you're finished with UVs.

Individually select the UVs for the right and left sides of the box, and rotate and position them to match Figure 7.133. Line up the sides to the top as closely as you can.

This was quite a tedious exercise. UV layout is a chore, but when it's completed, you're free to lay out your textures. You can check your work against the file boxTexture01.mb in the Scenes folder of the Decorative_Box project on the CD. You can also take a much needed breather. I sure hope you've been saving your work!

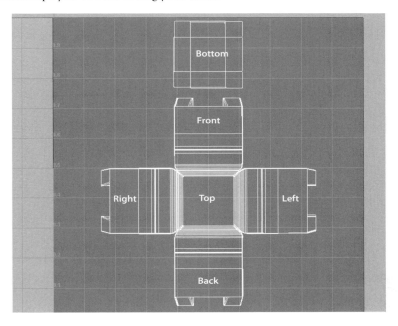

Figure 7.133

Place the sides of the box around the top, lining them up as closely as possible.

Color Mapping the Box

Now that you have a good UV layout, you can output a UV snapshot and get to work editing your photos of the box to make the color maps. Start with the following steps:

Figure 7.134

Setting the UV Snapshot options

1. Select the box, and open the UV Texture Editor window. From the UV Texture Editor menu, select Polygons → UV Snapshot. In the UV Snapshot window, set Size X and Y to 2048. Change Image Format to TIFF.

   Click the Browse button, and select a location for your UV snapshot image. Generally, the project's Sourceimages folder is the best place for it. Make sure you don't write over the UV snapshot already created for you. Type in a name for your UV snapshot, and click OK to create the image. Figure 7.134 shows the option box, and Figure 7.135 shows the UV snapshot image.

Figure 7.135

The UV snapshot for the decorative box, shown as black lines on white. You may see white lines on black in Photoshop.

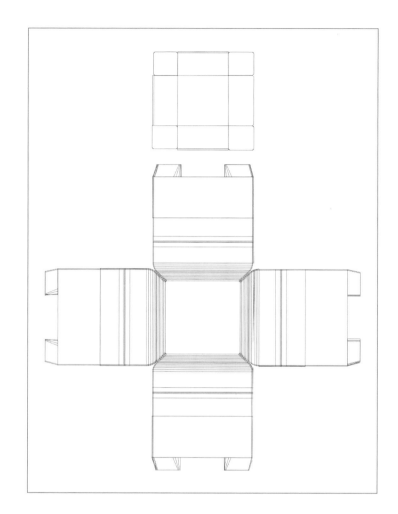

2. Open the UV snapshot image in Photoshop or your favorite image editor, and set it as its own layer. Rename the layer to UV Snapshot. I've done the heavy lifting for you and have prepared five photos of the decorative box that you can use to map the model. Figure 7.136 show the photos of the box. This image file is included as lineup .jpg in the Sourceimages folder in the Decorative_Box project on the CD.

Figure 7.136

Photos of the box

Top   Right   Left   Front   Back

3. As you've probably guessed, you need to copy and paste the photos to their respective views over the UV Snapshot layer. Open the `lineup.jpg` file in Photoshop alongside the UV snapshot. Marquee-select a box around the top image (the one at left in Figure 7.136), and copy it (Ctrl+C or Edit → Copy in Photoshop).

4. Go to the UV snapshot image in Photoshop, and paste the image on top. Rename the new layer to **Box Top**, and set the layer's Opacity to 50% so you can still see the UV layout, as shown in Figure 7.137.

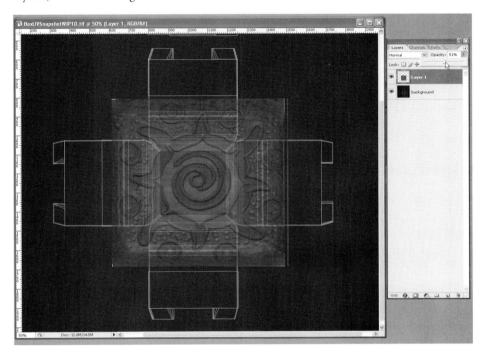

Figure 7.137

Paste the top image onto the UV snapshot image.

5. Use the Scale function in Photoshop (Edit → Transform → Scale) to move and scale the top image to fit over the top of the UV layout, as shown in Figure 7.138. Make sure you scale the box-top image uniformly to keep it from distorting. You can do this by holding the Shift key as you scale the image up or down.

These photo images of the box have been retouched and painted to create an overlap. This means that parts of the sides of the box show in the top image. As you can see in Figure 7.138, the top image extends slightly all around the four sides. This allows the different parts of the texture map (top and four sides) to overlap and blend with each other better when put on the model.

Save your work as `boxColorMapWork01.tif` in the project's `Sourceimages` folder. Make sure you're saving the TIF file with layers to preserve your layer work. You can also save the file as a PSD to preserve the layers.

Figure 7.138

Position and scale the top image in Photoshop to line up with the UVs of the top of the model. Notice the overlap of the sides and the top.

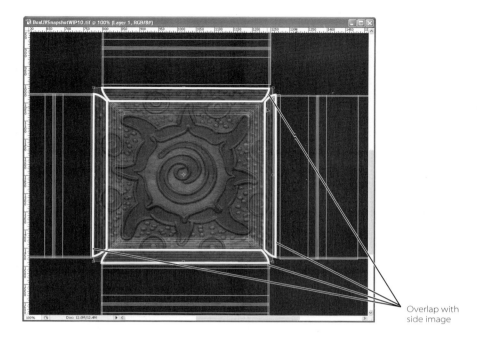

Overlap with side image

6. Marquee-select the right-side image of the box (immediately to the right of the top image in `lineup.jpg`), and copy it. Paste it into `boxColorMapWork01.tif` in Photoshop. Do your best to align the right-side image with the top image, using the features of the box to line them up, as you can see in Figure 7.139. You can fix this later by adjusting both the map and the UVs on the box for a tighter fit. For now, be fairly accurate, and leave the finesse for later. Save the file as `boxColorMapWork02.tif`.

Figure 7.139

Align the right-side image with the right-side UVs.

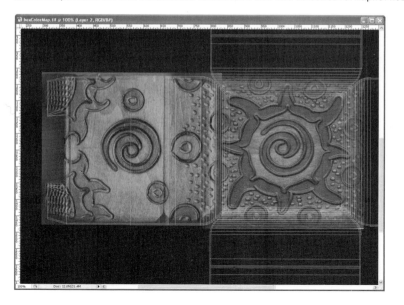

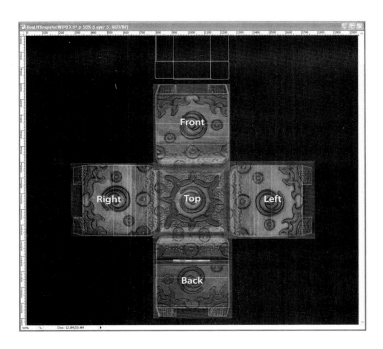

Figure 7.140

Figure 7.140

Copy, paste, and line up the box sides and the back to their respective UV areas.

7. Use the same procedures in Photoshop to line up the other sides of the box, as shown in Figure 7.140. Set the box-top image to be the topmost layer, make sure all the layers are at 100% opacity, and then turn off the UV Snapshot layer so it's not visible.

Figure 7.141

The color map layout

Save the final Photoshop file as boxColorMap.tif, again keeping all the layers. (Change the name if you don't wish to overwrite the file already created for you in the Sourceimages folder.) Then, resave the file as a JPEG called boxColorMap.jpg. This is the file you'll map. (See Figure 7.141.)

Mapping the Box

Let's map this color image to the box and see how it fits. Based on rendering the box, you can make adjustments to the UVs and the image map to get everything to line up. This, of course, requires more Photoshop and/or image-editing experience, which could be a series of books of its own. If you don't have enough image-editing experience, have no fear: the images have been created for you, so you can get the experience of mapping them and learn about the underlying workflow that this sort of texturing requires. Follow these steps:

1. Back in Maya, open the Hypershade window, and create a new Phong shader. Open the Attribute Editor, click the Map button (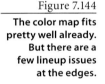) next to the Color attribute, and select File.

2. Double-click the file1 node to open the Attribute Editor. Click the folder icon next to the Image Name attribute, navigate to the Sourceimages folder for the project, and select the boxColorMap .jpg file (not the TIF file). The icon in the Hypershade doesn't show the image because it's a large file. (See Figure 7.142.)

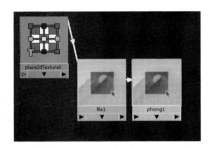

Figure 7.142

The color map's file node

3. Right-click the file1 node, and choose Refresh Swatch. The boxColorMap image is displayed as the file1 icon. (See Figure 7.143.)

4. Select the box, and assign the Phong shader it. Rename the Phong to **boxShader**. In the persp panel, press 6 for texture view. The color map is fairly well aligned on the model. Not bad! (See Figure 7.144.)

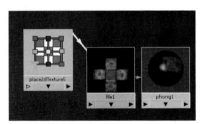

Figure 7.143

The icon is refreshed.

Figure 7.144

The color map fits pretty well already. But there are a few lineup issues at the edges.

Lineup issues

5. Render a frame to see how the box looks. Notice that there are small lineup issues at the edges where the sides meet and where the top meets the sides. Save your Maya scene.

This gives you a pretty good place to work from. You need to adjust the color map image to be more seamless. The scene file boxTexture02.mb in the Scenes folder of the Decorative_Box project on the CD will catch you up to this point.

Figure 7.145

A render of the box so far

Photoshop Work

This is where image-editing experience is valuable. From here on, it's all about working in Photoshop to line up the sides to the top and the sides to each other to minimize lineup issues and yield a seamless texture map. Although we won't get into the minutia of photo editing here, we'll show the progression of the images and the general workflow used in Photoshop to make the color map's different sides and top line up and or merge better. The images have already been created and are on the CD under the Sourceimages folder for this project.

First, using masking in Photoshop, spend some time feathering the intersection of the box's sides in boxColorMap.jpg so there is no hard line between the different sides and the top. Figure 7.146 shows a smoother transition between the different parts. This image has been created for you: it's boxColorMap02.jpg in the Sourceimages folder. Make sure you don't overwrite that file if you're painting your own.

In Maya, replace the original `boxColorMap.jpg` with `boxColorMap02.jpg`. Render and compare the difference. The top and front should merge a little better. In the persp panel, orbit around the box in Texture View mode (press 6) to see where else there are lineup issues. In some cases, as you can see in Figure 7.147, gray or black is mapped onto the box on its right side, and there is a warped area. Also, the crease where the lid meets the box is lower than you've modeled.

Figure 7.147

There are blank areas on the box as well as a little distortion.

The blank areas on the box are outside the bounds of the image in the Photoshop image and can be fixed by adjusting the UVs in Maya. The same goes for the distorted areas on the side of the box—you just need to adjust the UVs:

1. Select the box, and open the UV Texture Editor window. Figure 7.148 shows the primary areas for you to work on.

2. In the UV Texture Editor, select the UVs (right-click and choose UV) shown in Figure 7.149 on the left. Press W for the Move tool, and realign the UVs to the seam where the lid meets the box, as shown in Figure 7.149 on the right. As you make the changes in the UV Texture Editor, you should immediately notice them in the persp window (as long as you're in Texture View mode).

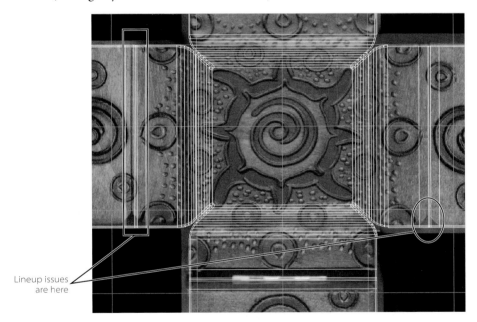

Lineup issues are here

Figure 7.148
Here are the main problems to fix.

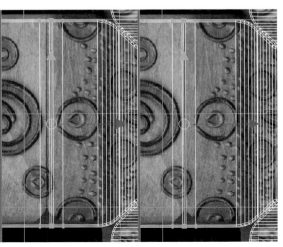

Figure 7.149
Move the UVs.

3. Look at the image on top in Figure 7.150. Move the appropriate UVs to align the edge of the UV layout to the image for the right side of the box, as shown on the bottom of Figure 7.150.

4. The box's distortion is gone, and the texture fits much better. But notice in the image on the left in Figure 7.151 that the right side of the box and the back of the box don't line up perfectly. Using the texture view in the persp window and the UV Texture Editor, go around the box in its entirety and adjust the UVs so that they all line up to the image in the UV Texture Editor and that the sides line up at the edges of the box. Figure 7.151's image on the right shows correctly lined up UVs for the right side/back side of the box.

Be careful when you're selecting the UVs of one side so you don't select UVs from an adjacent side in the UV Texture Editor.

Figure 7.150

Line up the UVs to the image for the right side of the box.

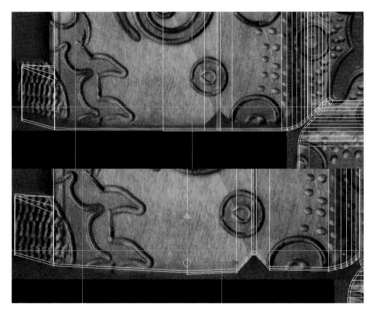

Figure 7.151

Line up the UVs for the right side/ back side edge of the box.

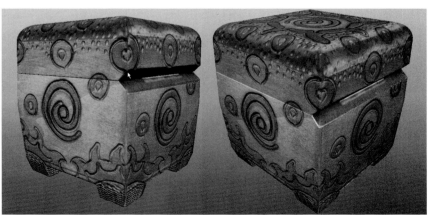

Figure 7.152 shows the UV Texture Editor and a persp view of the box with UVs lined up and ready to go. You can compare your work to the scene file boxTexture03.mb in the Scenes folder of the Decorative_Box project on the CD. Render a few different views to take in all the hard work. In Chapter 10, you'll light the box and prepare it for rendering; and in Chapter 11, you'll use displacement maps created from these photos to detail the indentations and carvings that are in the actual box. You've had enough excitement for one chapter.

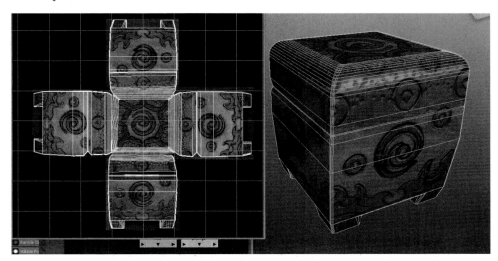

Figure 7.152

The UVs laid out for the decorative box

For Further Study

For a challenge and more experience, create new image maps for the wagon and try out your own decal designs. As previously suggested, you can try to create more realistic wood maps for the wagon's railings. In Chapter 10, you'll begin to see how shading and rendering go hand in hand; you'll adjust many of the shader attributes you created in this chapter to render the decorative box in Chapter 11.

You can also try to create textures to map onto the hand model you created in Chapter 4, using photos of your own hand with extensive UV manipulation.

Summary

In this chapter, you learned about the types of shaders and how they work. Each shader has a set of attributes that give material definition, and each attribute has a different effect on how a model looks.

To gain practice, you textured a NURBS axe model using various shaders, including the Layered shader, to create a wooden handle with a metal spike tip.

Next, you learned about the methods you can use to project textures onto a surface and how you can bake these projections onto an object to avoid "swimming." You learned about Maya's texture nodes, including PSD networks and the basics of UVs, and how to use them to place images onto your wagon model in a fairly detailed exercise exposing you to manipulating UVs and using Photoshop to create maps.

Texturing a scene is never an isolated process. Making textures work involves render settings, lighting, and even geometry manipulation and creation. Your work in this chapter will be expanded in Chapters 10 and 11 with discussions of lighting and rendering.

Just like everything else in Maya, it's all about collaboration—the more experience you gain, the more you'll see how everything intertwines.

However, for Maya to be an effective tool for you, it's important to have a clear understanding of the look you want for your CG. This involves plenty of research into your project, downloading heaps of images to use as references, and a good measure of trial and error.

The single best weapon in your texturing arsenal, and indeed in all aspects of CG art, is your eye, your observations of the world around you, and how they relate to the world you're creating in CG.

CHAPTER 8

Introduction to Animation

The best way to learn about animation is to start animating, so you'll begin this chapter with the classic exercise of bouncing a ball. You'll then take a closer look at the animation tools Maya software provides and how they work for your scene. You'll do that by throwing the axe you created earlier. Finally, you'll tackle animating a more complex system of parts when you bring your locomotive to life.

Topics in this chapter include:

- **Keyframe animation—bouncing a ball**
- **Throwing an axe**
- **Path animation**
- **Replacing an object**
- **Creating and deforming text along a path**
- **Rigging the locomotive, part 1**
- **Animating a catapult**

Keyframe Animation—Bouncing a Ball

No matter where you study animation, you'll always find the classic animation exercise of creating a bouncing ball. Although it's a straightforward exercise and you've probably seen it a hundred times on the Web and in other books, the bouncing ball is a perfect exercise with which to begin animating. You can imbue the ball with so much character that the possibilities are almost endless, so try to run this exercise as many times as you can handle. You'll improve with every attempt.

Animating a bouncing ball is a good exercise in real-world physical motion as well as in cartoon movement. First, you'll create a rubber ball and create a proper animation hierarchy for it. Then, you'll add cartoonish movement to accentuate some principles of the animation techniques discussed in the ultra-fabulous Chapter 1, "Introduction to Computer Graphics and 3D."

Creating a Cartoon Ball

First, you need to create the ball, as well as the project for this exercise. Follow these steps:

1. In a new scene, begin with a poly sphere, and then create a poly plane. Scale the plane up to be the ground plane.

2. Press 5 for Shaded mode.

3. Move the sphere 1.0 unit up in the *Y*-axis so that it's resting on the ground and not halfway through it, as shown in Figure 8.1.

4. Choose Modify → Freeze Transformations to set the ball's resting height to 0, as opposed to 1. This action sets the ball's Translate attribute back to 0, effectively resetting the object. This is called *freezing the transforms.* This is useful when you position, scale, and orient an object and need to set its new location, orientation, and size as the beginning state.

5. Choose File → Project → New to create a new project. Call the project **bouncing_ball**, and place it in the same parent folder as your Solar System project folder. Click the Use Defaults button to create the necessary folders in your project, and then click Accept. Save the scene file into that project.

Figure 8.1

Place the ball on the ground.

Setting Up the Hierarchy

To make life easier, you'll set up the ball with three null nodes above it, listed here from the top parent node down: translate, scale, rotate. All the animation will be placed on these three nodes, and not the sphere itself. This will allow you to easily animate the ball bouncing, squashing, and stretching, and moving forward in space.

1. Select the sphere and press Ctrl+G to create the first group. In the Outliner, call this new group **rotate**.

2. With the rotate node selected, press Ctrl+G to create the scale group, and name it accordingly.

3. With the scale group selected, press Ctrl+G one last time to create the translate group and name it accordingly. Figure 8.2 shows the hierarchy.

Figure 8.2

The ball's hierarchy

As you animate, you'll quickly see why you've set up a hierarchy for the ball, instead of just putting keys on the sphere itself.

Animating the Ball

Your next step is to keyframe the positions of the ball using the nodes above the sphere. As introduced in Chapter 1, *keyframing* is the process of setting positions and values at particular frames of the animation.

You'll start with the *gross animation*, which is the overall movement scheme, a.k.a. *blocking*. First, you'll move the ball up and down to begin its choreography in these steps:

1. Press W to open the Translate tool, select the translate node, and move it up to the top of the frame, say about 10 units up in the *Y*-axis and 8 units back in *X*-axis at (-8,10,0). Place the camera so that you'll have some room to work in the frame.

2. Instead of selecting the Translate attributes in the Channel Box and pressing S as you did in Chapter 2, "Jumping in Headfirst, with Both Feet," to set keyframes on the planets, you'll set keyframes for translation in an easier way.

   Press Shift+W to set keyframes on Translate X, Translate Y, and Translate Z at frame 1 for the top node of the ball (named translate). To make sure your scene is set up properly, set your animation speed to 30fps by choosing Window → Settings/Preferences → Preferences to open the Preferences window or by clicking the Animation Preferences button (⬚) next to the Auto-Key button. In the Settings category of the Preferences window, set Time to NTSC (30fps). A frame range of 1 to 120 is good for now. Figure 8.3 shows the ball's start position.

Figure 8.3

Start the ball here and set a keyframe on the translate node.

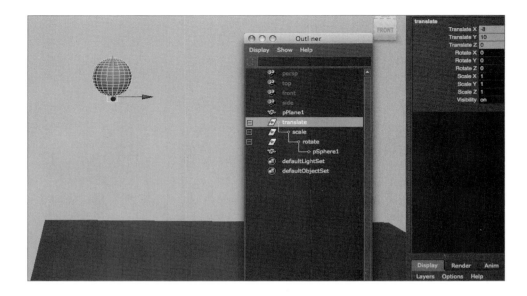

3. Click the Auto Keyframe button ( ) to turn it on; it turns red. Auto Keyframe automatically sets a keyframe at the current time for any attribute that has changed since its last keyframe for the selected object or node.

> For the Auto Keyframe feature to work, you have to set an initial keyframe manually for each of the attributes you want to animate.

4. Disregarding any specific timing, go to frame 10, and move the ball down in the Y-axis until it's about one-quarter through the ground plane. Because you'll be creating squash and stretch for this cartoon ball (see Chapter 1 for a brief explanation), you need to send the ball through the ground a little bit. Then, move the ball about 3 units to the right, to about (-5,-0.4, 0). The Auto Keyframe feature sets a keyframe in the X and Y axes at frame 10. Remember, this is all on the translate node.

5. Move to frame 20, and raise the ball back up to about half of its original height and to the right about 2.5 units (-2.5,4,0). Auto Keyframe sets X and Y Translation keyframes at frame 20 and will continue to set keyframes for the ball as you animate.

6. At frame 30, place the ball back down a little less than one-quarter of the way through the ground and about 2 units to the right, at about (−0.5, −0.3,0).

7. At frame 40, place the ball back up in the air in the Y-axis at a fraction of its original height and to the right about 1.5 units, at about (1.1,1.85,0).

8. Repeat this procedure every 10 frames to frame 110 or so, so that you bounce the ball a few more times up and down and to the right (positive in the X-axis). Make sure you're decreasing the ball's height and traveling in X with each successive bounce and

decreasing how much the ball passes through the ground with every landing until it rests on top of the ground plane. Open the Graph Editor for a peek into the ball's animation curves (see Figure 8.4). (Choose Window → Animation Editors → Graph Editor.)

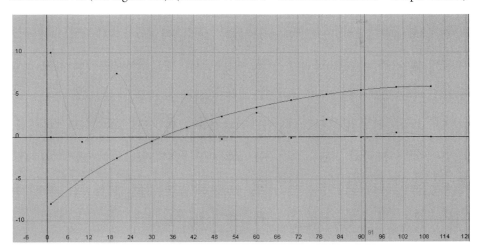

Figure 8.4

The Graph Editor curves for the ball's translate node

By holding down the Shift key as you pressed W in step 2, you set a keyframe for Translate. Likewise, you can keyframe Rotation and Scale. Here's a summary of the keystrokes for setting keyframes:

Shift+W   Sets a keyframe for the selection's position in all three axes at the current time

Shift+E   Sets a keyframe for the selection's rotation in all three axes at the current time

Shift+R   Sets a keyframe for the selection's scale in all three axes at the current time

You'll resume this exercise after a look at the Graph Editor.

The Graph Editor

The Graph Editor is a critical tool for an animator. You provide most of an animation's finesse through work in this window. As a matter of fact, you can animate a number of objects solely through this window. (See Chapter 3, "The Maya 2011 Interface," for an introduction to the Graph Editor.) Using its graph view of where in space and time each keyframe lies, you can conveniently control your animation. Move a keyframe in time to the right, for example, to slow the action. Move the same keyframe to the left in time to speed up the action.

Reading the Curves in the Graph Editor

Understanding what animation curves do in the Graph Editor is crucial to getting your animation right. Using the Graph Editor to *read animation curves*, you can judge an object's direction, speed, acceleration, and timing.

As you'll see later in this chapter with the axe-throwing tutorial, you'll invariably come across problems and issues with your animation that require a careful review of their curves. The ability to see a curve and translate it into what your object is doing comes with time and practice. Be patient, and don't be afraid to open the Graph Editor and animate through it as much as you can. Here are a couple of key concepts to keep in mind.

First, the curves in the Graph Editor are like the NURBS curves you've modeled with so far. Instead of CVs on a NURBS curve controlling the curvature, points directly on an animation curve represent keyframes and control the curvature with their *tangency handles*. By grabbing one end of a key's handle and dragging it up or down, you adjust the curve.

Second, the graph is a representation of an object attribute's position (vertical) over time (horizontal). Every place on the curve represents where the object is in that axis; there needn't be a keyframe on the curve. Not only does the placement of the keys on the curve make a big difference, so does the shape of the curve itself. Here is a quick primer on how to read a curve in the Graph Editor and, hence, how to edit it.

In Figure 8.5, the object's Translate Z attribute is being animated. At the beginning, the curve quickly begins to move positively (that is, to the right) in the Z-axis. The object shoots off to the right and comes to an *ease-out*, where it decelerates to a stop. The stop is signified by the flat part of the curve at the first keyframe at frame 41. The object then quickly accelerates in the negative Z direction (left) and maintains a fairly even speed until it hits frame 62, where it suddenly changes direction and goes back right for about 45 frames. It then slowly decelerates to a full stop in an ease-out.

Consider a single object in motion. The shape of the curve in the Graph Editor defines how the object moves. The object shown in Figure 8.6 is moving in a steady manner in one direction.

Figure 8.5

An animation curve

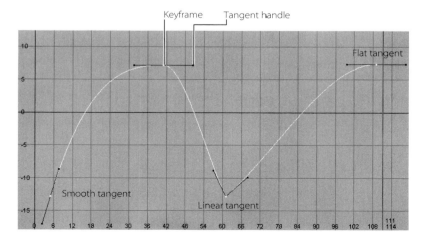

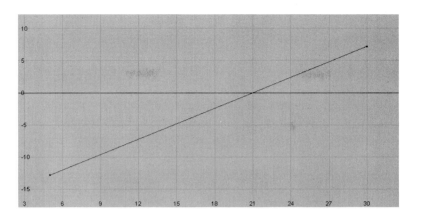

Figure 8.6
Linear movement

Figure 8.7 shows the object slowly accelerating toward frame 30, where it suddenly comes to a stop. If there is nothing beyond the end of the curve, there is no motion. The one exception deals with the *infinity* of curves, which is discussed shortly.

The object in Figure 8.8 begins moving immediately and comes to a slow stop by frame 27, where the curve first becomes flat.

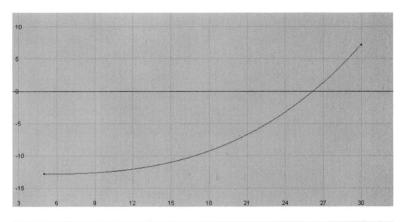

Figure 8.7
**Acceleration
(ease-in)**

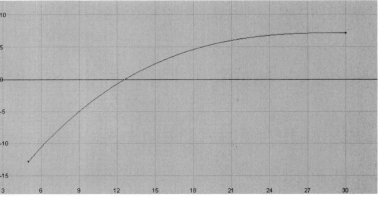

Figure 8.8
**Deceleration
(ease-out)**

Cartoon Ball

Now, let's apply what you've learned about the Graph Editor to the bouncing ball. Follow these steps:

1. Open the Graph Editor, and look at the ball's animation curves. They should be similar to the curves in Figure 8.4, shown earlier.

2. Notice how only the *X* and *Y* axes' translates have curves, and yet Translate Z has a single keyframe but no curve. It's from the initial position keyframe you set at frame 1. Because you've only moved the sphere in the *X* and *Y* axes, Auto-Key hasn't set any keys in the *Z*-axis. This is better than pressing S to set keys on everything, so if you don't have animation on something, it doesn't get keys. Keep your scene clean.

3. Play back the animation, and see how it feels. Be sure to open the Animation Preferences window. Click the Animation Preferences icon (🔳) to set the playback speed to Real-Time (30fps). You'll find this icon in the Playback section in the Timeline category.

4. Timing is the main issue now, so you want to focus on how fast the ball bounces:

   - The ball is falling too fast initially, although the second and third bounces should look fine.

   - To fix the timing, move the keyframes in the Graph Editor. For the *X* and *Y* axes, select the keyframes at frame 10 and all the others beyond on both curves. Move them all back two frames. (See Figure 8.9.)

As the ball's bounce decays over time, it goes up less but still takes the same amount of time (10 frames) to go up the lesser distance. For better timing, adjust the last few bounces to occur faster. Select the keys on the last three bounces and move them, one by one, a frame or two to the left to decrease the time on the last short bounces. (See Figure 8.10.)

Figure 8.9

Move all the keyframes for both curves to the right to slow the initial fall by two frames, but leave the timing the same for the rest.

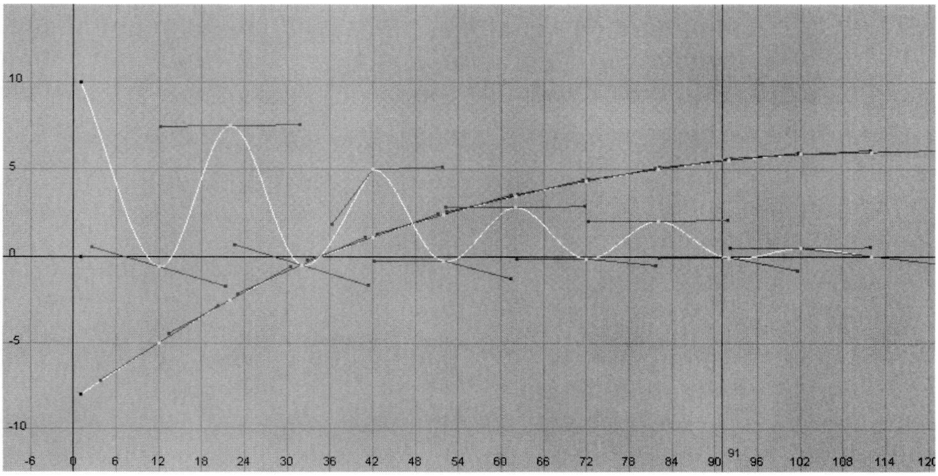

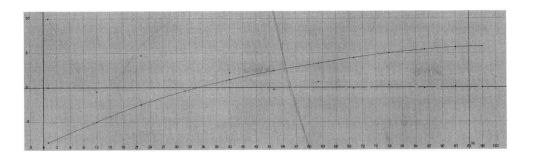

Figure 8.10

Move the keys to make the final short bounces quicker and the bounce height feel right.

To move a key in the Graph Editor, press W to open the Move tool, MMB+click, and drag the cursor in the Graph Editor window. Press the Shift key, and drag the cursor left and right or up and down to lock the movement to either horizontal or vertical to make it easier to control.

Understanding Timing

In animation, timing is all about getting the keyframes in the proper order. Judging the speed of an object in animation is critical to getting it to look right, and that comes down to timing. The more you animate, the better your timing will be, which is why the bouncing ball is such a popular exercise.

Load the file ball_v01.mb from the Bouncing_Ball project on the CD to get to this point.

When you play back the animation, it should look more natural. But it still looks fake, as if it's rising and falling on a wave as opposed to really bouncing. You need to edit the timing of the ball. The problem with the animation is that the ball eases in and out as it rises and falls. By default, setting a key in Maya sets the keyframes to have an ease-in and ease-out in their curves, meaning their curves are smooth like a NURBS curve.

Because of the smooth animation curve, the ball doesn't look natural in its timing. You need to accelerate the ball as it falls with a sharp valley in the curve, and you need to decelerate it as it rises with smooth peaks. Follow these steps:

1. In the Graph Editor, select the Translate Y entry in the left panel of the window to isolate your view to just that curve in the editor panel on the right. Select all the landing keyframes (the ones in the valleys of the curve) and change their *interpolation* from smooth to linear by clicking the Linear Tangents button ().

2. Likewise, select all the peak keyframes at the ball's rise, and change their tangents to flat by clicking the Flat Tangents icon (⬡) to make the animation curve like the one shown in Figure 8.11.

3. When you play back the animation, the ball seems to be moving more realistically. If you need to, adjust the keys a bit more to get the timing to feel right to you, before you move on to squash and stretch and rotation.

Figure 8.11

The adjusted timing of the bounce

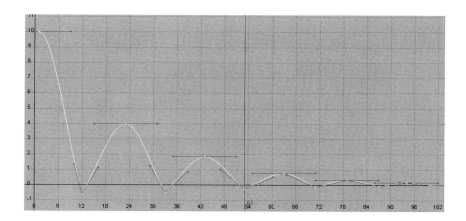
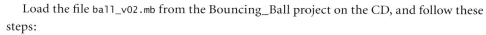

Squash and Stretch

The concept of *squash and stretch* has been an animation staple for as long as there has been animation. It's a way to convey the weight of an object by deforming it to react (usually in an exaggerated way) to gravity and motion.

In Maya, you use the Scale tool to squash and stretch your object—in this case, your ball, using only the scale node, not the sphere or translate node.

Load the file `ball_v02.mb` from the Bouncing_Ball project on the CD, and follow these steps:

1. Select the scale node, and select Modify → Center Pivot. This places the scale pivot point in the middle of the ball.

2. At frame 9, press R to set initial scale keyframes on the scale node of the ball, a couple of frames before the ball impacts the ground.

3. To initiate squash and stretch, go to frame 12, where the ball hits the floor the first time. With the scale node selected, press R to open the Scale tool; scale the ball down in the Y-axis until it no longer goes through the floor (about 0.6), as shown in the image on the left in Figure 8.12. Set a keyframe for scale by pressing Shift+R.

Figure 8.12

Squashing and Stretching the ball to react to bouncing on the floor

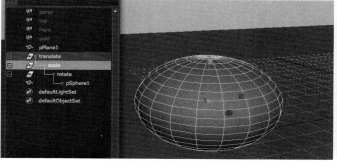
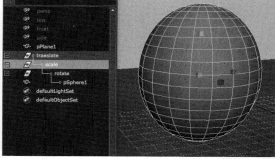

4. Move ahead in the animation about three frames to frame 15. Scale the ball up in the Y-axis slightly past normal to stretch it up (about 1.15) immediately after its bounce, as shown in the image on the right in Figure 8.12. Three frames later, at frame 18, set the Y-axis scale back to 1 to return the ball to its regular shape

5. Scrub your animation, and you should see the ball begin stretching even before it hits the ground. That's a bit too much exaggeration, so open the Graph Editor and move the Y-axis scale key from 9 to 11. Now, the ball squashes when it hits the floor and stretches as it bounces up.

6. Repeat this procedure for the remaining bounces, squashing the ball as it hits the floor and stretching it as it bounces up. Remember to decay the scale factor as the ball's bouncing decays to a stop, as when you decayed the height of the ball's bounce earlier. The final bounce or two should have very little squash and stretch, if any.

Load the file ball_v03.mb from the Bouncing_Ball project on the CD to get to this point. And now, let's rotate the ball as it bounces.

Rotation

Let's add some roll to the ball in these steps:

1. Select the ball's rotate node, and select Modify → Center Pivot to set that node's pivot at the center of the ball.

2. At frame 1, press Shift+E to set keys for rotation at (0,0,0).

3. Scrub to the end of your animation (frame 100 in this example), and set a value of -480 for Rotate Z in the Channel Box, as shown in Figure 8.13.

4. Open the Graph Editor to see the rotation curve on the ball's rotate node. It's a linear (straight) line angled down from 0 to -480. You need the rotation to slow to a stop at the end of the animation, so select the final keyframe and click (▭) to make it a flat tangent.

Figure 8.13

Setting a roll for the ball

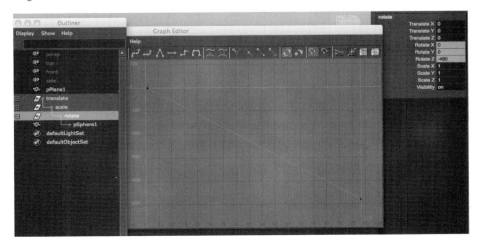

Load the file ball_v04.mb from the Bouncing_Ball project on the CD to see an example of the finished bouncing ball. Although the bouncing of this ball looks okay, it could definitely use some finesse, a little timing change, and so on. Open the file, open the Graph Editor, and edit the file to get a feel for how the ball bounces and rolls. For example, it could continue rolling with no bouncing for another 20 frames or so.

Throwing an Axe

This next project will exercise your use of hierarchies and introduce you to creating and refining motion to achieve proper animation for a more complex scene than the bouncing ball. The workflow is simple but standard for properly setting up a scene for animation, also known as *rigging*, especially for more complex objects, as you'll see later in this and the next chapter when you rig the locomotive for animation. First, you'll model an axe and a target, and then you'll set up the grouping and pivots for how you want to animate. Then, you'll throw your axe!

Why won't you throw the NURBS axe you've already created and textured? Because later in this chapter, you'll need it for an exercise on importing and replacing an object in Maya while keeping the animation intact.

The Preproduction Process

To begin the animation right away, you'll create a basic axe, focusing on the animation and the technique. Toward this end, connect to the Internet if you can, and look up axes and the art of axe throwing to get more familiar with the task at hand. You'll also need to create a simple bull's-eye target at which to throw your axe, so look for some references for a target as well.

Create a new project; choose File → Project → New. Place this project in the same folder or drive as your other projects, and call it Axe. Click the Use Defaults button to fill in the rest, and click Accept. Click the Animation Preferences button, and set the frames per second to 30fps. Later, you'll replace this simple axe with a finer NURBS axe model to learn how to replace objects and transfer animation properly in Maya.

Setting Up the Scene

To get started, model the axe and target from primitives, and set up their grouping and pivots. When your scene is set up properly, you'll animate. It's important to a healthy workflow that you make sure the scene is set up well before you begin animating.

Making the Axe

The axe will be made of two polygon primitives: a cylinder and a cube. Follow these steps:

1. Choose Create → Polygon Primitives → Cube ❑. Set Width Divisions to 4, and click Create.

2. Call this cube **axe_head**.

3. Choose Create → Polygon Primitives → Cylinder to create a cylinder to be the handle for your axe, and call it **handle**.

4. Scale the cylinder so that it's about one-half unit across and about 14 units tall.

5. Move the cube to the top of the cylinder, leaving just a little of the tip showing, and scale it so that it's about 2.5 units high and 4 units wide in the front view. (See Figure 8.14.)

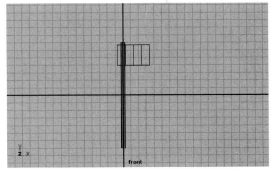

Figure 8.14

Placing the axe's head on the handle

6. Scale the cube in the *Z*-axis so that it's just a little thicker than the handle.

7. To put a sharp edge on the axe, go into Component mode (F8), and select the four vertices on the very end of the cube:

    *   Press R to activate the Scale tool.

    *   Scale the vertices down in the Z-axis to a sharp edge, and scale them slightly up in the *Y*-axis.

    *   Select the next four vertices in from the edge. Scale them down in the *X*-axis about halfway, and scale them up slightly in the *Y*-axis. (See Figure 8.15.)

8. Press F8 to get back into Object mode, and select both pieces.

Figure 8.15

Creating a sharp edge for the axe

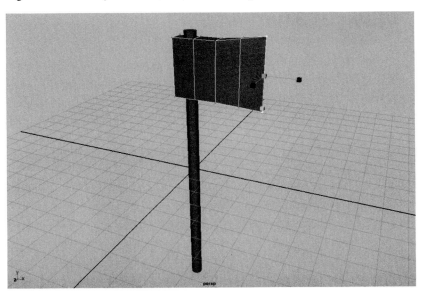

Most animation work doesn't depend on precise measurements. The key is using proportions and relative sizes. You can almost always use Maya's generic units (which are set to centimeters by default). The scope of your project will determine if greater precision is necessary.

9. Choose Edit → Group to group the pieces into one hierarchy, and call it **axe**.

   Now, you need to identify the *center of balance* for this axe. Doing so will give you the place for your pivot point. Because the heaviest part of this axe is the head, the center of balance is toward the top of the handle. In addition, the axe head protrudes in only one direction, so the balance point is a unit or two away from the handle.

10. Press Insert to activate the Pivot manipulator, and move the pivot just under the axe head and about 1 unit from the handle, as in Figure 8.16.

    Your scene should now look like the file axe_v1.mb in the Scenes folder of the Axe project on the CD.

Figure 8.16

Find the axe's center of balance to determine the proper place for its pivot point.

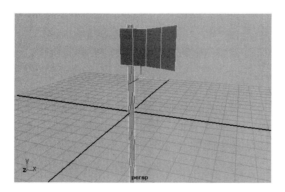

Making the Target

Move the axe about 40 units in the negative *X*-axis away from the origin to make some room for the throw, and move it about 15 units up in the *Y*-axis. Now, you need to create a simple target for your axe to hit. Follow these steps:

1. Start with a polygonal cylinder.

2. Scale down the cylinder's height to make it squat, and rotate it just a bit past being perpendicular to the ground, facing somewhat toward the sky.

3. Scale the cylinder up about seven times its original size.

   You also need to create a simple stand upon which to rest the target. Follow these steps:

1. Choose Create → Polygon Primitives → Cube for the base.

2. Scale the cube so that the target fits on the base with some room to spare.

3. Choose Create → Polygon Primitives → Cylinder to create two cylinders, to make a cross brace for the back of the target.

4. Scale, rotate, and position the cylinders to fit behind the target and into the back of the base. Figure 8.17 shows the positions of the pieces to make up the target.

5. When you're happy with the target, group the four objects together and name the group **Target**.

6. Move the target about 40 units in the positive *X*-axis away from the origin, and move it up in the *Y*-axis so its base is basically on the ground plane.

7. Press Insert to move the target's pivot point to the bottom of the base, right where the cross beams connect to it. Figure 8.18 shows the proper pivot placement.

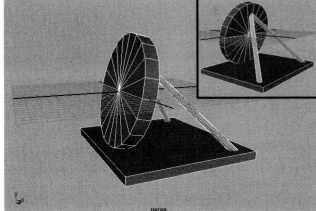

Figure 8.17

Positioning the cross braces for the target

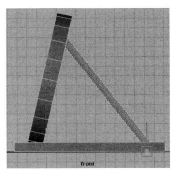

Figure 8.18

The proper placement of the target's pivot point

You place the pivot point at that location because the target will jerk up and back a little bit when the axe hits it. This is the best point for you to rotate around to lift the front of the base up a little to make it look like the axe is really hitting it. Save your file as your next version number. The scene is now ready for animation.

Preproduction: Keyframes and Motion Study

What separates good animation from bad animation is the feeling of weight that the audience infers from the animation. Being lifelong observers of natural physics, people instinctively understand how nature works in motion. You see an object in motion, how it moves, and how it affects its surroundings. From that, you can feel the essence of its motion, with its weight making a distinct, albeit subliminal, impression on you. As it pertains to animation, that essence is simply called *weight*, and its observation is called *motion study*.

Unfortunately, merely knowing how something should look while moving isn't all you need to animate it properly. Giving the axe believable weight is your primary job as an animator. You need to make the audience feel as if that CG axe is really moving. Modeling, texturing, and lighting are small parts of it, but motion can make or break the animation. Creating a convincing scene takes compelling motion, and creating compelling motion requires close observation.

A good feeling of weight in animation depends on timing and follow-through, which require practice.

It's a good idea first to try out an action you want to animate. It may upset the cat if you grab a real axe and start throwing it around your house, but you can take a pen, remove its cap, and lob it across the room. Notice how it arcs through the air, how it spins around its center of balance, and how it hits its mark. Now put the cap on the pen, lob it again, and notice the subtle yet instrumental differences in motion caused by the cap's mass.

As an animator, this experimentation is part of your preproduction and motion study. It's important to have as thorough an understanding of your subject matter as possible. Just try not to take out anyone's eye with the pen.

According to some Internet research, the perfect axe throw should contain as few spins as possible. This is good information to know, because it will shape your animation and come in handy if you're ever cornered in a hatchet shop.

Animating the Axe: Keyframing Gross Animation

The next step is to keyframe the positions of the axe, starting with the *gross animation*— that is, the movement from one end of the axe's trajectory to the other.

Setting Initial Keyframes

You can start in your current scene or load the unanimated, premade axe and target from the CD (axe_v2.mb in the Scenes folder of the Axe project). Follow these steps:

1. Select the axe's top group node—not just the pieces. To make selecting groups such as this easier, display the object's selection handle. To do so, select the axe's top node, and choose Display → Transform Display → Selection Handles. Doing so displays a small cross, called a *selection handle* (✛), at the axe's pivot point. You need only select this handle to select the top node of the axe.

> As you'll see later, in this chapter's catapult exercise, you can use selection handles to select the children of a group as well as the top node.

Because this node is the parent node of the axe, the selection handle displays as a hollow cross at the node's current pivot point.

> You can turn on selection handles for practically any object in Maya—no matter where it is in a group's hierarchy—whether it's a child or a parent. If it isn't the top node, the selection handle appears as a regular cross (✛).

2. With the axe selected, go to frame 1, and set a keyframe for the rotation and translation.

3. Hold down the Shift key, press W for the axe's translation keyframe, and then press E for the axe's rotation keyframe. You don't need to set a scale keyframe on the axe by pressing Shift+R because you won't be changing its size. When you're finished, you have the initial keyframes for the axe at its start position.

Creating Anticipation

Instead of the axe just flying through the air toward the target, you'll animate the axe moving back first to create *anticipation*, as if an invisible arm were pulling the axe back before throwing it. Follow these steps:

1. Go to frame 15.

2. Move the axe back in the *X*-axis about 8 units, and rotate it counterclockwise about 45 degrees.

3. The Auto Keyframe feature sets keyframes for the position and new rotation at frame 15.

    Because you've only moved the axe back in the *X*-axis and made the rotation on the *Z*-axis, Auto Keyframe sets keyframes only for Translate X and Rotate Z. The other position and rotation axes aren't keyframed because their values didn't change.

4. Scrub through the animation, and notice how the axe moves back in anticipation.

> Auto Keyframe inserts a keyframe at the current time for the selected object's changed attributes only.

5. Go to frame 40, and move the axe so that its blade cuts into the center of the target.

    Notice that you have to move the axe in the *X*- and *Y*-axes, whereas before you only had to move it back in the *X*-axis to create anticipation. This is because the axis of motion for the axe rotates along with the axe. This is called the *Local axis.* The Local axis for any given object shifts according to the object's orientation. Because you angled the axe back about 45 degrees, its Local axis rotated back the same amount.

The file axe_v3.mb in the Scenes folder of the Axe project on the CD will catch you up to this point in the animation.

This last step reveals a problem with the animation. If you scrub your animation now, you'll notice that the axe's movement back is different from before, setting a keyframe at frame 40.

This is because of the Auto Keyframe feature. At frame 1, you set an initial keyframe for all axes of translation and rotation. Then, at frame 15, you moved the axe back in the *X*-axis only (in addition to rotating it in the *Z*-axis only).

TROUBLESHOOTING AND AGGRAVATION

Why should you intentionally go through steps that create a problem, such as the axe's movement back? Understanding how to troubleshoot is the biggest challenge in learning a CG program. A good CG artist needs to know how to diagnose issues with their scene and be able to find a way to fix them. Your first forays into CG may be highly frustrating—riddled with simple troubles and issues that you just don't understand. When you can't figure out why things went wrong, you may turn red with aggravation and want to walk away. This is where you start molding yourself as a CG artist. Instead of giving up, ponder the steps you've taken, and see if you can spot where your CG has taken a weird turn. You'll probably find yourself in such spots several times as you study this book. Instead of throwing the baby out with the bathwater, stay patient and try, try again. You'll learn more from your mistakes and missteps in the tutorials in this book than you will if you follow everything to the letter.

Auto Keyframe set a keyframe for Translate X at frame 15. At frame 40, you moved the axe in *both* the X and Y axes to strike the target. Auto Keyframe set a keyframe at 40 for Translate X and Translate Y. Because the last keyframe for Translate Y was set at 1 and not at 15 as in the case of Translate X, there is now a bobble in the Y position of the axe between frames 1 and 15.

With the axe selected, open the Graph Editor (choose Window → Animation Editors → Graph Editor) to see what's happening. As you saw in the Bouncing_Ball exercise, using the Graph Editor is crucial, and the more practice you get with it, the better.

When you open the Graph Editor for this scene, you should see red, green, and blue line segments running up and down and left and right. You'll probably have to zoom your view to something more intelligible. By using the Alt key (or the Alt/Option key on a Mac) and mouse-button combinations, you can navigate the Graph Editor much as you can any of the modeling windows.

The hotkeys A and F also work in the Graph Editor. Click anywhere in the Graph Editor window to make sure it's the active window, and press A to zoom all your curves into view. Your window should look something like Figure 8.19.

Figure 8.19

The Graph Editor displays the axe's animation curves.

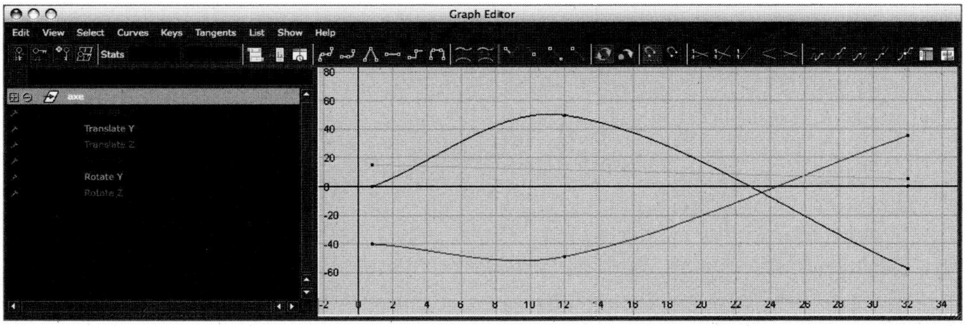

The curves in the Graph Editor represent the values of the axe's position and rotation at any given time. The three axes are in their representative red, green, or blue color, and the specific attributes are listed much as they are in the Outliner in the left column. Selecting an object or an attribute on the left displays its curves on the right.

You should also notice that the curves are all at different scales. The three rotate curves range in value from about −45 to 45, the Translate Y curve ranges from about 15 to 5, and Translate Z looks flat in the Graph Editor. It's tough to edit a curve with low values and still be able to see the timings of a larger value curve.

You can select the specific attribute and zoom in on its curve to see it better, or you can *normalize* the curves so that you can see them all in one view, with all their values in check. Click the Enable Normalized Curve Display icon in the top icon bar of the Graph Editor (⬚). Doing so *normalizes* the view of all the curves within a scale of −1 to 1 to allow you to see the relative movement of all the curves at once.

Figure 8.20 shows the Graph Editor from Figure 8.19 after the curves have been normalized. Keep in mind that this doesn't change the animation in the slightest. All it does is allow you to see all the curves and their relative motion. You can denormalize the view by pressing the Disable Normalized Curve Display icon in the Graph Editor (⬚). Normalizing your view is particularly helpful in busy scenes when you want to adjust the smallest scale of values alongside the largest scale of values without having to zoom in and out of the Graph Editor constantly to see the appropriate curves.

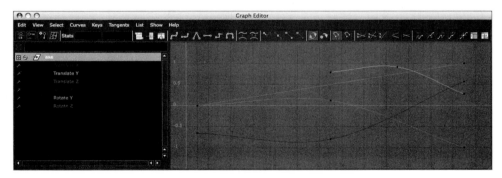

Figure 8.20

The normalized view in the Graph Editor lets you see all the curves of an animation together in the same scale.

Notice that the Scale attributes on the axe aren't shown in this window; only animated attributes appear here.

Also notice that the curve for Translate Y has keyframes only at frames 1 and 40. The animation dips in the first 15 frames because there is no keyframe at frame 15 as there is for Translate Z. That dip wasn't there before you set the end keyframe at frame 40.

Continue the exercise by fixing this issue:

1. Move the first keyframe of Translate Y from frame 1 to frame 15 to fix the dip:

   - Press W to activate the Move tool in Maya, or click the Move Nearest Picked Key Tool icon (⬚) in the Graph Editor.

- Click the Time Snap On/Off icon () to toggle it on.
- Select the offending Translate Y keyframe at frame 1, and MMB+click and drag it to the right until it's at frame 15.

Scrub your animation, and the backward movement looks as it did before. You might have prevented this problem by manually setting your keyframes for the axe instead of using Auto Keyframe. The more you work with Maya, the more valuable you'll find Auto Keyframe (although plenty of people get by without it just fine).

The axe now needs an arc on its way to the target.

2. Go to the middle of the axe's flight, frame 27.

3. Move the axe up in the Y-axis a bit using the green handle of the Tool manipulator.

   If the axe is slightly rotated in frame, Auto Keyframe can set a key for both Translate Y and Translate X, although you were perhaps expecting only a key in Translate Y. Because the Move tool is on the axe's Local axis, and because the axe was slightly rotated at frame 27, there is a change in the *Y* and *X* positions in the World axis, which is the axis represented in the Graph Editor.

4. Select the Translate X key at frame 27, if one was created, and press Delete to delete it.

5. Now you'll add a full spin to the axe to give the animation more reality and life. You can spin it in one of two ways:

   - Go to frame 40, select the axe, and rotate it clockwise a full 360 degrees positive. Auto Keyframe enters a new rotation value at frame 40, overwriting the old value. You should see the Rotate Z curve angle down steeply as soon as you let go of the Rotate manipulator.
   - In the Graph Editor, make sure you're at frame 40, grab the last keyframe on the Rotate Z curve, and MMB+click and drag it down, probably past the lower limit of the window. If you keep the middle mouse button pressed as you move the mouse, the keyframe keeps moving as you move the mouse, even if the keyframe has left the visible bounds of the Graph Editor.

If you hold down Shift as you MMB+click and drag the keyframe to move it in the Graph Editor, the keyframe will move in only one axis (up or down, left or right).

By moving the keyframe down, you change the Rotate Z value to a lower number, which spins the axe clockwise. Before you try that, though, move your Graph Editor window so you can see the axe in the Perspective window. As you move the Rotate Z keyframe down in the Graph Editor, you see the axe rotate interactively. Move the keyframe down until the axe does a full spin.

6. Play back the animation by clicking the Play button in the playback controls. If your animation looks blazingly fast, Maya's playback speed is probably set to Play Every Frame. Open the Animation Preferences window by clicking its icon (), and set Playback Speed to Real-Time (30fps).

> Changing the playback speed of an animation through the Animation Preferences window doesn't alter the timing of your animation. It only changes the speed at which Maya plays the animation back to you in its windows. To change the playback speed, choose Window → Setting/Preferences → Preferences to open the Preferences window, choose Settings → Working Units, and select the proper setting.

Now, when you play back the animation, it should look slow. Maya is playing the scene back in real time, as long as the options in the Animation Preferences window are set to play back properly at 30fps. Even at 30fps, the scene should play back slowly, and this means the animation of the axe timing is too slow.

7. All you need to do is tinker in the Graph Editor a bit to get the right timing. For a good result in timing, move the first set of keyframes from 15 to 13. Then, grab the Translate Y keyframe at frame 27 and move it to 19. Finally, grab the keyframes at frame 40 and move them all back to frame 25. Play back the scene.

Adding Follow-Through

Load the axe_v4.mb file from the Axe project on the CD, or continue with your own file.

The axe is missing weight. Nothing much in this scene indicates that this is a heavy axe. You can add some finesse to the scene using follow-through and secondary motion to give more weight to the scene.

In the axe scene, follow-through motion is the axe blade driving farther into the target a little beyond its initial impact. Secondary motion is the recoil in the target as the momentum of the axe transfers into it. As you increase the amount of follow-through and secondary motion, you increase the axe's implied weight. You must, however, walk a fine line; you don't want to go too far with follow-through or secondary motion. The Graph Editor is great for adding these nuances to the axe. Follow these steps:

1. Select the axe in the scene using its selection handle, and open the Graph Editor.

2. Because you'll add three frames to the end of this animation for follow-through, go to frame 28 (25 being the end of the current animation).

3. In the Perspective window, rotate the axe another 1.5 degrees in the *Z*-axis.

4. Rotating the axe in step 3 moves the axe's blade down a bit in the *Y*-axis. To bring the axe back up close to where it was before the extra rotation, move the axe up slightly using the Translate Y manipulator handle. This also digs the axe into the target a

little more. You'll see a keyframe for Translate Y and most probably for Translate X, as well as Rotate Z.

If you play back the animation, the follow-through doesn't look good. The axe hits the target and then digs into it as if the action were done in two separate moves by two different animators who never talked to each other. You need to smooth out the transition from the axe strike and its follow-through in the Graph Editor.

5. Highlight the Rotate Z attribute in the Graph Editor to get rid of the other curves in the window. Figure 8.18 shows the Rotate Z curve of the axe after the follow-through animation is added.

6. Focus on the last three frames of the curve, and zoom into that range only. The curve, as it is now, dips down past where it should and recoils back up a small amount.

When you set keyframes, you create animation curves in the Graph Editor for the axe. These curves are Bézier splines, which stay as smooth as possible from beginning to end. When you set the new keyframe, rotating the axe about 1.5 more degrees for follow-through, the animation curve responds by creating a dip, as shown in Figure 8.21, to keep the whole curve as smooth as possible.

Figure 8.21

The normalized Rotate Z curve of the axe after the follow-through animation

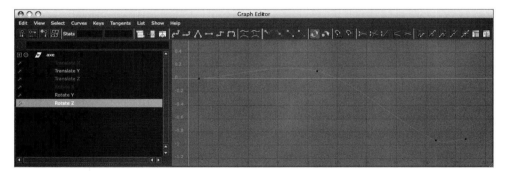

SECONDARY MOTION AND FOLLOW-THROUGH

Secondary motion in animation comprises all the little things in a scene that move because something else in the scene is moving. For example, when a superhero jumps from a tall building and his or her cape flutters in the wind, the cape's undulation is secondary motion.

Follow-through is the action in animation that immediately follows an object's or a character's main action. For example, after the superhero lands from their jump, his or her knees buckle a little, and the superhero bends at the waist, essentially squashing down a bit. That squashing motion is follow-through. The more follow-throughs, the more cartoon-like the animation appears.

The axe needs to hit the target with force and dig its way in, slowly coming to a stop. You need to adjust the curvature of the keyframes at frame 25 by using the keyframe's tangents. *Tangents* are handles that change the amount of curvature influence of a point on a b-spline (Bézier spline). Selecting the keyframe in question reveals its tangents. (See Figure 8.22.)

7. Select the Out tangent for the Rotate Z attribute's key at frame 25, and MMB+click and drag it up to get rid of the dip. Notice that the tangency for the In tangent also changes.

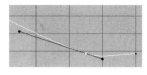

Figure 8.22

The tangent handles of a keyframe. The handle to the left of the keyframe is the In tangent, and the handle to the right is its Out tangent.

8. Press Z to undo your change. You need to break the tangent handles so that one doesn't disturb the other.

9. Select the Out handle, and click the Break Tangents icon ( ) to break the tangent.

10. Move the handle up to get rid of the dip so that the curve segment from frame 25 to frame 28 is a straight line, angled down. Figure 8.23 is zoomed into this segment of the curve after it's been fixed.

Figure 8.23

Zoomed into the end segment of the Rotate Z animation curve after the dip is fixed

Now, to get the axe to stop slowly as it digs into the target, you need to curve that end segment of the Rotate Z curve to flatten it out.

11. Grab the last frame to reveal its handles. You can manually move the In handle to make it horizontal, or you can click the Flat Tangents icon ( ) on the left side of the icon bar, under the menus in the Graph Editor.

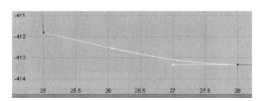

Figure 8.24

Zoomed into the end segment of the Rotate Z animation curve. Notice how the curve now smoothly comes to a stop by flattening out.

The curve's final segment for Rotate Z should now look like Figure 8.24.

12. Adjust the keyframe tangents similarly for the axe's Translate Y and Translate X curves. (See Figure 8.25.)

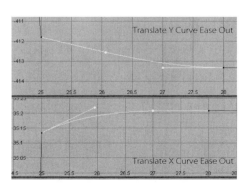

Figure 8.25

Smoothed translate curves to ease out the motion

13. Play back the animation, and you should see the axe impact the target and sink into it a bit for its follow-through.

Now, you need to polish things up more.

Adding Secondary Motion

Load axe_v5.mb from the Axe project on the CD, or continue with your own scene file.

For secondary motion, you'll move the target in reaction to the impact from the axe's momentum.

An object in motion has momentum. Momentum is calculated by multiplying the mass of an object by its velocity. So, the heavier and faster an object is, the more momentum it has. When two objects collide, some or all momentum transfers from one object to the other.

In a game of pool, for example, when the moving cue ball collides with a stationary eight ball, the cue ball transfers some of its momentum into the eight ball, setting it in motion; the cue ball uses the rest of its own momentum to ricochet off in another direction.

In the axe scene's impact, the axe lodges in the target, and its momentum is almost fully transferred to the target. But because the target is much more massive than the axe, the target moves only slightly in reaction. The more you make the target recoil, the heavier the axe will seem.

First, group the axe's parent node under the target's parent node. The axe will be left behind to float in midair if you animate the target's parent node without grouping the axe under it. By grouping the axe under the target, you'll move the target to recoil while keeping the axe lodged in it. The animation on the axe won't change when you group the axe and target under a new node.

Grab the parent node of the target (called Target), and reset its attributes to 0 by freezing its transforms as you did with the ball. This sets the target node's Translate and Rotate attributes back to 0 and its Scale attributes back to 1:

1. To freeze the transforms, select the target node, and then choose Modify → Freeze Transformations.

2. In the Outliner, MMB+click and drag the axe node to the target node to group it under. You can also MMB+click and drag the nodes in the Hypergraph to group the axe node under the target node.

3. Go to frame 25, the moment of impact, and set the position and rotation keyframes on Target.

4. Go to frame 28, rotate the target node in the Z-axis about 2.5 degrees, and move it up and back slightly in the Y and X axes, as shown in Figure 8.26.

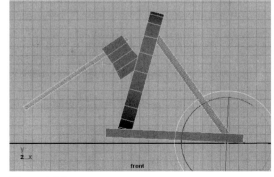

Figure 8.26

The front panel display of the target reacting to the impact of the axe

5. Go to frame 31. Rotate the target node back to 0 in the Z-axis, move it down to 0 in the Y-axis, and move it back a bit more in the X-axis.

6. Go to frame 35 and repeat step 4, but only move it half as much in Rotate Z, Translate X, and Translate Y.

7. Go to frame 40 and repeat step 5, but move Target back only slightly in the X-axis.

If you don't freeze the transforms on the target's parent node before grouping the axe under it, the axe's animation will change and yield undesirable results.

The preceding steps should give you an animation similar to axe_v6.mb in the Axe project on the CD.

Motion Trails

You can see a moving object's trajectory, or *motion trail*—that is, its path of motion. Follow these steps:

1. Select the axe through its selection handle, and then choose Animate → Create Motion Trail ☐. (See Figure 8.27.)

2. Select Line for Draw Style, and make sure the Show Frame Numbers check box is checked.

3. Click Apply, and then click Close to close the window.

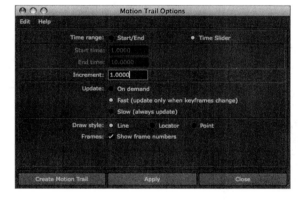

Figure 8.27

The Motion Trail Options window

The motion trail is useful for fine-tuning motion. Editing the animation curves in the Graph Editor and watching the motion trail adjust in the work panels shows you the precise trajectory of the axe throughout its movement. Play back your animation a few times to get a good sense of how the scene looks.

4. Select the axe, and open the Graph Editor.

5. Try adding more arc to the axe in the middle of its trajectory to the target.

6. In the Graph Editor, focus on the Translate Y curve, and select the keyframe at frame 19.

7. Move the keyframe up about 2 units, and watch the motion trail adjust to show you the higher arc.

8. Replay the animation with the higher arc in the middle.

Notice that the axe seems a little more solid than before. The extra height in the trajectory really helps give the axe more substance. Figure 8.28 shows the axe and its motion trail after more height is added to its arc.

Figure 8.28

The axe and its motion trail

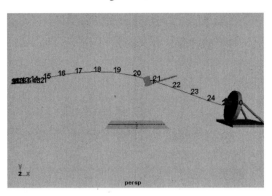

You can toggle the frame-number display on/off and change the display type of the motion trail from curve to points or locators through the motion trail's Attribute Editor. To get rid of the motion trail, select it and press Delete.

Path Animation

As an alternative to keyframing the position of the axe, you can animate it on a path. *Path animation* allows you to assign an object to move along the course of a curve, called a *path*.

Load axe_v7.mb from the Axe project on the CD. This is the finished axe animation. You'll delete most of your hard work by removing the translation animation on the axe, but you'll keep the rotation and everything else. You'll replace the translation keyframes you set up with a motion path instead. Follow these steps:

1. In the front window, and with the motion trails turned on, trace the motion trail with a CV curve (choose Create → CV Curve Tool) from the beginning of the trail to the end, as shown in Figure 8.29. Make sure the CV Curve tool is set to make cubic (3) curves.

Figure 8.29

Trace the motion trail.

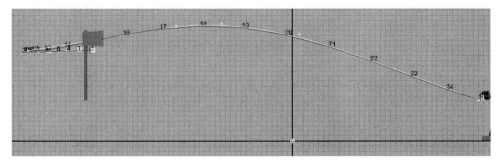

2. Take note of the frames on which you set important keyframes for the axe's position (for example, when it recoils and releases at frame 10 and when it hits the target at frame 25). Select the axe's top node (axe), and delete its translation animation. Select all three Translate attributes in the Channel Box, and right-click to display the shortcut menu. Choose Break Connections to delete the animation from those channels. The axe now spins around, and it and the target recoil at the moment of impact, but the axe doesn't actually move.

3. Keep the motion trail in the scene for now to help with the timing you've already created.

4. Select the top axe node, and then Shift+select the path curve. In the Animation menu set, choose Animate → Motion Paths → Attach to Motion Path ❐.

5. In the Options window, turn off the Follow check box.

   The Follow feature orients the object on the path so that its front always points in the direction of travel. Because the axe moves backward in anticipation before it's thrown forward, Follow would cause it to turn around twice, so turn this option off.

   Now the axe will follow the curve end to end from frame 1 to frame 60. Of course, you have to adjust the timing to fit it, as before.

6. Select the motion trail, and move it down in the window to get it out of the way; but keep it lined up vertically with the path curve so you can figure out the timing again.

   The file axe_path_v1.mb in the Axe project will bring you up to this point.

7. Select the top axe node, and open the Graph Editor to see the axe's curves. The rotation curve is still intact, although the translation curves are missing. Click motionPath1 in the Channel Box to highlight it; the motionPath1.U Value curve that took the place of the translation curves appears in the Graph Editor. On the left side of the Graph Editor, select the motionPath1.U Value curve to display only that. Zoom into it. (Press A to view all.)

8. The curve is an even, linear curve from 1 to 60. You need the axe to hit at frame 25, so move the end of the curve to frame 25 from frame 60.

9. Retime the backward movement. Scrub the animation until the axe moves all the way back (frame 4). Using the Insert Keys tool (▧), insert a keyframe at frame 4. Select the animation curve, click the tool, and MMB+click the curve to create a key on it. You can MMB+click and drag the cursor to place the key precisely at frame 10 before releasing the mouse button.

10. Move this new keyframe to frame 10 (the frame where backward movement originally ended).

11. Scrub the animation, and the timing is just about right. You'll have to adjust the tangents a bit to make the axe move more like before, but the movement is essentially there with path animation.

The file axe_path_v2.mb in the Axe project will bring you up to this point.

Path animation is extremely useful for a number of tasks, but particularly for animating an object along a particular course. By adjusting the resulting animation curve in the Graph Editor, you can readjust the timing of the path animation easily.

A good path-animation exercise is to create an atom and draw CV curves around the nucleus for the paths of the electrons. Then, animate all the electrons orbiting the nucleus with the paths. Also, try reanimating the Solar_System exercise with paths instead of the keyframes you set on the rotations.

> **GHOSTING**
>
> To see the position of an animated object a few frames before and after its current position, you can enable ghosting in Maya. For example, select the animated axe in your scene and, in the Animation menu set, choose Animate → Ghost Selected. Maya will display the axe's three frames before and after the current time. To turn off ghosting, choose Animate → Unghost Selected.

Axe Project Summation

In the Axe example, you furthered your use of layered animation by beginning with the gross animation to cover the basic movements of the axe. After those timings were set, you completed most of the remaining work in the Graph Editor by moving keyframes here and there to add detail to the motion. You added more keyframes to create follow-through and secondary movement to insinuate weight into the axe and target.

Without secondary movement in the target, the axe would seem to weigh nothing. With too much movement, however, the axe would seem too heavy, and the scene wouldn't look right. Subtle nuances can make stunning differences in the simplest of animations. You also went back into the animation and replaced the animation method entirely with path animation. This illustrates the multiple ways to accomplish a task in Maya; finding your own comfort zone with a workflow is one of the goals in learning Maya.

Replacing an Object

Aside from the need to model objects and texture them, there is the task of animation setup. Check your pivots, your geometry, and your grouping to make sure your scene will hold up when you animate it.

It's also common practice in setup to animate a *proxy* object—a simple stand-in model that you later replace. The next exercise will show you how to replace the axe you already animated with the fully textured NURBS axe from the previous chapter and how to copy an animation from one object to another.

Replacing the Axe

Load your completed, keyframed axe-animation scene (not the one using path animation), or switch to the Axe project and load the scene file axe_v7.mb from the CD. Now, follow these steps:

1. Choose File → Import.

2. Locate and import the Axe_Replace.ma scene file from the Scenes folder of the Axe project on the CD. The new axe appears at the origin in your scene.

Transferring Animation

To assume all the properties and actions of the original axe requires some setup. Follow these steps:

1. Move the pivot on the new axe to the same relative position as the pivot on the original animated axe (up toward the top and a little out front of the handle, just under the blade). This ensures that the new axe has the same spin as the old axe. If you don't make sure the pivots line up, the animation won't look right when transferred to the new axe.

2. Rotate the new axe's top node 180 degrees in *Y* to get it to face the right direction.

3. Use grid snap to place the top node of the new axe at the origin.

4. Freeze transforms on the new axe group to reset all its attributes.

5. Choose Display → Transform Display → Selection Handles to turn on the selection handle of the new axe.

6. Go to frame 1. Select the original axe, open the Graph Editor, and choose Edit → Copy.

7. Select the new axe to display its curves in the Graph Editor. It has no curves to display yet. With the axe node selected in the Graph Editor, choose Edit → Paste. As shown in Figure 8.30, the new axe is slightly offset from the original axe.

> When you copy and paste curves in the Graph Editor, make sure you're on the first frame of the animation. Pasting curves places them at the current frame. Because the animation of the original axe started at frame 1, make sure you're at frame 1 when you paste the curves to the new axe.

8. Move the new axe to match the original. Because it's already animated, move it using the curves in the Graph Editor as opposed to moving it in the viewport. With the new axe selected, in the Graph Editor, select the Translate Y curve; move it up to match the height of the original axe.

9. Select the Translate X curve, and move it to match the axe's *X* position, as shown in Figure 8.31. Line up the axe handle as a guide.

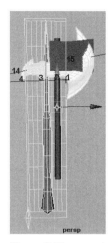

Figure 8.30

The new axe placed next to the original

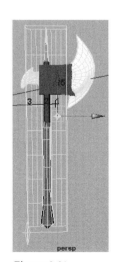

Figure 8.31

Lining up the two axes

Scrub the animation, and notice that the new axe has the same animation except at the end when it hits the target. It doesn't have the same follow-through as the original axe. Remember that you grouped the original axe under the target node for follow-through animation. Place the new axe under this node as well.

The file `axe_v8.mb` in the Axe project on the CD has the new axe imported and all the animation copied. It will get you caught up to this point.

10. After you scrub the animation and make sure the new axe animates properly, select the original axe's top node and delete it.

Animating Flying Text

It's inevitable. Sooner or later, someone will ask you to animate a flying logo or flying text for something or other. As late-1980s as that may sound, animating flying text—at least, the way you'll do it here—can teach you a thing or two about path animation and lattice deformers. You can use the following steps to animate pretty much anything that has to twist, wind, and bend along a path; this technique isn't just for text.

First, you'll need to create the text. To do so, follow these steps:

1. In a new scene, select Create → Text ❑. In the option box, enter your text, and select a font to use (see Figure 8.32). In this case, stick with Times New Roman. Set the Type to Bevel.

> Setting the Type attribute to Poly for your text creates curve outlines for the text and planar faces for the letters, for a flat-text effect. Setting the Type Creation option to Curves gives you just the curve outlines. Finally, using Trim to create your text makes the letters out of flat planar NURBS surfaces. However, no surface history is created with text. To allow you to edit the text later, you must re-create the text and/or font type as needed.

2. Leave the rest of the creation methods at their defaults. Doing so creates the text as beveled faces to make the 3D text, as shown in Figure 8.33.

3. When you have the text, you need to create a curve for it to animate along. Using either the CV or EP Curve tool, create a winding curve like a roller coaster for the logo, as shown in Figure 8.34.

4. Just as you did with the axe exercise, you'll assign the text object to this curve. Set your frame range to 1–100. Select the text, Shift+select the curve, and, in the Animation menu set, choose Animate → Motion Paths → Attach to Motion Path ❑. Set the Front Axis to X and the Up Axis to Y, and select the Bank check box, as shown in Figure 8.35.

Depending on how you create your curve and text, you may need to experiment with the Front Axis and Up Axis attributes to get the text to fly the way you want. Notice that history is created with the path animation, so you can adjust the axes' attributes after the fact to see how they work on the curve you have.

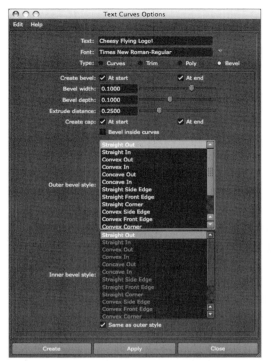

Figure 8.32

The Text Curves Options window

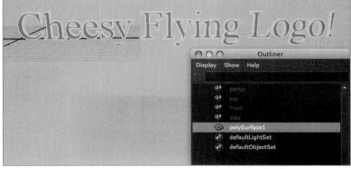

Figure 8.33

Creating the 3D text for the flying logo

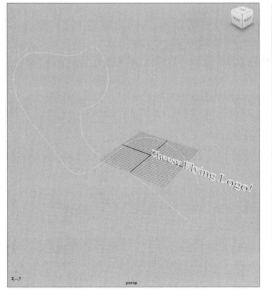

Figure 8.34

Create a curve path for the text to follow.

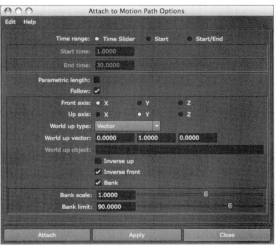

Figure 8.35

The Attach to Motion Path Options window

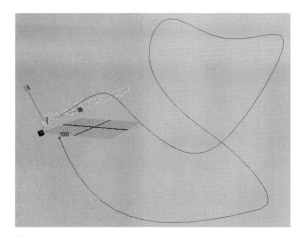

Figure 8.36
The text is on the path.

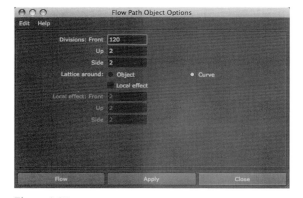

Figure 8.37
The Flow Path Object Options window

Figure 8.38
The geometry doesn't fit the lattice well.

5. Orbit the camera around to the other side, and you can see the text on the path, as shown in Figure 8.36. Notice the U Value attribute: this is the position of the text along the curve from 0 to 1. Scrub the animation, and the text should glide along the curve.

6. The text isn't bending along with the curve at all yet. To accomplish this, you need to add a lattice that bends the text to the curvature of the path. Select the text object, and choose Animate → Motion Paths → Flow Path Object ❒.

7. In the option box for the Flow Path Object, shown in Figure 8.37, set Divisions: Front to 120, Up to 2, and Side to 2, and select Curve for Lattice Around. Make sure the Local Effect box is unchecked. Doing so creates a lattice that follows the curve, giving it 120 segments along the path. This lattice deforms the text as it travels along the path.

8. Scrub your animation, and you see a fairly strange result: parts of the text explode out from the lattice, as shown in Figure 8.38.

9. The geometry is going outside the influence of the lattice, and this is causing the strange behavior. To fix the situation, select the lattice and base node, and scale up the lattice *and* its base node together to create a larger size of influence around the path (see Figure 8.39).

Scrub your animation to check the frame range and how well the text flies through the lattice. When the lattice and its base are large enough to handle the text along all of the path's corners and turns, voilà—Cheesy Flying Logo! (See Figure 8.40.)

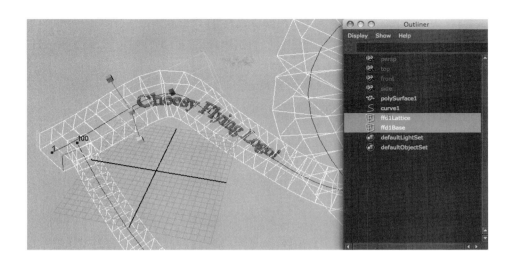

Figure 8.39

Scale the lattice and its base node to accommodate the flying text.

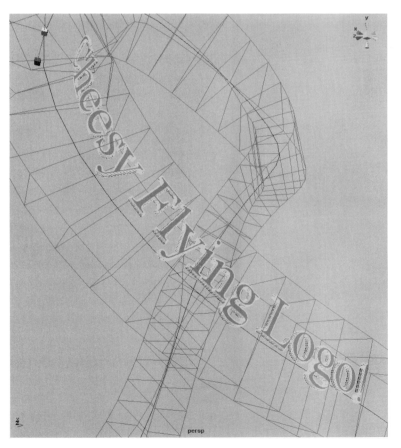

Figure 8.40

Cheesy Flying Logo! makes a nice turn.

Rigging the Locomotive, Part 1

In this section, you'll return to the locomotive you modeled in Chapter 4, "Beginning Polygonal Modeling," and put your new animation skills to use.

Load the file `locomotive_model_v4.mb`, which is the completed model of the locomotive from the Polygon Modeling exercise in Chapter 4. You can find it in the Scenes folder of the Locomotive project on the CD.

The Scene Setup

It's important to keep animation in mind as you build a model. In particular, making a good scene hierarchy is crucial to getting a smooth animation workflow going. That's

Figure 8.41

The locomotive's Outliner view

why, when you built the locomotive in Chapter 4, you used the Outliner to make sure the objects in your scene were grouped logically. Now you're going back in to make sure you have good organization before beginning the task of rigging this thing for animation.

Figure 8.41 shows the organization of the locomotive as it stands from Chapter 4. Later, you'll use a more finely detailed and prettier locomotive model to rig that is already grouped properly, using the intentions outlined here. This scene is in fairly good shape, but you have to identify the parts of the locomotive that you need to rig, determine how they will move, and decide what is the best hierarchy for the model from there.

The major moving parts of the engine are the wheels and the steam pump drive mechanism. The wheels, of course, need to rotate, as wheels do, and the steam pump drives the wheel arms back and forth, which is what drives the main wheels to rotate. Aside from animating some steam pumping out of parts of the engine, which we'll cover in Chapter 12, "Maya Dynamics and Effects," this is the basic rigging for the locomotive. First, you need to make sure the hierarchies are settled well and the pivot points are in their proper places.

The `locomotive_model_v4.mb` scene file has a well-organized hierarchy, but it needs some help to make rigging easier. Be sure all the individual wheel arms have their pivots at the base, as shown in Figure 8.42. Use Insert (or the Home key on a Mac—MacBook users also need to press the fn [function] key to access the Home function using the arrow key) to move the pivots as needed. You'll rig these wheel arms using IK bones in the next chapter.

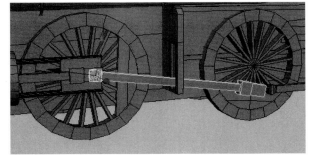

Figure 8.42

Check the pivot points.

Be sure all the elements that make up a wheel are grouped and that the group's pivot point is centered for all the wheel groups, as shown in Figure 8.43.

Finally, for this simple rig, make sure the steam pump arm elements are properly grouped and that the pivot is placed as shown in Figure 8.44.

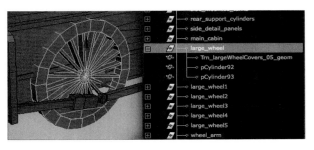

Figure 8.43

Check the hierarchy and pivot placement for the wheel.

If your locomotive is in organizational disarray, identify all the moving parts first, and then begin grouping them logically. Place pivots appropriately, and you're all set. The scene file `locomotive_anim_v1.mb` in the Locomotive project on the CD has the locomotive scene file with the pivots and grouping already finished, as discussed earlier.

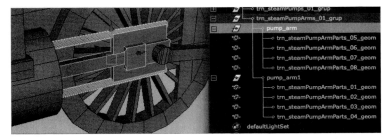

Figure 8.44

Place the pivot for the pump arm.

If the pivots and groupings are off, you'll notice as soon as you begin to animate; things just won't rotate on the correct axis, and pieces won't follow properly. The wheels, for example, may wobble around their axle.

For more practice in grouping and hierarchies, you can load `locomotive_anim_v1.mb` from the CD, ungroup everything in the scene, and piece it all back together. To ungroup everything, select the top node of the locomotive, and choose Edit → Ungroup. Doing so ungroups the major parts of the locomotive. With those groups selected, ungroup again to flush out individual geometry. You can also load `locomotive_anim_v1_B.mb` from the CD; it has all the major groupings removed. Then, regroup and repivot everything. This will be great practice and boatloads of fun!

Selection Handles

Using selection handles makes selection easier and work flow faster, so turn on selection handles for each of the groups you're animating. Select the wheel groups in the Outliner, and then choose Display → Transform Display → Selection Handles. Select the wheel arm

Figure 8.45

Selection handles make selecting a group of objects much easier.

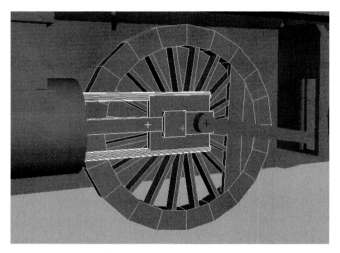

groups, and turn on their selection handles as well. Figure 8.45 shows the selection handles enabled for the wheel, pump arm, and wheel arm.

How selection handles work depends on Maya's selection order. *Selection order*, which you can customize, sets the priority of one type of object over another when you try to select in a work window.

After the selection handles for the locomotive's wheels and drive arms are turned on, only the handles will be selected (and not the whole locomotive) when you make a marquee selection that covers the entire locomotive. Handles have a high selection priority by default, so they're selected above anything else.

Animating the Locomotive

Animating most of the locomotive is straightforward. Simple rotations will make the wheels turn. Translating the locomotive's top node will move the entire object. This, however, leaves out the drive mechanism with the steam pump and the wheel and pump arms. You'll rig these to animate automatically in the next chapter, using IK handles and connections.

Animating a Catapult

As an exercise in animating a system of parts of a model, before you continue to animate the locomotive in the next chapter, you'll now animate a catapult. This catapult model is straightforward to animate. You'll turn its winch to bend back the catapult arm, which shoots the projectiles, and then you'll fire and watch the arm fly up.

First, let's get acquainted with the scene file and make sure its pivots and hierarchies are set up properly. The scene file `catapult_anim_v1.mb` in the Catapult_Anim project on the CD has everything in order, although it's always good to make sure. Figure 8.46 shows the catapult with its winch selected and ready to animate.

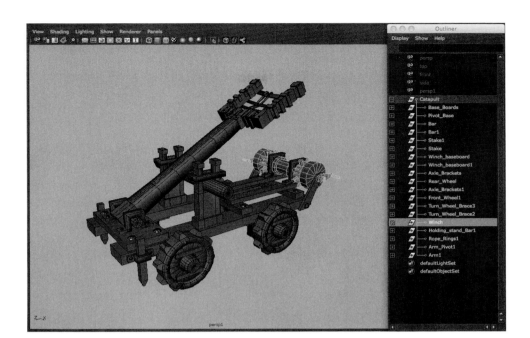

Figure 8.46

The catapult's winch is ready to animate.

Get a timing put down for the winch first, and use that to pull back the arm to fire. Follow these steps:

1. Select the Winch group with its selection handle. At frame 1, set a keyframe for rotation. If the selection handle isn't turned on, select Winch from the Outliner and turn on the selection handle by choosing Display → Transform Display → Selection Handles. To keep it clean as you go along, instead of pressing Shift+E to set a key for all three axes of rotation, select only the Rotate X attribute in the Channel Box, right-click to open the shortcut menu, and choose Key Selected. There only needs to be rotation in *X* for the winch.

2. Jump to frame 60.

3. Rotate the winch backward a few times, or enter **–400** or so for the Rotate X attribute.

4. Open the Graph Editor, ease in the curve a bit, and ease out the curve a lot so that the rotation starts casually but grinds to a stop as the arm becomes more difficult to pull back.

   Obviously, you're missing the rope between the winch and the arm. Because animating a rope is a fairly advanced task, the catapult is animated without its rope; but the principle of an imaginary rope pulling the arm down to create tension in the arm drives the animation.

5. To accentuate the more difficult winding at the end, add a key to the X-axis rotation through the Graph Editor. To do so, select the curve, and click the Insert Keys Tool icon () in the upper-left corner of the Graph Editor. Your cursor changes to a cross.

6. MMB+click frame 42 to add a keyframe already on the curve at frame 42. You can drag the key back and forth on the curve to place it directly at frame 42. It may help to turn on key snapping first. (See Figure 8.47.)

7. Move that keyframe down to create a stronger ease-out for the winch. Be careful not to let the curve dip down so that the winch switches directions. Adjust the handles to smooth the curve. You can also add a little recoil to the winch by inserting a new keyframe through the Graph Editor at frame 70. (See Figure 8.48.)

Figure 8.47

Insert a keyframe at frame 42.

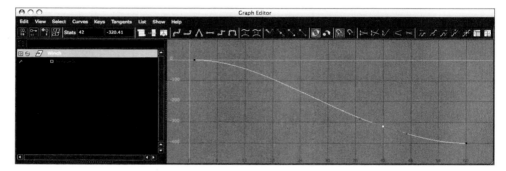

Figure 8.48

Creating a greater ease-out and adding a little recoil at the end

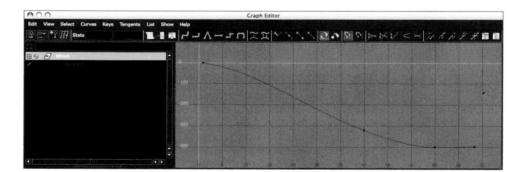

Animating with Deformers

It's time to animate the arm coiling back, using the winch's timing as it's driving the arm. Because the catapult's arm is supported by a brace, and the whole idea of a catapult is based on tension, you have to bend the arm back as the winch pulls it.

You'll use a nonlinear deformer, just as you did in the axe head exercise in Chapter 5, "Modeling with NURBS, Subdivisions, and Deformers"; but this time, you'll animate the deformer to create the bending of the catapult arm. Follow these steps:

1. Switch to the Animation menu set. Select the Arm1 group, and choose Create Deformers → Nonlinear → Bend to create a Bend deformer perpendicular to the arm. Select the deformer, and rotate it to line it up with the arm, as shown in Figure 8.49.

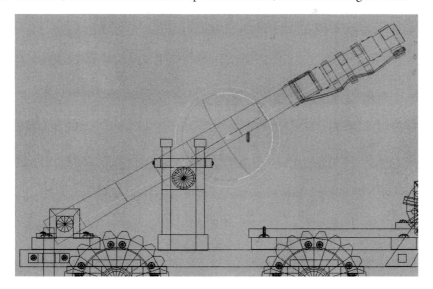

Figure 8.49

Align the Bend deformer with the catapult arm.

2. With the Bend deformer selected, look in the Channel Box for bend1 under the Inputs section, and click it to expand its attributes. Try entering **0.5** for Curvature. More than likely, the catapult arm will bend sideways. Rotate the deformer so that the arm is bending back and down instead. (See Figure 8.50.)

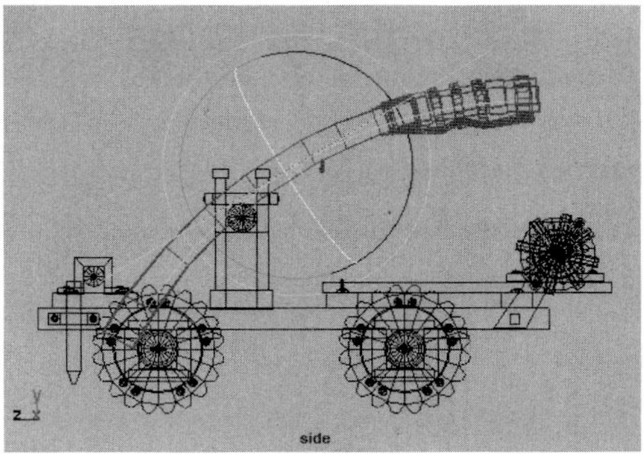

Figure 8.50

Orient the Bend deformer to bend the arm back and down.

3. You don't want the arm's base to bend back, just the basket side.

   You want it to bend at the brace point, not in the middle where it is now. Move the deformer down the length of the arm until the middle lines up with the arm's support brace.

4. To prevent the bottom of the arm from bending, change the Low Bound attribute to 0. To keep the basket from bending, set the High Bound attribute to 0.9.

The Low Bound and High Bound attributes control how far up and down the deformer the object is affected. The Envelope attribute for a deformer governs how much the object is affected overall, with 0 not affecting the geometry at all.

5. Instead of trying to match the speed, ease in and out of the winch and set the gross keyframes for the arm pulling back first. Reset Curvature to 0, and set a key for Curvature at frame 1. (Select bend1's Curvature in the Channel Box, right-click, and choose Key Selected from the shortcut menu.)

6. Go to frame 60, and set Curvature to 0.8. If Auto Key is turned on, this sets a keyframe; otherwise, set a key manually. (See Figure 8.51.)

Figure 8.51

Bend the arm back at frame 60 and set a keyframe.

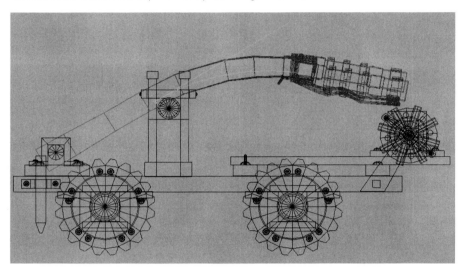

7. If you play back the animation, notice that the way the winch winds back and the way the arm bends don't match. In the Graph Editor, you can adjust the animation curve on the Bend deformer to match the winch's curve.

8. Insert a key on the Curvature curve at frame 42, and move it up to match the curvature you created for the winch.

9. Insert a new key at frame 70, and make the arm bend back up slightly as the winch recoils. Set Curvature to about 0.79 from 0.8. (See Figure 8.52.)

10. Go to frame 90, and set a key again at Curvature of 0. Set a key at 0.82 for frame 97 to create anticipation, and then keyframe at frame 103 to release the arm and fire the imaginary payload with a Curvature of −0.8.

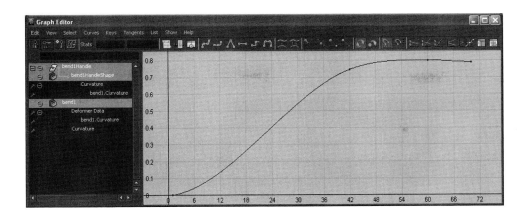

Figure 8.52

Try to match the relative curvature of the winch's animation curve with the Bend deformer's animation curve.

11. Add some rotation to the arm for dramatic effect. At about frame 100, during the release, the arm is almost straight. Select the Arm1 group, and set a rotation key on the *X*-axis. Go to frame 105, and rotate the arm 45 degrees to the left in the *X*-axis. If the starting rotation of the arm is at 30 (as it is in the sample file), set an *X*-axis rotation key of 75 at frame 105.

Figure 8.53

Group the deformer node under the Arm1 group node.

12. Notice that the arm is bending strangely now that it's being rotated. It's moving off the deformer, so its influence is changing for the worse. To fix this, go back to frame 100, and group the deformer node (called *bend1Handle*) under the Arm1 group, as shown in Figure 8.53. Now it rotates along with the arm, adding its own bending influence.

13. Work on setting keyframes on the deformer and the arm's rotation so that the arm falls back down onto the support brace and quivers until it becomes straight again. The animation curve for the Bend deformer should look like Figure 8.54. The rotation of the arm should look like Figure 8.55. Remember to make the tangents flat on the keys where the arm bounces off the brace linear and the peaks, like the ball's bounce from earlier in the chapter.

The file `catapult_anim_v2.mb` will give you a good reference to check out the timing of the arm bend and rotation.

Figure 8.54

The animation curve for the arm's vibration back and forth as it comes to a rest

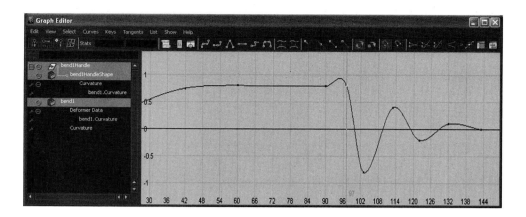

Figure 8.55

The animation curve for the arm's rotation as it heaves up and falls back down, coming to an easy rest on the brace

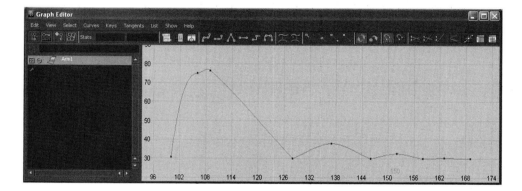

Without getting into a lot more detail, try your hand at animating the catapult on your own. Here are some items you can animate to make this a complete animation:

- Spin the winch around as the arm releases, as if its rope is being yanked away from it.

- Animate the entire catapult rocking forward and backward as the arm releases, similar to the way a car rocks when you jump onto the hood.

- Move the catapult forward on a road, spinning its wheels as best you can to match the distance it travels.

- Design and build your own catapult, and animate it along the same lines.

Summary

In this chapter, you began to learn the fundamentals of animating a scene. Starting with a bouncing ball, you learned how to work in the Graph Editor to set up and adjust timing as well as how to add squash and stretch to the animation. The next exercise, throwing an axe, showed you how to set up a scene for animation; expanded on your experience in creating timing in the Graph Editor, and showed you how to add anticipation, follow-through, and secondary motion to your scene. You then learned how to adjust animation using motion trails and how to animate the axe throw using path animation. You went on to learn how to replace a proxy object that is already animated with a different finished model and how to transfer the animation. Going back to the locomotive from Chapter 4, you began to set up the scene for rigging in the next chapter by setting proper pivots and hierarchy. Finally, you used a catapult to animate with deformers and further your experience in the Graph Editor.

Animating a complex system, such as a catapult or a locomotive, involves creating layers of animation based on facets of the mechanics of the system's movement. With the catapult, you tackled the individual parts separately and then worked to unify the animations. You'll use rigging concepts in the next chapter to automate some of that process for the locomotive.

The same is true of the Bouncing_Ball and Axe_Throwing exercises. The different needs of the animation were addressed one by one, starting with the gross animation and ending with finishing touches to add weight. Finally, the art of timing brought the entire effort into a cohesive whole.

Even when animation is already applied, it's simple to change *how* the animation is accomplished, as you did with path animation, or even to replace the animated object entirely.

Animation is the art of observation, interpretation, and implementation. Learning to see how things move, deciphering why they move as they do, and then applying all that to your Maya scene is what animation is all about.

CHAPTER 9

More Animation!

Now that you have a little more animation experience, you can get into some more involved animation practices and toolsets, taking further the principles covered in this book and its examples. Animation is a growing exploration, and you should use this book as a stepping-off point. For everything you're being exposed to here, there are many more techniques to discover.

Topics in this chapter include:

- Skeletons and kinematics
- Skeletons: the hand
- Inverse Kinematics
- Basic relationships: constraints
- Basic relationships: Set-Driven Keys
- Application: rigging the locomotive

Skeletons and Kinematics

In your body, your muscles move your bones; and as your bones move, parts of your body move. Bones are your internal framework.

In CG animation, a *skeleton* is an armature built into a 3D model that drives the geometry when the bones are moved. You insert a skeleton into a CG model and attach or bind it to the geometry. The skeleton's bones are animated (typically with rotations), which in turn move the parts of the geometry to which they're attached. By using a skeleton, Maya allows bending and deformation of the attached geometry at the skeleton's *joints*. A skeleton is, of course, useful for character work, but skeletons have many other uses. Any time you need to drive the geometry of a model with an internal system, such as fly-fishing line or a tree bending in the wind, you can use skeletons. You'll use them to drive the locomotive later in this chapter.

Skeletons and Hierarchy

Skeletons rely on hierarchies. Bones are created in a hierarchical manner, resulting in a *root joint* that is the parent of all the joints beneath it in the hierarchy. For example, a hip joint can be the root joint of a leg skeleton system in which the *knee joint* is the leg's child, the *ankle joint* belongs to the knee, and the five *toe joints* are the ankle's children. (See Figure 9.1.)

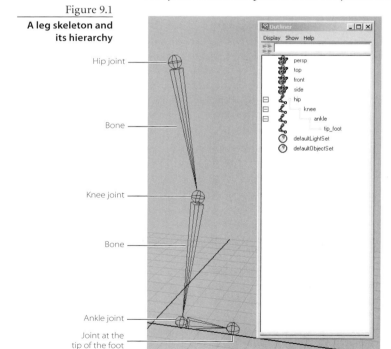

Figure 9.1

A leg skeleton and its hierarchy

Hip joint

Bone

Knee joint

Bone

Ankle joint

Joint at the tip of the foot

Using skeletons, you can easily create an immediate hierarchical system with which to animate. Furthermore, pieces of geometry need not deform to be attached to a bone system. Objects can be grouped with or under joints. They move under their parent joint and rotate around that joint's pivot as opposed to their own pivot point.

A skeleton is really just a collection of grouped and properly positioned pivot points called *joints* that you use to move your geometry, whether it deforms or not. A *bone* is the length between each joint; bones only show you the skeletal system.

Inverse Kinematics (IK) and *Forward Kinematics (FK)* are the methods you use to animate a skeletal system. FK rotates the bones directly at their top joint to assume poses.

This method resembles *stop-motion animation,* in which a puppet, along with its underlying armature, is posed frame by frame. With FK, the animator moves the character into position by rotating the joints that run the geometry.

The rotation of a joint affects the position of the bones and joints beneath it in the hierarchy (see Figure 9.2). If you rotate the hip up, the knee and ankle swing up as if the character is kicking. If you rotate the knee down, the ankle pivots down as if this character is seated. This form of motion moves the way you would expect it to move in hierarchies and is, therefore, called Forward Kinematics.

IK uses a more complex, but often easier, system of *IK handles* that are attached to the tip of a joint system. The corresponding base of the IK system is attached further up the skeleton hierarchy to a joint determined to be the root of that IK segment. It need not be the root joint of the entire skeleton, though.

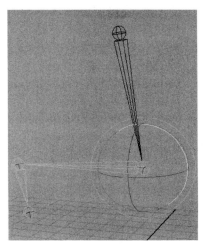

Figure 9.2

In Forward Kinematics, the joints are rotated directly.

The bones and joints in the IK chain are affected only by movement of the IK handle. When the handle moves, an *IK solver* figures out how to rotate all the joints to accommodate the new position of the IK handle. Moving an IK handle causes the bones to rotate around their joints to accommodate a new position.

The effect is as if someone grabbed your hand and moved it. The person holding your hand is similar to an IK handle. Moving your hand causes the bones in your arm to rotate around the shoulder, elbow, and wrist. As you can see in Figure 9.3, the animation flows up the hierarchy and is, therefore, called Inverse Kinematics.

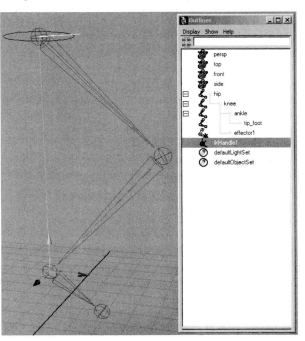

Figure 9.3

In Inverse Kinematics, the joints rotate in response to the IK handle's position.

Forward Kinematics: The Block Man

To understand skeletal hierarchy, look at the simple biped (two-legged) character made of primitive blocks, shown in Figure 9.4. He's called Block Man. (Surprise!) Each block represents a part of the body, with gaps between the blocks representing points where the body pivots.

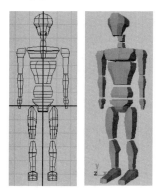

The pivot of each block is placed to represent the appropriate joint location. For example, the shin's pivot is located at the knee. Each block is grouped up the chain so that the foot moves with the shin, which moves with the thigh, which moves with the pelvis.

The hands are grouped under the arms, which are grouped under the shoulders, and so forth down the spine to the pelvis. The head groups under the first neck block, and so on down the spine to the pelvis. The pelvis is the center of the body, which is known as the *root* of the figure.

The way this figure is grouped (see Figure 9.5) represents how the hierarchy of a character works for the most part. Each body part is attached and becomes the child of the part above it in the chain.

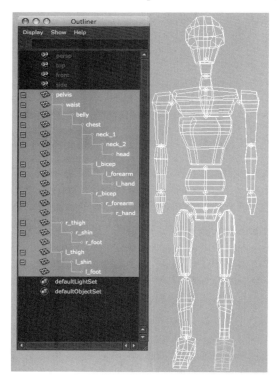

Load the file `block_man_v02.mb` from the Block_Man project folder on the CD for a good reference of the grouping structure. This file shows you what a skeleton hierarchy does.

In the Hypergraph Hierarchy window, choose Options → Layout → Freeform Layout to position the nodes any way you want. To make selections easier, you can arrange the nodes as if they were on a body (see Figure 9.6). You can toggle between freeform and automatic, and your freeform layout will be retained.

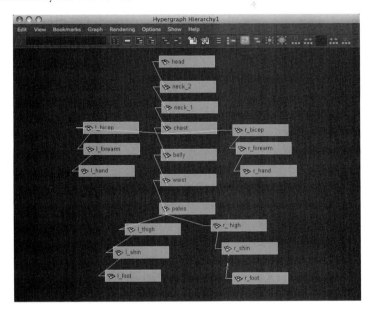

Figure 9.6

A freeform layout in the Hypergraph Hierarchy window

Creating the Skeleton

The basis of how the block man is laid out and grouped is what skeletons are all about. Skeletons make character animation easier by automating, at the very least, the hierarchy and pivot placement described earlier.

THE PELVIS AS ROOT

Traditionally, the pelvis is the basis of all biped setups. The root of any skeletal system (whether using bones or geometry as the example) is the character's pivot point—the center of balance. Because a biped character centers itself on two feet, its pelvis becomes the root of its skeletal system. In CG, the pelvis becomes the parent node of the whole system and is the node used to move or orient the entire character. In a skeleton system, this would be the root joint.

The root is then the top parent of the system below it and runs the entire chain. Therefore, selecting character parts straight from the Outliner or the Hypergraph is sometimes easier. You can see that a good naming convention is always important with character setups.

You'll use the block man to create a skeleton. Load `block_man_v01.mb` from the Block_Man project. This is the same as `block_man_v02.mb`, but this version isn't grouped.

1. Maximize the Front view window. Switch to the Animation menu by using the drop-down menu or by pressing F2.

2. Activate the Joint tool by choosing Skeleton → Joint Tool. Your cursor turns into a cross.

3. Click in the middle of the pelvis to place the first joint, the root joint of the skeleton.

4. Shift+click up to the space between the pelvis and the waist.

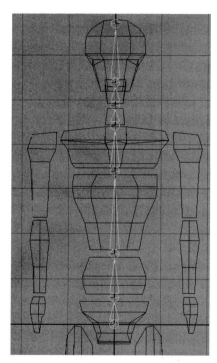

Figure 9.7

Place spine joints straight up the middle of the body.

The joint display sizes in your Maya window may not match those shown in the book. This isn't a problem; however, you can change the joint sizes by clicking Display → Animation → Joint Size.

By pressing Shift as you click, you create a joint in a straight line from the last joint placement. A bone is created between the two joints as a visual guide to the skeleton. The placement of the joints depends on the active view, so placing a second joint in a different view may place the joint in an awkward location.

5. Click more joints up the spine at the gaps between the body parts, as shown in Figure 9.7.

6. You need to start a new branch of joints leading into the legs and arms. Begin with the arms. With the Joint tool still active, press the Up arrow key three times to move up the hierarchy of joints to the one between the neck and chest parts.

Pressing the Up arrow key takes you up one node in a hierarchy. Pressing the Down arrow key takes you down one node in a hierarchy. This approach also applies to skeletons, because they're hierarchies.

7. Stay in the front view. Now, from this joint between the neck and chest, click to place a joint at the top of the right bicep at the shoulder. Click down to create joints at the elbow, the wrist, and the tip of the model's right hand.

8. Press the Up arrow to *pick walk up* the chain to the neck/chest joint, and repeat step 7 to create the joints for the left arm as shown in Figure 9.8.

> *Pick walking* is when you select one object or component in Maya and then use the Up or Down arrow key to pick the next object higher (or lower) in the hierarchy. You can use the Left or Right arrow key to pick-walk select any siblings of the currently selected object in its hierarchy.

9. To start another string of joints in the first leg, pick walk back up the skeleton until you're at the pelvis root joint. (See Figure 9.9.)

10. From the root joint at the pelvis, click to create a joint at the tip of the right thigh, and work down to the knee and ankle. Place the ankle joint halfway down the foot, as shown in Figure 9.10, as opposed to the gap between the shin and the foot. Press the spacebar to return to the four-way view from the front view, and maximize the side view. Click to create a joint at the tip of the foot. This allows you to place a joint in the proper axis in the side view. (See Figure 9.11.)

11. Return to the front view, and press the Up arrow to get back to the pelvis joint. Repeat step 10 to create joints for the left leg. After you place your joints, press Enter. Figure 9.12 shows the skeleton.

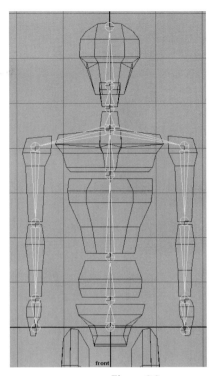

Figure 9.8

Place joints for the torso.

Figure 9.9

Start the leg series of joints from the root pelvis joint.

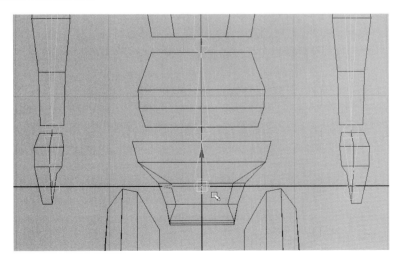

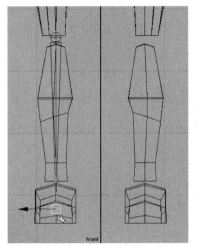

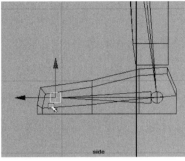

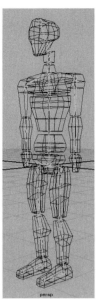

Figure 9.10

Place a joint inside the foot, not in the gap between the foot and the shin.

Figure 9.11

In the Side view panel, create a joint at the tip of the foot.

Figure 9.12

The full skeleton for the block man

Attaching to the Skeleton

You now have a full skeleton for your character. To attach the geometry, all you need to do is parent the body parts under their appropriate joints. Before you get to that, take a few minutes and name all the joints in the Outliner to make the scene easier to manage. Figure 9.13 shows the names used in the project on the CD.

 You can also load the `block_man_skeleton_v01.mb` file from the Block_Man project to get to this point.

To parent the block man's geometry to the skeleton, follow these steps:

1. Starting with the right foot, parent it under the right ankle joint (rt_ankle) by MMB+clicking and dragging it to rt_ankle in the Outliner or the Hypergraph. You don't want to parent it under the right foot joint (rt_foot), because you need the foot geometry to pivot with that foot bone and inherit the rotations from the ankle above it. Parent the left foot under the left ankle (lt_ankle). (See Figure 9.14.)

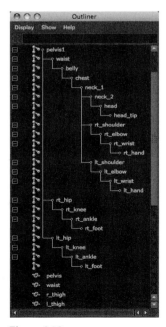

Figure 9.13

Use a consistent naming scheme for the joints to make it easy to keep track of them.

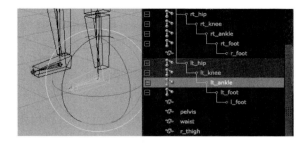

Figure 9.14

Begin organizing the hierarchy by grouping the block man's parts into the skeleton.

2. Parent the rest of the body parts (see the following list) under their respective joints, as shown in Figure 9.15:

- Shins under the knees, and thighs under the hips
- Hands under the wrists, and forearms under the elbows
- Biceps under the shoulders
- Head under the head joint (the joint between the head and the top neck geometry)
- Top neck geometry under the joint between the two neck pieces
- Bottom neck geometry under the joint between the chest and the neck
- Chest under the joint between the chest and belly pieces
- Belly under the joint between the belly and waist
- Pelvis with the root joint

The Block Man: Walk Cycle

A *walk cycle* is an animation that takes the character through a few steps that can be repeated many times so that the character seems to be taking numerous steps. In a cycle, make sure the position of the first frame matches the position of the last frame so that when the animation sequence is cycled, no "pop" occurs in the motion at that point.

Now, try animating this character's walk cycle using FK on the skeleton. You'll find the workflow straightforward, as if you were adjusting positions on a doll.

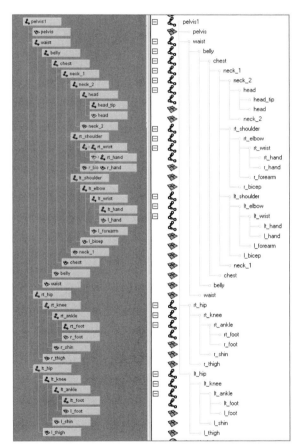

Figure 9.15

Views of the skeleton and geometry hierarchy in the Outliner and the Hypergraph

Load the `block_man_skeleton_v02.mb` file from the Block_Man project on the CD for the properly grouped model and skeleton.

Use the key poses in the following figures to guide you in animating the body as it walks. You'll key at five-frame intervals to lay down the gross animation. You can go back and adjust the timing of the joint rotations in the Graph Editor to make the animation better. The white leg and arm are behind the body, farther from the camera.

This animation is also called *pose animation* because you're posing the character from keyframe to keyframe.

Starting Out: Frames 1 and 5

Figure 9.16 shows the character's starting position. Here you'll set a key for this position and then begin the walk cycle by moving the joints into their second position and key-framing that:

1. At frame 1, set a key for the rotation of all the joints. The easiest way is to select all the joints in the Outliner or the Hypergraph. With this pose animation, make sure all the joints are keyframed at every step, even if Auto Keyframe is turned on.

   Also set a position keyframe for just the pelvis joint.

   A quick way to select all the joints, and only the joints, is to filter the Outliner view to show only joints. In the Outliner, choose Show → Objects → Joints. To reset the Outliner, choose Show → Show All.

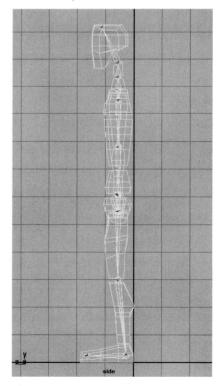

2. Go to frame 5. Rotate the back leg (the block man's right, white leg) back, and rotate the foot to make it level again. Lower the body (select and move the pelvis joint) to line up the back heel with the ground. This will keep the man on the ground as he goes through the walk cycle, although he won't actually move forward yet.

3. Rotate the near leg (the man's left leg) forward, bend the knee, and pivot the foot up a bit.

4. Rotate the back arm forward, and rotate the near arm back (opposite from the legs). Bend the arms at the elbows.

Figure 9.16

The character's starting position

5. Bend the man forward at the waist, bend neck_1 forward, and tilt the head back up to compensate a little. Figure 9.17 shows the pose at this point.

6. Select everything in the Outliner, and set a rotation key. You're setting a pose for all the joints, which will ensure that all the body parts are in synch.

If you don't key everything every step of the way, some parts of the body won't key with Auto Keyframe properly because the last time they moved may have been two steps previous.

Frame 10

Figure 9.18 shows the position you'll keyframe at frame 10; it's approximately midstride for the first leg:

1. Go to frame 10. Rotate the back leg out farther, and level the foot. Lower the body to place the man on the ground.

2. Rotate the front leg out, straighten the knee, and flatten the foot to place it on the ground. This is midstride. Swing the arms in their current direction a touch more. Bend the torso forward some more. Make sure you set a key for all the joints.

Frame 15

Figure 9.19 shows the position you'll keyframe at frame 15. At this point, the character begins to shift his weight to the front leg as it plants on the ground, and the character also begins lifting the back leg:

1. Go to frame 15. Rotate the front leg back toward the body, and raise the body as the man steps to keep the front foot flat on the ground. Rotate the back knee up to lift the foot, and rotate the foot down to make him push off the toe.

2. Start swinging the arms in the opposite direction. Start straightening the torso back up, but bend the head forward a bit.

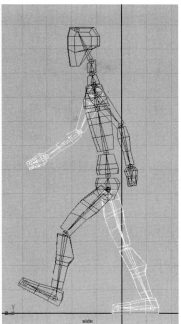

Figure 9.17

The second pose (frame 5)

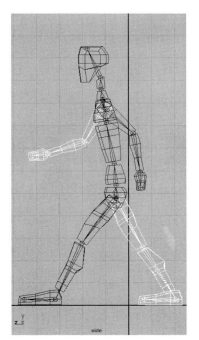

Figure 9.18

The third pose (frame 10)

Figure 9.19

The fourth pose (frame 15)

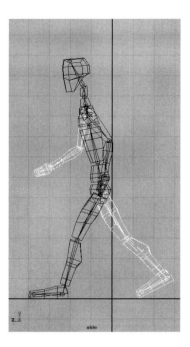

Frame 20

At frame 20, the man will shift all his weight onto the front leg and move his body over that leg, lifting his rear leg to begin its swing out front to finish the stride. Figure 9.20 shows the pose. Follow these steps:

1. Rotate the front leg almost straight under the man, and lift up the body to keep the front foot on the ground. Lift the rear leg, and swing it forward.

2. Straighten the torso, and keep the arms swinging in their new direction. Key all the joints.

Frame 25

Now, the man will swing his whole body forward, pivoting on the left leg (the dark one) to put himself off center and ready to fall forward into the next step. Figure 9.21 shows the pose. Here are the steps:

1. Go to frame 25.

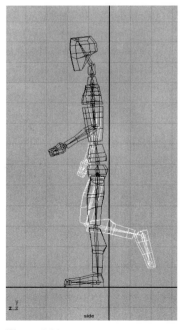

Figure 9.20

The fifth pose (frame 20)

2. Rotate the front (dark) leg back behind the man, and swing the white leg up and ready to take the next step. Lower the body to keep the now rear foot (the dark one) on the ground.

Frame 30

Use Figure 9.22 as a guide for creating the next pose. Notice that it's similar to the pose at frame 10 (in Figure 9.18). As a matter of fact, the only major differences are which leg and arm are in front. Everything else should be about the same. You'll want some variety in the exact positions to make the animation more interesting, but the poses are very similar.

Completing the Cycle

You've finished a set of poses for the character's first step. The next set of poses for your walk cycle corresponds to the first set, but now the other leg and arm correspond to these positions. For example, you animated the left leg taking a step forward in the first series of poses. The next series of poses has to do with the right leg. The pose at frame 35 corresponds to the pose at frame 15. Frame 40 matches frame 20. You can start a new series of poses with the left leg.

When a 30-frame section is complete, you need to return to the animation through the Graph Editor. Adjust all the keyframes that you set at five-frame intervals to make the animation more realistic. Right now, you have only the gross keyframes in place, so the timing is off. Your next step is to time the frames properly. This is ultimately a matter of how the animation looks to you.

Logistically speaking, some poses take a little less time to achieve than the evenly spaced five frames you used. For example, achieving the second pose from the start position should take four frames. The third pose

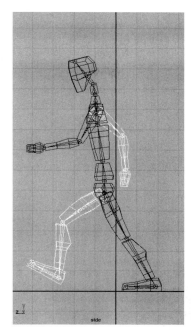

Figure 9.21

The sixth pose (frame 25)

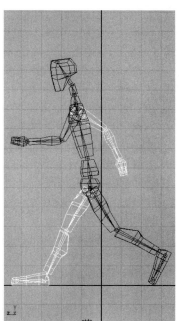

Figure 9.22

The seventh pose (frame 30)

(see Figure 9.18, earlier in the chapter) from frame 5 to frame 10 should take four frames. The next frame section, originally from frame 10 to 15 (the fourth pose; see Figure 9.19, earlier in the chapter), should take only three frames. To accomplish this easily, follow these steps:

1. Select the top node of the skeleton (the pelvis), and open the Graph Editor. On the pelvis node in the left side of the Graph Editor, Shift+click the plus sign to open the entire tree of nodes beneath the pelvis. All the animated channels show their curves to the right, as shown in Figure 9.23.

Figure 9.23

The Graph Editor shows the walk cycle animation curves.

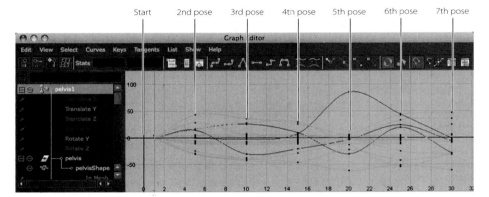

2. Marquee-select all the keyframes on the curves beyond frame 1, but not including those at frame 1. Press the W key to activate the Translate tool. Shift+MMB+click in the Graph Editor (so you can move only in one axis), and drag the keys horizontally to move them all 1 unit (frame) to the left. All the keyframes move, and the second pose now goes from frame 5 to frame 4.

3. Deselect the keys now at frame 4 by holding down the Ctrl key (you also use the Ctrl key on a Mac) and marquee-deselecting all those keys at frame 4. Shift+MMB+click, and drag the remaining selected keys 1 unit to the left again. The third pose goes from being at frame 9 to frame 8.

4. Deselect the keys now at frame 8, and Shift+click and drag the other selected keys to the left two frames so that the fourth pose animates between frame 8 and frame 11. Deselect the frame 11 keys, and move the rest over two frames to the left again so that the next section runs from frame 11 to frame 14. The following section should go from frame 14 to frame 18. The final section should go from frame 18 to frame 22. Figure 9.24 shows the new layout for the curves.

5. Continue to set and adjust keys for another cycle or two of the walk. The majority of time spent in animating something like this involves using the Graph Editor to time

out the keyframes to make the animation look believable. Also try offsetting some of the arm rotations a frame to the left or right to break up the monotony that arises from having everything keyed on the same frame.

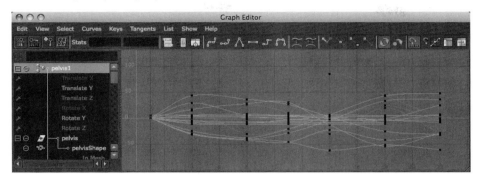

Figure 9.24

The keyframes are repositioned.

Load the file `block_walk_v01.mov` or `block_walk_v01.avi` of this walk cycle from the `Images` folder of the Block_Man project on the CD to see the animation in motion. It's a rough cycle, and you have to keep adjusting the character's height to keep the feet on the ground. This is where IK comes in handy, as you'll see later in this chapter. Also, the file `block_man_skeleton_walk_v01.mb` in the Block_Man project has the keyframed cycle for you to play with and continue animating.

Walk Cycle Wrap-Up

This walk cycle animation is more about getting comfortable with keyframing and skeletons than it is about creating great walk cycles, so take some time to practice and get better. Animating walk cycles is a good way to hone your animation skills. Several great books are devoted to character rigging and animation alone, and you can research the field for ways to become more proficient. But keep in mind that movement and timing are what make animation good, not the setup or the model.

Skeletons: The Hand

For another foray into a skeletal system, you can give yourself a hand—literally. You'll use a skeleton to deform the geometry and animate it as a hand would move.

Load the file `poly_hand_skeleton_v01.ma` from the Poly_Hand_Anim project on the CD. The hand is shown in Figure 9.25.

You'll use it to create a bone structure to make the hand animate. This is called *rigging*.

Figure 9.25

The hand mesh

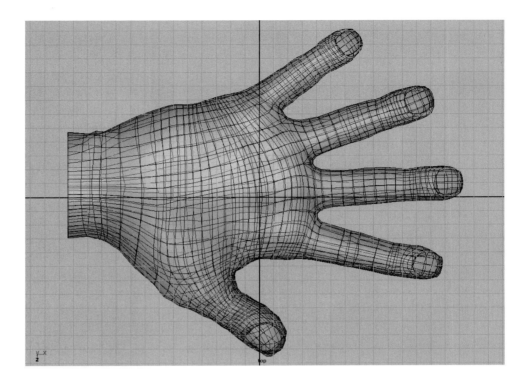

Rigging the Hand

To create the first bones of the hand, follow these steps:

1. Maximize the Top view window. Switch to the Animation menu by using the drop-down menu or by pressing F2.

2. Activate the Joint tool by choosing Skeleton → Joint Tool. Your cursor turns into a cross.

3. Click at the base of the wrist to place the first joint. This will be the root joint of the hand.

4. Shift+click the bottom part of the palm.

5. Place joints down through the thumb from this second joint, according to the corresponding bones in Figure 9.26.

6. To start another string of joints into the palm, press the Up arrow key four times until you're at the second joint at the base of the palm.

7. The next joint you place will be a branch from this joint. Place that joint in the middle of the palm. Place another joint up farther along the palm, and then branch it out to the index finger. Press the Up arrow key to return to that upper palm joint, and start a new branch into the middle finger.

Repeat this procedure to place joints for the remaining fingers, as shown in Figure 9.27. With these joints placed, you have a simple skeleton rig for the hand. This rig allows you quite a bit of hand and finger movement.

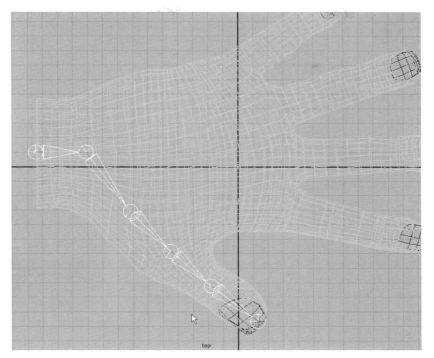

Figure 9.26

Place the joints through to the tip of the thumb.

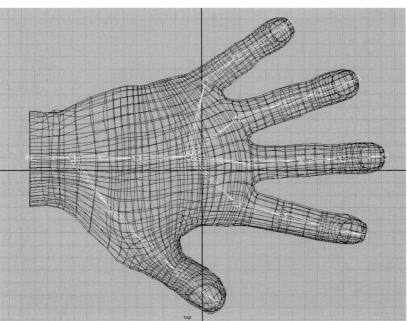

Figure 9.27

The joints in the hand

Check the other views (see Figure 9.28) to see where you need to tweak your joint positions to fit the hand. Ideally, you want the joints to be set inside your intended geometry in the same way that real bones are laid out.

Figure 9.28

Four views of the hand with initial placement of the joints

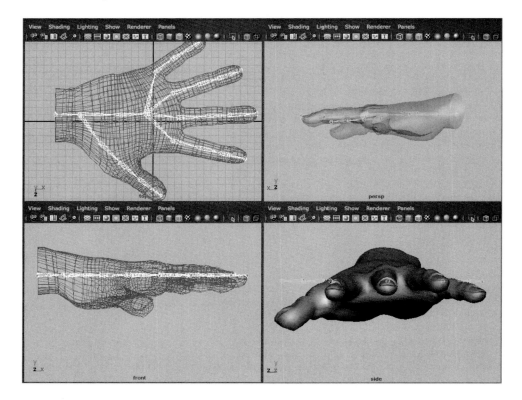

To position the joints, you can use either of two Maya tools: Move or Move Pivot. First, you'll try the Move tool. Select the tip joint for the pinkie. It needs to be lowered into the pinkie itself. Select the Move tool (press W), and move it down into the tip of the pinkie. Now, move on to the top pinkie knuckle. Notice that if you move the knuckle, the tip moves as well. That's not such a great idea.

Instead, it's best to move joints as pivots. Because joints are nothing more than pivots, go into Move Pivot mode (press the Ins key, or the Home key on a Mac) to move joints. Select the top pinkie-knuckle joint, and move it with Move Pivot instead (press Ins or Home). Only the joint moves, and the bones adjust to the new position. Set the positions on the remaining joints to be inside the hand properly, as shown in Figures 9.29 and 9.30.

Figure 9.29

The joints of the hand placed properly in the geometry

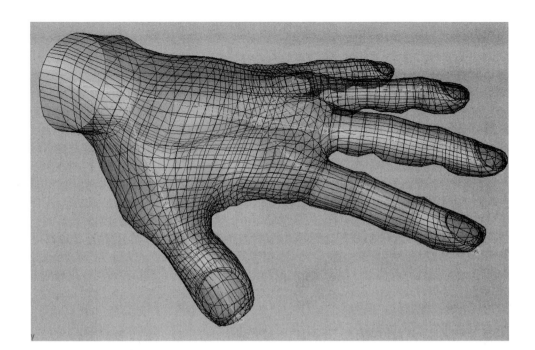

Figure 9.30

Second view of the hand's skeleton

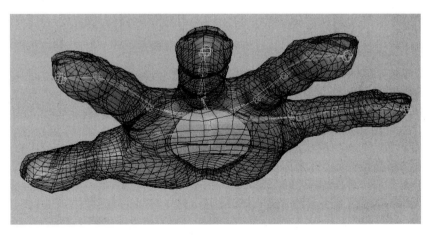

Binding to Geometry

An integral part of rigging a character or an object with a skeleton is *binding*, also known as *skinning*. Binding is another way to attach geometry to a skeletal system. With the block man, you directly attached the whole pieces of geometry to the bones through parenting, whereas binding involves attaching *clusters,* or groups of vertices or CVs, of the geometry to the skeleton to allow the skeleton to deform the model. This is typically how skeletons are used in character animation work. (For more on grouping and parenting, refer to the Solar_System exercise in Chapter 2, "Jumping in Headfirst, with Both Feet.")

The basic technique of binding a character is easy. However, Maya gives you tremendous control over how your geometry deforms.

Binding Overview

Binding is, in theory, identical to the Lattice deformer you saw in Chapter 5, "Modeling with NURBS, Subdivisions, and Deformers." A lattice attached to an object exerts influence over parts of the model according to the sections of the lattice. Each section affects a NURBS surface's CVs or a polygon surface's vertices within its borders; and as a section of the lattice moves, it takes those points of the model with it.

Skeletal binding does much the same thing. It attaches the model's points to the bones, and as the bones pivot around their joints, the section of the model that is attached follows.

By attaching vertices or CVs (depending on your geometry) to a skeleton, you can bend or distort the geometry. When a bone moves or rotates about its joint, it pulls with it the points that are attached to it. The geometry then deforms to fit the new configuration of the bones bound to it.

You can directly bind geometry to a skeleton in two ways: using Smooth Bind and using Rigid Bind. You can indirectly deform geometry using deformers and lattices attached to skeletons, but here you'll use the direct methods. Figure 9.31 shows a rigid bind, and Figure 9.32 shows a smooth bind.

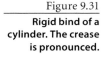

Figure 9.31

Rigid bind of a cylinder. The crease is pronounced.

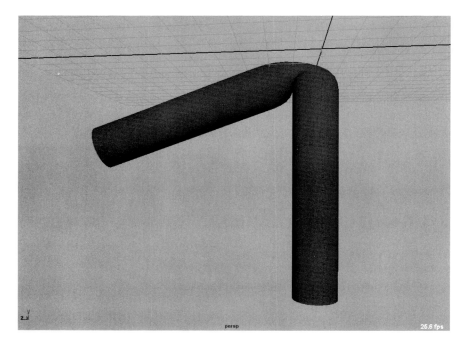

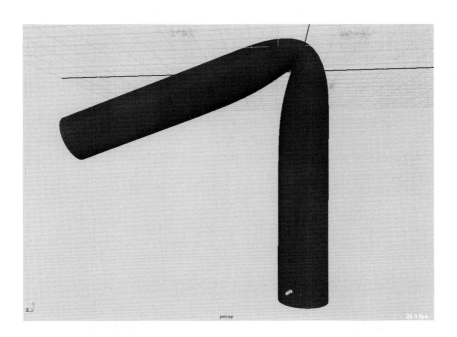

Figure 9.32

Smooth bind of the cylinder shown in Figure 9.31. The crease is smoother, yet less defined.

Create a tall NURBS cylinder, with a span of 16 or more. The more spans you have in the deformable model, the better it will bend. Duplicate the cylinder, and move it over in your window. Now, in the front view, create a four-bone (five-joint) skeleton that starts at the bottom of the first cylinder and goes straight up the middle, ending at the tip. Duplicate the skeleton, and move it to the center of the second cylinder.

CREATING A RIGID BIND

A rigid bind is the simpler of the two, because only one surface point (vertex or CV) is affected by a joint at a time. A *rigid* bind groups the CVs of a NURBS or the vertices of a polygon into *joint clusters* that are then attached to the bones. No one surface point is influenced by more than one joint.

Bending a model about a joint with a rigid bind yields a more articulate crease than a smooth bind. A smooth bind allows more than one joint to affect the CV or vertex, resulting in a more rounded and smooth bend.

To create a rigid bind, select the first skeleton and Shift+click its cylinder. In the Animation menu, choose Skin → Bind Skin → Rigid Bind ❐.

In the option box, you'll find that almost everything you need is already set to the default. The Bind To parameter lets you rigid-bind the entire skeleton to the geometry or rigid-bind only the joints selected. Using Selected Joints gives you the option of using just part of a skeleton system to rigid-bind, which also gives you flexibility in how your rig affects the model. Leave that option set to Complete Skeleton to attach the whole thing.

Click the Color Joints check box to set a different color for each joint in the bind, which can make for an easier workflow. The Bind Method parameter deals with how the points in the model are attached. The default, Closest Point, organizes the points into skin point sets according the joint to which they're closest. They're then assigned to be influenced by that joint only.

The Partition Set option lets you define your own points before you bind and select which points are set to which joints. If you define a partition set for each joint you have, Maya assigns each set to the nearest joint. For example, you can define some points at the top of the surface to be a part of a set controlled by a joint in the bottom part. Closest Point is the best option for most work.

Use the defaults, turn on Color Joints, and click the Bind Skin button in the option box. The root of the skeleton is selected and the cylinder turns magenta, signifying that it has input connections (such as history).

CREATING A SMOOTH BIND

A *smooth bind* allows a joint to influence more than one skin point on the model. This lets areas of the model farther from the joint bend when that joint rotates. Joints influence points to varying degrees between 0 and 1 across the surface, decreasing in influence the farther the point is from the joint. The multiple influences on a point need to add to 1 across all the joints that influence it. Maya automatically generates the proper influence amounts upon binding, although the animator can change these values later.

To create a smooth bind, select the second skeleton and its cylinder, and choose Skin → Bind Skin → Smooth Bind ❏.

In the option box, you'll find the familiar Bind To parameter. You'll also find, under the Bind Method drop-down menu, the options Closest in Hierarchy and Closest Distance. Choosing Closest in Hierarchy assigns the skin points to the nearest joint in the hierarchy. This option is most commonly used for character work, because it pays attention to the way the skeleton is laid out. For example, a surface point on the right leg wouldn't be affected by the thigh joint on the left leg simply because it's near it on the model. Closest Distance, on the other hand, disregards a joint's position in the hierarchy of the skeleton and assigns influences according to how far the point is from the joint.

Max Influences sets a limit on how many joints can affect a single point. Dropoff Rate determines how a joint's influence diminishes on points farther from it. For example, with Smooth Bind, one shoulder joint can influence, to varying degrees, points stretching down the arm and into the chest and belly. By limiting these two parameters, you can control how much of your model is pulled along by a particular joint.

Using all the defaults is typically best. So, click Bind Skin in the option box to smooth-bind your second cylinder to the bones.

Bend both cylinders to get a feel for how each creases at the bending joints. Figure 9.33 shows the difference.

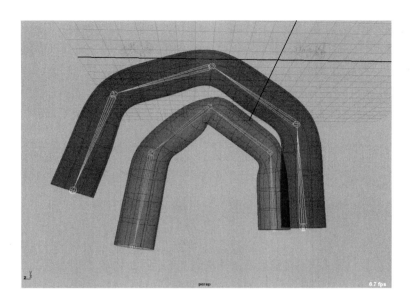

Figure 9.33

Rigid- and smooth-bound cylinders. The smaller cylinder is rigid bound, and the larger is smooth bound.

DETACHING A SKELETON

If you want to do away with your binding, select the skeleton and its geometry and choose Skin → Detach Skin. The model will snap to the shape it had before the bind was applied and the joints were rotated. It's common to bind and detach skeletons several times on the same model as you try to figure out the exact configuration that works best for you and your animation.

If you need to go back to the initial position of the skeleton at the point of binding it to the model, you can automatically set the skeleton back to the bind pose after any rotations have been applied to any of its joints. Simply select the skeleton and choose Skin → Go to Bind Pose to snap the skeleton and model into the position they were when you bound them together. It's also best to set your skeleton to the bind pose whenever you edit your binding weights.

A MODELING TRICK USING A SKELETON

An easy way to create bends and creases in a model is to create the surface without the bend and use a skeleton to deform it the way you want. You can then detach the skin and bake the history so that the surface retains its deformation but loses its connection to the skeleton. Bind your geometry to the skeleton chain using Smooth Bind or Rigid Bind. Bend the skeleton to deform the geometry, and then choose Skin → Detach Skin ❑. In the option box, set the History parameter to Bake History, and click Detach. The model will retain its deformed state but will lose all connections to the skeleton. This is just like using a Nonlinear or Lattice deformer on an object and then deleting the object's history to rid it of the deformer. With a detached skin, however, you won't lose any other history already applied to that object as you would if you deleted history through the Edit menu.

Binding the Hand: Rigid

Because you want definitive creases at the finger joints, you'll use Rigid Bind for the hand.

Load your hand and positioned skeleton, or use the file poly_hand_skeleton_v02.ma from the Poly_Hand_Anim project on the CD. Now, follow these steps to rigid-bind the hand:

1. Select the skeleton's root at the wrist, and Shift+click the top node of the hand. If you're using the file from the CD, select the hand's top node (handTopNode) to make sure you select the fingernails as well, as shown in Figure 9.34.

2. Choose Skin → Bind Skin → Rigid Bind □. Turn on Color Joints, and click the Bind Skin button in the option box. You're bound and ready to animate the hand. The joints take on colors to help you identify them.

3. Select some of the finger joints, and rotate them. Notice how the model creases at the knuckles, as shown with the index finger in Figure 9.35. If you rotate far enough, the model will fold in over itself.

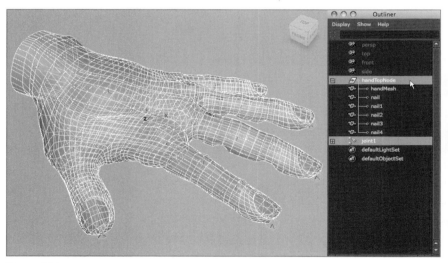

Figure 9.34

Select the root joint as well as the top node of the hand.

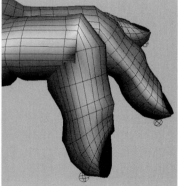

Figure 9.35

The crease at the knuckle is severe, and the geometry folds over into itself.

Editing a Rigid Bind

Having a rigid bind doesn't mean your creases always have to be this hard. With *flexors* (basically lattices, as discussed in Chapter 5), you can smooth out specific areas of a joint for a better look. This is useful at shoulder joints or hip joints, where a crease such as on an elbow isn't desired. In this case, it will help smooth out the knuckles so the geometry doesn't fold over itself, as in Figure 9.35:

1. Choose Skin → Go to Bind Pose to reset your skeleton.

2. Select the middle knuckle of the index finger, and choose Skin → Edit Rigid Skin → Create Flexor to open the Create Flexor option box (Figure 9.36).

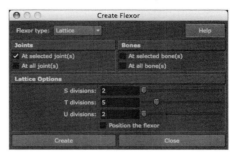

Figure 9.36

Creating a flexor

3. Notice that these options are similar to the lattice you created in Chapter 6, "Practical Experience," to edit the model. You can adjust the number of divisions later through the Attribute Editor, so you don't need to know exactly what you require before you create the flexor. Click Create to display a lattice at the joint position, as shown in Figure 9.37.

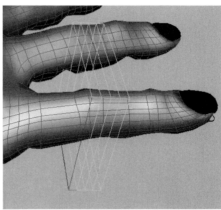

Figure 9.37

Creating a flexor at the middle knuckle

4. In the Outliner, drill down to the joint-Ffd1LatticeGroup node now attached under that knuckle joint in the hierarchy. Select the lattice as well as its base so you can adjust the size and, if need be, position of the flexor, just as you did on the lattice work earlier. Resize the flexor so that it better conforms to the knuckle, and elongate it so that it covers more of the finger, as shown in Figure 9.38.

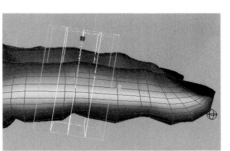

Figure 9.38

Scaling the flexor to fit better on the knuckle

5. Scaling and positioning the flexor (when both lattice and base nodes are selected) makes the joint bend more smoothly, without affecting it more than necessary. By elongating the flexor here, you smooth out the knuckle's bend, prevent the polygons from bending over each other, and still maintain a crisp crease, as shown in Figure 9.39.

6. Create flexors for the other knuckles that need them. Be sure to scale the flexors to make the most efficient use of them and fit them only where they need to be fitted. Figure 9.40 shows how the finger reacts when bending with flexors at each joint.

Figure 9.39

The knuckle's crease is now sharp, but the geometry doesn't fold over itself as before.

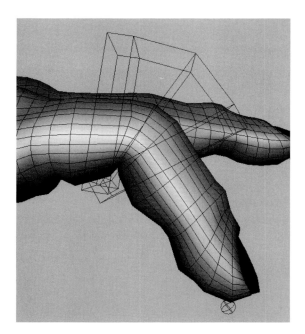

Figure 9.40

Flexors along the index finger

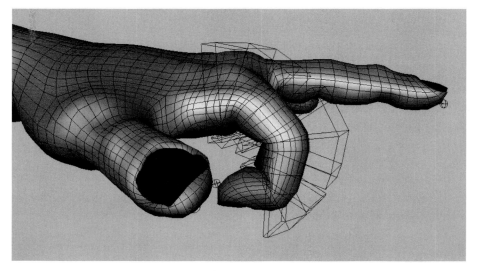

 For reference, the scene `poly_hand_skeleton_v03.ma` from the Poly_Hand_Anim project on the CD has the hand rigid-bound with flexors on one finger. Start with it to create flexors for the rest of the fingers, and animate the hand, making some sign language positions, grabbing a pencil, or pressing a button.

Binding the Hand: Smooth

Now, try skinning the hand with Smooth Bind.

Load your prebound hand or `poly_hand_skeleton_v02.ma` from the Poly_Hand_Anim project on the CD. Now, follow these steps to smooth-bind the hand:

1. Select the root at the wrist and the top node of the hand (if you're using the hand from the CD, make sure you have the nails as well). Choose Skin → Bind Skin → Smooth Bind.

2. Try rotating some of the knuckle joints to see how the fingers respond. Go back to the bind pose when you're done.

3. Rotate the middle knuckle of the index finger down. Notice how the knuckle gets thinner the more you bend the finger there. Go to the top knuckle of the index finger, and rotate that joint. Notice that part of the hand moves with the finger. This is again exaggerated because the hand is polygonal, so its deformations seem more severe than a NURBS model of the same hand. Figure 9.41 shows the result of bending at the index finger.

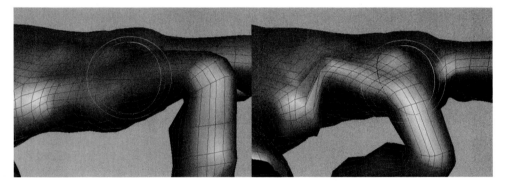

Figure 9.41

Bending at the index finger causes some unwanted deformation.

Editing a Smooth Bind

You usually edit a smooth bind by *painting skin weights*. Because points on the model are influenced by multiple joints in a smooth bind, you need to adjust just how much influence is exerted by these joints on the same points:

1. Make sure you're in Shaded mode (press 5). Select the hand, and then choose Skin → Edit Smooth Skin → Paint Skin Weights Tool □.

> You paint skin weights on the affected geometry and not on the joints themselves, so you need to select the model and not the skeleton before invoking this tool.

2. Your hand should turn black, with a bit of light gray at the wrist. The option box appears, listing the joints that are connected to the hand, as shown in Figure 9.42.

3. The color value (between white and black) determines how much binding influence the selected joint in the option box is exerting on that part of the geometry. It's best to name your joints properly so that selecting from this window is easier and more intuitive. If you loaded the file from the CD, you need to name the joints yourself to organize the scene and make working with it easier.

4. In the option box, make sure the Paint Operation button under the Paint Weights section is set to Replace. Change the Value slider to 0. In the Tool Settings section, Radius(U) and Radius(L) govern the size of your brush. In the Influence section, make sure the Opacity slider is set to 1.

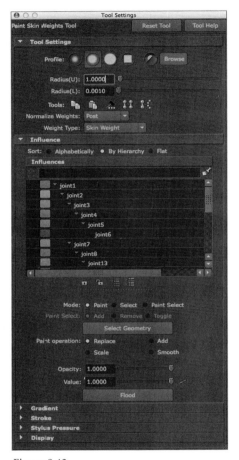

Figure 9.42

The option box for the Paint Skin Weights tool

> To change the size of your Artisan Brush while you're painting weights, you can hold down the B key and drag the mouse left or right to adjust the radius of the brush interactively.

5. Click and paint the black value around parts of the hand and palm that shouldn't be affected by the index finger bending at its top knuckle, as shown in Figure 9.43.

> Skin weights must always be normalized in a smooth bind, meaning the values have to add up to 1. When you reduce the influence of a joint on an area of the surface, the influence amount is automatically shifted to other joints in the hierarchy that have influence over that area; those joints are now more responsible for its movement.

6. Smooth out the area where it goes from white to black. In the Tool Settings window, set Paint Operation to Smooth. Right-click to smooth the area around the knuckle for a cleaner deformation. Your index knuckle should now bend beautifully.

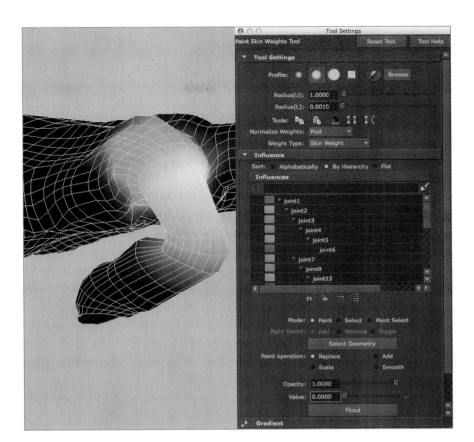

Figure 9.43

Paint the new weights to avoid unwanted deformations in the hand.

You can exit the Paint Skin Weights tool by selecting another tool (press W for Translate, for example), and your view will return to regular Shaded mode. Try bending the rest of the fingers and painting their influences; then, animate the hand, making gestures or grabbing an object using FK animation to set keys on the rotations.

When you paint weights on polygons, keep in mind that you're painting using the UVs. You may need to re-create the UVs of a polygonal mesh with a UV projection map for the Paint Weights tool to function properly, especially when you're importing and exporting the weight maps from one mesh to another (a procedure you won't encounter until later in your Maya experience).

The scene poly_hand_skeleton_v04.ma from the Poly_Hand_Anim project on the CD has the hand smooth-bound with painted weights on the index finger for your reference. Try painting the other knuckles as needed for your animation.

Rigging work is essential for getting a good animation from your model. In a professional shop, it usually falls under the domain of a technical director (TD) who oversees the setup of characters and may also model their geometry. The more time I spent rigging scenes for the animators when I was a TD on the television show *South Park*, the easier and faster they were able to accomplish their animations.

Inverse Kinematics

With IK, you have tools that let you plant a foot where it needs to be so you're not always moving the skeleton or model to compensate and keep the heel in place.

For legs, IK is nothing short of a blessing. There is no clearly preferable workflow to suggest when dealing with rigging arms and hands, however. Many people use IK on hands as well, but it can be better to animate the legs with IK and animate every other part of the body with FK. IK is best used when parts of the body (such as the feet) need to be planted at times. Planting the hands isn't necessary for a walk cycle, and having IK handles on the arms may create additional work while animating them.

Rigging the IK Legs

Back to the block man. Switch to that project, and load your version or the `block_man_skeleton_v02.mb` file from the Block_Man project on the CD.

You'll create an IK chain from the hip to the ankle on each foot. Creating the IK from the hip to the toe won't work as well.

Because IK automatically bends the joints in its chain according to where its *end effector*, or IK handle, is located, it has to choose which way to bend at a particular joint. To prevent IK from choosing the wrong way, you'll first nudge the knees slightly to let the IK solver know which way that joint is supposed to go. Follow these steps:

1. Select the two knee joints. In Pivot mode (press Ins; press the Home key on a Mac), move the knees forward a bit to create a slight crook in the leg, as a natural knee would bend.

2. Open the IK Handle tool by choosing Skeleton → IK Handle Tool. Your cursor changes to a cross.

3. Select the start joint for the IK chain. This will be the root of this chain. Click the left thigh joint, and then pick your end effector at the heel joint. Repeat this procedure for the other leg. Figure 9.44 shows handles on both ankles.

   If for some reason you can't manage to pick a joint for the IK tool, make sure Show → Pivots is turned on in your view panel. Also, if you have difficulty seeing the handles, you can increase their size by choosing Display → Animation → IK Handle Size.

4. Move the IK handles around, and see how the legs react. When you're done, reset the IK handle positions.

5. Grab the top joint of the skeleton, which is the pelvis joint. Move the joint, and the entire body moves with it. Select both ankle IK handles, and set a translation key for them (press Shift+W). Grab the pelvis joint again, and move it. The feet stick to their positions on the ground. Move the pelvis down, and the legs bend at the knees. Notice how the feet bend into the ground, though (see Figure 9.45 on the left).

6. Move the pelvis back to the origin. You can create an IK handle for the foot so that the foot stays flat on the ground. Open the IK Handle tool. For the start joint, select the ankle; for the end effector, select the joint at the tip of the foot. Repeat for the other foot.

You can invoke the last tool you used by pressing Y.

7. Set a translate key for the foot IK handles. Move the pelvis down; the legs bend at the knees and the ankle, keeping the feet flush on the ground (see Figure 9.45 on the right).

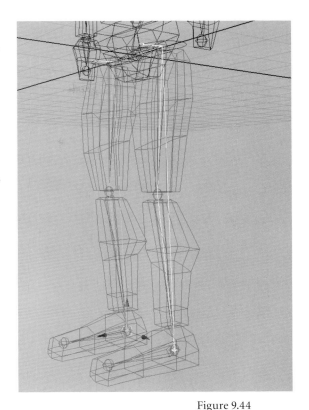

Figure 9.44

IK handles on both ankles with the roots at the hip joints

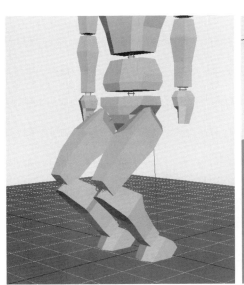

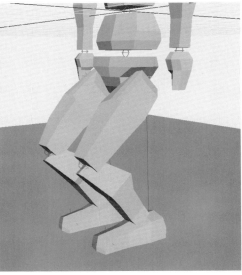

Figure 9.45

Creating another IK chain from the ankle to the tip of the foot and setting keyframes makes the feet stay on the ground (right) and not rotate into the ground (left).

Creating an IK Walk Cycle

Because the block man's feet will stick to the ground, creating a walk cycle with IK animation is far easier than using FK. Making the animation look good is still a tough job that requires a lot of practice.

Load the scene file block_man_IK_v01.mb from the Block_Man project on the CD, or use your own IK-rigged block man with handles at the ankles and feet. The white leg and arm are again on the far side of the character. You'll set keys every five frames again for the gross animation. To keep this short, we'll just discuss setting poses with the feet. You can always return to the scene to add animation to the upper body with FK, as you did earlier in this chapter. Follow these steps:

1. On frame 1, set translate keys on the pelvis joint and all four IK handles for their start position.

2. Go to frame 5, and move the pelvis forward about 1 unit. The legs and feet lift off the ground a bit and strain to keep their position. Lower the pelvis to get the feet flat on the ground again. Set a key for the pelvis. Because Auto Keyframe is turned on, all keys are set for this animation. (With the FK animation, you set keys for everything at every pose.)

3. Grab the near IK handles for the ankle and foot, and move them forward and up to match the pose shown in Figure 9.46.

4. Go to frame 10. Move the front foot forward, and plant it on the ground. Move the pelvis another three-fourths of a unit. Set translation keys for the rear ankle and foot handles where they are. Be sure to place the pelvis so that the rear foot is almost flat on the ground. Match the pose shown in Figure 9.47.

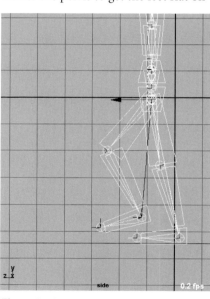

Figure 9.46
Step 3's pose

5. Go to frame 15. Move the pelvis another 2 units to center the body over the front foot. Lift the rear ankle and foot IK handles up to bend the knee, and bring the knee up a bit. Match the pose shown in Figure 9.48.

6. Go to frame 20. Move the pelvis forward 1 unit, and swing the white leg forward as in the pose shown in Figure 9.49.

7. Move the pelvis three-fourths of a unit forward, and plant the front leg down. Set keys for the rear leg and foot where they stand. Match the pose shown in Figure 9.50.

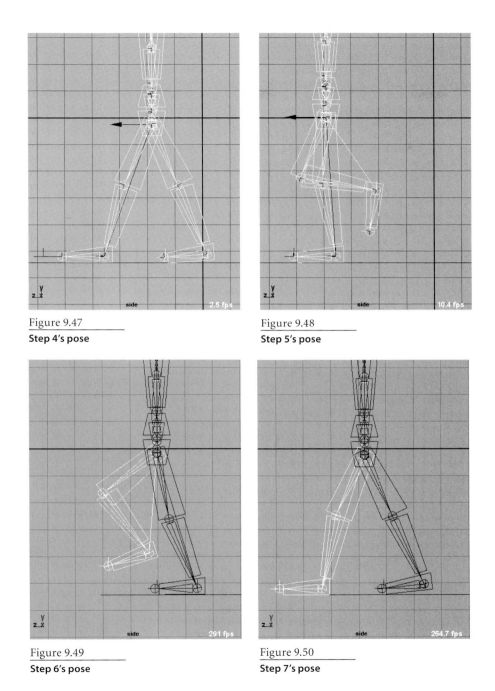

Figure 9.47
Step 4's pose

Figure 9.48
Step 5's pose

Figure 9.49
Step 6's pose

Figure 9.50
Step 7's pose

The next pose should match the pose in frame 10, although with the other leg. Continue the cycle, with each successive pose matching the one 15 frames before it on the opposite side. Don't forget to add FK animation to the top of the body to give your character some weight. Some rotation at the waist and shoulders to make the block man shift his weight as he walks would be a good start.

Further Uses for IK Chains

Many animators use IK chains more often in effects animation than in character work. IK chains can drive whips and ropes, flutter flags, bounce ponytails, and pump pistons as well as move legs and arms. For example, you can use a different type of IK chain, the

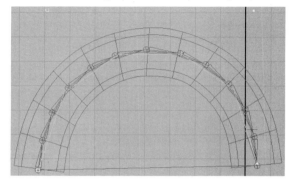

Figure 9.51

A spline IK chain is driven by the curvature of a NURBS spline. Adjusting the curve's CVs moves the joints.

spline IK chain, to control the shape of your bone chain with a NURBS spline. This is great for snakes and other long, deforming objects.

To create a spline IK chain, choose Skeleton → IK Spline Handle Tool, and then select your top joint and end effector. Maya creates a spline running the length of the bone chain. Adjusting the curvature of the spline in turn drives the bones, which in turn drive the geometry bound to them. Figure 9.51 shows a spline curve affecting the curvature of the bones in its spline IK chain.

Basic Relationships: Constraints

As you know, Maya is all about the relationships between object nodes. You can create animation on one object based on the animation of another object by setting up a relationship between the objects. The simplest way to do that (outside of grouping) is to create a *constraint*. For example, you can "glue" one object to another's position or rotation through a constraint.

A constraint creates a direct relationship between the source and the target object's Translate or Rotate attributes. This section explores six types of constraints: point, orient, scale, aim, geometry, and normal.

The Point Constraint

To attach a source object to a target object but have the source follow only the position of the target, use a *point constraint*. A point constraint connects only the Translate attributes of the source to the target. To use this method, select the target object(s) and then Shift+click the source object. In the Animation menu, choose Constrain → Point ❐.

The options allow you to set an offset that creates a gap between the source and the target. Constraints are based on the pivots of the objects, so a point constraint snaps the source at its pivot point to the pivot point of the target. Offset would dictate the distance between their pivots in any of the axes.

You can constrain the same source to more than one target object. The source then takes up the average position between the multiple targets. By setting the Weight slider in the option box, you can create more of an influence on the source by any of the targets.

In Figure 9.52, a cone has been point-constrained to a sphere. Wherever the sphere goes, the cone follows. This is different from parenting the cone to the sphere in that only its translations are affected by the sphere. If you rotate or scale the sphere, the cone won't rotate or scale with it.

Although you can blend keyframe animation with constraint animation, as a beginner to Maya, consider that after you set a point constraint like that shown in Figure 9.52, you're unable to control the cone's Translate attributes because they're being driven by the sphere's translations.

Point constraints are perfect to animate a character carrying a cane or a sword, for example. The rotations on the sword are still free to animate, but the sword is attached to the character's belt and follows the character throughout the scene.

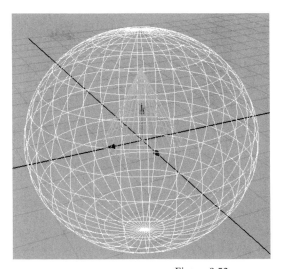

Figure 9.52

A cone point that is constrained to a sphere follows that sphere's position.

The Orient Constraint

An *orient constraint* attaches the source's Rotation attributes to the target's Rotation attributes. Select the target object(s) first, and then Shift+click the source object. In the Animation menu, choose Constrain → Orient ❑.

The Offset parameter allows you to set an offset in any axis. Otherwise, the source assumes the exact orientation of the target. In the case of multiple targets, the source uses the average of their orientations. Figure 9.53 shows the cone's orientation following an elongated sphere (the target).

A rotation constraint saves a lot of hassle when you have to animate an object to keep rotating in the same direction as another object. For example, if two speedboats are cruising along neck and neck and one turns, the other can turn to match, keeping them both on course. You can also set offsets and animate them to make the second boat look as if it's reacting to the other so that the animation doesn't look too perfect.

Figure 9.53

The cone's rotations match the sphere's rotations.

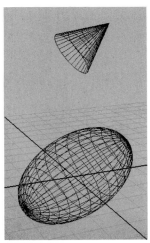

The Scale Constraint

A *scale constraint* attaches the source's Scale attributes to the target's Scale attributes. Select the target object(s) first, and then Shift+click the source object. In the Animation menu, choose Constrain → Scale ❑.

The Offset parameter allows you to set a scale offset in any axis. Otherwise, the source assumes the exact scale of the target. The source uses the average of the scales of multiple targets. Figure 9.54 shows the cone's scale matching the target sphere.

The scale constraint is good for matching the sizes of objects. For example, if an air hose is inflating a string of balloons, constraining the balloons to one target saves you the hassle of animating all their Scale attributes in unison. If a cartoon character's eyes are bugging out at something, you can scale-constrain one to the other so that both bug out in the same time and proportion.

The Aim Constraint

The *aim constraint* adjusts the source's rotations so that the source always points to the target object. Select the target object(s) first, and then Shift+click the source object. In the Animation menu, choose Constrain → Aim ❑.

The aim constraint has more options than the other constraints because you need to specify which axis of the source is to point to the target. You do so using the Aim Vector and Up Vector settings.

The Aim Vector setting specifies which axis of the source is the "front" and points to the target. In the cone and sphere examples, you set the Aim Vector of the cone to (0,1,0) to make the Y-axis the front so that the cone's point aims at the sphere. If Aim Vector is set to (1,0,0), for example, the cone's side points to the sphere. Figure 9.55 shows the cone pointing to the sphere with an Aim Vector setting of (0,1,0).

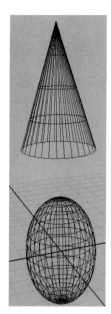

Figure 9.54

The cone now matches the sphere's scale.

Figure 9.55

The cone aiming at the sphere

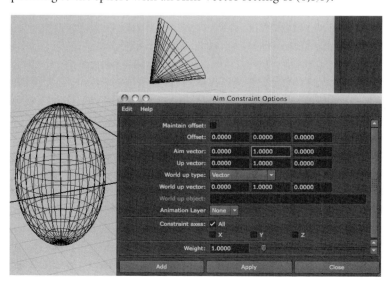

The Offset values create an offset on the source's Rotation attributes, tilting it one way or another. The Up Vector setting specifies which way the cone faces when it's pointing to the sphere.

Aim constraints are perfect for animating cameras to follow a subject, such as a car at a racetrack.

Geometry and Normal Constraints

The *geometry* and *normal constraints* constrain the source object to the surface of the target object (as long as it's a NURBS or poly mesh).

With a geometry constraint, the source object attaches at its pivot point to the surface of the target. It tries to keep its own position as best it can, shifting as its target surface changes beneath it. Again, select the target, select the source object, and choose Constrain → Geometry.

Using a geometry constraint is useful when you want to keep an object on a deforming surface, such as a floating boat on a lake. Figure 9.56 shows the cone after it has been geometry-constrained to a NURBS plane that is being deformed by a Wave deformer (choose Create Deformers → Nonlinear → Wave). The cone sits on the surface as the waves ripple through, but it doesn't rock back and forth to stay oriented with the surface.

To get the cone to orient itself so that it truly floats on the surface, you need to use a normal constraint. Using a normal constraint rotates the cone to follow the surface's normals, keeping it perpendicular to the surface.

A *surface normal* is an imaginary perpendicular tangent line that emanates from all surfaces to give the surface direction.

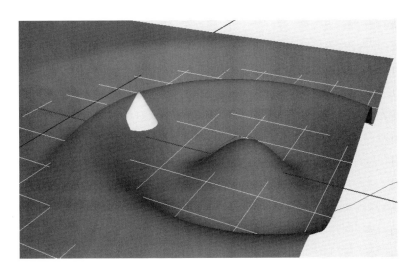

Figure 9.56

With a geometry constraint, the cone sits on the deforming surface.

The normal constraint is similar to the aim constraint, and its options are similar. Using the Aim Vector setting, you specify which way is up for the object, to define the orientation that the source should maintain. However, this setting doesn't constrain the location of the source to the target. If you want a floating effect, use geometry and a normal constraint to get the cone to bob up and down and roll back and forth as the waves ripple along (see Figure 9.57).

Figure 9.57

The cone now animates to float on the water surface, using both geometry and normal constraints.

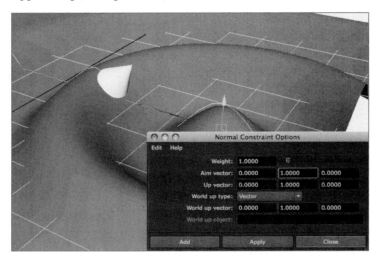

Parent, Tangent, and Pole Vector Constraints

Three more constraints are possible in Maya: the parent, tangent, and pole vector constraints. A *parent constraint* constrains an object's translation and rotation to another object by mimicking a parent-child relationship without actually parenting the objects. This keeps objects aligned without worrying about any grouping issues. You'll have a firsthand look at this in the exercise where you rig the locomotive later in this chapter. Lucky you!

A *tangent constraint* keeps an object's orientation so that the object always points along a curve's direction. This constraint is usually used with a geometry constraint or path animation to keep the object traveling along a curve pointed in the right direction, no matter the direction of the curve. *Pole vector constraints* are used extensively in character animation rigs to keep IK joints from flipping beyond 180 degrees of motion.

Basic Relationships: Set-Driven Keys

A favorite feature for character riggers is the *set-driven key* (SDK). A set-driven key establishes a relationship for objects that lets you create controls that drive certain features of a character or an object in a scene.

Before you can use an SDK, you must create extra attributes and attach them to a character's top node. These new attributes drive part of the character's animation. The term *character* is used broadly here. For example, you can set up a vehicle so that an SDK turns its wheels.

Let's start with a simple SDK relationship between two objects. You'll create a relationship between a ball and a cone. As the ball moves up in the Y-axis, the cone spins in the X-axis. As the ball descends, the cone spins back. You'll then revisit the hand and set up an SDK on the skeleton that animates the model.

Creating a Set-Driven Key

To create a simple SDK to make a sphere control the animation of a cone's rotation, follow these steps:

1. Create a NURBS sphere and a cone in a new scene. Move the cone to the side of the sphere, and lay it on its side, as shown in Figure 9.58.

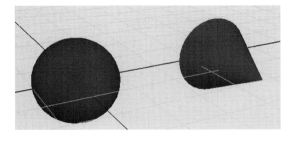

Figure 9.58

Lay out a cone and a sphere.

2. Select the sphere, and in the Animation menu, choose Animate → Set Driven Key → Set. The Set Driven Key window opens with the nurbsSphere1 object selected in the lower half of the window (the Driven section). Its attributes are listed on the right, as you can see in Figure 9.59.

Figure 9.59

The Set Driven Key window

3. You want the sphere to drive the animation of the cone, so you need to switch the sphere to be the driver and not what's driven. Click the Load Driver button to list the sphere in the top half of the window.

4. Select the cone, and click the Load Driven button to display the cone's attributes in the bottom half of the window.

5. In the Driver section, select the sphere's translateY attribute. In the Driven section, select the cone's RotateX attribute. Click the Key button to set an SDK that essentially says that when the sphere is on the ground (Y = 0), the cone's X rotation is 0 because both

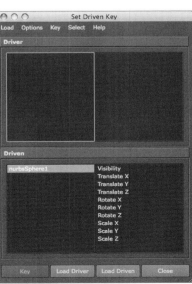

attributes are currently 0. The cone's RotateX attribute turns orange in the Channel Box, meaning a driven key has been set.

6. Select the sphere, and raise it in *Y* to a height of 5. Select the cone, and rotate it in *X* to 1800 to make it spin properly. Click the Key button in the Set Driven Key window to specify that when the sphere is at a height of 5, the cone's RotateX attribute is 1800 degrees. As the sphere's height increases from 0 to 5, the cone spins from 0 to 1800 in *X*.

An Advanced Set Driven Key: The Hand

Automating some animations on a character is indispensable to an animator. This can't be truer than when setting up an SDK for hand control. After you model and bind a hand to a skeleton, you're ready for an SDK.

   Open the scene `poly_hand_skeleton_v05.ma` from the Poly_Hand_Anim project on the CD, or use your own file that has the hand and its skeleton and is bound (either smooth or rigid) to the skin. Your file shouldn't have animation, though. Set your hand to the bind pose before you begin.

Creating a New Attribute

First, you'll create a new attribute called index_pull to control a contracting finger:

1. Select the hand. (It's best to select the top node handTopNode instead of just the poly mesh of the hand.) In the handTopNode tab of the Attribute Editor, click the Extra Attributes section. For now, at least, this section is empty.

2. In the Attribute Editor menu, choose Attributes → Add Attributes to open the Add Attribute window, which is shown in Figure 9.60. In the Long Name field, enter **index_pull**. Maya will automatically display that attribute as "Index Pull" in the UI. Make sure the Make Attribute Keyable check box is checked and that the Float option is selected in the Data Type section. In the Numeric Attribute Properties section, set Minimum to 0, set Maximum to 10, and set Default to 0. Click OK.

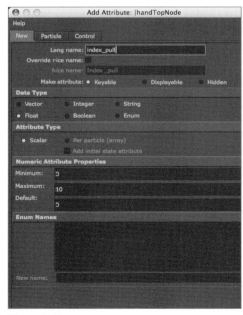

Figure 9.60

The Add Attribute window

After you click OK, the Index_Pull slider appears in the Attribute Editor and the Channel Box. This attribute alone will control the entire index finger.

Assigning the Set Driven Key

To set up the relationships with the SDK, follow these steps:

1. With the top hand node selected, open the Set Driven Key window (choose Animate → Set Driven Key → Set). Click Load Driver to specify that the hand should drive the animation.

2. Because you're animating the index finger pulling back, you want to drive the rotations of the top three knuckles. Shift+click all three knuckles on the index finger. Click the Load Driven button. All three knuckles appear on the bottom.

3. Select the hand's Index Pull attribute and the three knuckles' RotateY attributes, as shown in Figure 9.61.

4. With the rotations of the knuckles at 0 and the index_pull attribute at 0 as well, click the Key button to set the first relationship. When index_pull is at 0, the finger is extended.

5. Select the top hand node, and set the index_pull attribute to 5.

6. Select the fingertip's knuckle (joint11 in the CD file), and rotate it in *Y* to 20. Select the next joint up the chain (the middle knuckle, joint10), and rotate it to 35 in the *Y*-axis. Select the final index knuckle (joint9), and rotate it in the *Y*-axis to 5. Click the Key button. When the index_pull attribute is at 5, the finger assumes this bent position.

7. Select the top hand node, and set index_pull to 10.

8. Select each of the three knuckles. Set the tip to rotate to 65 in Y. Set the middle knuckle to 60. Set the last knuckle to 50. Click the Key button to see the result shown in Figure 9.62.

Select the top hand node, and change the value of the index_pull attribute to animate your finger. All you need to do to pull the finger is to set keys on that attribute,

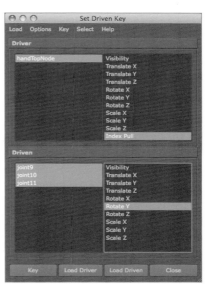

Figure 9.61

The Set Driven Key window for the hand

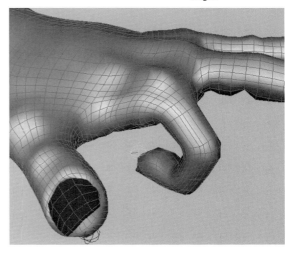

Figure 9.62

The bent index finger

without having to rotate the knuckles constantly. Furthermore, you can set up a single SDK to control the bending of all the fingers at once, or you can set up one SDK for each finger for more control.

Open the scene poly_hand_skeleton_v06.ma from the Poly_Hand_Anim project on the CD to see the hand with the SDK set up on the index finger.

Application: Rigging the Locomotive

Let's get back to our locomotive. In the previous chapter, you made sure the hierarchy and pivot placements were proper. In this exercise, you can use your own locomotive scene or the locomotive_anim_v1.mb file from the previous chapter. You can also use a fancy version of the locomotive, called fancy_locomotive_anim_v1.mb; it's set up similarly to locomotive_anim_v1.mb for the exercise. This scene is shown in Figure 9.63.

Familiarize yourself with the scene file first. To give yourself more modeling practice, you can use this scene file to remodel your own fancy locomotive if you like. All the parts of this fancy locomotive were made using the basic tools and procedures laid out in Chapter 4, "Beginning Polygonal Modeling."

Figure 9.63

The fancier locomotive model

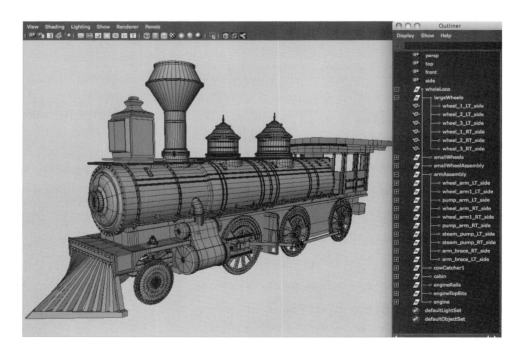

Setting Up Wheel Control

Your goal here is to rig the scene to animate all the secondary movements automatically based on some simple controls, such as you did for the hand earlier this chapter. In real-ity, the locomotive's steam pump drives the arms that then turn the wheels on the locomotive. You'll work backward, however, and use one wheel to drive the animation of everything else.

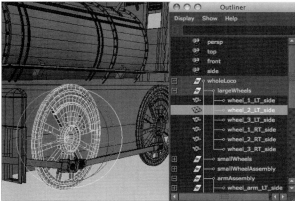

Because all the large wheels have the same diameter, they rotate the same as the locomotive moves. In this case, you'll use the Connection Editor to attach the *X* Rotation on all the wheels to your main control wheel. You'll pick the middle wheel to be the control. To set up the locomotive, follow these steps:

1. Select the middle wheel on the left side of the locomotive (node wheel_2_LT_side), as shown in Figure 9.64. Open the Connection Editor (choose Window → General Editors → Connection Editor). Click the Reload Left button to load the attributes of the selected middle wheel. Now, select the front wheel on the left side, and click the Reload Right button.

Figure 9.64

Select the middle wheel.

Figure 9.65

Connect the rotations of the two wheels.

2. Scroll down in the Connection Editor until you find Rotate in both columns. Click to highlight Rotate in the left column, and then click to highlight Rotate in the right column. Doing so connects the two rotations so that they both rotate at the same time, effectively letting you drive the animation of both wheels from just the center wheel. Figure 9.65 shows the Connection Editor.

3. Select the back wheel on the left side (wheel_3_LT_side). Click the Reload Right button in the Connection Editor. Connect the Rotate attribute for the middle and the back wheels. Close the Connection Editor, and select just the middle wheel. When you rotate the wheel, all three wheels rotate together.

4. Repeat this procedure to connect the rotations of the three wheels on the other side to this middle wheel as well. Now all six wheels rotate in synch with the one control wheel. When you select that left-side middle wheel (the control wheel), the other five wheels turn magenta, signifying a connection between these objects.

If you get strange results when you connect the rotations of objects (for example, if the wheels flip over or rotate the opposite direction of the control wheel), try disconnecting all the connections, freezing transforms, and reconnecting the attributes.

Controlling the Wheel Arms

You've now automated the animation of the wheels. Next, you'll figure out how to connect the wheel arms to the wheels and drive their motion as well. To do so, follow these steps:

1. Create a single joint that lines up with the first wheel arm. The root joint is placed where the wheel arm meets the middle wheel (control wheel), and the end joint is placed where the wheel arm meets the pump arm, as shown in Figure 9.66. The pump arm has been templated in this graphic (displays in light gray wireframe) to show you the entire wheel arm and joint.

Figure 9.66

Create a joint from the middle wheel to the pump arm at the first wheel.

2. Group the joint under the control wheel's node, as shown in the Outliner in Figure 9.67. Then, group the wheel arm under the top joint. This way, the joint rotates with the control wheel, also shown in Figure 9.67, albeit incorrectly for the pump arm.

3. As you saw in Figure 9.67, the joint isn't rotating properly to make the pump arm work right. The other end of it needs to attach to the pump arm in front of the front wheel, not fly up in space. You can use an IK handle for this. Make sure the rotation of the control wheel and the joint/wheel arm are set back to 0 to place them in the original position. In the Animation menu, choose Skeleton → IK Handle Tool. Make sure the settings are reset for the tool. Select the root joint as the start joint for the IK Handle. Select the other tip of the bone as the end effector. You now have an IK handle at the tip where the wheel arm connects to the pump arm, as shown in Figure 9.68.

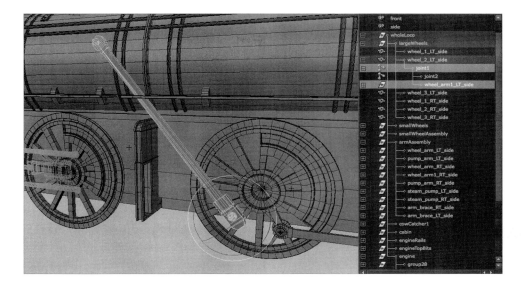

Figure 9.67
Group the top joint under the wheel, and then group the wheel arm under the top joint.

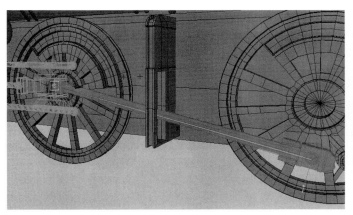

Figure 9.69

Group the IK handle under the locomotive's top node.

Figure 9.68

Place the end effector where the pump arm and the first wheel connect.

4. If you rotate the control wheel now, the wheel arm still separates from the pump arm. This is because the IK handle you just created needs a keyframe to keep it in position—that is, attached to the pump arm. Select the IK handle, and, at frame 1, set a position keyframe. Now, if you rotate the control wheel, the joint and wheel arm pump back and forth.

5. Group the IK handle (ikHandle1) under the top node of the locomotive (wholeLoco), as shown in Figure 9.69.

Controlling the Pump Arm

Next, you need to attach the pump arm to the wheel arm so that it pumps back and forth as the control wheel turns. If you simply group the pump arm with the end joint of the wheel arm's bone, the pump arm will float up and down as it pumps back and forth. You need to use a constraint to force the pump arm to move back and forth only in the Z-axis:

1. Make sure the control wheel is set back to 0 rotation. Select the pump arm, templated in Figure 9.70 so that you can see through to the wheel arm and joint, and line up its pivot with the end joint of the wheel arm bone.

2. Select the end joint (called joint2), Ctrl+click the pump arm group in the Outliner (called pump_arm_LT_side), and, in the Animation menu, choose Constrain → Point ❏. In the option box, uncheck All under Constraint Axes, select only Z to constrain the pump arm only in the Z-axis, and click the Add button. Now, if you rotate the control wheel, you see the pump arm and wheel arm connected. The pump arm pumps back and forth, although you'll immediately notice a need to adjust the model to make the piece fit when it animates. Figure 9.71 shows that the pump arm's geometry isn't yet quite right for animation. This is very normal for this process and luckily needs only a quick fix.

Figure 9.70

Line up the pivot of the pump arm with the end joint of the wheel arm joint.

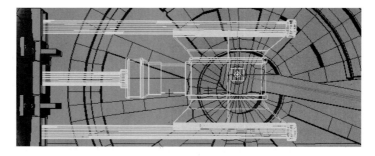

Figure 9.71

The pump arm is too short!

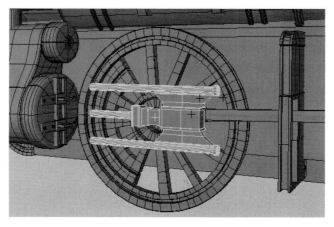

3. To fix the pump arm, select the vertices on the ends of the cylinders, and extend them to make them longer, as shown in Figure 9.72. Now the pump arm won't pull out of the steam pump assembly.

4. Adjust the pump arm so that the geometry fits when the pump pushes in as well.

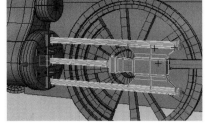

Figure 9.72

Use vertices to extend the pump arm.

The scene file `fancy_locomotive_anim_v2.mb` will catch you up to this point. Compare it to your work.

Controlling the Back Wheel

All that remains is to control the animation of the back wheel and its wheel arm. To set up the wheel arm animation, follow these steps:

1. Using the methods described in the steps in the "Controlling the Wheel Arms" section, create a joint to follow along the wheel arm between the middle control wheel and the back wheel. The root of the joint is set at the control wheel, as shown in Figure 9.73.

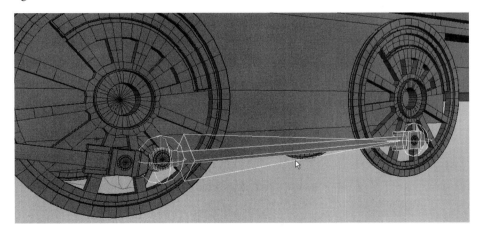

Figure 9.73

Create a joint to control the back wheel arm.

2. As before, create an IK handle for the end joint of this new bone, where it meets the back wheel, as shown in Figure 9.74. Make sure the handle is at the back wheel, not the middle control wheel.

3. Group the new joint under the master wheel, and then group the wheel arm under this new joint. If you rotate the control wheel, the wheel arm rotates with the joint and wheel but doesn't connect to the back wheel yet. You need to attach the IK handle you just created for that joint to the back wheel.

Figure 9.74

Create an IK handle to attach the wheel arm and the back wheel to the control wheel.

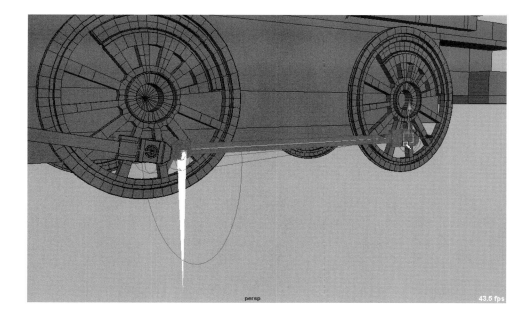

If you group the IK handle, as shown in Figure 9.75, you'll run into a problem when you animate. Let's try it: Group the IK handle (ikHandle2) under the end back wheel, as shown in Figure 9.75, and then rotate the control wheel. The wheel arm pumps back and forth along with the back wheel, but every now and then the wheel arm geometry flips over backward. This isn't good.

Fixing this is easy. The grouping of the IK handle to the back wheel is causing the issue. Although that is pretty much what you want to do, parenting the IK handle under the wheel is problematic. Here is where the parent constraint becomes extremely helpful. It gives you the desired result without the geometry flipping.

Figure 9.75

The wheel arm geometry flips over if you group the IK handle under the back wheel.

4. Make sure your control wheel is back to 0 rotation first. MMB+click in the Outliner, and place the IK handle outside the hierarchy of the locomotive to remove the IK handle from under the back wheel's node. You may also undo your past actions to the point before you grouped the IK handle (ikHandle2) under the back wheel. You gotta love Undo.

5. Select the back wheel, Shift+click the IK handle (ikHandle2), and choose Constrain → Parent. Now, if you rotate the control wheel, everything works great.

6. Group the IK Handle (ikHandle2) under the top node of the locomotive (wholeLoco). You can use `fancy_locomotive_anim_v3.mb` to compare your work.

> Again, seeing procedures go slightly awry, as when the wheel arm flipped over, is important. Doing so gives you a taste of trouble and a chance to fix it. Troubleshooting is an integral skill for a good CG artist.

Finishing the Rig

You're almost home free with the locomotive wheel rigging. Everything works great when you rotate the control wheel. If you select the top node of the locomotive and translate the train back and forth, everything should work perfectly. Repeat the steps in the previous few sections to connect the wheel arms and wheels on the other side of the locomotive, and you're finished! Figure 9.76 shows the completed and rigged locomotive.

Figure 9.76

The rigged fancy locomotive

Summary

In this chapter, you extended your experience with animation and learned about rigging techniques and automation. Starting with a simple block man, you learned how to set up a hierarchy for Forward Kinematics animation to create a walk cycle. Then, you revisited the hand model and used a skeleton to rig the hand for animation. Next, you learned how to bind the geometry of the hand to the skeleton using rigid and smooth binds and how to edit the binding. You also learned how to create an IK system to drive the joints in the block man for an IK walk-cycle animation. After that, you learned how constraints can be used in rigging and how to set up driven keys to create easy controls to animate the hand. Finally, you put all these rigging tricks together to rig the wheels of the locomotive to automate the animation of that complex system with a single control based on the middle wheel.

The true work in animation comes from recognizing what to do in the face of certain challenges and how to approach their solutions. Maya offers a large animation toolset, and the more familiar you become with the tools, the better you'll be able to judge which tools to use in your work. Don't stop with this chapter; experiment with the features not covered here, and see what happens.

Animation is about observation and interpretation. The animator's duty is to understand how and why something moves and to translate that into their medium without losing the movement's fidelity, tenacity, or honesty.

CHAPTER 10

Maya Lighting

Light shapes the world by showing us what we see. It creates a sense of depth, it initiates the perception of color, and it allows us to distinguish shape and form. For a scene to be successful in CG, these realities of light need to be reproduced as faithfully as possible. The trick is learning to see light and its astonishing effects on the world around us.

Topics in this chapter include:

- Basic lighting concepts
- Maya lights
- Light linking
- Adding shadows
- Raytracing soft shadows
- mental ray lighting
- mental ray Physical Sun and Sky
- Lighting effects
- Lighting the decorative box
- Further lighting practice
- Tips for using and animating lights

Basic Lighting Concepts

It's no surprise that Maya's lighting resembles actual direct-lighting techniques used in photography and filmmaking. Lights of various types are placed around a scene to illuminate the subjects as they would for a still life or a portrait. Your scene and what's in it dictate, to some degree at least, which lights you put where. The *type* of lights you use depends on the desired effect.

At the basic level, you want your lights to illuminate the scene. Without lights, your cameras have nothing to capture. Although it seems rather easy to throw your lights in, turn them all on, and render a scene, that couldn't be further from the truth.

Lighting is the backbone of CG. Although it's technically easy to insert and configure lights, it's *how* you light that will make or break your scene. Knowing how to do that really only comes with a good deal of experience and experimentation, as well as a good eye and some patience.

This chapter will familiarize you with the basic techniques of lighting a scene in Maya and start you on the road to finding out more.

Learning to See

There are many nuances to the real-world lighting around us that we take for granted. We intuitively understand what we see and how it's lit, and we infer a tremendous amount of visual information without much consideration. With CG lighting, you must re-create these nuances for your scene. That amounts to all the *work* of lighting.

The most valuable thing you can do to improve your lighting technique is to relearn how you see your environment. Simply put, refuse to take for granted what you see. Question why things look the way they do, and you'll find that the answers almost always come around to lighting.

Take note of the distinction between light and dark in the room you're in now. Notice the difference in the brightness of highlights and how they dissipate into diffused light and then into shadow.

When you start understanding how real light affects objects, you'll be much better equipped to generate your own light. After all, the key to good lighting starts with the desire to create an interesting image.

What Your Scene Needs

Ideally, your scene needs areas of highlight and shadow. Overlighting a scene flattens everything and diminishes details. This is perhaps the number-one mistake of beginners. Figure 10.1 shows a still life with too many bright lights that only flatten the image and remove any sense of color and depth.

Similarly, underlighting your scene makes it muddy, gray, and rather lifeless, and it covers your details in darkness and flattens the entire frame. Figure 10.2 shows the still life underlit. The bumps and curves of the mesh are hardly noticeable.

Figure 10.1
An overlit still life

Figure 10.2
An underlit still life

Finding a good middle ground to lighting your scene is key. Like a photographer, you want your image to have the full range of exposure. You want the richest blacks to the brightest whites in your frame to create a deep sense of detail. Even though you may not have an absolute black to white in the rendered image, the concept is appealing. As in Figure 10.3, light and shadow complement each other and work to show the features of your surface.

Three-Point Lighting

Because your scene needs to be rendered, and lighting can be a fairly heavy computational process when it comes to rendering, your lighting needs to be efficient. That means not using dozens of lights for every part of the scene.

Figure 10.3
Balanced lighting creates a more interesting picture.

The traditional approach to lighting an object efficiently, culled from filmmaking and television, starts with *three-point lighting.* In this setup, three distinct roles are used to light the subject of a shot. More than one light can be used for each of the three roles, but the scene should, in effect, seem to have only one primary, or *key,* light, a softer light to fill the scene, and a back light to pop the subject out from the background.

Three-point lighting ensures that the primary subject's features aren't just illuminated, but featured with highlights and shadow. Using three directions and qualities of light creates the best level of depth. Figure 10.4 shows a schematic of a basic three-point setup.

Figure 10.4

A three-point lighting schematic

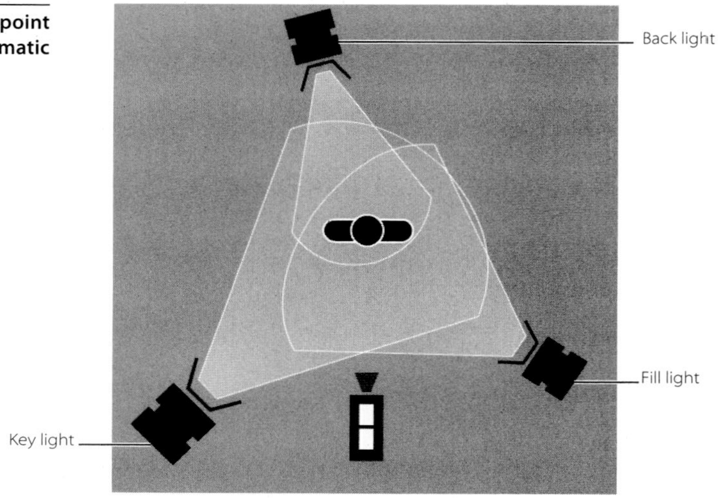

Back light

Fill light

Key light

Key Light

A *key light* is placed in front of the subject and off to the side to provide the principal light on the subject. Because it's usually off center, the key light creates one side of brighter light, increasing the depth of the shot. This light also provides the primary shadows and gives the important sense of lighting direction in the shot.

Although it's possible for several lights to fulfill the role of key light in a scene—for example, three ceiling lights overhead—one light should dominate, creating a definitive direction. Figure 10.5 shows the subject being lit by only a key light, although it's physically composed of two lights.

Figure 10.5

Key light only

The direction of the two lights remains the same, and one takes intensity precedence over the other and casts shadows. The effect creates a single key light, which produces a moody still life.

Fill Light

A more diffused light than the key light, the *fill light* seems directionless and evenly spread across the subject's dark side. This fills the rest of the subject with light and decreases the dark area caused by the key light.

The fill light isn't meant to cast any shadows onto the subject or background itself and is actually used to help soften the shadows created by the key light. Figure 10.6 shows the still life with an added fill light. Notice how it softens the shadows and illuminates the dark areas the key light misses.

Figure 10.6

A fill light is now included.

Typically, you place the fill light in front of the subject and aim it so that it comes from the opposite side of the key light to target the dark side of the subject. Even though the still life in Figure 10.6 is still a fairly moody composition, much more is visible than with only the key light in Figure 10.5.

Back Light

The *back light*, or rim light, is placed behind the subject to create a bit of a halo, which helps to pop the subject out in the shot. Therefore, the subject has more presence against its background. Figure 10.7 shows how helpful a back light can be.

The back light brings the fruit in this still life out from the background and adds some highlights to the edges, giving the composition more focus on the fruit.

Don't confuse the back light with the background light, which lights the environment behind the subject.

Using Three-Point Lighting

The three-point lighting system is used for the primary subject of the scene. Because it's based on position and angle of the subject to the camera, a new setup is needed when the camera is moved for a different shot in the same scene. Three-point lighting is, therefore, not scene-specific but shot-specific.

After the lighting is set up for the subject of a shot, the background must be lit. Use a directed primary light source that matches the direction of the key light for the main light, and use a softer fill light to illuminate the rest of the scene and soften the primary shadows.

Figure 10.7

A back light makes the subject pop right out.

Practical Lighting

Practical lighting is a theatrical term describing any lights in a scene that are cast from lighting objects within the scene. For example, a desk lamp on a table in the background of a scene would need practical lighting when it's on. You never want the practical lighting to interfere with the main lighting of the scene, unless the scene's lighting is explicitly coming from such a source.

Each light-emitting object in your CG scene doesn't necessarily need its own Maya light. Rendering tricks such as *glow* (for glow effects, see "Lighting Effects" later in this chapter) can simulate the effect that a light is turned on without actually having to use a Maya light. Of course, if you need the practical light to illuminate something in the scene, you need to create a light for it.

Maya Lights

Six types of light are available in Maya: Ambient, Directional, Point, Spot, Area, and Volume. These lights are also used when rendering in mental ray. How you use each dictates whether they become key, fill, or rim lights. Each light can fill any of those roles, although some are better for certain jobs than others. The most commonly used light types for most scenes are Spot, Directional, and Ambient. All of these Maya lights render in Maya software as well as mental ray.

To create each light, choose Create → Lights, and click the light type.

Common Light Attributes

Figure 10.8

A typical light's Attribute Editor

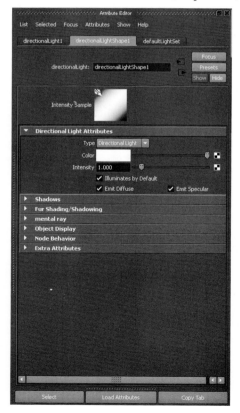

Lights in Maya are treated like any other object node. They can be transformed, rotated, scaled, duplicated, deleted, and so forth and are visible as nodes in the Hypergraph and Outliner alongside other objects in the scene. Like any other node, lights have attributes that govern how they function. Figure 10.8 shows the Attribute Editor for a typical light.

When you select any light type and then open the Attribute Editor, you'll see the following attributes and options:

Type This drop-down menu sets the type of light. You can change from one light type to another (for instance, from Spot to Point) at any time.

Color This attribute controls the color cast by the light. The darker the color, the dimmer the light will be. You can use Color in conjunction with Intensity to govern brightness, although it's best to leave that to Intensity only.

Intensity This attribute specifies how much light is cast. The higher the intensity, the brighter the illumination will be.

Illuminates by Default This check box deals with *light linking,* or the ability to illuminate specific objects with specific lights. Clearing this check box causes the light not to illuminate all objects by default, requiring you to link the light to objects you do want it to light. Keep this check box checked unless you're linking lights to specific objects. This chapter will briefly touch on light linking later.

Figure 10.9

Lights can render diffuse or specular components if needed.

Full render   Diffuse only render   Specular only render

Emit Diffuse and Emit Specular These two check boxes aren't available with the Ambient light type. For all other light types, they toggle on or off the ability to cast diffuse lighting or specular highlights on an object (see Figure 10.9). This is useful for creating specific lighting effects. For example, if lighting an object makes it too shiny, you can disable the specular emission from one or more of the lights on that object to reduce the glare.

Light Types

Beyond the common light attributes, each light type carries its own attributes that govern its particular settings.

Ambient Lights

Ambient lights cast an even light across the entire scene. These lights are great for creating a quick, even illumination in a scene; but, as you can see in Figure 10.10, they run the risk of flattening the composition. They're perhaps best used sparingly and at low intensities as fill lights or background lights.

The Ambient Shade slider in the Attribute Editor governs how flat the lighting is. The lower the value, the flatter the lighting. Figure 10.11 shows the effect of two contrasting Ambient Shade settings.

Figure 10.10

Ambient light

Figure 10.11

A low Ambient Shade setting flattens the image.

Ambient Shade = 0.1   Ambient Shade = 1.0

Directional Lights

Directional lights cast a light in a general direction evenly across the scene (see Figure 10.12). These lights are perhaps second to Spot lights as the most commonly used light type.

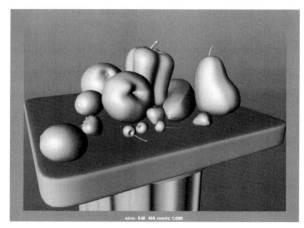

They're perfect for sunlight or general indoor lighting, for key lights, and for fill and back lights. They give an accurate sense of direction without having to emanate from a specific source.

Point Lights

A *Point light* casts light from a single specific point in space, similar to a bare light bulb. Its light is spread evenly from the emission point (see Figure 10.13).

Using the Decay Rate drop-down menu in the Attribute Editor, you can set how a Point light's intensity diminishes over distance. With No Decay, the Point light illuminates an object far away as evenly as it does up close.

Figure 10.12
Directional light

This is the most common setting for most applications.

Setting the Decay Rate to Linear, Quadratic, or Cubic requires you to increase the intensity level exponentially to compensate for the decay. You can use Decay Rate settings to illuminate nearby objects and to leave distant ones unaffected. In reality, lights have decay rates. But in CG, they don't really need to decay unless the falloff effect is needed, as shown in Figure 10.14. Clever lighting can easily avoid this cumbersome calculation.

Point lights are good for effects such as candlelight or setting a mood.

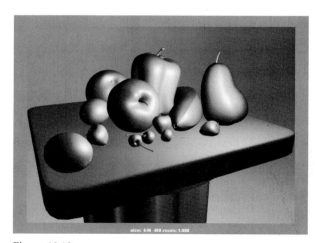

Figure 10.13

A Point light placed in the front right of frame

Figure 10.14

A Point light with a Decay Rate set

Spot Lights

Spot lights are arguably the most-used lights in Maya because they can be used for keys, fills, or rims; and they're highly efficient, casting light in specific areas, just like real spotlights.

Similar to Directional lights, Spot lights emphasize direction. But these lights emit from a specific point and radiate out in a cone shape, whereas a Directional light emits from an infinite source from a certain direction. As such, Spot lights can create a circular focus of light on the geometry much like a flashlight on a wall; Directionals spread the light evenly. Figure 10.15 shows a Spot light on the still life.

Figure 10.15
Using a Spot light

The following attributes govern the behavior of Spot lights:

Decay Rate Specifies the rate at which the light's intensity falls off with distance, as with the Point light. Again, the intensity needs to increase exponentially to account for any decay.

Cone Angle Sets the width of the cone of light emitted by the Spot light. The wider a cone, the more calculation intensive it becomes.

Penumbra Angle Specifies how much the intensity at the edges of the cone and hence the circular focus dissipates. (See Figure 10.16.) A negative value softens the light into the width of the cone, decreasing the size of the focus; a positive value softens away from the cone.

Dropoff Specifies how much light is decayed along the distance of the cone. The higher the dropoff, the dimmer the light gets farther along the length of the cone. This effect is much better to use than a decay rate, and it gives similar results.

Most practical lights are created with Spot lights. For example, a desk lamp's light is best simulated with a Spot light. Spot lights are also the lights of choice to cast shadows. You'll find more on shadows later in the chapter.

Figure 10.16

The Penumbra Angle attribute controls the softness of the edge of a Spot light.

Penumbra = 0   Penumbra = –10   Penumbra = 10

Area Lights

Area lights emit light from a flat rectangular shape only (see Figure 10.17). They behave similarly to Point lights, except they emit from an area and not from a single point. You can still set a decay rate, just as you can with Point lights. Area lights are the only lights whose scale affects their intensity. The larger an Area light, the brighter the light.

Because you can control the size of the area of light being emitted, these lights are good for creating effects such as a sliver of light falling onto an object from a crack in a door, as in Figure 10.18, overhead skylights, or the simulation of large diffused lighting fixtures such as overhead office lights. Use Area lights when you need to light a specific area of an object.

Volume Lights

Volume lights emit light from a specific 3D volumetric area as opposed to an Area light's flat rectangle (see Figure 10.19). Proximity is important for a Volume light, as is its scale.

Figure 10.17

An Area light and its placement

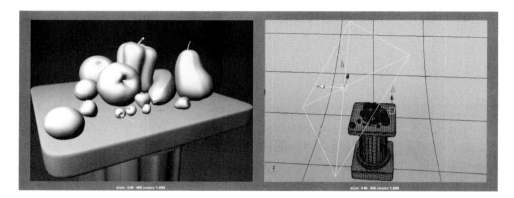

Figure 10.18

An Area light as a sliver, and its placement

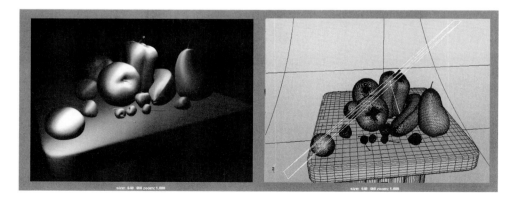

Figure 10.19

**A Volume light
and placement**

A Volume light can have the following attributes:

Light Shape A Volume light can be in the shape of a sphere, a box, a cylinder, or a cone. You select a shape from the Light Shape drop-down menu.

Color Range This section of attributes sets the color of the light using a built-in ramp. The ramp (from right to left) specifies the color from inside to outside. For instance, a white-to-black ramp from right to left creates a white light at the center of the Volume light that grades down to black toward the outer edge.

Volume Light Dir This attribute sets the direction for the light's color range. Outward lights from inside out, Inward lights from the volume's edge into the center, and Down Axis lights as a gradient in an axis of the light.

Arc and Cone End Radius This attribute defines the shape for the volume.

Penumbra For cylinder and cone shapes, this attribute adjusts how much the light dims along the edge of its length.

Use Volume lights when you need to control the specific area in which light is cast or when you need an object to move into and out of a particular area of light. Volume lights are also great for creating volumetric lighting effects such as areas of lit fog. For volumetric effects, see the section "Volumetric Lighting" later in this chapter.

Lighting a Scene

It's best to start with just a couple types of light, such as Directional and Spot, before turning to the more sophisticated types, such as Area and Volume.

Getting the essence of lighting is far more important in the beginning than understanding the nuances of all the attributes of a light. At first, limit yourself to Spots and Directionals, and try to avoid any Ambient light use.

Light Linking

You can control which lights illuminate which objects by using Maya's *light linking*. Inevitably, a time will come when you want to create a special light for a part of your scene but not for all of it. You'll need to create a special relationship, a connection from a special light or lights to specific objects and not to others.

Figure 10.20

The Light
Linking window

By default, lights created in your scene illuminate all objects in the scene. The easiest way to create an exclusive lighting relationship is first to create a light and turn off Illuminates by Default in the light's Attribute Editor. This ensures that this light won't cast light on any object unless specifically made to do so through light linking.

To assign your new light to the object(s) you want to illuminate exclusively, choose Window → Relationship Editors → Light Linking → Light-Centric. This opens the Relationship Editor and sets it for light linking. Light-Centric means the lights are featured in the left side of the panel as shown in Figure 10.20, and the objects in your scene that will be lit are on the right.

As you can see in Figure 10.21, the still life is lit evenly, and adding a new light with Illuminates by Default disabled won't increase the light level in the scene.

Figure 10.21

All of the scene's
lights illuminate
the scene.

Now, select the light you want to link—in this case, the directionalLight2 you just created—and the objects in the scene you'd like to link to—in this case, the apple and the pepper, as shown in Figure 10.22. Notice that no other objects on the right side of the Relationship Editor are selected; this means they will receive no illumination from this light source. When you render your scene, the objects you linked are e lit by the new light. In this case, the apple and the pepper are brighter than the other fruit in the still life. (See Figure 10.23.)

When you're in Lighted mode (press 7 in the Shaded panel), however, keep in mind that linked lights aren't taken into account in the view panel displays. The linking comes through in the render. Light linking works with Maya Software rendering and mental ray rendering.

Figure 10.22

Select the scene objects to link to the Directional light.

Figure 10.23

A linked light creates extra light for only the apple and the pepper behind it. The other objects aren't illuminated by that light.

Adding Shadows

Don't be too quick to create an abundance of light in your scene—eager to show off your models and textures. Shrouding objects in darkness and shadow is just as important as revealing them in light. You can say a lot visually by not showing parts of a whole, leaving some interpretation to the audience.

A careful balance of light and dark is important for a composition. As Figure 10.24 shows, the realism of a scene is greatly increased with the simple addition of well-placed shadows. Don't be afraid of the dark. Use it liberally, but in balance.

Figure 10.24

Darkness and shadow help add a sense of realism, depth, and mood to an otherwise simple still life.

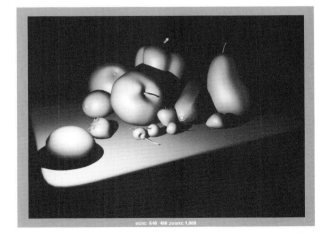

Creating Shadows in Maya

Maya lights don't cast shadows by default; you need to enable this feature in the light's Attribute Editor. When you do that, however, lights can cast shadows in one of two ways, depending on how the scene is rendered.

The more common method of the two is to create shadows by using Depth Map shadows. When you enable *shadow maps* (by clicking the Use Depth Map Shadows check box in the Shadows area of a light's

Figure 10.25

A Directional light with Depth Map shadows renders faster and is usually detailed enough.

Figure 10.26

A Directional light with raytraced shadows produces more detailed shadows but sometimes renders more slowly.

Attribute Editor), Maya generates shadow maps that locate where shadows fall by following the path of the light backward from the lighted object to the light itself. Shadow maps create fast, fairly accurate shadows through Maya's renderer. See the next section on how to create shadow map shadows.

The second method for casting shadows is achieved by raytracing with Maya's software renderer. *Raytracing* involves tracing a ray of light from every light source in all directions and tracing the reflection to the camera lens. Therefore, you can create more accurate shadows with raytracing. However, this render can take longer to calculate, particularly when using soft shadows. Later in this chapter, you'll learn how to create raytraced as well as soft shadows.

You need to turn on raytraced shadows for each light when you want more accurate shadows: either soft and diffused or sharp and crisp-edged, as well as enabling raytracing in the Render Settings window. See Figures 10.25 and 10.26.

Shadow Map Shadows

For every light type except Ambient, you can turn on shadow maps through the light type's Attribute Editor, as shown in Figure 10.27.

The depth-map Resolution defaults at 512. The higher this resolution, the better defined the shadows. Figure 10.25 was rendered with a depth map Resolution of 4096, a very high value. Figure 10.28 is the same render with a depth map Resolution of 768. Most shadows are detailed enough with a depth map Resolution of 1024.

Directional lights aren't the best lights to use for detailed shadow-map shadows because they require a high resolution for the maps; however, their raytraced shadows are extremely well done, as shown in Figure 10.26.

Spot lights create shadow maps with greater accuracy at lower depth-map Resolution settings and faster render times. As such, Spots are preferred to Directionals for shadow-casting lights. Figure 10.29 shows the same render with a Spot light and a depth map Resolution setting of only 1024, one-fourth the size of the Directional light's depth-map Resolution.

Figure 10.28

The depth map Resolution setting affects shadow quality for shadow maps.

Figure 10.27

Turning on shadow maps in the Attribute Editor for a Directional light

Figure 10.29

Spot lights cast faster and more detailed shadow-map shadows.

Trying to squeeze a detailed shadow map from a Directional light with an absurdly high depth-map Resolution setting can even crash your system. In these cases, it's wiser to use raytraced shadows.

Raytraced Shadows

To enable raytraced shadows, turn on the light's Use Ray Trace Shadows setting in the Attribute Editor (see Figure 10.27 earlier in this chapter), and enable the Raytracing

Figure 10.30

The Spot light shown in Figure 10.29, now has raytraced shadows.

check box under the Raytracing Quality heading in the Render Settings window. Choose Window → Rendering Editors → Render Settings, or click the Render Settings icon ( ) in the Status line.

Figure 10.30 shows the Spot light from Figure 10.29, this time rendered with a raytraced shadow. Notice that there isn't much difference in the renders at this point with simple shadows like these. However, as you'll see with soft shadows later in this chapter, raytracing shadows can make a big difference in the look of your renders.

For an object that has a transparency map applied to its shader, however, only raytraced shadows can cast proper shadows. On the left in Figure 10.31 is a plane with a mapped checkerboard transparency casting a raytraced shadow over the still life. On the right is the same light using shadow maps instead of raytraced shadows.

Figure 10.31

Only raytraced shadows work with transparencies.

Raytraced Shadow   Shadow Map Shadow

Controlling Shadows per Object

To better control your lighting, you can specify whether an object can cast and receive shadows in Maya. For example, if you have geometry casting light in front of a shadow, but you don't want it to cast a shadow, you can manually turn off that feature for that object only.

To turn off shadow casting for an object, select the object and open its Attribute Editor. In the Render Stats section is a group of check boxes that control the render properties of the object, as shown in Figure 10.32. Clear the Casts Shadows check box. If you don't want the object to receive shadows, clear the Receive Shadows check box.

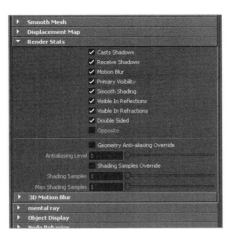

Figure 10.32

You easily can set whether an object casts or receives shadows.

Raytracing Soft Shadows

One interesting feature of shadows is that they can diffuse or soften as the shadow falls from its casting object. This small detail can greatly enhance the reality of any render. In Figure 10.33, you can see the still life rendered with sharp raytraced shadows.

However, softening shadows even in a small scene like this can help the look of the render. In Figure 10.34, you see the same render but this time with softening shadows. Notice how the shadow softens more toward the edge of the shadow; the shadow is still sharp at the point of contact.

This gives a much nicer feeling of depth to the scene. There is an increase in render time—it's important to evaluate how much softening you need so you don't overdo the look or increase the render time too much.

Figure 10.33

Regular raytraced shadows

Figure 10.34

Softening the shadows creates a nice effect.

Using soft shadows is easy. Simply select the light, and open its Attribute Editor. Under the Shadows heading, in the Raytrace Shadow Attributes heading, enable Use Ray Trace Shadows, and then set a Light Radius as shown in Figure 10.35. The higher the radius value, the softer the shadow will become. For Directional lights, however, the attribute is called Light Angle.

Figure 10.35

Create a soft shadow with Light Radius.

Whenever you increase the Light Radius, you must also increase the number of Shadow Rays to compensate for quality issues. Figure 10.36 shows the soft shadows with a Shadow Rays value of only 1 (default value). To achieve the smoothness of the render shown in Figure 10.34, Light Radius was increased to 0.30 and Shadow Rays was increased to 12.

Make sure you enable Raytracing in the Render Settings, of course. These soft ray-traced shadows work both in Maya Software rendering as well as mental ray rendering.

Figure 10.36

Increase the Shadow Rays value to better the quality; this render had only 1 Shadow Ray with a Light Radius of 0.3.

mental ray Lighting

mental ray lighting and rendering opens up a large range of possibilities within Maya. As with all rendering, lighting plays the primary role. We'll cover mental ray rendering more in the next chapter; but because rendering and lighting go hand in hand, it's tough to ignore it in this chapter. This section is a primer on mental ray light functionality.

Open the Render Settings window by choosing Window → Rendering Editors → Render Settings. If you don't see the mental ray for Maya (or any other, such as the Vector) option in the Render Using drop-down menu, you need to load the plug-in. Choose Window → Settings/ Preferences → Plug-in Manager to open the Plug-in Manager. Make sure Mayatomr.mll is checked for Loaded as well as for Auto Load to ensure that it loads by default.

Two important functions that mental ray brings to the Maya table are caustics and global illumination (GI). *Caustics* is the scattering of light reflections off and through semitransparent objects, such as the light that shines on the ceiling of an indoor pool or the sunshine at the bottom of an outdoor pool. *Global illumination* is the effect of light reflected from one object to another. For example, if you place colored spheres inside a gray box and shine a light into the box, the walls and floor of that box pick up the color of the spheres. The light from the spheres reflects onto the walls and tints them with the spheres'

Figure 10.37

The Maya Software render of the box of spheres scene

color. Furthermore, the light from the floor of the box bounces and helps illuminate the underside of the balls.

For example, Figure 10.37 shows a scene file that has a dozen or so glass spheres inside an enclosed box. The box has four holes in the top, and two spotlights with shadows turned on are positioned outside the box, shining in through the holes. Figure 10.37 shows a typical software render. The spheres under the holes are visible, and the rest of the box is in shadow.

However, when rendering through mental ray for Maya (see Figure 10.38), the light that enters the box bounces around the scene and illuminates the other spheres. The color of the spheres also colors the area immediately around them due to GI. Additionally, the light shines through the semitransparent spheres and casts caustic highlights on the floor. (You can see the full effect in the color section of this book.)

Figure 10.38

The mental ray for Maya render of the scene in Figure 10.37

Global Illumination: A downloadable PDF Exercise

Global illumination and caustics are both advanced lighting effects and won't be covered in this book. However, a short GI exercise from a previous version of this book is available for download from www.sybex.com/go/intromaya2011. However, all the scene files for this exercise are on the book's CD for your reference. Once you download the exercise, you can use Adobe Acrobat and the scene files on the CD to run through this living-room exercise, where you use simple GI techniques to explore this powerful rendering option in mental ray.

Image-Based Lighting

mental ray also brings image-based lighting (IBL) to Maya. This method of lighting uses an image, typically a High Dynamic Range Image (HDRI), to illuminate the scene using Final Gather or GI. Final Gather is a form of global illumination that relies on direct as well as indirect illumination. Direct illumination calculates the amount of light coming directly from lights in the scene and renders the result. However, it misses an important aspect of real-life lighting: diffuse reflections of light. Indirect illumination happens when light bounces off objects in a scene in order to reach and therefore light the rest of the scene—that is, diffuse reflections. Final Gather is typically a faster way than GI to get indirect illumination in a scene.

We'll briefly touch on Final Gather here as we explore Physical Sun and Sky lighting in the next section. However, we'll cover both IBL and Final Gather in depth in Chapter 11 when you light the decorative box model and apply displacement maps for its details.

mental ray Physical Sun and Sky

An impressive function in mental ray for Maya has been the implementation of a Physical Sun and Sky lighting methodology. In this method, mental ray for Maya creates nodes in your scene to simulate an open-air sunlight effect for your scene lighting. It's a quick way to create a nice-looking render. You'll place the textured red wagon into an open scene and apply a Physical Sun and Sky (PSAS) in the following exercise.

Figure 10.39

Enable mental ray rendering in Render Settings.

You can use your own scene with the textured red wagon from Chapter 6, or set your project to the RedWagon project and then load WagonSunlight_v01.ma from the Lighting project on the CD to follow along. Keep in mind that if you use your own scene, your camera angles and look won't be an exact match to the figures in the book. Follow these steps:

1. The camera for this scene is already set up for a somewhat interesting angle of the wagon in the persp panel. Switch to mental ray rendering in the Render Using pull-down menu at the top of the Render Settings window, as shown in Figure 10.39.

2. Open the Render Settings, and click the Indirect Lighting tab. In the Environment heading, click the Create button next to Physical Sun and Sky. The Attribute Editor opens for the mia_physicalsky1 node you just created, as shown in Figure 10.40.

3. Render a frame in the Perspective window, and compare to Figure 10.41. It's a bit bright, but there's something very nice about this render. Notice that the metal handlebar takes on a good look right off the bat.

4. The render is too bright, and the wood slats for the railings shouldn't be reflective. Your render should also show that the fire-engine red of the wagon is a bit washed out.

   Let's first address the wood railings. Open the Hypershade, and double-click the first Wood shader. Set Reflectivity down to 0.1 from 0.5. Repeat for the second Wood shader.

5. In the Render View window, click and drag a box region around the wood railings, as shown in Figure 10.42. Click the Render Region button ( ) to render that part of the frame only.

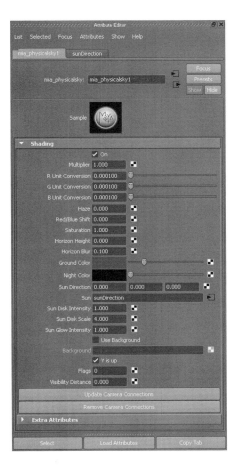

Figure 10.40
The physicalsky1 node.

Figure 10.41
The first PSAS render doesn't look too shabby.

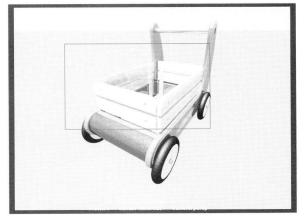

Figure 10.42
Render this region to check the reflection in the wood railings.

6. The wood looks much better now, so let's move on to the brightness of the scene. Open the Render Settings window, and go into the Indirect Lighting tab. Click the Input arrow next to the Physical Sun and Sky attribute's button (Figure 10.43). Doing so opens the Attribute Editor for the Physical Sun and Sky.

7. Set Multiplier to 0.5 from 1.0, and re-render the frame. The brightness comes down nicely, and the wagon is less blown out than your previous renders. See Figure 10.44.

Figure 10.43

Click to open the attributes for the daylight system.

Figure 10.44

Bringing down the brightness of the Sun

8. Let's play with the direction of the Sun. Look in your persp panel, and you see a Directional light sitting smack in the middle of the scene. Maya uses this light to set the direction of the sunlight, and it doesn't contribute to the lighting of the scene in any other way. Only its rotation is important to PSAS. Its intensity, color, and other attributes are irrelevant. In this scene, the Directional light is called sunDirection and is in the wagon behind the third texture placement node, as you can see in Figure 10.45. The light is currently pointing sunlight almost straight down, as if the Sun is high in the sky. It seems as if it's about noon. RotateY for the sunDirection light is -75.

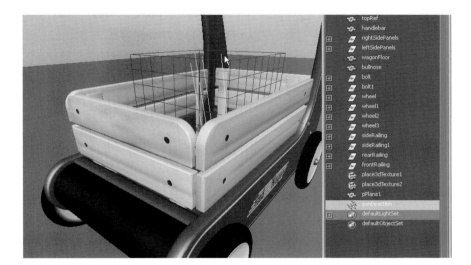

Figure 10.45

The sunDirection light adjusts only the direction of the sunlight in the scene.

9. That third texture placement node is getting in the way. To turn off its display easily, in the persp panel, click Show → Textures to uncheck it. The green box disappears in this view until you turn it back on through the Show menu. Now that you can see the Directional light better, you see that the Sun is pointed slightly toward the back of the wagon. Rotate the light so that it's angled away from the camera even more, as shown in Figure 10.46. The sunDirection's RotateY should be about -25.

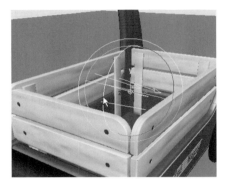

Figure 10.46

Angle the Sun further away from the camera.

10. Render the frame, and you'll see quite a difference in the scene. Maya automatically adjusts PSAS settings to make the render appear as if the Sun is about to set. This is because of the new angle. The scene (shown in Figure 10.47) not only shows a new lighting direction (the shadows fall toward the back and are longer) but also is a darker and warmer light, as if it were mid-to-late afternoon.

11. Angle the sunDirection light even more (so RotateY is at about -2.5), almost parallel with the ground plane, and render a frame. Now the Sun has all but set, and it's dark dusk, just before night falls on the scene. See Figure 10.48.

Figure 10.47

Now it's late afternoon.

Figure 10.48

It's getting late; you should get home before nightfall.

12. Rotate the sunDirection even more so that it's at a RotateY of about 15. It's now dark, and you can barely make out the wagon. See Figure 10.49. Time to go home before your mom gets mad. Remember, you can adjust the overall brightness of the scene by adjusting the mia_physicalsky1 node attributes, as you did in steps 6 and 7.

You can add lights to the scene as well; you aren't limited to the system's results. For example, Figure 10.50 shows a render of the wagon with the Sun beginning to rise behind it, making the foreground a bit dark. Figure 10.51 shows the same render, but with an added Directional light (with an Intensity of just 0.25) pointing toward the front of the wagon. This helps define the front of the wagon, hinting that there is another light source, perhaps a porch light behind the camera.

Figure 10.49

Ooh, it's dark—Mom's gonna be mad.

Figure 10.50

The sun also rises!

The PSAS system is pretty slick. It can get you some fairly nice results quickly. Keep experimenting with different sunDirection angles as well as the attributes for the system to see what results you can get for your scene. Add lights to create areas of detail in your model.

Unbeknownst to you, when you invoked the PSAS system, Maya turned on Final Gather in the mental ray settings. This enabled indirect lighting to work in the scene. We'll explore Final Gather in the next chapter.

We'll also explore conventionally lighting the wagon scene and bringing out its details for rendering starting at the end of this chapter and continuing into the next chapter. There, we'll introduce HDRI and image-based lighting for a fairly photoreal rendering of the wagon.

This is the perfect time for a break, so save your work (as if I have to tell you that at this point!) and go grab some iced tea and rest your eyes for a bit. In the next section, we'll go over various special lighting effects before returning to the wagon.

Figure 10.51

Adding a light to illuminate the front of the wagon in this sunrise scene from Figure 10.50

Lighting Effects

In CG, you must fake certain traits of light in the real world. Using certain methods, you can create smoky light beams, glowing lights, and lens flares. Although some of these effects fall under the domain of rendering and shader tricks, they're best explored in the context of lighting, because they're created by light in the real world.

Volumetric Lighting

How do you create an effect such as a flashlight beam shining through fog? This lighting effect is called *volumetric lighting,* and you can use it to create some stunning results that can sometimes be time consuming to render.

You can't apply volumetric effects to Ambient and Directional light types. To add a volumetric effect to any of the other types of lights, select the light and, in the Attribute Editor under the Light Effects section, click the checkered Map button to the right of the Light Fog attribute. This creates a new render node that appears in the Hypershade window. After you click the Map button, the Attribute Editor takes you to the lightFog node.

Maya handles volumetric lights by attaching a lightFog node to the light. The Color and Density attributes under this node control the brightness, thickness, and color of the fog attached to that light. Furthermore, in the light's Attribute Editor, you can control the fog with the Fog Spread and Fog Intensity settings. Fog Intensity increases the brightness of the fog, and Fog Spread controls how well the fog is defined within its confines. For example, a Spot light with a fog shows the fog in its cone. Figure 10.52 shows how Fog Spread affects the conical fog shape.

Figure 10.52

Fog Spread affects how the fog dissipates to the edges of the cone.

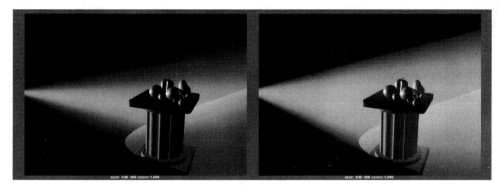

Fog Spread = 0.5   Fog Spread = 2.0

To remove a fog effect, right-click the Light Fog label in the light's Attribute Editor, and choose Break Connection from the shortcut menu.

If you want the light fog-cast shadows to make rays of light within the fog, check Use Depth Map Shadows for the light. You'll have to increase the depth-map Resolution for a higher-quality image.

Lens Flare

Lens flare and *light glow*, as illustrated in Figure 10.53, mimic the real-world effect created when light strikes a lens or when the light source is visible in the frame. The flare is created when the light hits the lens at a particular angle and causes a reflection of itself in the optics of the lens.

Figure 10.53

Light glow and lens flare turned on for the back light

To enable a light glow, under the Light Effects section in the light's Attribute Editor, click the checkered Map button next to the Light Glow attribute to create an OpticalFX node that appears in the Hypershade. The Attribute Editor shifts focus to that new node, which controls the behavior of the light glow and lens flare. The OpticalFX node contains the following attributes and settings:

Glow Type Setting this attribute specifies the kind of glow: Linear, Exponential, Ball, Lens Flare, and Rim Halo. These define the size and shape of the glow from the light.

Figure 10.54
**Glow Radial
Noise attribute**

Glow Radial Noise = 0   Glow Radial Noise = 0.5

Halo Type Specifying a halo creates a foggy halo around the light in addition to the glow. You can find controls for the halo under the Halo section in the Attribute Editor.

Star Points Setting this attribute specifies the number of star points the glow generates.

Rotation Setting this attribute rotates the orientation of the star points.

Radial Frequency Used in conjunction with the Glow Radial Noise attribute (see the next item) in the Glow section, this attribute defines the smoothness of any added glow noise.

Glow Radial Noise Setting this attribute adds noise to the glow effect, creating light and dark patches within the glow for a more random look, as shown in Figure 10.54.

Glow Color Setting this attribute specifies the color of the glow.

Glow Intensity and Spread Setting these attributes specifies the brightness and thickness of the glow and how well it fades away.

To turn on a lens flare along with the light glow, click the Lens Flare check box at upper right in the Attribute Editor for OpticalFX. The attributes under the Lens Flare section control the look of the flare.

Light glows and flares can be highly effective in scenes, adding credibility to the lighting; but they're often misused or, worse, overused in CG. Used sparingly and with subtlety, lens flares can go a long way toward adding a nice touch to your scene.

Shader Glow Effects

To create a glowing effect, it's sometimes better to place a glow on a geometry's shader instead of the light itself. Because a light must be seen in the shot and pointed at the camera to see any light glow and flare, a shader glow is sometimes more desirable. This process will composite a glow on the object assigned the Glow shader to simulate a volumetric light, such as a street lamp on a foggy night. Shader glows have far less render cost than true volumetric lights.

Try This To light a still-life scene, follow these steps:

1. Open the still_life_v03.mb file in the Lighting project on the CD. Create a Spot light, place it over the still life, and aim it directly down onto the fruit, as shown in Figure 10.55. Turn on Use Depth Map Shadows for the light, and set Resolution to 1024. Set Penumbra Angle to 10 and Intensity to 1.5. Press 7 for Lighted mode in the Camera1 view panel to see how the light is being cast.

2. The Spot light provides the practical light in the scene. You'll place a bare bulb on a wire directly above the fruit. Create a NURBS sphere, and position it right over the fruit but in the frame for camera1 to see. In the Render Stats section of the Attribute Editor for the sphere, turn off Casts Shadows.

3. Create a long, thin cylinder for the light bulb's wire, and position it as if the bulb were hanging from it, as shown in Figure 10.56. Turn off Casts Shadows for the cylinder as well.

Figure 10.55

Aim a Spot light down toward the fruit.

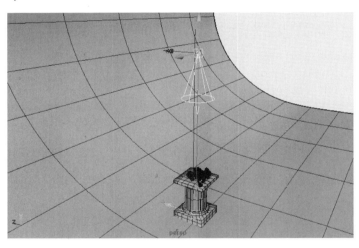

Figure 10.56

Place a bulb on a wire over the fruit pedestal.

4. Create a black Phong E shader to assign to the cylinder.

5. Create a Phong shader for the bulb, and assign it to the NURBS sphere. Set its Color to a pale, light yellow, and make it about 50 percent transparent.

6. Select the Spot light, and set its Color to the same yellow. You can do this easily through the Color Chooser. With the shader for the bulb selected, open the Color Chooser by clicking the pale yellow color you just made. Click the right arrow to place the yellow color in the swatches to the right of the main color swatch, or right-click any of the swatches.

7. Pick the Spot light, and click its Color attribute to set the Color Chooser to that color. Click the yellow swatch you created to get the same color on the light. For detail's sake, make the light's color less saturated. Click Accept to close the Color Chooser window.

Figure 10.57

The bare light bulb over the still life is created with a shader glow.

8. To make the shader glow for the bulb, open the Hypershade and select the bulb's Phong material. In the Attribute Editor's Special Effects section, drag the Glow Intensity slider from 0 to 1.0. If you render the frame, you see that the glow isn't quite enough to make a convincing light bulb. In the Hypershade, select the shaderGlow1 node; this node controls all the glows in the scene.

9. Set Quality to 0.1. In the Glow Attributes section, set Glow Intensity to 6.0, set Glow Spread to 0.5, and set Glow Radial Noise to 0.2.

The scene file `still_life_v04.mb` on the CD contains the full scene for your reference. See Figure 10.57 for the final result.

Lighting the Decorative Box

In this section, you'll set up the Decorative Box scene with lights so that you can render them in the next chapter using displacement maps, HDRI, mental ray, and Final Gather to match the lighting in a photo of the real box. Because most of your "lighting" look results from using an HDR image, the lighting you'll start with will be basic for now.

The lighting conditions you'll use as a starting point are shown in Figure 10.58 as well as in the Color Section of this book. You can see that there is a primary key light coming from the right side of the image, slightly from the front, with a good fill from the left side and from top back, which also gives a bit of a rim light. These lights will be easy to set up to get the general feel first. The finesse of this exercise will come from rendering through mental ray in the next chapter, using an HDR IBL, adding reflections to the box, adding displacement maps for the intricate carvings, and adjusting the shaders to taste. In the following exercise, you'll create a basic lighting setup for the decorative box and get a direct lighting solution first.

Figure 10.58

Lighting the decorative box using this practical lighting as reference.

Set your current project to the Decorative_Box project, which you should have already copied to your hard drive from the CD. To begin lighting, open the boxLighting01.mb scene file from the Scenes folder of the project. Then, follow these steps:

1. Create a new camera that you can use to render the scene. You'll keep using the persp camera to navigate through the scene. In one of the other view panels, click Panels → Perspective → New. Persp1 is created. Then, choose View → Camera Attribute Editor. Maya shows you the persp1Shape tab.

    In the Output Settings heading, make sure the Renderable box is checked. Click the persp1 tab in the Attribute Editor, and rename the camera from persp1 to **renderCam** (persp1Shape is automatically renamed to renderCamShape).

    Select the original persp camera, and, in the Attribute Editor, make sure the Renderable box is unchecked. This ensures that only the correct camera (renderCam) will render.

2. Select the renderCam again, and set its Focal Length attribute to 50. This places a 50mm lens on the renderCam to better match the camera taking the photo in Figure 10.58. Setup the renderCam to approximate the same angle of view in that photo.

3. Press Ctrl+A to toggle off the Attribute Editor and show the Channel Box. In the Channel Box, select the renderCam's Translate and Rotate attributes, right-click, and select Lock Selected from the context menu shown in Figure 10.59. Doing so locks the camera in place, disallowing you from moving it. This way, you won't accidentally mess up the view. To be able to move that camera again, highlight those attributes, right-click them, and select Unlock Selected from the context menu.

Figure 10.59

Lock the camera in place.

4. In the renderCam panel, press 6 for textured display and then 7 for lighted and textured display. This way, you can more easily see how you orient the lights.

5. Using the persp view, create a Directional light for the key light, and place it on the right side of the box, slightly in front, and angled down at about 45 degrees as shown in Figure 10.60. Set the Intensity to 1.5, and turn on Use Ray Trace Shadows under the Shadows → Raytrace Shadow Attributes heading.

Figure 10.60

Create the key light, and place it as shown.

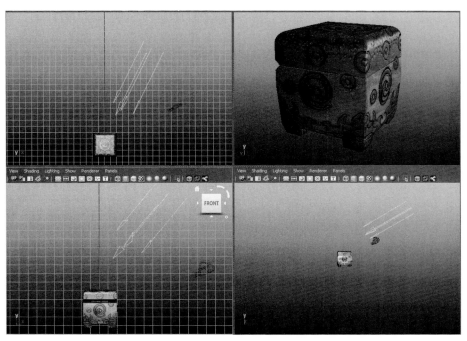

6. Create another Directional light, and place it as the fill light from the opposite angle from the left side and a bit higher and angled down more than the key light, as shown in Figure 10.61. Set Intensity to 0.35, and turn on Use Ray Trace Shadows. Isn't this exciting?

7. Create a third Directional light. Place it behind the box on its left side, almost diametrically across from the camera, and a bit higher than the box, as shown in Figure 10.62, so you get a nice light grazing across the top of the box. Set Intensity to 0.5.

Figure 10.61

Create the fill light.

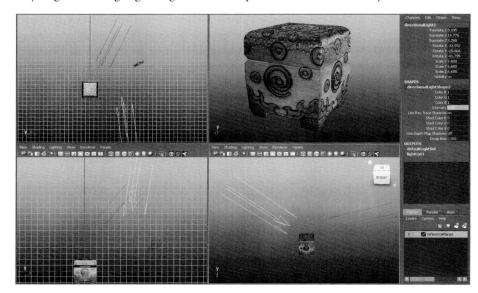

Figure 10.62

Create the back light.

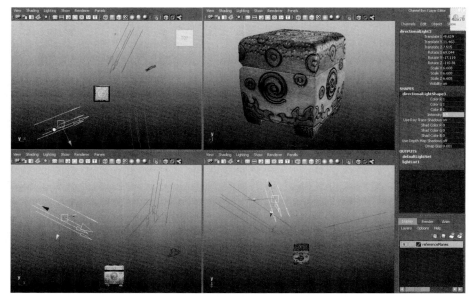

8. Create a poly plane, and scale it up to 50 in *X* and *Z*. Place it under the box to make a floor. Its default gray Lambert shader is fine for now. (See Figure 10.63.)

Figure 10.63

Create a floor plane.

9. Open the Render Settings window, and select mental ray as the renderer. This also automatically turns on raytracing, which you need for the shadows from the key and fill lights. Render a frame in the renderCam view.

   Figure 10.64 shows the first render with these three lights. Notice that the gray floor is reflecting in the box because you have a Phong shader assigned to it. You can use texture maps to adjust the reflective areas of the box and dial in the proper reflections in the next chapter as you render.

10. Select the key light (directionalLight1), and open the Attribute Editor. In the Raytrace Shadow Attributes heading, set a Light Angle of 3.5 and Shadows Rays of 64. Render. The primary shadowing on the floor looks much nicer.

    Select the fill light (directionalLight2), and set its Light Angle to 7 with Shadow Rays of 72 (see Figure 10.65). Play with the radii and number of rays to get the shadows to your liking. Notice how much longer the render takes with soft shadows enabled. You can temporarily use fewer Shadow Rays on your lights until you're ready for final renders, to save yourself some time. Just don't forget to turn those attributes back up to their full-quality looks!

Figure 10.64

The render doesn't look too bad with just the three-point lighting.

Figure 10.65

Much nicer shadows on the floor

11. You may be bothered by the low-quality settings on the render and the slight fuzziness of the wood texture on the box. Open the Hypershade, and click the Textures tab in the top part of the window to show the texture nodes in the scene. Select the box's color texture node (file1), and open the Attribute Editor. At the top, change Filter Type from the default Quadratic to Off. This prevents the renderer from slightly blurring the texture image to smooth it. (See Figure 10.66.)

12. Open the Render Settings window ( ), and click the Quality tab. Set Max Sample Level from 0 to 1. (See Figure 10.67.)

Figure 10.66

Turn off filtering for the color texture image.

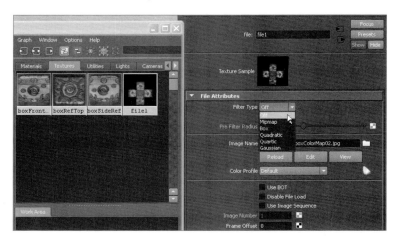

Figure 10.67

Select a slightly better render quality in the Render Settings window.

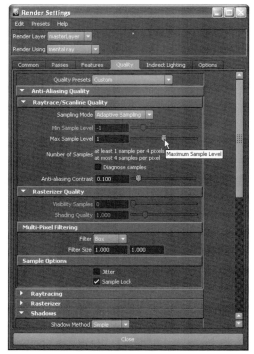

13. Save your previous render in the buffer by clicking the Keep Image icon () in the Render View window. A scroll bar appears at the bottom of the Render View win-

dow. Render a frame of the persp panel now that you've turned off filtering for the texture file and increased a quality setting. Use the scroll bar in the Render View to scrub back and forth between the older fuzzy render and the new unfiltered render. The box's decorative carvings and lines appear much stronger and crisper, as shown in Figure 10.68. It may be tough to compare the quality levels of the two renders in the book's black-and-white images, but you should notice them clearly in your Render View.

Figure 10.68

The render is much crisper and a bit cleaner.

You'll pick this exercise up from this point in Chapter 11, where you'll add more texture maps to control reflections as well as add carving detail and enable Final Gather to use an HDR image to light the scene. Woo!

The scene file boxLighting_v02.mb in the Scenes folder of the Decorative_Box project gives you this lighting setup.

Further Lighting Practice

Lighting professionals in the CG field are called on to find the most efficient way to light a scene and bring it to the peak of its beauty. Again, this only comes from experience. The best way to learn about lighting is to light some scenes. The best way to become a cracker-jack lighting artist is to spend months and years honing your eye and practicing the latest procedures, such as HDR lighting.

The file still_life_v01.mb in the Lighting project on the CD contains the scene of the still life with no lights so you can play with lighting and shadow methods as well as light linking to create some extra focus on some parts of the frame. The file still_life_v02.mb contains the same scene, but with three-point lighting already set up.

Notice in the still_life_v02.mb file that two lights make up the key light (spotLight1 and spotLight2). One light makes up the fill light (directionalLight1), and two lights (spotLight3 and spotLight4) make up the back light.

For practice, download some models from the Internet, and arrange them into your own still-life scenes to gain more lighting experience. Set up scenes, time the rendering process, and try to achieve the same lighting look using faster lighting setups that may not be as taxing on the renderer. Also, try taking pictures of situations and trying to match the lighting in the photo, as you're doing with the decorative box.

Try setting up simple scenes. Start with an indoor location that is lit by a single light bulb. Then, try the same scene in the following locations to expand your lighting repertoire:

1. A photography studio

2. Outside in the morning on a bright summer day

3. Outside at dusk in the fall

4. Outside at night under a street lamp

5. Inside on a window ledge

6. At the bottom of a closet lit by a nearby hallway light

Tips for Using and Animating Lights

When you're lighting a scene, invoking a lighting mode in your Perspective or Camera view panel will give you great feedback regarding the relative brightness and direction of your lights. Most computer system's graphics cards can handle a maximum of eight lights in Lighted mode; some professional cards can handle more.

You invoke Lighted mode by pressing the number 7 on your keyboard (not through the number pad on the side). You must first be in Shaded mode (press 5) or Texture mode (press 6) for Lighted mode. Remember that Lighted mode displays linked lights as if they're lighting the entire scene. This can cause some confusion, so it's wise to take notes on any light linking in your scene.

Maya's IPR renderer is also useful when lighting a scene. This almost-real-time updating renderer will give you a high-quality render of your scene as you adjust your lights. Chapter 11 will explore the IPR renderer.

Animating a Light

Any attribute of a light can be animated in the same way that you animate any other object attribute. You can't, however, animate a light's type. To edit a light's animation, you need only select the light and open the Graph Editor to access its keyframes. You can set keyframes on Intensity, Penumbra Angle, Color, and so on within the Channel Box or the Attribute Editor. Right-click the name of the attribute, and choose Key Selected from the shortcut menu.

By animating a light's intensity, you can simulate the real-world appearance of a light turning on or off. To turn on a light, create a quickly increasing curve so that its brightness arcs up slowly at first before climbing to full brightness. This animation mimics the way real lights turn on and off better than simply enabling or disabling them in your scene.

Animating the color of a light, as well as the color of a shader, sets keyframes for the color's RGB values as three separate keyframes. The Graph Editor shows a separate curve for the red, green, and blue channels of color when you animate a light's color. You can set all three keys at once by right-clicking the color attribute in the Attribute Editor and choosing Set Key from the context menu, as shown in Figure 10.69.

In addition, lights can be animated to be moved, scaled, and rotated like any other object. For further study, try animating the lighting for the simple scene(s) you set up to practice lighting from the previous section. Try creating animated lights to simulate a candle illuminating your scene, or a campfire, or the flashing emergency lights you would find in your average space-station airlock.

Figure 10.69

Set a key for the light.

Using the Show Manipulator Tool for Lights

An easy way to manipulate lights is to use their special manipulator (invoked by pressing T). For example, pressing T, or clicking the Show Manipulator icon () in the Tool Box, to select the Show Manipulator tool with a Spot light selected gives you two Translate manipulators in the view panel, as shown in Figure 10.70.

This allows you to move the source or target of the light to aim it better. By clicking the cyan circle that appears below the source's Translate manipulator, you can toggle through a number of manipulators to adjust the Spot light's settings, such as cone angle (two clicks clockwise) and penumbra angle (three clicks clockwise). The manipulator for cone angle is shown in Figure 10.71.

A Source and Target Translate manipulator is available for all light types through the Show Manipulator tool as well.

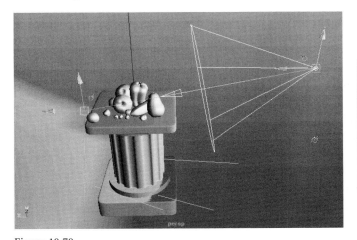

Figure 10.70

Using special manipulators to place and orient the Spot light

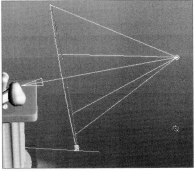

Figure 10.71

Adjusting the cone angle interactively with the special manipulator

Summary

This chapter explored lighting in Maya, beginning with basic concepts that included the three-point lighting technique. You then learned about the different lights in Maya, how they work, and how you can use light linking to control your scene better. Shadows are an important part of lighting and were covered next in this chapter, followed by a quick exploration of the Physical Sun and Sky system with mental ray and then lighting effects such as lens flare and light glows. You then created a simple lighting for the decorative box for a still rendering. Finally, you learned how to begin animating lights for use in your scenes.

Lighting is truly the linchpin of CG. It can make or break a scene with the flick of a switch. As you'll see in the next chapter, lighting goes hand in hand with rendering and shading, and the more you understand about all three functions, the better your scenes will look.

As mentioned, the trick to lighting is understanding how light works in the real world and how to approximate its effects in Maya. That comes with practice, so don't be afraid to experiment with lighting and shading schemes on all your projects.

CHAPTER 11

Maya Rendering

Rendering is the last step in creating your CG work. It's the process by which the computer calculates the surface properties, lighting, shadows, movement, and shape of objects, and it saves a sequence of images. Although the computer does all the thinking at this point, you still need to set up your cameras and the render to get exactly what you want.

This chapter will show you how to render out your scene using Maya's software renderer and how to create reflections and refractions. It will also introduce you to Maya's other rendering methods. In this chapter, you'll use a wine bottle and a still life from previous chapters, and you'll animate a camera to render out a sequence.

Topics in this chapter include:

- Rendering setup
- Previewing your render: the Render View window
- Reflections and refractions
- Using cameras
- Motion blur
- Batch rendering
- Rendering the wine bottle
- mental ray for Maya
- Render layers
- Final Gather
- Ambient occlusion
- HDRI
- Rendering the decorative box: displacement mapping, image-based lighting, and depth of field

Rendering Setup

When your scene is complete, you've had a celebration smoothie for your hard work, and you're ready to start a render, you'll need to set up how you want it rendered. Although this is the last part of the CG process, from now on you should be thinking about rendering all the way through your production. When you create models and textures with the final image in mind, and gear the lighting toward showing off the scene elegantly, the final touches are relatively easy to set up.

First, you decide which of the render engines included with Maya you'll use: Maya Software, Maya Hardware, mental ray for Maya (the most popular), or Maya Vector. Each engine has its own particular workflow and can yield entirely different results, although mental ray and Maya Software are close in look if you don't use the special features of mental ray. The choice of a rendering method depends on the final look you want and sometimes on the number of machines and licenses with which you can render. Maya's own Software rendering comes with an unlimited number of licenses, which means you can render on any machine you have (with Maya installed), although you can work with the Maya application only on as many machines for which you have licenses. There are also third-party developers in the CG field who have created other render engines that plug right into Maya, such as Vray for Maya, Maxwell, and Pixar's RenderMan for Maya.

No matter which renderer you use, the lighting and general setup are fairly common across the board. It's true, however, that some steps in the creation of your scene, from modeling to lighting, depend on which render engine you plan to use. It's a good idea to choose your render engine as you begin creating your scene. All in all, it's best to begin with Maya Software or basic mental ray to pick up the fundamentals of lighting, texturing, and rendering before you venture into mental ray's special features or try other renderers.

Regardless of the type of render, you need to specify a set of common attributes in the Render Settings window. As Figure 11.1 shows on the left, you use the options in this window to set up all your rendering preferences, including the resolution, file type, frame range, and so forth. Choose Window → Rendering Editors → Render Settings to open the Render Settings window.

The Render Settings window for Maya Software Rendering has two tabs: the Common tab and the Maya Software tab. The Common tab contains the settings common to all the rendering methods, such as image size. The Maya Software tab gives you access to render-specific attributes, such as quality settings, raytracing settings, motion blur, and so on.

If you switch the Render Using pull-down menu from the default Maya Software setting to mental ray, you'll notice several tabs: Passes, Features, Quality, Indirect Lighting, and Options, as shown on the right in Figure 11.1. These tabs give you access to all the settings for the incredibly powerful mental ray renderer.

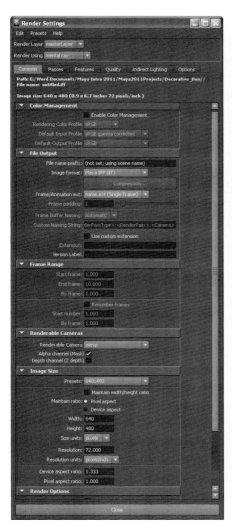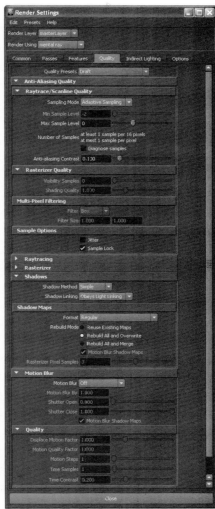

Figure 11.1

The Render Settings window

You may notice that some of the render engines don't show up in the Render Settings window right away. In this case, the renderers' respective plug-ins must be loaded first. We'll discuss this further in the section on mental ray for Maya in this chapter.

Choosing a Filename

Rendered images are identified by a filename, a frame number, and an extension, in the form *name.#.ext*: for example, `stilllife.0234.tif`.

In the File Name Prefix text box, enter the image sequence name. If you don't enter anything in this text box, Maya automatically names your rendered images after your scene file (`stilllife` in the example). When you're dealing with numerous scene files, this is the preferred naming convention; using it, you can immediately identify the scene file from which a particular image file was rendered. This is the preferred naming convention for most production houses, and using it is a good habit to establish.

The frame number portion of an image sequence name (0234 in the example) identifies which frame in the sequence the image represents. In the Frame/Animation Ext drop-down list box, select name.#.ext to render out a sequence of files. If you leave this setting at the default of *name.ext*, only a single frame will render, no matter what the animation range is in the Time slider.

> *Name.#.ext* is perhaps the most commonly used convention, as opposed to *name.ext.#* or *name.#*, because it allows you to identify the file type easily in Windows. Although Macintosh OS X isn't as picky about the order of number and extension, most Mac compositing software applications (such as After Effects and Shake) want filenames that end in the three-letter extension. Therefore, it's best for both Mac and Windows to use the *name.#.ext* format.

The extension portion of the image name is a three-letter abbreviation for the type of file you're writing to disk. By specifying in the Frame/Animation Ext drop-down list box that you want an extension appended to each image filename, you ensure that you can identify the file type.

Image Format

In the Image Format drop-down list box, select the type of image file you want to render. Maya will add the appropriate extension to the filename.

You can save your images in a wide range of formats. The format you choose depends on your own preference and your output needs. For example, Joint Photographic Experts Group (JPEG) files may be great for the small file sizes preferred on the Internet, but their color compression and lack of alpha channel (a feature discussed later in this chapter) make them undesirable for most professional CG work beyond test renders and *dailies*, a meeting in which the day's (or week's) work on a production is looked at and discussed for direction.

It's best to render a sequence of images rather than a movie file for two reasons. First, you want your renders to be their best quality with little or no image compression. Second, if a render fails during a movie render, you must re-render the entire sequence. With an image sequence, however, you can pick up where the last frame left off. The best file type format to render to is Tagged Image File Format (TIFF). This format enjoys universal support, has little to no compression, and supports an alpha channel. Almost all image-editing and compositing packages can read Targa- and TIFF-formatted files, so either is a safe choice most of the time. Also, the Silicon Graphics Image (SGI) and Maya Image File Format (IFF) formats are good, although some older versions of image editors may not be able to load them without a plug-in. For more on image formats, see Chapter 1, "Introduction to Computer Graphics and 3D."

Frame Range

Choosing the frame range ensures that your entire animation is rendered out. Maya defaults to the range 1–10, which you may often need to change to render your entire sequence. If you still have the Frame/Animation Ext attribute set to Name (Single Frame), the Frame Range text boxes will be grayed out. You must choose a naming convention other than Name (Single Frame) first. This is a common oversight when people first try to render their animations and see that only a single frame renders.

After you've selected a naming convention other than Name (Single Frame), enter the Start Frame and End Frame attributes for part of the sequence or the entire sequence. These attributes are also helpful if you need to render parts of the sequence at different times. By specifying new start and end frames, you can render different portions of a sequence or pick up where a previous render left off.

The By Frame attribute specifies the intervals at which the sequence will render. For example, if you want to render only the odd-numbered frames, set the Start Frame attribute to 1 and set the By Frame attribute to 2. If you want to render only even-numbered frames, set Start Frame to 2, set By Frame to 2, and so on. Typically, you leave By Frame set to 1 so that Maya renders each frame. In certain cases, such as in previsualization work or in rendering tests of a scene, it may be necessary to render only every second, third, or even tenth frame instead.

The Frame Padding attribute and slider have to do with the way an operating system, such as Windows or Mac OS X, orders its files by inserting leading zeros in the frame number. If Frame Padding is set to 2, for example, a single zero precedes every single-digit frame number in the filename. In this case, frame 8 is name.08.tif as opposed to name.8.tif (which is set to a padding of 1). If Frame Padding is set to 4, the filename contains three leading zeros; therefore, frame 8 is name.0008.tif.

Large sequences of files are easier to organize if they all have a frame padding of at least 3. Figure 11.2 shows an image sequence without padding and with padding. The files without padding aren't in numeric order. Because rendering can generate a large number of files, it's important to be able to manage them efficiently.

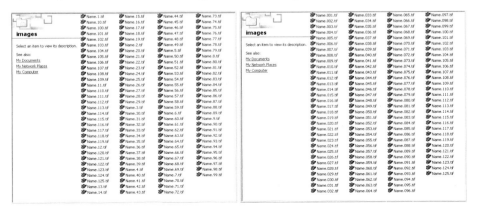

Figure 11.2

Images rendered without frame padding (left). Frame padding makes file sequences easier to organize (right).

Camera

Under the Renderable Cameras heading, you can choose the camera to render.

Image files are composed of red, green, and blue channels. Each channel specifies the amount of the primary additive color (red, green, or blue, respectively) in the image.

Figure 11.3

This wine bottle's transparency renders with a gray alpha channel.

(See Chapter 1 for more on how computers define color.) In addition, some file formats can save a fourth channel, called the *alpha channel*. This channel defines the image's transparency level. Just as the red channel defines how much red is in an area of the image, the alpha channel defines how transparent the image is when layered or composited on another image. If the alpha channel is black, the image is perfectly see-through. If the alpha channel is white, the image is opaque. The alpha channel is also known as the *matte*. An object with a transparency will render with a gray alpha channel, as shown in Figure 11.3.

The alpha channel can be displayed in the Render View window. As discussed later in this chapter, your test renders also display in this window.

To view an image's alpha channel in the Render View window, click the Display Alpha Channel icon ( ). To reset the view to RGB (full-color view), click the Display RGB Channels icon ( ).

Most renders have the alpha channels selected, so leave the Alpha Channel (Mask) check box checked at all times. Note, however, that JPEG, Graphics Interchange Format (GIF), and Windows bitmap files don't support alpha channels, regardless of whether the Alpha Channel (Mask) check box is checked as shown in Figure 11.4.

Only a few file formats, such as Maya IFF, support the depth channel. This grayscale channel resembles the alpha channel but conveys depth information: that is, the distance of an object from the camera. The Depth Channel (Z Depth) setting is typically used when compositing images.

Figure 11.4

Output an alpha channel.

Setting Resolution

The Width and Height attributes set the pixel size of the image to be rendered, a.k.a. the image *resolution*. In the Image Size section of the Render Settings window, you can select a resolution from the Presets drop-down list box. The commonly used resolution for professional broadcast is 720 × 486 National Television Standards Committee (NTSC), which appears as CCIR 601/Quantel NTSC in the Presets list. To composite Maya CG into a home-shot digital video (DV) movie, you use the standard DV resolution of 720 × 480 to render your scene, but you must enter that resolution manually in the Width and Height fields. (For more on resolutions, see Chapter 1.)

The Device Aspect Ratio and Pixel Aspect Ratio attributes adjust the width of the image to accommodate certain professional output needs; you need not adjust them here.

> Make sure your Pixel Aspect Ratio attribute is set to 1 before you render, unless you need to render CCIR 601/Quantel NTSC or DV for television needs; otherwise, your image may look squeezed or widened compared to any live-action footage you use to composite.

The higher your resolution, the longer the scene will take to render. Doubling the resolution may quadruple the render time. With large frame sequences, it's advisable to render tests at half the resolution of the final output or less to save time.

In addition to the image resolution, the image quality of a render also dictates how long a render will take. In addition to turning down the resolution for a test, you can use a lower-quality render. Each rendering method has its own set of quality settings, which are explained in the following sections.

Selecting a Render Engine

Maya allows you to select a render engine in the Render Settings window. Although mental ray for Maya is most commonly used, the other rendering methods give you flexibility in choosing a final look for your project.

Maya Software

Maya Software, the default software rendering method, can capture just about everything you want in your scene, from reflections to motion blur and transparencies. You can use the software rendering method in a couple of ways.

USING RAYTRACING

Raytracing, a topic introduced in Chapter 10, "Maya Lighting," is used to incorporate two optical effects into a rendering that the default software rendering method can't handle. *Raytracing* traces rays of light from each light source to every object in the shot and then traces the light's reflection from the object to the camera's lens. This allows true *reflections* and *refractions* to appear in the render as well as highly defined shadows (for more on shadows, see Chapter 10):

True Reflections True reflections occur when every object in the scene is viewed in a reflective surface, as a reflection of course. You can also have objects with reflections explicitly turned off through the Render Stats section in the Attribute Editor in case you don't want a particular reflection, which is common. Although it's possible to simulate reflections in Maya Software using *reflection maps*, true reflections can be generated only through raytracing. (In Chapter 7, "Maya Shading and Texturing," the axe project shows how to apply reflection maps.)

Refractions *Refractions* occur when light bends as it passes through one medium into another medium of different density. For example, a pencil in a glass of water appears to be broken. The light bouncing off the pencil refracts as it travels from the water into the air, bending a bit during the transition. That displaces the view of the pencil under the water, making it seem broken.

You saw in the previous chapter that raytracing is also a vital component of mental ray for Maya as well as the Maya Software renderer.

Because the default software renderer renders the same image without true reflections or refractions and can generate detailed shadows with shadow maps, the only reason to use raytracing is for reflective and refractive surfaces (as well as raytraced shadows) or to enable some of mental ray's features, such as Final Gather.

As with raytraced shadows, raytraced reflections need to be enabled. To do so, click Raytracing in the Raytracing Quality section of the Maya Software tab in the Render Settings window. Unlike raytraced shadows, however, raytraced reflections need not be explicitly turned on through the lights.

As soon as raytracing is enabled, any reflective surface receives a true reflection of the objects and environment in the scene. Even objects with reflection maps reflect other objects in addition to their reflection maps. For more on reflection maps, see the section "Reflections and Refractions" later in this chapter.

RENDER QUALITY

With software rendering, the render quality depends most noticeably on *anti-aliasing*. Anti-aliasing is the effect produced when pixels appear to blur together to soften a jagged edge on an angled line. Increasing the anti-aliasing level of a render produces an image that has smoother angles and curves. The Render Settings window contains presets that specify this level and a few others to set the quality of your render. Follow these steps:

1. In the Render Settings window, make sure Maya Software is selected in the Render Using drop-down list box, and click the Maya Software tab.

2. In the Anti-aliasing Quality section, select either Preview Quality or Production Quality from the Quality preset drop-down list box.

Figure 11.5 shows the fruit still life from Chapter 10 rendered with the Preview Quality preset and the same image with the Production Quality preset.

Figure 11.5

With Preview Quality (left), the edges of the fruit are jagged. With Production Quality (right), the jaggedness is gone.

Of course, the higher the quality, the longer the render will take. As you become more experienced, you'll be better able to balance uncompromised quality with efficient render times.

Maya Hardware

The hardware rendering method uses your graphic card's processor to render the scene. Hardware renders are similar to what you see when you play a 3D video game. The data output by the game is fed directly into the graphics pipeline of your hardware setup and is rendered on the fly as you play.

This method results in faster render times, but it lacks some of the features and quality you get from a software render. In Figure 11.6, the first image shows a wine bottle as rendered through hardware. The render time is blazingly fast, but the quality suffers. The second image shows the software render of the same frame. Hardware rendering becomes a good way to test render a scene, although only a few professional video cards fully support Maya's hardware rendering.

To use the Maya Hardware renderer, in the Render Settings window, make sure Maya Hardware is selected in the Render Using drop-down list box. To specify hardware quality, select a level from the Number of Samples drop-down list box under the Maya Hardware tab.

Figure 11.6

The hardware-rendered wine bottle (left) lacks some subtleties. The software-rendered wine bottle shows better specularity and surface detail (right).

mental ray for Maya

mental ray for Maya has become a standard for rendering through Maya, supplanting the Maya Software renderer due to its stability and quality results. The mental ray for Maya rendering method also can let you emulate the behavior of light even more realistically than the other rendering methods, as you saw in the previous chapter's Physical Sun and Sky exercise. Based on raytracing, mental ray takes the concept further by adding photon maps to the light traces. That is, it projects photon particles from lights and records their behavior and trajectory. The end result allows the phenomena of light *caustics* and *bounce,* also known as *radiosity* and *global illumination.*

The mental ray for Maya renderer can be an advanced and intricate rendering language with shaders and procedures all its own. This chapter briefly covers one of the popular mental ray methods called Final Gather using an HDR lighting dome; this should, in addition to the previous chapter's exercise, give you a primer on rendering Final Gather with mental ray for Maya. mental ray is becoming an overall rendering solution as well as a tool for renders that require a highly sophisticated lighting look. To use it, you still need to be experienced with the basics of lighting and rendering. At its base, mental ray will give you results similar to that of Maya Software, without any of the mental ray bells and whistles enabled. A scene lighted and set up for Maya Software will render out pretty much the same through a base mental ray render, although some of the quality settings are slightly different (and covered later in this chapter).

Maya Vector

Vector rendering lets you render your objects with an illustrated or cartoon look. You can render "ink" outlines of your characters to composite over flat-color passes. Figure 11.7 shows the fruit still life rendered with Maya Vector. This rendering method is different than Maya's Toon Shading feature, which is briefly covered in Chapter 12, "Maya Dynamics and Effects."

Maya Vector can output animated files in Adobe Flash format for direct use in web pages and animations, as well as Adobe Illustrator files and the usual list of image formats. To specify the attribute settings for Maya Vector, you use the Maya Vector tab in the Render Settings window (see Figure 11.8).

Figure 11.7

The fruit still life as a vector render

In the Fill Options section, click the Fill Objects check box, and select the number of colors for each object to set the look of the render. If you want the renderer to include an outline of the edges of your geometry, in the Edge Options section, click the Include Edges check box and set the line weights.

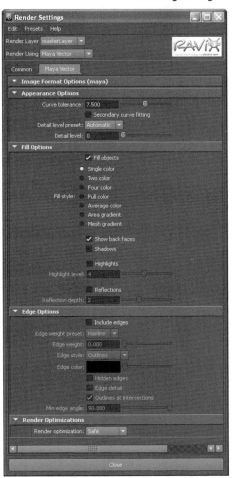

Figure 11.8

The Maya Vector rendering settings

Previewing Your Render: The Render View Window

The Render View window automatically opens when you test-render a frame, as you've already seen in your work through this book. To open it manually, choose Window → Rendering Editors → Render View. Your current scene renders in the Render View window. Figure 11.9 shows the important icons in this window:

Redo Previous Render Renders the last-rendered view panel.

Render Region Renders only the selected portion of an image. To select a portion of an image, click within the image in the Render View window, and drag a red box around a region.

Open Render Settings Window Opens the Render Settings window (also known as the Render Globals window in previous versions of Maya).

Display RGB Channels Displays the full color of the image.

Display Alpha Channel Displays only the alpha matte of the render as a black-and-white image.

Display Real Size Resets the image size to 100 percent to make sure the image displays properly. When the Render View window is resized, or when you select a new render resolution, the image renders to fit the window, and the image is resized if needed. If your render looks blocky, make sure the Render View window is displaying at real size before adjusting the options in the Render Settings window.

Select Renderer Lets you select the rendering method. This is the same as selecting it in the Render Settings window.

Information Readout At the bottom of the Render View window is a readout of information about the frame rendered. This information tells you the resolution, renderer used, frame number, render time, and camera used to render. This readout is a huge help in comparing different render settings and different frames as you progress in your work, especially when you keep images in the buffer (as explained later).

Figure 11.9

**The Render
View window**

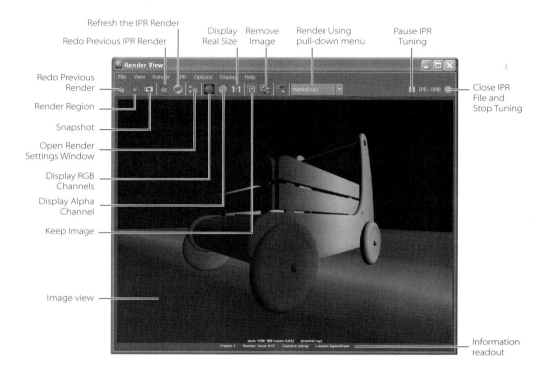

Refresh the IPR Render

Redo Previous IPR Render

Display Real Size

Remove Image

Render Using pull-down menu

Pause IPR Tuning

Redo Previous Render

Render Region

Snapshot

Open Render Settings Window

Display RGB Channels

Display Alpha Channel

Keep Image

Image view

Close IPR File and Stop Tuning

Information readout

Figure 11.9

The Render
View window

Saving/Loading an Image

Although you typically use the Render View window to test a scene, you can also use it to save single frames by choosing File → Save Image to save in all Maya's supported image formats. Likewise, choose File → Open Image to display any previously rendered image file in this window. If your task in Maya is to create a single frame, this is the best way to render and save it.

Keep/Remove Image

The Render View window is a prime place to see adjustments to various parts of your scene. You can store images in its buffer by clicking the Keep Image icon. When you do, a scroll bar appears at the bottom of the window, and you can scroll through any saved images. This is handy for making a change, rendering it, and scrolling back and forth between the old saved image and the new render to make sure the change is to your liking. You can store a number of images in the buffer. For a faster way to preview changes, use IPR rendering as discussed next.

IPR Rendering

As you saw in Chapter 7, a fast way to preview changes to your scene is to use Maya's Interactive Photorealistic Rendering (IPR). After you IPR-render a view panel, specify the region you want to tune by dragging a box around that area of the image in the Render View window. Maya updates that region every time you make a shader or lighting change to the scene. Figure 11.10 shows the fruit still life as an IPR render as the color and specular levels are being fine-tuned.

IPR is perfect for finding just the right lighting and specular levels. It will, however, register raytracing elements such as refractions and true reflections only if the scene is set to render through mental ray for Maya. Overall, IPR quality is fairly close to that of a full render while still allowing you to watch your tuning in near real time.

Figure 11.10

IPR rendering lets you fine-tune your textures and lighting with near real-time feedback.

Reflections and Refractions

You can either map or raytrace reflections.

As you saw in Chapter 7, creating a reflection map for an object is pretty simple. Simply assign a Phong, Phong E, Blinn, or Anisotropic material to your object, and make sure the Reflectivity attribute is greater than zero. Then, click the Reflected Color map button to add a texture or a file as a map to create the reflection. (See the axe project in Chapter 7 for more on reflection maps and shaders.)

To generate true reflections, however, you'll need to enable raytracing in either Maya Software or mental ray for Maya. Mapping textures to the reflected color isn't necessary when raytracing is enabled, because Maya reflects any objects in the scene that fall in the proper line of sight.

> **RAYTRACING WITH MENTAL RAY**
>
> Enabling raytracing in mental ray is as simple as checking the Raytracing box in the Render Settings window in the Features tab.

Raytraced Reflections

To enable raytraced reflections, use a material with a Reflections attribute, such as a Phong, and open the Render Settings window. Choose Maya Software, and in the Maya

Software tab, click the Raytracing check box in the Raytracing Quality section. (See Figure 11.11.)

The sliders control the quality of the render by specifying how many times to reflect or refract for any given object. Setting Reflections to 2, for example, enables an object's reflection in a second object to appear as part of its reflection in a third object.

Figure 11.11

Enabling raytracing in Maya Software rendering

The first image in Figure 11.12 shows the still life reflecting onto the surface of its table. In this case, Reflections is set to 1. If you increase Reflections to 2, however, you see the reflections of the pieces of fruit in each other also reflecting in the surface of the table.

Figure 11.12

(left) Reflections set to 1; (right) Reflections set to 2

Notice the difference in the reflections of the fruit in the table between the two renders. Raytraced reflections can consume valuable render resources and time, so it's a good idea to make your scene efficient. You don't want to reflect more than necessary.

You can control the number of reflections on a per-object basis as opposed to setting limits on the entire scene through the Render Settings window. To access a shader's reflection limits, select the shader in the Hypershade, and open the Attribute Editor. In the Raytrace Options section, drag the Reflection Limit slider to set the maximum number of reflections for that shader. The lower value (either this value or the Reflections value in the Render Settings window) dictates how many reflections are rendered for every object attached to that shader. The default shader reflection limit is 1, so make sure you change the Reflections value as well as each shader's value if you want more than one level of reflection.

Furthermore, you may not want some objects to cast reflections in a scene with raytraced reflections. To specify that an object doesn't cast reflections, select the object in a Maya panel, and open the Attribute Editor. In the Render Stats section, clear the Visible in Reflections check box.

Rendering Refractions

Refractions are also a raytraced-only ability. Refractions require that an object be semi-transparent so that you can see through it to the object (or objects) behind it that is being refracted. To control refractions, use the shader.

To enable refractions, select the appropriate shader in the Hypershade, and open the Attribute Editor. In the Raytrace Options section, click the Refractions check box. Now you need to set a refractive index for the shader and a refraction limit, similar to the reflection limit.

The refractive index must be greater or less than 1 to cause a refraction. Typically, a number within 0.2 of 1 is perfect for most refraction effects. The first image in Figure 11.13 is raytraced with a refractive index of 1.2 on the wine bottle and glasses; the second image has a refractive index of 0.8 on both bottle and glasses.

You can specify whether an object is visible in a refracting object by clicking or clearing the Visible in Refractions check box in the Render Stats section of the object's Attribute Editor.

Figure 11.13

(left) Refractive index of 1.2; (right) Refractive index of 0.8

Using Cameras

Cameras capture all the animation fun in the scene. In theory, Maya's cameras work the same way as real cameras. The more you know about photography, the easier these concepts are to understand.

The term *camera*, in essence, refers to the perspective view. You can have as many cameras in the scene as you want, but it's wise to have a camera you're planning to render with placed to frame the shot and another camera acting as the perspective work view so you can move around your scene as you work. The original persp panel fits that latter role well, although it can be used as a render camera just as easily.

You can also render any of your work windows to test render orthogonal views of your model the same way you render a perspective view.

Creating a Camera

The simplest way to create a new camera is to choose Panels → Perspective → New, as you've seen in a previous exercise. This creates a new camera node in Maya and sets that active panel to its view.

You can select a camera and transform it (move it, rotate it, scale it) just as you would select and transform any other object in Maya to be animated or positioned. Furthermore, you can move a camera and rotate it using the Alt/Option key and mouse button combinations.

For example, click inside a new Maya Scene Perspective window to make it active. Select that view's camera by choosing View → Select Camera. The camera's attributes appear in the Channel Box. Try moving the view around using the Alt/Option key and mouse button combinations. Notice how the attributes change to reflect the new position and rotation of the camera. You can animate the camera—for example, zoom in or out or pan across the scene—by setting keyframes on any of these attributes.

Camera Types

You can create three types of nonstereo cameras for your scene: Camera; Camera and Aim; and Camera, Aim, and Up (also known as single-node, two-node, and three-node cameras, respectively). To create any of these cameras, choose Create → Cameras. You can also change the type of these cameras at any time through the Attribute Editor. The other two options for creating cameras are Stereo Camera and Multi Stereo Rig to allow for a stereoscopic effect, although they aren't covered in this book.

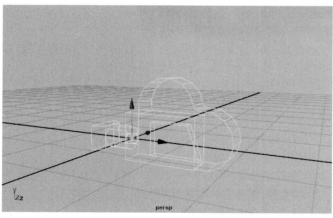

The single-node camera (*Camera*) is the most common (see Figure 11.14). This camera consists of a single camera node that you move and rotate as you would any other object for proper positioning. The persp panel's camera is a single-node camera.

The two-node camera (Camera and Aim) consists of the camera node and an aim node. You use the aim node to point the camera as opposed to rotating it to orient it properly. This is useful for animating a camera following an object. You animate the movement of the aim node to follow your object much as a car around a racetrack. The camera pivots to follow its aim point and, hence, the object. (See Figure 11.15.)

Figure 11.14
A single-node camera

The three-node camera (Camera, Aim, and Up) has a camera node, an aim node, and an up node. The additional up node is to orient the camera's up direction. This gives you the ability to animate the side-to-side rotation of the camera as well as its aim direction. (See Figure 11.16.)

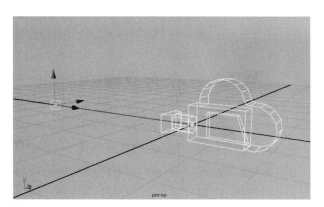

Figure 11.15
A two-node camera

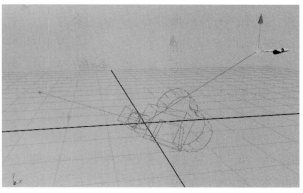

Figure 11.16
A three-node camera

Camera Attributes

As an example, set your project to Lighting, and load the still_life_render_v02.mb scene from the Lighting project on the CD. You'll see a green box in the persp panel that displays the resolution (set to 640 × 480) and the name of the camera (camera1).

Special attributes control the function of camera nodes. To set these attributes, follow these steps:

1. With camera1 selected, open the Attribute Editor (press Ctrl+A or choose View → Camera Attribute Editor).

2. At the top of the window, select the type of camera controls you want. The Controls attribute sets the type of camera from single- to two- to three-control nodes. Figure 11.17 shows the Attribute Editor for the camera.

Focal Length

The Focal Length attribute specifies the length of the lens. The lower the focal length (a.k.a. short lens), the wider the view. At very low numbers, however, the image is distorted, as you can see in the comparison in Figure 11.18. The higher the focal length, the closer the subject seems to the camera.

Figure 11.17
The Attribute Editor for the camera

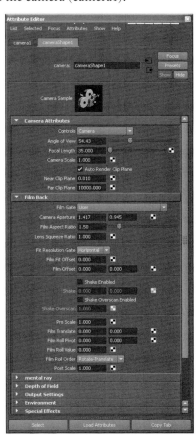

Focal Length = 35   Focal Length = 8   Focal Length = 60

Figure 11.18

Different focal lengths

Although adjusting the Focal Length attribute of a camera zooms in and out, it isn't the same as moving the camera closer to your subject using the Alt+right-click procedure to zoom in view panels. Focal-length zooming can create optical distortions, such as can be created with a fish-eye lens.

When you want to animate your camera getting closer to the subject of your shot, it's best to animate the camera and not the focal length. However, if you need to match some CG element in Maya to a photograph or video you've imported as an image plane, set your camera's focal length to match that of the real camera used for the background.

Clipping Planes

All cameras in Maya have clipping planes that restrict the amount of information that can be seen through them. The clipping plane is defined by the Near Clip Plane and Far Clip Plane attributes. These set the minimum and maximum distance, respectively, of the clipping plane. Any object or portion of an object that passes beyond these distances won't show in the window and should not render.

If you notice objects disappearing as you move your camera and create a scene, it may be because of the clipping plane. Increase the Far Clip Plane attribute, and the objects should reappear in the view.

Film Back

The Film Back attributes concern the type of output you'll be dealing with after your renders are finished and you're ready to put your animation on tape, DVD, film, or what have you:

Film Gate Defines the aspect ratio of your camera's view. Most images that are output to television have an aspect ratio of 1:1.33, exemplified by the 35mm TV Projection selection in the Film Gate drop-down list box, which is preferred for broadcast video. (For more on aspect ratios, see Chapter 1.)

Fit Resolution Gate Allows you to align footage you may have imported as an image plane to match up CG properly to live action.

Overscan

Found under the Display Options section for the camera's Attribute Editor, Overscan lets you resize the view without changing the film gate that will render. For example, the scene on the left in Figure 11.19 is set up with an Overscan setting of 1.3, allowing you to see more than what will render, which is defined by the outline box. The scene on the right in Figure 11.19 is set up with an Overscan setting of 2, which increases even more how much you see in the camera1 panel but doesn't change the view when rendered.

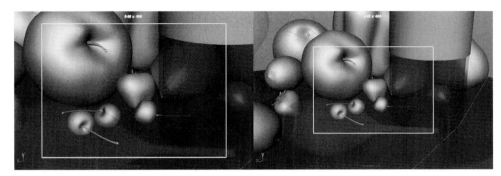

You can turn the green box in the panel on and off through the camera's Attribute Editor. Also in the Display Options section are Display Film Gate and Display Resolution check boxes, shown in Figure 11.20. Ideally, these two green boxes should align perfectly in the view pane. If the resolution box (the solid green line) doesn't line up with the film gate box (the dashed green line), change your film gate selection to match the resolution's aspect ratio in the Render Settings window. A resolution of 640 × 480, for example, has an aspect ratio of 1.33, the same as the 35mm TV Projection film gate currently selected for this scene.

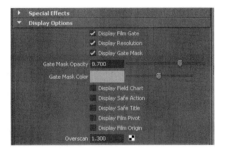

Environment

In the Environment section, you'll find attributes to adjust the background color that renders and to create an image plane as shown in Figure 11.21.

If you want to use a solid color as the camera's background when you render, click the color swatch next to Background Color to change the background color in your renders using the Color Chooser. The slider allows you to control the value, or brightness, of the current color. Neither changes the background color of your view panels, however.

CAMERA IMAGE PLANES

A camera image plane isn't like the reference planes you used for modeling the red wagon in Chapter 6. In this case, an image plane is created to be a background specific for that particular camera or view panel, but it's typically also used as a reference much like the planes you created and mapped in Chapter 6. Camera image planes are useful when you're matching your scene to existing footage or an image. For example, if you need to animate a flying saucer to a home video of a family gathering, you would import the video as an image sequence into Maya through a perspective camera to be able to line up your UFO properly to zap your cousins.

You can import an image plane by clicking the Create button in the Environment section of the Attribute Editor (see Figure 11.21) or directly through a view panel's menu, as you'll see in the next exercise.

In this exercise, we'll show you how to import a sketch of an axe into the Front view panel for a modeling assignment. (You won't actually model the axe, however.) The image, a sketch of a simple axe design, is to be used as a template for outlining the model. You can find the file Axe_outline_1.tif in the Sourceimages folder of the Axe project on the CD; it's shown in Figure 11.22. Follow these steps:

1. Choose File → New Scene.

2. Import the sketch of the axe into Maya as a camera image plane for the Front view panel. In your Front window, choose View → Image Plane → Import Image.

3. Point to Axe_outline_1.tif in the Axe project's Sourceimages folder, and load it. The sketch displays full screen in your Front window and as a plane in the Perspective window (see Figure 11.23).

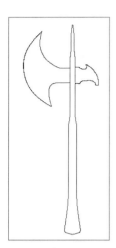

Figure 11.22

An image to import as a camera image plane

Figure 11.23

Importing a camera image plane into the Front view panel

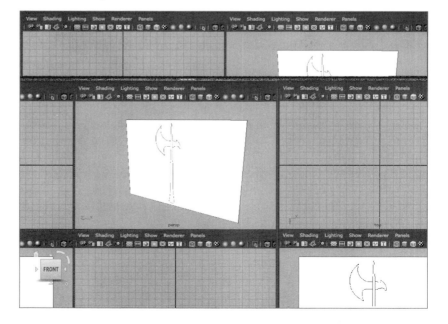

Now you'd be ready to trace the outline of the axe easily in the Front view panel, if you were going to model the axe.

If you can't see the image plane, click Show in the view panel, and make sure Cameras is checked.

IMAGE PLANE SEQUENCE

A movie file or a sequence of files can also be brought in to animate or to track motion (a.k.a. *matchmoving*) as a camera image plane. It's generally best to use a frame sequence, however. When you bring in an image for an image plane, check the Use Image Sequence box in the image plane's Attribute Editor window, as shown in Figure 11.24. Maya will automatically load the image to correspond to the frame number in the scene. For example, at frame 29 in your Maya animation, Maya loads frame 29 of your image sequence. But your image file sequence must be numbered correctly (such as `filename.###.jpg`). You can import an image plane into any perspective view in exactly the same way.

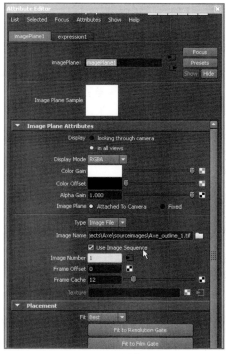

If the clutter of seeing a camera image plane in the other windows bothers you, under the Image Plane Attributes in the Attribute Editor, change the radio button selection next to Display from In All Views to Looking Through Camera. This setting removes the image plane from the other windows.

Motion Blur

Motion blur is an optical phenomenon that occurs when an object moves fast in front of a camera: the object looks blurred as it crosses the frame. Maya Software rendering renders out motion blur in two ways—2D blur or 3D blur—although neither will render as reflections:

Figure 11.24

Importing a sequence of image files as a camera image plane

- In the 2D blur process, Maya calculates after the frame is rendered. Any objects moving in the frame are blurred with a 2D filter effect. The 2D blur is effective for most applications and faster than 3D blur.

- The 3D blur process is calculated while a frame of the sequence is rendering. Every motion-blur-enabled object is blurred with typically better results than 2D blur, but at a cost of a much longer render time.

We'll briefly cover motion blur in mental ray for Maya later in the chapter.

To enable motion blur for the Maya Software renderer, open the Render Settings window. In the Motion Blur section in the Maya Software tab, click the Motion Blur check box. Then, choose 2D or 3D blur.

Typically, you control the amount of blur rendered for 2D and 3D by setting the Blur By Frame attribute—the higher the number, the greater the blur. Using additional controls, however, you can increase or decrease the 2D blur effect in the render. The Blur Length attribute affects the streakiness of the blur to further increase or decrease the amount of motion blur set with the Blur By Frame attribute.

Use motion blur sparingly in most scenes. It takes a careful eye to choose the right blur amount for an object.

Setting a camera's Shutter Angle attribute (in the camera's Attribute Editor in the Special Effects section) also affects the amount of blur rendered—the higher the number, the greater the blur.

Batch Rendering

So far, you've used single-frame rendering numerous times to see a scene in the Render View window. But how do you start rendering an animation sequence to disk? This is called *batch rendering* in Maya, whichever renderer you use. To batch-render an entire scene, follow these steps:

1. Open the Render Settings window.

2. Choose Maya Software to use to render, enter the start and end frames of your animation, and select your image format. Select your quality and resolution settings. Finally, set the camera you want to render in the Renderable Camera attribute.

Be sure to select *name.#.ext* in the Frame/Animation Ext drop-down list box to render out a sequence of files. Remember, if you leave the default setting, which is *name.ext*, only a single frame renders.

3. In the main Maya window under the Rendering menu set, choose Render → Batch Render ❐ to open the Batch Render Animation dialog box (or the Batch Render Frame box when rendering a single image). Figure 11.25 shows the Maya Software rendering batch options on top, and the image below shows the batch options for mental ray rendering.

4. If you have a multiprocessor, hyper-threading, or dual-core machine, select how many CPUs you would like to use to render your scene.

5. Click Batch Render to render the frame range you specified in the Render Settings window. The render occurs in the background, and you see progress updates in the Command line at the bottom of your Maya screen and in the Script Editor window if you open it.

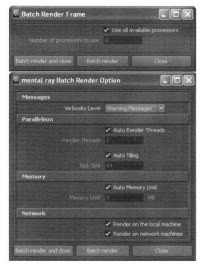

Figure 11.25

The Batch Render Frame dialog box for Maya Software (above) and mental ray rendering (below)

Figure 11.26

The Render Settings window shows you to where the images will be rendered.

To see a frame as the batch render progresses, choose Render → Show Batch Render. To cancel a batch render, choose Render → Cancel Batch Render.

When you batch render, your image files are written to the Images folder of the current project. Make sure your project is properly set; otherwise, your files will end up in an unexpected folder. You can always see the render path and the image name at the top of the Render Settings window, as shown in Figure 11.26.

Rendering the Wine Bottle

In this section, you'll set up and render an animated camera to move over 25 frames of a wine bottle still life.

Set your current project to Lighting, and then load `still_life_render_v01.mb` from the Lighting project on the CD. You'll adjust your render settings and some shader properties to make the wine bottle look more like glass.

Selecting Render Settings Options

Set your resolution and quality settings in the Render Settings window:

1. Open the Render Settings window, and select Maya Software. Click the Maya Software tab.

2. From the Quality drop-down list box, select Production Quality. This presets the appropriate settings to produce a high-quality render.

3. Click the Common tab. Set Frame/Animation Ext to `name.#.ext`, set Start Frame to 1, set End Frame to 25, and set Frame Padding to 2.

4. From the Image Format drop-down list box, select TIFF.

5. Make sure Renderable Camera is set to camera1. In the Image Size section, set Presets to 640 × 480.

Setting Up the Scene

Now, set up some of the objects in the scene. The wine bottle has been imported into the still life scene, and three wine glasses have been added. All the lights are in place, as is the camera.

Start by setting up this scene to raytrace to get true reflections and refractions:

1. Turn on refractions for the Glass shaders. In the Hypershade, select the Glasses material, and open the Attribute Editor. In the Raytrace Options section, click the Refractions check box, and set Refractive Index to 1.2. Set Reflection Limit to 2. Select the Wine_Bottle material, and repeat the previous steps.

2. Because your lights' shadows are set to shadow maps, you need to change them to raytraced shadows. Remember that semitransparent objects cast solid shadows unless shadows are raytraced, so the glasses and wine bottle will cast shadows as if they were solid and not glass. In the Outliner, select spotLight1. In the Attribute Editor, in the Shadows section, enable Use Ray Trace Shadows. Notice that the shadow map options turn off. Repeat these steps for the remaining two shadow-casting lights: spotLight4 and spotLight3. Figure 11.27 shows the three shadow-casting lights in the scene in white.

3. Open the Render Settings window, and turn on raytracing in the Raytracing Quality section. Set Reflections to 2.

Figure 11.27

Shadow lights

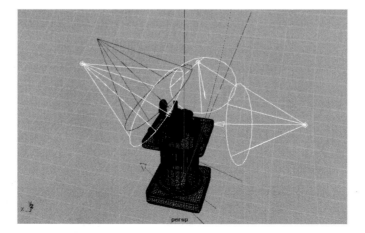

You can't select all three lights at once to turn on raytraced shadows in the Attribute Editor. Any adjustments you make in the Attribute Editor affect only the most recently selected object, not multiple selections.

Setting Up the Camera

Next, you'll set up the camera to render the scene:

1. Open the camera's Attribute Editor through the camera1 panel (choose View → Camera Attribute Editor).

2. Select the Display Film Gate option in the Display Options section to turn on a dashed green box in the camera1 panel. Enable the Display Resolution option. Notice that the two boxes aren't aligned.

3. Because the resolution is 640 × 480, you'll use a 1.33 aspect ratio. Select 35mm TV Projection from the Film Gate drop-down list box. The two green boxes now align. Although it's not absolutely necessary to match the resolution with the film gate, it's definitely good practice to do so, especially if you'll later insert CG in live-action videos.

4. As soon as you change the film gate, the framing of the scene changes. You must move the camera out to frame the entire still life. If you try to use the Alt key and mouse button combinations to zoom out, you'll notice that you can't move the camera in this scene: the movement attributes for the camera have been locked to prevent accidental movement that would disrupt the shot.

5. To unlock the camera, choose View → Select Camera. The camera's attributes appear in the Channel Box. Some are grayed out, signifying that they're locked and can't be changed. Highlight the locked attributes, and right-click Unlock Selected in the Channel box.

Figure 11.28

The camera view at the beginning of the animation

6. Create an animated camera move to pull out and reveal the still life slowly over 25 frames. Set your Range slider to 1 to 25 frames. Go to frame 1. The camera1 view should be similar to that shown in Figure 11.28. Select all three Translate and Rotate channels in the Channel Box, and right-click Key Selected to set keyframes for the first camera position.

7. Zoom (actually, truck) the camera out by pressing Alt+right-click to a wider framing to reveal the entire still life. Highlight the

Translate and Rotate channels again in the Channel box, and set keyframes for them. (See Figure 11.29.)

Scrub your animation, and you'll see a pullout revealing the full scene.

You can lock the camera to prevent accidentally moving the view after you set your keyframes, especially if Auto Keyframe is on. Select the Translate and Rotate attributes in the Channel Box, and right-click Lock Selected.

Figure 11.29

Pull out the camera.

Batch Rendering and Playing Back the Sequence

Now, you're ready to render out the 25-frame sequence. Choose Render → Batch Render.

Because you're raytracing this scene at full resolution, this render should take anywhere from 20 minutes to an hour. To chart the progress of the render, open the Script Editor by clicking its icon on the Help line or by choosing Window → General Editors → Script Editor.

To see the frames play back, you'll need a program that can load the images in sequence and play them back for you. You can also import the image sequence into a compositing or editing program, such as Adobe After Effects or Premiere, to play back as a clip and edit as you like.

You can also use FCheck, a frame viewer that is included with Maya. This small and surprisingly powerful program plays back your images in real time so that you can judge your finished animation. To use FCheck, follow these steps:

1. In Windows, choose Start → All Programs → Autodesk → Autodesk Maya 2010 → FCheck to open the FCheck window, as shown in Figure 11.30.

Figure 11.30

FCheck, shown here with a sample image, plays back your rendered sequence.

2. Choose File → Open Animation.

3. In the file browser, find your Images folder in your project, and click the first frame of the sequence you want to play back. FCheck loads the images frame by frame into RAM and then plays them back in real time. Just set your playback speed and use the VCR controls to play back your sequence.

Figure 11.31

Use the Plug-in Manager to load mental ray for Maya.

mental ray for Maya

You had some experience with mental ray rendering in the last chapter as you lighted using Physical Sun and Sky, which automatically used Final Gather to render. In this part of the chapter, we'll discuss mental ray options to begin to scratch the surface of this incredibly powerful renderer.

First, if you haven't done so already, be sure that mental ray is loaded. When you first start up, mental ray for Maya may not load because it's considered a plug-in. Choose Window → Settings/Preferences → Plug-in Manager to open the Plug-in Manager, shown in Figure 11.31. Make sure both the Loaded and Auto Load check boxes for Mayatomr.mll are checked so that mental ray for Maya loads by default.

With mental ray for Maya, you'll most often use Scanline or Raytracing for your renders. The Rasterizer renderer with mental ray is often used for fast motion and transparencies in a scene and isn't covered in this book. We'll cover the Scanline and Raytracing algorithms for the mental ray for Maya renderer.

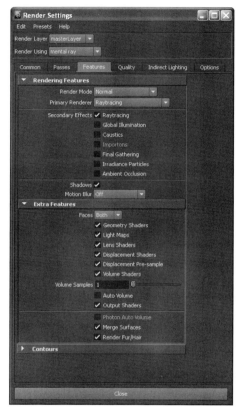

Figure 11.32

The Render Settings window for mental ray, showing the Features tab

To render with mental ray, open the Render Settings window, and change the Render Using drop-down menu selection to mental ray, as shown in Figure 11.32 (shown with the Features tab selected). The Render Settings window now has the Common tab along with five other mental ray–specific tabs: Passes, Features, Quality, Indirect Lighting, and Options.

mental ray Quality Settings

As with Maya's Software renderer, the primary quality settings for mental ray's renderer center on anti-aliasing. However, mental ray for Maya offers you finer control over how you set the quality levels through the Render Settings window. Under the Anti-Aliasing Quality → Raytrace/Scanline Quality heading in the Quality tab, you'll find these attributes:

Sampling Mode This drop-down menu sets the type of sampling mental ray performs in the render. *Sampling* is the number of times mental ray reads and compares the color values of adjacent pixels in order to smooth the resulting render to avoid jagged lines. The choices are Fixed Sampling, Adaptive Sampling (default), and Custom Sampling. Adaptive Sampling is generally the best choice because it sets the best range based on the Max Sample Level you set. If you choose Custom, you can set your own sampling range with the Min and Max Sample Levels.

Number of Samples These Min and Max Sample Level values set the number of times mental ray samples a pixel to determine how best to anti-alias the result. The higher the number, the finer the detail and the smoother the appearance of your rendered lines will be. These settings are *exponential*, so a small increase yields a much greater quality and much longer render time. You won't need to set the Max Sample Level above 2 for most uses. Both Max and Min Samples Level can be set into the negative numbers for fast renders, although you'll notice jagged edges. A good setting for most renders is 2 for the Max Sample Level with the Adaptive Sampling mode.

What determines the exact sample level within the min and max range set by these attributes is dependent on the Color and Alpha Contrast Thresholds, which are explained later.

Anti-aliasing Contrast Anti-aliasing Contrast values determine when mental ray turns up the number of samples in a particular region of the frame. If the contrast level from one pixel to its neighbor is below the threshold value, mental ray turns up the number of samples for that pixel to render a higher-quality result. Therefore, the *lower* the values set here, the *higher* the sample rate will be (within the Min and Max levels set).

Rather than setting high sample rates with just the Min and Max Sample Level attributes, lower the Anti-aliasing Contrast value to force mental ray to use a sample rate closer to the Max sample rate only where it needs to do so. You'll see this in action in the next section.

Multi-Pixel Filtering Heading When the Max Sample Level attribute is set to a value higher than 0, filtering is done on the results of the sampling of pixels to blend the pixels of a region together to form a coherent image. A high filter size tends to blur the image, whereas low filter values may look overly crisp. Box is the default filter and is the fastest to render, whereas Gaussian (Gauss) gives a slightly softer result with the slowest render times. Usually, render times don't vary much between different filter modes—it's not as if Gaussian takes four times longer to render the same frame over the Box filter type.

Sample Options Heading The Sample Lock and Jitter attributes are turned on to reduce noise and artifacts in rendered sequences with lots of movement.

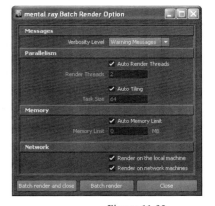

Figure 11.33

mental ray Batch Render options

When you're ready to render your scene to disk, you still use Batch Rendering; however, the options in the Batch Render Option window are different (Figure 11.33) than they are for Maya Software.

Render Settings in Action!

In this section, we'll look at how Anti-Aliasing Contrast values and Number of Samples work together to determine the quality of the render of a toy wagon. You can find the scene (`RedWagonRenderSettings.ma`) to render in the RedWagon project on the CD. This scene is set up to use Final Gather with an IBL using an HDR image. We'll cover these methods later in this chapter.

The render quality settings are low at first (Min Sample Level of -2 and Max Sample Level of 0 in Custom Sampling mode), with Anti-aliasing Contrast of 0.1 (default). This gives the render shown in Figure 11.34. You can see jagged highlights on the wagon, especially the white lines on the side body, the reflections in the front black nose, and on the back wheel.

Figure 11.34

A toy wagon rendered with low anti-aliasing values. Notice the jagged highlights on the white decal lines and the back wheel.

Figure 11.35

Better anti-aliasing improves the wagon's appearance.

If you enter Custom Sampling mode and increase Max Sample Level to 2 and Min Sample Level to 0, you see an immediate increase in quality (especially in the reflections of the wagon and the white decal lines) and a noticeable increase in render time (about twice as long), as shown in Figure 11.35.

Figure 11.36

The wagon has still better anti-aliasing because the Anti-aliasing Contrast Threshold was set lower. You'll see it better in your own renders.

You can get an even cleaner render. But rather than crank up the sample levels to the heavens, it's much better to lower the contrast thresholds to force mental ray to sample difficult areas closer to or at the max value of 2. Figure 11.36 shows the same frame with the Anti-aliasing Contrast value set to 0.04 instead of the default of 0.1. Also, the Min Sample Level is set to 1, but the Max Sample Level is left at 2. The render times increase, but at a more acceptable margin than if the Max Sampling Level were increased beyond a value of 2. The reflections of the wagon in the checker floor are markedly nicer in this render. Your results as you render the scene on your own computer will be more noticeable than the images shown here.

Finding the right levels to set is important to a quality render and an acceptable workflow. It's easy enough to crank the numbers to the sky, but render times will very quickly become unacceptable, especially when you have a supervisor or client breathing down your neck for the hundreds of frames you have to render by the time you have waffles the next day.

Motion Blur with mental ray

Now that you have a primer on quality settings in mental ray for Maya, let's see how motion blur works. In Maya Software rendering, as you saw previously, turning on motion blur is easily done through the Render Settings window. It's the same with mental ray.

Try this:

1. Load the `Planets_motionBlur.ma` scene file from the Solar_System project on the CD. This is an animated scene of the Solar System with just the first few planets and moons, as shown in Figure 11.37. A blast from the past!

Figure 11.37

The Solar System project is back!

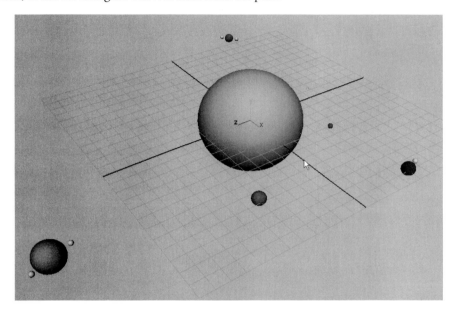

2. Open the Render Settings window. The scene should already be set to render with mental ray. If your scene isn't, make sure the mental ray for Maya plug-in is loaded, and set the scene to render with mental ray.

3. In the Common tab, set Frame/Animation Ext to name.#.ext, Frame Padding to 3, Start Frame to 1, and End Frame to 100.

4. Set the Image Size to 640 × 480 for now, and leave the renderable camera to persp.

5. Go to frame 75, and render a frame from the persp panel. Figure 11.38 shows the result.

6. In Render Settings, click to open the Features tab. In the Rendering Features heading, select No Deformation in the Motion Blur drop-down menu, as shown in Figure 11.39. This setting is the faster

Figure 11.38

A render of frame 75 shows the planets in motion without any motion blur.

size: 640 480 zoom: 1.000   (mental ray)
Frame: 75   Render Time: 0:03   Camera: persp

of two motion-blur methods and works for objects that move in the scene without deformation. *Deformations* are when the mesh or surface of an object changes, such as when you use a lattice or a skeleton rig like IK to drive a character. For deforming objects, you need to use Full as the Motion Blur setting.

7. Click to open the Quality tab in Render Settings. In the Motion Blur heading, set the Motion Blur By attribute from 1.0 to 3.0 for quite a bit of blur. Render a frame at frame 75. (See Figure 11.40.)

8. The render shows quite a bit of blur; however, the quality is low. You see a lot of graininess in your render, especially with the yellow and red planets at the bottom of the screen. In the Quality tab of the Render Settings, leave Sampling Mode at Adaptive Sampling, but change Max Sample Level to 2 (which also changes Min Sample Level automatically to 0 from -2).

Figure 11.39
Turn on motion blur.

9. Set the Anti-aliasing Contrast attribute to 0.03, and change Filter to Gauss. Render frame 75 again (see Figure 11.41). This render should be much cleaner, with a smooth motion blur for the planets. Notice, however, that the render time increases by about 50 percent! You control the amount of blur in your scene with the Motion Blur By attribute (step 7) for your scene; but the higher the blur amount, the higher sampling you'll need to use, and the higher the resulting render times.

Figure 11.40
Render a frame with motion blur turned on.

Figure 11.41
Motion blur looks much better with higher sampling levels.

Render Layers

An important notion to keep in mind is that a CG image need not be created entirely in a single render. Most of the time, it's better to composite different elements together to form the final image. Professional CG workflow almost always requires multiple render passes that are composited together later for the maximum in efficiency and quality.

Maya does a great job of making rendering in layers much easier with render layers. As you saw earlier in this book, using Display layers helps a lot in keeping your scene organized. Render layers operate in basically the same way, although they function by separating different elements of the scene into separate renders.

The functionality behind render layers is very powerful. We'll address the most basic and commonly utilized here: separating objects into different renders. You'll select elements in a scene and assign them to different render layers. When you batch-render the scene, Maya will render each of the layers separately and save the files into their own subfolders in the Images folder of your current project. You'll then need to load all the different rendered layers into a compositing program, such as Apple Shake or Adobe After Effects, and composite the layers together.

Render Passes in mental ray

Two powerful features in mental ray rendering, Render Passes and Pass Contribution Maps, make rendering in layers much more efficient. This mental ray–specific workflow is fairly advanced and requires an existing knowledge of rendering as well as rendering in simple passes (such as you did with render layers) to grasp fully. As such, we won't cover these features in this book; however, you should be aware of this mental ray rendering pipeline as you move beyond this introduction and continue rendering with mental ray in your own work.

Rendering the Still Life in Layers

In this example, you'll separate a scene into different layers for rendering with Maya Software rendering.

To separate a scene into different layers, follow these steps:

1. Open the still life scene (still_life_v02.mb from the Scenes folder of the Lighting project on the CD) to start there. The lights and a camera are already set up in this scene. Set your camera view to camera1. Open Render Settings, and make sure Maya Software is the current renderer and not mental ray.

2. Separate the scene into different renders. To do so, in the Layer Editor, click the Render tab to switch to the render-layers view. Select the foreground lemon, and click the Create New Layer and Assign Selected Objects icon (). This creates a new render layer called layer1 and assigns the lemon to it. (See Figure 11.42.)

Figure 11.42

**The newly created
render layer with
the foreground
lemon assigned**

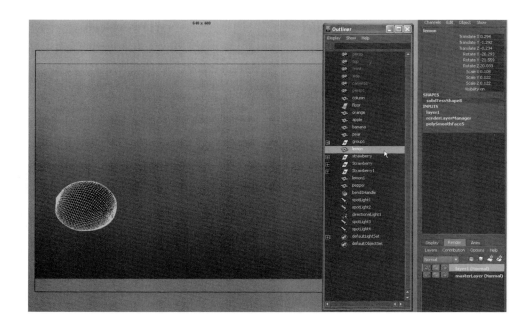

3. Click layer1, and everything but the lemon disappears from the scene (see Figure 11.42). Double-click layer1 in the Layer Editor and rename it **lemonPass,** as shown in Figure 11.43.

4. If you test-render a frame, the frame should turn black. You need to assign your lights to the render layer as well. Select all the lights in the scene using the Outliner, as shown in Figure 11.44. Right-click the lemonPass layer in the Layer Editor, and select Add Selected Objects from the shortcut menu. If you render a test frame now, the lemon renders as shown in Figure 11.45.

5. Create a render layer for the column and floor. Select the column, the floor, and all the lights in the scene. As you did with the lemon, click the Create New Layer and Assign Selected Objects icon (![icon]), and then click the new layer to select and display it. Double-click the layer name to rename the render layer **columnPass** (see Figure 11.46).

Figure 11.43

**Rename the render layer
to lemonPass.**

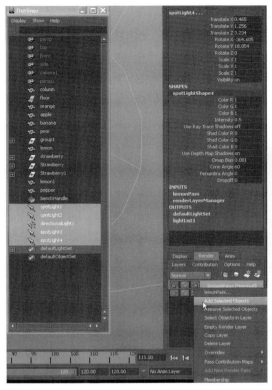

Figure 11.44

Add the lights to the lemonPass render layer.

Figure 11.45

The lemon rendered on its very own layer

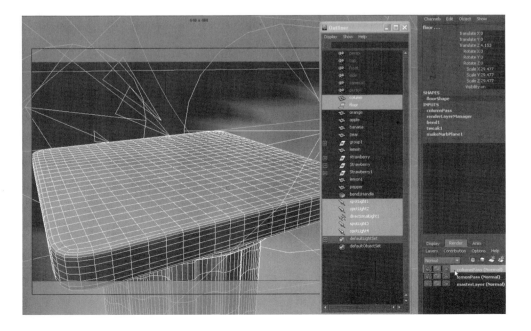

Figure 11.46

The background is assigned to its own render layer.

Figure 11.47

The newly created fruitPass render layer

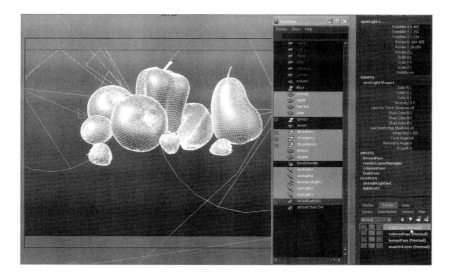

6. Select all the rest of the pieces of fruit, as shown in Figure 11.47, and create their render layer called **fruitPass**. You should now have three render layers and the default masterLayer. The masterLayer is always present to house all the elements of the scene. It switches to being not renderable as soon as you create a new render layer, as evidenced by the little red X in its Renderable icon ().

7. The first icon on each of the render layer entries in the Layer Editor toggles whether that layer will render or not. Make sure all your render layers are renderable, and leave the masterLayer off. Because all the elements of the scene are assigned to one render layer or another, the whole scene is covered. The masterLayer nonetheless is always present, because it represents all the objects in the scene, assigned to layers or not.

8. With the fruitPass render layer selected, test-render a frame, as shown in Figure 11.48. You should see just the fruit and not the background, column, or foreground lemon.

Figure 11.48

Rendering the rest of the fruit

Test-Rendering Everything Together

By default, Maya renders only the selected visible render layer. You can, however, tell Maya to test-render and show you all the layers composited together, to give you a pre-view of what you'll end up with when you composite all the layers together after batch-rendering the scene.

Figure 11.49

**Turn on Render
All Layers.**

To test-render all the layers together, click the Options menu in the Layer Editor, as shown in Figure 11.49, and toggle on Render All Layers by clicking the check box if it isn't already selected.

Now, if you test-render a frame, Maya will render each layer separately and then composite them together. Test-render a frame with Render All Layers enabled, and you should notice that the foreground lemon is missing, as in Figure 11.50.

Figure 11.50

**Rendering all the
layers together**

This is because the render layers in the Layer Editor need to be reordered so that columnPass is on the bottom, fruitPass is in the middle, and lemonPass is on top. This is the layer order-ing for the composite. You can reorder the render layers by MMB+clicking a layer and dragging it up or down to its new location in the Layer Editor, as in Figure 11.51.

Figure 11.51

**Reorder the
render layers.**

If you render the frame with Render All Layers enabled, you see the scene properly placed, as shown in Figure 11.52.

Figure 11.52

Now the lemon appears in the render.

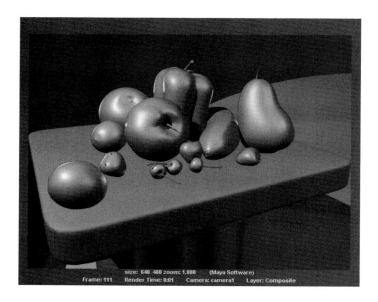

Creating a Shadow Pass

Where are the shadows? If you recall from earlier in this chapter, this scene renders with shadows; and now some of the shadows, particularly the ones that fall on the column, are gone. This is because the shadow-casting objects are on different layers than the column. Shadows can't be cast from one layer onto another. You'll need to create a layer for shadows to composite on top of everything.

Rendering everything in layers requires a workflow in which you essentially assemble everything in composite after your CG work is done and rendered. Creating a whole render pass for shadows is one step in this workflow. Just as you created different layers for the different objects in the scene, you'll create a new render layer to handle a shadow pass. A *shadow pass* in Maya is a render of only the shadows in the scene.

Keep in mind that this example works with Maya Software rendering and not mental ray. To create a shadow pass, follow along with these steps:

1. Select all the objects and lights in the scene, and create a new render layer by clicking the Create New Layer and Assign Selected Objects icon ( ). Rename the layer **shadowPass**, as shown in Figure 11.53.

2. Select the shadowPass, right-click it in the Layer Editor, and choose Attributes from the context menu that pops up. In the Attribute Editor, open the Render Pass Options heading, as shown in Figure 11.54; uncheck the Beauty check box, and check the Shadow check box.

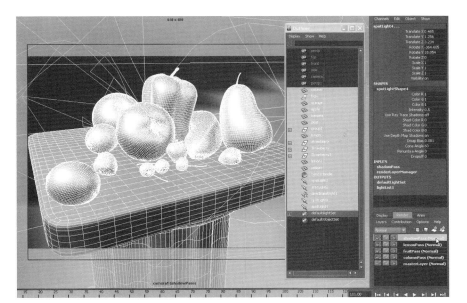

Figure 11.53
**Creating the
shadowPass layer**

This shadowPass layer now has a Render Override applied to it. All the objects in the layer will obey certain render settings that, in this case, will force Maya to render only the shadows for those objects.

3. In the Layer Editor, choose Options → Render All Layers to toggle it off for now. You just want to see the shadowPass test render. With the shadowPass selected, test-render a frame. You should see nothing but black in the Render View window, as shown in Figure 11.55. In such a pass, shadows render only in the alpha channel of the image.

4. Click the Display Alpha Channel icon (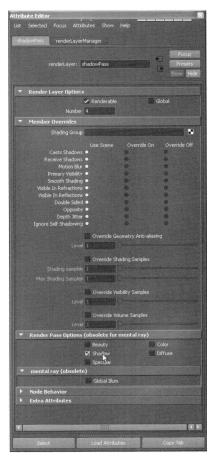) in the Render View window to show the shadows in the alpha channel, as you can see in Figure 11.56.

5. Re-enable Options → Render All Layers, and render the scene to see how the still life looks when Maya composites everything together for your test render, as shown in Figure 11.57.

Figure 11.54
Turn off the beauty pass, and turn on the shadow pass for the shadowPass layer.

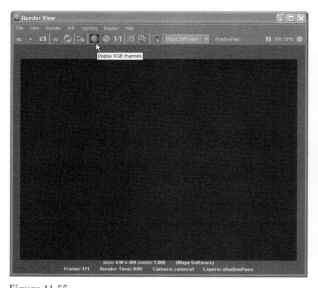

Figure 11.55

Nothing but black! Where are the shadows?

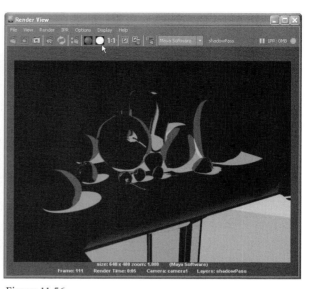

Figure 11.56

The shadows render into the alpha layer.

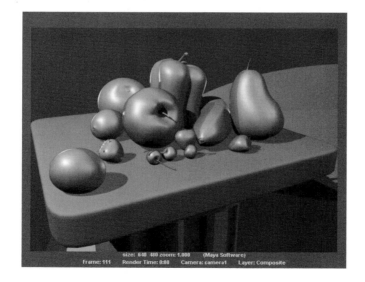

Figure 11.57

The still life rendered in layers and composited together in a test render with shadows

Figure 11.58

Check to make sure the layers you want to render are enabled.

Batch Rendering with Render Layers

Now that you have everything separated out into render layers, let's talk about batch rendering the scene out to composite later. Make the render layer you want to render out renderable by making sure the Renderable icon next to each render layer is enabled, as shown in Figure 11.58.

In the Render Settings window, make sure the Renderable Camera is set to camera1, as shown in Figure 11.59. Then, choose Render → Batch Render to render the scene. Because render layers are enabled here, Maya renders the scene out into different subfolders under the Images folder of your current project. Each render layer gets its own folder in the Images folder, as shown in Figure 11.60.

Render layers are a very powerful function of Maya's rendering workflow. We have only begun to scratch the surface here. When you get the hang of rendering, and as your CG needs begin to grow, you'll find a plethora of options when rendering with layers and rendering with passes through mental ray. This section and the "Ambient Occlusion" section later in this chapter are here only to familiarize you with the basic workflow of render layers. You can find a wealth of information about rendering in layers and passes in Maya's online documentation under the Help menu.

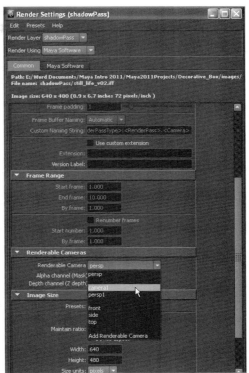

Figure 11.59

Select camera1 as your renderable camera in the Render Settings window.

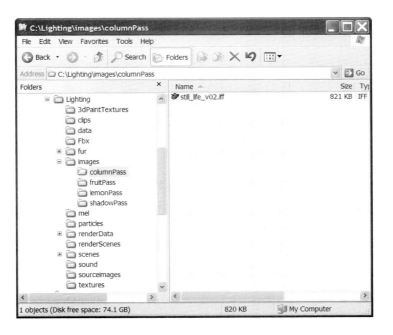

Figure 11.60

Render layers batch-render into subfolders under the Images folder of your project.

Final Gather

Final Gather (FG) is a type of rendering with mental ray that includes a single light bounce within the scene. Final Gather traces light as it reflects off surfaces to illuminate the scene for a nicely realistic render that takes into account color bleed of light from one surface to another. For example, a red wall casts a red hue on the surface right next to it. This is achieved easily with FG. FG is an intricate dance of settings and numbers that lets you get perfect renders. It's tough to cover in an introductory text such as this; however, this section will give you a primer to start using FG. In a follow-up section, you'll use a combination of lights and HDRI with Final Gather to render the red wagon.

The basic premise is that FG uses the illumination in the scene from lights as well as objects with color and incandescence set in their shaders to create a soft natural light. Its base settings will give you nice results right from the start.

To render the still life fruit scene with FG, begin by creating a dome light, which evenly illuminates a scene from a dome around the scene. (The term *dome light* is a bit of a misnomer, because a dome light isn't itself a light.) You'll construct a simple NURBS sphere, cut it in half to create a dome, and give it an Incandescent shader to provide the light for the scene. This type of quick FG setup is extremely useful for rendering out soft lighting and shadows to show off a model or a composition.

To light and render with FG, follow these steps:

1. Ensure that mental ray for Maya is loaded.

2. Load the still life scene file `still_life_mentalray_v01.mb` from the Lighting project from the CD. In the persp view (not the camera1 panel), create a NURBS sphere, and scale it up to enclose the entire scene. In the Channel Box, click the makeNurbSphere1 heading to select that node, and set the End Sweep attribute to 180 to cut the sphere in half. Rotate the dome to fit over the scene, as shown in Figure 11.61.

3. Add an Incandescent shader to the dome to give the scene some illumination through FG. To do so, in the Hypershade, create a new Lambert shader. Turn up its incandescence to a middle to light gray. Assign the new shader to the dome.

4. Maya has a feature that automatically creates a general default light in a scene that has no lights when you try to render it. Using this feature, you can test-render your scene quickly. However, because this incandescent dome light should be the only light source in the FG render, you have to turn off the default light feature before you render. Open the Render Settings window and, in the Common tab's Render Options heading (at the bottom of the Attribute Editor), turn off the Enable Default Light check box.

Don't forget to turn Enable Default Light back on when you're done with this FG exercise.

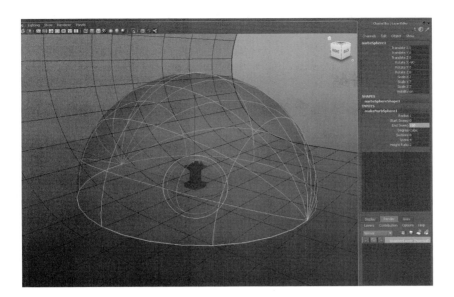

Figure 11.61

Create a sphere to act as the dome light.

5. At the top of the Render Settings window, switch the Render Using attribute to mental ray. You can keep the settings in the Common tab to render at 640 × 480. Choose the Quality tab to access its settings. Set Quality Presets to Preview: Final Gather to load the preset. This gives quick results using FG. Notice that raytracing is enabled under the Raytracing heading. Figure 11.62 shows the Quality tab of the Render Settings.

6. Click to open the Indirect Lighting tab, and click the Final Gathering heading to expand its attributes. Notice that Final Gathering is enabled. You can leave the settings at their defaults for your first render. Figure 11.63 shows the Indirect Lighting tab for the Render Settings window.

7. You need to make sure the sphere you're using as a dome light doesn't render out in the scene. Select the

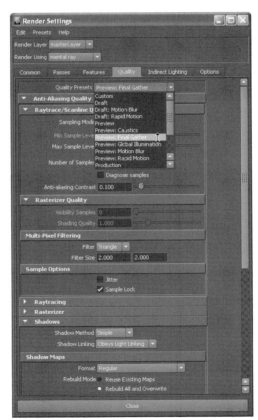

Figure 11.62

The Quality tab

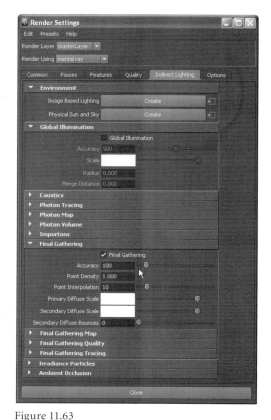

sphere, and, in its Attribute Editor under the Render Stats heading, turn off Primary Visibility. Highlight the camera1 panel, and render the frame. Maya makes two passes at the scene and shows you something like Figure 11.64. You can control the brightness of the scene with the Incandescence attribute value of the dome's shader—the whiter the incandescence, the brighter the scene.

Figure 11.63

The Indirect Lighting tab accesses all the Final Gather settings.

Figure 11.64

The Final Gather render of the still life

You can adjust the level of lighting by increasing or decreasing the amount of incandescence on the light dome's shader. The proximity of the sphere also affects the light amount, so moving the sphere closer or farther away will change the lighting level of the still life as well. You can also insert lights into the scene as you see fit. Using this sort of setup with only a light dome, however, gives you a quick and evenly lit render that is great for showing off models.

You can improve the quality of the render by adjusting either of the following two settings in the Indirect Lighting tab under the Final Gathering section of the Render Settings window:

Accuracy Increase this number for a more accurate render. Don't increase it too much, however, because it will slow down your render. Figure 11.64 shows the still life rendered with the default Accuracy setting of 100. In Figure 11.65, which uses a setting of 500, the soft shadows are noticeably smoother. Accuracy dictates the number of FG rays that are cast into the scene. The more rays, the better the quality of the render, although at a cost of rendering time.

Primary Diffuse Scale Use this setting to adjust the overall lighting level globally in the scene. The higher the value of this color, the brighter the scene. You can type values greater than 1 in the Color Chooser.

The Point Density and Point Interpolation attributes, along with several other attributes under the Final Gathering section, optimize and further control the FG settings for optimum efficiency and results, especially with animated scenes. Consider using the basic settings shown in this chapter to become familiar with mental ray for Maya, and then use FG to crank out fast and elegant renders to show off your models until you get more comfortable with mental ray.

When you get into complicated and intricate mental ray renders, you should consult the Maya documentation to learn more about its advanced settings. For now, however, using FG with basic settings will get you going. Final Gather is a tough nut to crack; it will take you some time to become proficient at rendering with FG in scene files and especially with animated scenes.

Later in this chapter, you'll try your hand at using FG, HDRI, and regular lights to render the decorative box from the previous chapters.

Figure 11.65

Accuracy set at 500 increases the smoothness of the soft shadows. It's hard to see here, but you'll notice it in your own render.

Ambient Occlusion

Ambient Occlusion is a special render pass that helps add depth and reality to a render. Ambient Occlusion goes by the premise that when two objects or surfaces are close to each other, they reduce the amount of light at the intersection. Ambient Occlusion passes make for great contact shadows and bring out the definition in surface creases and corners very nicely. Figure 11.66 shows an Ambient Occlusion pass for the living room scene from the PDF Global Illumination exercise included on the book's CD.

Figure 11.66

The Ambient Occlusion pass is black and white and is used to darken areas of the original color render.

How the composite works is very simple. Ambient Occlusion gives you a black-and-white pass of the same geometry you've already rendered. This pass is then multiplied over the color render. That means a brightness value of white (a value of 1) in the Ambient Occlusion pass won't change the color of the original render (when the original color of the render is multiplied by 1, it stays the same color). The black parts of the frame (with a brightness value of 0) turn those parts of the original render black (when the original color of the render is multiplied by 0, it goes to black). The gray points of the multiplying image darken the original render. It sounds confusing, but when you see it, it makes much better sense.

The Living Room

You'll now take the living room render made in the PDF file exercise on the CD and add an Ambient Occlusion pass using render layers. You don't have to read the PDF exercise to understand the concepts and practices for making an ambient occlusion pass here. However, if you'd like to understand how to light the living room scene with Global Illumination, you may wish to read that exercise on the CD now and then return to the following.

Set your current project to the Livingroom project you copied from the CD, open the livingRoom_v2.mb file from the Scenes folder, and follow these steps:

1. Make sure mental ray is loaded, of course, and that Render Settings is set to render with mental ray. As you did earlier, you need to create a new render layer for the Ambient Occlusion. This layer requires all the objects in the scene but the lights to be assigned to it. In this scene, the only light is a single directional light. In the Outliner, select all the top nodes of the scene, but leave out the light, as shown in Figure 11.67.

2. Click the Render radio button in the Layer Editor to switch to Render, and then click the Create New Layer and Assign Selected Objects icon (). Doing so creates a new layer (layer1) along with the preexisting masterLayer, as shown in Figure 11.68.

3. Click the new layer (layer1) to activate it. Everything in the scene should display as it did before, although the light disappears from view. Double-click layer1 to rename it **ambientOcclusion**.

4. You're going to use a preset to create a material override. This takes all the objects in the scene and assigns a single material to them: in this case, an Ambient Occlusion shader that generates the Ambient Occlusion pass for the entire scene. Right-click the ambientOcclusion layer, and select Attributes. In the Attribute Editor, click and hold down the Presets button. From the menu that appears, select Occlusion, as shown in Figure 11.69.

If you're in Shaded mode, everything should turn black in the view panels. This is normal, because everything now has the Ambient Occlusion Surface Shader

Figure 11.67

Select the scene objects for your Ambient Occlusion pass.

Figure 11.68

Create a new render layer.

assigned, and that shader displays black in Maya panels. If you click the masterLayer, everything pops back into place.

5. When you select Occlusion from the Presets menu, your Attribute Editor window should display a new shader called surfaceShader1. Figure 11.70 shows the new Ambient Occlusion shader that is assigned throughout the scene. Rename that shader to **ambOcc-Shader**. Don't worry if you don't see the surfaceShader1 in your Attribute Editor; you come back to it in later steps.

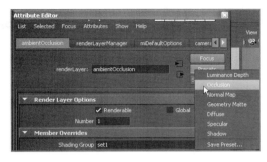

Figure 11.69

Setting an Occlusion preset for the layer

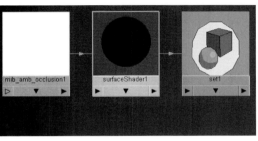

Figure 11.70

The Ambient Occlusion shader in the Hypershade

6. While still in the ambientOcclusion layer, render a frame. You should see something like Figure 11.71. You needn't worry about most of the settings in the Render Settings window; the layer preset takes care of it all. Well, almost all. It doesn't turn off the Global Illumination pass that you used for the original color render in the PDF exercise (which you can find on the CD); you need to turn that off manually in the next step.

7. In the Render Settings window, under the Indirect Lighting tab, you need to turn off Global Illumination, but just for the ambientOcclusion layer. With ambientOcclusion still selected in the Layer Editor, right-click the Global Illumination check box in Render Settings, and choose Create Layer Override. The attribute lettering turns orange to signify that it's being overridden for that render layer. Uncheck the box. It doesn't turn off GI for the masterLayer pass. You don't need to spend the time calculating any GI for this pass.

Figure 11.71

The first render from the Ambient Occlusion pass doesn't look great. It's too dark.

8. The render is mostly black, which darkens the original color render to black almost everywhere. You need the Ambient Occlusion shader to render mostly white with some darkening at the corners and where objects contact each other. You can adjust the Ambient Occlusion shader to fix this.

Open the Hypershade window, and click ambOccShader (or surfaceShader1, if you didn't rename it earlier in step 5—rename it now).

9. Notice that the Out Color attribute has a texture connection to it (signified by the 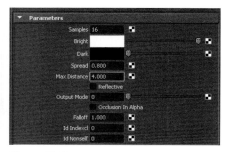 icon). Click this button to display the mib_amb_occlusion1 texture node in the Attribute Editor, as shown in Figure 11.72.

10. Set the Max Distance attribute to 4.0, as shown in Figure 11.73, and render the frame again. Your Ambient Occlusion layer should look like Figure 11.74. It should have also taken less than half as long to render as the darker render from Step 6.

Figure 11.72

The Ambient Occlusion shader attributes

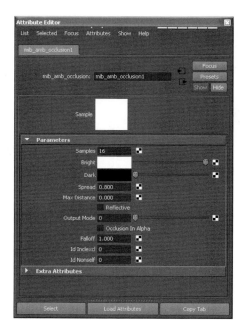

Figure 11.73

Set Max Distance to 4.

Figure 11.74

The Ambient Occlusion layer pass looks much better, but you aren't done yet!

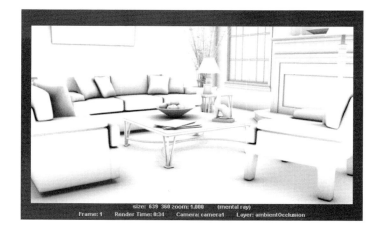

11. Notice that the glass in the window and the glass on the coffee table have shadows on them. Because glass is clear, they shouldn't have any Ambient Occlusion applied to them; it would look odd in the final composite. Select those pieces of geometry (Figure 11.75 shows the Outliner view for those pieces).

12. With the glass geometry selected, select Display → Hide → Hide Selection. Now the glass won't render in the Ambient Occlusion pass. But because you hid the objects only in this render layer, they still appear in the masterLayer; they will still render as glass in the color pass.

13. Render the frame, and you should have something similar to Figure 11.76. This is the Ambient Occlusion pass you need to composite.

Figure 11.75

The Outliner view of the glass geometry in the scene

Figure 11.76

The Ambient Occlusion pass

Rendering the Results

> Remember to check out the PDF exercise on the CD if you'd like to learn how this scene was lighted with Global Illumination.

You could save the image you just rendered in the Render View window to use in the composite, and then render the masterLayer for the color pass in the Render View and save that frame as well. Instead, let's batch-render the scene to show how Maya handles rendering with layers enabled. To batch-render the scene, follow these steps:

1. Turn on the Renderable icon box (![icon]) for the masterLayer, and make sure it's on for the ambientOcclusion layer as well.

2. Click to activate the masterLayer. Open the Render Settings window, and, in the Common tab, verify all the settings to render a single frame (name.ext.# in the Frame/Animation Ext field) at 639 × 360 (which is half 720p HD resolution). Also, select camera1 as the renderable camera.

3. If you batch-render (by choosing Render → Batch Render), Maya renders both render layers into the Images folder of your project in separate folders, as shown in Figure 11.77.

If for some reason your renders don't show up in your project's Images folder, open the Script Editor window, and look at the batch-render report. The render feedback shows you where the rendered images were saved, as shown in Figure 11.78. You may also want to make sure you set your project to the Livingroom project from the CD.

Figure 11.77

Maya renders the layers into their own folders by default.

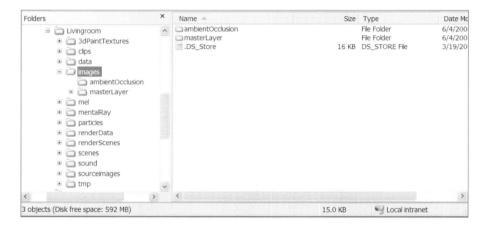

Figure 11.78

The Script Editor gives you feedback on the progress of the batch render.

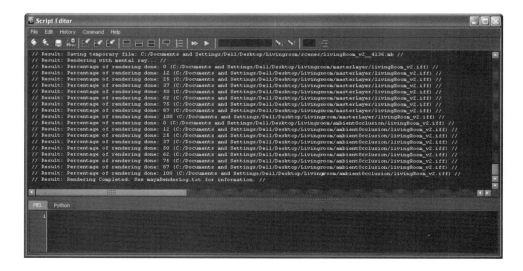

Compositing the Results

Now that the two layers are rendered in their respective folders, load them into your favorite compositing package. You'll layer the Ambient Occlusion pass over the color render using a Multiply Transfer mode. This exercise uses Adobe After Effects 7.0 to demonstrate how the Ambient Occlusion pass is composited over the original color render.

Figure 11.79 shows After Effects with the masterLayer color pass loaded. Figure 11.80 shows the ambientOcclusion pass layered on top of the color layer. Finally, Figure 11.81 shows the ambientOcclusion pass changed to a Multiply Transfer mode (as it's called in After Effects). Notice how the dark areas of the Ambient Occlusion pass help give contact shadows and depth to the color pass. Voila!

This is a prime example of rendering different passes to achieve a more realistic result. Remember, you needn't get everything in on a single pass. Use different layers to put your final images together in composite. The more you work with CG, the easier it will be to manage and plan.

You can see the difference Ambient Occlusion made to the living room image in the color section of this book and on the CD.

Figure 11.79

The masterLayer render pass is loaded into After Effects.

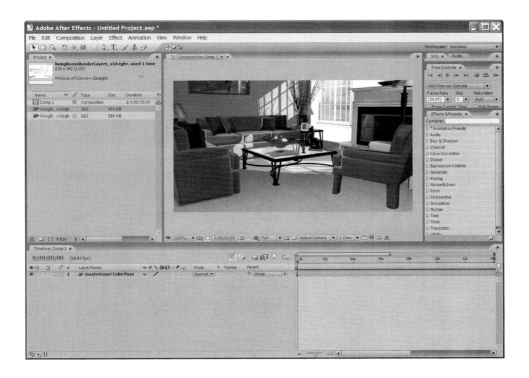

Figure 11.80

The ambient-
Occlusion render
pass is loaded into
After Effects.

Figure 11.80

The ambient-
Occlusion render
pass is loaded into
After Effects.

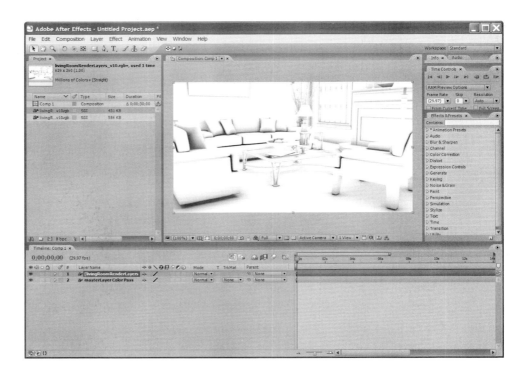

Figure 11.81

The ambient-
Occlusion pass is
multiplied over the
color pass and
creates a more real-
istic image.

HDRI

As you saw in the Final Gather section, FG rendering is based on the illumination in the scene from lights as well as the brightness of objects in the scene, such as a light dome. In the previous section, you used an incandescent dome to light the still-life scene. But what if you were to use an image instead of just white for the light dome?

Furthermore, what if the image you used was an High Dynamic Range Image (HDRI)? In Chapter 1, we briefly discussed HDR images. Several photos at varying exposures are taken of the same subject, ranging from very dark (low exposure) to highlight only the brightest parts of the scene, all the way up to very bright (overexposure) to capture the absolute darkest parts of the scene. When these images (usually five or seven images) are compiled into an HDR image, you get a fantastic range of bright to dark for that one subject.

How does this help you light? With image-based lighting (IBL), mental ray creates an environment sphere in your scene to which you assign an image, usually an HDRI. That environment sphere, much like the white dome in the Final Gather exercise earlier in the chapter, uses the brightness of its image to cast light in your Maya scene.

The best type of image to capture for an IBL is sometimes called a *light probe*. This is a picture of an environment, such as the office reflected in a chrome ball shown in Figure 11.82. You can also take a light probe using a fish-eye camera lens capable of capturing a field of view of close to 180 degrees.

Figure 11.82 shows the middle exposure of five exposures taken of the same office. Figure 11.83 shows the range from underexposed (dark) to overexposed (bright) of the five photos that were used to compile the HDRI of the desk you'll be using to light the decorative box in the next section.

The photos are compiled in an HDR image file (called DeskHDR.hdr in the Sourceimages folder of the Decorative_Box project on the CD) for the next section's IBL lighting exercise and as shown in Figure 11.84. You won't be able to see the

Figure 11.83

The five exposures that make up the HDRI of the desk to be used in the next section.

Figure 11.84

The images compiled into an HDR file and cropped to the ball

extensive range of the HDR, because the great majority of computer displays are limited to a display of 8-bit color. But you'll see that the image is cropped to the chrome ball's edges, because the ball's reflection of the office is what you're really after, not the desk.

Figure 11.84

The images compiled into an HDR file and cropped to the ball

The HDR will be mapped onto an IBL sphere. This is a large sphere that surrounds the environment in your Maya scene. Although you could use the simple DeskHDR.hdr and map it to the IBL sphere, it wouldn't be very accurate, because the corners of the square image show through to the desktop and background. The image first needs to be converted to a rectangular image file in which the sphere is unwrapped, as shown in Figure 11.85. This layout is called *LatLong* (Latitude/Longitude) and is just as if a geographic map on a school room globe was unwrapped into a rectangular sheet of paper. You can do this with a tool like HDRShop, available online. This LatLong image will now map more accurately onto the IBL sphere; only the reflection of the office in the ball will be used in the scene's lighting.

We won't get into the details of creating the HDRI, because it's an advanced topic using Photoshop CS3 or CS4; however, it's good to know the origins of HDR images and how they come to be used in IBL.

Figure 11.85

The chrome ball image is unwrapped and turned into a LatLong rectangular image.

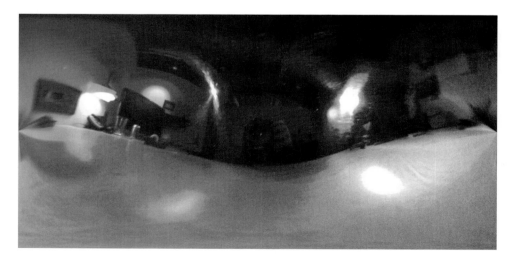

Rendering the Decorative Box

You're all grown up and ready to light a full scene using Final Gather, IBL with HDRI, and regular lights to get the best bang for your buck out of mental ray rendering. In the previous chapter, you briefly lit the decorative box with key, fill, and rim lights (the

three-point lighting system). In this exercise, you'll take this concept a few steps further, so take a deep breath, call your mother and tell her you love her, and let's get started! Open the boxLighting02.ma file in the Scenes folder of the Decorative_Box project. This has the lights and soft shadows created in Chapter 10 and is set to render through mental ray with raytracing enabled already. Let's take a critical look at the render from the previous chapter in Figure 11.86.

Most obviously, the carved details in the box need more detail. In the current render, the grooves are flat and shiny, whereas in the real box, they're carved into the wood and aren't glossy like the rest of the box.

Figure 11.86

The decorative box's current render from Chapter 10

Reflection Map

Just as you use a map to put color on the box, you can use similar maps to specify where and how much the box will reflect. Figure 11.87 shows the color map you used to texture the box in Chapter 7 side-by-side with a black-and-white map that shows only the carved regions of the box. This map was created with elbow grease and hard work to manually isolate just the carved areas of the box in Photoshop. See how much I do for you?

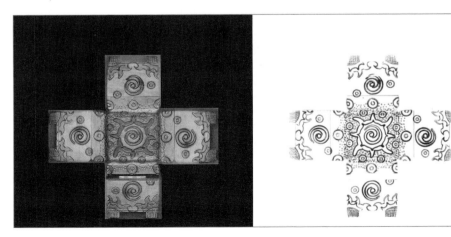

Figure 11.87

The black-and-white map on the right shows only the carved areas of the box.

You'll first take the reflections out of the carved areas in the following steps:

1. In the boxLighting02.mb scene, open the Hypershade. In the Create Bar on the left, click 2D Textures under the Maya heading, and choose File to open a new image file node (called file2). See Figure 11.88.

2. Double-click the file node, and navigate to find and choose the boxCarvings.jpg file in the Sourceimages folder of the Decorative_Box project. See Figure 11.89.

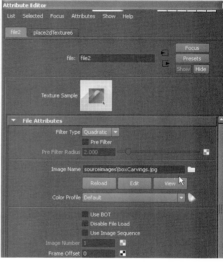

Figure 11.88

Create a new file node.

Figure 11.89

Select the proper image file.

3. Notice that the sample swatch at the top of the Attribute Editor for the file2 node doesn't show the image you just selected. This is because the image is too large for Maya to create a thumbnail swatch automatically, for expediency's sake. The file node in the Hypershade is also blank. Right-click the file node, and choose Refresh Swatch from the marking menu. Figure 11.90 shows the swatch with the black-and-white image as a thumbnail. This isn't necessary, but it makes it easier for you to identify what file map is where.

Figure 11.90

The swatch now shows a thumbnail of the image you're using.

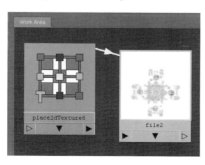

Figure 11.91

Map the new image file to the reflectivity attribute.

4. MMB-drag the phong1 node from the top of the Hypershade window down to the work area, alongside the file2 node. Double-click the phong1 node to open the Attribute Editor. MMB-drag the file2 node onto the Reflectivity attribute for the Phong2 shader, as shown in Figure 11.91.

5. Notice the connection line in the Hypershade between the file2 and phong1 nodes. The white areas of the map tell the phong1 shader to have a reflectivity of 1, whereas the black areas have zero reflectivity. This effectively removes reflections from the box's carvings. Render a frame of the box in the renderCam view, and compare to Figure 11.92. In the Render View window, click the Keep Image icon ( ) to store this render in the render buffer. Doing so allows you to easily compare renders to see the changes you make as you continue.

Figure 11.92

The reflections are stronger; the entire box looks like a mirror!

6. The box's reflections are now stronger all over, and the carvings still reflect. You need to turn on one switch. Select the file2 node, and open the Color Balance heading in the Attribute Editor. Check the box for the Alpha Is Luminance attribute. This instructs Maya to use the luminance values (basically the brightness) of the image to output to the reflectivity attribute of the phong1 shader. The box renders properly and the carvings have no reflections, as shown in Figure 11.93. Save this render into the render buffer with the Keep Image icon ( ).

7. You need to reduce the reflections on the rest of the box. Double-click the file2 node to open the Attribute Editor. In the Color Balance heading, set Alpha Gain to 0.4,

as shown in Figure 11.94. This sets the brightest part of the reflections to be capped at .4 and not the previous 1.0. Render, and you see a much better reflection in the box and no reflections in the carvings. (See Figure 11.95.) Save this to the render buffer.

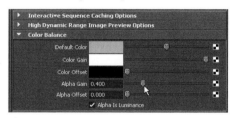

Figure 11.94

Set Alpha Gain to 0.4.

8. Rename the file2 node to reflectionMap and the phong1 node to boxShader, and save your work.

You can open the scene file boxRendering01.ma from the Scenes folder in the Decorative_Box project to catch up to this point or to check your work so far.

Figure 11.95

The reflections look much better now.

Displacement Mapping

Now that the reflections are set up, you'll use the same image map to create displacements in the box to sink the carvings into the box. Isn't that convenient?

1. In the Hypershade, click to create a new file node, and select the boxCarvings.jpg file in the Sourceimages folder again. You don't want to reuse the same file node as you did for the reflections (reflectionMap node), because you need to change some of its attributes. Name the new file node displacementMap.

2. Double-click the boxShader node to open the Attribute Editor. MMB-drag the new displacementMap node onto the boxShader node in the Hypershade, and select Displacement Map from the context menu that pops up, as shown in Figure 11.96.

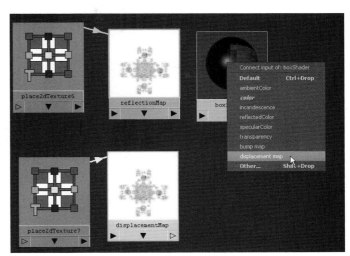

Figure 11.96

Add the new image map to the Displacement Map attribute.

3. A new node appears called displacementShader1, but there is no connection apparent to the boxShader. Select the boxShader, and choose the Input and Output connections icon at the top of the Hypershade (⬛). The Hypershade shows you the entire shader network, including the displacement map connection, as seen in Figure 11.97. Notice that the displacement connects to the phong1SG node and not directly to the boxShader node. This is normal and how it's always done.

Occasionally, when you click to view the input and outputs of a shader as you did in step 3, the Hypershade will put some nodes on top of others. If you don't see any of the nodes shown in Figure 11.96, try clicking and dragging some of the nodes around in the Hypershade to see if there are any accidentally hidden nodes. These little touches make Maya extra fun!

4. Render the box and see what happens now that you have a displacement map applied. Figure 11.98 shows how the box seems to have exploded!

Not to worry, this is to be expected. The values coming from the black-and-white map dictate how much of the geometry is displaced (moved). Obviously, you don't have an image that works well for the amount of displacement, although it does look like the displacements are in the proper place to correspond to where the carvings are on the box.

Figure 11.97

The shader network for the box

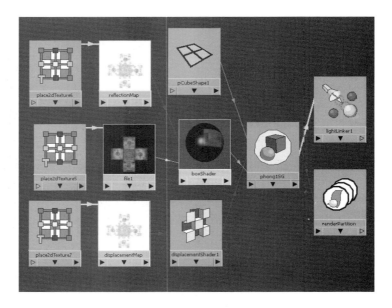

Figure 11.98

Oh no, the box has exploded!

5. Double-click the displacementMap node. In the Attribute Editor, open the Effects heading, and turn on the Invert check box. This turns the background to black and the carvings to white. Set Alpha Gain to 0.1 in the Color Balance heading, and make sure Alpha Is Luminance is also checked. (See Figure 11.99.) The Alpha Gain value reduces the amount of displacement, and inverting the image lets the rest of the box outside of the carvings not be displaced.

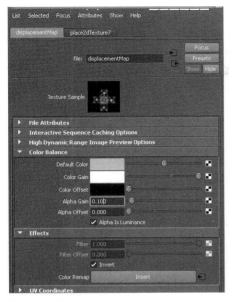

Figure 11.99

Set the attributes for the displacement image.

Figure 11.100

The carvings are displacing outward.

6. Render a frame, and compare it to Figure 11.100. It's not looking very good. The box isn't exploding anymore, and only the carvings are displacing, which is good. However, the carvings are sticking out, instead of in.

7. Set the Alpha Gain attribute to -0.05 to push the carvings in a little instead of out. Render, and compare to Figure 11.101. The carvings are set into the wood as they should be, but the render looks bad. The displacements are very jagged and ill-defined.

Figure 11.101

The carvings are inset into the wood, but they don't look good yet.

8. The jagged look of the carvings has to do with the tessellation of the box—that is, the detail of the box's polygonal mesh. There are advanced ways to deal with how mental ray deals with displacements; however, the most basic method is to adjust the detail of the box's mesh. Figure 11.102 shows the current box's mesh. Notice that the sides of the box are very simply detailed. To increase the box's faces to add detail, select the box, and then, in the Polygons menu set, choose Edit Mesh → Add Divisions ❑. Set the options to Exponentially and Division Levels of 3, as shown in Figure 11.103. Click Add Divisions to execute.

9. Figure 11.104 shows the newly tessellated box. It's far more detailed in the mesh. When you render, it gives a result similar to Figure 11.105.

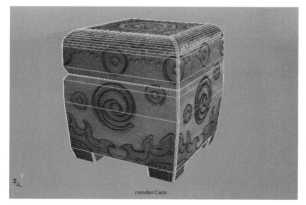

Figure 11.102
The current box's mesh isn't detailed enough.

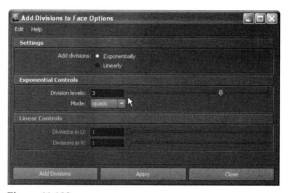

Figure 11.103
Set the Add Division values.

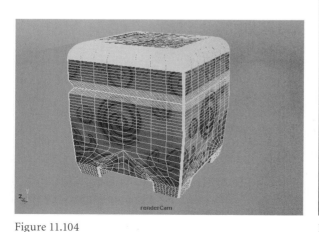

Figure 11.104
Added divisions

Figure 11.105
The displacements render much better now.

Notice that the render times have gone up because you increased the detail on the mesh. This is normal, but it can become a problem if the mesh is too divided and has more faces than you need. This box has fairly detailed carvings, so the level to which you set Add Divisions in Step 8 gives a good result without being too detailed. As your experience increases in Maya and mental ray rendering, you'll learn how to use functions such as mental ray's Approximation Editor to keep the overall detail low on the mesh, but with smooth displacement results when you render. This is an advanced technique, so we won't cover it in this book. You've taken in quite a lot by this point already.

The next time you select the box and open the Attribute Editor, you'll see a new tab called polySubdFace1. This is the node added with the Add Divisions function in Step 8. Feel free to adjust the Subdivision Levels in that tab and rendering to see how the detail levels affect the final render. Also try better quality settings in Render Settings, as you did with the red wagon earlier in this chapter, to clean up the render to your satisfaction.

Figure 11.106

Click to create an IBL.

You can open the scene file boxRendering02.ma from the Scenes folder in the Decorative_Box project to catch up to this point or to check your work so far. You'll next add an IBL sphere and use the HDR image you saw earlier in the chapter.

Adding an IBL

Here's where things get fun. You'll add an IBL node to the scene and add the office desktop HDR image to that IBL. First, make sure you have mental ray selected as your renderer in the Render Settings window, and then follow along with these steps:

1. In the Render Settings window, click the Indirect Lighting tab. At the top, in the Environment heading, click the Create button for Image Based Lighting, as shown in Figure 11.106.

2. The Attribute Editor opens to a view of the newly created IBL (named mentalrayIblShape1), as shown in Figure 11.107.

3. Click the folder icon () next to the Image Name attribute. Navigate to the Sourceimages folder of the Decorative_Box project on your system, and select the file DeskHDRLatLong.hdr. You see in your view panes that a large yellow sphere is created in your scene. The office light probe HDR image is mapped. (See Figure 11.108.)

Figure 11.107

The Attribute Editor for the IBL node

Figure 11.108

The IBL is in place and mapped to the office chrome ball HDRI.

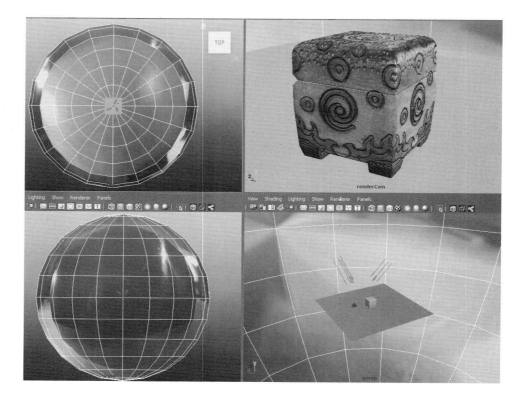

4. If you render a frame, you see the light probe in the background and in the reflections; however, the lighting is unchanged from before. This is because you need to enable Final Gather to take advantage of the IBL and the HDRI mapped to it. In the Render Settings window's Indirect Lighting tab, check the Final Gathering check box in the Final Gathering heading. Leave the settings at their defaults, and render a frame.

   Figure 11.109 shows a marked change in the look of the box from previous renders (as well as a longer render time). Save the image into your Render View buffer (▣), and compare it to your earlier render before the IBL. Also notice the bounced light on the gray floor, which is a nice touch, albeit splotchy right now.

5. Let's remove the IBL from the background of the render. Select the IBL sphere and, in the Attribute Editor under the Render Stats heading, turn off Primary Visibility. The background renders black without the IBL.

6. Because the IBL is doing some of the heavy lifting for the lighting, you can turn down the intensities of the direct lights. Set the key light (directionalLight1) intensity to 1.25 and the directional rim light (directionalLight3) to 0.35. The orientation of the IBL affects the lighting in the scene, although it's fine as it is now.

Figure 11.109

The IBL contributes to the lighting.

Figure 11.110

The box looks pretty good now, although still noisy.

Render the frame, and compare to Figure 11.110 and your previous renders. Feel free to select the IBL and change its rotation to a different orientation to see how it changes the look of the box. Just don't forget to return it to its current orientation to stay consistent with the results shown in Figure 11.110 and the following steps.

ORIENTING THE IBL

The image (HDRI or otherwise) used in an IBL and the IBL's orientation are huge factors in the lighting of a scene. Play around with the rotations of the IBL to see how the lighting differs until you settle on a look you like.

7. The render looks nice, except it's noisy. Notice the blotches of color all over the floor. This is from having low-quality settings for FG. In the Render Settings' Indirect Lighting tab, increase Accuracy to 300 under the Final Gathering heading. Also set Point Density to 2.0 and Point Interpolation to 30. Doing so dramatically increases the render time for the frame (almost doubling the previous time); however, it makes the box look much better—practically eradicating the blotchy nature of the previous renders. The box has a nice glossy look to it. (See Figure 11.111.) Save the image to your Render View buffer.

You can open the scene file boxRendering03.ma from the Scenes folder in the Decorative_ Box project to catch up to this point or to check your work so far.

Figure 11.111

Using higher-quality settings for FG makes a big difference.

FG is a difficult beast to tame, especially with an IBL. It takes a lot of experience and practice to be able to use this powerful feature of mental ray successfully in scenes. Experiment with different HDR images that you can download from the Internet as well as adjusting the lights in the scene.

Blurring Reflections

Let's tweak the render a little more by making a new desktop for the box to sit on:

1. Open the Hypershade, and create a new Blinn shader for the desktop. Call it **desk-Shader**, and assign it to the floor plane of the box scene.

2. Click the map icon next to the Color attribute for the deskShader, create a new file node, and choose the deskWood.jpg image from the project's Sourceimages folder.

3. Create two polygonal planes to make the corner of two walls behind the box, as shown in Figure 11.112, to have something in the background. Assign a light gray Lambert to the walls. Adjust the desk shape to be more of a rectangle, to make the wood image map look nicer.

Figure 11.112

Create walls and a wood desktop.

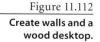

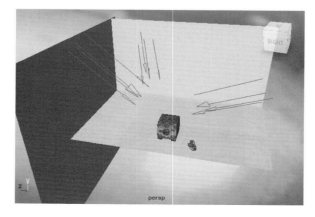

4. Render a frame, and compare it to Figure 11.113. The reflections are too glossy and apparent; you want to mimic a semi-gloss desktop table. Also, the lighting on the box has changed, because the new, shiny desktop shader is bouncing more light than the earlier default gray plane. This is why indirect lighting can be more photo-real, if not more tricky to control.

5. Select the deskShader, and turn down Reflectivity to 0.25. Open the mental ray heading, and set Mi Reflection Blur to 4. Set Reflection Rays to 8, as shown in Figure 11.114.

6. While you're at it, select the boxShader and set its reflections to be blurred, with a Mi Reflection Blur value of 2. Set Reflection Rays to 4. Render, and check against Figure 11.115. You'll see better results on your own screen, because the differences in reflections are subtle. And that's the point: the more finesse and attention you pay to the minor details, the better your image(s). You can play with the Reflection Rays for your desktop to get a softer look than in Figure 11.115.

Figure 11.113

The reflections look too perfect and glossy.

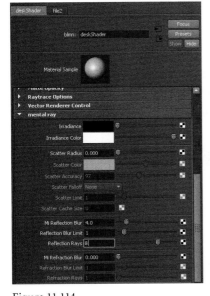

Figure 11.114

Create blurred reflections for the desk.

Figure 11.115

Blurred reflections on the desktop and the box make the image more real.

Adding Depth of Field

One last item of interest is adding a depth of field (DOF) to the image. This effect adds blur to the render for the areas of the image that may be out of the lens' focal depth. It can greatly add to the photo-realism of a rendered image.

Select the renderCam, and open the Attribute Editor. In the Depth of Field heading, check the Depth of Field attribute. Set Focus Distance to 11, because the box is about 11 units away from the camera, and set F Stop to 9.0. This setting, as with a real lens, sets how much is in focus around the focal distance. With a higher F Stop value, the focus runs deeper than with a low F Stop value.

Figure 11.116 shows the final render of the box with DOF enabled. Your render times will be longer; and for a better render, you'll need to increase your Sample settings. Figure 11.116 was rendered with Min Samples of 0, Max Samples of 1, and Anti-Aliasing Contrast of 0.04.

The scene file boxRendering04.ma from the Scenes folder in the Decorative_Box project will take you to this point.

Notice from the render that the back end of the box is thrown out of focus, along with the back of the desktop and the walls. Depending on the need and the size of the render, you'll have to set the sampling levels to suit your needs; but be warned that your rendering times will dramatically increase, easily tripling depending on the quality settings. There are several ways to create DOF in a render that are faster or more controllable than we've covered here. You can render out a depth pass to use with a lens filter in a compositing package such as Nuke, to keep render times down. There are also more accurate DOF methods in mental ray and its lens shaders that you can experiment with when you've comfortably grasped the overall workflow presented here.

Finally, adding an Ambient Occlusion pass isn't absolutely necessary for this render, although it will enhance the look of the contact shadows.

Figure 11.116

The decorative box is done!

Wrapping Up the Decorative Box

When you've learned a lot more about lighting and gained confidence with the processes of lighting, rendering, and compositing, you'll find a wealth of options when you render in several different layers. For example, if this decorative box were a professional job, its render would most likely be split into a flat color pass, a reflection pass, a specular high-light pass, a shadow pass, an Ambient Occlusion pass, a depth pass, and several different matte passes that separate parts of the scene to give the compositor the ultimate control in adjusting the image to taste.

You may not know what all those passes do right now, but understanding will come with time as long as you continue practicing your CG Kung Fu. Rendering your own color passes and ambient occlusions will give you some beautiful renders even without all the other passes. Keep in mind that small changes and additions can take you a long way toward a truly rich image.

Summary

In this chapter, you learned how to set up your scene for rendering. Starting with the Render Settings window and moving on to the different render engines available, you learned how to render your scene for a particular look. Then, we covered how to preview your render and how to use IPR for fast scene feedback. We moved on to how to render reflections and refractions, how to create and use cameras, and how to render motion blur. You tested your skill on a wine bottle scene; and, to batch-render it out into a sequence of images, you checked it in a program such as FCheck. You also used Maya's render layers and rendering and an Ambient Occlusion pass to make your renders more realistic. Finally, you applied this knowledge to rendering the decorative box using Final Gather and an HDR.

Getting to this point in a scene can take some work, but when you see the results playing back on your screen, all the work seems more than worth it. Nothing is more fulfilling than seeing your creation come to life, and that's what rendering is all about. But don't consider the rendering process a mere push-button solution when planning your animations. Always allow enough time to ensure that your animations render properly and at their best quality. Most beginners seriously underestimate the time needed to complete this step properly in CG production.

After you create numerous scenes and render them out, you'll begin to understand how to construct your next scenes so that they render better and faster. Be sure to keep on top of your file management: rendering can produce an awful lot of files, and you don't want to have them scattered all over the place.

CHAPTER 12

Maya Dynamics and Effects

Autodesk's Maya is renowned for creating special effects animations that simulate not only physical phenomena, such as smoke and fire, but also the natural movements of colliding bodies. Behind the latter type of animation is the Maya dynamics engine, which is the sophisticated software that creates realistic-looking motion based on the principles of physics.

Another powerful Maya animation tool, Paint Effects, can create dynamic fields of grass and flowers, a head full of hair, and other such systems in a matter of minutes. Maya also offers dynamic simulations for hair, fur, and cloth. In this chapter, we'll cover the basics of dynamics in Maya and let you practice working with particles by making steam.

Topics in this chapter include:

- **An overview of dynamics and Maya Nucleus**
- **Rigid and soft dynamic bodies**
- **Animating with dynamics: the pool table**
- **nParticle Dynamics**
- **Emitting nParticles**
- **Animating an nParticle effect: locomotive steam**
- **Introduction to Paint Effects**
- **Where do you go from here?**

An Overview of Dynamics and Maya Nucleus

Dynamics is the simulation of motion through the application of the principles of physics. Rather than assigning keyframes to objects to animate them, with Maya dynamics you assign physical characteristics that define how an object behaves in a simulated world. You create the objects as usual in Maya, and then you convert them to *dynamic bodies*. Dynamic bodies are defined through dynamic attributes you add to them, which affect how the objects behave in a dynamic simulation.

Dynamic bodies are affected by external forces called *fields*, which exert a force on them to create motion. Fields can range from wind forces to gravity and can have their own specific effects on dynamic bodies. You'll learn how to use fields later in this chapter.

In Maya, dynamic objects are categorized as bodies, particles, hair, and fluids. Dynamic bodies are created from geometric surfaces and are used for physical objects such as bouncing balls. *Particles* are points in space that have renderable properties and that behave dynamically. Particles are used for numerous effects, such as fire and smoke; they're also useful in tons of other situations and, as such, are a specialty of their own for professional animators. We'll cover particle basics in the latter half of this chapter. *Hair* consists of curves that behave dynamically, such as strings. *Fluids* are, in essence, volumetric particles that can exhibit surface properties. You can use fluid dynamics for natural effects such as billowing clouds or plumes of smoke.

Nucleus, which was introduced in Maya 8.5 with nCloth, is a more stable and interactive way of calculating dynamic simulations in Maya than the traditional dynamics engine. Nucleus speeds up the creation and increases the stability of some dynamic effects in Maya, including particle effects and cloth simulation (through nCloth).

In the Maya 2009 release, Autodesk introduced nParticles. They're closely related to traditional particles in Maya but have been made easier to create and manage, requiring less explicit expression controls than before.

We'll introduce nParticles (instead of traditional particles) later in this chapter; however, soft bodies, hair, nCloth, and fluid dynamics are advanced topics and won't be covered in this book.

Rigid and Soft Dynamic Bodies

The two types of dynamic bodies are rigid and soft. *Rigid bodies* are solid objects, such as a pair of dice or a baseball, that move and rotate according to the dynamics applied. Fields and collisions affect the entire object and move it accordingly. *Soft bodies* are malleable surfaces that deform dynamically, such as drapes in the wind or a bouncing rubber ball. In brief, this is accomplished by making the surface points (NURBS, CVs, or polygon vertices) of the soft body object dynamic instead of the whole object. The forces and collisions of the scene affect these surface points, making them move to deform their surface.

In this section, you'll learn about rigid body dynamics.

Creating Active and Passive Rigid Body Objects

Any surface geometry in Maya can be converted to a rigid body. After it's converted, that surface can respond to the effects of fields and take part in collisions. When one Maya object hits another in a dynamic simulation, Maya calculates the animation of the colliding objects according to their velocity and other dynamic properties such as mass. Sounds like fun, eh?

The two types of rigid bodies are active and passive. An *active rigid body* is affected by collisions and fields. A *passive rigid body* isn't affected by fields and remains still when it collides with another object. A passive rigid body is solely used as a surface against which active rigid bodies collide.

The best way to see how the two types of rigid bodies behave is to create some and animate them. In this section, you'll do that in the classic animation exercise of a bouncing ball.

To create a bouncing ball using Maya rigid bodies, switch to the Dynamics menu and follow these steps:

1. Create a polygonal plane, and scale it to be a ground surface.

2. Create a poly sphere, and position it a number of units above the ground, as shown in Figure 12.1.

3. Make sure you're in the Dynamics menu set (choose Dynamics from the Status Line drop-down bar). Select the poly sphere, and choose Soft/Rigid Bodies → Create Active Rigid Body. The sphere's Translate and Rotate attributes turn yellow. There will be a dynamic input for those attributes, and, as such, you can't set keyframes on any of them. The dynamics engine drives the movement and rotation of the active rigid body sphere.

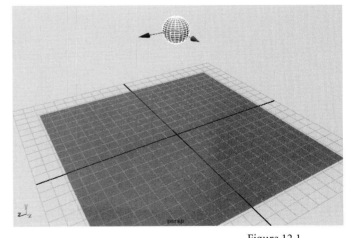

Figure 12.1

Place a poly sphere a few units above a poly plane ground surface.

4. Select the ground plane, and choose Soft/Rigid Bodies → Create Passive Rigid Body. This sets the poly plane as a passive rigid body to serve as the floor on which to bounce your active rigid ball. For this exercise, stick with the default settings and ignore the various creation options and Rigid Body attributes; you'll explore the most important of those later in this chapter.

5. To put the ball into motion, you need to create a field to affect it. Select the sphere, and choose Fields → Gravity. By selecting the active rigid object(s) while you create the field, you connect that field to the objects automatically. Fields affect only the

active rigid bodies to which they're connected. If you hadn't established this connection initially, you could still do so later, through the Dynamic Relationships Editor. You'll find out more about this process later in this chapter.

If you try to scrub the timeline, you'll notice that the animation doesn't run properly. Because dynamics simulates physics, no keyframes are set. You must play the scene from start to finish for the calculations to execute properly. You must also play the scene using the Play Every Frame option. Click the Animation Options button to the right of the Range slider, or choose Window → Settings/Preferences → Preferences. In the Preferences window, choose Time Slider under the Settings header. Choose Play Every Frame from the Playback Speed menu. You can also set the maximum frames per second that your scene will play back by setting the Max Playback Speed attribute.

To play back the simulation, set your frame range from 1 to at least 500. Go to frame 1, and click Play. Make sure you have the proper Playback Speed settings in your Preferences window; otherwise, the simulation won't play properly.

When the simulation plays, you'll notice that the sphere begins to fall after a few frames and collides with the ground plane, bouncing back up.

As an experiment, try turning the passive body plane into an active body using the following steps:

1. Select the plane, and open the Attribute Editor.

2. In the rigidBody2 tab, select the Active check box. This switches the plane from a passive body to an active body.

3. Play the simulation. The ball falls to hit the plane and knock it away. Because the plane is now an active body, it's moved by collisions. But because it isn't connected to the gravity field, it doesn't fall with the ball.

To connect the now-active body plane to the gravity field, open the Dynamic Relationships Editor window, shown in Figure 12.2 (choose Window → Relationship Editors → Dynamic Relationships).

Figure 12.2

The Dynamic Relationships Editor window

You can also connect a dynamic object to a field by selecting the dynamic object or objects and then the desired field and choosing Fields → Affect Selected Object(s). This method is more useful for connecting multiple dynamic objects to a field.

On the left is an Outliner list of the objects in your scene. On the right is a list from which you can choose a category of objects to list: Fields (default), Collisions, Emitters, or All. Select the geometry (*pPlane1*) on the left side, and then connect it to the gravity field by selecting the gravityField1 node on the right.

When you connect the gravity field to the plane and run the simulation, you'll see the plane fall away with the ball. Because the two fall at the same rate (the rate set by the single gravity field), they don't collide. To disconnect the plane from the gravity field, deselect the gravity field in the right panel.

RELATIONSHIP EDITORS

The Relationship Editors, such as the Dynamic Relationships window, are a means to connect two nodes to create a special relationship. The Dynamic Relationships Editor window specializes in connecting dynamic attributes so that fields, particles, and rigid bodies can interact in a simulation. Another example of a Relationship Editor is the Light Linking window, which allows you to connect lights to geometry so that they light only that specific object or objects. These are fairly advanced topics; however, as you learn more about Maya, their use will become integral in your workflow.

Turning the active body plane back to a passive floor is as simple as returning to frame 1, the beginning of the simulation, and clearing the Active attribute in the Attribute Editor. By turning the active body back to a passive body, you regain an immovable floor upon which the ball can collide and bounce.

Moving a Rigid Body

Because Maya's dynamics engine controls the movement of any active rigid bodies, you can't set keyframes on their translation or rotation. With a passive object, however, you can set keyframes on translation and rotation as you can with any other Maya object. The object isn't active, so the dynamics engine doesn't regulate its movement with fields or collisions. But you can easily keyframe an object to be either active or passive for the widest of options.

Now, any movement that the passive body has through regular keyframe animation is translated into momentum, which is passed on to any active rigid bodies with which the passive body collides. Think of a baseball bat that strikes a baseball. The baseball bat is a passive rigid body that you have keyframed to swing. The baseball is an active rigid body that is hit by (collides with) the bat as it swings. The momentum of the bat is transferred to the ball, and the ball is sent flying into the stadium stands.

You'll see an example of this in action in the next tutorial.

Rigid Body Attributes

To make an object a rigid body, you add several attributes that help govern how it behaves in a dynamic simulation. Here is a rundown of the more important attributes for both passive and active rigid bodies as they pertain to collisions:

Mass Sets the relative mass of the rigid body. Set on active or passive rigid bodies, *mass* is a factor in how much momentum is transferred from one object to another. A more massive object pushes a less massive one with less effort and is itself less prone to movement when hit. Mass is relative, so if all rigid bodies have the same mass value, there is no difference in the simulation.

Static and Dynamic Friction Sliders Set how much friction the rigid body has while at rest (static) and while in motion (dynamic). *Friction* specifies how much the object resists moving or being moved. A friction of 0 makes the rigid body move freely, as if on ice.

Bounciness Specifies how resilient the body is upon collision. The higher the *bounciness* value, the more bounce the object has upon collision.

Damping Creates a drag on the object in dynamic motion so that it slows down over time. The higher the *damping*, the more the body's motion diminishes.

Animating with Dynamics: The Pool Table

This exercise will take you through the creation of a scene in which you'll use dynamics to animate a cue ball striking two balls on a pool table.

Creating the Pool Table and the Balls

You'll create a simple pool table as a collision surface for the pool balls. To create the table, follow these steps:

1. Create a polygonal plane for the surface of the table. Scale it to 10 along its height and length.

2. To create the pocket holes, make two holes in opposite corners. The easiest way is to duplicate the tabletop plane and offset it slightly in both directions, as shown in Figure 12.3. Doing so creates a pair of square holes in the corners for the ball to drop through. For this exercise, it will do perfectly well.

3. Create a polygonal cube, and scale it to fit one edge of the plane to create a rail. Duplicate the cube three times, and then move and rotate the pieces to create the rails around the table, as shown in Figure 12.4.

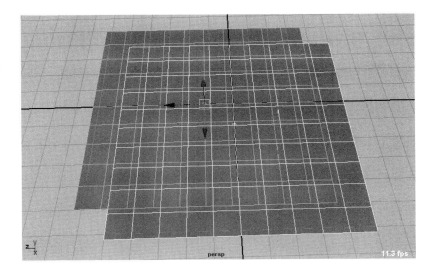

Figure 12.3

Duplicate the table-top plane, and offset it slightly in both directions.

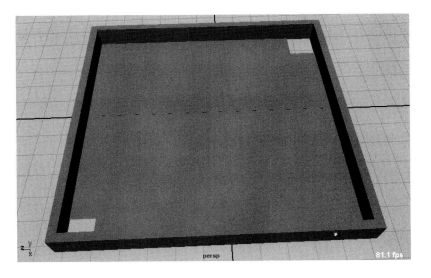

Figure 12.4

A simple pool table

4. Create three poly spheres, and then scale and place them as shown in Figure 12.5. It's important to place them slightly above the pool table surface. Although it's not imperative to have the exact location shown in the figure, it's a good idea to get close to the layout shown.

5. Shade your pool balls to make each one different. The figures in this exercise show a solid white ball, a striped ball (it will be yellow on your screen), and a black eight ball, as shown in Figure 12.6.

Figure 12.5

Scaling and placing the three spheres

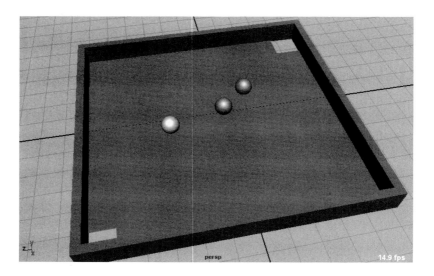

Figure 12.6

The pool balls in texture view

The spheres are placed a bit over the table surface so that their geometries' surfaces aren't accidentally crossing each other, an effect known as *interpenetrating*. When surfaces interpenetrate, the dynamics that result are usually as welcome as sand in your eyes. Starting all colliding rigid bodies slightly away from each other should guarantee that their surfaces don't interpenetrate. Using the simple pool table that you've set up will make the dynamics calculations quick and easy.

Use the file Table_v1.mb in the Scenes folder of the Pool_Table project on the CD as a reference or to catch up to this point.

Creating Rigid Bodies

Define the pool table as a passive rigid body, and define the pool balls as active rigid bodies. Follow these steps:

1. Select the two planes that make up the tabletop and the four cubes that are the side rails. Choose Soft/Rigid Bodies → Create Passive Rigid Body.

2. Select the three balls, and choose Soft/Rigid Bodies → Create Active Rigid Body to make them active rigid bodies.

3. With all three pool balls selected, create a gravity field by choosing Fields → Gravity. The gravity field automatically connects to all three balls.

4. Run the simulation. You should see the balls fall slightly onto the tabletop. Check to see that none of them interpenetrate the table surface. If any of them do, Maya will select the offending geometry and display an error message in the Command Feedback line, turning it red.

Animating Rigid Bodies

If you need to, enable texture view in your view panel by pressing 6.

The next step is to put the cue ball (the white sphere) into motion so that it hits the striped ball into the black eight ball to sink it into the corner pocket. The easiest way to do this is to keyframe the cue ball's translation from its starting point to hit into the striped ball. However, because active rigid bodies can't be keyframed, you have to turn the cue ball into a passive rigid body. To do that, follow these steps:

1. Select the cue ball (the white ball). Notice the Active attribute in the Channel Box. (You may have to scroll down; it's at the bottom.) It's set to On.

2. Rewind your animation to the first frame. Choose Soft/Rigid Bodies → Set Passive Key. Notice that the Active attribute turns a dark yellow. You've set a keyframe for the active state of the cue ball, and it now says Off. You can toggle rigid bodies between passive and active. Maya has also set translation and rotation keyframes for the cue ball.

3. Go to frame 10. Move the cue ball with the Translate tool so that its outer surface slightly passes through the yellow-striped ball, as shown in Figure 12.7. Choose Soft/Rigid Bodies → Set Passive Key.

4. Go to frame 11, and choose Soft/Rigid Bodies → Set Active Key. This turns the cue ball back into an active rigid body in the frame after it strikes the striped ball.

Figure 12.7

Move the cue ball with the Translate tool.

By animating the ball as a passive rigid body, keyframing its translation, and then turning it back to active, you set the dynamic simulation in motion. The cue ball animates from its starting position and hits the striped ball. Maya's dynamics engine calculates the collisions on that ball and sets it into motion; the ball then strikes the black eight ball, which should roll into the corner pocket. The dynamics engine, at frame 11, also calculates the movement of the cue ball after it strikes the striped ball, so you don't have to animate its ricochet.

Go to the start frame, and play back the simulation. The cue ball knocks the striped ball into the eight ball. The eight ball rolls into the corner, and the striped ball bounces off to the right. If the eight ball doesn't go into the corner, you'll have to edit your cue ball's keyframes to hit the striped ball at the correct angle to hit the eight ball into the corner pocket.

At the current settings, however, the eight ball bounces out of the corner without falling through the hole. You need to control the bounciness of the collisions:

1. Go back to the first frame. Select all three balls. In the Channel Box, change the Bounciness attribute from 0.6 to 0.2. After you set the attribute value in the Channel Box, Maya sets the value for all three spheres concurrently.

   Changing the Bounciness attribute through the Attribute Editor changes the value for only one sphere even when they're all selected. You have to change the value for each sphere individually in the Attribute Editor. This is true for all values changed on multiple objects through the Attribute Editor.

2. Play back the animation, and you'll see that the balls don't ricochet off each other and the sides of the pool table with as much spring. The eight ball should now fall through the hole. (See Figure 12.8.) You may need to increase your frame range if your ball doesn't quite make it by frame 120; try 200 frames instead.

Figure 12.8

The eight ball falls through the hole.

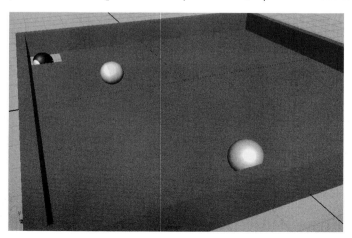

You can load the scene file `Table_v2.mb` from the Pool_Table project on the CD to compare your work.

Additional Rigid Body Attributes

In addition, while using the pool table setup without any animation, try playing with the rigid body attributes to see how they affect the rigid body in question. Some of these attributes are defined here:

Initial Velocity Gives the rigid body an initial push to move it in the corresponding axis.

Initial Spin Gives the rigid body object an initial twist to start the rotation of the object in that axis.

Impulse Position Gives the object a constant push in that axis. The effect is cumulative; the object will accelerate if the impulse isn't turned off.

Spin Impulse Rotates the object constantly in the desired axis. The spin will accelerate if the impulse isn't turned off.

Center of Mass (0,0,0) Places the center of the object's mass at its pivot point, typically at its geometric center. This value offsets the center of mass, so the rigid body object behaves as if its center of balance is offset, like trick dice or a top-weighted ball.

Creating animation with rigid bodies is straightforward and can go a long way toward creating natural-looking motion for your scene. Integrating such animation into a final project can become fairly complicated, though, so it's prudent to become familiar with the workings of rigid body dynamics before relying on that sort of workflow for an animated project. You'll find that most professionals use rigid body dynamics as a springboard to create realistic motion for their projects. The dynamics are often converted to keyframes and further tweaked by the animator to fit into a larger scene.

Here are a few suggestions for scenes using rigid body dynamics:

Bowling Lane The bowling ball is keyframed as a passive object until it hits the active rigid pins at the end of the lane. This scene is simple to create and manipulate.

Dice Active rigid dice are thrown into a passive rigid craps table. This exercise challenges your dynamics abilities as well as your modeling skills if you create an accurate craps table.

Game of Marbles This scene challenges your texturing and rendering abilities as well as your dynamics abilities.

Baking Out a Simulation

Frequently, a dynamic simulation is created to fit into another scene, perhaps to interact with other objects and such. In instances such as this, you want to exchange the dynamic properties of the dynamic body you have set up in a simulation for regular, good old-fashioned animation curves that you can edit along with the rest of the animated scene, if need be. You can easily take a simulation that you've created and bake it out to curves. As much fun as it is to think of cupcakes, *baking* is a somewhat catchall term used to describe converting one type of action or procedure into another; in this case, you're baking dynamics into keyframes.

You'll take the simulation you set up with the pool balls earlier and turn them into keyframes to give you a quick idea of how it can be done and the curves that you'll get. Dynamics is a deep layer of Maya, and there is a lot to learn about it. Keep in mind that you can use this introduction as a foundation for your own explorations.

To bake out the rigid body simulation of the pool balls, follow these steps:

1. Open the scene file `Table_v2.mb` from the Pool_Table project on the CD; or, if you prefer, open your scene from the previous exercise. You'll bake out the motion of all three pool balls on the table to see their keyframes.

2. Because the simulation is already set up and working to your liking, you can jump right to it. Select all three pool balls, and choose Edit → Keys → Bake Simulation ❑. In the option box, as shown in Figure 12.9, set Time Range to Time Slider (which should be set to 1 to 150). This, of course, sets the range you would like to bake into curves.

3. Set Hierarchy to Selected, and set Channels to From Channel Box. This ensures that you have control over which keys are created. Make sure Keep Unbaked Keys and Disable Implicit Control are checked and that Sparse Curve Bake is turned off. Before clicking the Bake or Apply button, select the Translate and Rotate channels in the Channel Box. Click Bake.

4. Maya runs through the simulation. Scrub the timeline back and forth. Notice how the pool balls move around normally as if the dynamic simulation were running—except that you can scrub in the timeline, which you can't do with a dynamics simulation. If you open the Graph Editor, you'll see something similar to Figure 12.10.

Figure 12.9

The Bake Simulation Options window

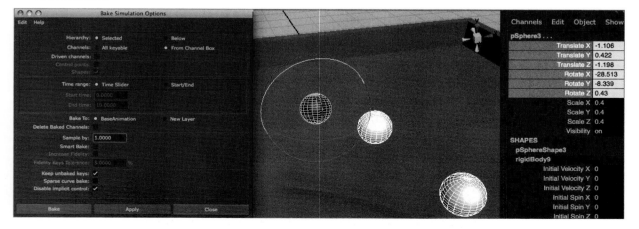

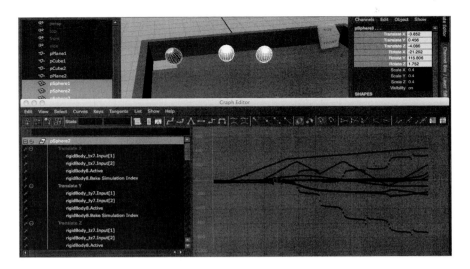

Figure 12.10

The pool balls have animation curves.

5. The curves are crowded; they have keyframes at every frame. A typical dynamics bake gives results like this. But you can set the Bake command to sparse the curves for you; that is, it can take out keyframes at frames that have values within a certain tolerance, so that a minor change in the ball's position or rotation need not have a keyframe on the curve.

6. Let's go back in time and try this again. Press Z (Undo) until you back up to right before you baked out the simulation to curves. You can also close this scene and reopen it from the original project, if necessary. This time, select the balls, and choose Edit → Keys → Bake Simulation ❐. In the option box, turn on the Sparse Curve Bake setting, and set Sample By to 5. Select the channels in the Channel Box, and click Bake. You're telling Maya to only look at every five frames of the simulation to set keyframes.

7. Maya runs through the simulation again and bakes everything out to curves. This time it makes a sparser animation curve for each channel because it's looking at five-frame intervals, as shown in Figure 12.11. If you open the Graph Editor, you'll notice that the curves are much friendlier to look at and edit.

Figure 12.11

Sampling by fives makes a cleaner curve.

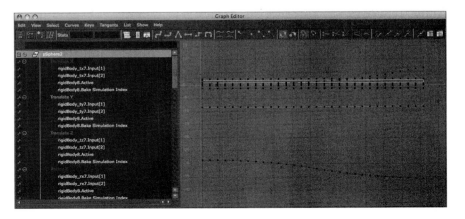

Sampling by fives may give you an easier curve to edit, but it can overly simplify the animation of your objects; make sure you use the best Sampling setting for your simulation when you need to convert it to curves for editing.

Simplifying Animation Curves

Despite a higher Sampling setting when you bake out the simulation, you can still be left with a lot of keyframes to deal with, especially if you have to modify the animation extensively from here. One last trick you can use is to simplify the curve further through the Graph Editor. You have to work with curves of the same relative size, so you'll start with the rotation curves, because they have larger values. To keep things simple, let's deal with one ball: the black eight ball. To simplify the curve in the Graph Editor, follow these steps:

1. Select the black eight ball, and open the Graph Editor. In the left Outliner side, select Rotate.X, Rotate.Y, and Rotate.Z to display only these curves in the graph view. Figure 12.12 shows the curves.

Figure 12.12

The Graph Editor displays the rotation curves of the eight ball.

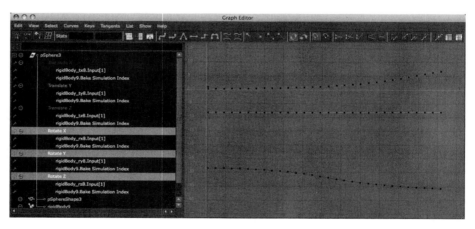

2. In the left panel of the Graph Editor, select the rigidBody_rx8.Input(1) nodes displayed under the Rotate *X, Y,* and *Z* entries for all three curves, as shown in Figure 12.13. In the Graph Editor menu, choose Curves → Simplify Curve ❒. In the option box, set Time Range to All, set Simplify Method to Dense Data, set Time Tolerance to 0.2, and set Value Tolerance to 0.5. These are fairly high values, but because you're dealing with rotation of the ball, the degree values are high enough. For more intricate values such as translation, you would use much lower tolerances when simplifying a curve.

3. Click Simplify, and you see that the curve retains its basic shape but loses some of the unneeded keyframes. Figure 12.14 shows the simplified curve, which differs little from the original curve with keys at every five frames.

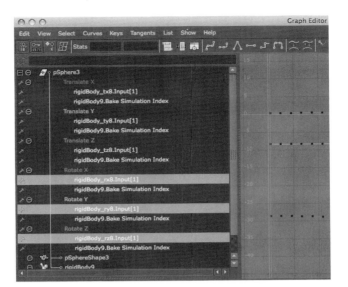

Figure 12.13

Select the curves to simplify them.

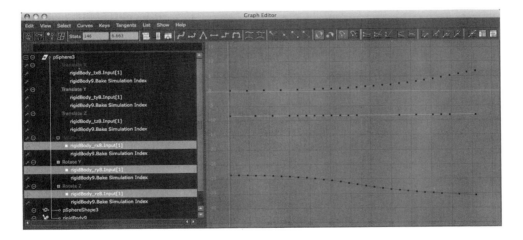

Figure 12.14

A simplified curve for the rotations of the eight ball

Simplifying curves is a handy way to convert a dynamic simulation to curves. But you can also use this method to simplify other animation curves, to make it easier to edit them as you animate the scene. Keep in mind that you may lose fidelity to the original animation after you simplify a curve, so use this technique with care.

With this methodology, you can bake out the animation of any simulation, from dynamics (as you just did) to constraints and some scripts. The curve simplification works with good old-fashioned keyframed curves as well; if you inherit a scene from another animator and need to simplify the curves, do it just as you did here.

nParticle Dynamics

Like rigid body objects, particles are moved dynamically using collisions and fields. In short, a *particle* is a point in space that is given renderable properties—that is, it can render out. When particles are used en masse, they can create effects such as smoke, a swarm of insects, fireworks, and so on. nParticles are an implementation of particles through the Maya Nucleus solver, which provides better and easier simulations than traditional Maya particles.

Although particles (and nParticles) can be an advanced and involved aspect of Maya, it's important to have some exposure to them as you begin to learn Maya.

Much of what you learned about rigid body dynamics transfers to particles. However, it's important to think of particle animation as manipulating a larger system rather than as controlling every single particle in the simulation. You control fields and dynamic attributes to govern the motion of the system as a whole.

For example, with the pool table, you control the motion of the cue ball and let Maya dynamics calculate the motion of the other balls after they collide. Each ball is a distinct part of the scene and renders out as a distinct object in the frame. Particles are most often used together in large numbers so that the entirety is rendered out to create an effect. To control a particle system, you create an emitter and define fields and attributes that control the particles' movement.

Emitting nParticles

A typical workflow for creating an nParticle effect in Maya breaks out into two parts: motion and rendering. First, you create and define the behavior of particles through *emission*. An *emitter* is a Maya object that creates the particles. After you create fields and adjust particle behavior within a dynamic simulation, much as you would do with rigid body motion, you give the particles renderable qualities to define how they look. This second aspect of the workflow defines how the particles come together to create the desired effect, such as steam. You'll make a steaming locomotive pump later in this chapter.

To create an nParticle system, follow these steps:

1. Make sure you're in the nDynamics menu set, choose nParticles → Create nParticles, and select Cloud. Choose nParticles → Create nParticles → Create Emitter ❑. The option box gives you various creation options for the nParticle emitter, as shown in Figure 12.15.

   The default settings create an Omni emitter with a rate of 100 particles per second and a speed of 1.0. Click Create. A small round object (the emitter) appears at the origin.

2. Click the Play button to play the scene. As with rigid body dynamics, you must also play back the scene using the Play Every Frame option. You can't scrub or reverse-

play particles unless you create a cache file. You'll learn how to create a particle disk cache later in this chapter. But for the most part, particles need to be played back to run properly.

You'll notice a mass of round circles streaming out of the emitter in all directions (see Figure 12.16). These are the nParticles.

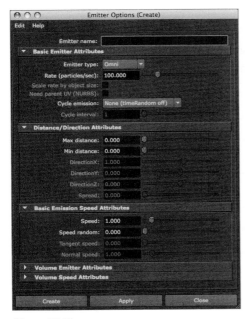

Figure 12.15

Creation options for an nParticle emitter

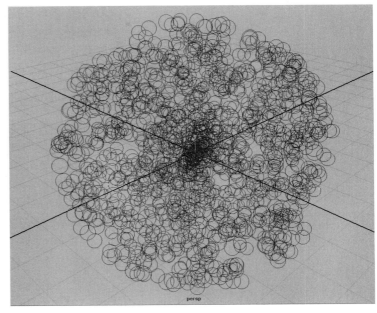

Figure 12.16

An Omni emitter emits a swarm of cloud particles in all directions.

Emitter Attributes

You can control how particles are created and behave by changing the type of emitter and adjusting its attributes. Here are the most often used emitters:

Omni Emits particles in all directions.

Directional Emits a spray of particles in a specific direction, as shown in Figure 12.17.

Volume Emits particles from within a specified volume, as shown in Figure 12.18. The volume can be a cube, a sphere, a cylinder, a cone, or a torus. By default, the particles can leave the perimeter of the volume.

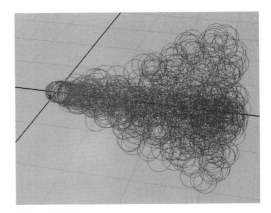

Figure 12.17

Cloud nParticles sprayed in a specific direction

Figure 12.18

Cloud nParticles emit from anywhere inside the emitter's volume.

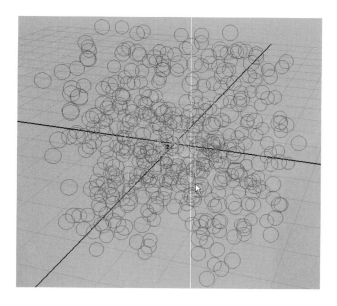

After you create an emitter, its attributes govern how the particles are released into the scene. Every emitter has the following attributes to control the emission:

Rate Governs how many particles are emitted per second.

Speed Specifies how fast the particles move out from the emitter.

Speed Random Randomizes the speed of the particles as they're emitted, for a more natural look.

Figure 12.19

An emitter with a Min and Max Distance setting of 3 emits Cloud nParticles three units from itself.

Min/Max Distance Emits particles within an offset distance from the emitter. You enter values for the Min and Max Distance setting. Figure 12.19 shows a Directional emitter with a Min and Max Distance setting of 3.

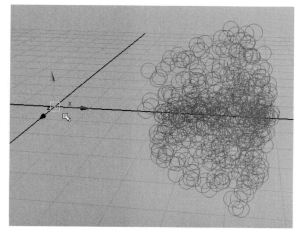

nParticle Attributes

After being created (or born) and set into motion by an emitter, nParticles rely on their own attributes and any fields or collisions in the scene to govern their motion, just like rigid body objects.

In Figure 12.20, the Attribute Editor shows a number of tabs for the selected particle object. Particle1 is the particle object node. This has the familiar Translate, Rotate, and Scale attributes, like most other object nodes. But the shape node, particleShape1, is where all the important attributes are for a particle, and it's displayed by default when you select a particle object. The third tab in the Attribute Editor is the emitter1 node that belongs to the particle's emitter. This makes it easier to toggle back and forth to adjust emitter and particle settings.

The Lifespan Attributes

When any particle is created, or born, you can give it a *lifespan*, which allows the particle to die when it reaches a certain point in time. Giving particles a lifespan is a good idea for a variety of reasons. As you'll see with the steaming locomotive later in the chapter, a particle that has a lifespan can change over that lifespan. For example, a particle may start out as white and fade away at the end of its life. A lifespan also helps keep the total number of particles in a scene to a minimum, which helps the scene run more efficiently.

You use the Lifespan mode to select the type of lifespan for the nParticle:

Live Forever The particles in the scene can exist indefinitely.

Constant All particles die when their Lifespan value is reached. Lifespan is measured in seconds, so upon emission, a particle with a Lifespan of 1.0 will exist for 30 frames (in a scene set up at 30fps) before it disappears.

Random Range This type sets a lifespan in Constant mode but assigns a range value via the Lifespan Random attribute to allow some particles to live longer than others for a more natural effect.

LifespanPP Only This mode is used in conjunction with expressions that are programmed into the particle with Maya Embedded Language (MEL). Expressions are an advanced Maya concept and aren't used in this book.

The Shading Attributes

The Shading attributes determine how your particles look and how they will render. Two types of particle rendering are used in Maya: software and hardware. *Hardware particles* are typically rendered out separately from anything else in the scene and are then composited with the rest of the scene. Because of this compound workflow for hardware particles, this book will introduce you to a software particle called *Cloud*. Cloud, like other *software particles*, can be rendered with the rest of a scene through the software renderer.

With your particles selected, open the Attribute Editor. In the Shading section, you'll find the Particle Render Type drop-down menu (see Figure 12.21).

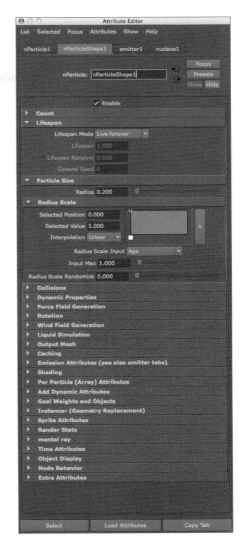

Figure 12.20

nParticle attributes

Figure 12.21

The Particle Render Type drop-down menu

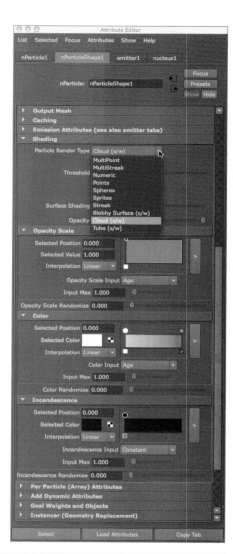

Figure 12.22

Dots on the screen represent Point particles.

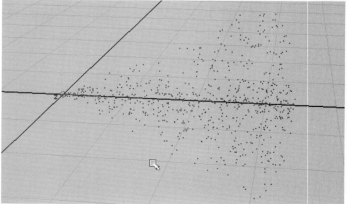

The three render types listed with the (s/w) suffix are software-rendered particles. All the other types can be rendered only through the hardware renderer. Select your render type, and Maya adds the proper attributes you'll need for the render type you selected.

For example, if you select the Points render type from the menu, your particles change from circles on the screen to dots, as shown in Figure 12.22.

Several new attributes that control the look of the particles appear when you switch the Particle Render Type. Each Particle Render Type has its own set of render attributes. Set your nParticles back to the Cloud type. The Cloud particle type attributes are Threshold, Surface Shading, and Opacity. (See Figure 12.23.)

In the Shading heading, shown in Figure 12.24 for the Cloud nParticles, are controls for the Opacity Scale, Color, and Incandescence attributes. They control how the particles look when simulated and rendered. Notice how each of these controls is based on ramps.

nParticles are already set up to allow you to control the color, opacity, and incandescence during the life of the particle. For example, by default, the Color attribute is set up with a white to cyan ramp. This means that each of the particles will begin life white in color and will gradually turn cyan toward the end of its lifespan, or Age.

Likewise, the Particle Size heading in the Attribute Editor contains a ramp for Radius Scale that works much the same way as the Color attribute just described. In this case, you use the Radius Scale ramp to increase or decrease the size of the particle along its Age.

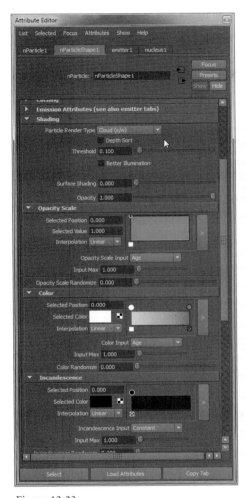

Figure 12.23

Each Particle Render Type displays its own set of attributes.

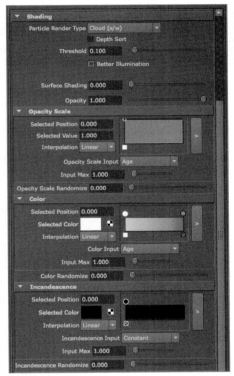

Figure 12.24

Controls for Opacity Scale, Color, and Incandescence attributes

nCaching Particles

It would be nice to turn particles into cash, but I can only show you how to turn your particles into a cache. You can cache the motion of your particles to memory or to disk to make playback and editing of your particle animation easier. To cache particles to your system's fast RAM memory, select the nParticle object you want to cache, and open the Attribute Editor. In the Caching section, under Memory Caching, select the Cache Data check box. Play back your scene, and the particles cache into your memory for faster playback. You can also scrub your timeline to see your particle animation. If you make changes to your animation, the scene won't reflect the changes until you delete the cache from memory by selecting the particle object and unchecking the Memory Cache check box in the Attribute Editor. The amount of information the memory cache can hold depends on your machine's system RAM.

Although memory caching is generally faster than disk caching, creating a disk cache lets you cache all the particles as they exist throughout their duration in your scene and ensures that the particles are rendered correctly, especially if you're rendering on multiple computers or across a network. You should create a particle disk cache before rendering.

> If you make changes to your particle simulation but you don't see the changes reflected when you play back the scene, make sure you've turned off any memory or deleted any disk cache from previous versions of the simulation.

Creating an nCache on Disk

After you've created a particle scene, and you want to be able to scrub the timeline back and forth to see your particle motion and how it acts in the scene, you can create a *particle nCache* to disk. This lets you play back the entire scene as you like, without running the simulation from the start and by every frame.

To create an nCache, switch to the nDynamics menu, select the nParticle object, and choose nCache → Create New Cache. Maya will run the simulation according to the timeline and save the position of all the particle systems in the scene to cache files in your current project's data\cache folder. You can then play or even scrub your animation back and forth, and the particles will run properly.

If you make any dynamics changes to the particles, such as emission rate or speed, you'll need to detach the cache file from the scene for the changes to take effect. Choose nCache → Delete Cache. You can open the option box to select whether you wish to delete the cache files physically or merely detach them from the current nParticles.

Now that you understand the basics of particle dynamics, it's time to see for yourself how they work.

Animating a Particle Effect: Locomotive Steam

You'll create a spray of steam puffing out of the steam pump on the side of the locomotive that drives the wheels on the model you started creating in Chapter 4, "Beginning Polygonal Modeling," and Chapter 5, "Modeling with NURBS, Subdivisions, and Deformers." You'll use the more detailed locomotive model from Chapter 8, "Introduction to Animation," and Chapter 9, "More Animation!"

Emitting the nParticles

The first step is to create an emitter to spray from the steam pump and to set up the motion and behavior of the nParticles:

1. In the nDynamics menu, choose nParticles → Create nParticles. Cloud should still be checked in the Create nParticles menu. If it isn't, select Cloud, and then choose nParticles → Create nParticles → Create Emitter ☐. Set Emitter Type to Directional, and click Create. Place the emitter at the end of the pump, as shown in Figure 12.25.

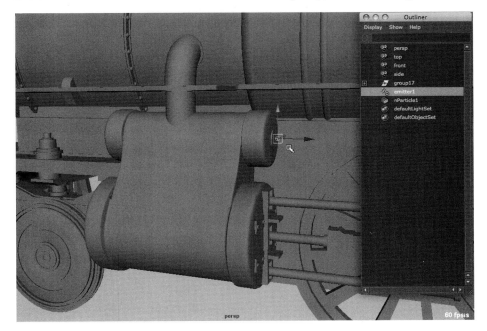

Figure 12.25

Place the emitter at the end of the pump.

2. To set up the emission in the proper direction, adjust the attributes of the emitter. In the Distance/Direction Attributes section, set Direction Y to 0, Direction X to 0, and Direction Z to 1. This emits the particles straight out of the pump over the first large wheel and toward the back of the engine.

> The Direction attributes are relative. Entering a value of 1 for Direction X and a value of 2 for Direction Y makes the particles spray at twice the height (Y) of their lateral distance (X).

3. Play back your scene. The Cloud nParticles emit in a straight line from the engine, as shown in Figure 12.26.

    You can load the file Locomotive_Steam_v1.ma from the Locomotive project on the CD to check your work.

Figure 12.26

Cloud nParticles emit in a straight line from the pump.

4. To change the particle emission to more of a spray, adjust the Spread attribute for the emitter. Click the emitter1 tab in the particle's Attribute Editor (or select the emitter to focus the Attribute Editor on it instead), and change Spread from 0 to 0.30. Figure 12.27 shows the new cloud spray.

The Spread attribute sets the cone angle for a directional emission. A value of 0 results in a thin line of particles. A value of 1 emits particles in a 180-degree arc.

Figure 12.27

The emitter's Spread attribute widens the spray of particles.

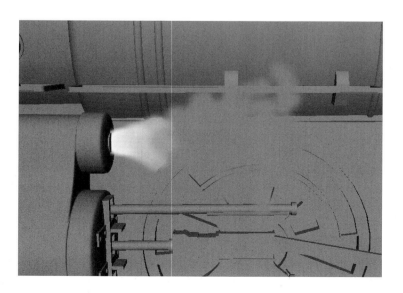

5. The emission is rather slow for hot steam being pumped out as the locomotive drives the wheels, so change the Speed setting for the emitter from 1 to 2.0, and change Speed Random from 0 to 1. Doing so creates a random speed range between 1 and 3 for each particle. These two attributes are found in the emitter's Attribute Editor in the Basic Emission Speed Attributes section.

6. So that all the steam doesn't emit from the same point, keep the emitter's Min Distance at 0 but set its Max Distance to 0.3. This creates a range of offset between 0 and 0.3 units for the particle to emit from, as shown in Figure 12.28.

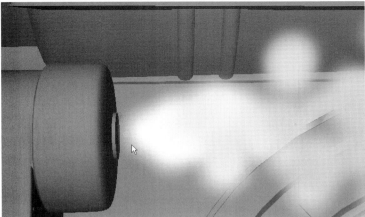

Figure 12.28

A range of offset between 0 and 0.3 units creates a more believable emission.

Setting nParticle Attributes

It's always good to get the particles moving as closely to what you need as possible before you tend to their look. Now that you have the particles emitting properly from the steam pump, you'll adjust the nParticle attributes. Start by setting a lifespan for them, and then add rendering attributes:

1. Select the nParticle object, and open the Attribute Editor. In the Lifespan section, set Lifespan Mode to Random Range. Set Lifespan to 2 and Lifespan Random to 1. This creates a range of 1 to 3 for each particle's lifespan. (This is based on a lifespan of 3, plus or minus a random value from 0 to 1.)

2. You can control the radius of the particles as they're emitted from the pump. Under the Particle Size heading in the Attribute Editor, set a Radius attribute of 0.50. Set the Radius Scale Randomize attribute to 0.25. This allows you to have particles that emit with a radius range between 0.25 and 0.75. Figure 12.29 shows the attributes.

3. If you play back the simulation, you see the particles are quite large initially. Because steam expands as it travels, you need to adjust the size (radius) of your nParticles to make them smaller at birth; they will grow larger over their lifespan and produce a good look for your steam.

Figure 12.29

The initial radius settings for the steam nParticles

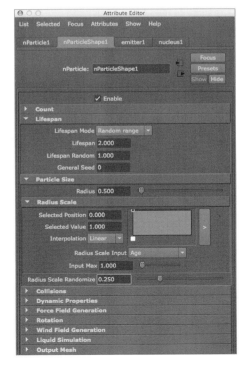

4. In the Radius Scale heading in the Attribute Editor, click the arrow to the right of the ramp to open a larger view of the ramp, as shown in Figure 12.30.

5. Click and drag the ramp's first and only handle (an open circle at the upper-left corner of the Ramp window) down to a value of about 0.25, as shown in Figure 12.31. The particles get smaller as you adjust the ramp value.

Figure 12.30

Open the Radius Scale ramp.

Figure 12.31

Decrease the Radius of the nParticles using the Radius Scale ramp.

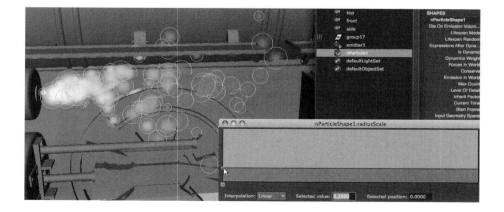

6. To allow the particles to grow in size, add a second handle to the scale curve by clicking anywhere on that line, and drag to a value of 1.0 and the position shown in Figure 12.32. The particles toward the end of the spray get larger.

7. You can set up collisions so the nParticle steam doesn't travel right through the mesh of the locomotive. Select the meshes shown in Figure 12.33, and choose nMesh → Create Passive Collider.

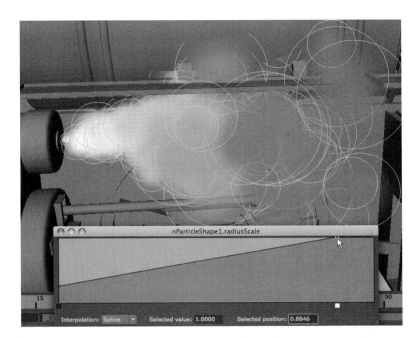

Figure 12.32

Adjust the Radius Scale ramp to grow the particles.

Figure 12.33

Select the meshes with which the nParticles will collide.

8. In the Outliner, select the three nRigid nodes that were just created, and set the Friction attribute in the Channel Box to 0.0 from the default of 0.10. Play back your scene, and your particles now collide with the surface of the locomotive. (See Figure 12.34.)

Figure 12.34

The particles now react very nicely against the side of the locomotive.

 If you want to check your work, load the file `locomotive_steam_v2.ma` from the Locomotive project on the CD.

Setting Rendering Attributes

After you define the nParticle movement to your liking, you can create the proper look for the nParticles. This means setting and adjusting their rendering parameters. Because Maya has several types of particles, the particles are set up according to their type; the following workflow applies only to the Cloud particle type:

1. Select the nParticle object, and open the Attribute Editor. Expand the Shading heading, and look at the Color ramp. By default, the particles go from white to light blue in color. Click the cyan color's circle handle on top of the ramp. The Selected Color attribute next to the ramp shows the cyan color. Click in the swatch to open the Color Chooser, and change the color to a very light gray.

2. Click the arrow bar to the right of the Opacity Scale ramp to open a larger ramp view. Grab the first handle in the upper-left corner, and drag it down to a value of 0.12.

3. The steam needs to be less opaque at its birth, grow more opaque toward the middle of its life, and fade completely away at the end of the particle's life. Click to create new handles to create a curve for the ramp, as shown in Figure 12.35. The values for the five ramp handles shown from left to right are 0.12, 0.30, 0.20, 0.08, and 0.

4. In the Render Settings window, set Image Size to 640 × 480. In the Maya Software tab, set Quality to Intermediate Quality. Run the animation, and stop it when some steam has been emitted. Render a frame. It should look like Figure 12.36. The steam doesn't travel far enough along the engine; it disappears too soon.

   With the steam nParticles selected, open the Attribute Editor and, in the Radius Scale, change the first handle's value from 0.25 to 0.35 to make the steam particles a bit larger. Below the Opacity Scale ramp is the Input Max slider; set that value to 1.6.

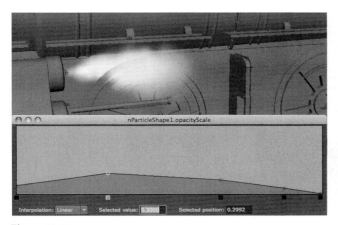

Figure 12.35

Creating an Opacity ramp for the steam

Figure 12.36

The steam seems too short and small.

5. Select the emitter1 tab, and change the Spread for the emitter to 0.2. Change Rate (Particles/Sec) to 200 and Speed to 3.0. Play back the simulation, and render a frame to compare to Figure 12.37.

6. The Color ramp in the nParticle's Attribute Editor controls the color of the steam, and a shader is assigned to the particles. Select the steam nParticle object, and open the Hypershade window. In the Hypershade, click the Graph materials on the selected object's icon (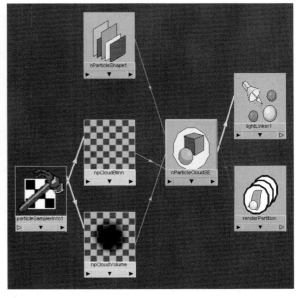), as shown in Figure 12.38.

Figure 12.37

A better emission, but a bit too solid

Figure 12.38

The shaders assigned to the Cloud nParticle

7. In the Hypershade, select the npCloudVolume shader, and open the Attribute Editor. Notice that the Common Material Attributes section's attributes all have connections. The ramp controls in the nParticle Attribute Editor are controlling the attributes in this Particle Cloud shader.

8. Under the Transparency heading in the Attribute Editor for the shader, set Density to 0.35. Try a render; the steam should look better. (See Figure 12.39.)

Batch-render a 200-frame sequence of the scene at a lower resolution, such as 320 × 240, to see how the particles look as they animate. (Check the frames with FCheck. Refer to Chapter 11, "Maya Rendering," for more on FCheck.)

Load the file locomotive_steam_v3.ma from the Locomotive project on the CD to check your work.

Experiment with the steam by animating the Rate attribute of the emitter to make the steam pump out in time with the wheel arm. Also, try animating the Speed values and

size: 640 480 zoom: 1.000   (Maya Software, Region)
Frame: 120   Render Time: 0:08   Camera: persp

Figure 12.39

The steam is less flat and solid.

playing with different values in the Radius and Opacity ramps. The steam you'll get in this tutorial looks pretty good, but it isn't as lifelike as it could be. You can do a lot more as you continue to learn about Maya, but those techniques are beyond the scope of this book. Particle animators are always learning new tricks and expanding their skills, and that comes from always trying new things and retrying the same effects with different methods.

When you feel comfortable with the steam exercise, try using the Cloud nParticle to create steam for a mug of coffee. That steam moves much more slowly and is less defined than the blowing steam of the locomotive, and it should pose a new challenge. Also try your hand at creating a smoke trail for a rocket ship or a wafting stream of cigarette smoke, or even the billowing smoke coming from the engine's chimney.

Cloud nParticles are the perfect particle type with which to begin. As you feel more comfortable animating with clouds, experiment with the other render types. The more you experiment with all the types of nParticles, the easier they will be to harness. You'll quickly find that Maya nParticles can create a wild array of realistic and stylized effects for your animations more easily than traditional Maya particles.

Introduction to Paint Effects

One of the tools in Maya's effects arsenal is called Paint Effects. Using Paint Effects, you can create a field of grass rippling in the wind, a head of hair or feathers, or even a colorful aurora in the sky. Paint Effects is a rendering effect found under the Rendering menu. It has incredible dynamic properties that can make leaves rustle in the wind or trees sway in a storm. Although it doesn't use the same dynamics engine as particles or rigid bodies, Paint Effects uses its own dynamics calculations to create natural motion. It's one of Maya's most powerful tools, with features that go far beyond the scope of this introductory book. Here you'll learn how to create a Paint Effects scene and how to access all the preset brushes to create your own effects.

Paint Effects uses brushes to paint effects into your 3D scene. The brushes create strokes on a surface or in the Maya modeling views that produce tubes, which render out through Maya's software renderer. These Paint Effects tubes have dynamic properties, which means they can move according to their own forces. Therefore, you can easily create a field of blowing grass.

Try This Create a field of blowing grass and flowers; it will take you all of five minutes.

1. Start with a new scene file. Maximize the perspective view. (Press the spacebar with the Perspective window active.)

2. Switch to the Rendering menu set (press F6). Choose Paint Effects → Get Brush to open the Visor window. The Visor window displays all the preset Paint Effects brushes that automatically create certain effects. Select the Grasses folder in the Visor's left panel to display the grass brushes available (see Figure 12.40). You can navigate the Visor window as you would navigate any other Maya window, using the Alt key and the mouse buttons.

3. Click the grassWindWide. mel brush to activate the Paint Effects tool and set it to this grass brush. Your cursor changes to a Pencil icon.

Figure 12.40

The preset grass brushes in the Visor window

4. In the Perspective window, click and drag two lines across the grid, as shown in Figure 12.41, to create two Paint Effects strokes of blowing grass. If you can't see the grass in your view panel, increase Global Scale in the Paint Effects Brush Settings to see the grass being drawn onto the screen.

5. To change your brush so you can add some flowers between the grass, choose Paint Effects → Get Brush, and select the flowers folder. Select the dandelion_Yellow.mel brush. Your Paint Effects tool is now set to paint yellow flowers.

6. Click and drag a new stroke between the strokes of grass, as shown in Figure 12.42.

Figure 12.41

Click and drag two lines across the grid.

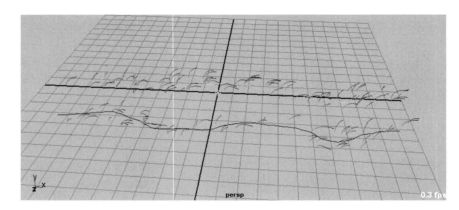

Figure 12.42

Add new strokes to add flowers to the grass.

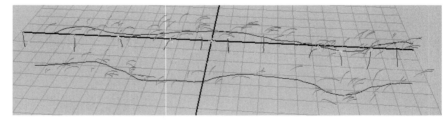

7. Position your camera, and render a frame. Make sure you're using Maya Software and not mental ray to render through the Render Settings window and that you use a large enough resolution, such as 640 × 480, so that you can see the details. Render out a 120-frame sequence to see how the grass animates in the wind. Figure 12.43 shows a scene filled with grass strokes as well as a number of different flowers.

After you create a Paint Effects stroke, you can edit the look and movement of the effect through the Attribute Editor. You'll notice, however, that there are a large number of attributes to edit with Paint Effects. The next section introduces the attributes that are most useful to the beginning Maya user.

Figure 12.43
**Paint Effects
can add realistic
flowers and grass
to any scene.**

Paint Effects Attributes

It's best to create a single stroke of Paint Effects in a blank scene and experiment with adjusting the various attributes to see how they affect the strokes. Select the stroke, and open the Attribute Editor. Switch to the stroke's tab to access the attributes. For example, for an African Lily Paint Effects stroke, the Attribute Editor tab is called africanLily1.

Each Paint Effects stroke produces tubes that render to create the desired effect. Each tube (you can think of a tube as a stalk) can grow to have branches, twigs, leaves, flowers, and buds. Each section of a tube has its own controls to give you the greatest flexibility in creating your effect. As you experiment with Paint Effects, you'll begin to understand how each attribute contributes to the final look of the effect.

Here is a summary of some Paint Effects attributes:

Brush Profile Gives you control over how the tubes are generated from the stroke; this is done with the Brush Width attribute. This makes tubes emit from a wider breadth from the stroke to cover more of an area.

Shading and Tube Shading Gives you access to the color controls for the tubes on a stroke.

> **Color1 and Color2** From bottom to top, graduates from Color1 to Color 2 along the stalk only. The leaves and branches have their own color attributes, which you can display by choosing Tubes → Growth.
>
> **Incandescence1 and 2** Adds a gradient self-illumination to the tubes.
>
> **Transparency1 and 2** Adds a gradient transparency to each tube.
>
> **Hue/Sat/Value Rand** Add some randomness to the color of the tubes.

In the Tubes section, you'll find all the attributes to control the growth of the Paint Effects effect. In the Creation subsection, you can access the following:

Tubes per Step Controls the number of tubes along the stroke. For example, this setting increases or decreases the number of flowers for the africanLily1 stroke.

Length Min/Max Controls how tall the tubes are grown to make taller flowers or grass (or other effects).

Tube Width1 and Width2 Controls the width of the tubes (the stalks of the flowers).

In the Growth subsection, you can access controls for branches, twigs, leaves, flowers, and buds for the Paint Effects strokes. Each attribute in these sections controls the number, size, and shape of those elements. Although not all Paint Effects strokes create flowers, all strokes contain these headings; some may or may not be active. Each stroke has its own settings.

The Behavior subsection contains the controls for the dynamic forces affecting the tubes in a Paint Effects stroke. Adjust these attributes if you want your flowers to blow more in the wind.

Paint Effects are rendered as a *post process*, which means they won't render in reflections or refractions as is. They're processed and rendered after every other object in the scene is rendered out. But they play back in the work panels to give you feedback on your dynamic settings.

You can also convert Paint Effects to polygonal surfaces that will render in the scene along with any other objects so that they may take part in reflections and refractions. To convert a Paint Effects stroke to polygons, select the stroke and choose Modify → Convert → Paint Effects to Polygons. The polygon Paint Effects tubes can still be edited by most of the Paint Effects attributes mentioned so far; however, some, such as color, don't affect the poly tubes. Instead, the color information is converted into a shader that is assigned to the polygons. It's best to finalize your Paint Effects strokes before converting to polygons, to avoid any confusion.

Paint Effects is a strong Maya tool and you can use it to create complex effects such as a field of blowing flowers. A large number of controls to create a variety of effects come with that complexity. Fortunately, Maya comes with a generous sampling of preset brushes. Experiment with a few brushes and their attributes to see what kinds of effects and strange plants you can create.

Toon Shading

Paint Effects has been developed into a toon-shading system to make your animations render more like traditional cartoons. Using Paint Effects, Maya renders outlines for the objects in your scene; and using a Toon shader, Maya renders the objects in the scene with a flat cartoon-color look. Next, we'll take a quick look at how to apply toon shading to the wagon scene to make it render like a cartoon.

Try This Set your project to the RedWagon project, and open the RedWagonModel_v08.ma scene file from the Scenes folder.

1. You'll see the wagon in a 3/4 view in the persp panel. Select all the parts of the body of the wagon without the railings, as shown in Figure 12.44.

2. Switch to the Rendering menu set, and select Toon → Assign Fill Shader → Shaded Brightness Two Tone. The Attribute Editor opens, focused on a Ramp shader as shown in Figure 12.45.

Figure 12.44

Select the main body of the wagon, without the wheels or the rails.

Figure 12.45

A Ramp shader is added to the scene and applied to the wagon's body.

3. Under the Color heading, set the color of the gray part of the ramp to a dark red, and set the white part of the ramp to a bright red. Your wagon should turn red in the persp panel if you're in shaded or texture view. Render a frame, and you should see the wagon in only two tones of red, but with gray railings and wheels (shown in grayscale in Figure 12.46).

4. Select the rail objects, and select Toon → Assign Fill Shader → Shaded Brightness Two Tone to create another Toon shader. Set the colors to a dark tan and a bright tan color in the Color ramp.

5. Select the handlebar and all four wheels and create another two-tone fill shader with a gray and white Color ramp (which is the default).

6. The frame, railings, and wheels now have a Toon shader as well. Notice the wheels in Figure 12.47 and how cool they look when toon shaded. Of course, adjust any of the colors to your liking.

Figure 12.46

The wagon now has a toon-shaded body. The front side of the wagon is a darker red than the front, due to the lighting in the scene.

Figure 12.47

The wagon has Toon shaders for the fill color applied.

7. Now for the toon outlines. Select all the parts of the wagon, and select Toon → Assign Outline → Add New Toon Outline. A black outline appears around the outside of the wagon's parts, and a new node called pfxToon1 appears in the Outliner or Hypergraph. The outlining is accomplished with Paint Effects.

8. Before you render a frame, set the background to white to make the black toon outlines pop. To do so, select the persp camera, and open the Attribute Editor. Under the Environment heading, set the Background Color to white.

Figure 12.48

The black outlines are applied, but they're too thick.

9. Open the Render Settings window, and set the renderer to Maya Software. Render a frame, and compare to Figure 12.48. The outlines are too thick!

> The mental ray renderer doesn't render Paint Effects by default. You have to render with Maya Software rendering to be able to see Paint Effects strokes. To see Paint Effects with mental ray, you must convert the paint effects to polygons, a procedure not covered in this introductory text.

10. Select the pfxToon1 node in the Outliner, and open the Attribute Editor window. Click the pfxToonShape1 tab to open the attributes for the outlines. Set the Line Width attribute to 0.03, and render a frame. Compare to Figure 12.49.

Figure 12.49

The cartoon wagon!

You can adjust the colors and the ramps of the Fill shader to suit your tastes, and you can try out the other Fill shader types, such as a three-tone shader to get a bit more detail in the coloring of the wagon. Adjust the toon outline thickness as you like, and have some fun playing with the toon outline's attributes to see how they affect the toon rendering of the wagon. This should be a quick primer to get you into toon shading. The rest, as always, is up to you. With some playing and experimenting, and you'll be rendering some pretty nifty cartoon scenes in no time.

Summary

In this chapter, you learned how to create dynamic objects and create simulations. Beginning with rigid body dynamics, you created a set of pool balls that you animated in the simulation to knock into each other. Then, you learned how to bake that simulation into animation curves for fine-tuning. Next, you learned about particle effects by creating a steam effect for the locomotive animation using nParticles. Finally, you learned a little about Maya's Paint Effects tool and how you can easily use it to create various effects such as grass and flowers.

To further your learning, try creating a scene on a grassy hillside with train tracks running through. Animate the locomotive, steam and all, driving through the scene and blowing the grass as it passes. You can also create a train whistle and a steam effect when the whistle blows, and you can create various other trails of smoke and steam as the locomotive drives through.

With power comes complexity of use. Maya dynamics has a rich feature set and compound controls. The best way to be exposed to Maya dynamics is simply to experiment once you're familiar with the general workflow in Maya. You'll find that the workflow in dynamics is more iterative than other Maya workflows, because you're required to experiment frequently with different values to see how they affect the final simulation. With time, you'll develop a strong intuition, and you'll accomplish more complex simulations faster and with greater effect.

Where Do You Go from Here?

It's so hard to say goodbye! But this is really a "hello" to learning more about animation and 3D!

Please explore other resources and tutorials to expand your working knowledge of Maya. Several websites contain numerous tips, tricks, and tutorials for all aspects of Maya, including the author's columns in HDRI3d magazine (www.hdri3d.com) and my occasional ramblings online at http://kooshspot.blogspot.com/. Of course, www.autodesk.com/maya has a wide range of learning tools. Check the bibliography in the absolutely fabulous Chapter 1, "Introduction to Computer Graphics and 3D," for some suggested reading materials. Now that you've gained your all-important first exposure, you'll be better equipped to forge ahead confidently.

The most important thing you should have learned from this book is that proficiency and competence with Maya come with practice, but even more so from your own artistic exploration. Treat this text and your experience with its information as a formal introduction to a new language and way of working for yourself; doing so is imperative. The rest of it—the gorgeous still frames and eloquent animations—come with furthering your study of your own art, working diligently to achieve your vision, and having fun along the way. Enjoy, and good luck.

About the Companion CD

Topics in this appendix include:

- **What you'll find on the CD**
- **System requirements**
- **Using the CD**
- **Troubleshooting**

What You'll Find on the CD

The following sections are arranged by category and provide a summary of the items you'll find on the CD.

If you need help installing the items provided on the CD, refer to the installation instructions in the "Using the CD" section of this appendix.

Project Files

The CD is organized into Project folders. Each folder contains all the scene and support files for that project. The folders are arranged as Maya projects, so you can copy them to your hard drive and then work directly from them. Working with files directly from the CD, however, is not encouraged.

System Requirements

You need to be running Maya 2011 to fully use all the files on the CD. Make sure your computer meets the minimum system requirements shown in the following list. If your computer doesn't match up to these requirements, you may have problems using the files on the companion CD:

- A PC running Microsoft Windows XP (SP2 or higher), Windows Vista, or Windows 7
- A Macintosh running Apple OS X 10.5.2 or later
- An Internet connection
- A CD-ROM drive

For the latest information on system requirements for Maya, go to www.autodesk.com/maya. Although you can find specific hardware recommendations on these web pages, there is some general information that will help you determine if you're already set up to run Maya: you need a fast processor, a minimum 2GB of RAM, and a workstation graphics card for the best compatibility (rather than a consumer-grade gaming video card).

> There is no Maya software provided on the CD. You need to already have a copy of Maya software to use the files on the CD.

Using the CD

To install the items from the CD to your hard drive, follow these steps:

1. Insert the CD into your computer's CD-ROM drive. The license agreement appears.

Windows users: The interface won't launch if autorun is disabled. In that case, click Start →
Run (for Windows Vista, Start → All Programs → Accessories → Run). In the dialog box that
appears, enter **D:\Start.exe**. (Replace D with the proper letter if your CD drive uses a different letter. If you don't know the letter, see how your CD drive is listed under My Computer.)
Click OK.

Mac users: The CD icon appears on your desktop; double-click the icon to open the CD, and
navigate to the files you want to copy to your hard drive.

2. Read through the license agreement, and then click the Accept button if you want to
   use the CD.

The CD interface appears. The interface allows you to access the content with just one
or two clicks.

Troubleshooting

Wiley has attempted to provide programs that work on most computers with the minimum system requirements. Alas, your computer may differ, and some programs may not
work properly for some reason.

The two likeliest problems are that you don't have enough memory (RAM) for the
programs you want to use or you have other programs running that are affecting installation or running of a program. If you get an error message such as "Not enough memory"
or "Setup cannot continue," try one or more of the following suggestions, and then try
using the software again:

Turn off any antivirus software running on your computer. Installation programs sometimes mimic virus activity and may make your computer incorrectly believe that it's
being infected by a virus.

Close all running programs. The more programs you have running, the less memory is
available to other programs. Installation programs typically update files and programs,
so if you keep other programs running, installation may not work properly.

Have your local computer store add more RAM to your computer. This is, admittedly, a
drastic and somewhat expensive step. However, adding more memory can really help the
speed of your computer and allow more programs to run at the same time.

Customer Care

If you have trouble with the book's companion CD-ROM, please call the Wiley Product Technical Support phone number at (800) 762-2974. Outside the United States, call +1(317) 572-3994. You can also contact Wiley Product Technical Support at http://sybex.custhelp.com. John Wiley & Sons will provide technical support only for installation and other general quality-control items. For technical support on the applications themselves, consult the program's vendor or author.

To place additional orders or to request information about other Wiley products, please call (877) 762-2974.

Should the need arise for an errata or replacement files, we will post them at www.sybex.com/go/intromaya2011.

Index

Note to the reader: Throughout this index **boldfaced** page numbers indicate primary discussions of a topic. *Italicized* page numbers indicate illustrations.

Wiley Publishing, Inc. End-User License Agreement

READ THIS. You should carefully read these terms and conditions before opening the software packet(s) included with this book "Book". This is a license agreement "Agreement" between you and Wiley Publishing, Inc. "WPI". By opening the accompanying software packet(s), you acknowledge that you have read and accept the following terms and conditions. If you do not agree and do not want to be bound by such terms and conditions, promptly return the Book and the unopened software packet(s) to the place you obtained them for a full refund.

1. **License Grant.** WPI grants to you (either an individual or entity) a nonexclusive license to use one copy of the enclosed software program(s) (collectively, the "Software," solely for your own personal or business purposes on a single computer (whether a standard computer or a workstation component of a multi-user network). The Software is in use on a computer when it is loaded into temporary memory (RAM) or installed into permanent memory (hard disk, CD-ROM, or other storage device). WPI reserves all rights not expressly granted herein.

2. **Ownership.** WPI is the owner of all right, title, and interest, including copyright, in and to the compilation of the Software recorded on the physical packet included with this Book "Software Media". Copyright to the individual programs recorded on the Software Media is owned by the author or other authorized copyright owner of each program. Ownership of the Software and all proprietary rights relating thereto remain with WPI and its licensers.

3. **Restrictions On Use and Transfer.** (a) You may only (i) make one copy of the Software for backup or archival purposes, or (ii) transfer the Software to a single hard disk, provided that you keep the original for backup or archival purposes. You may not (i) rent or lease the Software, (ii) copy or reproduce the Software through a LAN or other network system or through any computer subscriber system or bulletin-board system, or (iii) modify, adapt, or create derivative works based on the Software. (b) You may not reverse engineer, decompile, or disassemble the Software. You may transfer the Software and user documentation on a permanent basis, provided that the transferee agrees to accept the terms and conditions of this Agreement and you retain no copies. If the Software is an update or has been updated, any transfer must include the most recent update and all prior versions.

4. **Restrictions on Use of Individual Programs.** You must follow the individual requirements and restrictions detailed for each individual program in the About the CD-ROM appendix of this Book or on the Software Media. These limitations are also contained in the individual license agreements recorded on the Software Media. These limitations may include a requirement that after using the program for a specified period of time, the user must pay a registration fee or discontinue use. By opening the Software packet(s), you will be agreeing to abide by the licenses and restrictions for these individual programs that are detailed in the About the CD-ROM appendix and/or on the Software Media. None of the material on this Software Media or listed in this Book may ever be redistributed, in original or modified form, for commercial purposes.

5. **Limited Warranty.** (a) WPI warrants that the Software and Software Media are free from defects in materials and workmanship under normal use for a period of sixty (60) days from the date of purchase of this Book. If WPI receives notification within the warranty period of defects in materials or workmanship, WPI will replace the defective Software Media. (b) WPI AND THE AUTHOR(S) OF THE BOOK DISCLAIM ALL OTHER WARRANTIES, EXPRESS OR IMPLIED, INCLUDING WITHOUT LIMITATION IMPLIED WARRANTIES OF MERCHANTABILITY AND FITNESS FOR A PARTICULAR PURPOSE, WITH RESPECT TO THE SOFTWARE, THE PROGRAMS, THE SOURCE CODE CONTAINED THEREIN, AND/OR THE TECHNIQUES DESCRIBED IN THIS BOOK. WPI DOES NOT WARRANT THAT THE FUNCTIONS CONTAINED IN THE SOFTWARE WILL MEET YOUR REQUIREMENTS OR THAT THE OPERATION OF THE SOFTWARE WILL BE ERROR FREE. (c) This limited warranty gives you specific legal rights, and you may have other rights that vary from jurisdiction to jurisdiction.

6. **Remedies.** (a) WPI's entire liability and your exclusive remedy for defects in materials and workmanship shall be limited to replacement of the Software Media, which may be returned to WPI with a copy of your receipt at the following address: Software Media Fulfillment Department, Attn.: *Introducing Maya 2011*, Wiley Publishing, Inc., 10475 Crosspoint Blvd., Indianapolis, IN 46256, or call 1-800-762-2974. Please allow four to six weeks for delivery. This Limited Warranty is void if failure of the Software Media has resulted from accident, abuse, or misapplication. Any replacement Software Media will be warranted for the remainder of the original warranty period or thirty (30) days, whichever is longer.(b) In no event shall WPI or the author be liable for any damages whatsoever (including without limitation damages for loss of business profits, business interruption, loss of business information, or any other pecuniary loss) arising from the use of or inability to use the Book or the Software, even if WPI has been advised of the possibility of such damages. (c) Because some jurisdictions do not allow the exclusion or limitation of liability for consequential or incidental damages, the above limitation or exclusion may not apply to you.

7. **U.S. Government Restricted Rights.** Use, duplication, or disclosure of the Software for or on behalf of the United States of America, its agencies and/or instrumentalities "U.S. Government" is subject to restrictions as stated in paragraph (c)(1)(ii) of the Rights in Technical Data and Computer Software clause of DFARS 252.227-7013, or subparagraphs (c) (1) and (2) of the Commercial Computer Software - Restricted Rights clause at FAR 52.227-19, and in similar clauses in the NASA FAR supplement, as applicable.

8. **General.** This Agreement constitutes the entire understanding of the parties and revokes and supersedes all prior agreements, oral or written, between them and may not be modified or amended except in a writing signed by both parties hereto that specifically refers to this Agreement. This Agreement shall take precedence over any other documents that may be in conflict herewith. If any one or more provisions contained in this Agreement are held by any court or tribunal to be invalid, illegal, or otherwise unenforceable, each and every other provision shall remain in full force and effect.